Early Medieval Chinese Texts

CHINA RESEARCH MONOGRAPH 71

CENTER FOR CHINESE STUDIES

Early Medieval Chinese Texts
A Bibliographical Guide

Edited by

Cynthia L. Chennault
Keith N. Knapp
Alan J. Berkowitz
Albert E. Dien

A publication of the Institute of East Asian Studies, University of California, Berkeley. Although the institute is responsible for the selection and acceptance of manuscripts in this series, responsibility for the opinions expressed and for the accuracy of statements rests with their authors.

The China Research Monograph series is one of several publication series sponsored by the Institute of East Asian Studies in conjunction with its constituent units. The others include the Japan Research Monograph series, the Korea Research Monograph series, and the Research Papers and Policy Studies series.

Send correspondence and manuscripts to

Katherine Lawn Chouta, Managing Editor
Institute of East Asian Studies
1995 University Avenue, Suite 510H
Berkeley, CA 94720
ieaseditor@berkeley.edu

Library of Congress Cataloging-in-Publication Data

  Early Medieval Chinese Texts : a bibliographical guide / edited by Cynthia L. Chennault, Keith N. Knapp, Alan J. Berkowitz, Albert E. Dien.
    pages cm. — (China Research Monograph ; 71)
    Includes bibliographical references and index.
    ISBN 978-1-55729-109-7 (alk. paper)
    1. Chinese literature—221 B.C.–960 A.D.—Sources. 2. Chinese literature—Criticism, Textual. 3. China—Intellectual life—221 B.C.–960 A.D. I. Chennault, Cynthia Louise, editor of compilation. II. Knapp, Keith Nathaniel, editor of compilation. III. Berkowitz, Alan J., editor of compilation. IV. Dien, Albert E., editor of compilation.
  PL2284.5.E27 2014
  895.109′002—dc23   2014007573

Copyright © 2015 by the Regents of the University of California.
Printed in the United States of America.
All rights reserved.

Cover design by Mindy Chen.
Cover image: Traditionally attributed to Yan Liben, Chinese, about 600–673, *Northern Qi scholars collating classic texts* (detail), Chinese, Northern Song dynasty, 11th century, ink and color on silk, overall: 28.5 x 731.2 cm (11 1/4 x 287 7/8 in.), image: 27.5 x 114 cm (10 13/16 x 44 7/8 in.), Museum of Fine Arts, Boston, Denman Waldo Ross Collection, 31.123.

Contents

Introduction	ix
Chronology of Dynasties	xvii
Rulers and Reign Eras	xix

Texts

Bao Zhao ji 鮑照集—Su Jui-lung	1
Baopuzi 抱朴子—Matthew Wells	6
Bei Qi shu 北齊書—Kenneth Klein	13
Bei shi 北史—David Graff	18
Beitang shuchao 北堂書鈔—Damien Chaussende	24
Biqiuni zhuan 比丘尼傳—John Kieschnick	28
Bowu zhi 博物志—Roger Greatrex	32
Cao Zhi ji 曹植集—Qiulei Hu	39
Chen shu 陳書—Damien Chaussende	44
Chenggong Sui ji 成公綏集—Howard L. Goodman	48
Chuxue ji 初學記—Alexei Kamran Ditter	52
Diaoyu ji 琱玉集—Keith N. Knapp	58
Diwang shiji 帝王世紀—Monique Nagel-Angermann	62
Foguo ji 佛國記—Stuart H. Young	67
Fu Xuan ji 傅玄集—Kong Xurong	72
Gaoseng zhuan 高僧傳—John Kieschnick	76
Gaoshi zhuan 高士傳—Alan J. Berkowitz	81
Ge xianweng Zhouhou beijifang 葛仙翁肘後備急方—Fan Ka-wai	88
Guang Hongming ji 廣弘明集—Helwig Schmidt-Glintzer	95
Han Wei Liuchao baisanjia ji 漢魏六朝百三家集—Olga Lomová	98
He Chengtian ji 何承天集—Howard L. Goodman	102
He Xun ji 何遜集—Ping Wang	105

Hongming ji 弘明集—Helwig Schmidt-Glintzer	109
Hou Han shu 後漢書—Hans van Ess	112
Huanyuan ji 還冤記—Albert E. Dien	119
Huayang guo zhi 華陽國志—J. Michael Farmer	123
Jiankang shilu 建康實錄—Liu Shu-fen	131
Jin shu 晉書—Howard L. Goodman	136
Jing-Chu suishi ji 荊楚歲時記—Andrew Chittick	146
Jinlouzi 金樓子—Beatrice Spade	151
Kong Zhigui ji 孔稚珪集—Olga Lomová	158
Liang Jianwendi ji 梁簡文帝集—Xiaofei Tian	162
Liang shu 梁書—Damien Chaussende	167
Liang Wudi ji 梁武帝集—Xiaofei Tian	171
Liang Yuandi ji 梁元帝集—Xiaofei Tian	175
Liuzi 劉子—Lo Yuet Keung	179
Lu Ji ji 陸機集—Nicholas Morrow Williams	188
Lu Yun ji 陸雲集—Sujane Wu	193
Luoyang qielan ji 洛陽伽藍記—Victor Cunrui Xiong	198
Nan Qi shu 南齊書—William Gordon Crowell	202
Nan shi 南史—Mark Strange and Jakub Hruby	209
Niu Hong ji 牛弘集—Howard L. Goodman	217
Pan Yue ji 潘岳集—Nicholas Morrow Williams	220
Qieyun 切韻—Meow Hui Goh	225
Qimin yaoshu 齊民要術—Francesca Bray	232
Quan shanggu Sandai Qin Han Sanguo Liuchao wen 全上古三代秦漢三國六朝文—David R. Knechtges	242
Renwu zhi 人物志—Goh Kailing	245
Sanguo zhi 三國志—Robert Joe Cutter	250
Shanghan lun 傷寒論—Catherine Despeux	258
Shennong bencao jing 神農本草經—Catherine Despeux	264
Shenxian zhuan 神仙傳—Robert Ford Campany	269
Shi pin 詩品—John Timothy Wixted	275
Shiliuguo chunqiu 十六國春秋—David Brian Honey	289
Shishuo xinyu 世說新語—Qian Nanxiu	296
Shiyi ji 拾遺記—Lei Jin	302

Shu Xi ji 束皙集—Howard L. Goodman	306
Shuijing zhu 水經注—J. Henning Huesemann	311
Shuyi ji 述異記—Lily Xiao Hong Lee	318
Song shu 宋書—Andrew Chittick	320
Soushen ji 搜神記—Daniel Hsieh	324
Sui shu 隋書—Victor Cunrui Xiong	330
Sun Chuo ji 孫綽集—Zornica Kirkova	335
Taiping yulan 太平御覽—Johannes L. Kurz	342
Tao Yuanming ji 陶淵明集—Xiaofei Tian	347
Tong dian 通典—David Graff	355
Wang Shuhe Maijing 王叔和脈經—Catherine Despeux	362
Wei shu 魏書—Kenneth Klein	368
Wei Wendi ji 魏文帝集—Qiulei Hu	373
Wei Wudi ji 魏武帝集—Qiulei Hu	377
Wen xuan 文選—David R. Knechtges	381
Wenxin diaolong 文心雕龍—Antje Richter	389
Wu Jun ji 吳均集—Cynthia L. Chennault	401
Xiao Tong ji 蕭統集—Ping Wang	406
Xiaozi zhuan 孝子傳—Keith N. Knapp	409
Xie Huilian ji 謝惠連集—Olga Lomová	414
Xie Lingyun ji 謝靈運集—Wendy Swartz	418
Xie Tiao ji 謝朓集—Cynthia L. Chennault	422
Xu Gaoseng zhuan 續高僧傳—John Kieschnick	428
Xun Xu ji 荀勖集—Howard L. Goodman	432
Yanshi jiaxun 顏氏家訓—Albert E. Dien	436
Yezhong ji 鄴中記—Shing Müller	442
Ying Qu ji 應璩集—Pauline Lin	450
Yiwen leiju 藝文類聚—Jessey J. C. Choo	454
Yu Xin ji 庾信集—Albert E. Dien	465
Yuan Shu ji 袁淑集—Brigitta Lee	472
Yuefu shiji 樂府詩集—Joseph R. Allen	475
Yulin 語林—Lily Xiao Hong Lee	479
Yutai xinyong 玉臺新詠—Thomas Jansen	482
Yuzhu baodian 玉燭寶典—Ian Chapman	494

Zhang Hua ji 張華集—Howard L. Goodman	501
Zhang Rong ji 張融集—Olga Lomová	506
Zhou shu 周書—Scott Pearce	510
Zuo Si ji 左思集—Yue Zhang	514

Appendixes
- I: Cross-References to Alternate Titles — 519
- II: Common Literary Genres — 522
- III: Frequently Cited Sources and Collectanea — 524
- IV: Textual Transmission of the Standard Histories — 528
- V: Non-Western Periodical Titles — 536

Subject Index — 543

Introduction

The history of the Six Dynasties period, known also as early medieval China or the Northern and Southern Dynasties, has long been overshadowed by its contiguous Han and Tang dynasties and seen as the period of turmoil into which the Han descended and from which the Tang finally emerged. Some aspects of early medieval literature, art, thought, and religion have received due attention, but the overall perception has been encapsulated by the expression "Wu Hu luan Hua" 五胡亂華, "The Five Barbarians brought disorder to China." Yet a closer examination of the achievements during this eventful time reveals crucial developments across broad social, cultural, and political activities.

These accomplishments are revealed when one compares two surviving bibliographies, the first included in the *Han shu* (*juan* 30) and based on the work of Liu Xiang 劉向 (79–8 B.C.)[1] and his son Liu Xin 歆 (d. A.D. 23), and the second, the "Jingji zhi" 經籍志, which was compiled with other monographs from 641 to 656 to form the *Wudai shi zhi* 五代史志 and subsequently joined to the *Sui shu* (*juan* 32–35) as the bibliographic monograph of that history. The earlier bibliography lists 677 works while the later one lists 5,190 works, an increase that might be expected given the centuries that had elapsed between them, but the subsections into which the titles are divided, 38 as against 55, shows an expansion of horizons. We see that development most clearly in the field of history. The *Han shu* bibliography, whose contents were divided into six categories of subject matter, had classified historical writings merely as a subsection of the category "six arts" (*liu yi* 六藝), and recorded 11 titles of historical works in 45 *juan*. In the "Jingji zhi," which was likewise a six-part bibliography, history (*shi* 史) came to the fore as one of the major categories. Within the field's 13 subsections—including dynastic histories, local histories, family histories, records of officialdom's structure from the Han through Chen, biographies of exemplary individuals—there are 817 titles in 13,264 *juan*. This total is somewhat more than double the number of *juan* for the next most voluminous category, the collected writings of individual authors (*ji* 集).

Many writings from the Six Dynasties have not survived, but still there is enough of a corpus that a source guide should prove useful to those beginning their study of the period, to those already involved in its study but not acquainted with sources outside their own specializations, and to those who come to the

---

[1] Liu Xiang's dates have alternately been given as 77–6 B.C.

early medieval era from other periods in Chinese history. In recent years several reference works have been published, testifying to the increasing maturation of the field of Six Dynasties studies in the West. These include Albert E. Dien, *Six Dynasties Civilization* (New Haven, CT: Yale University Press, 2007); Victor Cunrui Xiong, *Historical Dictionary of Medieval China* (Lanham, MD: Scarecrow Press, 2009); *Ancient and Early Medieval Chinese Literature: A Reference Guide, Part One*, edited by David R. Knechtges and Taiping Chang (Leiden: Brill, 2010); *Classical Writers of the Pre-Tang Period*, edited by Curtis D. Smith as volume 358 in the series Dictionary of Literary Biography (Detroit: Gale, 2011), and *Early Medieval China: A Sourcebook*, edited by Wendy Swartz et al. (New York: Columbia University Press, 2014). For Daoist texts there is *The Taoist Canon: A Historical Companion to the Daozang*, edited by Kristopher Schipper and Franciscus Verellen (Chicago: University of Chicago Press, 2004). There are many such textual guides for the Buddhist Canon in a number of languages. However, there has been no one source guide about the authorship, contents, and history of texts that covers a wide spectrum of disciplines. For this reason, the decision was made at a meeting of the Early Medieval China Group in 2007 to compile such a guide, and the present editors were assigned to it.

Our task was greatly eased by *Early Chinese Texts: A Bibliographical Guide*, edited by Michael Loewe (Berkeley: The Society for the Study of Early China and the Institute of East Asian Studies, University of California, Berkeley, 1993), which in the first place suggested such a guide for the Six Dynasties, and which provided a model for us to emulate. There are differences in organization, to be sure, and certainly the level of excellence of the Loewe publication cannot be approached; we do wish to express our appreciation to Professor Loewe for showing us the way.

The ninety-three texts discussed in this volume were chosen in consultation with the list of works included in the Six Dynasties (Wei Jin Nanbeichao) portion of the *Chinese Ancient Texts Database* (CHANT) 漢達文庫, developed by the late professor D. C. Lau at the Research Centre for Chinese Ancient Texts, Institute of Chinese Studies, a division of The Chinese University of Hong Kong. We had hoped to represent the fullest spectrum possible of the important works and subjects of Six Dynasties texts. In some cases, however, when no one with the requisite familiarity with a text was available, the item was dropped. For still others, circumstances prevented the completion of the necessary contribution. Perhaps these missing texts can be included in a future supplement.

In a few cases, we included compilations of the post–Six Dynasties period that provide primary material for our period. The dynastic histories of the Six Dynasties commissioned by the Tang emperor Taizong (r. 626–649), the *Yuefu shiji* (Anthology of Music Bureau poetry) of Guo Maoqian (fl. 1084), and the *Xu Gaoseng zhuan* (Continuation of the Biographies of eminent monks) by Shi Daoxuan (596–667) are well-known examples. The *Jiankang shilu* (Veritable records of Jiankang), compiled circa 756, cites more than thirty pre-Tang and early Tang works that no longer survive. In the *Tong dian* (Comprehensive canons) by Du You (735–812), many essays in the section for rituals date from the Six Dynasties. Another encyclopedic work, the *Yiwen leiju* (Collection of literature arranged by categories), was conceived during the seventh century as an aid to composition but is now an indispensable resource for the collation of pre-Tang belletristic writings.

Our goal with this volume is to present information about the contents and transmission of specific texts. It is not a report on the current state of research in any particular field. To a certain degree, of course, the discussion of a text will have something to say about the wider aspects of scholarship that are involved, and the bibliographies that are included will certainly lead in that direction, but in an attempt to keep the volume within a reasonable size, the editors asked the contributors to concentrate on the texts and not the wider issues.

Organization of the entries

Entries are arranged alphabetically by their Chinese titles. If a work was issued under more than one title, other names by which it was known will be found in the essay's first paragraph or in the description of the work's history. The collected writings of individuals very often carried multiple titles. It seemed expedient to organize these by the author's surname and given name. We made an exception for the collections of emperors; we use the rubric of the dynasty's name followed by the ruler's posthumous title (*shihao* 謚號), since this form was predominately used during premodern times. Appendix I (Cross-References to Alternate Titles) gives variations of the titles of individual collections and other works. The cross-listing is for leading the reader to relevant information; it does not mean that works with different titles necessarily have identical contents.

As for the essays' contents, we asked the contributors to address certain topics in a prescribed order but recognized that a work's character or questions concerning it might call for departures from the model. Contributors were at liberty to add to the recommended topics and, naturally, to omit any that were not pertinent to the work. They sometimes found it practical to change the usual order of a topic's placement or to combine two topics under a single heading. In general, the entries are organized by the topical headings given next.

The INTRODUCTION provides an English translation of the title, the date of the work's compilation or the dates of its author, basic facts about the subject matter, and often a sketch of the author's life. There may be additional information in the introduction to situate the work's subject or special features in a historical or disciplinary frame. Especially where a focused elaboration is useful, the entry may organize the introductory information under separate headings such as AUTHORSHIP, AUTHENTICITY, DATING, and COMPILATION.

The CONTENTS section describes the structure of the work as it exists today, typically by identifying the kinds of materials contained within particular *juan* or other parts (including translations of the subdivisions' titles, if any). In descriptions of the contents of an individual's collected writings, most genres are identified by standard English translations of their names. Appendix II (Common Literary Genres) matches translated terms with Chinese characters and *pinyin*

xii   *Introduction*

romanization for the thirty genres of poetry and prose that were found by the editors to occur with most frequency. When a less common genre is mentioned, the character and *pinyin* are included in the entry. Three genres were so ubiquitous and generally recognized by the *pinyin* terms in studies of Chinese belles-lettres—the rhapsody (also called rhyme-prose), lyric poetry, and Music Bureau poetry—that we let these stand as *fu, shi,* and *yuefu,* respectively, when contributors referred to them as such. Appendix II is not a complete list of the types of compositions written during the Six Dynasties. For a comprehensive overview of early medieval genres that also encompasses earlier periods, readers should turn to the entry for the *Wen xuan* (Selections of refined literature) and, for prose alone, to the entry for the *Quan shanggu Sandai Qin Han Sanguo Liuchao wen* (Complete prose of high antiquity, the Three Dynasties, Qin, Han, Three Kingdoms, and Six Dynasties).

Next are SOURCES, and then TRANSMISSION AND EARLY HISTORY OF THE TEXT. These sections trace the text's history from its first appearance through later centuries of its reception, usually up to the early woodblock editions. Many but not all works underwent changes in their original form. A good number were reconstructed during the Song dynasty or later. A general trend was a reduction in the work's number of *juan,* yet the decrease did not always mean a loss of content. In the example of the *Huayang guo zhi* (Records of the south of Mount Hua), minor discrepancies in the records were probably due to different methods of counting the *juan.* Also, despite the work's being listed in the *Jiu Tan shu*'s bibliographic monograph as containing only three *juan,* a comparison with other bibliographies suggests that the number was a scribal error for thirteen. The *Huayang guo zhi*'s contents appear to have been relatively stable over time. On the contrary, the *Shanghan lun* (Treatise on cold pathogenic diseases) presents a complex case of revision. Some of its *juan* were removed at an early stage to form a new work, the *Jingui yaolüe.* There was also a third text, the *Jingui yuhan jing,* that recombined the original *juan,* at least in part. From an analysis of the surviving evidence, it can be deduced that the *Shanghan lun*'s initial version, which contained sixteen *juan,* had been organized according to therapeutic methods and the appropriate occasions to apply them, rather than the "six modalities of *yin* and *yang*" by which the six *juan* of the work now called the *Shanghan lun* are titled. All three of the differently titled works, which were revised under imperial auspices during the eleventh century, represent a part of the original text's contents.

Some of the materials upon which the contributors drew to describe a text's transmission were prefaces by the authors or later editors, comments about the work, passages quoted from it, and fragmentary manuscripts. Additionally, or in the absence of these kinds of evidence, the contributors referred to the bibliographic monographs of the dynastic histories, large-scale catalogs of books, encyclopedias, literary anthologies, and other compilations. To conserve space, the Chinese characters for resources repeatedly cited are not given in the entry proper. Upon their first occurrence in an entry, these are marked by an asterisk (e.g., *Chongwen zongmu*, Shi tong*, Wenguan cilin**) to indicate that the reader can find them in Appendix III (Frequently Cited Sources and Collectanea), which supplies the characters for titles and of authors or compilers, and also gives an example of a modern printing of each resource.

The section PRINCIPAL EDITIONS focuses on editions that are currently available. These range from single copies of woodblock and manuscript versions held in collections of rare books to ones that are in wide circulation because they were selected for a Qing or modern collectanea. For some entries, there is reason to note NEWLY DISCOVERED MANUSCRIPTS. The discussion of existing editions compares differences among them in respect to completeness and reliability. The survival of an early copy of the text often enters into judgments about an edition's authoritativeness. One of the few pre-Tang literary collections to have survived relatively intact is the *Tao Yuanming ji* (Collection of Tao Yuanming), for which four woodblock editions from the Southern Song survive, as well as a fifth printed during the Yuan that contains commentary by Song literati. By contrast, no consensus has been reached on which of two distinct editions of the *Shenxian zhuan* (Traditions of divine transcendents) more faithfully reflects the original. The *Shenxian zhuan* is known to have been lost during the Ming, and its reconstruction toward the end of that dynasty resulted in versions of disparate lengths and contents. The main difference in editions of another work by Ge Hong (ca. 283–343),[2] the *Baopuzi* (The master embracing the unhewn), is the variations in its subdivisions. Although the original work may not have survived in its entirety, no questions have been raised about the authenticity of the contents that have been transmitted. Readers today benefit from well-annotated collations of the *Baopuzi*'s "Inner Chapters" and "Outer Chapters" that were produced from the mid Qing on, as well as from extensive notes added by contemporary editors.

Thirteen of the dynastic histories are discussed in this volume: *Bei Qi shu*, *Bei shi*, *Chen shu*, *Hou Han shu*, *Jin shu*, *Liang shu*, *Nan Qi shu*, *Nan shi*, *Sanguo zhi*, *Song shu*, *Sui shu*, *Wei shu*, and *Zhou shu*. From the Song dynasty on, the histories were printed in groups—such as the "Seven Histories" sets printed during the first half of the twelfth century for the seven that fell within the Six Dynasties period. Over the centuries, revisions drew upon different sources, and a few private editions were added to those issued under state sponsorship. Appendix IV (Textual Transmission of the Standard Histories) presents an overview of the editions' sources and features, from the first woodblock printings through the punctuated and fully collated "Twenty-five Histories" published during the period 1959–1974 by Zhonghua shuju in Beijing.

Following the description of principal editions, TRADITIONAL ASSESSMENTS provides evaluative judgments about the work by premodern scholars. In some entries, annotated editions of the work or selections from it with notes, whether traditional or modern, are treated under the headings TEXTS WITH COMMENTARIES or COMMENTARIES AND NOTES WITHOUT THE COMPLETE TEXT.

SELECTED STUDIES provides a bibliography of modern scholarship about the work. Due to space limitations, this section prioritizes secondary literature that is

---

[2] Ge Hong's dates have alternately been given as 284–364.

cited earlier in the entry or research that bears directly on the topics discussed. The bibliography is not intended to be comprehensive. For the *Shishuo xinyu* (A new account of tales of the world), *Shi pin* (Poetry gradings), *Wenxin diaolong* (The literary mind and the carving of dragons), and various other groundbreaking works of the Six Dynasties, there may exist hundreds of valuable studies. The editors are grateful to the contributors of such entries for limiting their selection to only a few of the important readings. Appendix V (Non-Western Periodical Titles) lists in alphabetic order the romanized titles of the Chinese and Japanese journals cited in the volume, followed by the Chinese characters or *kana* for them. Characters for the names of modern non-Western publishers are not given in this appendix, nor are these given in the entry itself.

Lastly, the entry provides bibliographies of TRANSLATIONS of the work into English and other languages and, also, INDICES or other kinds of RESEARCH AIDS for the work.

Conventions

1. Any Chinese title that is not followed by characters in an entry but by the abbreviation "q.v." (*quod vide*) has its own entry in the volume, where the title's characters can be found.

2. As mentioned previously, any Chinese or Japanese title in an entry that is followed by an asterisk (*) is a resource listed in Appendix III (Frequently Cited Sources and Collectanea), where the characters for the title and name of the author or compiler can be found.

3. Citations of the standard histories are to the Zhonghua shuju edition (Beijing); the years of publication for individual titles are given in Appendix IV (Textual Transmission of the Standard Histories). It was not considered necessary to mark the histories with an asterisk when cited in an entry, nor to give the Chinese characters for their titles. Histories with entries of their own are marked with "q.v."

4. Chinese characters for personal names are given on each occurrence across the entries, unless these are supplied in Appendix III.

5. Chinese characters for the names of dynasties, reign eras, and the posthumous and personal names of emperors can be found in "Rulers and Reign Eras." This list also provides the year dates for reign eras.

6. The form of Chinese characters used throughout the volume is the full, traditional style and not the simplified, even for modern books and articles published in simplified characters. Japanese forms that differ from the Chinese are not necessarily observed in all Japanese titles. Romanization is in *pinyin*, not Wade-Giles. Japanese names and titles are in the modified Hepburn romanization system.

Acknowledgments

We wish to thank William Crowell for his helpful advice during the planning of this bibliographic project, and to thank Norman Harry Rothschild for his reading of the draft manuscript and thoughtful suggestions for revision. When it was time to proof the galley, the assistance of Eric R. I. Casanas was invaluable. Naturally, we are indebted as well to the contributors for their patience during the years it has taken to see *Early Medieval Chinese Texts* to completion. Lastly, we express our appreciation to Katherine Lawn Chouta and Keila Diehl, our editors at the Institute of East Asian Studies, University of California, Berkeley. We are most grateful for their care and diligence.

Cynthia L. Chennault

May 2015

Chronology of Dynasties

HAN

Former/Western Han (206 B.C.–A.D. 24)   Later/Eastern Han (25–220)

THREE KINGDOMS

Shu (221–263)   Wei (220–265)   Wu (220–280)

JIN

Western Jin (265–317)   Eastern Jin (318–420)

SIXTEEN STATES OF NORTH CHINA (304–439)

NORTHERN DYNASTIES AND SOUTHERN DYNASTIES

Northern Wei (386–534)

Eastern Wei (534–550)   Western Wei (535–557)   [Liu-]Song (420–479)
[Northern] Qi (550–577)   Northern Zhou (557–581)   [Southern] Qi (479–502)
                                                    Liang (502–557)
                                                    Chen (557–589)

SUI (581–618)

TANG (618–906)

FIVE DYNASTIES AND TEN STATES (907–960)

SONG

Northern Song (960–1126)   Southern Song (1127–1279)

JIN (1115–1235)

YUAN (1280–1368)

MING (1368–1644)

QING (1644–1911)

Rulers and Reign Eras

Only the emperors and eras mentioned in the entries are listed. The beginning of an emperor's rule is given here as the year of accession to the throne, which may differ from the year that the title of a new reign era (*nianhao* 年號) was declared. The name of the dynasty precedes the ruling family's surname; the posthumous temple name (*miaohao* 廟號) or memorial name (*shi* 謚) precedes the years of rulership and the personal name.

Han

Later/Eastern Han 後/東漢: Liu 劉
    Guangwudi 光武帝, r. 25–57; Xiu 秀
    [Xiao 孝] Shundi 順帝, r. 125–144; Bao 保
    [Xiao 孝] Xiandi 獻帝, r. 189–220; Xie 協
        era: Xingping 興平 (194–195)
        era: Jian'an 建安 (196–220)

Three Kingdoms

Wei 魏: Cao 曹
    Wudi 武帝, r. 190–220; Cao 操
    Wendi 文帝, r. 220–226; Pi 丕
        era: Huangchu 黃初 (220–226)
    Mingdi 明帝, r. 226–239; Rui 叡
        era: Taihe 太和 (227–233)
        era: Jingchu 景初 (237–239)
    Qi wang 齊王 (Shaodi 少帝), r. 239–254; Fang 芳
        era: Zhengshi 正始 (240–248)

Jin

Western Jin 西晉: Sima 司馬
    Wudi 武帝, r. 266–290; Yan 炎
        era: Taikang 泰康 (280–289)
Eastern Jin 東晉: Sima 司馬
    Yuandi 元帝, r. 318–323; Rui 睿

Sixteen States of North China

Later Zhao 後趙: Shi 石
    Gaozu 高祖, r. 319–333; Le 勒
    Taizu 太祖, r. 334–349; Hu 虎

Northern Dynasties

[Northern] Wei 北魏: Tuoba 拓跋
    Daowudi 道武帝, r. 377–409; Gui 珪
    Xianwendi 獻文帝, r. 466–470; Hong 弘
    Xiaowendi 孝文帝, r. 471–499; Hong 宏
        era: Taihe 太和 (477–499)
[Northern] Qi 北齊: Gao 高
    Wenxuandi 文宣帝, r. 550–559; Yang 洋
[Northern] Zhou 北周: Yuwen 宇文
    Wendi 文帝, b. 505–d. 556; Tai 泰

Southern Dynasties

[Liu-]Song [劉]宋: Liu 劉
    Shaodi 少帝, r. 422–424; Yifu 義符
    Wendi 文帝, r. 424–453; Yilong 義隆
        era: Yuanjia 元嘉 (424–453)
    Xiaowudi 孝文帝 (453–464); Jun 駿
        era: Daming 大明 (457–464)
    Qian Feidi 前廢帝, r. 464–465; Ziye 子業
[Southern] Qi 南齊: Xiao 蕭
    Gaodi 高帝, r. 479–482; Daocheng 道成
    Wudi 武帝, r. 482–493; Ze 賾
        era: Yongming 永明 (483–493)
    Mingdi 明帝, r. 494–498; Luan 鸞
    Donghun hou 東昏侯, r. 498–501; Baojuan 寶卷
Liang 梁: Xiao 蕭
    Wudi 武帝, r. 502–549; Yan 衍
    Jianwendi 簡文帝, r. 549–551; Gang 綱
    [Xiao 孝] Yuandi 元帝, r. 552–555; Yi 繹
Chen 陳: Chen 陳
    Wudi 武帝, r. 557–559; Baxian 霸先
    Houzhu 後主, r. 582–589; Shubao 叔寶
        era: Zhenming 禎明 (587–589)

Rulers and Reign Eras xxi

Sui

Sui 隋: Yang 楊
　Wendi 文帝, r. 581–604; Jian 堅
　Yangdi 煬帝, r. 604–617; Guang 廣
　Gongdi 恭帝, r. 617–618; You 侑

Tang

Tang 唐: Li 李
　Gaozu 高祖, r. 618–626; Yuan 淵
　Taizong 太宗, r. 626–649; Shimin 世民
　　era: Zhenguan 貞觀 (627–649)
　Wu Hou 武后 (Wu Zetian 武則天), r. 690–705; Zhao 曌
　Xuanzong 玄宗, r. 712–756; Longji 隆基
　　era: Tianbao 天寶 (742–756)

Five Dynasties and Ten States

Southern Tang 南唐 (937–975)

Song

Northern Song 北宋
　Taizu 太祖, r. 960–976
　　era: Kaibao 開寶 (968–976)
　Taizong 太宗, r. 976–997
　Zhenzong 真宗, r. 997–1022
　　era: Xianping 咸平 (998–1003)
　　era: Jingde 景德 (1004–1007)
　Renzong 仁宗, r. 1022–1063
　　era: Tiansheng 天聖 (1023–1031)
　Huizong 徽宗, r. 1100–1126
　　era: Daguan 大觀 (1107–1110)
Southern Song 南宋
　Gaozong 高宗, r. 1127–1162
　　era: Shaoxing 紹興 (1131–1162)
　Guangzong 光宗, r. 1189–1194
　　era: Shaoxi 紹熙 (1190–1194)
　Ningzong 寧宗, r. 1194–1224
　　era: Qingyuan 慶元 (1195–1200)

Yuan 元

era: Zhizheng 至正 (1341–1368)

Ming 明

era: Zhengde 正德 (1505–1521)
era: Longqing 隆慶 (1567–1572)
era: Wanli 萬曆 (1573–1620)
era: Chongzhen 崇禎 (1628–1644)

Qing 清

era: Qianlong 乾隆 (1736–1796)
era: Guangxu 光緒 (1875–1908)

Texts

Bao Zhao ji 鮑照集

Introduction

The collection of Bao Zhao, styled Mingyuan 明遠 (414–466?), is also known as *Bao Canjun ji* 鮑參軍集 (Collection of Military Adjutant Bao) and has additionally appeared as *Baoshi ji* 鮑氏集 and *Bao Mingyuan ji* 鮑明遠集. Bao was appointed to the position of military adjutant during the last stage of his career, and this title became attached to his works centuries later, during the Southern Song. Together with Xie Lingyun 謝靈運 (385–433) and Yan Yanzhi 顏延之 (384–456), he is known as one of the three great masters of poetry of the Yuanjia 元嘉 era (424–453). Although accomplished in other genres, Bao is especially famous for his *yuefu* poetry and parallel prose; he is considered one of the most important *yuefu* poets of the Southern Dynasties.

Hailing from a declining scholar-class family, Bao Zhao strove all his life for success in his career. Although some men of his time were able to overcome the disadvantage of a humble birth and rise to high office through clever political maneuvering or opportunities that presented themselves, Bao enjoyed neither fortuitous happenstance nor deftness with politics. He never managed to hold an office above the seventh rank. Liu Yiqing 劉義慶 (403–444), the Prince of Linchuan 臨川, most appreciated Bao's talent but met an untimely death at the age of forty-one. Throughout long service to Liu Jun 濬 (fl. 436–453), the Prince of Shixing 始興 and a son of Emperor Wen (407–453), Bao remained an "attendant gentleman" without promotion. Bao was fortunate to have left Liu Jun's establishment before 453, when the prince became involved with Liu Shao's 劭 (426–453) assassination of Wen. Other literati did not survive the political intrigues of this period.

Bao's literary talent later made him a target of the jealousy of Emperor Xiaowu (r. 453–464). After Xiaowu's death, Bao became entangled in a web of political machinations that began with the ascent to power of Liu Ziye 子業 (referred to posthumously as the "First Deposed Emperor"; r. 464–465). Bao was then serving as military adjutant under the Prince of Linhai 臨海, Liu Zixu 子頊 (d. 466), who was only a young child. Soon after the murder of Liu Ziye, Bao became implicated in a rebellion led by supporters of the Prince of Jin'an 晉安, Liu Zixun 子勛 (456–466). The uprising was quickly crushed, and two local commanders of Jingzhou 荊州 (modern Hubei), Song Jing 宋景 and Yao Jian 姚儉, took advantage of this turn of events to lay siege to the provincial center, Jiangling 江陵. During their raid, Bao and other clerks were killed. Bao could not have escaped execution since the rebellion was led not by the young princes but by their aides and administrators. These political ups and downs in Bao's life provide the background for many of his works.

Contents

Some twenty years after Bao's death, most of his works were lost or scattered. Xiao Changmao 蕭長懋 (458–493), Crown Prince Wenhui of the Southern Qi, ordered Yu Yan 虞炎 (fl. 483–493) to collect and compile them. The widely circulated *Bao Canjun ji* that was produced during the Ming dynasty was based upon a Southern Song edition titled *Baoshi ji* 鮑氏集. This is the earliest edition available and contains ten untitled *juan* whose contents are as follows:

1. Rhapsodies
2. Rhapsodies
3. *Yuefu* poems (each poem title is preceded by the word *dai* 代, "in place of")
4. Literary imitations
5. Miscellaneous lyric poems
6. Miscellaneous lyric poems
7. Miscellaneous lyric poems and contemporary *yuefu* poems of the categories *Wuge* 吳歌 (Wu songs) and *Xiqu* 西曲 (Western tunes)
8. Miscellaneous lyric poems and *yuefu* poems, among which the most famous is "Ni Xinglu nan" 擬行路難 (In imitation of "The wayfaring is hard")
9. Petitions, and proposals (*shu* 疏)
10. Eulogies, inscriptions, and miscellaneous prose works

There are only two *juan*, however, in the popular *Bao Canjun ji* compiled during the seventeenth century by Zhang Pu for inclusion in his *Han Wei Liuchao baisanjia ji*, q.v. The first *juan* includes all the rhapsodies and prose works, and the second contains both lyric and *yuefu* poems. There are two other Ming editions: the *Bao Canjun ji* in six *juan*, compiled by Zhang Xie (1574–1640), and the *Bao Mingyuan ji* in ten *juan*, by Wang Shixian 汪士賢 (Ming dynasty, dates unknown). The former is not available but the latter is identical to the Song edition (*Baoshi ji*) in its arrangement of the content.

The best edition to date and the one most widely used in academia is the *Bao Canjun ji zhu* 鮑參軍集注 (Annotated collection of Military Adjutant Bao), compiled and annotated by Qian Zhonglian 錢仲聯 (1908–2003), who continued the project of his grandfather Qian Zhenlun 振倫 (1816–1879) to annotate Bao's works. Probably because *Sui shu*, q.v., 35:1535, recorded that during the Liang dynasty there existed six *juan* of Bao Zhao's works, Qian used the same number for his edition, whose contents are organized by generic category as follows:

1. Rhapsodies; petitions, proposals
2. Official letters; personal letters; eulogies; inscriptions; essays
3. *Yuefu* poems
4. *Yuefu* poems
5. Lyric poems
6. Lyric poems

Authenticity and transmission of the text

Yu Yan's preface to his compilation during the Southern Qi of Bao's works states that only about half of Bao's poems could be recovered. *Sui shu* 35:1535 records a *Bao Canjun ji* in ten *juan* and mentions that there was a six-*juan* version in the Liang dynasty. *Jiu Tang shu* 47:2068, *Xin Tang shu* 60:1592, and *Song shi* 208:5329 all list a *Bao Zhao ji* in ten *juan*. There is no evidence, however, that any text was cited from the *Bao Zhao ji* or *Bao Canjun ji* before the Song. It seems that the text and its title became stabilized only in the Southern Song, since the *Bao Canjun ji* was cited as a book title in a poetic title found in *juan* 4 of the *Jianquan ji* 澗泉集 by Han Biao 韓 淲 (1159–1224).

Chongwen zongmu* 5:32a (751) records a *Bao Zhao ji* in one *juan* (*zhao* 照 was written as 昭 to avoid the name taboo of the empress Wu Zetian 武則天 [r. 690–705]). Both *Junzhai dushuzhi** (dated 1151), 819–820, and *Zhizhai shulu jieti**, compiled by Chen Zhensun 陳振孫 (fl. 1211–1249), 16:464, list the text as having ten *juan*. Later in the Yuan, *juan* 230 of Ma Duanlin's 馬端臨 (1254–1323) *Wenxian tongkao* 文獻通 考 lists a *Bao Canjun ji* in ten *juan*.

No scholars have doubted the authenticity of the *Bao Canjun ji*, though it is no longer identical to the original version from the Liang. The *Siku quanshu zongmu tiyao** points out that one of Bao's lines cited by Zhong Rong (ca. 468–518) in his *Shi pin*, q.v., is missing from the *Siku quanshu** edition in ten *juan* of the *Bao Canjun ji*: "Rizhong shichao man" 日中市朝滿 (At noon the market and the court are full). The *Siku quanshu* adopted the edition compiled by Zhu Yingdeng 朱應登 (1477–1526).

Principal editions

All modern editions derive from the Southern Song compilation that was titled *Baoshi ji*. The most accessible printing of this earliest text is that in the *Sibu congkan**. Qian Zhonglian's *Bao Canjun jizhu*, first published in 1957, is also based on the Song edition. Additionally, there are:

Baoshi ji. Ten *juan*. Collated by Mao Fuji 毛斧季 (1640–?). Taipei: Taiwan shangwu yinshu guan, 1967. Mao Fuji's edition is based mainly on the text that Zhu Yingdeng published in 1510.

Bao Mingyuan ji. Ten *juan*. Collated by Wang Shixian (Ming dynasty), proofread by Wang Fengzhou 王鳳洲 (Ming dynasty); postface of 1510; in *Han Wei Liuchao ershiyi mingjia ji** and reprinted in *Siku quanshu cunmu congshu bubian** 27:642–81 and 28:1–10.

Bao Canjun ji. Two *juan*. In *Han Wei Liuchao baisanjia ji*, q.v., compiled by Zhang Pu.

Bao Zhao ji. Two *juan*. In *Quan shanggu Sandai Qin Han Sanguo Liuchao wen*, q.v., "Quan Song wen," *juan* 46–47. Compiled by Yan Kejun.

Bao Zhao ji jiaobu 校補. One *juan*. Collated by Lu Wenchao 盧文弨 (1717–1796). *Congshu jicheng chubian**, vols. 61–70.

Modern complete and partial editions

Cao Minggang 曹明綱. *Tao Yuanming, Xie Lingyun, Bao Zhao shiwen xuanping* 陶淵明, 謝靈運, 鮑照詩文選評. Shanghai: Shanghai guji chubanshe, 2002.

Hu Dalei 胡大雷. *Xie Lingyun, Bao Zhao shixuan* 謝靈運鮑照詩選. Beijing: Zhonghua shuju, 2005.

Huang Jie 黃節 (1874–1935). *Bao Canjun shi zhu* 鮑參軍詩注. In *Huang Jie zhu Han Wei Liuchao shi liuzhong* 黃節注漢魏六朝詩六種. Beijing: Zhonghua shuju, 2008.

Qian Zhonglian. *Bao Canjun jizhu*. Shanghai: Shanghai gudian wenxue chubanshe, 1957; rpt., Zhonghua shuju, Shanghai bianji suo, 1958; Shanghai guji chubanshe, 1980. Although the annotator has identified almost all of the allusions in Bao's works, he does not attend to the interpretation of Bao's poetic diction and phrasing where it is most difficult for the reader.

Zhu Sixin 朱思信. *Bao Zhao shiwen xuanzhu yu yanjiu* 鮑照詩文選注與研究. Wulumuqi: Xinjiang daxue chubanshe, 1997.

Selected studies

Cao Daoheng 曹道衡. "Bao Zhao." In *Zhongguo lidai zhuming wenxuejia pingzhuan* 中國歷代著名文學家評傳, ed. Lü Huijuan 呂慧鵑, Liu Bo 劉波, and Lu Da 盧達, 459–82. Ji'nan: Shandong jiaoyu chubanshe, 1985.

———. "Lun Bao Zhao shige de jige wenti" 論鮑照詩歌的幾個問題. *Shehui kexue zhanxian* (1981.2): 270–86. Rpt., *Zhonggu wenxue shi lunwenji*, 211–41.

Chang, Sun Kang-i. "Bao Zhao: In Search of Expression." In *Six Dynasties Poetry*, 79–111. Princeton, NJ: Princeton University Press, 1986.

Chen Jingjie 陳敬介. *Jun yi Bao canjun: Nanchao Yuanjia sandajia zhi Bao Zhao shi yanjiu* 俊逸鮑參軍: 南朝元嘉三大家之鮑照詩研究. Taipei: Duce wenhua shiye youxian gongsi, 2000.

Chen Yixin 陳貽焮. "Bao Zhao he tade zuopin" 鮑照和他的作品. *Wenxue yichan*, supplement 1 (增刊一集) (1957): 182–90.

Ding Fulin 丁福林. *Bao Zhao nianpu* 鮑照年譜. Shanghai: Shanghai guji chubanshe, 2004.

Fujii Mamoru 藤井守. "Hō Shō no fu" 鮑照の賦. *Hiroshima daigaku bungakubu kiyō* 34 (1975): 230–44.

Knechtges, David R. "Pao Chao's 'Rhapsody on the Ruined City': Date and Circumstances of Composition." In *Qingzhu Rao Zongyi jiaoshou qishiwu sui lunwenji* 慶祝饒宗頤教授七十五歲論文集, ed. Zheng Huxin 鄭會欣, 319–29. Hong Kong: Chinese University of Hong Kong, 1993.

Kotzenberg, H. "Der Dichter Pao Chao (466): Unterschungen zu Leben und Werk." Ph.D. diss., Rheinische Friedrich-Wilhelms-Universitat zu Bonn, 1971.

Lin Wenyue 林文月. "Bao Zhao yu Xie Lingyun de shanshui shi" 鮑照與謝靈運的山水詩. *Wenxue pinglun* 2 (1980): 1–21.

Liu, Hsiang-fei. "The Hsing-ssu Mode in Six Dynasties Poetry: Changing Approaches to Imagistic Language." Ph.D. diss., Princeton University, 1988.

Su Jui-lung 蘇瑞隆. "Lun Liu-Song zhuwang dui Bao Zhao yuefu chuangzuo de yingxiang—yi qiyanti yu juejuti weizhu de tantao" 論劉宋諸王對鮑照樂府創作的影響—以七言體與絕句體為主的探討. *Hanxue yanjiu* (Taipei) 20.2 (2002): 141–63.

———. "Patrons' Influence on Bao Zhao's Poetry." In *Studies in Early Medieval Chinese Literature and Cultural History*, ed. Paul W. Kroll and David R. Knechtges, 303–29. Boulder: T'ang Studies Society, University of Colorado, 2003.

———. *Bao Zhao shiwen yanjiu* 鮑照詩文研究. Beijing: Zhonghua shuju, 2006.

Zhong Youmin 鍾優民. *Shehui shiren Bao Zhao* 社會詩人鮑照. Taipei: Wenjin chubanshe, 1994.

Translations

English

Chen, Robert Shanmu (陳山木). "A Study of Bao Zhao and His Poetry with Complete English Translation of His Poems." Ph.D. diss., University of British Columbia, 1989.

Frodsham, J. D., with the collaboration of Ch'eng Hsi. *An Anthology of Chinese Verse: Han Wei Chin and the Northern and Southern Dynasties*. London: Oxford University Press, 1967. Pp. 142–56.

Su, Jui-lung. "An Annotated English Translation of Bao Zhao's 'Letter to My Younger Sister upon Ascending the Bank of Thunder Lake'" 登大雷岸與妹書. *Renditions* 41 and 42 (1994): 18–24.

———. "Versatility within Tradition: A Study of the Literary Works of Bao Zhao (414?–466)." Ph.D. diss., University of Washington, 1994.

Japanese

Suzuki Toshio 鈴木敏雄. *Hō sangun shishū* 鮑参軍詩集. Tokyo: Hakuteisha, 2001.

Su Jui-lung

Baopuzi 抱朴子

Introduction

The *Baopuzi* (The master embracing the unhewn), by Ge Hong 葛洪 (ca. 283–343), is a seminal work of broad scope from the early medieval period that defies easy classification. Part religious apology, part social criticism, the text is also a major source for social commentary, literary criticism, medicine, popular culture, and religious practice from the early fourth century. The varied content of the *Baopuzi* reflects the biography of its author, whose life was divided between the social and political world of the literati on the one hand, and practices associated with the textual and religious traditions of the Jiangnan 江南 area, such as Great Clarity (*taiqing* 太清) Daoism, on the other. Ge was born in Jurong 句容 (near modern Nanjing) shortly after the Western Jin conquered the southern kingdom of Wu. He fought bandits and rebels in command of a regional militia around 304, and lived in semireclusion for a tumultuous decade during which Sima Rui (276–322) rose to power in the south and ultimately established the Eastern Jin in 318. Although Ge served the Eastern Jin court in an official capacity, he seems to have been equally dedicated to esoteric traditions for formulating elixirs of divine transcendence, transmitted in part through his family lineage. In his surviving writing, Ge often mentions his desire to live in total reclusion in pursuit of elixirs of transcendence; he would eventually retire from official life around 331 to pursue religious practice near Luofu Mountain (in Guangdong Province) before his death in 343.

Contents

The *Baopuzi* is divided into two distinct sections that cover different materials, and the majority of the bibliographical works mentioned herein regard these sections as two separate texts. In Ge's own words, the *Neipian* 內篇 (Inner chapters) is chiefly concerned with "Daoist" (道) topics such as immortality, transcendence, and elixirs, while the *Waipian* 外篇 (Outer chapters) discusses "Confucian" (儒) or literati topics such as the successes and hazards of political life. In reality, neither section fits neatly into any particular bibliographic category, and the text as a whole seems to imitate Qin-Han texts such as the *Huainanzi* 淮南子, which combines sweeping political and social theories with cosmological and religious speculation. The *Neipian*'s vigorous defense of religious transcendence through concocting and imbibing elixirs remains the single most important source for the texts and esoteric practices of the Jiangnan area during the late third and early fourth centuries. The *Waipian* is a sophisticated work of political, social, and literary commentary that draws freely from Han canonical texts but also bears the hallmarks of Ge's own historical context. The text continues to be a significant source of inspiration for modern scholarship in both Asia and the West.

The *Baopuzi neipian* is divided into twenty sections:

1.	Chang xuan 暢玄	Illustrating the abstruse
2.	Lun xian 論仙	On transcendent beings
3.	Dui su 對俗	Responding to popular conceptions
4.	Jin dan 金丹	The gold elixir
5.	Zhi li 至理	The utmost principle
6.	Wei zhi 微旨	The meaning of subtlety
7.	Sai nan 塞難	Countering objections
8.	Shi zhi 釋滯	Resolving hesitations
9.	Dao yi 道意	The meaning of the Way
10.	Ming ben 明本	Illuminating the root
11.	Xian yao 仙藥	Transcendent medicine
12.	Bian wen 辨問	Discerning questions
13.	Ji yan 極言	Ultimate speech
14.	Qin qiu 勤求	Seeking diligently
15.	Za ying 雜應	Miscellaneous responses
16.	Huang bai 黃白	Yellow and white
17.	Deng she 登涉	Climbing [mountains] and crossing [rivers]
18.	Di zhen 地真	Earthly perfected
19.	Xia lan 遐覽	Broad overview
20.	Qu huo 袪惑	Allaying doubts

The *Baopuzi waipian* is divided into fifty sections:

1.	Jia dun 嘉遯	Praise of eremitism
2.	Yi min 逸民	Recusants
3.	Xu xue 勗學	Encouraging study

4.	Chong jiao 崇教	Venerating the teachings
5.	Jun dao 君道	The Way of the ruler
6.	Chen jie 臣節	The integrity of the ministers
7.	Liang gui 良規	Good regulations
8.	Shi nan 時難	Averting difficulties at the right time
9.	Guan li 官理	The right order among the officials
10.	Wu zheng 務正	The correct [conduct] of affairs
11.	Gui xian 貴賢	Esteeming sages
12.	Ren neng 任能	Employing the capable
13.	Qin shi 欽士	Admiring scholars
14.	Yong xing 用刑	Using punishments
15.	Shen ju 審舉	Examining promotions
16.	Jiao ji 交際	Social intercourse
17.	Bei que 備闕	Precautions against deficiencies
18.	Zhuo cai 擢才	Promoting talents
19.	Ren ming 任命	Employing orders
20.	Ming shi 名實	Reputation and reality
21.	Qing jian 清鑒	The pure mirror
22.	Xing pin 行品	Categories of behavior
23.	Mi song 弭訟	Ending disputes
24.	Jiu jie 酒誡	Admonitions on alcohol
25.	Ji miu 疾謬	Detesting erroneous [practices]
26.	Ji huo 譏惑	Censuring confusion
27.	Ci jiao 刺驕	Criticizing pride
28.	Bai li 百里	One hundred *li*
29.	Jie shu 接疏	Accepting neglected [talent]
30.	Jun shi 鈞世	Equalizing generations
31.	Sheng fan 省煩	Decreasing vexations
32.	Shang bo 尚博	Valuing breadth of learning

33.	Han guo 漢過	The faults of Han
34.	Wu shi 吳失	The failings of Wu
35.	Shou qi 守㙷	Holding to destitution
36.	An pin 安貧	Peace in poverty
37.	Ren ming 仁明	Benevolence and brilliance
38.	Bo yu 博喻	Broad analogies
39.	Guang pi 廣譬	Comprehensive examples
40.	Ci yi 辭義	Style and content [of literature]
41.	Xun ben 循本	Following the root
42.	Ying chao 應嘲	Responding to derision
43.	Yu pi 喻蔽	Clarifying obscurities
44.	Bai jia 百家	The Hundred Schools
45.	Wen xing 文行	Cultivated behavior
46.	Zheng Guo 正郭	Correcting Guo
47.	Tan Ni 彈禰	Impeaching Ni
48.	Jie Bao (Jingyan) 詰鮑	Interrogating Bao
49.	Zhi zhi 知止	Knowing when to stop
	Qiong da 窮達	Failure and success
	Chong yan 重言	Grave speech
50.	Zi xu 自敘	Authorial postface

Authenticity and transmission of the text

Internal evidence from the *Baopuzi waipian* suggests that Ge Hong had completed a version of the text by 318, and scholars continue to debate whether he made later additions and revisions. The text underwent several reorganizations after Ge's time. His postface to the *Waipian* states that the *Neipian* consisted of twenty *juan* and the *Waipian* of fifty *juan*, while his official biography in *Jin shu*, q.v., 72:1912, states that the text consisted of 116 *pian*. Exactly how many *pian* constituted a *juan* is unclear in this instance, but regardless the official tally of sections was fairly elastic through time. *Jiu Tang shu* (47:2029, 2033) lists the *Neipian* as having twenty *juan* and the *Waipian* with fifty *juan*, while *Xin Tang shu* (59:1516, 1534) lists the *Neipian* as having ten *juan* and the *Waipian* as having twenty *juan*. *Chongwen zongmu** (1034–1038) 3:13a–b lists both sections together as having twenty *juan*. Two Ming bibliographies, the *Tianyi ge shumu* 天一閣書目 and the *Shishantang shumu* 世善堂書目, list the *Neipian* in twenty *juan* and the *Waipian* in ten *juan*.

Daoist compilations frequently included the whole *Baopuzi* or fragments of the text, perhaps as early as the Northern and Southern Dynasties period. The modern *Daozang* 道藏 (mid-fifteenth century) contains the *Waipian* (fasc. 871–873) in fifty *juan* and the *Neipian* in twenty (fasc. 868–870). Most early bibliographies list the two sections of the text in separate sections; thus, the *Neipian* is often listed under the heading for Daoist texts (道家類) while the *Waipian* is typically listed under the heading for miscellaneous texts (雜家類). Although editions appear to have varied with regards to the subdivisions of the work, no real challenge has been made to the overall authenticity of the *Baopuzi* as it exists today, although some have wondered whether the complete Jin text survives in its entirety.

Principal editions

The survival of older editions and the scholarly interest in collating, annotating, and editing the text in the early nineteenth century has resulted in several excellent modern editions. Besides the *Daozang* edition, a Song copy of the text still exists, preserved in the Liaoning provincial library. Modern editions of the *Baopuzi neipian* derive from the mid Qing and the editorial efforts of Sun Xingyan 孫星衍 (1753–1818), Fang Weitian 方維甸 (d. ca. 1819), and Gu Guangqi 顧廣圻 (1776–1835), who collated an authoritative edition of the *Neipian* around 1812 based on earlier texts, including the *Daozang* edition. Sun's preface to the *Baopuzi* was included in his *Pingjin guan congshu* 平津館叢書 edition, which would later be the basis of the *Sibu congkan** edition as well as the *Zhuzi jicheng* 諸子集成 edition.

A collated and edited version of the *Waipian* was produced through the efforts of the noted Qing scholar Yan Kejun 嚴可均 (1762–1843) under the patronage of Ji Chang 繼昌 around 1817. Yan also researched the *Neipian* and produced an *yi wen* 佚文 chapter for each section consisting of quotations and fragments not found in available editions.

In recent years, excellent critical editions have been produced in the People's Republic and in Taiwan. Wang Ming's annotated and edited *Baopuzi neipian* (1985) takes Sun Xingyan's edition as its basis, but the final text and extensive notes reflect his use of the preceding commentarial tradition and many different editions of the text. Wang's edition also includes Yan Kejun's *Neipian yiwen*, the *Neipian xu* 序, the *Waipian zixu* 自叙, Ge Hong's biography (*Jinshu Ge Hong zhuan* 晉書葛洪傳), and the prefaces of Sun Xingyan and Fang Weitian. Yang Mingzhao's edited and annotated *Baopuzi waipian* (1991) is similarly extensive, relying on many editions and providing copious notes. Yang concludes his edition with biographical sources for Ge Hong, bibliographic information for the *Baopuzi*, Yan Kejun's *Waipian yiwen*, several prefaces from previous editions including that of Yan, and a discussion concerning Ge's time line and biography. Chen Feilong's *Baopuzi neipian* (2001) and *Baopuzi waipian* (2002) are less extensive but notable for their annotation of

Ge's references to Han canonical texts, an informative and interesting translation into modern Chinese, and a well-researched *nianpu* 年譜 (chronology) of Ge.

Texts with commentaries and notes

Chen Feilong 陳飛龍, ed. *Baopuzi neipian jinzhu jinyi* 抱朴子內篇今註今譯. Taipei: Taiwan shangwu yinshuguan, 2001.

———. *Baopuzi waipian jinzhu jinyi* 抱朴子外篇今註今譯. Taipei: Taiwan shangwu yinshuguan, 2002.

Wang Ming 王明, ed. *Baopuzi neipian jiaoshi* 抱朴子內篇校釋. Beijing: Zhonghua shuju, 1996.

Yang Mingzhao 楊明照, ed. *Baopuzi waipian jiaojian* 抱朴子外篇校箋. 2 vols. Beijing: Zhonghua shuju, 1997.

Selected studies

Chen Feilong 陳飛龍. *Ge Hong zhi wenlun ji qi shengping* 葛洪之文論及其生平. Taipei: Wenshizhe chubanshe, 1980.

Hu Fuchen 胡孚琛. *Wei-Jin shenxian daojiao: Baopuzi neipian yanjiu* 魏晉神仙道教: 抱朴子內篇研究. Beijing: Xinhua, 1991.

Kojima Sukema 小島祐馬. "Hōbokushi to dōka shisō" 抱朴子と道家思想. *Shinagaku* 1.9 (1921): 697–708.

Lai, Chi-Tim. "Ko Hung's Discourse of *Hsien* Immortality: A Taoist Configuration of an Alternate Ideal Self-Identity." *Numen* 45 (1998): 183–220.

Lin Lixue 林麗雪. *Baopuzi nei wai pian sixiang xilun* 抱朴子內外篇思想析論. Taipei: Xuesheng shuju, 1980.

Needham, Joseph, ed. *Science and Civilisation in China*. Cambridge: Cambridge University Press, 1976. Vol. 5, part 3.

Poo, Mu-chou. "A Taste of Happiness: Contextualizing Elixirs in Baopuzi." In *Of Tripod and Palate: Food, Politics, and Religion in Traditional China*, ed. Roel Sterckx, 123–39. New York: Palgrave MacMillan, 2005.

Pregadio, Frabrizio. *Great Clarity: Daoism and Alchemy in Early Medieval China*. Stanford, CA: Stanford University Press, 2006.

Robinet, Isabelle. *Daoism: Growth of a Religion*. Trans. Phyllis Brooks. Stanford, CA: Stanford University Press, 1997.

Sivin, Nathan. "On the *Pao p'u tzu nei p'ian* and the Life of Ko Hung (283–343)." *Isis* 60.3 (Autumn 1969): 388–91.

Wang Liqi 王利器. *Ge Hong lun* 葛洪論. Taipei: Wunan tushu chubanshe, 1997.

Wells, Matthew. "Self as Historical Artifact: Ge Hong and Early Chinese Autobiography." *Early Medieval China* 9 (2003): 71–103.

———. *To Die and Not Decay: Autobiography and the Pursuit of Immortality in Early China*. Ann Arbor, MI: Association for Asian Studies, 2009.

Translations and partial translations

Western languages

Balázs, Etienne. Translation of a chapter from the *Waipian*. In *Chinese Civilization and Bureaucracy*, ed. Arthur F. Wright, 243–46. New Haven, CT: Yale University Press, 1964.

Che, Philippe. *La Voie des Divins Immortels, les chapitres discursifs du Baopuzi neipian*. Paris: Gallimard, 1999.

Davis, T. L., and Lu-Ch'iang Wu. "Ko Hung on the Gold Medicine and on the Yellow and the White." *Proceedings of the American Academy of Arts and Sciences* 70 (1935–1936): 221–64. Translates *Baopuzi neipian* chapters 4 and 16.

Davis, Tenney, and Guofu Chen. "The Inner Chapters of *Pao-p'u-tzu*." *Proceedings of the American Academy of Arts and Sciences* 74.10 (1941): 297–325.

Feifel, Eugene. "Pao P'u-tzu Nei-P'ien, Chapters I–III." *Monumenta Serica* 6 (1941): 113–211. Translates *Baopuzi neipian* chapters 1–3.

Pregadio, Fabrizio. *Ko Hung, le Medicine della Grande Purezza*. Rome: Edizioni Mediterranee, 1987.

Sailey, Jay. *The Master Who Embraces Simplicity: A Study of the Philosopher Ko Hung*. San Francisco: Chinese Materials Center, 1978.

Ware, James. *Alchemy, Medicine, and Religion in the China of A.D. 320*. Boston: MIT Press, 1966.

Japanese

Honda Wataru 本田済. *Hōbokushi* 抱朴子. Tokyo: Heibonsha, 1990.

Ishijima Yasutaka 石島快隆. *Hōbokushi* 抱朴子. Tokyo: Iwanami shoten, 1942.

Chinese

Chen Feilong 陳飛龍, ed. *Baopuzi neipian jinzhu jinyi* 抱朴子內篇今註今譯. Taipei: Taiwan shangwu yinshuguan, 2001.

———. *Baopuzi waipian jinzhu jinyi* 抱朴子外篇今註今譯. Taipei: Taiwan shangwu yinshuguan, 2002.

Li Zhonghua 李中華, ed. *Baopuzi* 抱朴子. 2 vols. Taipei: Sanmin shuju, 1996.

Index

This text is included in the Chinese Text Project (http://ctext.org/) with full-text search capability.

Matthew Wells

Bei Qi shu 北齊書

Introduction

The *Bei Qi shu* (History of the Northern Qi), compiled by Li Baiyao 李百藥 (565–648), is the record of the Northern Qi dynasty (550–577) from the founding of its predecessor state, the Eastern Wei (534–550), until its defeat by the Northern Zhou state in 577. Together with the Western Wei/Northern Zhou state, the Eastern Wei/Northern Qi state supplanted the Northern Wei state and contended for overall control of the north. The Eastern Wei/Northern Qi state was established in the northeast by Gao Huan 高歡 (d. 547) and his sons, who claimed to be ethnically Han but were more likely to have been Xianbei (see Holmgren, "Family Marriage and Political Power"), or even Kŏguryan (see Yan, "Gao Huan zuyuan tanwei").

The *Bei Qi shu* was commissioned and compiled under authorization of a Tang emperor but, due primarily to its parochial voice and tone, it was denounced soon after it was issued, as were several other dynastic histories of the regionally fragmented period that existed prior to the unification under the Sui state. The *Bei shi*, q.v., was commissioned in order to present a more balanced interpretation, drawing heavily and largely verbatim from the previous individual histories. As a result, the *Bei Qi shu* suffered from considerable neglect during its years as a manuscript and, in fact, came close to disappearing.

Contents

The *Bei Qi shu* consists of fifty *juan*, the first eight of which present the imperial annals (*di ji* 帝紀), the simple chronology of the regime, based on events during the successive rulers' lives and periods in power. *Juan* 1 through 3 relate the careers of Gao Huan and his eldest son, Cheng 澄, during the Eastern Wei period, and *juan* 4 through 8 cover those of Gao Yang 洋, Huan's second son and the founder of the Northern Qi, and his successors. The remaining forty-two *juan* consist fully of biographies of Northern Qi empresses (*juan* 9), princes (*juan* 10–14), and notable personages. Only two are devoted to single individuals, those for the atheist writer Xing Shao 邢邵 (*juan* 36) and for Wei Shou 魏收 (*juan* 37), best known for his authorship of the *Wei shu*, q.v. Other *juan* include biographies of descendants of rulers of the Northern Wei (*juan* 28 and 38), the Southern Liang (*juan* 33), and the Northern Yan and Xia (*juan* 40). There are also *juan* devoted to Confucians (*juan* 44), literary persons (*juan* 45), upright officials (*juan* 46), cruel officials (*juan* 47),

Northern Qi imperial in-laws (*juan* 48), astrologers and other diviners (*juan* 49), and court favorites (*juan* 50). In twelve of the *juan*, Li includes postscripts, which often provide valuable additional information or perspective.

Authorship

In 629, Tang Taizong (r. 627–649) commissioned Li to compile the history of the Northern Qi dynasty. During the Sui dynasty, several scholars had begun the work, most notably Li's father, Li Delin 李德林 (531–591), whose work was titled *Qi shu* 齊書. Others included Wang Shao's 王劭 *Qi zhi* 齊志 and Cui Zifa's 崔子發 *Qi ji* 齊紀. Li Baiyao used the foundation provided by these previous works, particularly that of his father, for his own project, which he completed in the year 636. Authorship is often attributed jointly to father and son.

Liu Zhiji (661–721), in his *Shi tong**, criticized Li Baiyao for neglecting the distinction between the annals—properly used for relating the narrative of major events—and the biographies, province of the smaller details of history (*Shi tong* 2:38). He also faulted Li for using such things as altered posthumous names, having bad judgment in what topics and events were worthy of emphasis (17:499), and his overly favorable treatment of Wei Shou, the author of the *Wei shu*, q.v. (7:198).

Transmission of the text

According to an analysis of the *Bei Qi shu*—or *Qi shu*, as it was originally called—by the Qing scholar Qian Daxin 錢大昕 (1728–1804), by the time of the first printing of the work, in the Song period, only eighteen of the original fifty *juan* had survived (*Nian'ershi kaoyi*, 2:1). By the twentieth century, historian Tang Changru 唐長孺 counted only seventeen (Xu and Liu, "*Bei Qi shu* jizhuan yinian lu," 14). Most of the rest of the history had been reimported from the *Bei shi*. Qian's contemporary Wang Mingsheng 王鳴盛 (1722–1798) pointed out that another source of the restored text was the *Gaoshi xiaoshi* 高氏小史, written by Tang writer Gao Jun 高峻 (*Shiqishi shangque, juan* 66) *in the ninth century*. Since the authors of the *Bei shi* had drawn directly from Li Baiyao's work for those sections dealing with the Northern Qi, changing only the voice and some terminology, the importation of these sections back into the reconstructed set produced a text that was likely close to the original. It cannot, however, be regarded as the full history compiled and completed by Li Baiyao.

The *juan* that have been fully transmitted, according to Qian Daxin, are the following: *juan* 4 (biography of Gao Yang), *juan* 13, *juan* 16–25, *juan* 41–45, and 50 (*Nian'ershi kaoyi*, 2:1), though this last now seems also to have come from the *Bei shi*.

Chao Gongwu's *Junzhai dushu zhi** (1151) 5:190 includes an entry for the *Bei Qi shu* (published as such to distinguish it more clearly from the *Nan Qi shu*, q.v., the history of the Southern Qi state), indicating that the first known printing of the work had been completed sometime in the early twelfth century. An edition of Chao's work, printed in 1250, has a note that parts of the history were already missing. The earliest surviving edition of the *Bei Qi shu* was printed in the Yuan and Ming period, relying on an extant imprint from the Southern Song. This printing is referred to as the Sanchao edition (三朝本). Two editions dating from the Ming dynasty's Wanli era (1573–1620), one printed in Nanjing—the Nan edition (南本)—and the other in Beijing—the Bei edition (北本)—have survived, as has another Ming edition printed by the Jiguge 汲古閣, known as the Ji edition (汲本). The edition printed at the Wuyingdian 武英殿 within the Imperial Palace (1739–1747) survives and is known as the Dian ben 殿本, or Palace edition. Another edition was printed in 1874 by the Jinling shuju and is referred to as the Ju edition 局本.

For an overall account of the textual history of this and the other Six Dynasties standard histories, see appendix IV (Textual Transmission of the Standard Histories).

Principal editions

The Commercial Press published an edition of the *Bei Qi shu*, the Baina edition (百衲本), between 1930 and 1937. The text up to *juan* 34 is a photolithographic reproduction of the Sanchao edition, while that from *juan* 34 through 50 consists of photolithographic reproductions of remnants of various Song editions.

Zhonghua shuju published a punctuated edition of the *Bei Qi shu* in 1973, based on a close comparison of the Baina edition with the various extant pre-1900 editions, but also with relevant parts of the *Taiping yulan*, q.v., *Cefu yuangui* 冊府元龜, *Bei shi*, *Zizhi tongjian* 資治通鑑, and *Tong zhi** (Xu and Liu, "*Bei Qi shu* jizhuan yinian lu," 58).

Electronic text versions of the *Bei Qi shu*, based on the Zhonghua shuju edition, can be accessed through various academic and commercial providers, including the Academia Sinica in Taiwan, and the China National Knowledge Infrastructure, or CNKI (Zhongguo zhishi jichu sheshi gongcheng 中國知識基礎設施工程), in China.

Early commentaries

Zhao Yi 趙翼 (1724–1814) wrote commentaries on several topics gleaned from the Bei Qi shu, noting in a couple of items comparisons with records in the Wei shu, Zhou shu, q.v., and Sui shu, q.v., but most of his comments were on specific issues he found in the Bei Qi shu itself (*Nian'ershi zhaji*, 287–335).

Selected studies and bibliography

Gardiner, Kenneth Herbert James. "Standard Histories, Han to Sui." In *Essays on the Sources for Chinese History*, ed. Donald D. Leslie, Colin Mackerras, and Wang Gungwu, 42–52. Canberra: Australian National University Press, ca. 1973.

Holmgren, Jennifer. "Family Marriage and Political Power in Sixth Century China: A Study of the Kao Family of Northern Ch'i, c. 520–550." *Journal of Asian History* 16.1 (1982): 1–50.

Li Yan 李研. "Zhonghua shuju ben *Bei Qi shu* jiaokan ji buzheng" 中華書局本北齊書校勘記補正. *Gudian wenxianxue yanjiu* (2009.6): 58–60.

Qian Daxin 錢大昕. *Nian'ershi kaoyi* 廿二史考異. Taipei: Dezhi chubanshe, 1963. *Juan* 31.

Wang Mingsheng 王鳴盛. *Shiqishi shangque* 十七史商榷. Taipei: Guangwen shuju, 1960. Vol. 3, *juan* 66.

Xu Fuqian 許福謙 and Liu Yong 劉勇. "*Bei Qi shu* jizhuan yinian lu" 北齊書紀傳疑年錄. *Shoudu shifan daxue xuebao, Shehui kexue ban* 126 (1991): 14–23.

Yan Hai 閻海. "Gao Huan zuyuan tanwei" 高歡族源探微. *Bowuguan yanjiu* 93 (2006.1): 23–7.

Yi Kyemyŏng 李啓命. "Pukcheso sanon ul t'onghiso bon Yi Paekyo ui yoksagwan" 北齊書史論을통해서본李百藥의歷史觀. *Chonnam sahak* 13 (1999.12): 59–92.

Zhao Yi 趙翼. *Nian'ershi zhaji* 廿二史札記. Taipei: Huashi chubanshe, 1977.

Zhou Wenying 周文英. *Bei Qi shu* 北齊書. In *Zhongguo shixue mingzhu pingjie* 中國史學名著評介, ed. Cang Xiuliang 倉修良, vol. 1, pp. 353–66. Ji'nan: Shandong jiaoyu chubanshe, 1990.

Zhu Qingru 朱清如. "Ping Liu Zhiji lun *Bei Qi shu*" 評劉知幾論北齊書. *Changde shifan xueyuan xuebao, Shehui kexue ban* 24.6 (1999): 48–50.

Translations

In addition to those listed in Hans H. Frankel, *Catalogue of Translations from the Chinese Dynastic Histories for the Period 220–960* (Berkeley: University of California Press, 1957), 118–20, there are the following.

English

Jamieson, John Charles. "The Biography of Wei Shou." Master's thesis, University of California, Berkeley, 1964. Translation of *juan* 37.

Dien, Albert E. *Pei Ch'i shu 45: Biography of Yen Chih-t'ui*. Bern: Herbert Lang, 1976. Translation of *juan* 45.

Japanese

Watabe Takeshi 渡部武. "*Hokuseisho* Gan Shisui den no 'Kan gasei fu'ni tsuite" 北斉書顔之推伝の観我生賦について. In *Chūgoku seishi no kisoteki kenkyū* 中国正史の基礎的研究, 181–97. Tokyo: Waseda daigaku shuppanbu, 1984.

Modern Chinese

Huang Yongnian 黄永年, trans. *Bei Qi shu xuanyi* 北齊書選譯. Chengdu: Ba Shu shushe, 1991.

Indices

Chen Zhongan 陳仲安, Tan Liangyi 譚兩宜, and Zhao Xiaoming 趙小鳴. *Beichao sishi renming suoyin* 北朝四史人名索引. 2 vols. Beijing: Zhonghua shuju, 1988.

Jian Xiuwei 簡修煒. *Beichao wushi cidian* 北朝五史辭典. 2 vols. Ji'nan: Shandong jiaoyu chubanshe, 2000.

Liang Qixiong 梁啓雄. *Niansishi zhuanmu yinde* 廿四史傳目引得. Shanghai: Zhonghua shuju, 1936.

Mao Huayang 毛華陽. *Ershiwushi jizhuan renming suoyin* 二十五史紀傳人名索引. Shanghai: Shanghai guji chubanshe, 1990.

Yang Jialuo 楊家駱. *Xinjiao ben Bei Qi shu, fu suoyin* 新校本北齊書, 附索引. Taipei: Dingwen shuju, 1980.

Zhang Chenshi 張忱石 and Wu Shuping 吳樹平. *Ershisishi renming suoyin* 二十四史人名索引. 2 vols. Beijing: Zhonghua shuju, 1990.

Kenneth Klein

Bei shi 北史

Introduction

The *Bei shi* (History of the Northern Dynasties) is a privately compiled work that relates the fortunes of the various regimes that held power in the north of China between 386 and 618, primarily the Northern Wei, its eastern and western successor states, and finally the Sui dynasty. A product of the first three Tang reigns, it was begun by Li Dashi 李大師 (572–628) and completed by his son Li Yanshou 延壽 (exact dates unknown). Although based in large part on earlier histories that are extant, it is nevertheless a valuable source for this period because it incorporates much material from works that have not survived.

Contents

Inspired by the *Wu Yue chunqiu* 吳越春秋 (Spring and autumn annals of Wu and Yue), Li Dashi adopted the chronicle (*bian nian* 編年) format when he began work on this project. This was later converted by Li Yanshou to the composite annal-biography form (*jizhuan ti* 紀傳體) pioneered by Sima Qian 司馬遷 (145?–86? B.C.) in the *Shi ji* 史記. Li's work also resembles the *Shi ji* in that it is not limited to a single dynasty. The *Bei shi* consists of 100 *juan*, with 12 *juan* of annals and 88 *juan* devoted to biographies. Although Li was a member of the team of official historians that compiled the *Wudai shi zhi* 五代史志 (Monographs for the histories of the Five Dynasties) eventually incorporated in the *Sui shu*, q.v., and had access to that material when he was completing his own book, the *Bei shi* does not include any monographs (*zhi* 志). The contents of the *Bei shi* are as follows:

Juan 1–5. Wei annals, including Eastern Wei and Western Wei

6–8. Northern Qi annals

9–10. Northern Zhou annals

11–12. Sui annals

13–14. Biographies of empresses and consorts

15–19. Biographies of the Wei royal family

20–50. Other Wei biographies

51–52. Biographies of the Northern Qi royal family

53–56. Other Northern Qi biographies

57–58. Biographies of the Northern Zhou royal family

59–70. Other Northern Zhou biographies

71. Biographies of the Sui royal family

72–79. Other Sui biographies

80. Biographies of royal affines (*waiqi* 外戚)

81–82. Biographies of Confucian scholars (*rulin* 儒林)

83. Biographies of literati (*wenyuan* 文苑)

84. Biographies of exemplars of filial conduct (*xiao xing* 孝行)

85. Biographies of exemplars of loyalty and righteousness (*jieyi* 節義)

86. Biographies of good officials (*xunli* 循吏)

87. Biographies of harsh officials (*kuli* 酷吏)

88. Biographies of recluses (*yinyi* 隱逸)

89–90. Biographies of diviners (*yishu* 藝術)

91. Biographies of famous women (*lienü* 列女)

92. Biographies of royal favorites (*enxing* 恩幸)

93. Accounts of lesser northern regimes: Xia, Yan, Later Qin, Northern Yan, Western Qin, Northern Liang, and Later Liang

94–99. Foreign states and peoples

100. Li Yanshou and his forebears

The apparently chronological sequencing of the majority of the biographical chapters in the scheme belies the fact that many of the individual biographies are arranged along genealogical lines, with individuals who lived in different periods grouped together on account of kinship. This principle, reflecting the familial ethos of the authors' time, reaches an extreme in the book's final chapter, containing biographies not only of Li Dashi and Li Yanshou, but also of their putative ancestors as far back as Qin and Han times.

Authorship

Li Yanshou and Li Dashi claimed membership in the Guzang 姑臧 branch of the illustrious Longxi 隴西 Li choronym, but the family's more immediate place of origin was Xiangzhou 相州, today's Anyang, Henan (for Li Dashi, see *Bei shi* 100:3341–43; for Li Yanshou, see *Bei shi* 100:3343–45 and *Jiu Tang shu* 73:2600–1 and 72A:2462). Li Dashi served the Sui dynasty as a member of the senior administrative staff in several prefectures, and when the Sui faltered he took office with one of the many contenders for the imperial mantle, the Hebei warlord Dou Jiande 竇建德. After falling into the hands of Dou's Tang rivals in 620, Li was exiled to the northwest (today's Gansu), where a chance friendship with the Tang Liangzhou 涼州 area commander Yang Gongren 楊恭仁, and access to Yang's well-stocked library, enabled him to begin working toward the realization of his long-cherished ambition to produce a universal history of the period of division that would transcend the biases and blind spots of the existing regionally focused histories. After his death in 628, the work was continued by his son Yanshou, who had the advantage of being first an assistant (*zhi guoshi* 直國史) and then a compiler (*xiu guoshi* 修國史) in the Historiography Institute (Shiguan 史館) during the reigns of Tang Taizong (r. 626–649) and Tang Gaozong (r. 649–683). Li Yanshou is known to have participated in the compilation of the *Jin shu*, q.v., and the monographs attached to the *Sui shu*, and he eventually rose to hold the substantive office of "court gentleman for the imperial seals" (rank 6b1) in the Chancellery concurrently with his historiographical position (*Xin Tangshu* 58:1456–57 and 102:3986; Zhang Rongfang, *Tangdai de shiguan yu shiguan*, 253). Although the exact date of Li's passing is unknown, it is certain that he died before 680 (*Jiu Tang shu* 5:105; *Tang huiyao* 36:657).

Composition

In composing the *Bei shi*, Li Yanshou borrowed heavily from earlier histories to which he had access, including not only works such as Wei Shou's *Wei shu*, q.v., but also the many official dynastic histories compiled during his own tenure in the Historiography Institute; in his autobiography in *juan* 100, he reports that he had to make his own manuscript copies of these books. Li did not, however, leave his sources unaltered. He made a point of excising the many memorials and other primary documents quoted at length in the earlier histories, so as to produce a much tighter narrative structure, and added new material gleaned from his reading of unofficial, miscellaneous histories (*zashi* 雜史) totaling—he claimed— more than one thousand *juan* (*Bei shi* 100:3344). Although Li inherited from his father a single project embracing both north and south, he eventually divided the work into two books, the *Bei shi* of 100 *juan* dealing with the north, and the *Nan shi*, q.v., of 80 *juan* dealing with the south. The two are sometimes given the collective appellation *History of the Southern and Northern Dynasties* (*Nanbei shi* 南北史).

Dating

The *Bei shi* was completed in 659, when Li Yanshou presented it to the throne together with the *Nan shi* (*Tang huiyao* 63:1092). Li's memorial presenting his two histories is appended to his autobiography at the end of the *Bei shi*. The *Nan shi* was, however, the first to be finished, and was submitted to Li's superior in the

Historiography Institute, Linghu Defen 令狐德棻 (583–666), for screening. Li claimed to have spent sixteen years working on the combined project; if we take 659 as the end date, he must have begun work in earnest around 643, the same year that he started to work on the *Wudai shi zhi* in his official capacity (Wang Shumin, *Shibu yaoji jieti*, 85; *Bei shi* 100:3343–45).

Transmission of the text

Although the *Bei shi* was not universally well received at first, to some extent because of the author's youth and low rank (*Xin Tangshu* 100:3986), it seems to have circulated widely in the Tang period. Gaozong himself favored it with a preface (no longer extant), and in the mid-eighth century the prominent scholar Liu Zhi 劉秩 suggested that it and the *Nan shi* be included in the curriculum for the *jinshi* 進士 examination (*Tang huiyao* 63:1092; *Tong dian*, q.v., 17:423). The *Bei shi* is listed in the *Chongwen zongmu**, 2:19b (166), and in the bibliographical monographs of both the *Jiu Tangshu*, 46:1990, and the *Xin Tangshu*, 58:1458. While the *Chongwen zongmu* (1034–1041) assigns it to the category of miscellaneous histories, the Tang histories considered it to be one of the standard histories (*zhengshi* 正史), a classification that continues to this day. Although fragments of a Northern Song printed edition are preserved in the Beijing Library, the earliest surviving edition of the *Bei shi* dates from the Dade 大德 era (1297–1307) of the Yuan dynasty. A photolithographic reprint of this edition was included in the Baina edition (百衲本) of the standard histories issued by the Shangwu yinshuguan (Commercial Press) in the 1930s, and this in turn provided the basis for the typeset, collated, and punctuated edition of the *Bei shi* published by Zhonghua shuju in 1974.

The text is not thought to have suffered serious damage in transmission, although it does appear that Li Yanshou's original annals for the emperor Sui Yangdi were lost and subsequently replaced with material borrowed wholesale from the corresponding annals in the *Sui shu* (Wang Shumin, *Shibu yaoji jieti*, 88; Yu Jiaxi, *Siku tiyao bianzheng*, 206–9).

For an overall account of the textual history of this and the other Six Dynasties standard histories, see appendix IV (Textual Transmission of the Standard Histories).

Principal editions

Bei shi, 100 *juan*. Xinzhou lu ruxue 信州路儒學 woodblock edition of Yuan Dade era (1297–1307). 32 *ce*. Shanghai: Shangwu yinshuguan photolithographic edition, 1935. Included in the series Baina ben Ershisi shi 百衲本二十四史 ["Hundred patches" edition of the twenty-four standard histories]. *Sibu congkan**.

Bei shi, 100 *juan*. Changshu, Jiangsu: Mao Jin 毛晉 Jiguge 汲古閣 woodblock edition of 1639, with supplement added in 1653. 24 *ce*.

Bei shi, 100 *juan*. Wuying dian ben 武英殿本 (Palace edition) of 1739. 6 vols. Taipei: Taiwan Zhonghua shuju photolithographic edition, 1965. *Sibu beiyao**.

Bei shi, 37 *juan*. Beijing: Beijing tushuguan chubanshe, 2003. 13 vols. published in the series Zhonghua zaizao shanben Tang Song bian, shibu 中華再造善本唐宋編, 史部 [Zhonghua reprints of rare Tang and Song editions, history section]; this is a photo-reprint of the surviving *juan* (13–49) of a Song woodblock edition in the Beijing Library.

Bei shi, 100 *juan*. 10 vols. Beijing: Zhonghua shuju, 1974. Typeset edition based on the Baina ben edition but collated with other editions; punctuated by Chen Zhongan 陳仲安.

Commentaries

Li Qing 李清 (1602–1683). *Nanbei shi hezhu* 南北史合注, 191 *juan*. Beijing: Quanguo tushuguan wenxian suowei fuzhi zhongxin, 1993. 4 vols. Photolithographic reproduction of a manuscript copy of the Qianlong period (1736–1796).

Lü Zuqian 呂祖謙 (1137–1181). *Donglai xiansheng Bei shi xiangjie* 東萊先生北史詳節, 28 *juan*. 6 vols. Shanxi buzhengsi 陝西布政司 edition of the Longqing period (1567–1572).

Shen Mingsun 沈名蓀 (*juren* 1690). *Bei shi shi xiao lu* 北史識小錄, 8 *juan*. 2 vols. Taipei: Taiwan shangwu yinshuguan, 1979. Photolithographic reproduction of the Wenyuange copy.

Selected studies

Gao Min 高敏. *Nanbei shi duosuo* 南北史掇瑣. Zhengzhou: Zhongzhou guji chubanshe, 2003.

Qu Lindong 瞿林東. *Nan shi he Bei shi* 南史和北史. Beijing: Renmin chubanshe, 1987.

Translations to modern Chinese

Diao Zhongming 刁忠明. *Bei shi xuanyi* 北史選譯. Chengdu: Ba Shu shushe, 1991.

Zhou Guolin 周國林, ed. *Bei shi* 北史. 4 vols. Shanghai: Hanyu da cidian chubanshe, 2004. Published in the series Ershisishi quan yi 二十四史全譯.

Translations to Western languages

Although there is no complete translation of the *Bei shi* into any Western language, several biographies, chapters, and substantial sections of chapters have been translated and published. These include the following.

The biography of Northern Wei Empress Wenming 文明, from *juan* 13, in A. G. Wenley, "The Grand Empress Dowager Wên Ming and the Northern Wei Necropolis at Fang Shan," *Freer Gallery of Art Occasional Papers* 1.1 (1947): 2–10.

The biography of Pei Ju 裴矩 from *juan* 38 in F. Jäger, "Leben und Werk des P'ei Kü," *Ostasiatische Zeitschrift* 9 (1920–1922): 87–107, 221–26.

The account of the Tujue 突厥 (Türks) from *juan* 99 in E. H. Parker, "The Early Turks," *The China Review* 24 (1900): 163–70; 25 (1901): 2–9, 69–76.

Numerous shorter excerpts have also been translated and published, many of them parallel passages from other standard histories. For a quite thorough list of work done before 1957, see Hans H. Frankel, *Catalogue of Translations from the Chinese Dynastic Histories for the Period 220–960*, Chinese Dynastic Histories Translations, supplement no. 1 (Berkeley: University of California Press, 1957): 156–70.

Indices

Chen Zhongan 陳仲安 et al., eds. *Beichao sishi renming suoyin* 北朝四史人名索引. 2 vols. Beijing: Zhonghua shuju, 1988.

Huang Huixian 黃惠賢, editor-in-chief. *Ershiwushi renming da cidian* 二十五史人名大辭典. 2 vols. Zhengzhou: Zhongzhou chubanshe, 1997.

Bibliography

Tang huiyao 唐會要. Comp. Wang Pu 王溥 (922–982), 961. Beijing: Zhonghua shuju, 1990.

Wang Shumin 王樹民. *Shibu yaoji jieti* 史部要籍解題, 84–88. Beijing: Zhonghua shuju, 1981.

Yu Jiaxi 余嘉錫. *Siku tiyao bianzheng* 四庫提要辨證, 201–9. Beijing: Kexue chubanshe, 1958.

Zhang Rongfang 張榮芳. *Tangdai de shiguan yu shiguan* 唐代的史館與史官. Taipei: Dong Wu daxue, 1984.

David Graff

Beitang shuchao 北堂書鈔

Introduction

The *Beitang shuchao* is the earliest encyclopedia (*leishu* 類書) that has survived as an integral work, though with some losses. It was compiled by Yu Shinan 虞世南 (558–638), who served the Sui dynasty as assistant in the Palace Library (*mishulang* 秘書郎). One of the buildings of the library was called the Northern Hall (Beitang 北堂); hence, the title of the book can be translated as *Excerpts from Books in the Northern Hall*.

Contents

The extant *Beitang shuchao* consists of 160 *juan* divided into 19 sections (*bu* 部), themselves subdivided into 850 categories (*lei* 類). A few examples of the subsection topics are listed next to give a sense of the scope:

1. Diwang 帝王 — Emperors and imperial princes (22 *juan*/75 categories): includes subsections on specific qualities such as "filial virtue" (*xiaode* 孝德) and "love for learning" (*haoxue* 好學)
2. Houfei 后妃 — Empresses and imperial consorts (4/26)
3. Zhengshu 政術 — Art of government (16/46)
4. Xingfa 刑法 — Punishment and law (3/13)
5. Fengjue 封爵 — Vasselage and ranks of nobility (3/14)
6. Sheguan 設官 — Institutions and official posts (31/182)
7. Liyi 禮儀 — Rites and ceremonials (15/42)
8. Yiwen 藝文 — Art and literature (10/56): includes subsections ranging from the classics to writing utensils
9. Yue 樂 — Music (8/29)
10. Wugong 武功 — Military forces (14/61)
11. Yiguan 衣冠 — Clothing (3/30)

12.	Yishi 儀飾	Instruments and ritual implements (2/15): includes subsections on water clocks and seals
13.	Fushi 服飾	Clothing and ornaments (5/86): includes subsections on screens and fans
14.	Zhou 舟	Ships (2/22)
15.	Che 車	Vehicles (3/25)
16.	Jiushi 酒食	Food and drinks (7/60)
17.	Tian 天	Celestial phenomena (4/25)
18.	Suishi 歲時	Calendar, seasons (4/28)
19.	Di 地	Terrestrial phenomena (4/16): with subsections on mud and sand

Sources

As the title suggests, the *Beitang shuchao* is fundamentally a collection of referenced and thematically arranged excerpts. Yu Shinan relied on more than eight hundred documents, from the most ancient (classics and pre-Han works) to quasi-contemporary books, such as the *Wei shu*, q.v., of Wei Shou (506–572). This encyclopedia is not generally useful to the researcher, but it is important as a depository of otherwise lost material and as an early example of an encyclopedia. It was rather clearly compiled with the intention of providing an aid to literary composition. Striking phrases culled from literature are arranged under appropriate sections and subsections, with an indication of source. In some cases, the original has been edited to make a better phrase.

Parts of encyclopedias having the same arrangement as the *Beitang shuchao* appear in some manuscripts found in Dunhuang (P2502, P3733, P5002, P3715).

Authenticity and transmission of the text

The *Beitang shuchao* has suffered much in the course of its transmission. The reason is that it was superseded by later encyclopedias, especially the *Taiping yulan*, q.v., compiled during the tenth century. The book is entered in the *Sui shu* bibliography as *Shuchao* 書鈔 in 174 *juan*, without the compiler's name (*Sui shu*, q.v., 34:1009; Kōzen and Kawai, *Zuisho keisekishi shōkō*, 557). It is cited with the complete title and the name of Yu Shinan in the bibliographies of the *Jiu Tang shu* (47:2046) and the *Xin Tang shu* (59:1563) as having 173 *juan*. The difference with the *Sui shu* may be the table of contents, one *juan* long, which may have not been counted in the *Jiu Tang shu* and *Xin Tang shu*. The *Chongwen zongmu** (1034–1041) 3:53b–54a (entered as *Shuchao* 書抄) also records it as having 173 *juan*, while the *Junzhai dushuzhi** (1151) 14:649 lists the work in 173 *juan* but specifies that the version in hand has only 120 *juan*. The *Beitang shuchao* is cited in the *Song shi* (compiled in 1345) in a 160-*juan* version (207:5293).

Principal editions

The earliest extant manuscript of the *Beitang shuchao* dates from the beginning of the Ming and was completed at the behest of Tao Zongyi 陶宗儀 (ca. 1316–1402). Based upon Song editions, this manuscript is conserved in the National Library of Beijing (Beijing tushuguan 北京圖書館).

The first printed edition is rather late and of poor quality. Chen Yumo 陳禹謨 (1548–1618), basing his edition on defective manuscripts, published it in 1600. During the eighteenth and nineteenth centuries, scholars felt the need for a more reliable edition of the *Beitang shuchao*. For this purpose, Sun Xingyan 孫星衍 (1753–1818), Yan Kejun 嚴可均 (1762–1843), and others collected many manuscripts, including Tao Zongyi's, from which they compiled a draft, but it was unfortunately not published during their lifetime. In 1888, Kong Guangtao 孔廣陶 (1832–1890) printed a movable-type edition based on that draft, adding further identifications and collational comments in notes introduced by the phrase *jin'an* 今案. This version is still the standard edition.

Texts with commentaries and notes

Siku quanshu*, reprinted in *Yingyin Wenyuange Siku quanshu** 889:1–907. Based on the Chen Yumo edition of the Ming.

Kong Guangtao edition of 1888; facsimile included in *Xuxiu Siku quanshu** 1212:46–650 and 1213:1–155. Reprinted also separately in facsimile by Wenhai chubanshe, Taipei, 1962.

Selected studies

Bauer, Wolfgang. "Encyclopedia in China." *Cahiers d'histoire mondiale* 9.3 (1966): 665–91, esp. 678.

Drège, Jean-Pierre. "Des ouvrages classés par catégories: Les encyclopédies chinoises." *Extrême-Orient, Extrême-Occident* 29 (2007): 19–38, esp. 25, 27.

Fang Shiduo 方師鐸. *Chuantong wenxue yu leishu zhi guanxi* 傳統文學與類書之關係. Taizhong: Donghai daxue, 1979. Pp. 199–212.

Hu Daojing 胡道靜. *Zhongguo gudai de leishu* 中國古代的類書. Beijing: Zhonghua shuju, 1982. Pp. 64–75.

Kaderas, Christoph. *Die Leishu der imperialen Bibliothek des Kaisers Qianlong (reg. 1736–1796)—Untersuchungen zur chinesischen Enzyklopädie*. Wiesbaden: Harassowitz, 1998. Pp. 60–63.

Kōzen Hiroshi 興膳宏 and Kawai Kōzō 川合康三. *Zuisho keisekishi shōkō* 隋書經籍志詳考. Tokyo: Kyūko shoin, 1995.

Lai Yuanhua 賴苑華. "Beitang shuchao yuebu yinshu chutan" 北堂書鈔樂部引書初探. *Leshan shifan xueyuan xuebao* 18.8 (2003): 137–40.

Qi Zhifen 戚志芬. *Zhongguo gudai de leishu, zhengshu yu congshu* 中國古代的類書, 政書與叢書. Taipei: Taiwan shangwu yinshuguan, 1994. Pp. 32–35.

Wang Jian 王鏗. "Shanjian xiangpin kao—Yi *Beitang shuchao* banben yiwen wei xiansuo" 山簡鄉品考—以北堂書鈔版本異文為線索. *Zhongguo shi yanjiu* (2005.3): 47–55, esp. 47–52.

Wang Sanqing 王三慶, ed. *Dunhuang leishu yanjiu* 敦煌類書研究. Taipei: Liwen wenhua shiye gongsi, 1993. Pp. 111–15, 463–97, 863–73.

Wu Shuping 吳樹平. "Cao Yin cangben *Beitang shuchao* shulüe" 曹寅藏本北堂書鈔述略. *Wenwu* (1984.7): 56–63.

———. "Jiang Guangyu cangben *Beitang shuchao* jilüe" 蔣光煦藏本北堂書鈔記略. *Zhonghua wenshi luncong* (1984.3): 127–43.

———. "Lu Yanchun cangben *Beitang shuchao* shulüe" 路衍淳藏本北堂書鈔述略. *Xuelin manlu* (1985.5–10): 149–61.

Zhu Taiyan 朱太岩. "*Beitang shuchao* xiaokao" 北堂書鈔小考. *Gansu shida xuebao, Zhexue shehui kexue* (1981.1): 29–37.

Index

Yamada Hideo 山田英雄. *Beitang shuchao yinshu suoyin* 北堂書鈔引書索引. Taipei: Wenhai chubanshe, 1975. A listing of the titles of books cited in the *Beitang shuchao*, with page references to the 1888 edition. At the back there is a list of the first characters of the book titles by stroke order, which serves as a finding list. This index would be useful primarily for someone collating the text of a book or seeking surviving passages from a work no longer extant.

Damien Chaussende

Biqiuni zhuan 比丘尼傳

Introduction

The *Biqiuni zhuan* (Biographies of *bikṣuni*), attributed to Shi Baochang 釋寶唱 (ca. 495–528), is a collection of sixty-five biographies of Buddhist nuns who lived between the early fourth century and the early sixth. Early bibliographies mention other collections of nuns' biographies for the period but none of these survives, making the *Biqiuni zhuan* the principal source for information about Buddhist nuns for the Six Dynasties period. The *Biqiuni zhuan* is, moreover, the main source for information about the first ordinations of women in China, a topic of great historical and contemporary significance, as the line of ordained women was long ago broken in Buddhist traditions in South Asia and in Tibet (Heirman, "Chinese Nuns," 2001).

The *Biqiuni zhuan*, though much shorter than the *Gaoseng zhuan*, q.v., is also a key source for information on monasticism, Buddhist practice, and the history of women during the Six Dynasties. Unlike the *Gaoseng zhuan*, the *Biqiuni zhuan* was not imitated by later authors. Despite the continued success and expansion of the monastic order for women in China, aside from the *Biqiuni zhuan*, biographical information about nuns before modern times is relatively scarce.

Contents

The text begins with a brief preface in which the author asserts the value of preserving records of worthy nuns who might serve as models for others and notes the sources he drew upon in compiling his history. After the preface, the biographies are arranged in chronological order and grouped according to dynasty. In a few instances, the biographies are supplemented with comments by the compiler, noting discrepancies in place-names or dates.

Authorship

From the eighth century on, the *Biqiuni zhuan* has been attributed to Baochang. The thirteenth-century *Shishi jigulüe* 釋氏稽古略 even confidently dates the text to 517, the sixteenth year of the Tianjian era of the Liang. Modern scholarship, however, has cast doubt on this attribution. The *Biqiuni zhuan* is not listed in early Buddhist bibliographies; it is only with the *Kaiyuan Shijiao lu* 開元釋教錄, compiled in 730, that the text is mentioned and attributed to Baochang. Nor is any mention of the

Biqiuni zhuan made in Daoxuan's 道宣 seventh-century biography of Baochang in the *Xu Gaoseng zhuan*, q.v. All of this has led some to suggest that it may not in fact be the work of Baochang (see De Rauw, "Baochang"; Tso, "Biqiu Shi Baochang shifou *Biqiuni zhuan* xuanren de yiwen"; Suzuki, "Shaku Hōshō Bikuniden ni kansuru gigi"). Kathryn Tsai, pointing out that part of the biography of the nun Feng overlaps with a surviving fragment of another of Baochang's works, the *Mingseng zhuan* 名僧傳, argues for the traditional attribution of the text to Baochang (*Lives of the Nuns*, 107). De Rauw in turn argues that the overlap between the *Mingseng zhuan* and the *Biqiuni zhuan* does not prove that they are works of the same author; the *Biqiuni zhuan* biography may have been based on the *Mingseng zhuan* account. Commentary by the compiler at a few points in the *Biqiuni zhuan* places the compiler at roughly the same time as Baochang, lending support to either the argument that Baochang was the compiler or, as De Rauw suggests, the argument that it may have been compiled by a disciple of Baochang.

The most thorough assessment of the authorship of the text is by Suzuki Keizō, who, in addition to noting the absence of the *Biqiuni zhuan* in early bibliographies, also examines subtle differences in language between the *Biqiuni zhuan* and surviving fragments of Baochang's *Mingseng zhuan*, as well as differences between the *Biqiuni zhuan* and works compiled by Baochang's teacher, Sengyou 僧祐 (445–518). All of this leads Suzuki to suggest that the *Biqiuni zhuan* was compiled some time after Baochang's death. In sum, the evidence for authorship is inconclusive. It is reasonable to assume that the *Biqiuni zhuan* was compiled in the sixth century, but Baochang's authorship of the text and its precise date of completion remain in dispute.

Most of what we know of Baochang derives from his biography in the *Xu Gaoseng zhuan*. He was a disciple of the prominent monk Sengyou, participated in several translation projects, and compiled a number of works including a commentary to the Nirvana Sutra and a catalog of Buddhist scriptures, fragments of which survive as quotations in later works. Aside from the *Biqiuni zhuan*, his only work to survive intact is the *Jinglü yixiang* 經律異相 (*Taishō shinshū Daizōkyō**, vol. 53, no. 2121), a collection of stories extracted from Buddhist scriptures. He is most famous for his *Mingseng zhuan*, a collection of biographies of monks that was influential in the composition of Huijiao's *Gaoseng zhuan*, but, except for a fragment (*Myōsōden chō* 名僧傳抄, in *Shinsan Dainihon zokuzōkyō* 新纂大日本續藏經 [Tokyo: Kokusho kankōkai, 1975–1989], vol. 77, no. 1523), the *Mingseng zhuan* is lost.

Composition

As with the collections of biographies of monks, the sources for the biographies of nuns appear to have been primarily previous collections of miracle tales, stele inscriptions, and some oral accounts collected by the compiler. Most of these sources are no longer extant, but some of the miracle tales that seem to have been the sources for some of the biographies survive in later quotations (Tsai, *Lives of the Nuns*, 108–9).

Transmission of the text

First mentioned in the *Kaiyuan Shijiao lu* in approximately 730, the *Biqiuni zhuan* was then entered into the Buddhist Canon and henceforth widely distributed both independently and as a part of the canon. Most references to the text in subsequent bibliographies list it as containing four *juan*, but some also refer to three- and five-*juan* versions. Wang Rutong has shown that these in fact refer to the same content, divided differently (*Biqiuni zhuan jiaozhu*, 2–7).

Principal editions

Modern editions of the *Biqiuni zhuan* for the most part derive from the Jin dynasty's Zhaocheng 趙城 edition (1139–1172) or the Korean edition (1236–1251) of the Buddhist Canon. The *Zhonghua dazang jing* 中華大藏經 edition (Beijing: 1984–), for instance, is based on the Zhaocheng, while the most commonly cited edition, the *Taishō shinshū Daizōkyō*, vol. 50, no. 2063, is based on the Korean printing, with annotation of discrepancies with some other editions. The *Taishō* edition is widely available in printed and digital forms and was the basis for the two English translations of the text listed herein.

Modern critical edition

Wang Rutong 王孺童, ed. *Biqiuni zhuan jiaozhu* 比丘尼傳校註. Beijing: Zhonghua shuju, 2006. The text is based on the *Taishō* edition, with annotation offering comparison with several other editions and an introduction containing analysis of the authorship and history of the text.

Selected studies

De Rauw, Tom. "Baochang: Sixth-Century Biographer of Buddhist Monks…and Nuns?" *Journal of the American Oriental Society* 125.2 (2005): 203–18.

Heirman, Ann. "Chinese Nuns and Their Ordination in Fifth Century China." *Journal of the International Association of Buddhist Studies* 24.2 (2001): 275–304.

Suzuki Keizō 鈴木啟造. "Shaku Hōshō Bikuniden ni kansuru gigi" 釋寶唱撰比丘尼傳に関する疑義. *Shikan* 89 (1973): 48–59.

Tso Sze-Bong (Cao Shibang) 曹仕邦. "Biqiu Shi Baochang shifou *Biqiuni zhuan* xuanren de yiwen" 比丘釋寶唱是否比丘尼傳撰人的疑問. In *Fojiao sixiang de chuancheng yu fazhan—Yinshun daoshi jiuzhi huadan zhushou wenji* 佛教思想的傳承與發展—印順導師九秩華誕祝壽文集, ed. Shi Hengqing 釋恆清. Taipei: Dongda tushu gongsi, 1995. Pp. 455–66.

Wu Jifei 吳季霏. "*Biqiuni zhuan* yanjiu" 比丘尼傳研究. *Faguang xuetan* 4 (2000): 105–23.

English translations

Li, Rongxi. *Biographies of Nuns*. In *Lives of Great Monks and Nuns*, vol. 76 of the BDK English Tripitaka. Berkeley, CA: Numata Center for Buddhist Translation and Research, 2002.

Tsai, Kathryn Ann. *Lives of the Nuns: Biographies of Chinese Buddhist Nuns from the Fourth to Sixth Centuries*. Honolulu: University of Hawai'i Press, 1994. In addition to the translation, appendices provide useful information on the authorship of and sources for the text.

John Kieschnick

Bowu zhi 博物志

Introduction

The *Bowu zhi* (Treatise on manifold topics) by Zhang Hua 張華 (232–300) is an enigmatic work, widely regarded as one of the earliest examples of *zhiguai xiaoshuo* 志怪小說 (stories of anomalies). However, on close examination, the work reveals itself to be a compilation of predominantly unattributed quotations, of varying length and regarding diverse topics, drawn from Han dynasty and third-century writings. The subjects of the quotations include geographical information, natural history, pharmaceutical substances and their uses, folklore, local and anecdotal history, prognostications, dreams, memorials, and inscriptions, among others. All in all, the book is a treasure trove of early medieval information. As noted by Dudbridge (*Religious Experience and Lay Society in T'ang China*, 32n57), the book's title echoes a remark, recorded in the *Zuozhuan* 左傳, that was made in 531 B.C. by an ailing Marquis of Jin (晉侯). Having heard a lengthy and profoundly erudite answer given by Gongsun Qiao 公孫僑 (d. 522 B.C.), also known as Zichan 子產, regarding the nature of his ailment, the marquis exclaimed, "You are a gentleman [knowledgeable in] manifold topics!" (博物君子也), and generously rewarded him.

Authorship

The author Zhang Hua, styled Maoxian 茂先, was born in Fangcheng 方城 in Fanyang 范陽 commandery, which lay 50 kilometers south of the modern Beijing. He began his official career in 253 and rose eventually to the position of minister of works (*sikong* 司空). Embroiled in the political struggle that engulfed the last decade of the third century, Zhang Hua and almost his entire family were executed on order of Sima Lun 司馬倫 (d. 301). Later generations regarded Zhang Hua as remarkably erudite; they honored him as the patron of such great literary talents as Chen Shou 陳壽 (233–297), author of the *Sanguo zhi*, q.v., Zuo Si 左思 (d. 306), author of the *Sandu fu* 三都賦, Lu Ji 陸機 (261–303), and Lu Yun 陸雲 (262–303). In addition to amassing a prodigious library himself, in 270 Zhang Hua was appointed Secretariat director (*zhongshuling* 中書令) and undertook, as a subordinate of Xun Xu 荀勖 (ca. 231–289), the reorganization of the imperial library, according to the system proposed by Liu Xiang 劉向 (57–6 B.C.). The library's catalog titled *Xinbu* 新簿 listed 1,885 books in a total of 29,935 *juan*.

Zheng Qiao 鄭樵 (1104–1162) expressed his opinion that Zhang Hua was so erudite because he had access to Han dynasty illustrated texts. Referring to a passage from the *Jinyang qiu* 晉陽秋 by Sun Sheng 孫盛 (302–373) that tells how accurately Zhang Hua described Jianzhang Palace (Mather, *Shih-shuo hsin-yü*, 42), Zheng wrote, "If Zhang Hua had not seen such illustrated texts, even if he had read every book written during the Han, he would not have been able to know the layout of the imperial chambers of former dynasties." Whether Zhang actually perused illustrated texts is not verifiable, but it seems at least that, when working together with Xun, he had the opportunity to read much of what was written during the Han dynasty. Furthermore, we can be certain that Zhang did have access to the vast imperially commissioned encyclopedia the *Huanglan* 皇覽 (Imperial readings), compiled by Liu Shao 劉劭 and others, completed in 222, since he includes passages from this work in the *Bowu zhi*.

Authenticity of the text

The original book appears to have been lost at an early date; the received text is in a corrupt state. Furthermore, more than two hundred passages attributed to the *Bowu zhi* are found in works from the fifth century onward, but they are not found within the present edition itself. This has led to the often-repeated opinion that the *Bowu zhi* as it exists today is a reconstruction and that it may suffer from later interpolations. Unlike texts presently available more or less in their original formats, the *Bowu zhi* does not therefore invite further study of its structure, content, style, or language. Consequently, neither premodern annotated nor commentated versions of the work exist. Modern scholarly interest has focused on problems of authenticity, identifying the sources of the text's passages, and placing the work in its contemporary intellectual context.

A few decades after Zhang Hua's death, a story concerning the composition of the *Bowu zhi* began to circulate. Wang Jia 王嘉 (d. ca. 386), in his *Shiyi ji*, q.v. (Beijing: Zhonghua shuju, 1981, 9:210–11), wrote that the original *Bowu zhi* was four hundred *juan*, but that Zhang was ordered by the emperor to reduce it in size and edit what remained into ten *juan*. Despite the dismissal of the *Shiyi ji* as a historical source by such later scholars as Wang Yinglin (1223–1296) and Hu Yinglin (1551–1602), the story that the original *Bowu zhi* was of vast size became accepted (*Kunxue jiwen* 困學紀聞 10:6a, and *Sibu zhengwei* 四部正偽 in *Shaoshi shanfang bicong* 32:318). It is repeated, for example, by Yin Wengui (*jinshi* 898) in his *Jinxiu wanhuagu qianji* (20:10b). The opinion was long-lived. When Zhu Guozhen (*jinshi* 1589, d. 1632) bewailed the fact that the *Yijian zhi* 夷監志 by Hong Mai 洪邁 (1123–1202) was originally in 420 *juan*, but that the edition that he had in hand was only 51 *juan* in length, he added, "It is just like the *Bowu zhi*, of which there remains only ten *juan*. How lamentable!" (*Yongchuang xiaopin* 18:7b; p. 2018.) Eventually, the whole story of the early history of the *Bowu zhi* was ridiculed by Yao Jiheng (1647–at least 1715), who wrote, "This book is shallow and not at all worth reading. It definitely is not Zhang Hua's original work, and Yin's statements were just an attempt to adorn this work's wretchedness. Anyway, how could any man living during the Wei-Jin period ever compose a work in four hundred chapters, and what criteria could he use to select ten *juan* from four hundred?" (*Gujin weishu kao*, 30). Despite this and other similar criticisms, notably by the editors of the late-eighteenth-century imperial collection *Siku quanshu* (*Siku quanshu zongmu tiyao** 142:2959–61; see also Yu Jiaxi, *Siku tiyao bianzheng*, 1154–58), the *Bowu zhi* has been widely drawn upon as a reliable source over the centuries and continues to be quoted in modern times. And when we consider that Zhang clearly had access to the *Huanglan*, an encyclopedia that consisted of more than one thousand sections and contained more than eight million Chinese characters (*Sanguo zhi* 2:88, and *Weilüe* 魏略 at *Sanguo zhi* 23:664), the impossibility of his producing a work in four hundred chapters cannot be taken for granted, and the size of the original *Bowu zhi* must remain a point of uncertainty.

Transmission of the text

The earliest mention of the *Bowu zhi* in the contents of a work is in the *Zichao* 子鈔 compiled by Yu Zhongrong 庾仲容 (476–549). This work itself is found in Gao Sisun's (1160–1220) *Zilüe* 子略 (1.15a–18b, esp. 18b; p. 46). The *Bowu zhi* is first quoted by name in Pei Songzhi's 裴松之 (373–450) commentary to the *Sanguo zhi*, q.v., completed in 429 (1:54 and 2:90). The first mention of the work in a dynastic history is when Chang Jing 常景 (ca. 478–550) is said to have "revised and edited the *Bowu zhi* by Zhang Hua" (*Wei shu*, q.v., 82:1808). In my 1987 translation, I suggest that certain passages in the text may be comments first introduced by Chang Jing. The book furthermore carries fragmentary annotations by two writers, Master Lu 盧氏 and Zhou Riyong 周日用. At the latest, Master Lu's annotations may be dated to 984 and those of Zhou Riyong to 1151. The *Bowu zhi* appears in the *zajia* 雜家 category of the *Sui shu*, q.v., 34:1006, the *xiaoshuojia* 小說家 category of the *Jiu Tangshu* 47:2036, and the *xiaoshuo* category of the *Xin Tangshu* 59:1539. The *Bowu zhi* continued to be cited in the Song: it is listed in the *xiaoshuo* categories of the *Chongwen zongmu** (dated between 1034 and 1038) 3:31a, the *Junzhai dushuzhi** (dated 1151) 13:543, and the thirteenth-century *Zhizhai shulu jieti** (10:303), and in the *jizhi* 記志 category of the *Zhongxing guange shumu* 中興館閣書目 (1178), cited in Wang Yinglin's *Yu hai* 57:32a. Thereafter, the work is entered in *Song shi* 205:5208 in the *zajia* category and in the *Wenxian tongkao** (1308) in the *xiaoshuo* category. In the Ming dynasty, the *Bowu zhi* was entered in the *Wenyuange shumu* 文原閣書目 (1441) in the *gujin zhi* 古今志 category, the *Baowentang shumu* 寶文堂書目 (mid-sixteenth century) in the *zajia* category, and the *Hongyulou shumu* 紅雨樓書目 (1602) in the *xiaoshuo* category. The ongoing indecisiveness displayed here as to how to classify the *Bowu zhi* well reflects the complex and diverse nature of its contents and how the work was regarded over the centuries.

Principal editions

There are two distinct editions of the *Bowu zhi*. The most widespread edition derives from the He Zhitong 賀志同 edition of 1505 that bears a postface by Du Mu 都穆 (1458–1525). The text in this edition has chapter headings and subheadings of the sort frequently found in Ming encyclopedia. Most modern editions derive from this edition. In 1804, Huang Pilie 黃丕烈 (1763–1825), in his *Shiliju* 士禮居 collectanea, published a variant edition of the *Bowu zhi* that he considered to be a Northern Song copy of the work. It is this edition that is reprinted in the *Sibu beiyao* 四部備要. However, the contents of the two editions are almost identical, albeit arranged in different sequences, and both editions are ten *juan* in length. The *Shiliju* edition lacks *juan* headings, while the He Zhitong edition is divided into thirty-nine subheadings:

1. Dililüe 地理略 — Geographical accounts
2. Di 地 — Land
3. Shan 山 — Mountains
4. Shui 水 — Watercourses
5. Shanshui zonglun 山水總論 — Comprehensive discussions of mountains and watercourses
6. Wufang renmin 五方人民 — Peoples of the five directions
7. Wuchan 物產 — Products
8. Waiguo 外國 — Foreign lands
9. Yiren 異人 — Extraordinary men
10. Yisu 異俗 — Extraordinary customs
11. Yichan 異產 — Extraordinary products
12. Yishou 異獸 — Extraordinary animals
13. Yiniao 異鳥 — Extraordinary birds
14. Yichong 異蟲 — Extraordinary insects
15. Yiyu 異魚 — Extraordinary fish
16. Yicaomu 異草木 — Extraordinary plants and trees
17. Wuxing 物性 — The nature of things
18. Wuli 物理 — The principles of things
19. Wulei 物類 — The categories of things
20. Yaowu 藥物 — Medicinal substances

21.	Yaolun 藥論	Discussions of medicines
22.	Shiji 食忌	Dietary warnings
23.	Yaoshu 藥術	Medical skills
24.	Xishu 戲術	Deceptive skills
25.	Fangshi 方士	Masters of techniques
26.	Fushi 服食	Taking [health-promoting] foodstuffs
27.	Bian fangshi 辨方士	Discussions of the masters of techniques
28.	Renming kao 人名考	Investigations of names
29.	Wenji kao 文籍考	Investigations of writings
30.	Dili kao 地理考	Investigations of geography
31.	Dianli kao 典禮考	Investigations of rituals
32.	Yue kao 樂考	Investigations of music
33.	Fushi kao 服飾考	Investigations of apparel
34.	Qiming kao 器名考	Investigations of the names of objects
35.	Wuming kao 物名考	Investigations of the names of things
36.	Yiwen 異聞	Extraordinary reports
37.	Shibu 史補	Supplements to the histories
38.	Zashuo: shang 雜說: 上	Miscellaneous commonplaces: A
39.	Zashuo: xia 雜說: 下	Miscellaneous commonplaces: B

While each section found in the He Zhitong edition purports to deal with a different topic, there is considerable confusion among the sections; the entire structure of subheadings reveals itself to be arbitrarily imposed upon the text. The *Shiliju* edition, however, displays a faint remnant of what may have been the structure of the original work or, failing that, the result of Chang Jing's editing. Rather than following a thematic structure, the *Shiliju* edition groups passages together by source. Thus, the composition of the work displays a sort of logical structure unnoticed by many modern scholars.

Texts with commentaries and notes

Fan Ning 范寧. *Bowu zhi jiaozheng* 博物志校證. Beijing: Zhonghua shuju, 1980.
Tang Jiuchong 唐久寵. *Bowu zhi* 博物志. Taipei: Jinfeng chubanshe, 1987.
Wang Fuxiang 王富祥. "*Bowu zhi* shuzheng" 博物志疏證. *Taidong shizhuan xuebao* 4 (1976): 1–76.

Commentary and notes without the complete text

Tang Jiuchong 唐久寵. *Bowu zhi jiaoshi* 博物志校釋. Taipei: Taiwan xuesheng shuju, 1980.

Selected studies

Campany, Robert Ford. *Strange Writing: Anomaly Accounts in Early Medieval China*. Albany: State University of New York Press, 1996.

Cao Daoheng 曹道衡 and Shen Yucheng 沈玉成. *Zhonggu wenxue shiliao congkao* 中古文學史料叢考. Beijing: Zhonghua shuju, 2003.

Dudbridge, Glen. *Religious Experience and Lay Society in T'ang China*: *A Reading of Tai Fu's Kuang-i chi*. Cambridge: Cambridge University Press, 1995.

Gao Sisun 高似孫. *Zilüe* 子略. Taipei: Guangwen shuju, 1968.

Hu Yinglin 胡應麟. *Shaoshi shanfang bicong* 少室山房筆叢. Beijing: Zhonghua shuju, 1958; rpt., 1964.

Jiang Liangfu 姜亮夫. *Zhang Hua nianpu* 張華年普. Shanghai: Gudian wenxue chubanshe, 1957.

Li Jianguo 李劍國. *Tangqian zhiguai xiaoshuo jishi* 唐前志怪小說輯釋. Shanghai: Shanghai guji chubanshe, 1986.

———. *Tangqian zhiguai xiaoshuo shi* 唐前志怪小說史. Tianjin: Nankai daxue chubanshe, 1984.

Mather, Richard, trans. *Shih-shuo hsin-yü*: *A New Account of Tales of the World*. Minneapolis: University of Minnesota Press, 1976.

Nylander, R. "The Po-wu Chih of Chang Hua: A Short Textual History." Unpublished paper. University of Washington, 1974.

Straughair, Anna. *Chang Hua*: *A Statesman-Poet of the Western Chin Dynasty*. Occasional Paper 15. Canberra: Australian National University, 1973.

Tang Jiuchong 唐久寵. "Fan Ning *Bowu zhi* jiaozheng pinglun" 范寧博物志校證評論. *Zhongguo gudian xiaoshuo yanjiu zhuanji* 6 (1983): 315–31.

Wang Yinglin 王應麟. *Kunxue jiwen* 困學紀聞. *Sibu congkan**, 3rd series, 26th han 函.

———. *Yu hai* 玉海. Hangzhou: Zhejiang shuju, 1883; rpt., Taipei: Hualian chubanshe, 1964.

Yao Jiheng 姚際恆. *Gujin weishu kao* 古今僞書考. Hong Kong: Taiping shuju, 1962.

Yin Wengui 殷文圭. *Jinxiu wanhuagu qianji* 錦繡萬花谷前集. In *Yingyin Wenyuange Siku quanshu**, vol. 924.

Yu Jiaxi 余嘉錫 (1883–1955). *Siku tiyao bianzheng* 四庫提要辨證. Beijing: Zhonghua shuju, 1980.

Yuan Xingpei 袁行霈 and Hou Zhongyi 侯忠義. *Zhongguo wenyan xiaoshuo shumu* 中國文言小說書目. Beijing: Beijing daxue chubanshe, 1981.

Zhu Guozhen 朱國禎. *Yongchuang xiaopin* 湧幢小品. *Biji xiaoshuo daguan* 筆記小說大觀 edition. Taipei: Xinxing shuju, 1962.

Translations

English

Greatrex, Roger. *The Bowu zhi: An Annotated Translation*. Orientaliska Studier 20. Stockholm: Akademitryck AB, Täby, 1987.

Japanese

The *Bowu zhi* Project. "The *Bowu zhi*: Critical Edition and Commentaries (I)." *Tōhō gakuhō: Journal of Oriental Studies* 59 (1987): 463–590.

Chinese

Zhang Enfu 張恩富. *Bowu zhi*. Chongqing: Chongqing chubanshe, 2007.
Zhu Hongjie 祝鴻傑. *Bowu zhi quanyi* 博物志全譯. Guiyang: Guizhou renmin chubanshe, 1992.
———. *Bowu zhi xinyi* 博物志新譯. Shanghai: Shanghai daxue chubanshe, 2010.

Index

Lau, D. C. 劉殿爵, Chen Fong Ching 陳方正, and Ho Che Wah 何志華. *Renwu zhi zhuzi suoyin; Bowu zhi zhuzi suoyin* 人物志逐字索引; 博物志逐字索引. Hong Kong: Chinese University Press, 2007.

Roger Greatrex

Cao Zhi ji 曹植集

Introduction

Cao Zhi, styled Zijian 子建 (192–232), was the third son of Cao Cao 曹操 (Wei Wudi; r. 190–220) by his concubine née Bian 卞. He was a famous literary prodigy at an early age. A faction at court later tried to make him Cao Cao's heir. In 217, when Cao Cao decided upon Cao Pi 丕 (Wei Wendi; 187–226), his first son by Bian, the supporters of each brother created a serious rift between them. After Cao Pi became emperor in 220, he immediately started to weaken the power of his younger brother. Cao Zhi was put under surveillance, forced to move from one fief to another, and repeatedly demoted in rank.

Some scholars believe the recurrent image of drifting tumbleweeds (*zhuan peng* 轉蓬) in Cao Zhi's poetry symbolizes his personal situation. Although people tend to sympathize with his predicament, the claim that he was wronged by his father's not choosing him as his successor is difficult to support, for his elder brother was indeed the legitimate heir. Moreover, Cao Zhi's failure to gain Cao Cao's trust and his falling out of favor with his father were largely due to his own imprudent behavior. Cao Zhi's resentment over the decision and its consequences are not difficult to discern in some of his literary works. According to a poem he wrote after paying a visit in 223 to the capital Luoyang, "Presented to Biao, Prince of Baima" ("Zeng Baima wang Biao" 贈白馬王彪), he and his brother Biao were even forbidden to travel together on the way back to their respective fiefs. Cao Zhi's difficulties continued under the rule of Cao Pi's son Rui 叡 (Wei Mingdi; r. 226–239). Although Cao Zhi wrote petitions begging for official employment, all his appeals were denied. He died in his fief in 232 and was given the posthumous title "Prince Si of Chen" (Chen Si wang 陳思王).

Cao Zhi is regarded as the representative author of the Jian'an 建安 period (196–220), the last reign era of Emperor Xian of the Han dynasty. During these years, so many literati enjoyed the support of Cao family members that the period stands out as an ideal epoch of patronage by political leadership. The Jian'an period also saw the rise in popularity of poetry in the five-syllable line (*wuyan shi* 五言詩). Cao Zhi's literary reputation has much to do with his accomplishments in this new poetic form. Zhong Rong (fl. 502–519) ranked him in the highest category of the *Shi pin*, q.v.

Cao Zhi was also known for his rhapsodies, of which the most famous is the "Rhapsody on the Goddess of the Luo" ("Luoshen fu" 洛神賦). This work depicts an encounter with a dazzling immortal and ends with her departure and the frustration of the speaker's desire. According to Cao Zhi's preface, he was inspired (*gan* 感) by the "Rhapsody on the Goddess" ("Shennü fu" 神女賦) attributed to Song Yu 宋玉 (fl. third century B.C.). Yet, Cao Zhi's rhapsody differs from this and other works on the same topic in that his preface sets the event in the concrete time frame of his own life—specifically, during a journey back to his fief from Luoyang. The precise year, given in the existing version of the preface as the third year of the Huangchu era, may have been a copyist's error for the fourth year (223). The preface's realistic detail may account for the tendency of biographical interpretation among later readers. Although the object of the description was ostensibly Fufei 宓妃, the Luo River's goddess, a note quoted in Li Shan's 李善 (d. 689) commentary to the *Wen xuan*, q.v., states that this figure was actually a disguise for Cao Pi's principal wife, Empress Zhen 甄后. According to the same note, Cao Zhi had a secret affair with her. After her death, Cao Pi gave him her pillow, and on his journey back to his fief, Cao Zhi encountered her spirit when crossing the Luo River. Although not based on any historical record, this story has been closely associated with the rhapsody ever since. The work has also been read as a political allegory in the tradition of Wang Yi's 王逸 (89–158) interpretation of the "Li Sao" 離騷. Following this interpretive scheme, the beautiful goddess is taken as a reference to Cao Pi, and Cao Zhi's pursuit of a romantic relationship with her is understood as an expression of his loyalty and desire to serve the government.

Contents

The current "complete collection" of Cao Zhi was reconstructed entirely from miscellaneous sources. Apart from citations in commentaries, other major sources include literary anthologies such as the *Yutai xinyong*, q.v., the *Wen xuan*, and the *Yuefu shiji*, q.v.; encyclopedias such as the *Yiwen leiju*, q.v., the *Wenyuan yinghua**, and the *Taiping yulan*, q.v.; and the "Monograph on Music" ("Yue zhi" 樂志) of the *Song shu*, q.v., which preserves some of the *yuefu* poems.

Cao Zhi's collection curiously kept expanding in size, contrary to those of most writers in the early period. According to the *Jin shu*, q.v., 50:1390, false attributions to Cao Zhi were already made at the time of Emperor Wu (r. 265–290). A possible explanation is the tendency of scholars living in later ages to attribute anonymous poems to famous poets. For this reason, the assumed authorship of many poems, including some of Cao Zhi's "famous works," is dubious.

Zhao Youwen's 趙幼文 *Cao Zhi ji jiaozhu* 曹植集校注 (Beijing: Renmin wenxue chubanshe, 1984) contains 130 lyric poems, 46 rhapsodies, 12 dirges, 30 petitions and declarations, 4 personal letters, and 18 essays that include disquisitions, discourses, and other kinds of prose compositions. These are arranged chronologically in three sections corresponding to the Jian'an, Huangchu (220–226), and Taihe (227–233) reign eras.

Authorship and date of composition

Dating most of Cao Zhi's poems is an unsolvable puzzle. Scholars have long tried to arrange them in chronological order and link them to events in his life. Given the lack of reliable records, however, their efforts often follow a circular logic, that is, critics detect details of Cao Zhi's life in his poems and then arrange his poems according to the details they have deduced from them. This approach is made even more dubious by the presence of many poems in the collection of which the attribution is uncertain.

A telling example of problematic biographical interpretation is the reading of "Ballad on a Yellow Sparrow in the Wild Field" ("Yetian huangque xing" 野田黃雀行), which begins with the line, "In tall trees the gloomy winds are heavy" (高樹多悲風). The poem relates the story of a young man using his sword to save a sparrow trapped in a net. Although its first appearance in the tradition is suspiciously late—in the *Yuefu shiji*, q.v., by Guo Maoqian 郭茂倩 (fl. 1084)—it nevertheless has been firmly attached to Cao Zhi's name and included in almost every modern anthology of his poetry. Moreover, the poem is almost always interpreted as self-referential, with Cao Zhi himself as the brave youth, and his friends Ding Yi 丁儀 and Ding Yi 丁翼 represented by the sparrow. The Ding brothers were both executed by Cao Cao in 220 for their failed scheme to put Cao Zhi on the throne. This poem of dubious authenticity has thus been read as a hidden expression of frustration and resentment and, owing to its close association with an actual event, has been considered one of Cao Zhi's most representative works. Of course we cannot rule out the possibility that Guo Maoqian had a reliable source in hand that is no longer extant, but the poem's absence in all earlier sources suggests otherwise (Owen, *The Making of Early Chinese Classical Poetry*, 256–59).

Transmission and early history of the text

Quite exceptionally for such an early poet, Cao Zhi seems to have collected his own writings. Fragments of his self-preface that survive in the *Yiwen leiju* (*juan* 55) indicate that the original collection included seventy-eight rhapsodies. Another early collection of his works was made during the Wei dynasty's Jingchu (237–239) era by order of Emperor Ming. According to *Sanguo zhi* 19:576, this collection contained over a hundred pieces of poetry, rhapsodies, hymns, inscriptions, and miscellaneous essays. The bibliographic monograph of the *Sui shu*, q.v., 35:1059, lists a *Chen Si wang Cao Zhi ji* 陳思王曹植集 in thirty *juan*. *Jiu Tang shu* 47:2053 and *Xin Tang shu* 60:1579 each record two editions of the collection—one in twenty *juan* and the other in thirty *juan*. This information plausibly indicates a quantity of works larger than the previous number of "over a hundred" pieces. Unfortunately, both editions were lost by the Song dynasty.

Principal editions

According to *Siku quanshu zongmu tiyao** 29:3104, the earliest extant edition of Cao Zhi's collection and the basis of most later editions is a ten-*juan Cao Zijian ji* 曹子建集 compiled in the Southern Song dynasty, which included forty-four rhapsodies, seventy-four poems, and ninety-two pieces of miscellaneous writings (*zawen* 雜文). During the Ming dynasty, Zhang Xie (1574–1640) edited a ten-*juan Chen Si wang ji* in his *Qishi'er jia ji**; this has been reprinted in *Xuxiu Siku quanshu** 1584:65–173. Zhang Pu's (1602–1641) *Han Wei Liuchao baisan mingjia ji*, q.v., included a *Chen Si wang ji* in two *juan*. Both editions were collations from various early sources and provided materials for the work of Qing scholars, among which Ding Yan's 丁晏 (1794–1875) *Cao ji quanping* 曹集詮評 (preface dated 1875; rpt., Beijing: Wenxue guji kanxingshe, 1957) supplies the base text for versions widely used in modern times. In addition to Zhao Youwen's annotation of both prose and poems, the following modern editions are also widely available for the poetry alone.

Gu Zhi 古直 (1885–1959). *Cao Zijian shi jian* 曹子建詩箋. Shanghai: Zhonghua shuju, 1928; rpt., Taipei: Guangwen shuju, 1966.

Huang Jie 黃節 (1873–1935). *Cao Zijian shi zhu* 曹子建詩注. Beijing: Beijing daxue chubanzu, 1928; rpt., Beijing: Renmin wenxue chubanshe, 1957.

Selected studies

Cutter, Robert Joe. "Cao Zhi's (192–232) Symposium Poems." *Chinese Literature: Essays, Articles and Reviews* 6.1–2 (1984): 1–32.

———. "The Incident at the Gate: Cao Zhi, the Succession, and Literary Fame." *T'oung Pao* 71.2 (1985): 228–40.

Diény, Jean-Pierre. "Les sept tristesses (*Qi ai*): A propos deux versions d'un 'poéme à chanter' de Cao Zhi." *T'oung Pao* 65.1 (1979): 51–65.

Frankel, Hans H. "The Problem of Authenticity in the Works of Cao Zhi." *Essays in Commemoration of the Golden Jubilee of the Fung Ping Shan Library (1932–1982)*, ed. Chan Pingleung et al., 187–89. Hong Kong: Fung Ping Shan Library, Hong Kong University, 1982.

Holzman, Donald. "Cao Zhi and the Immortals." *Asia Major*, 3rd ser., 1.1 (1988): 15–57.

Kameyama Akira 龜山朗. "Kan Gi shi ni okeru gūiteki shizen byōsha Sō Shoku 'Kusahen' o chūshin ni" 漢魏詩における寓意的自然描写曹植'吁嗟篇'を中心に. *Chūgoku bungaku hō* 31 (1980): 1–28.

Kroll, Paul. "Seven Rhapsodies of Ts'ao Chih." *Journal of the American Oriental Society* 120.1 (2000): 1–12.

Owen, Stephen. *The Making of Early Chinese Classical Poetry*. Cambridge, MA: Harvard University Press, 2006. Pp. 75–77, 103–9 *passim*, 128–47 *passim*, 168–81 *passim*, 202–4, 256–59.

Roy, David. "The Theme of the Neglected Wife in the Poetry of Ts'ao Chih." *Journal of Asian Studies* 19 (1959): 25–31.

San Cao ziliao huibian 三曹資料彙編. Beijing: Zhonghua shuju, 1980.

Xu Gongchi 徐公持. "Cao Zhi shige de xiezuo niandai wenti" 曹植詩歌的寫作年代問題. *Wen shi* 6 (1979): 147–60.

Zhang Keli 張可禮. *San Cao nianpu* 三曹年譜. Ji'nan: Qi Lu shushe, 1983.

Zheng Yongkang 鄭永康. *Wei Cao Zijian xiansheng nianpu* 魏曹子建先生年譜. Taipei: Taiwan shangwu yinshuguan, 1981.

Zhong Youmin 鐘優民. *Cao Zhi xintan* 曹植新探. Hefei: Huangshan shushe, 1984.

Translations

English

Demiéville, Paul. *Anthologie de la poésie chinoise classique*. Paris: Gallimard, 1962. Pp. 118–22.

Dunn, Hugh. *Ts'ao Chih: The Life of a Princely Chinese Poet*. Taipei: China News, 1970.

Frodsham, J. D., with the collaboration of Ch'eng Hsi. *An Anthology of Chinese Verse: Han Wei Chin and the Northern and Southern Dynasties*. London: Oxford University Press, 1967. Pp. 35–50.

Kent, George. *Worlds of Dust and Jade: Forty-seven Poems and Ballads of the Third Century Chinese Poet Ts'ao Chih*. New York: Philosophical Library, 1960.

Owen, Stephen. *An Anthology of Chinese Literature: Beginnings through 1911*. New York: W. W. Norton, 1996. Pp. 194–97, 262, 265, 267–70, 282, 614–15.

Watson, Burton. *Chinese Rhyme-Prose: Poems in the Fu Form from the Han and Six Dynasties Periods*. New York: Columbia University Press, 1971. Pp. 55–60.

Japanese

Itō Masafumi 伊藤正文. *Sō Shoku* 曹植. Tokyo: Iwanami shoten, 1964.

Concordance

Diény, Jean-Pierre, et al. *Concordance des oeuvres complètes de Cao Zhi* (added title: *Cao Zhi wenji tongjian* 曹植文集通檢). Paris: l'Institut des Hautes Etudes Chinoises, Collège de France, 1977.

Qiulei Hu

Chen shu 陳書

Introduction

The *Chen shu* records the history of the Chen dynasty (557–589), beginning with the early life of its founder, Chen Baxian 陳霸先, posthumously Emperor Wudi (503–559, r. 557–559), and ending with the annexation of the Chen by the Sui in 589 during the reign of Chen Shubao 陳叔寶 (553–604), last emperor of the Chen, a dynasty with a duration of only some thirty-three years. The *Chen shu*, as well as the *Liang shu*, q.v., is the work of Yao Silian 姚思廉 (557–637).

Contents

The *Chen shu* consists of thirty-six *juan*; there are six imperial annals (*benji* 本紀) and thirty biographical accounts (*zhuan* 傳). As with the *Liang shu*, q.v., the *Bei Qi shu*, q.v., and the *Zhou shu*, q.v., all compiled in the same period, the *Chen shu* contains no tables (*biao* 表) or monographs (*zhi* 志). All these dynasties, as well as the Sui, were treated collectively in a work titled "Monographs of the History of the Five Dynasties" ("*Wudai shi zhi*" 五代史志) which came to be included in the *Sui shu*, q.v.

Date of compilation and authenticity

Yao Silian was commissioned to compile both the *Chen shu* and the *Liang shu* in 629 by Li Shimin, Emperor Taizong of the Tang (r. 626–649), who at the same time ordered other scholars to compile the *Bei Qi shu*, *Zhou shu*, and *Sui shu*. These commissions were part of the establishment of the Historiography Institute (Shiguan 史館), created to supervise and control the writing of history. The Historiography Institute was under the direction of Fang Xuanling 房玄齡 (578–648) and Wei Zheng 魏徵 (580–643); the latter not only supervised the compilation of the *Chen shu* but also wrote some parts of it (6:117, 7:131). The *Liang shu* and the *Chen shu* were completed in 636. It is generally assumed that the *Chen shu* text that we have today is the original text.

Sources

As Yao himself explained (*Chen shu* 27:354), he relied mostly on the work of his father, Yao Cha 姚察 (533–606), who had begun to write a *Chen shu* during the Sui dynasty. As evidence, there are two places in the *Chen shu* where the father is cited as author (2:40, 3:61). Yao Silian also relied on other materials, some of them written during the Chen dynasty itself. Gu Yewang 顧野王 (519–581) and Fu Zai 傅縡 (531–585) wrote the court diaries (*qijuzhu* 起居注) of Emperor Wu and his nephew and successor Chen Qian 陳蒨 (posthumously Wendi; r. 560–566). During the reign of Chen Xu 陳頊 (posthumously Xuandi; r. 569–582), Lu Qiong 陸瓊 extended these works and published a *Chen shu* in forty-two *juan*, listed in the bibliography of *Sui shu* 33:956 and cited in *Shi tong** 12:356.

After the collapse of the Chen in 589, the Sui emperor Yang Jian (posthumously Wendi; r. 541–604) ordered Yao Cha, a former Chen official, to revise and complete the work of Lu (*Chen shu* 27:352). Yao Cha died before his work was finished, but, in a dramatic scene on his deathbed, he had his son promise to complete the work. During the reign of Emperor Yang Guang (posthumously Yangdi; r. 605–617), Yao Silian was officially ordered by Yu Shiji 虞世基 (d. 618) to complete the *Chen shu* (*Chen shu* 27:354). Despite this it was still not completed when, together with Dou Jin 竇璡 and Ouyang Xun 歐陽詢 (557–641), Yao Silian was again given the commission to write the history by the Tang emperor Li Yuan (temple name Gaozu; r. 618–626) in 622 (*Tang dazhaoling ji* 81:466–67). Yao finally completed it alone after being reordered to do so by Tang Taizong, in 629 (*Tang huiyao* 63:1091).

Compared with the histories of the earlier dynasties, the *Chen shu* is written in a more concise style. Yet the biography of Yao Cha, who actually died during the Sui, is over 3,000 characters long, and includes much that is considered by critics to be irrelevant.

Transmission of the text

The earliest printed edition of the *Chen shu* that survives is (a) the Song Shaoxing 紹興 era (1131–1162) edition printed in Sichuan, known as the Song Shu ben 宋蜀本. Later editions include the following:

(b) Nanjian 南監, or Nanking Academy, edition of 1588;

(c) Beijian 北監, or Northern Academy, edition of 1605;

(d) Mao Jin's 毛晉 Jiguge 汲古閣 edition of 1631;

(e) Wuyingdian 武英殿, or "Palace," edition of 1739;

(f) *Siku quanshu* 四庫全書 edition of 1782;

(g) Jinling shuju 金陵書局 edition of 1872.

Principal editions

There are two principal editions consulted in modern times. The earlier one is the Baina 百衲 edition, a photolithographic reproduction of (a), the "Shu edition" of the Song dynasty's Shaoxing era, which was issued by Shangwu yinshuguan (1936). The second one, which is now the standard edition, was based on the (a)–(e) and (g) editions and was published by Zhonghua shuju (1972). For an overall account of the textual history of this and the other Six Dynasties standard histories, see appendix IV, "Textual Transmission of the Standard Histories."

Studies and research aids

Cui Lindong 崔林東. *Zhongguo shixueshi—Wei Jin Nan Beichao Sui Tang shiqi* 中國史學史—魏晉南北朝隋唐時期. Shanghai: Shanghai renmin chubanshe, 2006. Pp. 137–38, 145–47.

Jiang Boliang 蔣伯良. "*Liang shu, Chen shu* chuanwu bian" 梁書, 陳書舛誤辨. *Ningbo daxue xuebao, Renwen kexue ban* (2003.3): 62–65.

Kanai Yukitada 金井之忠. *Tōdai no shigaku shisō* 唐代の史學思想. Tokyo: Kōbundō, 1940.

Li Shaoyong 李少雍. "Yaoshi fuzi de wenbi yu shibi—du *Liang shu, Chen shu* zhaji" 姚氏父子的文筆與史筆—讀梁書陳書札記. *Wenxue yichan* (2002.6): 79–92.

Lin Rengqian 林礽乾. *Chen shu benji jiao zhu* 陳書本紀校注. Gudian wenxian yanjiu jikan 古典文獻研究輯刊, series 6, vol. 27. Taipei: Hua Mulan wenhua chubanshe, 2008.

———. *Chen shu jiaozheng* 陳書校證. Taipei: Wenjin chubanshe, 1975.

———. *Chen shu yiwen kaozheng* 陳書異文考證. Taipei: Wen shi zhe chubanshe, 1979.

MacMullen, David. *State and Scholars in T'ang China*. Cambridge: Cambridge University Press, 1988. Pp. 165–67.

Qian Yiji 錢儀吉. *Nanchao huiyao* 南朝會要. Shanghai: Shanghai guji chubanshe, 1996.

Twitchett, Denis. *The Writing of Official History under the T'ang*. Cambridge: Cambridge University Press, 1992. P. 52n3.

Wechsler, Howard. *Mirror to the Son of Heaven: Wei Cheng at the Court of T'ang T'ai-tsung*. New Haven, CT: Yale University Press, 1974. Pp. 111–13.

Wright, Arthur. *The Sui Dynasty: The Unification of China, A.D. 581–617*. New York: Alfred A. Knopf, 1978. Pp. 14–16.

Wu Tianren 吳天任. *Zhengshi daodu* 正史導讀. Taipei: Taiwan shangwu yinshuguan, 1990. Pp. 58–61.

Yuan Yingguang 袁英光 et al. *Nanchao wushi cidian* 南朝五史辭典. Ji'nan: Shandong jiaoyu chubanshe, 2005.

Zhao Jun 趙俊. "*Liang shu, Chen shu* de bianzuan deshi" 梁書, 陳書的編纂得失. *Zhongguo shehui kexue yanjiushengyuan xuebao* (1994.3): 17–24.

Zhu Mingpan 朱銘盤. *Nanchao Chen huiyao* 南朝陳會要. Shanghai: Shanghai guji chubanshe, 1986. Pp. 88–89.

Translations

Bielenstein, Hans. "The Six Dynasties, vol. I." *Bulletin of the Museum of Far Eastern Antiquities* 68 (1996): 227–46; this section is mainly based on the annals of the *Chen shu*.

Frankel, Hans H. *Catalogue of Translations from the Chinese Dynastic Histories for the Period 220–960*. Chinese Dynastic Histories Translations, supplement 1, 102–4. Berkeley: University of California Press, 1957.

Indices

Ershisishi renming suoyin 二十四史人名索引. Beijing: Zhonghua shuju, 1980.
Ershiwushi jizhuan renming suoyin 二十五史紀傳人名索引. Shanghai: Shanghai guji chubanshe and Shanghai shudian, 1990.
Ershiwushi renming suoyin 二十五史人名索引. Ed. Ershiwushi kanxing weiyuanhui 二十五史刊行委員會. Beijing: Zhonghua shuju, 1956.
Kubo Takuya 久保卓哉. *Chinsho hyōgo sakuin* 陳書評語索引. Fukuoka: Chūgoku shoten, 1990.
Zhang Chenshi 張忱石. *Nanchao wushi renming suoyin* 南朝五史人名索引. 2 vols. Beijing: Zhonghua shuju, 1985.

Bibliography

Tang dazhaoling ji 唐大詔令集. Comp. Song Minqiu 宋敏求 (1019–1079). Beijing: Shangwu yinshuguan, 1959.
Tang huiyao 唐會要. Comp. Wang Pu 王溥 (922–982). Beijing: Zhonghua shuju, 1990.

Damien Chaussende

Chenggong Sui ji 成公綏集

Introduction

Chenggong Sui, styled Zi'an 子安 (231–273), lived in the era from about 150 to 300 A.D., when scholars' private interests in antiquity, historiography, classical commentary, and poetry, as well as arts and technical skills, rose to new heights and were renewed especially after 220, following decades of interruption and political stress. Chenggong Sui thus shared many interests with his peers and associates, including Fu Xuan 傅玄 (217–278), Xun Xu 荀勖 (d. 289), Zhang Hua 張華 (232–300), and Shu Xi 束晳 (d. ca. 302). The collection of Chenggong Sui's writings contains, *inter alia*, the rhyme-prose pieces for which he is especially known.

The author's rhyme-prose displays a unique natural philosophy that was Daoist in both tone and worldview—as may be seen in his most famous works "Tiandi fu" 天地賦 (Rhapsody on heaven and earth) and "Xiao fu" 嘯賦 (Rhapsody on whistling), both of which were included in the *Wenxuan*, q.v. He was also a poet and an expert in music and calligraphy, arts that are reflected in several items of his literary collection (*wenji* 文集)—for example, a miscellaneous item titled "Lishu ti" 隸書體 (On the forms of the *li*-script), rhyme-prose pieces on the zither and the lute, and musicological speculation in the "Xiao fu." He was known by, and served alongside, politically powerful men during the formative years of the Jin dynasty, chiefly as a participant in court projects, but he was not a political factionalist or seeker of high office. He wrote no freestanding works of classical commentary or historiography, nor do we know of any weighty court policy memorials from his hand. Yet, he was prominent enough to have been commissioned to write lyrics for court rites and festivities, as discussed later.

Chenggong Sui's biography in *Jin shu*, q.v., 92:2371–75, is part of a set of biographies in the section titled "Garden of Literati" ("Wenyuan" 文苑). It is quite short, devoting most of its space to recording his two famous rhyme-prose pieces. Thus, we know very little of his life and career, but the biography does claim that he was from a poor family (there is no evidence that any of his antecedents had received noble title). Chenggong was recognized for writing only after becoming a protégé of Zhang Hua, who praised his writings and had him appointed to the office of chamberlain for ceremonials (*taichang* 太常) in 255; then, in around 260, Chenggong became assistant in the Imperial Library (*mishulang* 祕書郎). In 264 he served in the commission of the soon-to-be emperor of Jin, Wudi (Sima Yan;

235–290, r. 266–290), to revamp the Jin legal code. In around 269, holding the post of gentleman of the Secretariat (*zhongshulang* 中書郎), he participated in a court project to compose ritual lyrics for scheduled rites and feasts; his colleagues in this commission were Xun Xu, Zhang Hua, and Fu Xuan. There exists no further information on Chenggong Sui subsequent to this event. Biographies can be found in Knechtges (*Wen xuan*, 374–75), Brashier ("A Poetic Exposition on Heaven and Earth," 1–2), and Berkowitz ("Ch'eng-kung Sui," 7–8).

Contents

The extant, and fullest, edition of Chenggong's *wenji* is the version collected by Zhang Pu (1602–1641, *jinshi* 1631) for his anthology *Han Wei Liuchao baisanjia ji*, q.v., where it is titled *Chenggong Zi'an ji* 成公子安集. As is many other Six Dynasties *wenji*, it is a collection of prose items such as petitions, letters, disquisitions, epitaphs, and rhyme-prose; it also includes verse items such as songs (or chants, *ge* 歌) and lyric poems. The thirty-five items in the *Chenggong Zi'an ji* are in the following order:

Rhyme-prose, 20 titles (of which two are rhyme-prose prefaces only)

Eulogy, 2 titles

Inscription, 3 titles

Admonition, 1 title

Dirge, 1 title

Sevens (*qi* 七), 1 title

Miscellaneous, 2 titles (including "Lishu ti," which some have considered to be a rhyme-prose work; see Berkowitz, "Ch'eng-kung Sui," 7–9)

Court songs (*yuege* 樂歌), 2 titles (under the general rubric "Jin sixiang yuege" 晉四廂樂歌 [Songs for the Jin (palace) four side-rooms]; these are traditional subgenres of lyric for court festal, saltatory, and temple ritual occasions)

Lyric poetry, 3 titles (one with subdivisions)

Yan Kejun's (1762–1843) "Quan Jin wen" 59:1a–10b (part of his larger work *Quan shanggu Sandai Qin Han Sanguo Liuchao wen*, q.v.) collects only the prose but presents certain differences from *Chenggong Zi'an ji*. First, there are short fragments of four rhyme-prose titles that are not carried in *Chenggong Zi'an ji*, and the latter in addition has one rhyme-prose not found in Yan's collection (on the subject of wild geese, titled "Hongyan fu" 鴻雁賦). Moreover, the rhyme-prose material varies from the texts in *Chenggong Zi'an ji*. For example, "Tiandi fu" in "Quan Jin wen" has roughly fifteen more words and rearranges four words at the very beginning; "Yun fu" 雲賦 (Rhapsody on clouds) has sixteen more words;

and the title "Qi gubi fu" 棄古筆賦 (Rhapsody on discarding the ancient brush) in *Chenggong Zi'an ji* has the word "Qi" dropped in "Quan Jin wen," perhaps to conform to the earliest source, *Yiwen leiju*, q.v., 58:1055 (Shanghai guji chubanshe, 1985). "Quan Jin wen" also includes one title in the disquisition genre.

Transmission and early history of the text

In the limited material surrounding Chenggong Sui's life, there are no clues as to persons responsible for first collecting and transmitting his *wenji*. His seventh-century *Jin shu* biography says that "the poems, *fu*, and miscellaneous jottings that [Chenggong Sui] composed in over 10 *juan* were circulated" (92:2375). The *Sui shu*, q.v., bibliographic monograph, which was finished in 656 but based on early lists, records *Chenggong Sui ji* in nine *juan* (35:1061). *Sui shu*'s notes to this, based on pre-Sui catalogs, such as that compiled by Ruan Xiaoxu 阮孝緒 (479–536), state that the collection was not in whole form, and that during the Liang dynasty it had ten *juan*. Thus, it seems clear that a so-called original version of "ten *juan*" stayed integral well into Tang times. In fact, the *Jiu Tang shu* bibliographic monograph (completed in 945, but utilizing eighth-century records) gives ten *juan* for the *wenji* (47:2058). There are no records of it in Song catalogs. In Ming times, scholars such as Mei Dingzuo 梅鼎祚 (1549–1615), who collated Han- and Jin-era *wenji*, and Feng Weine (1513–1572), who compiled *Gushi ji**, were able to rely on surviving early texts, and their efforts then became the basis for the many pre-Tang *wenji* brought together in the *Han Wei Liuchao baisan jia ji*.

Principal editions

Chenggong Sui's *wenji* has never received a modern, critical edition. The edition of choice, in Zhang Pu's *Han Wei Liuchao baisanjia ji*, is titled "Chenggong Zi'an ji" in the 1879 re-cut edition (重刻本) of the Xinshutang 信述堂 printing (rpt., Jiangsu: Jiangsu guji shudian, 1990; 2:769–84) but titled "Chenggong Sui ji" in the *Siku quanshu** (*Yingyin Wenyuange Siku quanshu*, vols. 1412–1416:1–162). Today, there are modern punctuated versions for only certain items of Chenggong's verse; see Lu Qinli's *Xian Qin Han Wei Jin Nanbeichao shi** 1:584–85 (for lyric poetry only), and 1:823–24 for court songs. For modern punctuated versions of "Tiandi fu" and "Xiao fu," see *Jin shu* 92:2371–75.

Selected studies

Berkowitz, Alan. "Ch'eng-kung Sui." In *The Indiana Companion to Traditional Chinese Literature*, ed. William H. Nienhauser, Jr., with Charles Hartman and Scott W. Galer, 2:7–9. Bloomington: Indiana University Press, 1998.

Fan Rong 樊榮. "Xiao, 'Xiao fu' yu Wei Jin mingshi fengdu" 嘯、嘯賦與魏晉名士風度. *Changchun shifan xueyuan xuebao* 23.5 (2004): 70–73.

Lü Zeli 呂則麗. "Zhi qianqiu yi li xiang, si jimo zhi laihe: Chenggong Sui fu lun 指千秋以厲響, 俟寂寞之來和: 成公綏賦論." *Zaozhuang shifan zhuanke xuexiao xuebao* 21.3 (2004): 30–33.

Wang Fuli 王福利. *Jiaomiao yanshe geci yanjiu* 郊廟燕射歌辭研究. Beijing: Beijing daxue chubanshe, 2009. Briefly discusses Chenggong's court lyrics. This is one of very few modern studies that looks at the texts of this genre of post-Han lyric. Pp. 23–28.

Yu Jiang 余江. "Miaoyin jile, ziran zhihe: Chenggong Sui 'Xiao fu' lun 妙音極樂, 自然至和: 成公綏嘯賦論." *Hunan keji daxue xuebao (shehui kexue ban)* 8.1 (2005): 106–9.

Zhang Kefeng 張克峰. "Chenggong Sui 'Li shu ti' de wenxue tezheng yu shufa lilun jiazhi 成公綏隸書體的文學特徵與書法理論價值." *Sheke zongheng* 22.1 (2007): 97–98.

Translations

Brashier, Kenneth E. "A Poetic Exposition on Heaven and Earth by Chenggong Sui (231–273)." *Journal of Chinese Religions* 24 (1996): 1–46.

Holzman, Donald. "Written en Route." In *Landscape Appreciation in Ancient and Early Medieval China: The Birth of Landscape Poetry*, 110. Hsin-chu, Taiwan: College of Humanities and Social Sciences, National Tsing Hua University, 1996. Translates "Tu zhong zuo 途中作."

Knechtges, David R. *Wen xuan, or Selections of Refined Literature*. Princeton, NJ: Princeton University Press, 1996. Translates "Rhapsody on Whistling." Vol. 3, pp. 315–23.

White, Douglass A. "Rhapsody on Whistling." In *The Columbia Anthology of Traditional Chinese Literature*, ed. Victor H. Mair, 429–434. New York: Columbia University Press, 1994.

Zach, Erwin von. "Das Pfeifen." In *Die chinesische Anthologie*, 1:258–61. Cambridge, MA: Harvard University Press, 1958. Translates "Xiao fu."

Howard L. Goodman

Chuxue ji 初學記

Introduction

The *Chuxue ji* (Fundamentals of learning) by Xu Jian 徐堅 (d. 729) and others is one of only four extant *leishu* 類書 (commonly translated as "encyclopedia") from the Tang dynasty. It contains selections from texts written between the pre-Qin era and the early Tang, arranged into categories for easy reference. According to Liu Su's 劉肅 (fl. 806–820) *Da Tang xinyu* (New accounts of the Great Tang), the *Chuxue ji* was compiled at the behest of the Tang emperor Xuanzong as an easy-to-use writing textbook for his male heirs. According to Liu, Xuanzong addressed the official Zhang Yue 張說 (667–731) as follows:

> My sons will be learning to write compositions. They need to investigate affairs and learn to recognize genres. Texts like the *Imperial Readings* 御覽 are already enormous and looking up what you want in them is somewhat difficult. I would like you and the other scholars [of the Academy of Assembled Worthies] to compile a collection of key affairs and key writings that are organized by category. You should strive above all to make it convenient to use so that my sons can easily display their accomplishments. (*Da Tang xinyu* 9:137; for the *Imperial Readings*, see Dien, "A Note on Imperial Academies," 62–65.)

The *Chuxue ji* succeeded admirably in fulfilling the objectives delineated by Xuanzong, that it be both comprehensive and succinct. Its 23 categories and 313 topics are analogous to those of contemporary encyclopedias, but at 30 *juan* and approximately 600,000 characters, it is significantly shorter. It also fulfilled its objective of being a useful resource for composition; within each of its topics is a clear definition of terms, their origins, and their changing meanings over time, as well as examples of how they might be used within various genres of composition.

The *Chuxue ji* is an important text for scholars today for several reasons. First, it preserves fragments of texts from the Six Dynasties period that are no longer extant. Second, it provides evidence for what texts were extant and available at the time of its compilation in the early Tang. Third, it provides convenient access to historical and cultural information that may have been familiar to educated readers of that time. Fourth, the *Chuxue ji* serves as a record of changing literary and scholarly trends; its divergence from earlier *leishu* in terms of content, form, and organization points toward new tastes in terms of what earlier authors and

Chuxue ji

texts considered essential for contemporary textual practice. Fifth, as the account translated earlier demonstrates, *leishu* such as the *Chuxue ji* can offer us insight into the literacy education and training of the children of the elite.

Contents

The *Chuxue ji* is divided into twenty-three topical sections (*bu* 部):

1. Tian 天 — Heaven (cosmological and meteorological phenomena)
2. Suishi 歲時 — Seasons and important dates
3. Di 地 — Earth (various features of terrain)
4. Zhoujun 州郡 — Provinces and commanderies (administrative geography)
5. Diwang 帝王 — Rulers
6. Zhonggong 中宮 — The inner palace (empresses and concubines)
7. Chugong 儲宮 — Palaces of the crown princes
8. Diqi 帝戚 — Imperial relatives
9. Zhiguan 職官 — Imperial offices
10. Li 禮 — Rituals
11. Yue 樂 — Music (types of music and musical instruments)
12. Ren 人 — People (kinds and qualities of people)
13. Zhengli 政理 — Principles of government (from amnesty and reward to exile and imprisonment)
14. Wen 文 — Writing (classifications and instruments of writing)
15. Wu 武 — The military (military insignia and weaponry)
16. Dao Shi 道釋 — Daoism and Buddhism (ideas, architecture, and people)
17. Juchu 居處 — Buildings and places (from capitals and cities to parks, roads, and markets)
18. Qiwu 器物 — Objects I
19. Qiwu 器物 — Objects II [in some editions, this second section is titled *Fu shi* 服食, Clothing and food]
20. Baoqi 寶器 — Precious objects; also, flowers and fragrant grasses (*huacao fu* 花草附)

21.	Guomu 果木	Fruit-bearing trees
22.	Shou 獸	Animals
23.	Niao 鳥	Birds; also, scaled creatures and insects (*linjie chong fu* 鱗介蟲附)

Each section is further subdivided into subcategories treating altogether 313 "topics" (*zimu* 子目). These categories and subcategories are for the most part analogous to those found in earlier and contemporary encyclopedias.

Structure and arrangement

As mentioned previously, the *Chuxue ji* was commissioned as a composition primer for imperial princes, one that could be easily referenced. Thus, while the *Chuxue ji* contains many of the same categories and subcategories found in contemporary or later Tang *leishu*, it differs from these texts in the way that it organizes the information and texts included within it. Each of its 313 topics begins with a section titled "Definitions" (*xu shi* 敘事; literally, "describing the thing"). This section contains a listing of quotations from earlier texts—most often dictionaries such as the *Erya* 爾雅, *Shuo wen* 說文, and *Shi ming* 釋名, but also relevant passages from the classics (*jing* 經), histories (*shi* 史), and other texts—that define the terms titling the particular subcategory as well as how the usage of these terms changed over time. Following the definition is a section titled "Matched Phrases" (*shi dui* 事對). These are two-, three-, or four-character phrases arranged into parallel couplets followed by the texts or events to which they refer or from which these character phrases are derived. The final section of a topic consists of examples of writings that reference that topic. Typically referred to as "Poetry and Prose" (*shi wen* 詩文), it contains sections labeled separately by genre, most commonly rhyme-prose (*fu* 賦) and lyric poetry (*shi* 詩), but at times including examples from thirty different genres of prose composition as well.

The scholar Wen Yiduo wrote that "as a matter of fact, if one removes the 'Matched Phrases' section, then it becomes just like the *Yiwen leiju* [q.v.]. And if one further removes the poetry, prose, and rhyme-prose, it becomes just like the *Beitang shu chao* [q.v.]," ("Leishu yu shi," 4–5). The contemporary scholar Jiang Xiumei sees this as a process of evolution in which the later *leishu* improves upon the structure of the earlier (*Chuxue ji zhengyin jibu dianji kao*, 1:7).

Sources

According to Jiang Xiumei, the *Chuxue ji* contains extracts from more than 1,170 different texts. These break down according to the four traditional bibliographic categories as follows: 175 from the classics, 335 from the histories, 275 from philosophical writings of "Masters" (*zi* 子), and 388 from the collected works of individuals (*ji* 集). As mentioned earlier, the *Chuxue ji* preserves fragments of many texts that are no longer extant.

Authorship and date of composition

Received accounts for the dates of composition vary, with the earliest date given for when work began on the text being the seventh year of the Kaiyuan reign (719) and the latest for its completion being the sixteenth year (728) of the same era (Yan, *Chuxue ji yanjiu*, 24–26). The text is credited as a collaborative effort by seven scholars of the Jixian Academy in addition to Xu Jian: Zhang Yue 張說 (667–731), Wei Shu 韋述 (d. 757), Yu Qin 余欽 (dates unknown), Shi Jingben 施敬本 (dates unknown), Zhang Xuan 張烜 (dates unknown), Li Rui 李銳 (dates unknown), and Sun Jiliang 孫季良 (dates unknown).

Transmission and editions

The *Chuxue ji* has been well circulated since its initial composition. Liu Su, for example, noted that "this text was circulated among contemporaries" (*Da Tang xinyu*, 9:137). It was transmitted to Japan as well by no later than the ninth century (Yan, *Chuxue ji yanjiu*, 40–41n5). Fragments of a Tang dynasty manuscript copy have also been found among the texts preserved at Dunhuang (Duan, "*Chuxue ji* canpian bukao," 109–10). A woodcut edition of the text was produced by Wu Zhaoyi 毋昭裔 (dates unknown), a minister of the Latter Shu (Hou Shu 後蜀) dynasty. This edition was broadly circulated in its own time and was the edition upon which later Northern Song editions were based. It is no longer extant.

In the Song dynasty, the *Chuxue ji* was listed in the bibliography of the *Xin Tang shu* 59:1563, the *Chongwen zongmu** (dated between 1034 and 1038) 3:55a (p. 409), and the *Junzhai dushu zhi** (dated 1151) 14:651 as having thirty *juan*. One major edition of the text, the *Guozijian kanben* 國子監刊本 of the Northern Song, was printed in 1025. It is no longer extant. For its printing, see *Xu Zizhi tongjian changbian* 續資治通鑒長編, *juan* 103. This edition served as the base text for both the Southern Song's *Shaoxing dingmao kanben* 紹興丁卯刊本 edition and the Ming's *Jiajing bingshen Hu Yunzi ba kanben* 嘉靖丙申壺雲子跋刊本 edition.

A second major edition, the Southern Song's *Dongyang Chongchuan Yu sishisanlangzhai kanben* 東陽崇川余四十三郎宅刊本, was printed in 1147. This is the earliest extant printed version of the *Chuxue ji* and is currently held in Japan. Two reprint editions of this text have been published: *Riben gongneiting shulingbu cang Song Yuan ban Hanji yingyin congshu* 日本宮內廳書陵部藏宋元版漢籍影印叢書 (Beijing: Xianzhuang shuju, 2001; rpt., 2002, 156 vols) and *Song ben Chuxue ji* 宋本初學記 (Taipei: Yiwen yinshuguan, 1976), 10 vols.

Several editions of the *Chuxue ji* were printed in the Ming dynasty. The *Xishan Anguo* [1481–1534] *Guipoguan kanben* 錫山安國桂坡館刻本, first printed in 1531, is extant in several different reprints (Yan, *Chuxue ji yanjiu*, 45–53). It was based, at least in part, on the Southern Song *Dongyang Chongchuan Yu sishisanlangzhai kanben* edition. Note that questions over the source of this edition remain unresolved (Chen and Xiao, "Mingdai Jin Fan Xuyitang ben," 68). This edition seems to have been widely circulated. It was the base text for many other Ming editions of the *Chuxue ji* and has been extremely influential in the subsequent circulation of this text as well as providing the basis for the modern edition, which has an appended index.

Multiple copies of another Ming edition, the *Jinling Yang Long Jiuzhou shuwu kanben* 晉陵楊櫳九洲書屋刊本, printed in 1531, are also extant. Despite the date of printing, this edition appears to be based on the *Anguo* edition (Chen and Xiao, "Mingdai Jin Fan Xuyitang ben," 69). Other Ming editions include the 1534 *Jin Fan Xuyitang kanben* 晉藩虛益堂刊本, the 1536 *Zhengshi Zongwentang ba kanben* 鄭氏宗文堂跋刊本, the 1544 *Shen Fan kanben* 瀋藩刊本, the 1587 *San Wu Xu Shouming Ningshoutang kanben* 三吳徐守銘寧壽堂刊本, the 1597 *Chongchuan Chen Dake kan Wuling Gongshi buyiben* 崇川陳大科刊吳陵宮氏補遺本, and the 1605 *Hulin Shen Zongpei ke jinxiang ben* 虎林沈宗培刻巾箱本. Multiple copies of all these Ming editions are still extant.

During the Qing dynasty, an edition of the *Chuxue ji* was produced during the Qianlong reign period, the *Neifu ke Guxiangzhai xiuzhen ben* 內府刻古香齋袖珍本. According to *Siku quanshu zongmu tiyao* 26:2785–86, this edition was used in the *Siku quanshu** (*Yingyin Wenyuange Siku quanshu** 890:1–497). A reprint, the *Nanhai Kongshi Sanshiyousanwanjuantang Fuguxiangzhai ben* 南海孔氏三十有三萬卷堂復古香齋本, was produced in 1883. There is a modern reprint in Dong Zhi'an 董治安, ed., *Tangdai si da leishu* 唐代四大類書, vol. 3 (Beijing: Qinghua daxue chubanshe, 2003). A third Qing edition, the *Chengdu keben* 成都刻本, was produced during the Guangxu reign period. Multiple copies of all these Qing editions are still extant.

Two important variorum (*jiaoben* 校本) editions of the *Chuxue ji* were also issued during the Qing. The first was produced by Yan Kejun 嚴可均 (1762–1843) in 1815 and is titled *Wucheng Yan Kejun jiaoben* 烏程嚴可均校本. The second is Lu Xinyuan's 陸心源 (dates unknown) *Chuxue ji jiaobu* 初學記校補 produced during the Guangxu era. They differ in the base texts they use as well as their methodology in collating and correcting the different versions.

The most widely available modern edition is the *Chuxue ji* published by the Beijing Zhonghua shuju in 1962. This is based on the Qing dynasty's *Guxiangzhai* edition. It includes a table outlining differences between this text and the texts of the Ming dynasty *Anguo* edition and the *jiaoben* that were produced by Yan Kejun and Lu Xinyuan.

Traditional assessments

The text has been generally well regarded within Tang and later sources. Sima Guang 司馬光 (1019–1086) in his *Wengong xu shihua* 溫公續詩話 records the enthusiastic praise of one reader, Liu Ziyi 劉子儀 (dates unknown) of Zhongshan 中山, for this text: "It is not only for those beginning their studies; it can be regarded as recorded words that can be used throughout one's whole life!" (非止初學, 可為終身記也). The editors of the *Siku quanshu zongmu tiyao** also praised it highly: "In comparison to the other *leishu* written during the Tang dynasty, it does not match the *Yiwen leiju* [completed in 624, q.v.] in terms of its comprehensiveness, but in terms of the excellence of its selections it far surpasses it. As for the *Beitang shuchao* [q.v.] and the *Liutie* 六帖, they are by far inferior to it" (在唐人類書中, 博不及藝文類聚, 而精則勝之. 若北堂書鈔及六帖, 則出此書下遠矣; Yan, *Chuxue ji yanjiu*, 1; *Siku quanshu zongmu tiyao* 26:2786). Critiques of the text have also been made. These have typically focused on misattributions or incorrect characters in the texts cited, or on inconsistencies in the text's arrangement.

Commentaries and notes without the text

Fracasso, R. "Note introduttive al *Chuxue ji*." *Cina* 20 (1986): 93–121.

———. "Note integrative sul *Chuxue ji*." *Annali Instituto Universitario Orientale Napoli* 53.1 (1993): 102–8.

Hu Daojing 胡道靜. *Zhongguo gudai de leishu* 中國古代的類書. Beijing: Zhonghua shuju, 1982. Pp. 94–102.

Nakatsuhama Wataru 中津濱涉. *Shogakuki insho intoku* 初學記引書引得. Kyoto: Ibundō shoten, 1977.

Yan Qinnan 閻琴南. *Chuxue ji yanjiu* 初學記研究. N.p.: N.p., 1981.

Selected studies and bibliography

Chen Qinghui 陳清慧 and Xiao Yu 蕭禹. "Mingdai Jin Fan Xuyitang ben *Chuxue ji* kaolun" 明代晉藩虛益堂本初學記考論. *Tushuguan zazhi* 28.1 (2009): 64–69.

Dien, Albert E. "A Note on Imperial Academies of the Northern Dynasties." *Proceedings of the Second Biennial Conference, International Association of Historians of Asia*. Taipei, 1962. Pp. 57–69.

Duan Yuquan 段玉泉. "E cang Heishuicheng wenxian *Chuxue ji* canpian bukao" 俄藏黑水城文獻初學記殘片補考. *Ningxia shehui kexue* (2006.1): 109–10.

Jiang Xiumei 江秀梅. *Chuxue ji zhengyin jibu dianji kao* 初學記徵引集部典籍考. 2 vols. Yonghe, Taiwan: Hua Mulan wenhua chubanshe, 2006.

Liu Su 劉肅. *Da Tang xinyu* 大唐新語. Ed. Xu Denan and Li Dingxia. Beijing: Zhonghua shuju, 1984; rpt., 1997.

Sun Suting 孫愫婷. "*Chuxue ji suoyin* ding que" 初學記索引訂闕. *Guji zhengli yanjiu xuekan* (1988.1): 45–47.

Tang Guangrong 唐光榮. *Tangdai leishu yu wenxue* 唐代類書與文學. Chengdu: Ba Shu shushe, 2008.

Wen Yiduo 聞一多. "Leishu yu shi" 類書與詩. In Wen Yiduo and Fu Xuancong 傅璇琮, *Tangshi zalun* 唐詩雜論. Shanghai: Shanghai guji chubanshe, 1998.

Indices

Xu Jian 徐堅. *Chuxue ji fu suoyin* 初學記附索引. 3 vols. Taipei: Xinxing shuju, 1972.

Xu Yimin 許逸民. *Chuxue ji suoyin* 初學記索引. Beijing: Zhonghua shuju, 1980. (See also Sun Suting.)

Alexei Kamran Ditter

Diaoyu ji 琱玉集

Introduction

The *Diaoyu ji* (A collection of carved jade) was a privately compiled, popular encyclopedia that was probably designed to aid students preparing for low-level examinations. It was composed around the beginning of the eighth century and is of unknown authorship; about fifty years later it made its way to Japan. By the fourteenth century it had disappeared in China, but two of its *juan* have survived in Japan. Further, fifty years ago, Japanese scholars stated that a Dunhuang manuscript (Stein 2072) is almost certainly a fragment of an abbreviated version of this encyclopedia. The value of the *Diaoyu ji* is that it is a text for relatively unsophisticated readers that preserves fragments of not only lost early medieval texts but also those not found in more refined, officially sponsored Tang encyclopedias.

Contents

Unlike officially sponsored encyclopedias, such as the *Beitang shuchao*, q.v., *Yiwen leiju*, q.v., and *Chuxue ji*, q.v., the *Diaoyu ji* was privately compiled and was not meant for use by a highly literate audience. Its target was probably persons of modest origins who were attempting to elevate their status through increased literacy. By means of relating single, well-known anecdotes about certain people, its purpose was to teach students to recognize famous men and women of the past. The author was not fastidious about the source of his information. As Nishino Teiji and Kawaguchi Hisao have shown, unlike the authors of the aforementioned encyclopedias, the compiler of the *Diaoyu ji* sometimes took his material directly from other encyclopedias rather than from the original source. In other cases, the compiler attributed an anecdote to a dynastic history where, in fact, it does not appear. As an example, he labeled the tale of Tian Zhen 田真, who prevented his brothers from splitting the family's patrimony after their parents' death, as coming from the *Han shu*, whereas the *Chuxue ji* and *Yiwen leiju* state that it is from the *Zhou Jingshi Xiaozi zhuan* 周景式孝子傳. It thereby provides an example of a work meant for a more popular audience.

Like other Tang encyclopedias, the *Diaoyu ji* is important also because it preserves fragments of many lost texts, but, due to its popular nature, it preserves fragments of works found nowhere else, such as the *Wang Zhishen Song shu* 王智深

宋書, the *Cai Yan biezhuan* 蔡琰別傳, and the *Tongxian ji* 同賢記 (Records of men of shared worthiness). Nishino observes that this last text, which the *Diaoyu ji* quotes, is mentioned in no other medieval work except for one Dunhuang manuscript.

The two *juan* of the *Diaoyu ji* preserved in Japan are *juan* 12 and 14. The twelfth *juan* is divided into four *pian*: "Conghui" 聰慧 (Intelligent men), "Zhuangli" 壯力 (Men of physical might), "Jianshi" 鑒識 (Men of penetrating insight), and "Ganying" 感應 (Men who bring about sympathetic responses). *Juan* 14 is divided into eight *pian*: "Meiren" 美人 (Beauties), "Chouren" 醜人 (Homely people), "Feiren" 肥人 (Plump individuals), "Shouren" 瘦人 (Thin people), "Shijiu" 嗜酒 (Those who love alcohol), "Biewei" 別味 (Discriminating tasters), "Xiangrui" 祥瑞 (Those who attract auspicious signs), and "Guaiyi" 怪異 (Those who attract inauspicious signs). Altogether there are 164 accounts in these twelve *pian*.

At the head of each *pian*, there is a table of contents that consists of short, matching couplets of four or six characters, in which each person and his or her notable characteristic is encapsulated. For example, under the category of "Intelligent Men," we are told that "Wang Chong [27–97] had penetrating eyes; Zhongxuan [Wang Can 王粲; 177–217] could memorize steles" (王充寄目, 仲宣背碑). Wang Chong's account in the main text recounts how by reading a book just once he could recite it from memory; Wang Can's narrative tells us that after reading an inscription just once, he could reproduce the whole text without a single erroneous character.

Kawaguchi has pointed out that the characterization of famous men in brief and matching statements is similar to what one finds in the Tang primer *Mengqiu* 蒙求, which also uses anecdotes to teach students about famous people. Obviously, just as in the *Mengqiu*, students were meant to remember the historical figures mentioned in the text by memorizing the four- or six-character formulas, to recognize references to those persons, and to use the catchphrases appropriately.

Authorship, date of composition, and transmission

The *Diaoyu ji* appears in a few bibliographies but without credit to an author. The earliest listing is in the *Nihon genzai sho mokuroku* 日本現在書目録 (875–891), which merely states its title and that it has fifteen *juan*. The first Chinese bibliography that lists it is the *Chongwen zongmu** (dated 1041) 3:60a (419), which also cites no author for it and puts its length at twenty *juan*. The only other Chinese bibliographies that mention it are in the *Tong zhi** (69:814c), compiled by Zheng Qiao (1104–1162), and the *Song shi* (207:5295), which both list it as twenty *juan* in length. That an entry for it exists in the bibliography in the *Song shi*, of the fourteenth century, is not considered evidence that the item actually existed at that time, so the *Diaoyu ji* may well have disappeared in China sometime during the Song.

The two *juan* of this work that survived in Japan were located at the Shinpukuji 真福寺, a temple in Nagoya. At the end of each of these two *juan*, there is a colophon that states they were copied in the nineteenth year of the Tempyō 天平 reign (747), giving an *ante quam* for the compilation of the *Diaoyu ji*. Shibue Chūsai

澁江抽齋 (1805–1858) and Mori Yōchiku 森養竹 (1807–1885) first took note of this manuscript in their *Jingji fanggu zhi* 經籍訪古志 (Monograph on investigating ancient books). In 1884, Yang Shoujing 楊守敬 (1839–1915) reproduced this text in his *Guyi congshu* 古逸叢書 (Collectanea of ancient unedited books).

There are a number of different opinions as to how early the *Diaoyu ji* could have been written. Based on the *Diaoyu ji*'s style of writing, Li Ciming 李慈銘 (1830–1894), in his *Yuemantang riji* 越縵堂日記, proposed that it was written at the end of the Sui or the beginning of the Tang. Other scholars, though, point out that since it quotes the encyclopedia *Leilin* 類林 numerous times, it must postdate the work. There are, however, two works with this name: one was compiled by Pei Ziye 裴子野 (468–530) and the other by Yu Lizheng 于立政 (fl. 660). Due to the overlap of *pian* names between the *Diaoyu ji* and the *Leilin zashuo* 類林雜說, a Song expansion of Yu Lizheng's *Leilin* compiled in 1189, Wang Sanqing has argued that the *Diaoyu ji* was based on Yu Lizheng's text. Nonetheless, after comparing all of the tales attributed to the *Leilin* in the *Diaoyu ji* with their equivalents in the *Leilin zashuo*, due to their many discrepancies, Fukuda Toshiaki concludes that the *Diaoyu ji* quoted from Pei Ziye's work.

Assuming that Stein 2072 is a version of the *Diaoyu ji*, Nishino argued that a source cited for one of its stories, the *Zhanghuai taizi Xian zhu Hou Han shu* 章懷太子賢注後漢書, was written by Crown Prince Li Xian 李賢 (652–684) in 676. If one gives credence to this observation, that would mean that the *Diaoyu ji* was completed sometime after 676 and before 747. Nishino believes that it was compiled at the end of the seventh or in the early eighth century.

Newly discovered manuscripts

As stated previously, it has been proposed that Dunhuang manuscript Stein 2072, which appears to be a Tang dynasty work because it avoids Tang dynasty taboo words, is an abbreviated version of a portion of the *Diaoyu ji*. Nishino puts forth three reasons he believes this text is the *Diaoyu ji*. First, it cites its sources in the same way as do the two *juan* of the *Diaoyu ji* from the Shinpuku temple: the source comes at the end of the account and is headed by the word *chu* 出 ("from the … "). Second, S 2072 quotes from many of the same sources as the Shinpukuji *Diaoyu ji*; most particularly, it often cites the *Leilin*. Third, the twelfth-century Japanese work *Sangyō shiki* 三教指歸 has ten quotations from the *Diaoyu ji*. Two of these closely match, nearly word for word, two of the accounts found in S 2072. One difference between S 2072 and the Shinpukuji *Diaoyu ji*, though, is that the former is not organized into *juan*, only *pian*; moreover, each *pian* is missing the four- to six-character couplets that serve as the *pian*'s table of contents. Nishino thinks this is the case because S 2072 is an abbreviated version of the text.

The Dunhuang document is divided into fifteen *pian* that have 109 accounts. The *pian* titles are as follows: "Yinyue" 音樂 (Musicians), "Gongshu" 工書 (Calligraphers), "Shanshe" 善射 (Archers), "Fangshu" 方術 (Magicians), "Shanxiang" 善相 (Physiognomists), "Jianshi" 鑒識 (Men of penetrating insight),

"Jianbu" 鑒卜 (Diviners), "Zhanmeng" 占夢 (Diviners of dreams), "Gaoshi" 高士 (Men of lofty principle), "Qinxue" 勤學 (Diligent students), "Zhijie" 志節 (Men of ambition and resolution), and "Ruxing" 儒行 (Practitioners of Confucianism).

Principal editions

The primary edition of this work is the photolithographic reproduction of the Shinpukuji edition that Yang Shoujing published in his 1884 *Guyi congshu*. This is often published individually in reprints of the *Guyi congshu*, or in collections of lost works, such as Zhong Zhaopeng's 鍾肇鵬 *Guji congcan huipian* 古籍叢殘彙編 (Beijing: Beijing tushuguan chubanshe, 2001). In *Chōgyoku shū chūshaku*, Yanase Kiyoshi and Yahagi Takeishi have supplied a modern critical edition of these two *juan*.

As for the Dunhuang version (S 2072), Wang Sanqing has photographically reproduced it in his *Dunhuang leishu* (2:1157–72) and has created a critical edition of it (1:245–59).

Selected studies

Fukuda Toshiaki 福田俊昭. *Tonkō ruisho no kenkyū* 敦煌類書の研究. Tokyo: Daitō Bunka daigaku Tōyō kenkyūjo, 2003.

Kawaguchi Hisao 川口久雄. "Tonkōhon Ruirin to wagakuni no bungaku" 敦煌類林と我が国の文学. *Nihon Chūgoku gakkai hō* 22 (1970): 52–71.

———. "The *Lei-lin*, One of the Popular *Lei-shu* and the Varieties of the Same Pattern from Tun-huang." In the proceedings of the Twenty-ninth International Congress of Orientalists, Paris, 1973, pp. 195–205.

Nishino Teiji 西野貞治. "*Chōgyoku shū* to Tonkō sekishitsu no ruisho: Stein shūshū kanbun bunshochū no *Chōgyoku shū* zanken o megutte" 彫玉集と敦煌石室の類書: スタイン蒐集漢文文書中の彫玉集殘卷をめぐって. *Jinbun kenkyū* 8.8 (1957): 60–69.

Shi Jinbo 史金波, Huang Zhenhua 黃振華, and Nie Hongyin 聶鴻音. *Leilin yanjiu* 類林研究. Yinchuan: Ningxia renmin chubanshe, 1993.

Wang Sanqing 王三慶. *Dunhuang leishu* 敦煌類書. 2 vols. Kaohsiung, Taiwan: Liwen wenhua shiye, 1993.

Japanese translation

Yanase Kiyoshi 柳瀬喜代志 and Yahagi Takeishi 矢作武. *Chōgyoku shū chūshaku* 彫玉集注釈. Tokyo: Kyūko shoin, 1985.

Keith N. Knapp

Diwang shiji 帝王世紀

Introduction

The *Diwang shiji* (Genealogical records of emperors and kings) of Huangfu Mi 皇甫謐 (215–282) survives in fragments only. Therefore, it is not possible to give a clear and comprehensive picture of its original contents. Each fragment should be evaluated by the reliability of the source that quotes the *Diwang shiji*. Although some entries are transmitted by several sources, this does not mean these entries are more reliable, since later sources sometimes seem to be quoting isolated items from earlier ones instead of from an original, coherent manuscript of the *Diwang shiji*.

Contents

According to the transmitted fragments, the *Diwang shiji* appears to have been a universal history starting with cosmogony and ending with the last ruler of the Wei, close to Huangfu Mi's own time. Although the original structure of the text is unknown to us, it was probably chronologically organized according to the rulers. For each ruler, Huangfu Mi noted his full name, his parents's names, sometimes special birth circumstances or physical appearance, achievements and faults, reign length, and burial place. For each era or dynasty, the element of the cosmological phase is given. In addition to canonical scriptures, and philosophical and historical works, Huangfu Mi quoted many apocryphal texts to prove the legitimacy of several rulers. Reports of auspicious and inauspicious omens, together with entries on instances of miraculous conception without a human father, further stress the strong connection between heaven and these rulers and emphasize their special charisma. Emphasis was furthermore placed on topographic information. There are also some fragments dealing with astronomy, astrology, and demography. Even today, fragments of the *Diwang shiji* are quoted by scholars interested in Chinese mythology and early history, though without evaluation of the whole text.

Transmission of the text

It is difficult to trace the transmission of the *Diwang shiji* since there are several entries listing texts with similar titles or with the same title but by different authors in the literary catalogs of the dynastic histories. The *Diwang shiji* appears to have been lost after the Song.

Diwang shiji

The *Diwang shiji* of Huangfu Mi is recorded under that name in the bibliographical monograph of the *Sui shu*, q.v., as containing ten *juan* and listed in the category *zashi* 雜史 (miscellaneous histories). There it is said that the *Diwang shiji* starts with the San Huang 三皇 and ends with the Han and Wei (33:361). The bibliographic monograph of the *Jiu Tang shu* lists a *Diwang daiji* 帝王代記 compiled by Huangfu Mi (46:1996), while the *Xin Tang shu* has the title as *Diwang daiji* 帝王代紀 (48:1464); both agree with the *Sui shu* in the number of *juan* and category. The characters 記 and 紀 seem to be interchangeable and the character *shi* 世 was replaced by *dai* 代 due to a taboo during the Tang.

The category of *zashi*, which included historical and anecdotic works, was replaced in the *Song shi* by the title *bieshi* 別史 (unofficial histories), and the *Diwang shiji* was moved to the category *biannian* 編年 (annals) and listed at nine *juan* (203:5088). This change of category and the difference in the text's size indicate that from the Song period on, the transmission of the *Diwang shiji* as a coherent work had become uncertain. The Song scholar Wang Yinglin 王應麟 (1223–1296) informs us that Huangfu Mi from Anding 安定 regarded the *Hanji* 漢紀 (of Xun Yue 荀悅; 148–209) as incomplete, and therefore at the beginning of the Zhengshi 正始 era of the Jin he relied on the canonical texts and the records of the philosophical schools in order to compile the *Diwang shiji* and the *Nianli* 年歷 (Calendar) together in twelve *juan* (*Yu hai** 47:23a–b, p. 932). There is a problem, however, in Wang's dating of the compilation. The state of Wei during the Three Kingdoms period had a Zhengshi era (240–248) but there is none for the Jin; it is possible that Wang meant the Jin's Taishi 泰始 era (265–274). Both eras fall within Huangfu Mi's lifetime. Also according to Wang's description, the *Diwang shiji* started with Emperor Taihao 太昊 and ended with Han Xiandi (r. 189–220).

There is no entry for the *Diwang shiji* in the *Chongwen congmu** compiled by Wang Yaochen (1001–1056), in the private literary catalog *Junzhai dushu zhi** of Chao Gongwu (1151), nor in the *Zhizhai shulu jieti** (ca. 1235). The *Suichutang shumu**, a catalog of the collection of You Mou 尤袤 (1127–1193), is the last bibliography that lists the *Diwang shiji* (15b; *Yingyin Wenyuange Siku quanshu** 674:451).

Huangfu Mi did not explain his reason for writing the *Diwang shiji*. Apart from the entries in the biographies of several dynastic histories, only a small number of scholars have offered some insights concerning the *Diwang shiji*. In *Shi tong** 5:116, Liu Zhiji (661–721), who might have been able to see the complete *Diwang shiji*, criticized the *Diwang ji* 帝王紀 of Xuanyan 玄晏 (i.e., Huangfu Mi) for quoting many apocryphal texts (*tuchen* 圖讖) attached to the "six canonical works" (*liu jing* 六經). In general, the *Diwang shiji* is quoted and thereby transmitted in fragmentary form by a wide range of sources. Most fragments are transmitted in encyclopedias (*leishu* 類書), geographical works, commentaries on canonical and philosophical works, and commentaries on dynastic histories. These fragments do not comment on the structure of the whole text.

During the Qing, there was special interest in the *Diwang shiji* because of its extensive use of apocryphal texts, and Huangfu Mi was thought perhaps to have been involved in the forgery of a *Guwen Shangshu* 古文尚書. During the Zhengshi era of the Wei, the "Old Text" tradition of the *Shangshu* had become orthodox and was engraved in the "Three Stone Classics" (*San ti shijing* 三體石經). However, after the fall of the Western Jin in 317, the Three Stone Classics were lost; afterwards, Mei Ze 梅賾 (fl. 317–322) presented a text under the title *Kong Anguo Shangshu* 孔安國尚書 to Emperor Yuan (Sima Rui; r. 318–323) of the Eastern Jin. This version was accepted as the authentic *Shangshu* and in 653 was published under the nominal editorship of Kong Yingda 孔穎達 (574–648). Since Mei related that he had obtained his version from Zang Cao 藏曹, who had obtained it from Liang Liu 梁柳, a cousin of Huangfu Mi, the *Guwen Shangshu* was connected to Huangfu Mi. Careful study of all fragments does not, however, confirm this connection (Nagel-Angermann, *Das Diwang shiji*, 111–27).

Continuations and commentaries

He Maocai 何茂材 wrote a continuation of the *Diwang shiji* called the *Xu Diwang daiji* 續帝王代記 (*Jiu Tang shu* 46:1996 and *Xin Tang shu* 58:1465). The Japanese edition of the bibliography of the *Sui shu* gives his name as He Maolin 何茂林 (33:993). In the *Wei shu*, q.v., it is said that Yuan Yanming 元延明 of the Northern Wei wrote a commentary (*zhu* 注) for the *Diwang shiji* (20:530). Yu Chuo 虞綽 (sixth century) wrote a phonological commentary with the title *Diwang shiji yin* 帝王世紀音 in four *juan* (*Sui shu* 33:962). All these texts are lost.

Reconstructions and recompilations

The first reconstruction of the *Diwang shiji* goes back to Tao Zongyi 陶宗儀 (1316–1403), who collected only a small number of fragments without references (*Shuofu san zhong*, 5:2729). A number of Qing scholars tried to reconstruct the *Diwang shiji*: Wang Mo 王謨 (*jinshi* 1778), Zhang Shu 張樹 (1781–1847), Song Xiangfeng 宋翔鳳 (1776–1860), Gu Guanguang 顧觀光 (1799–1862), Qian Baotang 錢保塘, Wang Renjun 王仁俊 (1799–1826), and Zang Yong 臧庸 (1767–1811).

In contrast to the others, Wang Mo placed special emphasis on the *Diwang shiji*'s geographical and topographical entries. He collected fragments of the text and arranged them chronologically with reference to the work he quoted under the title *Diwang jingjie ji* 帝王經界紀 (Territorial records of the canon of emperors and kings) in his *Han Tang dilishu chao* 漢唐地理書鈔 (Collected geographical writings of the Han and Tang), 120–29.

Zhang Shu, in the foreword of his reconstruction of the *Diwang shiji*, defended Huangfu Mi against scholars who had criticized him for using unreliable sources such as apocryphal texts and had accused him of forgery. Zhang evaluated the fragments of the *Diwang shiji* and regarded Huangfu Mi as equal to Zheng Xuan 鄭玄 (127–200) in his canonical knowledge, to the calendrical expert Liu Xin 劉歆 (46 B.C.–A.D. 23), and to the geographer Pei Xiu 裴秀 (224–271).

Song Xiangfeng wanted to defend Huangfu Mi against the rumor that he was the author of the forged *Guwen Shangshu* (Xu Zongyuan, *Diwang shiji jicun*,

139–40). His reconstruction consists of ten chapters under the title *Diwang shiji* with an appendix (*fulu* 附錄) of one *juan* and another *juan* addendum (*buyi* 補遺). His reconstruction is included in the *Xunzuantang congshu* 訓纂堂叢書, in *Xuxiu Siku quanshu** 301:1–42.

Gu Guanguang collected fragments of the *Diwang shiji* and handed them over to Qian Xizuo 錢熙祚 (1801–1844), who wrote a preface for the resulting collection. Qian argued against the hypothesis that Huangfu Mi had written the *Diwang shiji* to promote the forged version of the *Guwen Shangshu*, which he is supposed to have obtained from his cousin Liang Liu. Qian compared the fragments of the *Diwang shiji* with the chapters of the allegedly forged *Guwen Shangshu* and came to the conclusion that Huangfu Mi did not rely on the forged text. Moreover, he praised Huangfu Mi for his topographical entries. The entries are arranged chronologically, with those treating topographical information at the end. This reconstruction can be found in *Baibu congshu jicheng* 54 (*Zhihai* 指海).

Qian Baotang differed from previous Qing scholars in taking a critical position toward the *Diwang shiji*. He was an adherent of the "New Text" school of the *Shangshu* and criticized Song Xiangfeng for his incomplete—according to Qian Baotang—reconstruction. In general, Qian considered the *Diwang shiji* to be partially unreliable. However, due also to the fact that much of the contemporary texts was lost, he found it difficult to evaluate the *Diwang shiji*. His reconstruction titled *Diwang shiji xubu kaoyi* 帝王世紀續補考異 is part of the *Xunzuan tang congshu* 訓纂堂叢書, *ce* 301 of the *Xuxiu Siku quanshu* (previously cited). The forewords of Zhang Shu, Song Xiangfeng, Qian Xizuo, and Qian Baotang are all included in Xu Zongyuan's edition (1964: 137–43). Xu indicates that the Qing scholar Zang Yong 臧庸 (1767–1811) also tried to reconstruct the *Diwang shiji*, but that work is not extant.

Principal edition and modern reconstructions

Xu Zongyuan's edition and compilation of the *Diwang shiji* fragments is based on previous collections and editions. His foreword gives some basic data about Huangfu Mi and an introduction to the textual history of the *Diwang shiji*. He arranges the fragments chronologically in ten chapters and gives a reference for each entry. At the end of the book, he provides a list with the titles and editions he used. If a given entry is transmitted by more than one source he tried to combine them; however, he indicates variants with small characters giving the exact reference as well. Xu's edition starts with the remote past ("From high antiquity to the Five Emperors") and goes on to the Xia, Yin-Shang, Zhou, Lieguo 列國, Qin, Han, and Wei. The ninth chapter is devoted to astronomical, geographical, and demographical entries. The tenth chapter gives some fragments without clear attribution. Xu tried to reconstruct the text by quoting the most comprehensive or perhaps the most reliable sources. His appendix supplies the biography of Huangfu Mi from *Jin shu*, q.v., 51:1409–18, with some annotations and references to other works.

Bibliography

Baibu congshu jicheng 百部叢書集成 [A hundred collectanea]. Compiled by Yan Yiping 嚴一萍. Taipei: Yiwen yinshuguan, 1965–1970.

Declerq, Dominik. *Writing against the State: Political Rhetoric in Third and Fourth Century China*. Leiden: E. J. Brill, 1998.

Guo Wei 郭偉. "Jiekai *Diwang shiji* yi shu er shuo zhi mi" 揭開帝王世紀一書二說之迷. *Xibei shidi* 4 (1997): 83–90.

Han Tang dili shuchao 漢唐地理書鈔. Comp. Wang Mo (ca. 1778). Beijing: Zhonghua shuju, 1961.

Knapp, Keith N. "Heaven and Death according to Huangfu Mi, a Third-Century Confucian." *Early Medieval China* 6 (2000): 1–31.

Liu Qiyu 劉起釪. *Shangshu yuanliu ji chuanben kao* 尚書源流及傳本考. Shenyang: Liaoning daxue chubanshe, 1987.

Minamizawa Yoshihiko 南澤良彥. "*Teiō seiki* no seiritsu to sono igi" 帝王世紀の成立とその意義. *Nihon Chūgoku gakkaihō* 44 (1992): 32–46.

Nagel-Angermann, Monique. "Looking for a Third-Century Concept of History—the *Diwang shiji* of Huangfu Mi." *In Papers from the XIII EACS Conference* ("The Spirit of the Metropolis," Torino, 30 August–2 September, 2000). Torino: Università degli Studi di Torino, 2002. CD-ROM.

———. "Eine Kompilation der übelsten Sorte: Das *Diwang shiji* des Huangfu Mi (215–282)." *Oriens Extremus* 43 (2002): 51–59.

———. "Das *Diwang shiji* des Huangfu Mi (215–282)." Ph.D. diss., University of Münster, 1999 (published 2008). Available at http://nbn-resolvinbf.de/urn:nbn:de:hbz:6-43599582520/.

Tao Zongyi 陶宗儀. *Shuofu san zhong* 說郛三種. 10 vols. Shanghai: Guji chubanshe, 1989.

Togawa Yoshiro 戶川芳郎. "Teiki to seiseiron" 帝紀と生成論. In *Chūgoku tetsugakushi no tenbō to mosaku* 中國哲學史の展望と摸索, 347–80. Tokyo: Sōbunsha, 1976.

Xu Zongyuan 徐宗元. *Diwang shiji jicun* 帝王世紀輯存. Beijing: Zhonghua shuju, 1964.

Monique Nagel-Angermann

Foguo ji 佛國記

Introduction

The *Foguo ji* (Record of Buddhist kingdoms), also known as the *(Gaoseng) Faxian zhuan* (高僧) 法顯傳 (Biography of [the eminent monk] Faxian) or *Liyou Tianzhu jizhuan* 歷遊天竺記傳 (Chronicle of an expedition through India), is the account of the journey Faxian (ca. 337–422) took from China to India and back. Traveling from 399 to 414, overland to the west and back east by sea, Faxian is the first known Chinese monk to undertake this pilgrimage and return to tell of it. He details the conditions of Buddhist monasteries through all the major kingdoms of South and Central Asia and recounts his experiences at Indian sites important to the life of the Buddha. Faxian's record was highly influential for medieval Chinese understandings of Buddhist India at a time when the religion was becoming enormously popular in China.

Contents

Since the nineteenth century, Western scholars have touted the *Foguo ji* as an invaluable record of Buddhism in India. Given the relative dearth of historical evidence about early Indian Buddhism, Chinese travel accounts such as this have long been mined for information about the development of Buddhism in the land of its birth. Medieval Chinese Buddhists shared this preoccupation, frequently citing Faxian's chronicle as authority in discerning the contours of Buddhist history, practice, and sacred geography through the so-called Western Regions (Xiyu 西域). Following the template of the travelogues in the *Shi ji* and *Han shu*, Faxian recounts the political geography of some thirty kingdoms beyond China's western passes, and in the tradition of the *Aśokāvadāna* (*Ayuwang zhuan* 阿育王傳, Biography of King Aśoka) he delineates the sacred geography of ancient India by retracing the steps of the historical Buddha Śākyamuni.

The *Foguo ji* is a short text of only one *juan*. It begins with Faxian's departure from Chang'an, together with four companions, through the frontier garrison of Dunhuang 敦煌 and into a number of Central Asian states across the Taklamakan Desert. Faxian takes note of the monastic populations of these states, their doctrinal affiliation (Mahāyāna or Hīnayāna), and emphasizes especially the enthusiasm with which local kings patronized these monastic institutions. The majority of the *Foguo ji*'s narrative takes place across northeastern India, at kingdoms made famous by great monasteries, royal patrons of the Dharma, and miraculous events that took place during the lifetime of the Buddha. In this setting, Faxian plays a role akin to the monk Upagupta in the *Aśokāvadāna*, ushering his readers on a pilgrimage through sacred Indian sites such as Kapilavastu, Śrāvasti, Kuśinagara, Pāṭaliputra, Rājagṛha, and Bodh Gayā. Like Upagupta, at each of these sites Faxian recounts tales of Śākyamuni's miraculous birth, enlightenment, final nirvana, and numerous other stories, as his party makes devotional offerings to the monuments and relics left behind. The *Foguo ji* also retells a number of stories directly from the *Aśokāvadāna*, such as Aśoka's past-life gift of dirt to Kāśyapa Buddha, his conversion to Buddhism, and his construction of 84,000 stupas, further indicating the influence of this classical Indian legend on Faxian's travel narrative. As he traverses these celebrated Indian kingdoms, Faxian continues his ethnography of the Buddhist institution, describing the constituency, teachings, and practices of numerous monasteries while highlighting their fidelity to traditional rules of discipline (Vinaya). He emphasizes throughout that a flourishing monastic community is the sine qua non of a prosperous state.

After several years roaming the Indian subcontinent, Faxian travels south to the island of Sri Lanka. He similarly records the conditions of local monasteries, legends of the Buddha's visits and of great Buddhist kings, while adding pertinent details concerning the local economy, climate, agriculture, and flora. From there Faxian sets sail for the Chinese port of Guangzhou, via the Malacca Strait between Sumatra and the Malay Peninsula, before being blown off course and eventually landing in Qingzhou 青州 on the Shandong Peninsula. All in all, Faxian was abroad for nearly fifteen years, having reached his late seventies by the time he returned to China. His *Foguo ji* solidified early Chinese impressions of Buddhist India as a highly civilized, prosperous, and magical land, and the Indian monastic community as a model of perfect Buddhist practice. This text also served as an important prototype for the Tang travelogues of Xuanzang 玄奘 (ca. 600–664) and Yijing 義淨 (635–713)—the *Da Tang Xiyu ji* 大唐西域記 (Great Tang record of the Western Regions) and *Nanhai jigui neifa zhuan* 南海寄歸內法傳 (Account of Buddhist practices sent home from the southern seas), respectively.

Authorship

According to Faxian, the purpose of his journey was to acquire monastic disciplinary codes from India, which were lacking in China up until the time of his departure. Although full Vinaya texts were brought to China while Faxian was abroad, rendering his mission somewhat extraneous, he nonetheless returned with the Vinaya of the sects of Mahīśāsaka (*Taishō shinshū Daizōkyō**, vol. 22, no. 1421) and Mahāsāṃghika (Taishō, vol. 22, nos. 1425 and 1427) and helped translate the latter into Chinese. He brought back a handful of other texts as well, and he translated some of these together with his colleagues—including most notably the renowned Indian missionary Buddhabhadra (Fotuobatuoluo 佛陀跋陀羅; 360–429)—at the Daochang 道場 Monastery in the Eastern Jin capital of Jiankang 建

康 (modern Nanjing, Jiangsu Province). It was apparently at the behest of these colleagues that Faxian recounted the *Foguo ji,* which according to its epilogue was completed in the twelfth year of the Eastern Jin Yixi 義熙 era (416).

Newly discovered manuscripts

Manuscripts of the *Foguo ji* have been found in a number of Japanese monastery collections, including those of Ishiyama-dera 石山寺, Kōshō-ji 興聖寺, Myōren-ji 妙蓮寺 (Matsuo-sha 松尾社), Nanatsu-dera 七寺, Nanzen-ji 南禪寺, Saihō-ji 西芳寺, and Shōsō-in 正倉院 (Shogozō 聖語蔵). The Ishiyama-dera manuscript has been dated to 1164 and the Nanzen-ji edition to ca. 1400; the others appear in collections copied during the Nara (710–794), Heian (794–1185), and Kamakura (1185–1333) periods (see Deeg, *Das Gaoseng-Faxian-Zhuan als religionsgeschichtliche Quelle*, 12; Nagasawa, *Hokken den,* iv; and *Nihon genson hachishu issaikyō taishō mokuroku, zantei dainihan*, 339). Nagasawa Kazutoshi has studied the Ishiyama-dera manuscript; Zhang Xun surveys the editions of Ishiyama-dera and Nanzen-ji. The other texts await further research. There are no known Dunhuang manuscripts of the *Foguo ji,* nor is it preserved among the stone sutra tablets at Fangshan Yunju 房山雲居 Monastery.

Principal editions

The primary edition of this work appears in the Japanese Taishō-era Buddhist Canon, *Taishō shinshū Daizōkyō**, vol. 51, no. 2085, an edition based on the *Gaoseng Faxian zhuan* from the second Koryŏ Canon, completed in 1251 (no. 1073 in *Koryŏ taejanggyŏng* 高麗大藏經, 47 vols. [photolithographic reprint, Seoul: Tongguk University Press, 1976]). The Koryŏ recension was copied from the first printed edition of the Chinese *Tripiṭika,* the Kaibao 開寶 Canon (971–983). The Taishō text also indicates variants in recensions from the Zifu 資福 Canon or Later Sixi 思溪 edition, completed circa 1239; the Puning 普寧 Temple edition, completed in 1290; the Jiaxing 嘉興 Canon or Jingshan 徑山 Canon, expanded until ca. 1684; and the "Palace edition" belonging to the Japanese Imperial Library—a copy of the Pilu 毗盧 Canon (or the Fuzhou 福州 edition), completed by 1176. There is considerable variance among these different recensions of the text. Several other xylographic editions of the *Foguo ji* are listed by Deeg (*Das Gaoseng-Faxian-Zhuan als religionsgeschichtliche Quelle*, 12, 14), who provides his own critical edition of the text as well (579–611). Also worth consulting is the variorum edition in the *Zhonghua Dazangjing* 中華大藏經 (Beijing: Zhonghua shuju, 1984–), vol. 61, no. 1178.

Selected studies

Adachi Kiroku 足立喜六. *Hokkenden Chūa Indo nankai kikō no kenkyū* 法顯傳中亞印度南海紀行の研究 [A study of the travelogue of Central Asia, India, and the southern seas in the biography of Faxian]. Tokyo: Chōeisha, 1940.

Boulton, Nancy Elizabeth. "Early Chinese Buddhist Travel Records as a Literary Genre." Ph.D diss., Georgetown University, 1982.
Deeg, Max. *Das Gaoseng-Faxian-Zhuan als religionsgeschichtliche Quelle*. Weisbaden: Harrassowitz, 2005.
Hazra, Kanai Lal. *Buddhism in India as Described by the Chinese Pilgrims AD 399–689*. New Delhi: Munshiram Manoharlal, 1983.
von Hinüber, Haiyan Hu. "Faxian's (法顯, 342–423) Perception of India: Some New Interpretation of his *Foguoji* 佛國記." *Annual Report of the International Research Institute for Advanced Buddhology at Soka University* 14 (2011): 223–47.
Liu, Xinru. *Ancient India and Ancient China:* Trade *and Religious Exchanges,* A.D. *1–600*. New Delhi: Oxford University Press, 1988.
Wang Bangwei 王邦維. "Faxian yu Faxian zhuan: Yanjiushi de kaocha" 法顯與法顯傳: 研究史的考察. *Shijie zongjiao yanjiu* (2003.4): 20–27.
Zhang Xun 章巽. *Faxian zhuan jiaozhu* 法顯傳校注. Shanghai: Shanghai guji chubanshe, 1985.
Zhu Huiwen 朱繪文. "Faxian Foguo ji yanjiu" 法顯佛國記研究. Ph.D. diss., Yunlin keji daxue (Taiwan), 2007.

Selected translations
English
Beal, Samuel. *Travels of Fah-Hian and Sung-Yun: Buddhist Pilgrims from China to India (400 A.D. and 518 A.D.)*. London: Trübner and Co., 1869.
Giles, H. A. *The Travels of Fa-hsien (399–414 A.D.), or Record of the Buddhistic Kingdoms*. London: Trübner and Co., 1877.
Legge, James. *A Record of Buddhistic Kingdoms—Being an Account by the Chinese Monk Fa Hien of Travels in India and Ceylon (AD 399–414) in Search of the Buddhist Books of Discipline*. Oxford: Clarendon Press, 1886.
Li, Rongxi. "The Journey of the Eminent Monk Faxian." In *Lives of Great Monks and Nuns*, 155–214. Berkeley: Numata Center for Buddhist Translation and Research, 2002.
Li, Yung-hsi. A Record of the Buddhist Countries by Fa-hsien. Beijing: Chinese Buddhist Association, 1957.

Other European languages
Deeg, Max. *Das Gaoseng-Faxian-Zhuan als religionsgeschichtliche Quelle*. Weisbaden: Harrassowitz, 2005. Pp. 505–77.
Rémusat, Abel, et al. *Foe-koue-ki, ou relation des royaumes bouddhiques: Voyage dans la Tartarie, dans l'Afghanistan et dans l'Inde*. Paris: l'Imprimerie Royale, 1836.

Japanese
Nagasawa Kazutoshi 長澤和俊. *Hokken den: Yakuchū kaisetsu—Hokusō-bon, Nansō-bon, Kōrai Daizōkyō-bon, Ishiyamadera-bon yonshu eiin to sono hikaku kenkyū* 法顯

伝: 訳註解說―北宋本, 南宋本, 高麗大蔵経本, 石山寺本四種影印とその比較研究. Tokyo: Yūzankaku, 1996.

Research aid

Nihon genson hasshu issaikyō taishō mokuroku, zantei dainihan 日本現存八種一切経対照目録, 暫定第二版 [Concordance of eight Buddhist manuscript canons extant in Japan, 2nd edition]. Tokyo: Kokusai Bukkyōgaku daigakuin daigaku, 2007. Available online at http://www.icabs.ac.jp/frontia/Hachishu.pdf/.

Stuart H. Young

Fu Xuan ji 傅玄集

Introduction

Fu Xuan, styled Xiuyi 休奕 (217–278), was a productive writer, a key composer of court music, and an influential figure during his time. He was born in Niyang 泥陽 (modern Ningxian 寧縣, Gansu) at the end of the Han dynasty and lived through the Wei and one decade of the Jin. His hometown in north China was in a key pass to a region inhabited by various non-Han peoples who often attacked Chinese settlements. Members of his upper-class family fought bravely against them. In particular, his grandfather Fu Xie 傅燮 died in 187 while defending Hanyang 漢陽 (Gangu 甘谷, Gansu). Fu Xie's staunch personality seems to have been handed down to Fu Xuan. Fu Xuan's father, Fu Gan 幹, was a famous scholar who served the state of Wei as grand administrator of Fufeng 扶風 commandery (Xianyang 咸陽, Shaanxi). He died when Fu Xuan was young, and his death marked the decline of the Fu family. Fu Xuan studied hard, however, and through his own ability was able to rise in the ranks of officialdom.

Fu Xuan's first office was as gentleman of the Interior (*lang zhong* 郎中); six years later, in 245, he was selected as an editor to assist in the compiling of a *Wei shu*. Subsequent positions during the Wei culminated in his being ennobled as baron of Chungu 鶉觚, the place to which his collection's traditional title, *Fu Chungu ji* 傅鶉觚集, refers. As his biography in *Jin shu*, q.v., 47:1317–23, describes:

> Afterwards, [Fu] served as an adviser on the staff of the General of Andong. He was then transferred to the position of Magistrate of Wen [Wenxian 溫縣, Henan]. Following this, [in 260] he was shifted to the office of Governor (*taishou* 太守) of Hongnong 弘農 [commandery] and presided in the office of Commandant of the Agriculture Office (*diannong xiaowei* 典農校尉).… [In 264] he was established in the fifth rank of the nobility as Baron (*nan* 男) of Chungu [Lingtai 靈臺, Gansu].

When Fu Xuan was on duty at Wen, the hometown of the Sima 司馬 clan, he established a good relationship with its members, which paved the way for his later prominence after Sima Yan (236–290) established the Jin dynasty in 265. The new emperor advanced Fu Xuan's noble stature to viscount (*zi* 子) and honored him with the post of cavalier attendant-in-ordinary (*sanji changshi* 散騎常侍). Later, he successively occupied other posts, ending with that of metropolitan commandant (*sili xiaowei* 司隸校尉) in 275.

Whatever positions Fu Xuan held, he repeatedly submitted documents and policy suggestions to the rulers, as noted in the *Jin shu* and as evident from his extant works. Fu's scholarship also brought him the opportunity to establish the music and rites used for the ceremonies of the new dynasty. Had he not been so "unyielding, straightforward, and unable to tolerate other people's shortcomings," which provoked jealous persons to attack him, he might have achieved still higher position. When Fu died at sixty-two *sui*, he was posthumously named "Unyielding" (Gang 剛) and later conferred with the title "Marquis of the Pristine Spring" (Qingquanhou 清泉侯). His friends were mostly accomplished literati, including Wang Chen 王沈 (d. 266), Yang Hu 羊祜 (221–278), Xun Xu 荀勖 (d. 289), Zhang Hua (232–300), Chenggong Sui 成公綏 (231–273), and Zhang Zai 張載 (ca. 250–ca. 310).

Contents

The edition of Fu Xuan's works reconstructed during the Ming dynasty was titled *Fu Chungu ji*. Its nineteen *juan* reflect the generic breadth of his compositions, particularly in prose writings presented at court:

1. Rhapsodies, 53
2. Grave-memoir inscription, 1
3. Commentaries (*shu* 疏), 3
4. Memorials/Petitions, 2
5. Presentation, 1
6. Opinions, 2
7. Prefaces, 5
8. Disquisition, 1
9. Encomiums, 6
10. Admonitions, 2
11. Inscriptions, 18
12. Commandment (*jie* 誡), 1
13. Eulogy, 1
14. Hypothetic (*shenan* 設難), 1
15. Dirge, 1
16. Sacrificial prayer (*zhuwen* 祝文), 1
17. Essays on clothing (*fu* 服), 2
18. *Yuefu* poems, 87
19. Lyric poems, 29

Transmission of the text

Collections of Fu Xuan's works are listed in the bibliographical treatises of the *Sui shu*, q.v., *Jiu Tang shu*, *Xin Tang shu*, and *Song shi*. None of the early collections are extant. Fortunately, two encyclopedias from the Tang dynasty preserved some of his prose. The *Yiwen leiju*, q.v., contains forty-seven fragments of his prose, among which thirty-one are from rhapsodies. The *Chuxue ji*, q.v., collects forty incomplete pieces, of which twenty are from rhapsodies. The *Chongwen zongmu** (compiled between 1034 and 1038) lists the work as having five *juan* and containing thirty-two pieces.

Principal editions

During the Ming and Qing dynasties, several reconstructed editions appeared. Zhang Pu's *Fu Chungu ji* in *Han Wei Liuchao baisanjia ji*, q.v., has five *juan*, containing ninety-four essays and 116 poems (eighty-seven *yuefu* and twenty-nine *shi*). Yan Kejun's (1762–1843) *Quan shanggu Sandai Qin Han Sanguo Liuchao wen*, q.v., includes Fu Xuan's prose in "Quan Jin wen," *juan* 45–50, which contain fifty-three rhapsodies and fifty-nine items of prose. The last four *juan* provide excerpts from the *Fuzi* (Master Fu), q.v., which was considered one of the greatest Confucian works of the early medieval period. Well-preserved during the Tang, this work began to disappear after the Song, and what survives today was reconstructed by Qing scholars.

In 1876, Fang Junshi 方濬師 (1830–1889) compiled the *Fu Chungu ji fu Fuzi jiaokan ji* 傅鶉觚集附傅子校勘記 (Collection of Fu Chungu with collations and notes on the *Fuzi*) in five *juan*. The first two *juan* and the supplement consist of the *Fuzi*. The third *juan* contains thirty-one rhapsodies, forty-five essays, and seventeen incomplete *fu*. The fourth *juan* contains seventy-nine *yuefu*, and the fifth contains thirty-five lyric poems and some collated lines. Ye Dehui 葉德輝 (1864–1927) produced a three-*juan* edition titled *Jin sili xiaowei Fu Xuan ji* 晉司隸校尉傅玄集 in his *Guangutang suo zhushu* 觀古堂所著書, dated 1891. This edition was based on Zhang Pu's edition but provides notes about the contents of the works and references they made. The first *juan* contains forty-nine rhapsodies, fifty-three lyric poems, and six collated items; the second, ninety-one *yuefu*; the third includes all other genres, containing fifty-five pieces in total. The standard modern collection of Fu Xuan's poetry is in the *Xian Qin Han Wei Jin Nanbeichao shi** edited by Lu Qinli (1911–1973), which contains seventy lyric poems and fifty-three *yuefu* verses ("Jin shi," 1:553–77).

Commentary and notes without the complete text

Jian Changchun 蹇長春 et al. *Fu Xuan Yin Keng shizhu* 傅玄陰鏗詩注 [Annotated poems of Fu Xuan and Yin Keng]. Lanzhou: Gansu renmin chubanshe, 1987.

Selected studies

Chen Zuolin 陳作林. "Lun Fu Xuan shi de sixiang yu yishu" 論傅玄詩的思想與藝術. *Beifang luncong* (1984.4): 36–41.

Jiang Jianyun 姜劍雲. "Lun Fu Xuan 'yin qi yuan er guang zhi' de wenti fengge guannian" 論傅玄'引其源而廣之'的文體風格觀念. *Wenyi lilun yanjiu* (2002.5): 86–90.

Kong Xurong. "Fu Xuan's (217–278) Rhapsodies on Objects (*Yongwu fu*)." Ph.D. diss., University of Wisconsin-Madison, 2005.

Liao Guodong 廖國棟. *Wei Jin yongwu fu yanjiu* 魏晉詠物賦研究. Taipei: Wen shi zhe chubanshe, 1990.

Liu Zhili 劉治立. "Fu Xuan ji qi shixue" 傅玄及其史學. *Shixueshi yanjiu* (1998.2): 38–44.

Mu Jiguang 穆紀光. "Fu Xuan ji qi zhexue sixiang" 傅玄及其哲學思想. *Xibei shidi* (1984.3): 94, 104–8.

———. "Lun Fu Xuan de meixue sixiang" 論傅玄的美學思想. *Shehui kexue* (Lanzhou) (1984.5): 33–37, 57.

Paper, Jordan D. *The Fu-tzu: A Post-Han Confucian Text*. Monographies du T'oung Pao 13. Leiden: Brill, 1987.

Sun Li 孫立. "Cong Fu Xuan dao Liu Xie: Guanyu erzhe de wenti yanjiu fangfa lun" 從傅玄到劉勰: 關於二者的文體研究方法論. *Zhongshan daxue xuebao* (1998.2): 42–48.

Wang Huijie 王繪絜. *Fu Xuan ji qi shiwen yanjiu* 傅玄及其詩文研究. Taipei: Wenjin chubanshe, 1997.

Wei Min'an 魏民安 and Zhao Yiwu 趙以武. *Fu Xuan pingzhuan* 傅玄評傳. Nanjing: Nanjing daxue chubanshe, 1996.

———. "Fu Xuan shi Taikang zuojia ma?" 傅玄是太康作家嗎? *Gansu shida xuebao, Zhexue shehui kexue* (1981.2): 69–75.

Zhao Yiwu 趙以武. "Shi lun Fu Xuan de yuefu shi" 試論傅玄的樂府詩. *Shehui kexue* (Lanzhou) (1984.3): 117–23.

Translations

Frodsham, J. D., with the collaboration of Cheng Hsi. *An Anthology of Chinese Verse: Han Wei Chin and the Northern and Southern Dynasties*. Oxford: Oxford University Press, 1967. Pp. 251–52.

Paper, Jordan D. "Fu Hsuan as Poet: A Man of His Season." In *Wen-lin: Studies in Chinese Humanities*, ed. Tse-tsung Chow, 45–60. Madison: University of Wisconsin Press, 1989.

Kong Xurong

Gaoseng zhuan 高僧傳

Introduction

The *Gaoseng zhuan* (Biographies of eminent monks), compiled by Shi Huijiao 釋慧皎 (497–554), is the primary source for information about monks in China from the beginnings of Chinese Buddhism in the first century until the book's completion in approximately 530. A number of collections of monks' biographies had appeared before the *Gaoseng zhuan*, but, with the exception of a few fragments, these are not extant. The *Gaoseng zhuan* can be mined for historical data about key figures, doctrines, monasteries, and events. Drawing on a wide variety of sources, the text further reflects generally held beliefs and perceptions of Buddhism and monks in the sixth century, including, for instance, conceptions of the spirit world and criteria for evaluating what was to be considered an "eminent" monk.

The influence of the *Gaoseng zhuan* extends well beyond the date of its composition. From the early sixth century on, the *Gaoseng zhuan* was avidly read and quoted by monks, laymen and even those with no Buddhist affiliation. The *Gaoseng zhuan* is also important in the development of Buddhist historiography in China. Regarding the criteria for inclusion, the organization of biographies, and the inclusion of commentaries by the historian, the *Gaoseng zhuan* served as the model for two later major collections of biographies of monks, the *Xu Gaoseng zhuan*, q.v., compiled by Daoxuan 道宣 in the seventh century, and the *Song Gaoseng zhuan* 宋高僧傳, compiled by Zanning 贊寧 at the end of the tenth. Although the style and principles of compilation of monastic biography subsequently underwent radical changes, the *Gaoseng zhuan* remained the most popular and admired collection of monastic biographies in Chinese Buddhist history.

Contents

The *Gaoseng zhuan* contains 257 major biographies. More than 200 subordinate biographies of figures Huijiao considered of lesser importance are attached to major biographies (there is divergence of opinion on how many subordinate biographies there because subordinate biographies, *fuzhuan* 附傳, were not marked off as such by Huijiao). The earliest account purports to describe events of A.D. 67, the last from 519. The biographies are divided into ten categories:

1. Yijing 譯經 — Translators
2. Yijie 義解 — Exegetes
3. Shenyi 神異 — Divine wonders (devoted to wonder-workers)
4. Xichan 習禪 — Practitioners of meditation
5. Minglü 明律 — Elucidators of the regulations (devoted to scholars of the Vinaya)
6. Wangshen 亡身 — Those who sacrificed themselves (i.e., monks who sacrificed their bodies in acts of charity or devotion). In Huijiao's preface he gives *yishen* 遺身 in place of *wangshen*.
7. Songjing 誦經 — Chanters of scriptures
8. Xingfu 興福 — Benefactors (literally, the "elicitation of merit," for monks who solicited funds for construction and other worthy enterprises)
9. Jingshi 經師 — Hymnodists (monks skilled in intoning liturgy)
10. Changdao 唱導 — Proselytizers

At the end of each section, Huijiao appended a disquisition (*lun* 論) in which he discusses the theme of the section. For instance, in his disquisition to the section on translators, Huijiao gives a brief history of the transmission of Buddhist scriptures and discusses the difficulties of translating Indian texts into Chinese. A preface to the book (in most editions appended to the last chapter) lists earlier collections of monastic biography (most no longer extant) and explains how Huijiao distinguished his work from them.

Authorship

Although Huijiao's authorship of the text is undisputed, we know very little about him. Other than the detail that he was a native of Kuaiji 會稽, we know nothing of Huijiao's early life or even his secular surname. As a monk he lived at a monastery in Kuaiji where he was said to have composed commentaries to the Nirvana Sutra and to the *Fanwang jing* 梵網經, an indigenous scripture on the monastic regulations. These works are not extant. Soon after Kuaiji's fall to Hou Jing 候景 in 549, Huijiao fled to Pencheng 湓城, near present-day Jiuzhang 九江 in Jiangxi, where he died in 554 at the age of fifty-eight. The *Gaoseng zhuan* is his only extant work.

Composition

Most of the biographies in the *Gaoseng zhuan* are taken in large part or completely from previous sources. In some cases, these sources are still extant. For instance,

Huijiao follows biographies in the *Chu sanzang jiji* 出三藏記集 very closely. This is the only work that Huijiao drew upon that is extant in complete form. In most cases, it is not possible to examine his sources and determine the extent to which he differed from them. From Huijiao's comments in his preface and occasional notes in the biographies themselves, we can at least determine the types of sources he employed, chiefly inscriptions, biographies of individual monks that circulated independently, prefaces to translations, collections of biographies of monks, and collections of miracle tales.

Transmission of the text

The *Gaoseng zhuan* is recorded in the major premodern Buddhist and non-Buddhist bibliographies from the early seventh century on. Most bibliographies attribute the text to Huijiao and record it as having fourteen *juan*. Chen Yuan 陳垣 in his *Zhongguo fojiao shiji gailun mulu* 中國佛教史籍概論目錄 (Beijing: Zhonghua, 1962, p. 22) attributes discrepancies in the bibliographies that list different authors or number of *juan* as clerical errors. The *Junzhai dushu zhi** 9.389–90 lists two works under the title *Gaoseng zhuan*, one in six *juan* and one in fourteen. It is most likely that the first refers to an edition of the first two chapters of the *Gaoseng zhuan* ("Translators" and "Exegetes") that circulated independently. The *Gaoseng zhuan* was included in printed versions of the Buddhist Canon from the early twelfth century, and through seventeen later printed editions from the Song into the twentieth century.

Principal editions

Modern editions of the *Gaoseng zhuan* for the most part derive from the Zhaocheng 趙城 (1139–1172), the Qisha 磧砂 (1225–1233), or the Korean edition (1236–1251) of the canon. The *Zhonghua Dazang jing* 中華大藏經 edition (Beijing: Zhonghua shuju, 1984–1996), for instance, is based on the Zhaocheng, while the most commonly cited edition, the *Taishō shinshū Daizōkyō**, vol. 50, no. 2059, is based on the Korean printing, with annotation of discrepancies with some other editions in the notes. The *Taishō* edition is widely available in printed and digital forms. There is as yet no consensus among scholars as to which edition is superior.

Modern critical editions

We await an edition of the text that rigorously compares all of the major editions and explains all discrepancies. The most commonly cited critical edition currently available is that of Tang Yongtong 湯用彤, edited by Tang Yijie 湯一介, published posthumously as *Gaoseng zhuan* 高僧傳 (Beijing: Zhonghua shuju, 1992). The text is based on the *Taishō* edition with punctuation and some annotation. An edition by Zhu Hengfu 朱恒夫 et al., *Xinyi Gaoseng zhuan* 新譯高僧傳 (Taipei: Sanmin, 2005), has the original text (based on the Qisha edition), extensive annotation, and translation into modern Chinese of the entire text.

Studies of the text

Major studies

Ji Yun 紀贇. *Huijiao Gaoseng zhuan yanjiu* 慧皎高僧傳研究. Shanghai: Shanghai guji chubanshe, 2009.

Makita Tairyō 牧田諦亮. "Kōsōden no seiritsu" 高僧傳の成立. *Tōhō gakuhō* 44 (1973): 101–25, and 48 (1975): 229–59.

Naomi Gentetsu 直海玄哲. "Kōsōden seiritsujō no mondaiten—Donmushin no jirei o tsūjite" 高僧傳成立上の問題點―曇無讖の事列を通じて. *Tōyō shien* 26.27 (March 1986): 63–82.

Wright, Arthur. "Biography and Hagiography: Hui-chiao's *Lives of Eminent Monks*." In *Silver Jubilee Volume*, 383–432. Kyoto University: Jimbun kagaku kenkyū-sho, 1954. Reprinted in *Studies in Chinese Buddhism*, ed. Robert M. Somers, 73–111, 150–72. New Haven, CT: Yale University Press, 1990. This remains the best study of the sources and composition of the text.

Xu Yanling 徐燕玲. *Huijiao Gaoseng zhuan ji qi fenke zhi yanjiu* 慧皎高僧傳及其分科之研究. Taipei: Hua Mulan wenhua gongzuofang, 2006.

Zheng Yuqing 鄭郁卿. *Gaoseng zhuan yanjiu* 高僧傳研究. Taipei: Wenjin chubanshe, 1990.

Works on particular chapters or themes

Mizuo Genjo 水尾現誠. "Shashin ni tsuite—Ekō no tachiba" 捨身について―慧皎の立場. *Indogaku bukkyōgaku kenkyū* 22 (1963): 174–75.

Murakami Yoshimi 村上嘉實. "Kōsōden no shin-i ni tsuite" 高僧傳の神異について. *Tōhō shukyō* 17 (1961): 1–17.

Tanaka Keishin 田中敬信. "Ryōkōsōden ni okeru shin-i" 梁高僧傳における神異. *Indogaku bukkyōgaku kenkyū* 20.1 (1972): 291–93.

Historiography and hagiography

Kieschnick, John. "Buddhism: Biographies of Buddhist Monks." In *The Oxford History of Historical Writing*, vol. 1, *Beginnings to AD 600*, ed. Andrew Feldherr and Grant Hardy, 535–52. Oxford: Oxford University Press, 2011.

———. *The Eminent Monk: Buddhist Ideals in Medieval Chinese Hagiography*. Honolulu: University of Hawai'i Press, 1997.

Kiriya Seiichi 桐谷征一. "Ryō Shaku Ekō ni okeru rekishi, ishiki tokuni kankai ishiki no igi ni tsuite" 梁釋慧皎における歷史,意識特に鑑戒意識の意義について. *Indogaku bukkyōgaku kenkyū* 20.2 (1971): 298–301.

Poo, Mu-chou. "The Images of Immortals and Eminent Monks: Religious Mentality in Early Medieval China (4–6 c. A.D.)." *Numen* 42 (1995): 172–96.

Shinohara Koichi. "Two Sources of Chinese Buddhist Biographies: Stupa Inscriptions and Miracle Stories." In *Monks and Magicians: Religious Biographies in Asia*, ed. Phyllis Granoff and Koichi Shinohara, 119–228. London: Mosaic Press, 1988.

Translations in European languages

Berkowitz, Alan J. "Account of the Buddhist Thaumaturge Baozhi." In *Buddhism in Practice*, ed. Donald S. Lopez, Jr., 578–85. Princeton, NJ: Princeton University Press, 1995.

Kieschnick, John. "Biography of the Jin Monk Bo Sengguang 帛僧光 of Hermit Peak in Shan." In *Buddhist Scriptures*, ed. Donald S. Lopez, 286–88. London: Penguin Books, 2004.

Liebenthal, Walter. "A Biography of Chu Tao-sheng." *Monumenta Nipponica* 11.3 (1955): 64–96.

Link, Arthur. "Biography of Shih Tao-an." *T'oung Pao* 46 (1958): 1–48.

Link, Arthur, and Hirai Shunei 平井俊榮. "Kōsōden no chūshakuteki kenkyū" 高僧傳の注釋的研究. *Komazawa daigaku bukkyōgakubu ronshū* 駒沢大学仏教学部論集 23 (1992): 443–56 (Biographies of Dharmaratna, Dharmakāla, Kang Sengkai 康僧凱, Tandi 曇帝, Boyan 帛延); 24 (1993): 436–70 (Biographies of Kang Senghui 康僧會 and Zhi Qian 支謙); 25 (1994): 414–28 (Biography of Dharmarakṣa); 26 (1995): 313–32 (Biographies of Śrīmitra, Saṅghabhadra, and Buddharakṣa). *Komazawa daigaku bukkyōgakubu kenkyū kiyō* 駒沢大学仏教学部研究紀要 49 (1991): 170–84 (Biography of Shemoteng 攝摩騰); 53 (1995): 333–50 (Biographies of Boyuan 帛遠, Fazuo 法祚, and Wei Shidu 衛士度). Note that these pieces include Arthur Link's translations of some of the biographies of monks in the first *juan* together with Japanese translation and annotation by Hirai Shunei. Altogether, six installments were published in the 1990s.

Shih, Robert. *Biographies des moines éminents (kao seng tchouan) de Houei-kiao*. Louvain: Université de Louvain, Institut Orientaliste, 1968. Shih translates only the "Translators" chapter.

Wright, Arthur. "Fo-t'u-teng, A Biography." *Harvard Journal of Asiatic* Studies 11 (1948): 321–71.

Japanese annotations and translations

Hirai Shunei. See in previous section under Link.

Suwa Gijun 諏訪義純 and Nakajima Ryūzō 中嶋隆蔵. *Kōsōden* 高僧傳. Tokyo: Chūō kōronsha, 1991. (Biographies of Kumarajīva, Dao'an, and Zhu Daosheng.)

Yoshikawa Tadao 吉川忠夫 and Funayama Tōru 船山徹. *Kōsōden* 高僧傳. Tokyo: Iwanami shoten, 2009. This is a four-volume Japanese translation of the entire text with notes, the most comprehensive translation of the text to date.

John Kieschnick

Gaoshi zhuan 高士傳

Introduction

The *Gaoshi zhuan* (Accounts of high-minded men), compiled by Huangfu Mi 皇甫謐 (215–282), is the standard resource for accounts of practitioners of reclusion from legendary antiquity into the Wei (220–265). That is, it has been the text most often quoted implicitly or explicitly through the centuries as the source for information and anecdotes concerning the most renowned recluses, moral exemplars, and political recusants who were celebrated for their strong individualism, or their often idealistic or contrarian conduct, or as foils and counterweights to the largely Confucian scholarly ethos of bettering the world through participation in state governance.

In contradistinction to men who held official positions, men in reclusion (*yinzhe* 隱者) commonly were referred to by such terms as *yinshi* 隱士 (hidden men), *yimin* 逸民 (disengaged persons), *chushi* 處士 (scholars-at-home) and, especially, *gaoshi* 高士 (high-minded men). *Gaoshi* were said to loftily exalt their inner principles and decline appointments to serve in official capacity within the imperial bureaucracy. Indeed, one explanation of the term is that it refers to the *Yi jing* 易經: "He does not serve a king or lord; he elevates in priority his [own] affairs" (不事王侯, 高尚其事; no. 18, "Gu" 蠱, line text for "Nine at the Top"). Huangfu Mi's understanding of the term may be implied in his "Preface" where he writes that in accordance with classical practice, "men who loftily renounce [worldly position] (高讓之士) are those whom the king's governing body would advance." Accordingly, a great many of the accounts mention the renunciation of offers to serve in government. Some scholars maintain that Huangfu Mi collected the accounts as support for his own repeated refusals to take office. Still, it may also be that he simply followed a conventional usage, referring generally to men of lofty, high-minded ideals and conduct. (Those who would see a titular affinity to the *Gaoseng zhuan*, q.v., should keep in mind that Huangfu Mi's work preceded it by more than two centuries.) There are no separate accounts of high-minded women in Huangfu Mi's collection, perhaps reflecting the overall backgrounding of the contrast of choice of individual proclivity over official service.

Contents

The *Gaoshi zhuan* contains more than ninety accounts of high-minded men in three *juan*, organized in roughly chronological order. More than half are from the pre-Qin period, taking up the first one and two-thirds *juan* (fifty individuals under forty-six headings), with accounts of Former Han individuals (eighteen men in seventeen headings) filling the remainder of the second *juan*, the largest of the three. The third *juan* contains twenty-five accounts of Later Han individuals and three accounts of men from the Three Kingdoms. There is an innate imprecision in the chronological division of the entries and the exact number of individuals in each period as well as the total number treated in the compilation, since some individuals span more than one dynastic division and several accounts describe more than one individual (for example, the Four Hoaryheads, Si hao 四皓). Also, some editions lack a heading for Yan Zun 嚴遵 of the Former Han. Accounts generally are brief, around 200 characters; the longest is 421 characters (Liang Hong 梁鴻 of the Later Han), and the shortest 58 characters (the Farmer of Stone Gate, Shihu zhi nong 石戶之農). The *Gujin yishi* 古今逸史 version of the text includes a verse appraisal for each entry, all consisting of eight four-character lines in rhyming couplets. Huangfu Mi's preface precedes the accounts in all editions, and some editions also include a postface by the prolific editor Wang Mo 王謨 (ca. 1731–ca. 1817) of Rushang 汝上 (Wang's postface is not in the *Gujin yishi* edition).

In Huangfu Mi's collection, the most celebrated men in reclusion are predominantly the ones who appear in the great books of old, that is, the classics and the writings of the various pre-Han Masters, and in Han historical and literary works. The accounts illustrate a broad spectrum of mind-sets and behaviors that were characteristic of the portrayal of reclusion, and for the most part they follow in chronological order. The early accounts include more enigmatic individuals than do the later accounts, which mostly concern historically verifiable men. These include anonymous recluses known by an epithet derived from their outer traces, such as appearance, locale, or métier—for instance, Chaofu 巢父 (the Nest-dweller), Yufu 漁父 (the Fisherman), and Heshang zhangren 河上丈人 (the Adept by the River). And there are luminaries of the so-called Confucian and Daoist traditions such as Yan Hui 顏回 and Zeng Shen 曾參, and Laozi 老子 and Zhuangzi 莊子, as well as celebrity recluses including Xu You 許由 and the Four Hoaryheads. It should be kept in mind that the *Gaoshi zhuan* is not a Daoist work per se, even while a fair number of the accounts embody attitudes and lifestyles often popularly associated with early "Daoist" thought, and some concern men revered in Daoist texts, including a sampling of gods in the Daoist pantheon. Rather, as expressed in the title, it is a work exemplifying men in reclusion. The *Gaoshi zhuan* is not included in the Daoist compendia, as are seemingly analogous compilations such as the *Liexian zhuan* 列仙傳 and the *Shenxian zhuan*, q.v.

Huangfu Mi mentioned in his preface that his may not have been the first work to group together stories about such individuals, but it was the first to be comprehensive in terms of temporal scope and the principles of collocation. That is, he considered his compilation to be the first to limit the scope of reclusion and who was to be considered a *gaoshi*, and what acts or attitudes constituted the conduct of a *gaoshi*. He ends his preface by relating that all of the men in his compilation "were not to be humbled by kings and lords, [and they were those] whose reputation has not diminished over time.... [Yet] as for those who held to their principles in the manner of Bo Yi 伯夷 and Shu Qi 叔齊, whose choice of action resembled that of the two men named Gong 龔: I have not recorded any of them." That is, Huangfu Mi specifically excludes from his collection, and thus also from the delimitation of who should be considered a *gaoshi*, those who chose suicide as an extreme demonstration of staunch adherence to principle and as an overt and indelible expression of preserving one's own pristine virtue. The well-known individuals in Huangfu Mi's accounts all demonstrated their high-mindedness through exemplary life-conduct: they were models of reclusion, and, as one particular sort of laudable and appropriate attitude and pursuit, reclusion was to be considered a constituent aspect of life in the Chinese cultural world.

Authorship and transmission

Huangfu Mi was a prominent scholar from what is now Gansu who composed influential and enduring works on history and medicine, as well as literary compositions in a wide variety of forms on a broad array of topics. His *Zhenjiu jiayi jing* 針灸甲乙經 (Fundamentals of acupuncture and moxibustion) remains a seminal and essential treatise on the subject. He steadfastly declined numerous official appointments, defending his disengagement and choice of lifestyle with deft and persuasive reasoning, replete with examples of men whose similar behavior was admired throughout history. His *Gaoshi zhuan* in effect supports his own decision not to serve in office. The *Gaoshi zhuan*'s accounts all concern men commonly cited in literature and familiar to all scholar-officials, as well as to the rulers, and such a collection of worthies implicitly justified both the noncareer, outsider stance of the individuals and the magnanimity of their rulers for sanctioning such conduct. Huangfu Mi's accounts on the whole are derivative, that is, he most often redacted and resituated materials from other sources, usually refining anecdotes and other descriptive accounts of individuals into pithy syntheses of lore that center on exemplifying in their portrayal the qualities and actions that made them memorable and representative as high-minded men.

Huangfu Mi's *Gaoshi zhuan* follows in the tradition of collected, categorized accounts of exemplary individuals that perhaps began with the *Liexian zhuan* (Arrayed accounts of transcendents), *Lieshi zhuan* 列士傳 (Arrayed accounts of noteworthy men), and *Lienü zhuan* 列女傳 (Arrayed accounts of noteworthy women), all three attributed to Liu Xiang 劉向 (79–8 B.C.). Huangfu Mi's younger contemporary Ji Kang 嵇康 (also romanized as Xi Kang; 223–262) compiled a similar work called the *Sheng xian gaoshi zhuan zan* 聖仙高士傳讚 (Accounts of sages, transcendents, and high-minded men, with encomiums), also known simply as the *Gaoshi zhuan*, and there is a good deal of debate about whose compilation came first. The question of antecedence remains unresolved, and indeed there is some overlap in the extant accounts. Huangfu Mi mentions in his preface that his work would correct lapses and inconsistencies in previous compilations of accounts of high-minded men, and as Ji Kang's work contains accounts of some men who served in office, this has been seen by some as evidence of the precedence of Ji Kang's compilation. Nevertheless, similar compilations that preceded the *Gaoshi zhuan* of both Huangfu Mi and Ji Kang also do not appear to have made the clear distinction that Huangfu Mi establishes in his preface and choice of entries. Huangfu Mi himself also compiled a work called the *Yishi zhuan* 逸士傳 (Accounts of disengaged men), and here too there is a fair amount of conflation in the attribution of excerpts of this work and those cited as coming from his *Gaoshi zhuan*.

The text's transmission is not entirely straightforward. Although there are records of separate editions of the *Gaoshi zhuan* existing since Huangfu Mi's time, virtually all modern editions derive from the three-*juan* version contained in the Ming compilation *Gujin yishi*. Yet bibliographic records have been discrepant over the centuries. The *Sui shu* bibliographic monograph lists the *Gaoshi zhuan* as containing six *juan* (*Sui shu* 33:975); the Tang bibliographies have seven (*Jiu Tang shu* 46:2002) or ten (*Xin Tang shu* 58:1481); and the several Song bibliographies all list ten. The number of *juan* does not necessarily correlate with or indicate the completeness or incompleteness of the text.

Much more problematic are the discrepancies in the number of accounts and the textual history of witnesses. Huangfu Mi's preface states that he included accounts of more than ninety men, and this also happens to be the number contained in modern editions of the work (ninety-one account headings, ninety-six total men). Song dynasty bibliographies mention ninety-six or eighty-seven men. One often quoted Southern Song source, the *Xu Bowu zhi* by Li Shi 李石, unequivocally states that there were seventy-two accounts, pressing the point that this equals the number of disciples of Confucius according to Kong Anguo 孔安國 (in the *Kongzi jiayu* 孔子家語), as well as the number of accounts in Liu Xiang's *Liexian zhuan* and the *Chenliu qijiu zhuan* 陳留耆舊傳 of Chen Changwen 陳長文. Thus, some bibliographers conclude that there were at least two versions circulating in the Song and that the version with ninety-six men is likely not Huangfu Mi's original, but a redaction of accounts from commonplace books, especially the *Taiping yulan*. If this is the case, then one must also cast suspicion on the transmission of Huangfu Mi's preface, as it specifies "more than ninety" accounts. Actually, Li Shi's statement about the number of accounts is directly derived from a declaration by Yang Xi 楊羲 (330–386) as recorded in the *Zhen gao* 真誥 (*juan* 17). This conclusively demonstrates that a recension of the *Gaoshi zhuan* with accounts of seventy-two men certainly circulated in the fourth century; nevertheless, we cannot know Huangfu Mi's original, and extant versions are likely to be Song or later reconstructions.

Commonplace books and collectanea since the Tang contain much of the material found in the extant editions of the work, but it would be difficult to ascribe the present text in its entirety as a single editor's later recompilation, due to lack of editorial evidence; attribution discrepancies; variant readings; and incomplete entry content. Luo Zhenyu 羅振玉 (1866–1940) collected accounts of seventy-three men from passages directly attributed to Huangfu Mi's *Gaoshi zhuan*, and he points out the problem of attribution for some accounts: more than a few of these are quoted in other sources as coming from Huangfu Mi's *Yishi zhuan*. Luo carried out his collation in 1887 but did not have it published until 1915; he ends his postface: "and I lament the increasing turbidity of these times; how to get to revive the men in these pages and pass my days in their company?" Huangfu Mi's *Gaoshi zhuan* spurred a dozen or so similar collections or sequels over the next several centuries and many others into modern times, many of which prominently include an account of Huangfu Mi himself. A number of artists later provided woodblock illustrations to accompany the text of the *Gaoshi zhuan*, and more recently a well-known seal carver produced a series of commemorative seals for each of the accounts.

Standard editions

1. The *Siku quanshu** edition is based on an unknown edition from Jiangsu submitted in 1781 but appears to derive from the *Gujin yishi* version (see later).

2. The *Sibu beiyao** edition indicates that it is based on a *Han Wei congshu* version, but that itself derives directly from the *Gujin yishi* text; the *Sibu beiyao* version is virtually identical to the *Gujin yishi* version, although lacking the rhymed-verse encomia.

3. Wu Guan 吳琯 (*jinshi* 1571), comp., *Gujin yishi* 古今逸史. The Shanghai Hanfenlou 上海涵芬樓 facsimile reprint of a Ming woodblock edition has a version of the text nearly identical to the *Sibu beiyao* and *Han Wei congshu* versions but also includes a verse appraisal for each entry, each one in eight four-character lines in rhyming couplets.

4. The *Han Wei congshu* edition, compiled in the late Ming, is virtually identical to the *Gujin yishi* version, although lacking the rhymed-verse encomia.

5. The *Congshu jicheng** *chubian* also is based on the *Gujin yishi*, including the verse encomia.

Other editions

Deng Sanmu 鄧散木 (1898–1963). *Deng Sanmu xiansheng Gaoshi zhuan yinpu* 鄧散木先生高士傳印譜. Hong Kong: Shanheshe, 1985.

Liu Xiaodong 劉曉東, ed. *Gaoshi zhuan* 高士傳. Shenyang: Liaoning jiaoyu chubanshe, 1998.

Luo Zhenyu carefully assembled passages directly attributed to Huangfu Mi's *Gaoshi zhuan* contained in commentaries and collectanea, with the large majority culled from the *Taiping yulan*, q.v. Luo's collated version of quotations was first printed as *Gaoshi zhuan* in his *Xuetang congke* 雪堂叢刻 (n.p., n.d.) and reprinted in various editions of his collected works; it is titled

Gaoshi zhuan jiben 高士傳輯本 in other editions of his collected works, such as in Zhang Benyi 張本義, ed., *Luo Xuetang heji* 羅雪堂合集 (Hangzhou: Xiling yinshe, 2005).

Ren Xiong 任熊 (1823–1857), illustrator. *Gaoshi zhuan huazhuan* 高士傳畫傳, a woodblock edition reprinted in *Huangfu Mi yizhu ji*. Full text, accompanied by a contextual portrait for each account.

Shi Xinghai 史星海, ed. *Huangfu Mi yizhu ji* 皇甫謐遺著集. Yangzhou: Guangling shushe, 2008. This edition also takes the *Gujin yishi* version as base text; it compares other editions and aims for a collated version but does not include emendations.

Wang Xiling 王錫齡 (fl. ca. 1858), ed. *Gaoshi zhuan tuxiang* 高士傳圖像. N.p., Wang shi Yanghetang 王氏養龢堂 woodblock edition, 1858; includes Ren Xiong's illustrations from the first *juan*, followed by the full text.

Selected studies and further readings

Berkowitz, Alan. "Huangfu Mi 皇甫謐 (215–282), *Accounts of High-Minded Men (Gaoshi zhuan* 高士傳)," in *Early Medieval China: A Sourcebook*, ed. Wendy Swartz, Robert Ford Campany, Yang Lu, and Jessey Choo, 333–49. New York: Columbia University Press, 2013. Includes translations of the preface and eighteen accounts.

———. *Patterns of Disengagement: The Practice and Portrayal of Reclusion in Early Medieval China*. Stanford, CA: Stanford University Press, 2000.

———. "Accounts of High-Minded Men by Huangfu Mi." In *Hawaii Reader in Traditional Chinese Culture*, ed. Victor Mair et al., 242–50. Honolulu: University of Hawai'i Press, 2005. Includes translations of the preface and thirteen accounts.

———. "Social and Cultural Dimensions of Reclusion in Early Medieval China." In *Philosophy and Religion in Early Medieval China*, ed. Alan K. L. Chan and Yuet-Keung Lo, 291–318. Albany, NY: SUNY Press, 2010.

Cai Xinfa 蔡信發. "Xilun Huangfu Mi zhi *Gaoshi zhuan*" 析論皇甫謐之高士傳. *Guoli Zhongyang daxue wenxueyuan yuankan* 1 (1983): 1–7.

Declercq, Dominik. *Writing against the State: Political Rhetorics in Third and Fourth Century China*. Leiden: Brill, 1998. Pp. 159–205.

Ishikawa Tadahisa 石川忠久. "Inshi Kōho Hitsu ron" 隱士皇甫謐論. *Kan Gi bunka* 7 (1968): 33–39.

Knapp, Keith N. "Heaven and Death According to Huangfu Mi, a Third-Century Confucian." *Early Medieval China* 6 (2000): 1–31.

Shi Xinghai 史星海, ed. *Huangfu Mi yanjiu quanji diyi juan, di'er juan* 皇甫謐研究全集第一卷, 第二卷. Beijing: Renmin ribao chubanshe, 2005, 2006.

Niwa Taiko 丹羽兌子. "Kōho Hitsu to Kōshi den" 皇甫謐と高士伝. *Nagoya daigaku bungakubu kenkyū ronshū* (shigaku) 50 (1970): 49–66.

Vervoorn, Aat. *Men of the Cliffs and Caves: The Development of the Chinese Eremitic Tradition to the End of the Han Dynasty*. Hong Kong: Chinese University Press, 1990.

Wei Ming'an 魏明安. "Huangfu Mi *Gaoshi zhuan* chutan" 皇甫謐高士傳初探. *Lanzhou daxue xuebao* (1982.4): 1–13.

See also the various entries at the dedicated website "Zhongguo Huangfu Mi wang" 中國皇甫謐網, http://www.huangfumi.com/.

Alan J. Berkowitz

Ge xianweng Zhouhou beijifang
葛仙翁肘後備急方

Introduction

The *Ge xianweng Zhouhou beijifang* (Immortal Ge's handy prescriptions for emergencies), hereafter abbreviated as *Zhouhou beijifang*, was compiled by Ge Hong 葛洪 (283–343). It is the earliest medical formulary of China that still exists; it records a variety of simple and user-friendly medical formulae that were inexpensive and easy to obtain. The *Zhouhou beijifang* plays an essential role in documenting medical prescriptions that have been in use since before the Western Jin dynasty, and in the development of Chinese medicine thereafter. Additionally, it served as a crucial reference book for the compilation of two of the most important works in traditional Chinese medical history: the *Beiji qianjin yaofang* 備急千金要方 by Sun Simiao 孫思邈 (ca. 581–682) and the *Waitai miyaofang* 外台秘要方 by Wang Tao 王燾 (ca. 670–755).

Contents

Apart from treatments for emergency medical cases such as apoplexy, fainting, drowning, and external injuries, the *Zhouhou beijifang* also includes cures for contagious diseases, such as typhoid and smallpox, as well as epidemics. It provides brief descriptions of these diseases' causes, symptoms, and treatments. The *Zhouhou beijifang* is one of a large number of medical formularies that appeared in the Six Dynasties. From the perspective of present-day medicine, these medical formularies include data on internal medicine, surgery, gynecology, pediatrics, external injuries, parasitic diseases, and maladies related to the ear, mouth, nose, and throat. Modern scholars generally agree that two of the *Zhouhou beijifang*'s most substantial contributions are its record of *wandouchuang* 豌豆瘡 (smallpox), the earliest detailed documentation of this disease in medical history, and the use of *qinghao* 青蒿 (Artemisia apiacea) as a drug to treat *nüe* 瘧 disease (malaria). Thanks to this record, medical researchers of contemporary China have developed a new drug to treat malaria.

In the modern edition, a total of seventy-three sections are found in the book's table of contents, but actually there are only sixty-nine sections because the thirty-seventh section has neither heading nor content, and the forty-fourth through forty-sixth sections have been lost. *Juan* 1 to 4, containing thirty-five sections, are mainly dedicated to treatments of internal illnesses, such as attacks of pestilence, abdominal pains, typhoid, epidemics, apoplexy, and the yellowing of hair. *Juan* 5 and 6 consist of seventeen sections that concern how to treat external illnesses, such as ulcers, sores, scabies, and ear and eye diseases. *Juan* 7, composed of twenty-one sections devoted to treatments of illnesses caused by poisons or other harmful substances and injuries inflicted by insects and beasts, is concerned with drugs and powdered medicines for hundreds of diseases and medical emergencies, as well as with veterinary medicine.

Sources of the work

According to the bibliographical monograph of the *Jiu Tang shu* and the *Zhouhou beijifang*'s own preface, this work was originally named the *Zhouhou jiucufang* 肘後救卒方 and had three *juan* organized into a total of eighty-six sections. The *Jin shu*, q.v., and the *Sui shu*, q.v., record a book written by Ge Hong titled *Zhouhou jiyaofang* 肘後急要方. Typically, the terms *beiji* 備急, *jiyao* 急要, and *jiucu* 救卒 bear similar meanings. In his preface and in the "Zaying pian" 雜應篇 of the *Baopuzi neipian* 抱朴子內篇, Ge Hong mentioned that he had collected five *Baocu beijifang* 暴卒備急方 and over five hundred *juan* of texts written by various medical experts, such as Hua Tuo 華佗 (d. ca. 208), Zhang Zhongjing 張仲景 (ca. second and third century), and Dai Ba 戴霸 (dates unknown).

Ge Hong studied all these texts and found that their contents were incomplete and poorly organized, with no reference to treatments of many critical diseases. He also noted that the authors tended to use expensive medicines in the formulae, making the text difficult for ordinary people to use. For instance, these books teach acupuncture therapies, but they mention only the names of the acu-points; their locations are not given, which renders the text useless to laypeople. Hoping to collect more medical formulae, Ge Hong traveled to various places, classifying the collected recipes into different categories and composing the *Yuhan fang* 玉函方. He then compiled the *Zhouhou jiucufang* from a selection of the most simple, user-friendly, and efficacious formulae in the *Yuhan fang*. These selected formulae could be used to treat critical diseases in emergency situations. Ge Hong claimed that, if people had these formulae, they would not need a physician. Based on his own testimony, the formularies for emergency medicine had been available before his compilation of these two books; Ge Hong merely reclassified and tested the formulae found in them.

Authorship and date of composition

Ge Hong was from a distinguished Daoist family in Danyang 丹陽 (in modern Jiangsu). His entry in *Jin shu* 72:1910–13 reports that he died at age eighty-one but it does not mention in which year. According to the textual research of Chen Guofu 陳國符, *Daozang yuanliukao* 道藏源流考 (Beijing: Zhonghua shuju, 1963), 95–99, Ge Hong was born in 283 and died in 343; hence, he actually died at age sixty-one. When he was young, he was particularly fond of studying the arts of transcendence, such as alchemy, physical exercises, and the sexual arts, leading him to become a student of Zheng Yin 鄭隱 and Bao Jing 鮑靚. He learned alchemy, pursued ways of becoming immortal, and studied medicine. Because of the political upheaval of the time, Ge Hong requested a government position in Guangzhou 廣州 (modern Guangdong) and stayed in the south for many years. After the establishment of the Eastern Jin Dynasty, he asked to become district magistrate of Goulou 勾漏 (near modern Hanoi in Vietnam), where minerals for his alchemy experiments were to be found. But on his way, the governor of Guangzhou insisted he remain there, so he stayed in the nearby Luofu 羅浮 Mountains and continued to refine his pill-making techniques until his death. He thus came to be known as Ge *xianweng*, *xianweng* being the term used to address an old Daoist priest.

In his *Baopuzi neipian*, Ge Hong mentioned that he had completed the *Zhouhou jiucufang*. Since it is believed that the *Baopuzi neipian* was initially completed in 317 and possibly revised around 333, and the *jiaoqi* 腳氣 disease, which was common after the establishment of the Eastern Jin, is recorded in the *Zhouhou beijifang*, the most probable time for Ge to have completed the *Zhouhou beijifang* is between 317 and 333.

Transmission and early history of the text

In the *Zhouhou beijifang*'s preface, Ge Hong mentions that the book contains three *juan*. However, other authors have given different numbers. Ruan Xiaoxu 阮孝緒 (479–536) of the Liang dynasty mentioned in his *Qilu* 七錄 that it had two *juan*, whereas the *Sui shu*'s bibliographical monograph states that it has a total of six. The *Jiu Tang shu* reports that the *Zhouhou fang* has only four *juan*. It is listed in *Zhizhai shulu jieti*** (ca. 1235) 13:386 as having three *juan*. Citations from the *Zhouhou fang* can also be found in *Qimin yaoshu*, q.v., *Yiwen leiju*, q.v., and *Ishinpō* 醫心方. The Yaofang 藥方 Cave of the Longmen 龍門 Grottoes contains fourteen medical prescriptions, carved into the wall during the early Tang, that are similar or identical to those found in the *Zhouhou fang*. Quotations from the *Zhouhou fang* can also be found in Wang Tao's *Waitai miyaofang* (Tang) and in the *Zhenglei bencao* 證類本草 by Tang Shenwei 唐慎微 (ca. eleventh and twelfth century). It is believed that the quotations in these two books are from an edition of the *Zhouhou fang* that was in circulation during the Tang and Song dynasties. The *Waitai miyaofang* notes that the *Zhouhou fang* has two editions, one of which with three *juan*, the other six.

Tao Hongjing 陶弘景 (456–536), a well-known Daoist priest and medical practitioner, greatly esteemed the *Zhouhou beijifang*, which was widely circulated after Ge Hong's death. However, he also noted its shortcomings, so he reorganized the book into 79 sections and added 22 more, making a total of 101 sections. He also amended the original text and added new information. For easy reference, he quoted the original text in black and added supplementary information in red. Tao's edition is divided into three *juan*: the first is on the treatments of internal illnesses, the second on external illnesses, and the third on illnesses caused by harmful matters. After Tao completed the revision of the book, he renamed this edition the *Buque Zhouhou baiyifang* 補闕肘後百一方. The reason that Tao included a total of 101 sections (not more or fewer) was because of Buddhist medical concepts. In Buddhist scriptures, earth, water, fire, and wind constitute the four elements of the human body, and each of these elements could trigger 101 diseases.

If we compare the prescriptions found in the modern edition of the *Zhouhou fang* with those found in the *Waitai miyafang* edition, we can find some discrepancies in terms of the wording and the *juan* in which they appear. After the Tang dynasty, a number of additions were made to the *Zhouhou fang* from medical books written after the Eastern Jin and Liang dynasties. During the Liao (916–1125) and in 1059 in Koryō 高麗 (modern-day Korea), the *Zhouhou fang* was reproduced using lithography. In 1144, during the Jin dynasty (1155–1234), Yang Daoyong 楊道用 used the edition printed in the Liao between 1101 and 1110 to rework the text, turning it into the modern edition of the *Zhouhou beijifang*. Yang expanded the *Zhouhou fang* to eight *juan*. He cited prescriptions of the *Zhouhou fang* found in the *Zhenglei bencao* and referred to them as "supplementary prescriptions" at the end of each section. After Yang had finished his revisions, he gave the *Zhouhou fang* the new title of *Fuguang Zhouhou fang* 附廣肘後方.

Principal editions

Modern editions are derived from those that appeared in the Ming dynasty.

1. Between 1368 and 1398 Yang Daoyong's *Fuguang Zhouhou fang*, which consisted of eight *juan*, was included in the *Daozang* 道藏, to which Zhao Nanyang's 趙南陽 *Waikefang* 外科方 was also attached. This is the earliest *Daozang* edition of the *Zhouhou fang*.

2. In 1574, while in the Wudang 武當 Mountains, Li Shi 李梴 extracted the *Fuguang Zhouhou fang* from the *Daozang* to form a separate manuscript. Since then, it has become the basic text for comparing different versions of the *Zhouhou fang* published during the Ming and Qing dynasties, and in Japan.

3. Yang Daoyong's *Fuguang Zhouhou fang* was also in wide circulation in Korea. Between 1443 and 1445, Kim Ye-mong 金禮蒙 edited the *Yifang leiju* 醫方類聚 and quoted the *Zhouhou baiyifang* 肘後百一方 in his book. The *Yifang leiju* contains fourteen more sections than the *Daozang* edition of the *Zhouhoufang*.

4. The *Siku quanshu zongmu tiyao** (19:2088) mentions that a Mr. Wu 烏 in the Yuan dynasty received Mr. Guo's 郭 edition of the *Zhouhou fang*. In 1336, Duan Chengji 段成己 wrote a preface for it. In 1551, Lü Yong 呂顒 printed this edition using lithography. In 1891, Cheng Yongpei 程永培 included this edition in his *Liulizhai yishu* 六醴齋醫書.

5. In 1955 the Commercial Press (Shangwu yinshuguan 商務印書館) reprinted the *Zhouhou fang* based on the edition found in the *Ming Zhengtong Daozang* 明正統道藏 that was in the collection of the Hanfenlou 涵芬樓.

6. In 1956, the Renmin weisheng chubanshe photocopied Li Shi's 1574 edition. The editor revised this edition by consulting seven others.
7. In 1992, the Ming edition of the *Zhouhou beijifang* 明版肘後備急方 was included in the twenty-seventh collection of the *Tōyō igaku zenpon sōsho* 東洋醫學善本叢書 published in Osaka by Tōyō igaku kenkyūkai 東洋医学研究会. This was a reprint of a copy in the collection of the Kokuritsu kōbunshokan naikaku bunko 國立公文書館內閣文庫.
8. Shang Zhijun 尚志鈞, an expert on herbology, compiled the *Buji Zhouhou fang* 補輯肘後方. He selected for his compilation a total of 1,265 prescriptions from medical books and encyclopedias of the Tang and Song periods that are not included in the modern edition.

Texts with commentaries and notes

Du Zuyi 杜祖貽 et al. *Zhongyi jiuzhishu jinghua: Ge Hong yu Tao Hongjing Zhouhou beijifang ji shu* 中醫救治術精華: 葛洪與陶弘景肘後備急方輯述. Hong Kong: Shangwu yinshuguan, 2007. This book is divided into three parts: (1) a selected commentary on the *Zhouhou beijifang*, in which twenty-four prescriptions are discussed and explained further; (2) a review of the *Zhouhou beijifang*, and (3) the original text of the *Zhouhou beijifang*.

Gao Meifeng 高美鳳 and Shi Qiwu 石啟武. "Ji yi ben *Zhouhou beijifang* buzheng" 輯佚本肘後備急方補正. *Nanjing zhongyiyao daxue xuebao* 2 (2000): 92–94. This article offers amendments and additional information to Shang Zhijun's work.

Ge Hong 葛洪. *Ge Hong Zhouhou beijifang* 葛洪肘後備急方. Beijing: Renmin weisheng chubanshe, 1963.

Shang Zhijun 尚志鈞. *Buji Zhouhou fang* 補輯肘後方. Hefei: Anhui kexue jishu chubanshe, 1996.

Wang Junning 王均寧. *Zhouhou beijifang* 肘後備急方. Tianjin: Tianjin kexue jishu chubanshe, 2000.

Yan Shiyun 嚴世芸 and Li Qizhong 李其忠, eds. *Buque Zhouhou baiyifang* 補闕肘後百一方. In *Sanguo Liang Jin Nanbeichao yixue zongji* 三國兩晉南北朝醫學總集. Beijing: Renmin weisheng chubanshe, 2009.

Commentaries and notes without the complete text

Andō Tuguo 安藤維男. "Katsu senō *Chūgo bikyūhō* ni tsuite" 葛仙翁肘後備急方について. *Tōhō shukyō* 41 (1973): 36–50.

Shi Yongchang 史永常. "Buque *Zhouhou baiyifang* de jiazhi he jiyi" 補闕肘後百一方的價值和輯佚. *Zhonghua yishi zazhi* 12.1 (1982): 42–48.

Shimomi Takao 下見隆雄. "Kakkō no chosho ni tsuite—*Chūgo bikyūhō*" 葛洪の著書について—肘後備急方. *Fukuoka joshi tandai kiyō* 7 (1973.12): 97–106.

Tōno Haruyuki 東野治之. "Heijōkyū mokkan naka no katsushi pō dankan" 平城宮木簡中の葛氏方斷簡. In *Nihon kodai mokkan no kenkyū* 日本古代木簡の研究, 185–207. Tokyo: Hanawa shobō, 1983.

Wang Ning 王寧. "*Zhouhoufang* he *Buque Zhouhou fang* pinglun" 肘後方和補闕肘後方評論. *Zhonghua yishi zazhi* 18.1 (1988): 58–61.

Selected studies

Ding Yizhuang 丁貽莊. "Shi lun Ge Hong de yixue chengjiu ji qi yixue sixiang" 試論葛洪的醫學成就及其醫學思想. *Sichuan daxue xuebao congkan* 25 (1985): 13–21.

Hu Naichang 胡乃長. "*Zhouhou fang* de waikexue chengjiu" 肘後方的外科學成就. *Zhonghua yi shi zazhi* 11.1 (1981): 25–28.

Jiang Pizheng 姜丕政 and Zhang Zhibin 張志斌. "*Zhouhou beijifang* zhong de chuanranbing renshi" 肘後備急方中的傳染病認識. *Zhonghua yi shi zazhi* 34.4 (2005): 224.

Kosoto Hiroshi 小曾戶洋. "Chūgo bikyūhō" 肘後備急方. In *Chūgoku igaku koten to Nihon: shoshi to denshō* 中国医学古典と日本: 書誌と伝承, 334–45. Tokyo: Hanawa shobō, 1996.

Ma Jixing 馬繼興. "Zhouhou beijifang" 肘後備急方. In *Zhongyi wenxian xue* 中醫文獻學, 159–61. Shanghai: Shanghai kexue jishu chubanshe, 1990.

Mei Quanxi 梅全喜 and Wu Huifei 吳惠妃. "Shilun *Zhouhou beijifang* zai yiyaoxue shang de gongxian" 試論肘後備急方在醫藥學上的貢獻. *Zhongyiyao xue kan* 23.7 (2005): 1194–97.

Murakami, Yoshimi 村上嘉實. "Kanbo shinhatsugen no isho to *Hōbokushi*" 漢墓新發現の醫書と抱朴子. *Tōhō gakuhō* 53 (1981): 387–421.

Qin Qingfu 秦慶福 and Nian Li 年莉. "*Zhouhou beijifang* de fangjixue chengjiu" 肘後備急方的方劑學成就. *Tianjin zhongyiyao daxue xuebao* 27.1 (2008): 9–10.

Sakade Yoshinobu 坂出祥伸. "Kakkō no iyakukan to *Chūgo bikyūhō* kaidai, kenkyū" 葛洪の医薬観と肘後備急方解題, 研究. In *Tōyō igaku zenpon sōsho* 東洋医学善本叢書, ed. Kosoto Hiroshi 小曾戶洋 et al., 29:26–44. Osaka: Oriento shuppan, 1996.

Sivin, Nathan. "On the *Pao P'u Tzu Nei Pien* and the Life of Ko Hong (283–343)." *Isis* 60 (1976): 388–91.

Sun Yixin 孫益鑫. "*Zhouhou beijifang* zhixue sixiang chutan" 肘後備急方治學思想初探. *Nanjing zhongyiyao daxue xuebao* 2 (1997): 62–63.

Xie Suzhu 謝素珠. "Ge Hong yiyaoxue chengguo zhi tantao" 葛洪醫藥學成果之探討. *Dao jiao xue tansuo* 8 (1994): 85–145.

Yang Dianhui 楊佃會 and Zang Shouhu 臧守虎. "*Zhouhou beijifang* jiufa xueshu sixiang tanxi" 肘後備急方灸法學術思想探析. *Shandong Zhongyiyao daxue xuebao* 25.1 (2001): 14–15.

Yin Biwu 尹必武. "Qianlun *Zhouhou beijifang* dui Zhongyi jizheng zhenzhi de gongxian" 淺論肘後備急方對中醫急症診治的貢獻. *Zhongguo Zhongyi ji zheng* 9.1 (2000): 37.

Yu, David C. *History of Chinese Daoism.* Lanham, MD: University Press of America, 2000. Vol. 1. In this translated work, an extensive chapter is devoted to Ge Hong, including an introduction to his contributions on medicine.

Translation

Hao Jinda 郝近大 and Hu Xiaofeng 胡曉峰. *Zhouhou beijifang jinyi* 肘後備急方今譯. Beijing: Zhongguo Zhongyiyao chubanshe, 1997.

Electronic research aid

Klein, Kenneth. "Bibliography of Western Works on Early Medieval China, Religion, Taoism, Ge Hong." Available at http://www.earlymedievalchinagroup.org/wjbiblio.htm#gehong/.

Fan Ka-wai

Guang Hongming ji 廣弘明集

Introduction

The *Guang Hongming ji* was compiled by the Vinaya teacher Daoxuan 道宣 (596–667), who in his later years regarded himself as an incarnation of Sengyou 僧祐 (445–518). It is not just a continuation of the *Hongming ji*, q.v., but encompasses a broader scope; it contains documents from periods before the compilation of the *Hongming ji*. Each of the openings of the ten sections of the *Guang Hongming ji* refers to certain texts of the *Hongming ji*.

Contents

The thirty *juan* of the *Guang Hongming ji* are divided into ten sections. These are the following:

1. Guizheng 歸正 — Committing oneself to the correct [doctrine]
2. Bianhuo 辯惑 — Discourse on delusions
3. Fode 佛德 — Buddha-virtue
4. Fayi 法義 — The meaning [or truth] of the Dharma
5. Sengxing 僧行 — The conduct of the sangha
6. Ciji 慈濟 — Compassion and salvation
7. Jiegong 戒功 — Precepts and merit
8. Qifu 啟福 — Clarifying blessedness
9. Huizui 悔罪 — Repenting sinfulness
10. Tonggui 统歸 — Submission and commitment [to the doctrine]

Each section starts with a preface followed by a list of texts from the *Hongming ji* that, according to the compiler, belong to the section. The organization and categorization of the material in the *Guang Hongming ji* and in the *Hongming ji* have not yet been studied; it would be worthwhile to include in such a comparison the categories set out by Huijiao for the *Gaoseng zhuan*, q.v., and by Daoxuan for his *Xu Gaoseng zhuan*, q.v. Daoxuan places himself in the tradition of compiling material relevant for the history of Buddhism in China.

Authorship

As is the case with other works by Daoxuan, he might have worked on this collection even after the completion of its preface, dated 664. In the preface for his *Xu Gaoseng zhuan* 續高僧傳, Daoxuan makes clear that his collection of biographies covers the period of time from the early Liang dynasty (502–557) to Zhenguan 19 (645) of the Tang (*Taishō shinshū Daizōkyō**, no. 2060 [50:425b, 21–22]). Although by 664 he might have completed the initial version of this collection, he apparently continued to write new biographies of "eminent monks," probably until his death in 667. It seems that he approached the *Guang Hongming ji* in a similar way.

Composition

The *Guang Hongming ji* is a compendium of a great variety of documentary material encompassing texts of literary as well as doctrinal and even purely polemical character all related to the discourses on the question of the appropriateness of Buddhism for China. With this compilation Daoxuan took "a lead role in negotiating the relationship between the secular state and the Buddhist church" (Strange, "Representations of Liang Emperor Wu," 82).

Transmission of the text

The *Guang Hongming ji*, together with the *Hongming ji*, is recorded in the major premodern Buddhist and non-Buddhist bibliographies from the early seventh century on. An example from the Tang dynasty is its listing in the *Kaiyuan shijiao lu* 開元釋教錄 (Kaiyuan catalog of Buddhist teachings), compiled in 730 by Zhisheng 智昇 (*Taishō shinshū Daizōkyō*, nos. 2154–55 [55:742a–b]).

Principal edition

Taishō shinshū Daizōkyō, no. 2103 (52:97–361). This is still the most commonly cited edition of the *Guang Hongming ji*. It indicates a wide number of textual variations in earlier editions and is also available in a digital version. There is a Japanese translation (see *Kokuyaku issaikyō* in the following).

Modern critical editions

As is the case with other texts of the era, we await an edition of this text that compares all of the major editions and explains all discrepancies.

Selected studies

Schmidt-Glintzer, Helwig. *Das Hungming chi und die Aufnahme des Buddhismus in China*. Wiesbaden: Steiner, 1976. Pp. 149–59.

Strange, Mark. "Representations of Liang Emperor Wu as a Buddhist Ruler in Sixth- and Seventh-Century Texts." *Asia Major*, 3rd series, 24.2 (2011): 53–112, esp. 82–89.

Translation

Kokuyaku issaikyō 国訳一切経. Trans. Ōta Teizō 大田悌藏. *Wa-Kan senjutsubu* 和漢選述部, vol. 94 (1936; rpt. 1960), 348–418; vol. 95 (1936; rpt. 1961); vol. 96 (1963). Tokyo: Daitō shuppansha.

Helwig Schmidt-Glintzer

Han Wei Liuchao baisanjia ji
漢魏六朝百三家集

Introduction

The *Han Wei Liuchao baisanjia ji* (One hundred and three masters of the Han, Wei, and Six Dynasties) is a comprehensive Ming dynasty collection of individual literary collections (*bie ji* 別集) containing both poetry and prose. It begins with Jia Yi 賈誼 (200–168 B.C.) of the Han dynasty and ends with Xue Daoheng 薛道衡 (A.D. 540–609) of the Sui. Before the twentieth century, the *Han Wei Liuchao baisanjia ji* was the most complete primary source for literature of the early imperial period. The *Liuchao* in this case includes both the north and the south during the Period of Disunion. In cases where a modern critical edition is lacking, it remains an important source even now (Mu, *Wei Jin Nanbeichao wenxue shiliao shulüe*, 10).

The compiler of the anthology, Zhang Pu 張溥, styled Tianru 天如 (1602–1641; *jinshi* 1631), was a native of Taicang 太倉 in Jiangsu. A leading scholar of the late-Ming's Fushe 復社 society, he was an editor and publisher of books as well. The *Han Wei Liuchao baisanjia ji* was his largest project.

Contents

The *Han Wei Liuchao baisanjia ji* is divided into 118 *juan* (the total number is in fact 124 *juan*; some are divided into two or three parts, yet they are counted as one). Individual collections, each preceded by a colophon, are arranged chronologically and according to the dynasties:

Juan 1–22: Han

Juan 23–26: Wei

Juan 27–62: Jin

Juan 63–72: Liu-Song

Juan 73–79: Qi

Juan 80–101: Liang

Juan 102–106: Chen

Juan 107–108: Northern Wei

Juan 109–110: Northern Qi

Juan 111–113: Northern Zhou

Juan 114–108: Sui

Within each individual's collection the writings are arranged according to their form. Usually a collection begins with *fu* 賦 and is followed by various prose genres. Lyric poetry (*shi* 詩) and *yuefu* 樂府 come next. Fragments of compositions are also included.

The text includes the collections of nearly all the important figures of pre-Tang literature. In short colophons (*tici* 題辭), the editor makes a critical assessment of the personality and writings of each author. In his preface (*xu* 叙), Zhang Pu claims that he has included only *belles lettres* (*wenti* 文體); however, his critics in *Siku quanshu zongmu tiyao** 38:4213–14 point out that he is not always consistent in this respect and occasionally also includes pieces belonging to the classics, historiography, or philosophy. Despite Zhang Pu's often anachronistic views that were shaped primarily by his own late-Ming agenda, the colophons together make "a collective portrait of Six Dynasties writers" (Ke, "*Han Wei Liuchao baisanjia ji*") and have also often been used separately as a source for the study of Six Dynasties literature.

Sources of the work

Zhang Pu based his anthology on earlier Ming collections and anthologies of pre-Tang poetry and prose. Since in Zhang's time many individual collections from the pre-Tang period were no longer in circulation, these had to be reconstructed by "gathering up" (*ji* 輯) the material from various sources. Zhang Pu used Zhang Xie's (1574–1640) *Qishi'er jia ji** as his base text; at the same time, he used as complementary sources earlier Ming anthologies, such as the *Gu shiji** by Feng Weine (1513–1572) and the *Liang wen ji** by Mei Dingqi (1549–1615), as well as writings scattered in the histories, encyclopedias, various collectanea, and sometimes also Buddhist and Taoist collections.

Authenticity and transmission of the text

Zhang Pu printed the collection in eighty volumes (*ce* 冊) during the Chongzhen era (1628–1644), and this first edition became known as the Loudong Zhang family edition (*Loudong Zhangshi keben Han Wei Liuchao baisanjia ji* 婁東張氏刻本漢魏六朝百三家集). The exact year of the first printing is uncertain (sometimes 1628 is given as the publication date). There was at least one other Ming dynasty private printing of the book (see Ke, "*Han Wei Liuchao baisanjia ji*"). Later the collection was included in the *Siku quanshu** (see the following).

Principal editions

In the preface, Zhang Pu called the work by a slightly longer title: *Han Wei Liuchao baisan ming* (名) *jia ji*. Later editions use either of the two titles. In the *Siku quanshu* the shorter title occurs.

During the late Qing's Guangxu era (1875–1908) and the early Republic, there were several printings of the *Han Wei Liuchao baisan (ming) jia ji*. Until recently, the most widely used edition was the *Chongjiao jingyin Han Wei Liuchao baisan mingjia ji* 重校精印漢魏六朝百三名家集 (Taipei: Wenjin chubanshe, 1979), which is a reprint from a woodblock edition published by the famous Saoye shanfang 掃葉山房 publishing house in 1925. In 1987 this book was published in a reduced format (*suoyin ban* 縮印版) by the Shanghai guji chubanshe. Another edition of the *Han Wei Liuchao baisan mingjia ji* was published in 1990 by the Jiangsu Guangling guji keyinshe of Yangzhou. This is a photofacsimile reprint of a Guangxu *jimao* 己卯 (1879) five-volume edition published by Peng Maoqian 彭懋謙 in his *Xinshu tang* 信述堂. Another reprint, in six volumes, was published by the Jiangsu guji chubanshe of Nanjing in 2002.

Other readily available editions are those included in photofacsimile reproductions of the *Siku quanshu*:

Yingyin Wenyuange Siku quanshu*, *ji bu* 集部, nos. 351–55, vols. 1412–16:1–162.
Chizaotang Siku quanshu huiyao 摛藻堂四庫全書薈要, *ji bu* 集部, nos. 121–25, vols. 468–72. Taipei: Shijie shuju, 1988.

Traditional assessments

The *Siku quanshu*'s editors acknowledged the *Han Wei Liuchao baisanjia ji* as the most comprehensive source of Six Dynasties literature. At the same time, they blamed Zhang Pu for being inconsistent in not limiting himself strictly to *belles lettres* and for mistakes regarding authorship and textual integrity. The gravest mistake in the view of the editors of the *Siku quanshu zongmu tiyao** (38:4214) was not including important authors such as the Jin dynasty's Zuo Si 左思 (ca. 253–ca. 307). In some cases they also point out questionable attributions. As a whole the collection is, however, highly valued.

Selected studies

Though the collection has been widely used as a source of primary data, it has been rarely an object of independent study. The first seminal study of the *Han Wei Liuchao baisanjia ji* is the brief entry in the *Siku quanshu zongmu tiyao*.

Shortly after Zhang Pu printed the book, his colophons started to circulate separately (see Ke, "Han Wei Liuchao baisanjia ji," for more bibliographical details about early editions). A modern and copiously annotated edition of the colophons, *Han Wei Liuchao baisanjia ji tici zhu* 漢魏六朝百三家集題辭注, was prepared by Yin Menglun 殷孟倫 and first published in 1960 (Beijing: Renmin wenxue chubanshe; second and third printing in 1963 and 1981, respectively, and by Zhonghua shuju in 2007). There is also a Shangwu yinshuguan edition (Hong Kong) from 1961, and reprints published in Taiwan, of which the most carefully done is the Muduo chubanshe edition (Taipei) from 1982.

Amendments to Yin Menglong's work, as well as critical remarks, were published in two articles:

Xiong Qingyuan 熊清元. "*Han Wei Liuchao baisanjia ji tici zhu* kuang bu" 漢魏六朝百三家集題辭注匡補. *Guji zhengli yanjiu xuekan* 6 (1995): 11–12.

———. "*Han Wei Liuchao baisanjia ji tici zhu* shangque" 漢魏六朝百三家集題辭注商榷. *Huanggang shizhuan xuebao* 3 (1996): 28–31.

Reference works, research aids, and bibliography

Jiang Yixue 蔣逸雪. *Zhang Pu nianpu* 張溥年譜. Ji'nan: Qi Lu shushe, 1982.

Ke Changli 柯昌禮. "*Han Wei Liuchao baisanjia ji*—Tici zhong de renwu piping" 漢魏六朝百三家集—題詞中的人物批評. Master's thesis, Shanghai shifan daxue, 2006. This is one of the most useful resources for students of early medieval China's literary thought. It contains a good bibliographical summary, including a list of early editions of the collection preserved in Chinese libraries.

Mu Kehong 穆克宏. *Wei Jin Nanbeichao wenxue shiliao shulüe* 魏晋南北朝文學史料述略. Beijing: Zhonghua shuju, 1997.

Index

No special index to the *Han Wei Liuchao baisanjia ji* exists. The electronic version of the *Wenyuan ge Siku quanshu* can be of help in the location of a document or quotation.

Olga Lomová

He Chengtian ji 何承天集

Introduction

He Chengtian, styled Hengyang 衡陽 (370–447), a native of Donghai 東海 (in southern Shandong), has biographies in *Song shu*, q.v., 64:1701–11, and *Nan shi*, q.v., 33:868–70. He was appointed erudite (*boshi* 博士) in the Imperial Academy of the Eastern Jin in the period 405–418. He wrote ritual lyrics for the court and at the beginning of the (Liu-)Song dynasty was also commissioned to compile administrative protocol; later in life, in 433, he was reappointed as academy erudite.

After about 440, with appointment to history-writing posts, He Chengtian wrote both a Song "National History" ("Guo shi" 國史) and treatises for the latter (noteworthy being the draft of "Lüli zhi" 律曆志, which was incorporated into the *Song shu*), as well as compilations of texts on the Rites. (On his historiography, see *Song shu*, 11:205–6, and 64:1704. On his overall literary output, see Liu, *Dong Jin Nanbeichao xueshu biannian*, 211–12; also Yin, *Han Wei Liuchao baisanjia ji tici zhu*, 164–65). During his long career, he served in both military positions and literary offices, but toward the end of his life he was impeached and cashiered.

Modern scholarship has focused on He Chengtian's mathematics and astronomy. Although the latter technical art throughout Chinese history served as a basis for prognostic astrology, we have no evidence that He practiced astrology officially at court. His calendar for the (Liu) Song dynasty, the Yuanjia Calendar (*Yuanjia li* 元嘉曆) of 445, attempted to correct previous calendars through the use of better gnomon and lunar-cycle observations. The Yuanjia Calendar served later as a basis of Sui Wendi's first calendar reform, but it was repeatedly challenged by technical experts during the Sui. (On He's calendrics, see *Song shu* 12:261ff; *Sui shu*, q.v., 17:426; Yabuuchi, *Zōtei Zui Tō rekihō shi no kenkyū*, 243–49).

The *wenji*, or collected works, as they have come down to us in the *Han Wei Liuchao baisanjia ji*, q.v., give much evidence of He Chengtian's court lyrics and his court memorials on policy matters such as law, the history and practice of imperial rites, and military concerns. They also contain his findings in astronomy and its methods (for instance, see "Qing gai louke zou" 請改漏刻奏, an explanation of improvements in clepsydra time-keeping). He was a fervent anti-Buddhist polemicist, often employing xenophobic rhetoric (Zürcher, *The Buddhist Conquest of China*, 1:15, 2:415n42).

Contents

The extant, and fullest, edition of choice for He Chengtian's *wenji* is the version collected in the late Ming by Zhang Pu (1602–1641) as *juan* 63 of his larger work *Han Wei Liuchao baisanjia ji*, q.v., which titles it *He Hengyangji* 何衡陽集. As with many other Six Dynasties *wenji*, He Chengtian's is a collection of prose items such as petitions, letters, disquisitions, epitaphs, and rhyme-prose, also including verse items. In the *Han Wei Liuchao baisanjia ji*, there are forty-seven items in all, in the following order:

1. Rhyme-prose, 1 title
2. Petition, 1 title
3. Opinion, 6 titles
4. Presentation, 3 titles
5. Disquisition, 9 titles
6. Inquiry (*wen* 問), 1 title
7. Personal letter, 6 titles
8. Eulogy, 3 titles
9. Encomium, 2 titles
10. Court song, 15 titles (all under the general rubric of "Guchuinao ge" 鼓吹鐃歌)

Yan Kejun's (1762–1843) "Quan Song wen" 全宋文, 22:4b–24:9b in his *Quan shanggu Sandai Qin Han Sanguo Liuchao wen*, q.v., collects the prose only and yields thirty-seven items, five more than the prose items in the *Han Wei Liuchao baisanjia ji*. There are considerable variations in genres and titles, and there are several more petitions, which Yan drew from other men's biographies in the *Song shu*. Moreover, "Quan Song wen" is considerably stronger than the *Han Wei Liuchao baisanjia ji* in isolating He's statements on astronomy and musicology, drawing from sources such as the *Tong dian*, q.v., and the standard histories.

Transmission and early history of the text

The bibliographic monograph of *Sui shu*, q.v., 35:1072, lists the *He Chengtian ji* as containing twenty *juan*, and the following small-character commentary, based on pre-Sui documents, says that "in Liang it was thirty-two *juan*, now lost." The *Jiu Tang shu* (completed in 945, but utilizing eighth-century records) lists the *He Chengtian ji* as containing thirty *juan* (47:2060). It would appear that twelve *juan* fell out of the collection that was listed in the imperial Sui catalog, but the total seen a century later was thirty. There are no mentions of the *wenji* in later catalogs. There is no way to know when He Chengtian's *wenji* dropped out of wide circulation after the Tang, before being reconstituted during the Ming.

Principal editions

The most complete edition of He Chengtian's *wenji* contains *juan* 63 of the *Han Wei Liuchao baisanjia ji*. The unpunctuated *Siku quanshu* edition is quite reliable relative to all the early *Han Wei Liuchao baisanjia ji* editions (see *Yingyin Wenyuange Siku quanshu* 1414:1–25; see also the 1879 traditionally punctuated edition [rpt., Jiangsu:

Jiangsu guji shudian, 1990], 3:267–96. For modern punctuated and annotated versions of Zhang's verse ("Guchuinao ge"), see Lu Qinli, *Xian Qin Han Wei Jin Nanbeichao shi**, "Song shi" section, 2:1204–10.

Concerning He's court statements on rites, astronomy, and musicology, the *Han Wei Liuchao baisanjia ji* and *Quan Song wen* both drew on his *Song shu* biography and the treatises there and in the *Sui shu* as well. Thus, today we may refer to those punctuated and annotated editions for certain items of He's prose, some of the more important quotations being *Song shu* 12:260–62 ("Lüli zhi," part 2) for "Shang li xinfa biao" 上歷新法表, 13:285 ("Lüli zhi," part 3) for "Qing gai louke zou," and 15:399–401 ("Li zhi," part 2) for "Yi gongzhu fu mu zou" 議公主服母奏, as well as *Sui shu* 19:511 ("Tianwen zhi," part 1) for "Lun Wang Fan huntian ti" 論王蕃渾天體.

Selected studies

Chen Yingshi 陳應時. "Shi'er pingjun lü de xianqu: He Chengtian xinlü" 十二平均律的先驅: 何承天新律. *Shenyang yinyue xueyuan xuebao* (1985.2): 44–47.

Holzman, Donald. "Songs for the Gods: The Poetry of Popular Religion in Fifth-Century China." *Asia Major*, 3rd series, 1 (1990): 1–20.

Kalinowski, Marc, ed. *Divination et société dans la Chine médiévale: Étude des manuscrits de Dunhuang de la Bibliothèque nationale de France et de la British Library*. Paris: Bibliothèque nationale de France, 2003.

Pan Fu'en 潘富恩 and Ma Tao 馬濤. *Fan Zhen pingzhuan, Fu He Chengtian pingzhuan* 范縝評傳, 附何承天評傳. Nanjing: Nanjing daxue Zhongguo sixiangjia yanjiu zhongxin and Nanjing daxue chubanshe, 1996.

Yabuuchi Kiyoshi 藪內清. *Zōtei Zui Tō rekihōshi no kenkyū* 增訂隋唐曆法史の研究. Kyoto: Rinsen shoten, 1989.

Yang Yinliu 楊蔭瀏. *Zhongguo gudai yinyue shigao* 中國古代音樂史稿. Beijing: Renmin yinyue chubanshe, 1980. Pp. 1–2.

Zheng Cheng 鄭誠. "He Chengtian suicha kao" 何承天歲差考. *Shanghai jiaotong daxue xuebao, Zhexue shehuikexue* (2007.1): 50–57.

Zürcher, Erik. *The Buddhist Conquest of China*. Leiden: Brill, 1959.

Reference works, research aids, concordances

Liu Rulin 劉汝霖, comp. *Dong Jin Nanbeichao xueshu biannian* 東晉南北朝學術編年. Shanghai: Shangwu yinshuguan, 1935; rpt., Shanghai: Shanghai shudian, 1991.

Yao Zhenzong 姚振宗 (1843–1906). *Suishu jingji zhi kaozheng* 隋書經籍志考證. Reprinted in vols. 915–16 of *Xuxiu Siku quanshu** (also printed in vol. 4 of *Ershiwu shi bubian* 二十五史補編 [Shanghai: Kaiming shudian, 1937]).

Yin Menglun 殷孟倫. *Han Wei Liuchao baisan jia ji tici zhu* 漢魏六朝百三家集題辭注. Beijing: Zhonghua shuju, 2007.

Howard L. Goodman

He Xun ji 何遜集

Introduction

The exact dates of He Xun, styled Zhongyan 仲言, are a matter of contention. The reconstruction of his biography by Li Boqi (*He Xun ji jiaozhu*) suggests the dates 466–519. One of the most talented poets of the Liang dynasty, He Xun came from a distinguished and learned family whose ancestral home was in Shandong. By his lifetime, however, the family's standing was more a subject of poetic lamentation than a source of tangible benefit. Through recommendation by local authorities, young He went to the southern capital, Jiankang (modern Nanjing), and embarked on an unimpressive yet laborious career, during which he mainly held secretarial positions in the establishments of royal family members.

Tiresome travels entailed by frequent changes of post appear to have been offset by the company of like-minded friends and beautiful scenery encountered along the Yangzi River. Many of He's poems concern separation, yet indications of friendships with kindred spirits and records of shared experiences bear out a lively community surrounding the constantly lonely and dejected man approaching old age, a persona He created for himself. Such an image is now often associated with the great poet Du Fu (712–770), who professed to have learned the art of poetry from He Xun.

He's depiction of the southern landscape is impressionistic: rivers meander into rosy clouds; mountains are cloaked with green trees; a single crane disappears into the sky; a pair of ducks rise, startled out of the waves. Things in nature are presented subjectively, and the mood is often pensive and mildly melancholic.

Contents

He Xun's collection has also been known as *He Zhongyan ji* or has been titled by the offices that he held, such as *He Shuibu ji* 何水部集 (Collection of Officer of the Bureau of Waterways He) and *He Jishi ji* 何記室集 (Collection of Record Keeper He). According to the 1980 Beijing Zhonghua shuju edition of the *He Xun ji*, which is based on Zhang Xie's (1574–1640) *Qishi'er jia ji** in consultation with other editions, there are altogether ninety-five poems, thirteen linked verses, one "sevens" (*qi* 七), one *fu*, one letter, and two memoranda. The *Qishi'er jia ji* edition has been reprinted in *Xuxiu Siku quanshu** 1587:331–67.

Sources of the work

He Xun's works were collected immediately after his death by Wang Sengru 王僧孺 (465–522), a fellow townsman and lifetime friend of the author. The work is recorded as early as in his biography in *Liang shu*, q.v., 49:698–99, where it was said to consist of eight *juan*. The bibliographic monograph of the *Sui shu*, q.v., notes a seven-*juan* collection, one *juan* shorter than in the *Liang shu* account. The bibliographic monographs *Jiu Tang shu* and *Xin Tang shu* both list He's collection as having eight *juan*.

Yet, the *Song shi*'s bibliographic monograph records a five-*juan* collection. Chao Gongwu's *Junzhai dushu zhi** (1151) 17:824 notes a two-*juan* collection. Chen Zhensun's (fl. 1211–1249) *Zhizhai dushu tijie** 16:465 records a three-*juan* collection. It seems that by the Southern Song, more than half of He's collection had been lost.

Principal editions

The following traditional editions are available in reprint.

He Shuibu ji 何水部集, edited by Zhang Hong 張紘 (1517). In *Yingyin Wenyuange Siku quanshu** 1063:691–712.

He Shuibu ji 何水部集, edited by Xue Yingqi (*jinshi* 1535). In *Liuchao shiji**; see *Xuxiu Siku quanshu** 1589:286–302.

He Jishi ji 何記室集, edited by Zhang Xie (1574–1670). In *Qishi'er jia ji*; *Xuxiu Siku quanshu* 1589:286–302.

He Jishi ji 何記室集, edited by Zhang Pu (1602–1641). In *Han Wei Liuchao baisan mingjia ji*, q.v., 5:31–59. 5 vols. Nanjing: Jiangsu guji chubanshe, 2001.

He Jishi ji xuan 何記室集選, edited by Wu Rulun 吳汝綸 (1840–1903). In *Han Wei Liuchao baisanjia ji xuan* 漢魏六朝百三家集選 (1917), vol. 14. 16 vols. Rpt., Hangzhou: Zhejiang guji chubanshe.

He Xun ji, in three *juan* with an appendix. Beijing: Zhonghua shuju, 1980. Includes five prose pieces, 117 poems, He Xun's biographies in the *Liang shu* and *Nan shi*, anecdotes, collected comments, and prefaces or postface by Zhang Hong, Zhang Pu, and Jiang Fang 江昉.

"He Xun," in *Quan shanggu Sandai Qin Han Sanguo Liuchao wen*, q.v., compiled in 1836 by Yan Kejun, vol. 7, "Quan Liang wen," 59:10a–11a. 9 vols. Taipei: Shijie shuju, 1982.

"He Xun," edited by Lu Qinli. In *Xian Qin Han Wei Jin Nanbeichao shi**, vol. 2, "Liang shi," 1678–1714.

Editions with commentaries

He Shuibu shi zhu 何水部詩注. Hao Liquan 郝立權. Ji'nan: Qi Lu daxue, 1937.

He Shuibu shi zhu 何水部詩注. He Rong 何融. N.p., 1947.

He Xun ji jiaozhu 何遜集校注. Li Boqi 李伯齊. Ji'nan: Qi Lu shushe, 1989. Rev. and rpt., Beijing: Zhonghua shuju, 2010.

He Xun ji zhu 何遜集注. Liu Chang 劉暢 and Liu Guojun 劉國珺. Tianjin: Guji chubanshe, 1988.

Traditional assessments

Shen Deqian 沈德潛 (1673–1769) commented in his *Gushi yuan* 古詩源 (*juan* 13): "Although Zhongyan is short on robustness and vigorousness (*fenggu* 風骨), the emotive and verbal effect of his poetry is subtle and long lasting. Even simple words from him can be profound. How proper that he was admired by Shen Yue and Fan Yun!" Shen Deqian also said, "Yin [Keng] and He [Xun] are named together, yet He was certainly more superb," and "there are many well-known lines from He Xun, and most of them closely approach the recent style" (i.e., regulated verse).

Selected studies

Cao Daoheng 曹道衡. "He Xun san ti" 何遜三題. *Zhonghua wenshi luncong* (1983.4): 317–22. Rpt., *Zhonggu wenxue shi lunwenji* 中古文學史論文集, 435–37. Beijing: Zhonghua shuju, 2002.
———. "He Xun shengzu nian wenti shikao" 何遜生卒年問題試考. *Wen shi* 24 (1985): 219–23. Rpt., *Zhonggu wenxue shi lunwenji*, 427–34.
Cheng Zhangcan 程章燦. "He Xun 'Yong zaomei' shi kao" 何遜'詠早梅'詩考. *Wenxue yichan* 5 (1995): 47–53.
Fan Ziye 范子燁. "He Xun yu Tao shi" 何遜與陶詩. *Wenxue yichan* (2008.2): 85.
Han Lei 韓磊. "He Xun yanjiu" 何遜研究. Master's thesis, Fujian shifan daxue, 2004.
He Shuiying 何水英. "Lun He Xun de xintai yu shige" 論何遜的心態與詩歌. Master's thesis, Guangxi shifan daxue, 2007.
Li Jinxing 李金星. *He Xun yanjiu* 何遜研究. Taipei: Huashi chubanshe, 1982.
Numaguchi Masaru 沼口勝. "Ka Son no 'Ryūsaku Hyakuitsu tai no shi' ni tsuite" 何遜の'聊作百一體の詩'について. *Kambun Gakkai kaihō* 34 (1975): 13–25.
Yamada Hideo 山田英雄. "Ka Son no shifu" 何遜の詩賦. *Nagoya daigakubu bungakubu kenkyū ronshū* 55 (1972): 362–76.
Yu Suxiang 于素香. "He Xun de shige yishu" 何遜的詩歌藝術. Master's thesis, Xizang minzu xueyuan, 2008.
Zhang Zhonggang 張忠綱. "He Xun" 何遜. In *Zhongguo lidai zhuming wenxuejia pingzhuan* 中國歷代著名文學家評傳, ed. Lü Huijuan 呂慧鵑 et al., 1:615–22. Ji'nan: Shandong jiaoyu chubanshe, 1983.

Translations

Birrell, Ann, ed. and trans. *New Songs from a Jade Terrace: An Anthology of Early Chinese Love Poetry*. London: George Allen and Unwin, 1982. Pp. 152–55, 278–79.

Frodsham, J. D., with the collaboration of Ch'eng Hsi. *An Anthology of Chinese Verse: Han, Wei, Chin, and the Northern and Southern Dynasties*. Oxford: Clarendon Press, 1967. Pp. 185–86.

Wang, Ping. "Ho Hsün and His Poems." Master's thesis, University of Colorado, 2000.

Index

Morino Shigeo 森野繁夫, Ogawa Tsuneo 小川恒男, and Hashida Kasumi 橋田佳純. *Ka Son shi sakuin* 何遜詩索引. Tokyo: Hakuteisha, 1999.

Ping Wang

Hongming ji 弘明集

Introduction

The *Hongming ji* (Collection on the dissemination and clarification [of Buddhism]) is the earliest surviving collection of Buddhist apologetic literature in China, dating from the early sixth century. The texts themselves date from the fourth century A.D. until the time of compilation. The collection documents the various disputes among the elite about the acceptability of Buddhism in the realm of Chinese culture. Issues include the immortality of the soul, the character of Buddhism, disputes between followers of Buddhism and Daoism, and the like. This collection reflects the changing role of the *sangha* during the fourth and fifth centuries and attempts to reconcile Buddhism and Confucianism.

Contents

The *Hongming ji* contains several treatises and includes disputes as well as correspondence among members of the elite in southern China concerning the nature and the acceptability of Buddhism in the Chinese realm. For most of the texts, the *Hongming ji* is the earliest source. The collection opens with a treatise that has been attributed by some to Mou Rong 牟融 or Mouzi 牟子 (d. A.D. 79), which is, in fact, a work written not earlier than the beginning of the fourth century. This text deals with nearly forty topics in order to prove the compatibility of the Three Teachings of Confucianism, Buddhism, and Daoism. The "Mouzi lihuo lun" 牟子理惑論 (Master Mou's treatise dispelling doubts) has remained through centuries the most prominent Buddhist apologetic text. Other texts in the collection exhibit not only the discourse about the relationships between the Three Teachings but also debates among Buddhist laypersons and the clergy.

Authorship

The author of the collection, completed in 513, is Sengyou 僧祐 (445–518), a Buddhist monk who is also famous as author of the earliest annotated catalog of Buddhist scriptures in China, the *Chu sanzang jiji* 出三藏記集.

Composition

The *Hongming ji* is only one of a series of compilations undertaken by Sengyou, of which the most prominent is the *Chu sanzang jiji*. In chapter 12 of that bibliographic collection, we find a list of Sengyou's literary works and compilations that mentions a *Hongming ji* in ten *juan*. It seems that, according to the lists given in the *Chu sanzang jiji*, Sengyou used an earlier collection titled *Falun* 法論 by Lu Cheng 陸澄 (between 465 and 572) when he compiled his *Hongming ji*. Before the final edition in fourteen *juan*, there seems to have been a collection in ten *juan*. The fourteen-*juan* version was apparently completed after the composition of the "Hongming lun" 弘明論, which is placed at the end to function as an "author's epilogue" and represent his main aims in compiling the collection.

Transmission of the text

The collection was from the beginning part of the Chinese Buddhist Canon. The earliest printed version is contained in the Song edition of the canon. The *Hongming ji* is recorded in the major premodern Buddhist and non-Buddhist bibliographies from the early sixth century on.

Principal edition

The most reliable of all editions seems to be the early print from Korea. The standard edition is still the *Taishō shinshū Daizōkyō**, no. 2102 (52:1–96).

Modern critical edition

Gumyōshū kenkyū: Chūsei shisōshi kenkyūhan, Gumyōshū kenkyūhan kenkyū hōkoku 弘明集研究: 中世思想史研究班, 弘明集研究班研究報告. 3 vols. Edited by Kyōto daigaku, Jimbun kagaku kenkyūjo 京都大学, 人文科学研究所. Kyoto: Kyōto daigaku, 1973–1975.

Studies of the text

Keenan, John P. *How Master Mou Removes Our Doubts: A Reader-Response Study and Translation of the Mou-tzu Li-huo lun*. Albany: State University of New York Press, 1994.

Kopecki, Andrew Joseph. "Cultural Adaptation in the Chinese Acceptance of Buddhism: Selections from the *Hung-ming chi*." Ph.D. diss., Harvard University, 1981.

Link, Arthur E. "Shih Seng-yu and His Writings." *Journal of the American Oriental Society* 80.1 (1960): 17–43.

Pelliot, Paul. "Meou-tseu ou les doutes levés." *T'oung Pao* 19 (1920): 255–433.

Schmidt-Glintzer, Helwig. *Das Hung-ming chi und die Aufnahme des Buddhismus in China*. Wiesbaden: Steiner, 1976.

Zürcher, Erik. *The Buddhist Conquest of China*. 2 vols. Leiden: E. J. Brill, 1972.

Translations in European languages

The following are translations of individual selections only, in English, French, and German.

Balazs, Stefan. "Der Philosoph Fan Dschen und sein Traktat gegen den Buddhismus. *Sinica* 7 (1932): 220–34.

Hurvitz, Leon. "'Render unto Caesar' in Early Chinese Buddhism: Hui-yüan's Treatise on the Exemption of the Buddhist Clergy from the Requirements of Civil Etiquette." *Sino-Indian Studies* (Liebenthal Festschrift, ed. Kshitis Roy) 5.3–4 (1957): 80–114.

Liebenthal, Walter. "The Immortality of the Soul in Chinese Thought." *Monumenta Nipponica* 8 (1952): 327–97.

———. "A Clarification (Yü-I lun)." *Sino-Indian Studies* 5.2 (1956): 88–99.

Link, Arthur E. "Cheng-wu lun: The Rectification of Unjustified Criticism." *Oriens Extremus* 8 (1961): 136–65.

Link, Arthur E., and Tim Lee. "Sun Ch'o's 'Yü-tao-lun': A Clarification of the Way." *Monumenta Serica* 25 (1966): 169–96.

Japanese annotated translation

Kokuyaku issaikyō 国訳一切経. Trans. Ōta Teizō 大田悌藏. Wa-Kan senjutsubu 和漢選述部 no. 94, pp. 1–339. Tokyo: Daitō shuppansha, 1936; rpt., 1960.

Helwig Schmidt-Glintzer

Hou Han shu 後漢書

Introduction

The *Hou Han shu* (History of the Later Han) by Fan Ye 范曄 (398–446) is our most important source for the history of the Later Han era. From a total of more than twenty histories of that period, only two have survived in their entirety: this work and the *Hou Han ji* 後漢紀 by Yuan Hong 袁宏 (328–376). As the *Hou Han shu* eventually was to become the standard history for the Later Han, it is a book that has received wide attention almost ever since it was written. It belonged to a canon of knowledge that literati not only in China but also in neighboring countries of East Asia were supposed to have read. In the commonly used expression "five canonical scriptures and three histories," the three histories signified Sima Qian's 司馬遷 *Shi ji*, Ban Gu's 班固 *Han shu*, and Fan Ye's *Hou Han shu*. It is thus clear that this is one of the most important texts written during the Six Dynasties.

Contents

The *Hou Han shu* we have today recounts the story of the Later Han dynasty in ten *juan* of annals (*benji* 本紀) and eighty accounts or biographies (*liezhuan* 列傳). Originally, Fan Ye also planned to write ten monographs (*zhi* 志); however, he never completed these. Later, thirty monographs were added to the text from a different history of the Later Han.

The annals describe in chronological arrangement the political history of nine emperors as well as of three minor emperors who died as children after less than a year on the throne. The style of these *juan* follows the example set by the earlier histories *Shi ji* and *Han shu*. They consist of short entries on the appointment and dismissal of high officers, military campaigns, sacrifices, imperial edicts on important matters of the state, and sometimes also short reports on deliberations that took place at court. By far the longest *juan* in this section is *juan* 1, on the first emperor of the Later Han, Liu Xiu 劉秀 (r. 25–57), who is known under his posthumous name Guangwudi. Because of the length of his annals, they are divided into two parts: *shang* and *xia* (commonly designated A and B). The same division is true also for *juan* 10, the annals that tell the story of the empresses who played important roles under the Later Han.

In the biographical section we first find biographies of important officials and generals of the Later Han as well as of competitors of Guangwu and of imperial relatives who became titulary kings. Usually, each *juan* is devoted to more than one person, but some persons who were considered especially important have an entire *juan* dedicated to them. In the cases of Ban Biao 班彪 (3–54) and Ban Gu (32–92) who composed the *Han shu*, a "double juan" with parts A and B is dedicated to their lives. Some *juan* contain collective biographies connected by events of the period, such as that which deals with the famous era of proscription against critical scholars (between 166 and 184); others, such as those devoted to reasonable and cruel officials (*xunli* 循吏 and *kuli* 酷吏) or to Confucian scholars (*rulin* 儒林), employ categories invented by Sima Qian in his *Shi ji*. Notable categories of collective biographies that originated with Fan Ye are *juan* 78 (*huanzhe* 宦者), which reflects the rise of the eunuchs at the court of the Later Han emperors; *juan* 80A and B (*wenyuan* 文苑), which contains altogether twenty-two short biographies of literary scholars; *juan* 81 (*duxing* 獨行), the biographies of twenty-four persons with "singular behavior"; *juan* 82A and B (*fangshu* 方術), the biographies of thirty-four magicians and doctors; *juan* 83 (*yimin* 逸民), the biographies of seventeen hermits; and *juan* 84 (*lienü* 列女), the biographies of seventeen exemplary women. *Juan* 85 to 90 are devoted to the countries and tribes surrounding the Han empire. Here we find accounts continuing those contained in the former histories but also ones that introduce a new country, as, for example, that on Japan.

The thirty monographs not authored by Fan Ye include those on the pitch pipes and the calendar (1–3), rites and ceremonies (4–6), state sacrifices (7–9), astronomy (10–12), the five elements (13–18), geography (19–23), the bureaucracy (24–28), and finally chariots and uniforms (29–30). Although most of these subjects had been dealt with by previous authors, these monographs constitute a rich mine of information about the Later Han period and beyond.

Authorship

Fan Ye (style Weizong 蔚宗), according to his biography in the *Song shu*, q.v., was a native of northwestern Hubei. His ancestors had been scholars and prominent officials for more than a hundred years. Probably the best-known member of the family before Fan Ye was his grandfather Fan Ning 范甯 (339–401), who wrote a commentary for the Guliang 穀梁 commentary to the *Spring and Autumn Annals*. This commentary was later universally recognized as the standard one for this work.

Fan Ye started to write the *Hou Han shu* as a result of bad behavior on his own part. While sitting with a friend during a state funeral, he had become intoxicated and mocked the funeral dirges. For this offense he was degraded in the official hierarchy and thereafter had no future in officialdom. At that point, he began to compile the *Hou Han shu* based on a number of earlier works. His chief source was the *Dongguan Han ji* 東觀漢記 (Eastern Lodge records of the Han) written under the Later Han by four successive committees (see Wu, *Dongguan Han ji jiaozhu*), but he also relied on histories written by other authors and on the work of philosophers such as Wang Fu 王符 (fl. mid-second century) and Zhongchang Tong 仲長統

(179–219). His biography states that he wanted to make out of them "the work of one family" (*wei yi jia zhi zuo* 為一家之作), which is clearly an allusion to Sima Qian, whose ambition with his *Shi ji* had been to "complete the teachings of one family" (*cheng yi jia zhi yan* 成一家之言). Fan Ye apparently was an extravagant person who did not like to stick to Confucian norms. His biography reports that when his mother died he did not observe the correct mourning rules but tarried and went to the funeral accompanied by a singing girl. Later, he was involved in a plot against the reigning emperor that led to his execution in A.D. 446.

Early commentaries

As mentioned previously, Fan Ye did not write the thirty *juan* of monographs in the *Hou Han shu*. These were written by his predecessor Sima Biao 司馬彪 (240–306), who had composed a sequel to Ban Gu's *Han shu* with the name *Xu Han shu* 續漢書. The thirty *juan* in the current text had originally been only eight *juan* but they were split up by Liu Zhao 劉昭, who, during the Liang dynasty, had written a commentary to Fan Ye's *Hou Han shu* and then added these monographs to make up for what he felt to be a serious omission. The commentary of Liu Zhao was afterwards lost with the exception of that on the monographs. A new commentary was commissioned in Tang times by the heir apparent Li Xian 李賢 (651–684), posthumously Zhanghuai Heir Apparent (章懷太子), whose team was also responsible for partitioning the history's longer *juan* into A and B sections.

Transmission of the text and textual history

Despite the textual development recounted previously, the first two printed editions of the *Hou Han shu*, produced in 994 and 1005, did not include Sima Biao's monographs. The first edition to do so was printed in 1022. Several more editions were commanded by imperial order under the Northern Song; of these there are, however, only a few fragments extant. A new edition known as the Shaoxing 紹興 edition after the name of the reign when it was commissioned (1131–1162) was apparently completed after that period because taboos of the names of both Emperor Gaozong (r. 1127–1162) and his successor Xiaozong (r. 1162–1189) were observed. Five *juan* of this edition were lost and have been replaced by *juan* taken from fragments of other editions. In the table of contents of the Shaoxing edition, the monographs were listed as coming between the annals and the biographies, which corresponds to the place that monographs occupy in other dynastic histories. However, they were actually printed after the biographies, a measure by which the editors stressed that they originally came from another work. It was only in editions produced in Ming times that the monographs were at last physically placed between the annals and the biographies. The same was true for the so-called palace edition of 1739 that included *kaozheng* 考證 remarks by Qing scholars after every *juan*. However, the tradition of keeping the monographs apart from Fan Ye's text continued with the Jiguge 汲古閣 edition of Mao Jin 毛晉 (1598–1659). These differing placements of course affect the sequential numbering of the *juan*, a matter to be considered where citations are concerned.

For an overall account of the textual history of this and the other Six Dynasties standard histories, see appendix IV, "Textual Transmission of the Standard Histories."

Principal editions

The three principal editions used in modern scholarship are as follows.

Hou Han shu, 90 plus 30 *juan*. In Baina ben *Ershisishi* 百衲本二十四史. Shanghai: Shangwu yinshuguan, 1930–1937. *Sibu congkan** edition.

Hou Han shu jijie 後漢書集解, with commentary by Wang Xianqian 王先謙 (1842–1918). Changsha, 1915. There are several reprints, among which the most readily available is that published in Beijing by Zhonghua shuju, 1984.

Hou Han shu, 90 plus 30 *juan*. Beijing: Zhonghua shuju, 1965.

The Shaoxing edition was photolithographically reproduced for the Baina edition, the standard source for scholars during the first half of the twentieth century. Of paramount importance is the richly annotated version by Wang Xianqian, who used the Ming Jiguge version as his base text. The popularity of the Baina text was superseded when in 1959 the Zhonghua shuju began printing a set of the twenty-four histories with modern punctuation; in 1965 the *Hou Han shu* was the third text published. Whereas this is the edition regularly cited, it is worth also checking Wang Xianqian's commentaries.

Traditional assessments

Fan Ye's *Hou Han shu* is mentioned in all major early book catalogs, although there are several discrepancies as far as its number of *juan* is concerned. Thus, we find that the bibliographic monograph of the *Sui shu*, q.v., states that the text includes ninety-seven *juan*, whereas those in the two Tang histories indicate that it had only ninety-two. However, the *Siku quanshu zongmu tiyao** editors (10:983) wrote that the text remained unaltered and that the diverging opinions could be reconciled by assuming different ways of counting.

Studies of the text and supplements

The Western scholar who has worked most on textual issues of the *Hou Han shu* is Hans Bielenstein, whose first volume of his seminal series of articles titled "The Restoration of the Han Dynasty," *Bulletin of the Museum of Far Eastern Antiquities* 26 (1954), is devoted to questions of the text's transmission and authenticity, and also of the credibility of its contents. Three more volumes of the "Restoration of the Han Dynasty" appeared in *BMFEA* 31 (1959), 39 (1967), and 51 (1979,) in which Bielenstein analyzed the text as a source for the history of the Later Han. A summary can be found in the *Cambridge History of China* (Cambridge: Cambridge

University Press, 1986), vol. 1, chap. 3, 223–90, a volume that also contains several other chapters based upon the *Hou Han shu*. There has been no attempt in Western scholarship to go beyond Bielenstein's findings as far as the historiography of the *Hou Han shu* is concerned. On the text, see also:

Gardiner, K. H. J. "Standard Histories, Han to Sui." In *Essays on the Sources for Chinese History*, ed. Donald D. Leslie, Colin Mackerras, and Wang Gungwu, 42–52. Columbia: University of South Carolina Press, 1975.

Mansvelt-Beck, Burchard J. *The Treatises of Later Han: Their Author, Sources, Contents, and Place in Chinese Historiography*. Leiden: E. J. Brill, 1990. Provides an extensive study of Sima Biao's monographs.

Nylan, Michael. "*Hou Han shu*." In *RoutledgeCurzon Encyclopedia of Confucianism*, ed. Xinzhong Yao, 1:260–61. London: RoutledgeCurzon, 2003.

Important studies in Chinese include:

Ershiwushi bubian 二十五史補編. Beijing: Zhonghua shuju, 1956. Vol. 2 contains a great number of tables and treatises for the Later Han.

Song Wenmin 宋文民. *Hou Han shu kaoshi* 後漢書考釋. Shanghai: Shanghai guji chubanshe, 1995.

Xiong Fang 熊方 (Song). *Hou Han shu Sanguo zhi bubiao sanshi zhong* 後漢書三國志補表三十種. 3 vols. Beijing: Zhonghua shuju, 1984.

Research aids

Crespigny, Rafe de. *A Biographical Dictionary of Later Han to the Three Kingdoms*. Leiden: E. J. Brill, 2007. Compiled largely on the basis of the *Hou Han shu*, this is the most important research aid for the text in a Western language.

Wu Shuping 吳樹平. *Dongguan Han ji jiaozhu* 東觀漢記校注. Beijing: Zhonghua shuju, 2008.

Zhang Shunhui 張舜徽, ed. *Hou Han shu cidian* 後漢書辭典. Ji'nan: Shandong jiaoyu chubanshe, 1994. A dictionary of the language of the *Hou Han shu*.

Translations

European languages

There is no translation of the *Hou Han shu* as a whole into a European language. Although some complete or partial translations of individual *juan* exist, no annals or monographs have been translated. The list here is incomplete but contains some of the most important contributions.

Excerpts of many biographies are to be found in Ch'ü T'ung-tsu, *Han Social Structure*, edited by Jack Dull (Seattle: University of Washington Press, 1972). Large parts of *juan* 30B are rendered into English in Rafe de Crespigny, *Portents of Protest in the Later Han Dynasty: The Memorials of Hsiang K'ai to Emperor Huan* (Canberra: Australia National University Press, 1976).

The chapters on Chinese relations with Central Asia and other foreign regions have received much attention. A French translation of *juan* 47 on the generals who re-conquered the Western Territories for the Han is by Édouard Chavannes, "Trois Généraux chinois de la dynastie des Han Orientaux, Chapitre LXXVII du *Heou Han chou*" (*T'oung Pao* 7 [1906]: 210–69). Gregory Young translates *juan* 65 in *Three Generals of Later Han*, Faculty of Asian Studies Monographs, new series, no. 6 (Canberra: Australian National University, 1984). Chavannes has also translated the account on the Western Territories, *Hou Han shu* 88, in "Les Pays d'Occident d'après le *Heou Han chou*" (*T'oung Pao* 8 [1907]: 149–244). The same chapter is also presented in John Hill's carefully annotated translation, "The Western Regions according to the *Hou Hanshu*," first published 2003, available at http://depts.washington.edu/silkroad/texts/hhshu/hou_han_shu.html. While not translating any relevant chapter in full, Rafe de Crespigny's *Northern Frontier: The Policies and Strategy of the Later Han Empire*, Faculty of Asian Studies Monographs, new series, no. 4 (Canberra: Australian National University, 1984) contains excerpts that, combined with other sources, are used to present an interpretative political and military history.

The chapter on the southern neighbors of the Later Han was translated by Johann Michael Streffer, *Das Kapitel 86 (76) des Hou Han Shu* (Göppingen, Germany: Verlag Alfred Kümmerle, 1971).

An English version of several passages of *juan* 85 is contained in Kenneth Gardiner, "The *Hou-Han-shu* as a Source for the Early Expansion of Koguryō," *Monumenta Serica* 28 (1969): 148–87.

As for personages of the Later Han, Étienne Balazs discusses three philosophers and translates large parts of *juan* 79 in "La crise sociale à la fin des Han" (*T'oung Pao* 39 [1948–1950]: 83–131); English translation in his *Chinese Civilization and Bureaucracy: Variations on a Theme*, translated by H. M. Wright and edited by Arthur F. Wright (New Haven, CT: Yale University Press, 1964), 187–225. The biography of Ma Rong, *juan* 60A, is fully translated by M. Künstler in *Ma Jong, Vie et oeuvre* (Warsaw: Państwowe Wydawn. Naukowe, 1969). Nancy Lee Swann's "Biography of the Empress Teng" (*Journal of the American Oriental Society* 51 [1931]: 138–59) deals with parts of *juan* 10A. Her monograph *Pan Chao: Foremost Woman Scholar of China* draws upon Ban Zhao's biography in *juan* 84 (New York: The Century Co., 1932; rpt., Center for Chinese Studies, University of Michigan, 2001).

Much of the chapter on the eunuchs in *Hou Han shu* 78 has been translated into German in *Politische Funktion und soziale Stellung der Eunuchen zur späteren Hanzeit (25–220 n. Chr.)* by Ulrike Jugel (Wiesbaden: Franz Steiner Verlag, 1976).

There is also a complete translation of *juan* 82 on the magicians in Ngo Van Xuyet, *Divination, magie et politique dans la Chine ancienne: Essai* (Paris: Presses universitaires de France, 1976). The same *juan* was again translated by Kenneth J. De Woskin, in *Doctors, Diviners, and Magicians of Ancient China: Biographies of Fangshih* (New York: Columbia University Press, 1983).

Burton Watson's "Biographies of Recluses," in *Renditions* 33–34 (1990): 35–51, is a partial translation of *juan* 83. These biographies have been studied in Aat

Vervoorn, *Men of Cliffs and Caves, The Development of the Chinese Eremitic Tradition to the End of the Han Dynasty* (Hong Kong: Chinese University Press, 1990).

Chinese

There are at least two translations into modern Chinese:

Ershisishi quanyi: Hou Han shu 二十四史全譯: 後漢書. 3 vols. Ed. Xu Jialu 許嘉璐. Shanghai: Hanyu dacidian chubanshe, 2004.

Hou Han shu quanyi 後漢書全譯. 5 vols. Ed. Dai Yi 戴逸. Zhongguo lishi mingzhu yizhu congshu 中國歷史名著譯注叢書 series. Guizhou: Guizhou renmin chubanshe, 1995.

Japanese

Zenyaku Go Kan sho 全譯後漢書. Ed. Watanabe Yoshiko 渡邉義浩, Ikeda Masanori 池田雅典, and Okamoto Hideo 岡本秀夫. Tokyo: Kyūko shoin, 2001– . Vols. 1–4, 8, 11–12, 14–16.

Go Kan sho kunchū 後漢書訓注, vols. 1–10, plus index. Ed. Yoshikawa Tadao 吉川忠夫. Tokyo: Iwanami shoten, 2001–2007.

Indices

While still useful for some purposes, the indices listed here have been superseded by searchable full-text databases of which the most important is the Scripta Sinica database of the twenty-five histories at Academia Sinica (Taipei) available at http://hanji.sinica.edu.tw/.

Gokanjo goi shūsei 後漢書語彙集成. 3 vols. Comp. Fujita Shizen 藤田至善. Kyoto: Jimbun kagaku kenkyūjo, 1960–1962.

Hou Hanshu diming suoyin 後漢書地名索引. Comp. Wang Tianliang 王天良. Beijing: Zhonghua shuju, 1988.

Hou Han shu ji zhushi zonghe yinde 後漢書及注釋綜合引得. Harvard Yenching Index 41. Peking, 1949; rpt., Taipei: Ch'eng-wen Publishing, 1966.

Hou Hanshu renming suoyin 後漢書人名索引. Comp. Li Yumin 李育民. Beijing: Zhonghua shuju, 1979.

Hans van Ess

Huanyuan ji 還冤記

Introduction

The *Huanyuan ji* (Record of returning grievances), originally titled the *Yuanhun zhi* 冤魂志 (Accounts of ghosts with grievances) and compiled by Yan Zhitui 顏之推 (531–at least 591), is at present a collection of stories, taken by Yan to be factual, that deal with supernatural retribution for unjust treatment that resulted in death. The theme has led to a general misunderstanding that the purpose of the compilation was to confirm Buddhist doctrines, but a closer examination of the nature of the stories and the cultural milieu of the time reveals a more complex situation. Unlike other contemporary collections that have a Buddhist orientation, this work has no accounts of miraculous events or the potency of the Buddha and Buddhist images. There is, in fact, almost no overt reference to Buddhism at all. Rather, Yan took for granted a general belief in the survival of souls after death, a feature in the belief system of popular Buddhism of that time, to warn that there were unfavorable consequences for those who misused their power and harmed those below them. In other words, the workings of karma were considered a given, not to be confused with such miraculous events as the direct intervention of the supernatural into human affairs. Yan wished to communicate this given, so his intent was not primarily religious proselytism, as some modern critics have supposed. Further, an examination of the current text reveals that it is probably a late-Ming recension and not, as has been maintained, an integral survival from the Six Dynasties period.

Transmission and early history of the text

The collection occurs under its original name of *Yuanhun zhi* in the bibliographic monograph of *Sui shu*, q.v., 33:981, in three *juan*, some sixty years after Yan's death, the *Sui shu* having been compiled in 656. A descendant of Yan's, the famous calligrapher Yan Zhenqing 顏真卿 (709–785), wrote a family temple inscription in 780 that also cites the *Yuanhun zhi* in three *juan* (*Jinshi cuibian* 101:25a). Both *Jiu Tang shu* 46:2006 (945) and *Xin Tang shu* 59:1540 (1041–48) describe the work as having three *juan*. However, the *Fayuan zhulin* 法苑珠林, compiled by Daoshi 道世 in 668, signals a change: depending upon the edition of the *Fayuan zhulin*, the *Yuanhun zhi* is listed as being in one or two *juan*. It may be that at some point another work of Yan Zhitui, the *Jiesha xun* 戒殺訓, was joined to the *Yuanhun zhi*, giving it the higher number of *juan*. The title of the *Jiesha xun* suggests a similar motif. One story included in the *Guang Hongming ji* (preface dated 664), q.v., by Daoxuan 道宣, has its source listed as the *Jiesha xun*, whereas the *Taiping guangji* 太平廣記 of 977–978 has the same story as coming from the *Yuanhun zhi*. Either there was an overlap in content or the two texts by Yan had been merged.

During the Song dynasty, there was a name change, and the text appears in bibliographies under the title *Huanyuan zhi* 還冤志 (Accounts of returning grievances). The listings include *Chongwen zongmu** (1034–1038), 3:34a, three *juan*, and *Zhizhai shulu jieti** (ca. 1235), 11:317, in two *juan*. The many stories included in the *Taiping guangji* list this new title as the source. The original text was lost sometime in the following centuries.

The modern text of the work, now titled *Huanyuan ji*, with *ji* 記 replacing *zhi* 志, is a recension most probably compiled by Chen Jiru 陳繼儒 (1558–1639) who copied out the stories in the sequence in which they appeared scattered over almost seventy *juan* in the *Fayuan zhulin*; he published the resulting work in his *Bagong youxi congtan* 八公遊戲叢談 and the *Baoyantang miji* 寶顏堂秘笈, the latter of which has a preface dated 1615. Tao Ting 陶珽 (*jinshi* 1610), whose expanded edition of the *Shuofu* 說郛 was first printed in 1621, seems to have used Chen Jiru's recension. The *Huanyuan ji* as included in the 1646 reprinting of the *Shuofu* is missing a portion of its text because the original blocks suffered some damage; since a number of collectanea that included the *Huanyuan ji* used the very woodblocks of the *Shuofu*, it is thus possible to ascertain which edition of *Shuofu* was used for this purpose. For example, the *Xu Baichuan xuehai* 續百川學海 was printed with blocks from the earlier edition, while the *Han Wei congshu* 漢魏叢書 of Wang Mo 王謨 has the faulty text. The *Huanyuan zhi* included in the *Siku quanshu* (*Yingyin Wenyuange Siku quanshu** 1042:561–72) is claimed by the editors to be based on the He Tang *Han Wei congshu* but in three *juan*; an examination of the copy in the Palace Museum in Taipei reveals it is in one *juan* with the same missing pages that characterize the *Han Wei congshu*.

A portion of a collection of stories, titled *Mingbao ji* 冥寶記, with an inscription dated 882, was found at Dunhuang. Since the fifteen stories contained in that fragment are all included in the *Huanyuan ji*, it has been suggested that it may be a portion of the original *Huanyuan ji* text with a different title. If so, then since the sequence of the stories differs from that of the modern text; this would confirm that the modern text is a recension drawing on the sequence of the *Fayuan zhulin* (see Wang Zhongmin's and Shigematsu Shunshō's works in the bibliography).

Nature of contents

The stories in the *Huanyuan ji* are about the spirits of the dead seeking vengeance for wrongs done them while alive. The earliest examples are drawn from classical texts such as the *Mozi* 墨子 and the *Zuo zhuan* 左傳; others range in time from the Han down to the Northern Zhou. In some cases a condemned person about to be unjustly executed will vow that, if there is cognition after death, vengeance will be sought. Some also ask for pen and paper to be placed in their graves so that they can file a complaint with the authorities in the afterworld. The method used to wreak retribution varies widely, either directly with a weapon or indirectly through a third party; in some cases the simple appearance of the spirit causes the guilty person to collapse and die.

While Chinese fiction stories, such as the *chuanqi* 傳奇 of the Tang, may well have had their origins in the collections of which the *Huanyuan ji* is an example, these stories were considered factual by their compilers. Names, places, and dates are supplied to support their authenticity, a characteristic taken on by their fictional derivatives. The modern reader of the *Huanyuan ji* may well doubt that these events actually transpired, still, for the audience at that time, these were credible happenings. There is evidence here of the position of slaves, of the vulnerability of those who worked the land for estate owners, and of the plight of lower-class women and of merchants, all of whom could be mistreated with impunity, and whose only recourse was to appear as vengeful ghosts. Much of this material does not appear in the standard historical sources and hence the *Huanyuan ji* is a valuable social and historical document.

Principal editions

Aside from the collectanea cited previously, the *Huanyuan ji* is also found in the *Tang Song congshu* 唐宋叢書 and *Wuchao xiaoshuo* 五朝小說, both Ming compilations, *Wuchao xiaoshuo daguan* 五朝小說大觀 (Shaoye shanfang lithograph edition; Shanghai, 1926), and *Gujin shuobu congshu* 古今說部叢書 (Shanghai: Guoxue fulunshe, 1911). The edition in the *Congshu jicheng** (Beijing: Zhonghua shuju, 1991), vol. 270, is a photolithographic reproduction of the *Tang Song congshu* edition. A selection of the stories is in the *Jiu xiaoshuo* 舊小說 (Shanghai: Shangwu yinshuguan,1957).

Selected studies

Zhou Fagao's "Yan Zhitui *Huanyuan ji* kaozheng" 顏之推還冤記考證 (1961) is a pioneering study of the *Huanyuan ji*. This was followed by a broader analysis of the text by Albert E. Dien, "The *Yuan-hun Chih* (Accounts of Ghosts with Grievances): A Sixth Century Collection of Stories" (1968), in which he established the origin of the modern text. Wang Guoliang 王國良, in the preface to his *Yan Zhitui Yuanhun zhi yanjiu* 顏之推冤魂志研究 (1995), largely bases his discussion of the text on the findings by Dien, and includes the text with notes concerning textual variants. Dien had located the sources of sixty-two stories, twenty-six beyond the thirty-six in Chen Jiru's version. Wang added an additional three stories. Alvin P. Cohen, in his *Tales of Vengeful Souls* (1982), provides a translation of the sixty-two stories that Dien identified with varying degrees of certainty as belonging to the original text by Yan Zhitui.

Translations

Cohen, Alvin P., trans. *Tales of Vengeful Souls: Yuan hun zhi—A Sixth Century Collection of Chinese Avenging Ghost Stories*. Variétés sinologiques, n.s., no. 68. Taipei: Ricci Institute, 1982.

Yang, Gladys, and Xianyi Yang. *Poetry and Prose of the Han, Wei, and Six Dynasties*. Beijing: China International Book Trading Co., 1986. Pp. 133–36.

Bibliography

Campany, Robert Ford. *Strange Writing: Anomaly Accounts in Early Medieval China*. Albany: State University of New York Press, 1996. Pp. 90–91, 378.

Dien, Albert E. "The *Yuan-hun Chih* (Accounts of Ghosts with Grievances): A Sixth Century Collection of Stories." In *Wen-lin*, ed. Tse-tsung Chou, 211–28. Madison: University of Wisconsin Press, 1968.

Ishii Kōsei 石井公成. "*Genji monogatari* ni okeru Gan Shisui sakuhin no riyō—*Ganshi kakun* to *Enkon-shi* 'Ō Hanshō'" 源氏物語における顔之推作品の利用—顔氏家訓,冤魂志'王範妾.' *Bukkyō ronshū* 9 (2003): 87–115.

Jinshi cuibian 金石萃編. Compiled by Wang Chang 王昶 (1725–1806). Taipei: Guolin shuchuban youxian gongsi, 1964; photolithographic reprint of woodblock print, Jingxuntang, 1805.

Katsumura Tetsuya 勝村哲也. "*Ganshi kakun* 'Kishin-hen' to *Enkon-shi* o megutte gakkai tembō" 顔氏家訓歸心篇と冤魂志をめぐって學界展望. *Tōyōshi kenkyū* 26 (1967): 104–16.

Kominami Ichirō 小南一郎. "Gan Shisui *Enkon-shi* o megutte—Rikuchō shikai shōsetsu no seikaku 顔之推冤魂志をめぐって—六朝志怪小説の性格." *Tōhōgaku* 65 (1983): 15–28.

———. "Ron Gan Shisui *Enkon-shi*: Rikuchō shōsetsu teki seikaku" 論颜之推冤魂志: 六朝志怪小说的性格. *Chūgoku kodai shōsetsu kenkyū* 1 (2005): 83–92.

Shigematsu Shunshō 重松俊章. "Tonkōhon *Ken'enki* zankan ni tsuite" 敦煌本還冤記殘卷に就いて. *Shien* 17 (1937): 120–39.

Wang Guoliang 王國良. *Yan Zhitui Yuanhun zhi yanjiu* 顔之推冤魂志研究. Taipei: Wen shi zhe chubanshe, 1995.

Wang Zhongmin 王重民. *Dunhuang guji xulu* 敦煌古籍敘錄. Rev. ed. Beijing: Shangwu yinshuguan, 1958.

Zhou Fagao 周法高. "Yan Zhitui *Huanyuanji* kaozheng" 顔之推還冤記考證. *Dalu zazhi* 22.9 (1961): 1–4; 22.10 (1961): 13–18; 22.11 (1961): 14–22.

Albert E. Dien

Huayang guo zhi 華陽國志

Introduction

The *Huayang guo zhi* (Records of the states south of Mount Hua) by Chang Qu 常璩 (ca. 291–ca. 361) is a comprehensive gazetteer of southwest China from its legendary prehistory to the middle of the fourth century. It stands as one of China's oldest extant works of local history and was taken as a model during the local history revival of the Ming and Qing periods. Moreover, it is an important repository of materials for the study of the history, geography, economy, and culture of early and early medieval Sichuan and surrounding areas.

Contents

The *Huayang guo zhi* is divided into twelve *juan*:

1. Ba zhi 巴志 (Records of Ba)
2. Hanzhong zhi 漢中志 (Records of Hanzhong)
3. Shu zhi 蜀志 (Records of Shu)
4. Nanzhong zhi 南中志 (Records of Nanzhong)
5. Gongsun Shu/Liu ermu zhi 公孫述/劉二牧志 (Records of Gongsun Shu and the two regional governors Liu)
6. Liu Xianzhu zhi 劉先主志 (Records of Former Sovereign Liu)
7. Liu Houzhu zhi 劉後主志 (Records of Later Sovereign Liu)
8. Datong zhi 大同志 (Records of the Great Unification)
9. Li Te, Xiong, Qi, Shou, Shi zhi 李特, 雄, 期, 壽, 勢志 (Records of Li Te, Xiong, Qi, Shou, and Shi)

10A. Xianxian shinü congzanlun 先賢士女總讚論 (Collected encomia and discourses on former worthy men and women)

10B. Guanghan shinü 廣漢士女 (Men and women of Guanghan)

10C. Hanzhong shinü 漢中士女 (Men and women of Hanzhong)

11. Houxian zhi 後賢志 (Record of later worthies)

12. Xuzhi 序志 (Postface)

The twelve *juan* can be grouped into four major sections. *Juan* 1–4 present the geography, history, and culture of specific local administrative units. Modeled on the "Yu gong" 禹貢 (Tribute of Yu) section of the *Shang shu* 尚書—from which the *Huayang guo zhi* takes its name (i.e., a reference to the region as Huayang, "lands south of Mount Hua")—and the "Geographic Treatises" of the *Han shu*, these four *juan* combine discussion of political and administrative matters such as the division and renaming of commanderies and districts, local uprisings, and so on with enumeration of the locale's unique characteristics, including flora, fauna, industry, and even prominent families. Stories linking the local sites with the centers of imperial power (e.g., the sage-king Yu's 禹 marrying two sisters of Tushan 塗山 in Shu, Liu Bang's 劉邦 watching local minorities dance at the Yu 渝 River in Ba) both add local color to the narration of local administrative history and also argue for the political and cultural inclusion of the region in the greater world of imperial Chinese polity. These geographically centered *juan* are generally regarded as the most important of the *Huayang guo zhi* for their details on local products and customs, including those of local ethnic minorities.

Juan 5–9 present the affairs of various independent regimes in the region in an annalistic manner similar to the *benji* 本紀 (basic annals) sections of the *Shi ji*, *Han shu*, and *Sanguo zhi*, q.v. Treated here are Gongsun Shu 公孫述 (d. 36), a supporter of Wang Mang 王莽, who proclaimed himself emperor of Chengdu in 35; Liu Yan 劉焉 (d. 194) and Liu Zhang 劉璋 (d. 219) who ruled nominally in the name of the Han court while preparing their own imperial regalia; Liu Bei 劉備 (161–223) and Liu Shan 劉禪 (207–271) and their state of Shu-Han 蜀漢 (220–264); the brief unification of the region under the Western Jin; and the five rulers of the Li 李 clan and their state of Cheng-Han 成漢 (302–347). These accounts often include details not found in the standard histories' narration of these rulers and their states, and, as such, are important supplements to the more commonly referenced histories.

Juan 10A–C and 11 present the lives of local worthies, both male and female. These biographies are organized geographically and chronologically, and they closely resemble those found in the standard histories. While there is some overlap in figures treated by the *Huayang guo zhi* and the *Shi ji*, *Han shu*, *Hou Han shu*, q.v., *Sanguo zhi*, and *Jin shu*, q.v., the text often contains details missing from the other accounts. In the cases of the *Hou Han shu* and *Jin shu*, the *Huayang guo zhi* is clearly the primary source of information for figures from the southwest, with the two later histories copying directly from Chang Qu's earlier work. Many of the figures given biographical treatment are found only in the *Huayang guo zhi*, though some are represented with nothing more than a terse encomium. Common themes running through the biographies are the manifestation of "Confucian" virtues in the lives of local men and women and the vitality of local intellectual traditions, especially that of the Yang 楊 clan from Guanghan and their disciples in the mantic arts of celestial observation and prophetic word-play.

Chang Qu's short and apparently truncated "Postface" is an important document in the argument for cultural legitimacy of the southwest. It opens with a brief account of the involvement of Ba and Shu in early Chinese imperial politics, a list of prior histories of the region, and mentions of the area in earlier historical writings from north China. Moreover, Chang Qu notes what he considers to be the *Huayang guo zhi*'s strengths: expounding the path of righteousness, laying out laws and punishments, linking the past and present, displaying meritorious service, and manifesting the worthy and able of the southwest. The "Postface" elaborates on the role of the region in the ancient affairs of the Zhou, Qin, and Han dynasties, then refutes any questions that might arise regarding the region's loyalty to the Chinese imperial project by noting the ultimate failure of the various regimes who relied upon the region's defenses and resources to establish their own states. Finally, the "Postface" contains summaries of the twelve *juan*, offered in rhymed verse, as well as Chang Qu's final poetic appraisal of the work.

Authorship

Little is known about the life and career of Chang Qu. He has no biography in the *Jin shu*, and the autobiographical information typically contained in prefaces and postfaces is missing in the "Postface" of the *Huayang guo zhi*. All that survives is a brief notice in Cui Hong's 崔鴻 (d. 525) *Shiliuguo chunqiu*, q.v., which reads, "Chang Qu, style Daojiang 道將, was a native of Chengdu in Shu [commandery]. As a youth he was fond of learning. He compiled the *Huayang guo zhi* in ten *pian*. It begins with the establishment of the state(s) [in the region] and ends with Li Shi. It is orderly in its presentation." Chang Qu served as cavalier attendant-in-ordinary at the court of Li Shi, and in 347 Chang urged his ruler to surrender to the Eastern Jin forces led by Huan Wen 桓溫 (312–373). Following the surrender, Chang Qu accompanied Huan Wen to Jiankang, where he awaited an official post in the Eastern Jin court, an appointment that never came. It is believed that while in Jiankang, Chang Qu completed his work on the *Huayang guo zhi*.

Composition

Chang Qu's motivation in compiling the *Huayang guo zhi* appears to stem from both personal and professional interests. Chang Qu's grandfather Chang Kuan 常寬 was said to have compiled at least three local histories, including a supplement to Chen Shou's *San guo zhi* called the *Shu hou zhi* 蜀後志 (Later records of Shu). Therefore, Chang Qu was likely following a family avocation of compiling history. Moreover, Chang was following an important regional tradition. In his "Postface," he notes several other Chengdu Plain natives who had compiled histories of the area. Although little remains of most of these histories (and in several cases there is no evidence to suggest that those named compiled any historical texts), Chang Qu clearly incorporates and expands on elements from two important early Sichuan historians: Qiao Zhou 譙周 (201–270) and Chen Shou 陳壽 (233–297). Chang directly quotes numerous passages from Qiao's local histories, most frequently in the first four *juan* of the *Huayang guo zhi*. He also incorporates material from Chen Shou's now-fragmented *Yibu qijiu zhuan* 益部耆舊傳 (Biographies of the elders of the Yi region). Professionally, Chang's position in the Cheng-Han bureaucracy may have provided not only access to source materials, but even an official charge to compile the history of the Li state that later circulated under the titles *Han zhi shu* 漢之書 (History of Han) and *Shu Li shu* 蜀李書 (History of the Li [clan] in Shu). The Eastern Jin historian Sun Sheng 孫盛 (ca. 302–ca. 375) called Chang Qu "the Historian of Shu" (Shu *shi* 蜀史), but it is unclear whether this was in reference to Chang's official position or rather an honorific recognizing Chang's contributions to writing the history of the southwest. In either case, it is likely, however, that Chang Qu's work on the *Huayang guo zhi* was a private venture and not state sponsored.

Dating

It is generally accepted that Chang Qu began compiling the *Huayang guo zhi* while in Chengdu prior to his move eastward in 347. Each section of the work offers concluding dates for the material covered, and these dates vary. Ren Naiqiang (*Huayang guo zhi jiaobutuzhu*) argues that the geographic sections (*juan* 1–4) were compiled first, with the work on these *juan* completed around 333. The *juan* on the Li clan's rule ends with the year 339 and was likely completed around that time. The biographies were the last sections to be compiled. Ren speculates that originally there were only encomia for these figures, but after Chang Qu's move to Jiankang he added full biographies for most. The entire work was most likely completed between 348 and 354. The extended period of compilation results in some anachronisms in the text, particularly in terms of administrative geography, with some place-names following old, outdated nomenclature (Ren, *Huayang guo zhi jiaobutuzhu*, 3–5).

Transmission of the text

The *Huayang guo zhi* appears to have circulated freely in the Lower Yangzi region during the Southern Dynasties period. The work was cited (sometimes under the title *Huayang guo ji* 記) in the works of several prominent southern historians, including Xu Guang's 徐廣 (352–425) *Jin ji* 晉紀, Fan Ye's 范曄 (398–445) *Hou Han shu*, Pei Songzhi's 裴松之 (372–451) *Sanguo zhi zhu* 三國志注, Liu Zhao's 劉昭 (fl. 502–520) *Xu Han shu zhu* 續漢書注, and Xiao Fang's 蕭方 (fl. sixth century) *Shisanguo chunqiu* 十三國春秋. The geographic *juan* of the work appear to have been known in the Central Plains, but the entire *Huayang guo zhi* was more difficult to obtain. In a memorial to the throne in the early sixth century, Cui Hong notes that his seven-year quest to find a copy of Chang Qu's history remained unsuccessful, and he asks for the court's assistance in locating a copy with which to complete his own historical project (*Wei shu*, q.v., 67:1504). Despite the limited availability, Cui Hong references the work in his *Shiliuguo chunqiu*, q.v., and Li Daoyuan 酈道元 (d. 527) relies upon it in his *Shuijing zhu*, q.v.

During the Tang, the *Huayang guo zhi* was cited or referenced in many of the major collectanea, including *Beitang shuchao*, q.v., *Yiwen leiju*, q.v., *Kuodi zhi* 括地志, *Chuxue ji*, q.v., and *Junxian tuzhi* 郡縣圖志. The work was also referenced by the historical critic Liu Zhiji (661–721) in his *Shi tong**, and it was a major source for Fang Xuanling's *Jin shu* on matters relating to southwest China. The *Huayang guo zhi* continued to be cited in the major collectanea of the Song, including the *Taiping yulan*, q.v., *Taiping guangji* 太平廣記, *Taiping huanyu ji* 太平寰宇記, *Cefu yuangui* 冊府元龜, and *Yudi guangji* 輿地廣記.

Entries in the bibliographic monographs of the standard histories provide evidence of the relative stability of the text. The *Sui shu*, q.v., bibliography classifies the *Huayang guo zhi* as a "History of Overlords" ("Ba shi" 霸史) and describes the text as consisting of twelve *juan* (33:963). The bibliography of the *Jiu Tang shu* includes the *Huayang guo zhi* under the category of "Unofficial History" ("Weishi" 偽史) and describes the text as consisting of three *juan* (46:1992). This claim is most likely a scribal error for "thirteen," since the *Xin Tang shu* bibliography similarly classifies the text as an "Unofficial History" in thirteen *juan* (58:1461). The *Huayang guo zhi* appears twice in the bibliography of the *Song shi*; first under the heading of "Unofficial History" ("Bieshi" 別史) in ten *juan* (203:5095) and again under the heading of "History of Overlords" in twelve *juan* (204:5166). The *Huayang guo zhi* is also included in several other traditional bibliographies, including the *Tong zhi**, the *Wenxian tongkao* 文獻通考, the *Junzhai dushu zhi** (preface dated 1151) of Chao Gongwu, the *Zhizhai shulu jieti** of Chen Zhensun (fl. 1211–1249), the *Yu hai**, and the *Siku quanshu zongmu tiyao**. The discrepancy among the bibliographies regarding the number of *juan* in the work is more likely the result of counting methods (i.e., subdividing the biographies into three *juan*, including or excluding the postface in the total, etc.) than due to any significant changes in the contents of the *Huayang guo zhi*. In this regard, the *Huayang guo zhi* appears to have been transmitted from the mid-fourth century into the thirteenth century with very little loss.

Principal editions

Between the eleventh and nineteenth centuries there were at least twenty-five printed editions of the *Huayang guo zhi*. The earliest known of these editions dates to 1078 and was printed by Lü Dafang 呂大方 of Chengdu. It is now lost. All later editions of the *Huayang guo zhi* are based on the critical edition prepared by Li Ji 李塈 in 1204. Eight different printed editions of the *Huayang guo zhi* were published during the Ming. An edition was produced for inclusion in the *Yongle dadian** in the early fifteenth century, but it is now lost. During the Jiajing period (1522–1566), Qian Gu 錢穀 prepared an edition that was later included in the *Siku quanshu* (*Yingyin Wenyuange Siku quanshu** 463:131–303). Two printed editions were produced in 1564, one by Liu Dachang 劉大昌 of Chengdu, now fragmented, and the other by Zhang Jiayin 張佳胤, now lost. In 1592 Wu Guan 吳琯 published an edition based closely on Zhang Jiayin's earlier edition. Wu Guan's edition was included in Cheng Rong's 程榮 *Han Wei congshu* 漢魏叢書. He Yunzhong 何允中 produced an edition in 1579 that was included in He Tang's 何鏜 edition of the *Han Wei congshu*. In 1626, Li Yigong 李一公 of Chengdu produced a "recarved" *Huayang guo zhi*, moving Chang Qu's postface to the beginning of the text. Finally, an edition based on the Wu Guan and He Yunzhong editions was printed by He Yu 何宇 (dates unknown) and circulated independently. Three printed editions were produced during the Qianlong period (1736–1795). One of these, printed by Li Diaoyuan 李調元 in 1782, was included in the *Han hai* 函海. In 1791 Wang Mo 王謨 produced an edition based on He Yunzhong's *Han Wei congshu* edition. A third edition, undated, was printed in Hangzhou and also based on the *Han Wei congshu* edition. Finally, in 1814 Liao Yin 廖寅 prepared an edition of the text at Nanjing. The *Huayang guo zhi* was frequently reprinted during the nineteenth century, and editions were included in revised publications of the *Han Wei congshu* (1876), in the *Han hai* (1881, 1882), and in the early twentieth-century collection *Longxi jingshe congshu* 龍溪精舍叢書 (1917). The edition contained in the *Sibu beiyao** is based on the Liao Yin edition; the edition contained in the *Sibu congkan** is based on the Qian Gu edition; the *Gujin yishi* 古今逸史 contains a reprint of the Wu Guan edition.

There are two important modern critical editions of the *Huayang guo zhi*:

Liu Lin 劉琳. *Huayang guo zhi jiaozhu* 華陽國志校注. 1984. Rpt., Chengdu: Ba Shu shushe, 2007.

Ren Naiqiang 任乃強. *Huayang guo zhi jiaobutuzhu* 華陽國志校補圖注. 1987. Rpt., Shanghai: Shanghai guji chubanshe, 2007.

The first contains commentary and glosses by Liu Lin. The second and most comprehensive modern critical edition contains a lengthy prolegomenon including a detailed history of the text, maps and tables, exhaustive glosses and interpretative commentary, and collated passages from all extant editions of the text. It has become the standard modern edition of the *Huayang guo zhi*.

Studies of the text

Gu Guanguang's 顧觀光 (1799–1862) *Huayang guo zhi jiaokanji* 華陽國志校勘記 collates variant passages from the Liao edition with passages from the He Yunzhong and Wang Mo editions of the *Huayang guo zhi* contained in the two *Han Wei congshu*. The work is available in two recent editions:

Gu Guanguang. *Huayang guo zhi jiaokanji*. Chengdu: Sichuan renmin chubanshe, 1957.

———. *Huayang guo zhi jiaokan*. In *Zhongguo yeshi jicheng xubian* 中國野史集成續編. Chengdu: Ba Shu shushe, 2000.

Selected studies

Farmer, J. Michael. "Qiao Zhou and the Historiography of Early Medieval Sichuan." *Early Medieval China* 7 (2001): 31–69.

Gu Jiegang 顧頡剛. "Shu wang benji yu *Huayang guo zhi* suo ji Shu guo shishi" 蜀王本紀與華陽國志所記蜀國史事. In *Shilin zashi* 史林雜識, 240–46. Beijing: Zhonghua shuju, 1963.

Huang Wei 黃葦. "Guanyu *Huayang guo zhi*" 關於華陽國志. In *Fangzhi xue* 方志學, ed. Huang Wei, 423–29. Shanghai: Fudan daxue, 1993.

Jin Qi 金其. "*Huayang guo zhi*." In *Zhongguo shixue mingzhu tijie* 中國史學名著題解, ed. Zhang Shunhui 張舜徽, 276–77. Beijing: Zhongguo qingnian chubanshe, 1984.

Li Youming 李有明. "*Huayang guo zhi* de zuozhe Chang Qu" 華陽國志的作者常璩. In *Sichuan gudai mingren* 四川古代名人, ed. Li Youming and Chen Hongtao 陳紅濤, 29–34. Chengdu: Sichuan sheng shehui kexue yuan chubanshe, 1984.

Liu Chonglai 劉重來. "Shuo *Huayang guo zhi*" 說華陽國志. *Shixue shi yanjiu* (1984.4): 28–38.

Liu Chonglai and Xu Shiduan 徐適端. *Huayang guo zhi yanjiu* 華陽國志研究. Chengdu: Ba Shu shushe, 2008.

Liu Lin 劉琳. "*Huayang guo zhi* jianlun" 華陽國志簡論. *Sichuan daxue xuebao, Zhexue shehui kexue ban* (1979.2): 82–87.

———. "Chang Qu jiqi *Huayang guo zhi*" 常璩及其華陽國志. In *Zhongguo fangzhi xuejia yanjiu* 中國方志學家研究, ed. Huang Desheng 黃德聲 and Fu Dengzhou 傅登舟, 1–14. Wuhan: Wuhan chubanshe, 1989.

Liu Xianxin 劉咸炘. "*Huayang guo zhi* lun" 華陽國志論. In *Tui shi shu* 推十書, 5.28a–31b. Chengdu: Chengdu guji shudian, 1996. Reprinted in *Tui shi shu: Zengbu quanben* 推十書：增補全本. Shanghai: Shanghai kexue jishu wenxian chubanshe, 2009. 3.1, pp. 566–69.

Zhao Yi 趙毅. "Lun *Shi ji* yu *Huayang guo zhi* de guanxi" 論史記與華陽國志的關係. In *Sichuan lishi yanjiu wenji* 四川歷史研究文集, ed. Jia Daquan 賈大泉, 53–66. Chengdu: Sichuan sheng shehui kexue yuan chubanshe, 1987.

Translations

Chinese

Wang Qiming 汪啓明 and Zhao Jing 趙靜, trans. *Huayang guo zhi yizhu* 華陽國志譯注. Chengdu: Sichuan daxue chubanshe, 2007. This is based on Ren Naiqiang's edition of the text and includes the original text, a rendition into modern Chinese, and minimal annotations.

European languages

There is no translation of the entire *Huayang guo zhi* into any Western language, but portions of the text have been translated in the following works:

Farmer, J. Michael. "A Person of the State Composed a Poem: Lyrics of Praise and Blame in the *Huayang guo zhi*." In *Chinese Literature: Essays, Articles, and Reviews* 29 (2007): 23–54. Farmer translates a portion of *juan* 1 dealing with poetry and historical narrative.

Kleeman, Terry F. *Great Perfection: Religion and Ethnicity in a Chinese Millennial Kingdom*. Honolulu: University of Hawai'i Press, 1998. Kleeman translates passages relating to the state of Cheng-Han during the fourth century, corresponding to *juan* 8 and 9 of the *Huayang guo zhi*, and adds relevant passages from other texts.

Sage, Steven F. *Ancient Sichuan and the Unification of China*. Albany: State University of New York Press, 1992. Sage translates passages relating to the earliest history of the region up to the Western Han period.

Japanese

Nakabayashi Shirō 中林史朗. *Kayō kokushi* 華陽国志. Tokyo: Meitoku shuppansha, 1995. Nakabayashi translates excerpts from the first four *juan* of the *Huayang guo zhi*. The volume provides the original Chinese text, explanatory glosses, and a narrative analytic commentary of the passages translated. Additionally, the preface contains a general introduction to the *Huayang guo zhi*, an extended genealogy of Chang Qu, and a bibliography of recent studies in both Chinese and Japanese. An index of personal names, place-names, and year-titles is included in the appendix.

Index

Taniguchi Fusao 谷口房男, ed. *Kayō kokushi jinmei sakuin, fu Kayō kokushi minzoku kankei goi sakuin* 華陽國志人名索引, 附華陽國志民族關係語彙索引 [Index of personal names in the *Huayang guo zhi*, supplemented with index of vocabulary related to peoples in the *Huayang guo zhi*]. Tokyo: Kokusho kankōkai, 1981.

J. Michael Farmer

Jiankang shilu 建康實錄

Introduction

The subject of the *Jiankang shilu* (The veritable records of Jiankang), by Xu Song 許嵩 (eighth century) is the city and region of Jiankang (modern-day Nanjing), the capital of six states in south China between the Han and the Tang dynasties, that is, Sun Wu, Eastern Jin, Song, Qi, Liang and Chen—hence the name Six Dynasties for the period. The standard histories aside, the *Jiankang shilu* is a very important work for the history of this period. It can be said to be a concise history of the Six Dynasties, as well as a prized work of historical geography. In a condensed manner it not only narrates the history of the dynasties but also emphasizes the geography of Jiankang and its environs, providing a record of the remains of the city, palaces, official offices, Buddhist temples, and so forth. An important feature of the book is its preservation of various historical records that have been lost. According to some scholars' calculations, the book cites over fifty pre-Tang and early Tang works, among which there are over thirty that have not survived, such as the *Song lue* 宋略 and *Liangjing xinji* 兩京新記, making it a very rare historical document. But because the *Jiankang shilu* had very few copies of block-printed editions available since its initial publication, not enough importance was attached to it until 1980.

Contents

The *Jiankang shilu* is a general history of some four hundred years with a focus on Jiankang as the political and economic center. The account starts with the first year of the Xingping reign of Emperor Xian of the Eastern Han (194) and ends with the third year of the Zhenming reign of the Last Ruler (Houzhu) of the Chen (589), but some records relating to the history of the Buddhist temples of Jiankang reach into the Tang. In addition, it records some common Tang sayings, and it uses the location of the Tang's Jiangning xian 江寧縣 (the name Jiankang was changed to Jiangning in 635) to indicate the locations of and relative distances between some sites of the Jiankang of the Six Dynasties period.

The *Jiankang shilu*'s style and contents differ from those of the usual history, and at it simultaneously uses both the annal-biography format and the chronological style of traditional historiography. As a result, it was criticized by later scholars for its "style not being pure." *Juan* 1 to 10 deal with events of the Sun Wu and

Eastern Jin dynasties in chronological order, and in taking the emperors as the basis of organization, they correspond to the annals of the standard histories. *Juan* 11 to 20 cover the history of the Song, Qi, Liang, and Chen, following the annal-biography format by first arranging the events concerning the emperors in chronological sequence and then supplying the biographies of eminent officials. As for the sections relating to each dynasty, those of the Sun Wu, Eastern Jin, and Song are relatively detailed, while those for the Qi, Liang, and Chen are rather cursory; this parallels the varying degrees of detail in the standard histories of those dynasties.

As for format, aside from the basic text, there is also a commentary by the author, in smaller-sized characters that appear below the main text. This commentary is abundant, preserving much important material, some of it from works no longer extant. It thus enables one to fill in lacunae and correct errors in the standard histories.

Authorship

Xu Song probably wrote the *Jiankang shilu* around the year 756. His ancestors were from Beixincheng 北新城, Gaoyang 高陽, Jizhou 冀州 (southwest of modern Xushui xian 徐水縣, Hebei). They may have moved to the south at the end of the Eastern Han. Xu Song himself, perhaps with his family, seems to have lived for an extensive period of time in Jiankang, and as a result he was quite familiar with the city and the surrounding area and knew the regional lore. The city's ancient geography, sites, and monasteries occupy quite a bit of space in the *Jiankang shilu*. Another work concerning the palaces of the Six Dynasties, the *Liuchao gongyuan ji* 六朝宮苑記 in two *juan*, no longer extant, is attributed to him in the bibliographic monograph of the *Song shi* (204:5154), but because neither the *Jiu Tang shu* nor the *Xin Tang shu* mention it, the modern scholar Zhang Chenshi thinks Xu Song may not have written such a work. Nonetheless, there is a special emphasis on the historical architecture of Six Dynasties palaces and gardens, official offices, residences, and Buddhist temples in the *Jiankang shilu* that provides important material for an understanding of changes in architecture and geographical locations. In 1160, Zhang Dunyi 張敦頤 compiled the *Liuchao shiji bianlei* 六朝事蹟編類, in which much of the content regarding ancient sites was gleaned from the *Jiankang shilu*.

The most important reason, and perhaps Xu Song's main impetus, for writing the *Jiankang shilu* was that after Emperor Wen of the Sui wiped out the Chen dynasty in 589, he had the city of Jiankang destroyed: "reduced to tilled fields." Consequently, the palaces, offices, and even some of the residences of the Six Dynasties did not survive. Shortly after, in 590, there was a great rebellion in the south, and among the five men who led the revolt was Li Leng 李稜, a native of Jiankang. When order was restored, Emperor Wen ordered that even the Buddhist temples of Jiankang were to be totally razed. These two rounds of destruction were greatly deplored, and many were saddened by the devastation of the proud city. During the following Tang period, poets wrote many Jinling *huaigu* 金陵懷古 poems (Jinling being another name for the Jiankang area) to chant and dwell upon Six Dynasties sites and culture. It was in that context that Xu Song would have personally visited many of the Six Dynasties historical remains. In the *Jiankang shilu*, the locations of official sites are often defined by the distances from some Tang landmark. Another characteristic of the work is its detailed histories of Buddhist temples. In this Xu Song may have been inspired by Yang Xuanzhi's *Luoyang qielan ji*, q.v., for Yang had used Buddhist temples as his basic organizational point of reference, to reflect the Northern Wei period's rise and fall. The *Jiankang shilu* also gives a detailed account of the establishment and subsequent history of each Buddhist temple, as well as their dimensions and interior murals, and so the work provides extremely important documentation for the history of Buddhism and Buddhist culture during the Six Dynasties.

Transmission of the text

The text has been transmitted in two formats: woodblock print and manuscript.

1. Block-printed editions

    a. Northern Song block print. The earliest print was issued by Jiangning department (Jiangning fu 江寧府; now Nanjing, Jiangsu), relying on a collation with Six Dynasties histories (including the *Sanguo zhi*, q.v., *Jin shu*, q.v., *Nan shi*, q.v., and *Bei shi*, q.v.), twenty *juan* in all, begun in the tenth month of 1058 and finished in the fifth month of 1059. This imprint has not survived intact; there are only fragmentary copies.

    b. Southern Song block print. Printed in the eleventh month of 1148, this was a recarving of the 1058 edition by the military commission (*anfu shisi* 安撫使司) of the Jing-Hu Northern circuit (Jing Hu bei lu 荊湖北路). There is a copy in the Beijing Library. In 1984 the Zhonghua shuju, Beijing, published a facsimile edition without color so that the seals added by collectors since the Song do not appear. In 2003 the Beijing Library, as a part of its series of rare-edition reprints, produced it in color so that these seals do appear.

    c. A Song edition of 1256 that has not survived.

    d. A Qing edition of 1808, of which the Nanjing Library has a copy.

    e. A Qing edition of 1902. Gan Yuanhuan 甘元煥 (1841–1897), a member of a distinguished Nanjing family, published a collated edition. Later, his grandson Ye Shunan 葉樹楠 had the blocks recarved. It was published in 1902. In 1993 the Ba Shu shushe, Chengdu, published a photolithographed edition.

2. Manuscript editions

The most accessible manuscript version at present is in the Wenyuange 文淵閣 copy of the *Siku quanshu**. In 1983 the Taiwan Commercial Press printed a photolithographed copy, which is volume 370 in *Yingyin Wenyuan Siku quanshu**. In addition, the Shanghai Library has a manuscript copy that has been studied by the Japanese scholar Yoshimori Kenkai (see later).

Concerning the various editions of the *Jiankang shilu*, Ji Zhongping 季忠平 has written a master's thesis, "*Jiankang shilu* banben yanjiu" 建康實錄版本研究 (Fudan University, 2001), that contains a detailed discussion; it is available on the Internet.

Modern critical editions

There are two punctuated and collated editions:

Zhang Chenshi 張忱石, ed. *Jiankang shilu*. Beijing: Zhonghua shuju, 1986.
Meng Zhaogeng 孟昭庚, Sun Shuqi 孫述圻, and Wu Taiye 伍貽業, eds. *Jiankang shilu*. Shanghai: Shanghai guji chubanshe, 1987.

Of these, the collated edition of Zhang Chenshi is quite extensive, has a very high scholarly value, and at present is considered the most authoritative.

Major studies

Because the received copies have many textual problems and, moreover, it was only from the 1980s that serious attention began to be paid to the *Jiankang shilu*, research to date has advanced only so far as the analysis of editions and collations. Zhang Chenshi's introduction, titled "Explanation of the Punctuation and Collation," is the first important research essay, narrating the life of author Xu Song, recounting the editions of the book, and also discussing the value of its documentation. Of the research in recent years, the more important studies are the following:

Bing Hong 冰鴻 (Xie Binghong, see later). "Jiankang shilu jiaoyi" 建康實錄校議. *Wenjiao ziliao* (2001.6): 114–21.
Gao Min 高敏 and Zhu Heping 朱和平. "Yibu jutese de guji dianjiao—Zhang Chenshi dianjiao *Jiankang shilu* shuping" 一部具特色的古籍點校—張忱石點校建康實錄述評 [A special work of punctuation and collation of an ancient book—A review of Zhang Chenshi's punctuation and collation of the *Jiankang shilu*]. *Xinyang shifan xueyuan xuebao, Zhexue shehui kexue ban* (1990.2): 49–51.
Ji Zhongping 季忠平. "*Jiankang shilu* banben yanjiu" 建康實錄版本研究. Master's thesis, Fudan daxue, 2001.
———. "*Jiankang shilu* Songben jiaokan chuyi" 建康實錄宋本校勘芻議. *Wenxian* (2001.3): 10, 23–31.
———. "*Jiankang shilu* jiaokan zhaji" 建康實錄校勘札記. *Guji zhengli yanjiu xuekan* (2002.3): 80–83.

Li Chengquan 酈承銓. "*Jiankang shilu* jiaoji" 建康實錄校記. *Jiangsu shengli guoxue tushuguan niankan* 6 (1933): 1–52; 7 (1934): 1–67.

Li Xiaoshu 李小樹. "Nanchao shoudu Fosi jianzao tedian lunxi—Cong *Jiankang shilu* de jizai tanqi" 南朝首都佛寺建造特點論析—從建康實錄的記載談起. *Xueshujie* (2004.2): 217–24.

Meng Wentong 蒙文通. "Songlue cunyu *Jiankang shilu* kao" 宋略存於建康實錄考. *Guoli Beiping tushuguan guankan* 8.5 (1934): 51–58.

Tang Bianjun 唐燮軍. "Bian *Jiankang shilu* ji Song shi quan ju Songlue wei lanben" 辨建康實錄記宋史全據宋略為藍本. *Zhongguoshi yanjiu* (2005.2): 42.

Tao Yuanzhen 陶元珍. "*Jiankang shilu* zhaji" 建康實錄札記. *Shixue niankan* 1.2 (1940): 99–111.

Wu Jinhua 吳金華. "*Jiankang shilu* shi'erti (shang)" 建康實錄十二題 (上). *Nanjing Xiaozhuang xueyuan xuebao* (2006.3): 21–32.

———. "*Jiankang shilu* shi'erti (xia)" 建康實錄十二題 (下). *Nanjing Xiaozhuang xueyuan xuebao* (2006.5): 18–28.

Wu Jinhua and Ji Zhongping. "*Jiankang shilu* jiaoyi" 建康實錄校議. *Guji yanjiu* (2000.3): 35–39.

Xie Binghong 謝秉洪. "*Jiankang shilu* jiaodu zhaji" 建康實錄校讀札記. Master's thesis, Nanjing shifan daxue, 2003.

———. "*Jiankang shilu* zuozhe yu chengshu shidai xinlun" 建康實錄作者與成書時代新論. *Nanjing shida xuebao, Shehui kexueban* (2004.5): 140–44.

Yang Xiaochun 楊曉春. "*Jiankang shilu* zhong de *Liangjing xinji* yiwen" 建康實錄中的兩京新記佚文." *Zhongguo difangzhi* (2008.1): 40.

Zhang Qimin 張琪敏. "*Jiankang shilu* jiaokan zhaji" 建康實錄校勘札記. *Nanjing shida xuebao, Shehui kexueban* (1991.1): 29–33.

Zhang Xunliao 張勛燎. "*Jiankang shilu* ji qi chengshu niandai wenti" 建康實錄及其成書時代問題. In *Guwenxian luncong* 古文獻論叢, 160–74. Chengdu: Ba Shu shushe, 1990.

Japanese annotations and translations

Yasuda Jiro 安田二郎. "Kyo Sū no *Kenkō jitsuroku*" 許嵩の建康實錄. *Rikuchō gakujutsu gakkai* 7 (2006.3): 125–38.

Yoshimori Kensukei 葭森健介. "Jōkai toshokanzō shōhon *Kenkō jitsuroku* kō" 上海圖書館藏鈔本建康實錄考. *Tokushima daigaku sōkai kagakubu kiyō* 5 (1992): 1–12.

Liu Shu-fen

Jin shu 晉書

Introduction

Jin shu (History of the Jin dynasty), consisting of 130 *juan*, is a sophisticated editorial product of early seventh-century court scholarship. It remains a primary, if not entirely defining, framework for interpreting historically the persons and actions of the Sima 司馬 family's Jin dynasty (8 February 266 to 7 July 420). This dynasty was later analyzed as Western and Eastern Jin, since in 317, six years after the capital at Luoyang fell, a Sima emperor was reestablished in Jiankang (modern Nanjing, known until 313 of the Western Jin as Jianye).

Contents

The *Jin shu* is an example of the composite, or *jizhuan* 紀傳, style of dynastic histories, following the pattern of the *Shi ji*, written during the Former Han. The *Shi ji* had pulled together older, traditional genres of narrative, thematic account, institutional chronology, and historian's judgment. Thus, in a similar way, the *Jin shu* contains the following sections:

1. Court annals (*ji* 紀). These ten *juan* are the chronological records of the political actions and policies of all Sima emperors during Jin, but they include at the beginning the records of two predynastic leaders, Sima Yi 司馬懿 (179–251) and his son Sima Shi 師 (211–265).

2. Monographs (*zhi* 志). These twenty *juan* are accounts of administrative institutions, each beginning with a synthetic historical overview: "Heaven's Patterns" (*tianwen* 天文, that is, mantic astronomy), "Land Organization" (*dili* 地理, administrative geography), "Harmonic and Celestial Systems" (*lüli* 律曆, metrology, pitch regulation, computational astronomy), "Rites" (*li* 禮), "Music" (*yue* 樂), "State Offices" (*zhiguan* 職官), "Carriages and Garments" (*yufu* 輿服), "Food and Money" (*shihuo* 食貨), "Five Phases" (*wuxing* 五行, mantic metaphysics), and "Punishment and Laws" (*xingfa* 刑法).

3. Biographies (*liezhuan* 列傳). The first of these *juan* covers imperial consorts and princes, then come the numerous important officials (and their sons and other associates). Next are collective biographies, among which are such categories as the "Filial and Devoted" (*xiaoyou* 孝友), "Loyal and True" (*zhongyi* 忠義), "Excellent Officials" (*liangli* 良吏), "Ritual Exegetes"

(rulin 儒林), "Literary Writers" (wenyuan 文苑), "Consorts' Influential Families" (waiji 外戚), "Recluses and the Disengaged" (yinyi 隱逸), "Artificers and Technicians" (yishu 藝術), "Exemplary Women" (lienü 列女), "Four Yi-Barbarian Groups" (siyi 四夷), and several *juan* devoted to traitorous figures.

4. Reports (*zaiji* 載記). These thirty *juan* represent a variant on the composite history format; they are reports covering non-Chinese states established by conquest throughout northern and western China (the so-called Sixteen States). By creating a separate subgenre, the editors clearly delegitimized these states' non-Chinese leaders (for discussion, see Rogers, *Chronicle of Fu Chien*).

The *Jin shu*, finished in the beginning years of the Tang dynasty, was the product of a new development in Chinese historiography. For the first time, scholarly committees under imperial commission undertook to revamp existing histories. They concentrated on all such writings that dealt with dynasties coming after the Three Kingdoms, having deemed them incomplete, or lacking in proper form and didactic style. We cannot determine precisely how the older proto–*Jin shu* materials were changed and refashioned in this process. Most of the pre-Tang sources for the *Jin shu* survive only as short quotations in encyclopedic works of the late Tang and Song, even though they were partly reconstructed by Qing-era scholars. Because the *Jin shu* was a notable Tang-court commission, and due as well to the rise of book printing soon after the end of Tang, the *Jin shu* has remained textually stable since its original compilation.

The *Jin shu* has received negative evaluations over the centuries, usually on the grounds of its overinclusiveness and indulgence in popular literature, for example, the long quotations of scholar-officials' *fu* rhapsodies, their letters, and anecdotes about the spirit world and mantic events that are quoted in the context of court policy and private lives. Moreover, the editors' set-piece judgments on individuals and groups are generally rendered in a flowery and obscure style. (See *Siku quanshu zongmu**, *juan* 45, "Tiyao" preface; Zhao Yi, *Nian'er shi zhaji*; and Zhang Lizhi, *Zhengshi gailun*.) Finally, scholars have pointed out another possible drawback—the Tang throne's keen interest in the *Jin shu* project. The early Tang emperors sought policy lessons (and ideological framing) in the events of the Jin era, especially since the Jin provided a political and military model for uniting north and south China. We get the sense that Tang foreign policies and wars, and internal matters of imperial legitimacy, influenced the shape of the annals and biographies of the *Jin shu*.

Composition

Prior to the early Tang commission to compile the *Jin shu*, the Tang throne had already commissioned other post–Three Kingdoms histories. In the 620s, the noted scholar Linghu Defen 令狐德棻 (582–666) successfully suggested to Tang

Gaozu that scattered and lost works be collected, and in 623 proposed that histories of the Southern and Northern Dynasties and Sui be collated and written. The 623 project was suspended; then, in about 630, it was restarted under Tang Taizong, with new offices and titles. William Hung sees this as the true beginning of regularized historiography bureaus staffed by scholars of relatively high status (see "T'ang Bureau of Historiography," 94–98; also Fairbank, "Ssu-ma I," 225–31). For the next phase of court historiography, on 24 April 646, Taizong ordered the compilation of the *Jin shu*, which was completed very rapidly, in 648 (some sources point to a possible beginning date of 644). Linghu and Fang Xuanling 房玄齡 (578–648) received major roles in the *Jin shu* project, in part because they were highly respected as literary stylists. Taizong, an avid poet and writer himself, wanted to work with excellent scholars whom he knew and whose progress he could monitor. It is usually agreed that the total number of scholars appointed in 646 by Tang Taizong was twenty-one, although some believe it was twenty-four. The overall editor was Fang Xuanling, but direct editing and writing of the biographies is thought to have been heavily undertaken by Xu Jingzong 許敬宗 (592–672). Taizong himself wrote four chapter-ending "pronouncements" (*chi* 敕), functioning as judgments on the lives of those particular Jin rulers and officials.

As remarked previously, versions of a history of the Jin dynasty, some in the standard-history composite format, had been written in the fourth and fifth centuries, but Taizong thought that they were inadequate. The *Jin shu* committee did, however, use several as bases for their new *Jin shu*. To the best of our knowledge, there were at that time fourteen extant compilations of Jin history. The chief ones among them by sheer size, all titled "Jin shu," were as follows:

> Zang Rongxu 臧榮緒 (415–488), 110 *juan*; the chief source of the Tang compilers.
>
> Yu Yu 虞預 (fl. early 300s), 44 *juan*.
>
> Xie Chen 謝沈 (d. ca. 345), over 30 *juan*.
>
> Xiao Ziyun 蕭子雲 (487–549), 110 *juan*.
>
> Wang Yin 王隱 (ca. 270–ca. 340), 93 *juan*.
>
> Gan Bao 干寶 (fl. 320s), 23 *juan*.
>
> Xu Guang 徐廣 (352–425), 46 *juan*.

In addition, there was the large work (78 *juan*) of He Fasheng 何法盛 titled *Jin zhongxing shu* 晉中興書. An extant collection that reconstructs some of these materials is that of Tang Qiu 湯球 (1804–1881), *Jiujia jiu Jin shu jiben* 九家舊晉書輯本. Other pre-Tang Jin materials, such as anecdotes and collections of scholars' writings, were also available to the Tang editors.

Transmission of the text

Both the *Jiu Tang shu* (*juan* 46) and the *Xin Tang shu* (*juan* 58), in their bibliographic monographs, list a *Jin shu* edited by the Tang committee in 130 *juan*, and subsequently there has been little problem tracing the integrity of the text. There has been no change in the number (130) or order of the *juan*, beginning from the earliest Song-era printing currently held in the Beijing Library. Originally in the collection of Zhou Xian 周暹, it has been reprinted in the Zhonghua zaizao shanben 中華再造善本 series as *Jin shu* (Beijing: Beijing tushuguan chubanshe, 2003). Another Song edition, with some *juan* missing and including a Qing-era postface, is in the Nanjing Library. A third, with some missing *juan* and a Qing-era postface by Qian Taiji 錢泰吉 (1791–1863) and others, is in the Beijing Library. There are numerous Yuan and Ming editions held in Chinese and American collections. Another Song edition is held at the Harvard-Yenching Library (see Harvard-Yenching Microfilm FC4171; v.1–10 missing), as well as a late-Ming Imperial Academy and Mao Jin 毛晉 (1599–1659) edition. (See further comments under "Principal Editions.")

A 130-*kan* edition was made in Japan, titled *Shinjo* 晉書; principal editors were Shimura Teikan 志村槇幹 and Ogyū Mokei 荻生茂卿 (*kutō* 句讀), published at Kōriyama 郡山, Shōkaidō 松會堂, and dated Genroku 元禄 14–15 (1701–1702). This is held in the Harvard-Yenching Rare Book Room (no. TJ 2570 3202). It includes the Tang-era pronunciation guide *Jin shu yinyi* 晉書音義 (J. *Shinjo ongi*) at the beginning (see later). The Japanese compilers added *kanbun* reading marks throughout and in various places made notes above the columns that explain orthographies. There are no commentarial remarks otherwise.

For an overall account of the textual history of this and the other Six Dynasties standard histories, see appendix IV, "Textual Transmission of the Standard Histories."

Principal editions

Jin shu. 20 *ce*. Shanghai: Shangwu yinshuguan, 1936. Photolithographic ed. of a Song imprint. Included in the series Baina ben *Ershisishi* 百衲本二十四史. *Sibu congkan** ed. This and the editions following are all attributed to Fang Xuanling et al. and contain 130 *juan*.

Jin shu. Photolithographic copy of the Wuying dian ben 武英殿本 (Palace ed.) of 1739. Taipei: Taiwan Zhonghua shuju, 1965.

Jin shu. Beijing: Zhonghua shuju, 1974. Punctuated. Based primarily on the late-Qing Jinling shuju 金陵書局 edition collated with the Wuyingdian Palace edition (1739) and the Baina edition (itself based on a Song edition), with further reference to the Yuan-era *Dade jiulu* 大德九路 edition and others, including the *Jiguge* 汲古閣 (1631). Several early modern and modern *jiaokanji* 校勘記 (variorum notes; some unpublished) were also consulted. Tang Taizong's edict to compile the *Jin shu* is printed at the end (see in the following, under "Translations"), as well as the Tang-era pronunciation guide,

Jin shu yinyi, 3 *juan*, by He Chao 何超, including a preface by He's son-in-law and student Yang Qixuan 楊齊宣, of Hongnong.

Critical scholarship

There were no early line-by-line commentaries to the *Jin shu*, but in modern times one was made in 1927 by Wu Shijian 吳士鑑 and Liu Chenghan 劉承幹, *Jin shu jiaozhu* 晉書斠注 (rpt., Taipei: Yiwen yinshuguan, 1956; also reprinted in *Xuxiu Siku quanshu** vols. 275–77). It is most effective for complete, verbatim quotations of supporting material from early florilegia and from Qing scholarship; it is less deep in regard to philological explanations and cross-connections to other *Jin shu* passages and episodes. (See Yang, "Notes on Economic History," 190.) A specific section of this commentary by Wu and Liu (concerning the *Jin shu* chapters on the "Siyi" peoples) is reprinted as *Jin shu jiaozhu: Si yi, Fuyu guo deng* 晉書斠注: 四夷, 夫餘國等 (Chengdu: Sichuan minzu chubanshe, 2002). Finally, there are reports of a new, perhaps still forthcoming, annotated edition: Zhu Dawei 朱大渭 and Fang Beichen 方北辰, *Jinzhu ben Jin shu* 今注本晉書.

Thirteen mostly Qing-era appendices and tables of *Jin shu* data are included in *Ershiwu shi bubian* 二十五史補編 (Shanghai: Kaiming shudian, 1936–1937), vol. 3. (For a thorough review of *kaozheng* scholarship on the *Jin shu* in general, see Zhu Dawei, "*Jin shu* de pingjie.") These chiefly are chronological and hierarchical tables of chief ministers, generals, non-Chinese peoples, and military regions, as well as *kaozheng*-style commentaries on existing *Jin shu* monographs such as geography and rites, and a supplemental Jin-era bibliographic monograph (a topic not treated in the *Jin shu*).

Ten other important *kaozheng* writings on the *Jin shu* are now collected and reprinted in an ongoing collational project for the standard histories: see Xu Shu 徐蜀, general editor, *Wei Jin Nan Bei chao zhengshi dingbu wenxian huibian* 魏晉南北朝正史訂補文獻彙編 (Beijing: Beijing tushuguan chubanshe, 2004), vols. 2 and 3. Volume 2 reprints these eight *Jin shu* items:

1. Sun Renlong 孫人龍, *Jin shu kaozheng* 晉書考證
2. Fu Yunlong 傅雲龍, *Jin shu kaozheng* 晉書考證
3. Ding Guojun 丁國鈞, *Jin shu jiaowen* 晉書校文
4. Zhou Jialu 周家禄, *Jin shu jiaokanji* 晉書校勘記
5. He Chao (Tang era), *Jin shu yinyi*. This item is also printed at the end of the Zhonghua edition and in the *Shinjo* edition (see earlier).
6. Tang Qiu, *Jin shu jiben* 晉書輯本. Also published as *Jiujia jiu Jin shu jiben* (see earlier). Shanghai: Shangwu yinshuguan, 1937.
7. Hang Shijun 杭世駿, *Jin shu bu zhuanzan* 晉書補傳贊
8. Ma Yulong 馬與龍, *Jin shu dilizhi zhu* 晉書地理志注

Vol. 3 reprints these two:

9. Zhao Zaihan 趙在翰, *Jin shu bubiao* 晉書補表; also available in vol. 22 of Chengdu: Sichuan minzu chubanshe, 2002 (earlier). A horizontal layout provides a chronological chart of court actions concerning non-Han activities. The print reproduction is relatively poor; many characters are hard to read. Some parts of the preface are "missing."

10. Zhang Daling 張大齡, *Jin Wuhu zhizhang* 晉五胡指掌

Modern studies of *Jin shu* monographs and biographies

Chen Lianqing 陳連慶. *Jin shu shihuozhi jiaozhu, Wei shu shihuozhi jiaozhu* 晉書食貨志校注, 魏書食貨志校注. Changchun: Dongbei shifan daxue chubanshe, 1999. Fairly comprehensive commentary; aimed at a slightly lower level than Nishijima's (following), and its range of contents differs. Printed in traditional characters and punctuated.

Chūbashi Masakazu 中鉢雅量 and Yasumoto Hiroshi 安本博. "*Shinjo* jurinden kenkyū (yakuchū hen II)" 晉書儒林伝研究 (訳注編 II). *Aichi kyōiku daigaku kenkyū hōkoku (jimbun kagaku)* 29 (1980.3): 193–206.

Ishiguro Noritoshi 石黑宣俊 et al. "*Shinjo* jurinden kenkyū (yakuchū hen)" 晉書儒林伝研究 (訳注編). Four parts. *Aichi kyōiku daigaku kenkyū hōkoku (jimbun kagaku)* 29 (1980.3): 207–20; 30 (1981.3): 204–18.

Kubota Morihiro 窪田守弘. "Gen Seki no seikaku to seikatsu taido, *Shinjo* no Gen Seki den yori" 阮籍の性格と生活態度, 晉書の阮籍傳より. *Aichi shukutoku daigaku ronshū, Bungakubu, Bungaku kenkyū-ka hen* 25 (2000): 1–16.

Kusuyama Shūsaku 楠山修作. "*Shinjo* Shokkashi no ichi kōsatsu" 晉書食貨志の一考察. *Tōhōgaku* 51 (1976.01): 28–39.

Rogers, Michael. *The Chronicle of Fu Chien: A Case of Exemplar History*. Berkeley: University of California Press, 1968. This is an important analysis of the accounts of the numerous non-Chinese states and the pre-Tang *Shiliu guo chunqiu*, q.v., see 16–22. It also reviews the structure and reception of *Jin shu* 14–15 (the "Monograph on Administrative Geography"), including an investigation of its early sources (297–302).

Saitō Kuniharu 斉藤国治. "*Shinjo* no naka no tenmon shiryō (A.D. 221–420) no tenmon nendaigaku teki na kenshō" 晉書の中の天文史料 (A.D. 221–420) の天文年代学的な検証. *Kagaku shi kenkyū* 145 (1983.4): 21–34.

Satō Toshiyuki 佐藤利行. "*Shinjo* Ka Go den ni tsuite" 晉書賈后傳について. *Chūgoku gaku ronshū* 12 (1996.1): 10–17.

Suzuki Katsura 鈴木桂. "Goko-jūryokugoku jidai ni kansuru shushiryō no kinen mujun to sono sei'in: Tō shū *Shinjo* Saiki o chūshin to shite" 五胡十六國時代に關する諸史料の紀年矛盾とその成因: 唐修晉書載記を中心として. *Shiryō hihan kenkyū* 4 (2000.6): 66–133.

Other secondary studies

Articles

Hung, William. "The T'ang Bureau of Historiography before 708." *Harvard Journal of Asiatic Studies* 23 (1960–1961): 93–107.

Li Bujia 李步嘉. "*Jin shu* jiaozhu shuwu guankui" 晉書斠注疏誤管窺. *Guizhou wenshi congkan* (1991.2): 98–106.

Li Ciming 李慈銘. *Jin shu zhaji* 晉書劄記; included in his *Yuemantang wenji* 越縵堂文集. Peking: Guoli Beijing tushuguan, 1930. I have been able to consult only Li's *Yuemantang dushu ji* 越縵堂讀書記 (Beijing: Zhonghua shuju, 1963), vol. 1, where Li's reading notes on sections of *Jin shu* appear on pp. 208–26.

Lin Ruihan 林瑞翰. "*Jinshu* shixi" 晉書試析. *Wen shi zhe xuebao* 32 (1983): 55–100.

Nagasawa Kikuya 長沢規矩也. "Wakokubon *Shinjo* ni tsuite (Haruyama Kasenō tsuitōgō)" 和刻本晋書について (春山霞仙翁追悼号). *Shoshi gaku* 26–27 (1981): 26, 35–36.

Ozaki Yasushi 尾崎康. "Sō Gen kan *Sangokushi* oyobi *Shinjo* ni tsuite" 宋元刊三国誌および晋書について. *Shidō bunko ronshū* 16 (1979): 315–57.

Peng Jiusong 彭久松. "*Jin shu* zhuanren kao" 晉書撰人考. *Sichuan shifan daxue xuebao* (1989.1): 45–51.

Peng Jiusong and Zhang Dake 張大可. "*Jin shu*" 晉書. In Cang Xiuliang 倉修良, ed., *Zhongguo shixue mingzhu pingjie* 中國史學名著評介, 493–507. Ji'nan: Shangdong jiaoyu chubanshe, 2006.

Shimizu Yoshio 清水凱夫. "Lun Tang xiu *Jin shu* de xingzhi" 論唐修晉書的性質. *Beijing daxue xuebao, Zhexue shehui kexue ban* (1995.5): 98–103.

Song Zhiying 宋志英. "Wang Yin *Jin shu* chutan" 王隱晉書初談. *Wenxian* (2002.3): 4–15.

Wu Zhuzhu 吳鉒鉒. "*Jin shu* de bianshu shijian: Zuozhe ji qi youguan de jige wenti" 晉書的編書時間: 作者及其有關的幾個問題. *Fujian xuekan* (1992.3): 59–64.

Yang Chaomin 楊朝民. "Tang xiu *Jin shu* de zhengzhi yinsu" 唐修晉書的政治因素. *Shixue shi yanjiu* (1989.4): 27–33.

Yang, Lien-Sheng. "Notes on the Economic History of the Chin Dynasty." *Harvard Journal of Asiatic Studies* 9.2 (1946): 107–85; rpt., *Studies in Chinese Institutional History*, 119–97 (Cambridge, MA: Harvard University Press, 1961). The first part of the article deals with the history of the compilation of the *Jin shu*.

Yue Chunzhi 岳純之. "Tang chao chunian chongxiu *Jin shu* shimo kao" 唐朝初年重修晉書始末考. *Shixue shi yanjiu* (2000.2): 38–42.

Zhao Yi 趙翼. *Nian'er shi zhaji* 廿二史札記. Beijing: Zhonghua shuju, 2008.

Zhu Dawei 朱大渭. "*Jin shu* de pingjia yu yanjiu" 晉書的評價與研究. *Shixue shi yanjiu* (2000.4): 44–52. This is a thorough account of Qing, Republican, and modern *kaozheng* works on the *Jin shu*. Zhu relied chiefly on early drafts of Liao Jilang's 廖吉郎 research (see later) and Li Ciming's (see earlier), as well as unpublished works, for example, Wu Shijian, "Bu *Jin shu* jingjizhi" 補晉書經籍志 (apparently not incorporated into Wu and Liu, *Jin shu jiaozhu*).

Books

Chaussende, Damien. *Des Trois Royaumes aux Jin: Légitimation du pouvoir impérial en Chine au IIIe siècle*. Paris: Les Belles Lettres, 2010. Pp. 81–93.

Fairbank, Anthony Bruce. "Ssu-ma I (179–251): Wei Statesman and Chin Founder. An Historiographical Inquiry." Ph.D. diss., University of Washington, 1994. See especially pp. 203–78. Appendix B is a finding index for the names of pre-Tang scholars who produced *Jin shu* drafts, as mentioned in *Shi tong**; appendix C gives all known pre-Tang *Jin shu* drafts in a deduced chronological order; appendix D lists titles of early collectanea, especially that of Tang Qiu, that gathered quotations from pre-Tang *Jin shu* versions.

Hao Runhua 郝潤華. *Liuchao shiji yu shixue* 六朝史籍與史學. Beijing: Zhonghua shuju, 2005. Esp. pp. 100–117.

Liao Jilang. *Liang Jin shibu yiji kao* 兩晉史部遺籍考. Taipei: Jiaxin shuini gongsi wenhua jijinhui, 1970; rpt., Taipei (Yonghe): Hua Mulan wenhua gongzuofang, 2008. This is a major study of sources for the history of historiography during Jin times, covering scholars who worked in all sorts of history genres. Chap. 3 deals specifically with the sources for Jin-era scholars who wrote and compiled Jin history.

Ochi Shigeaki 越智重明. *Shinjo* 晉書. Tokyo: Meitoku shuppansha, 1970. Studies themes encountered in various *Jin shu* chapters.

Yamano Yukio 山根幸夫, ed. *Chūgoku shi kenkyū nyūmon* 中国史研究入門. Tokyo: Yamakawa shuppansha, 1983. Vol. 1, pp. 278–79.

Zhang Lizhi 張立志. *Zhengshi gailun* 正史概論. Taipei: Taiwan shangwu yinshuguan, 1969. Pp. 58–62.

Translations

European languages

A finding list of short passages of the *Jin shu* that have been translated in a variety of secondary literature is in Hans H. Frankel, comp., *Catalogue of Translations from the Chinese Dynastic Histories for the Period 220–960* (Westport, CT: Greenwood Press, 1974; reprint of Berkeley: University of California Press, 1957, issued as supplement no. 1 of the Chinese Dynastic Histories series). Moreover, Dominik Declercq, *Writing against the State: Political Rhetorics in Third and Fourth Century China* (Leiden: Brill, 1998), especially chapters 3–8, translates and annotates several complete biographies and prose pieces, for example, those of Wang Chen, Huangfu Mi, Xiahou Zhan, and Guo Pu.

The following are translations of larger, integral passages or whole *juan*, not included in Frankel's catalog, and listed in order of the *juan* in the *Jin shu* (*JS*):

1. Taizong's order to compile the *Jin shu*; carried in the *Tang da zhaoling ji* 唐大詔令集, and also in *JS* 3305–6. Trans. Fairbank, "Ssu-ma I," 254–57 (see under "Books").

2. *JS* 1 ("Diji" 1, "Annals of Emperor Hsüan"); trans. Fairbank, "Ssu-ma I," chap. 6.

3. *JS* 11–13 ("Monograph on Mantic Astronomy"); trans. Ho Peng Yoke, *The Astronomical Chapters of the Chin Shu: With Amendments, Full Translation, and Annotations* (Paris: Mouton, with the collaboration of University of Malaya Press, 1966).

4. *JS* 26 ("Monograph on Food and Money"), trans. Yang, "Notes on Economic History," 137–85 (see under "Articles").

5. Biography of Zhang Hua (*JS* 36); trans. Anna Straughair, *Chang Hua: A Statesman-Poet of the Western Chin Dynasty*, Occasional Paper 15 (Canberra: Australian National University, Faculty of Asian Studies, 1973).

6. Biography of Fu Xuan (*JS* 47); trans. Jordan D. Paper, *The Fu-tzu: A Post-Han Confucian Text*, Monographies du T'oung Pao 13 (Leiden: Brill, 1987).

7. Biography of Lu Yun (*JS* 54); trans. Sujane Wu, "The Biography of Lu Yun (263–303) in *Jin shu* 54," *Early Medieval China* (2001): 1–38.

8. Biography of Gu Kaizhi (*JS* 92); trans. Chen Shih-hsiang, *Biography of Ku K'ai-chih* (Berkeley: University of California Press, 1961).

9. Preface and historian's judgment (*JS* 94); trans. Alan J. Berkowitz, *Patterns of Disengagement: The Practice and Portrayal of Reclusion in Early Medieval China* (Stanford, CA: Stanford University Press, 2000), 198–203.

10. Biography of Dai Yang (*JS* 95); trans. Kenneth J. DeWoskin, *Doctors, Diviners, and Magicians of Ancient China: Biographies of Fang-shih* (New York: Columbia University Press, 1983).

11. Biography of Liu Yuan (*JS* 101); trans. David B. Honey, "The Rise of the Medieval Hsiung-nu: The Biography of Liu Yüan," Papers on Inner Asia (Bloomington, IN: Research Institute for Inner Asian Studies, 1990).

12. Biography of Fu Jian (*JS* 113–14); trans. Rogers, *The Chronicle of Fu Chien* (see "Modern Studies").

13. Biography of Lü Guang (*JS* 122); trans. Richard B. Mather, *Biography of Lü Kuang* (Berkeley: University of California Press, 1959).

Japanese

Komatsu Hideo 小松英生. "Seishin Sha Shō den, *Shinjo* Sha Shō den yakuchū" 西晋謝尚伝, 晋書謝尚伝訳注. *Chūgoku chūsei bungaku kenkyū* 45–46 (2004.10): 44–61.

Nishijima Sadao 西嶋定生 (1919–1998), with Kubozoe Yoshifumi 窪添慶文 and Nakajima Satoshi 中嶋敏. *Shinjo shokkashi yakuchū* 晋書食貨志譯註. Tokyo: Tōyō bunko, 2007. This Japanese translation of *JS* 26 contains occasional *furigana*. Very brief bibliography of relevant secondary works on economics (16–17). This is an essential commentary to the monograph, giving locus classicus and philological comments. Notes are conveniently interspersed throughout the main text; well edited and produced.

Takahashi Akihisa 鷹橋明久. "Gen Kan den, *Shinjo* kan shijūku yakuchū (Rikuchō shi no goi oyobi hyōgen gikō no kenkyū) 阮咸伝, 晋書卷四十九訳注 (六朝詩の語彙および表現技巧の研究). *Chūgoku koten bungaku kenkyū* 1 (2003.12): 129–32.

———. "*Shinjo* San Tō den yakuchū" 晉書山濤伝訳注. *Gengo bunka* 3 (2005.12): 47–61.

Uchida Tomoo 内田智雄. "Yakuchū *Shinjo* Keihoushi" 訳注晉書刑法志. 11 parts. *Dōshisha hōgaku* 10 (1958): 74–90 to 13 (1961): 49–75.

Zen yonshi sensha retsuden kenkyū zeminaaru 前四史撰者列傳研究ゼミナール. "Zen yonshi sensha retsuden no kenkyū: *Shinjo* Chin Ju den yakuchū" 前四史撰者列傳の研究: 晉書陳壽傳譯注. *Shiteki* 25 (2003.12): 56–77.

Research aids and indices

Bielenstein, Hans. "The Six Dynasties, Vols. 1 and 2." *Bulletin of the Museum of Far Eastern Antiquities* 68 (1996): 5–324 and 69 (1997): 5–246. These contain useful tables and maps related to Jin (principally Eastern Jin) history, demography, solar eclipses, genealogies, and so on; they are useful guides when reading the *Jin shu* and other Jin-era materials.

Liu Naihe 劉乃和 and Zhu Zhongyu 朱仲玉, comps. *Jin shu cidian* 晉書辭典. Ji'nan: Shandong jiaoyu chubanshe, 2001. Capsule biographies, important terms, place-names, and the like are given entries. The biographies in themselves represent an important reference tool. Numerous cross-references lead to modern studies or to related places in the *Jin shu*. There is only one finding system (total strokes, subdivided by initial stroke type). The work gives the Zhonghua edition page number at the end of each entry for ease of finding.

Zhang Chenshi 張忱石. *Jin shu renming suoyin* 晉書人名索引. Beijing: Zhonghua, 1977. This has been the standard index for finding personal names since its appearance.

Howard L. Goodman

Jing-Chu suishi ji 荊楚歲時記

Introduction

Jing-Chu suishi ji (Festivals and seasonal customs of the Jing and Chu region) is one of the earliest accounts of seasonal festivities and observances in medieval China. It has been characterized as "extremely important in Chinese social history" and "the first real effort to describe the seasonal practices of common people" (Teiser, *Ghost Festival*, 57n13). Its format and contents set the template for subsequent compendia on seasonal festivals through the Tang and Song periods and beyond. However, the text has a complex provenance that makes it challenging to use properly.

Authorship and contents

The core text seems to have been originally titled *Jing-Chu ji* 荊楚記 (Record of the Jing-Chu region) and probably contained no more than a single *juan*, organized by the lunar calendar. Its author, Zong Lin 宗懍 (ca. 500–563), has a biography in *Zhou shu*, q.v., 42:759–60. He grew up in Jiangling 江陵, the most important urban center of the Jing-Chu region (approximately the modern central Yangzi provinces of Hubei and Hunan). In the fourth and early fifth centuries, his ancestors, along with numerous other families, migrated to Jiangling from the once-prosperous and powerful Nanyang area, at the northern edge of the region; by the early sixth century, their descendants were Jiangling's leading, educated elite. Zong served as a provincial administrator under the Liang dynasty, primarily in the service of Xiao Yi 蕭繹, Prince of Xiangdong 湘東, who was based at Jiangling. In response to Hou Jing's 侯景 rebellion (549–552), the prince declared himself Liang Emperor Yuan (r. 552–555). However, Jiangling's fall to the Western Wei state ended his reign, and many of the city's residents, including Zong Lin, were forcibly relocated to Chang'an 長安. Zong was honored by the northern regime and served in scholastic posts for about another decade until his death. It was probably in this period that he wrote the short text of *Jing-Chu ji*, described (by Chapman, "Carnival Canons," 48) as "a carefully framed portrait, for an outside audience, of a cherished locality through the prism of its festival customs." It is no longer extant in its original form.

Within a generation, the *Jing-Chu ji* made its way into the hands of Du Taiqing 杜臺卿 (see biography in *Sui shu*, q.v., 58:1421–22), a scholar-official in the Chang'an court with a strong interest in history and *yueling* 月令 (monthly ordinance) materials patterned on the "Yueling" chapter of the *Li ji*. He assembled a massive encyclopedia of *yueling* materials, the *Yuzhu baodian*, q.v., which consisted almost entirely of quotes from a wide variety of texts, including the *Jing-Chu ji*, with occasional speculations and observations from the editor. Taiqing's nephew, Du Gongzhan 杜公瞻 (fl. 600s–610s), appears to have drawn on a similar body of materials for a far more circumscribed project, an annotated edition of the *Jing-Chu ji*, which was retitled *Jing-Chu suishi ji*. The annotated text may have been two *juan*, twice as long as the original text; it included some material not found in the *Yuzhu baodian*, as well as some of Gongzhan's own comments and speculations on the festivals' origins and significance.

One challenge in reading any material from the *Jing-Chu suishi ji* is determining whether it came from Zong Lin's original or was added by Du Gongzhan. There are frequent markings for annotated material, using the character *an* 按 or *zhu* 注; some may be Zong Lin's, but a majority are probably Gongzhan's. These appended materials are often not specific to Jing-Chu, and neither Gongzhan nor his uncle are known to have visited the region, so the text cannot simply be read as if it were derived from firsthand experience of central Yangzi regional customs. And, as the transmission history makes evident, there is a strong possibility of substantial subsequent emendation or recompilation as well.

Early evidence of transmission

The *Jing-Chu suishi ji* is not noted in the Sui history's bibliographical monograph but is recorded by both Tang histories. The *Jiu Tang shu* lists a *Jing-Chu suishi ji*, authored by Zong Lin, as having ten *juan*, probably an error for one *juan*; the same line also mentions the existence of a two-*juan* version compiled by Du Gongzhan. The *Xin Tang shu* lists Zong Lin's *Jing-Chu suishi ji* in one *juan* and has a separate entry for the same title authored by Du Gongzhan, in two *juan*. The Song history has only a single entry for a version by Zong Lin, in one *juan*. Other bibliographies also record the text as the *Jing-Chu suishi ji* and credit it to Zong Lin alone; see, for example, *Chongwen zongmu** 2:64a, 255, which lists it in two *juan*, and *Zhizhai shulu jieti** 6:190, which lists six *juan*. *Junzhai dushu zhi** 12:530, which lists four *juan* (but other editions have one or two *juan*), appends an extended note that indicates that the complete text includes over twenty items.

The *Jing-Chu ji* is cited in numerous places in the *Yuzhu baodian*, but without the full *Jing-Chu suishi ji* title, suggesting that Du Gongzhan's annotated and retitled edition was not yet written when the *Yuzhu baodian* was compiled. Since the *Yuzhu baodian* has far fewer problems with textual transmission than the *Jing-Chu suishi ji*, these passages must be the earliest version we have of Zong Lin's material, and the most reliable. *Yiwen leiju*, q.v., cites both the *Jing-Chu ji* and the *Jing-Chu suishi ji*, suggesting that the original and the annotated versions were available to the compilers. More significantly, the *Jing-Chu suishi ji* appears to have greatly influenced the chapter in the *Yiwen leiju* on seasonal activities, *juan* 4, including the seasonal format, the selection of festivals to highlight, and the selection of quotations and sources to cite. A similar format and corpus of quotes, with some rearrangement and the addition of more material, was adopted by the respective sections on seasonal festivals in *Chuxue ji*, q.v., *juan* 4, and *Taiping yulan*, q.v., *juan* 29–33. The calendric format for recording provincial customs eventually became a genre in its own right, with such examples as the *Suihua jili* 歲華紀麗 (tenth century) and the *Suishi guangji* 歲時廣記 (thirteenth century).

Printed editions

Printed editions of the *Jing-Chu suishi ji* generally follow one of two basic texts. The earliest surviving printed edition, in one *juan*, is by Chen Jiru 陳繼儒 (style Meigong 眉公) in 1615; it is divided into forty-nine items. Also known as the Miji 秘笈 edition, it is considered the most authoritative, though there is considerable debate about the extent to which it represents something close to a transmitted edition (argued by Moriya Mitsuo), or whether it was compiled from fragmentary sources in the mid-Ming period (see Chapman, "Carnival Canons," 79–104, for a thorough discussion of this debate). The Miji edition was reprinted with some further alterations in the *Siku quanshu* (*Yingyin Wenyuange Siku quanshu** 589:13–27) and *Congshu jicheng** (1935). It serves as the basis for the modern punctuated and annotated edition by Wang Yurong 王毓榮, who also offers a list of various printed editions and carefully compares their variant readings.

Another late-Ming edition, somewhat condensed and arranged into only thirty-six (or thirty-seven) items, appears in Tao Ting's 陶珽 *Shuofu* 說郛 and He Yunzhong's 何允中 *Guang Han-Wei congshu* 廣漢魏叢書. It was reprinted in Wang Mo's 王謨 *Han-Wei congshu* 漢魏叢書 in 1791, which in turn was used for the *Sibu beiyao** edition published by Zhonghua shuju in 1934 and was further annotated by Chen Yunrong 陳運溶 for inclusion in his *Lushan jingshe congshu* 麓山精舍叢書. For those scholars who consider all post-Song editions of the text to be compilations of fragments, this edition offers a viable alternative starting point; it serves as the basis for the modern punctuated and annotated edition by Tan Lin.

Modern editions and translations

Jiang Yanzhi 姜彥稚, ed. *Jing-Chu suishi ji* 荊楚歲時記. Changsha: Yue Lu shushe, 1986. Assembled using the version of thirty-six items as a starting point.

Moriya Mitsuo 守屋美都雄. *Kōchū Keiso saijiki: Chūgoku minzoku no rekishiteki kenkyū* 校註荊楚歲時記: 中國民俗の歷史的研究. Tokyo: Teikoku shoin, 1950. A translation into Japanese, based on the version in the *Shuofu* and done prior to Moriya's work arguing for the superiority of the Miji edition.

Muramatsu Kazuya 村松一弥 and Baba Eiko 馬場英子, eds. "Keiso saijiki" 荊楚歲時記. *Higashi Ajia no kodai bunka* 東アジアの古代文化 (1974.2): 172–87; (1974.3): 174–88; (1975.1): 166–81. A translation into Japanese, based on the Miji edition.

Tan Lin 譚麟, ed. *Jing-Chu suishi ji yizhu* 荊楚歲時記譯注. Wuhan: Hubei renmin chubanshe, 1985. Based on the *Sibu beiyao* edition, with biographical introduction, explanatory footnotes, and translations into modern Chinese.

Wang Yurong 王毓榮, ed. *Jing-Chu suishi ji jiaozhu* 荊楚歲時記校注. Taipei: Wenjin chubanshe, 1988. Based on the Miji edition, with an introduction offering a history of the text, its editions, and a survey of its contents.

Xiang Linzhi 項琳之 and Chen Gaomo 陳皋謨, eds. *Jing-Chu suishi ji* 荊楚歲時記. Taipei: Yiwen yinshuguan, 1965.

Other studies and secondary literature

Chang Jianhua 常建華. *Suishi jieri li de Zhongguo* 歲時節日裏的中國. Beijing: Zhonghua shuju, 2006.

Chapman, Ian. "Carnival Canons: Calendars, Genealogy, and the Search for Ritual Cohesion in Medieval China." Ph.D. diss., Princeton University, 2007.

Eberhard, Wolfram. *The Local Cultures of South and East China*. Leiden: E. J. Brill, 1968.

Holzmann, Donald. "The Cold Food Festival in Early Medieval China." *Harvard Journal of Asiatic Studies* 46.1 (1986): 51–79.

Li Yumin 李裕民. "Zong Lin ji qi *Jing-Chu suishiji* kaoshu" 宗懍及其荊楚歲時記考述. In *Jing-Chu suishiji* 荊楚歲時記, ed. Song Jinlong 宋金龍, 1–22. Taiyuan: Shanxi renmin chubanshe, 1987.

Moriya Mitsuo 守屋美都雄. "*Keiso saijiki* no shoshigaku teki kenkyū (I, II)" 荊楚歲時記の書誌學的研究 (上,下). *Tōyō gakuhō* 36.3 (1953): 1–32; 36.4 (1954): 75–114.

———. "*Keiso saijiki* no shiryō teki kenkyū" 荊楚歲時記の資料的研究. *Ōsaka daigaku bungakubu kiyō* 3 (1954): 45–113.

———. Chūgoku kosaijiki no kenkyū; shiryō fukugen o chūshin to shite 中國古歲時記の研究; 資料復元を中心として. Tokyo: Teikoku shoin, 1963.

———. "*Keiso saijiki* no senja Sō Rin ni tsuite no oboegaki" 荊楚歲時記の撰者宗懍についての覚書. In *Iwai Hakushi koki kinen tenseki ronshū* 岩井博士古稀紀念典籍論集, 728–34. Tokyo: Iwai Hakushi koki kinen jigyōkai, 1963.

———. "*Keiso saijiki* ni miru Chūgoku no shōgatsu fūkei" 荊楚歲時記に見る中國の正月風景. *Kanbun kyōshitsu* 70 (1965): 18–22.

Nakamura Takashi 中村喬. *Chūgoku saijishi no kenkyū* 中国歲時史の研究. Kyoto: Hōyū shoten, 1993.

Sakamoto Tarō 坂本太郎. "*Keiso saijiki* to Nihon" 荊楚歲時記と日本. In *Wada hakushi kanreki kinen Tōyōshi ronsō* 和田博士還曆記念東洋史論叢, ed. Wada Hakushi kanreki kinen Tōyōshi ronsō hensan i-inkai 和田博士還曆記念東洋史論叢編纂委員會, 237–53. Tokyo: Dainihon yūbenkai kodansha, 1951.

Tan Yeting 譚業庭. *Zhongguo chuantong jieri caifeng* 中國傳統節日採風. Beijing: Yejin gongye chubanshe, 1999.

Teiser, Steven. *The Ghost Festival in Medieval China*. Princeton, NJ: Princeton University Press, 1988.

Turban, Helga. "Das Ching-Ch'u sui-shi chi, ein chinesischer Festkalender." Diss., Augsburg, 1971.

Wada Hisanori 和田久德. "*Keiso saijiki* ni tsuite" 荊楚歲時記について. *Tōa ronsō* 5 (1941): 397–437.

Xiao Fang 蕭放. *Jing-Chu suishi ji yanjiu lun chuantong Zhongguo minzhong shenghuo de shijian gainian* 荊楚歲時記研究論傳統中國民眾生活中的時間觀念. Beijing: Beijing shifan daxue chubanshe, 2000.

———. "*Jing-Chu suishi ji* yanjiu shulun" 荊楚歲時記研究述論. *Minsu yanjiu* (2000.2): 172–78.

———. *Suishi: Chuantong Zhongguo minzhong de shijian shenghuo* 歲時: 傳統中國民眾的時間生活. Beijing: Zhonghua shuju, 2002.

Zhang Chengzong 張承宗. *Zhongguo fengsu tongshi—Wei Jin Nanbeichao juan* 中國風俗統史—魏晉南北朝卷. Shanghai: Wenyi chubanshe, 2001.

Andrew Chittick

Jinlouzi 金樓子

Introduction

Xiao Yi 蕭繹, Emperor Yuan of the Liang (r. 552–555), completed the *Jinlouzi* (Book of the Golden Hall Master) in 553 after almost twenty-five years spent preparing the manuscript and a little more than a year before his death. A prolific writer of poetry and prose, Xiao Yi considered this book his magnum opus. He hoped it would form the basis of an independent school of thought and place him on the same level as Confucius. Following the examples of Ge Hong 葛洪 (283–363) and Huangfu Mi 皇甫謐 (215–282), Xiao Yi based the title of the book on his own sobriquet, Golden Hall Master. The text of the *Jinlouzi* contains a mixture of quotations from earlier authors selected by Xiao Yi and the personal reflections and writing of Xiao Yi himself. The book covers a wide range of historical and intellectual issues and includes autobiographical and biographical sketches, admonitions to Xiao Yi's children, directions for his burial, and many other topics. The *Jinlouzi* provides readers with a fascinating miscellany of scientific, literary, historical, and philosophical information, much of which is found nowhere else. It reflects the wide-ranging knowledge and interests of an intellectual in southern China in the sixth century.

Contents

Classification of the work has varied. The *Nan shi*, q.v., the *Sui shu*, q.v., the *Wenxian tongkao**, and the *Ming shi* list the *Jinlouzi* as "classical writing"; other works, such as the *Jiu Tang shu*, *Xin Tang shu*, and *Song shi* list it under "literary works"; while still others, including the *Siku quanshu* (*Yingyin Wenyuange Siku quanshu** 848:791–880), place it in the "miscellaneous" category. Genre classification also concerned Xiao Yi. Many sections of his book appear to be named for a genre of literary work popular in his own time period.

The major reconstituted editions of the *Jinlouzi* contain six *juan*, further divided into fourteen sections. Each section of the work originally contained a preface to the contents. According to early accounts, the book initially contained fifteen sections, but one section heading no longer survives in the reconstituted editions. The following chart indicates the names of the remaining sections, whether the preface remained intact, whether the body of the text remained intact, and the contents of each section:

Section Title	Preface intact? (Based on the Siku quanshu zongmu tiyao)	Body of text intact? (Based on the Siku quanshu zongmu tiyao)	Contents and comments (Siku quanshu zongmu tiyao* 23.2460–61)
Juan I			
1. Founding rulers (*xingwang* 興王)	no	yes	Describes successful founding rulers including Xiao Yi's father, Emperor Wu.
2. Cautionary warnings (*zhenjie* 箴戒)	no	no	Describes rulers who failed because of improper behavior.
Juan II			
3. Empresses (*houji* 后妃)	yes	no	Includes notes or biographies of empresses; the longest biography is that of Xiao Yi's mother.
4. Funeral instructions (*zhongzhi* 终制)	no	no	Xiao Yi quotes noted individuals who preferred simple burials and includes a few direct remarks to his children about his desire for a simple burial.
5. Admonitions to my children (*jiezi* 戒子)	yes	yes	Xiao Yi quotes cautionary warnings of other writers to their children and adds a few direct remarks to his own children.
6. Collecting books (*jushu* 聚書)	no	yes	Xiao Yi relates where, when, and how he collected books that formed his library.
7. The Two Regents and the Five Hegemons (*ernan wuba* 二南五霸)	no	no	Only three entries appear under this heading in the *Yongle dadian** and all are duplicated in section eight of the reconstructed *Jinlouzi*. *Siku quanshu* editors question whether this was an original section heading and believe that all three entries belong in section eight.
Juan III			
8. Discussing imperial relatives with provincial appointments (*shuofan* 說番)	no	yes	Addresses the issue of the moral behavior, scholarly achievements, military ability, and political loyalty of imperial relatives appointed to provincial posts. (Since Xiao Yi held provincial appointments for most of his life, this section would have had particular relevance for him.)

Jinlouzi

Section Title	Preface intact? (Based on the Siku quanshu zongmu tiyao)	Body of text intact? (Based on the Siku quanshu zongmu tiyao)	Contents and comments (Siku quanshu zongmu tiyao* 23.2460–61)
Juan IV 9. Establishing immortality through words (*liyan* 立言)	no	yes	Xiao Yi presents the essential aspects of his lifelong scholarship and thought and comments on literary matters, politics, social behavior, schools of thought, natural phenomena, and matters of scientific and technical interest.
Juan V 10. Writing books (*zhushu* 著書)	no	yes	Lists works Xiao Yi wrote, compiled, or commissioned. Since the original appears to have included prefaces to each of the works cited, the *Siku quanshu* editors have added prefaces when they could locate them.
11. Quick retorts (*jiedui* 捷對)	yes	yes	Contains examples of eloquent and witty responses of the type popularized by proponents of "Pure Talk" (*qingtan* 請談) and found in the *Shishou xinyu* and other works of the period.
12. Recording the unusual (*zhiguai* 志怪)	yes	yes	Based on a popular genre during this period, it describes uncommon mechanical and technical devices, rare natural phenomena, exotic people, plants, birds, fish, animals, and minerals, strange places, and fantastic happenings.
Juan VI 13. Miscellaneous accounts (*zazhi* 雜志)	no	no	Composed mainly, but not exclusively, of historically oriented anecdotes. Several entries are about Xiao Yi.
14. Autobiography (*zixu* 自序)	no	no	Fragmented entries of the autobiography provide some information about Xiao Yi's illnesses, pastimes, childhood, study habits, and attitudes.

Authorship

The author of the *Jinlouzi* was a member of the royal family that ruled in southern China from 502 to 557. Of the eight sons of Emperor Wu, the Liang dynasty's founder, Xiao Yi was the seventh. As such, Xiao Yi had little expectation of ascending the throne as emperor during most of his lifetime. This aspect of his life influenced the composition of the *Jinlouzi*. Without hope of making a name for himself as imperial ruler, Xiao Yi focused on the *Jinlouzi* as an alternate route to fame. He believed his scholarship would gain him recognition in his own time and in succeeding generations. He also displayed a special interest in royal relatives who served in provincial posts, devoting a whole section of the *Jinlouzi* to this subject.

Intellectually, Xiao Yi leaned toward eclecticism and syncretism. He read broadly over a wide range of works. He personally believed in Buddhism, but stressed those aspects of Daoism and Confucianism that could fit into a syncretic system. In undertaking rituals, he followed both Confucianism and Buddhism. He records in the *Jinlouzi* that he composed fourteen works himself, compiled one work jointly with another editor, wrote forewords for five works, and commissioned eleven other works.

After a career largely spent in the provinces as magistrate and governor in various posts, the unexpected chance to ascend the throne as emperor of the Liang dynasty came when the capital Jiankang 建康 was occupied by Hou Jing 侯景 in 549. Emperor Wu, Xiao Yi's father, died in captivity, and Xiao Yi's brother, the heir apparent, was killed after a short term as a puppet ruler. Xiao Yi, as the head of one of the most powerful provincial armies, was able to suppress the other brothers who were rivals for the throne, and his generals eventually defeated Hou Jing, who was killed by his own men while fleeing for his life in 553. Xiao Yi officially declared himself emperor on 13 December 552. Because the capital city, Jiankang, was largely destroyed, Xiao Yi decided to make Jiangling 江陵, where he had been governor, the new capital of the empire. By the time Xiao Yi became emperor, the territory under Liang rule was much diminished and the state was much weakened, remaining a target for ambitious rulers in the north. In early January of 555 the Western Wei defeated Xiao Yi's army and took him captive; soon after he was put to death.

Transmission of the text

Xiao Yi reported in the *Jinlouzi* that he had collected some 80,000 *juan* of books by 553. In addition, he moved the court library, which had survived the occupation of Hou Jing, from Jiankang to Jiangling, the new capital. When his defeat became obvious, he ordered assistants to burn the library. However, even after the great loss of books due to this conflagration, the *Jinlouzi* continued to circulate with ten *juan* and fifteen sections. The ten *juan* version of the book remained available into the Northern Song though few copies of it had survived. By the end of the Yuan and the beginning of the Ming, there appeared to be no complete copies of the work in circulation. At the beginning of the Zhizheng reign period (1341–1368) of the Yuan dynasty, Ye Senhen 葉森很 organized what he could of the book. His version of the *Jinlouzi* was apparently used by the editors of the massive encyclopedic work *Yongle dadian**, completed in 1408, as the source of their entries.

Qing scholars in the late eighteenth century redacted the *Jinlouzi* as best they could from the *Yongle dadian*'s encyclopedic entries. Zhou Yongnian 周永年 (1730–1791), a noted member of the Hanlin Academy (翰林院), read through some 9,000 *juan* of the *Yongle dadian* as he and 360 other scholars abstracted entries from the encyclopedia in an attempt to reconstruct works otherwise lost. The results of their work were published in the *Siku quanshu** completed in 1782. In 1777, Zhou sent a manuscript copy of the *Jinlouzi* to his friend, the noted bibliophile Bao Tingbo 鮑廷博 (1728–1814). The manuscript's perilous journey to Bao took almost two years. After receiving the manuscript, Bao published the *Jinlouzi* bearing a colophon date of 1781 in his collection of works called the *Zhibuzuzhai congshu* 知不足斎叢書 (Collected works from the "Know-Your-Deficiencies Studio"). The colophon date in the *Siku quanshu* edition of the *Jinlouzi* is also 1781. Later editions relied on one or the other, or on both of these two editions, themselves having been reconstructed from a common source—the *Yongle dadian*.

Almost a century later, Xie Zhangting 謝章鋌 (1820–1903) made a handwritten copy directly from the *Yongle dadian*, noting where it differed from the Bao edition that he had copied in 1881. This handwritten copy, preserved in the National Central Library in Taipei, was photocopied and published in 1959. One additional entry from the *Yongle dadian* not in the Bao edition is contained in the 797 surviving *juan* of the *Yongle dadian* published in 1986 by the Zhonghua shuju in Beijing. A full discussion of these items can be found in the book by Zhong Shilun (*Jinlouzi yanjiu*, 2004).

In addition to the two major editions based on the *Yongle dadian*, mentioned previously, there are scattered entries from the *Jinlouzi* found elsewhere. The *Shuofu* 說郛 compiled by Tao Zongyi 陶宗儀 (fl. 1360–68), a sort of sampler of many texts, contains twenty-three entries of the *Jinlouzi* in one *juan*. These entries were apparently copied from various reference works arranged by subject rather than from an original copy of the *Jinlouzi*. Most of the entries preserved in the *Shuofu* belong either to the section on "Recording the Unusual" or to the section on "Miscellaneous Accounts." The *Chen shu*, q.v., and reference collections like the *Taiping guangji* 太平廣記, *Yunxian sanlu* 雲仙散錄, *Leishuo* 類說, and *Taiping yulan*, q.v., also contain entries, some of which do not appear in either the *Siku quanshu* or Bao editions of the *Jinlouzi*.

Modern edition and monographic study

Zhong Shilun's *Jinlouzi yanjiu* contains the greatest number of items missing from the traditional editions, but most can also be found in the work by Xu Deping. Her collation and commentaries of the *Jinlouzi*, based on her graduate work at National Chengchi University in Taiwan, remains the major modern critical edition of the

Jinlouzi today. The text of the *Jinlouzi* has been digitized and is available as an e-book.

Xu Deping 許德平. *Jinlouzi jiao zhu* 金樓子校注. Taipei: Jiaxin shuini gongsi wenhua jijinhui, 1969.

Zhong Shilun 鍾仕倫. *Jinlouzi yanjiu* 金樓子研究. Bejing: Zhonghua shuju, 2004.

Selected studies

Cao Xu 曹旭. "Lun Xiao Yi de wenxueguan" 論蕭繹的文學觀. *Shanghai shifan daxuexue bao, Zhexue shehui kexuexuebao* (1999.1): 21–27.

Du Zhiqiang 杜志強. "Xiao Yi de sixiang yu renge" 蕭繹的思想與人格. *Hexi xueyuan xuebao* (2004.6): 37–41.

———. "Xiao Yi ji qi *Jinlouzi* yanjiushi shuping" 蕭繹及其金樓子研究史述評. *Xibei shifan daxue xuebao, Shehui kexue ban* 41.1 (2004): 56–59.

———. "Cong *Jinlouzi* kan Xiao Yi de wenlun" 從金樓子看蕭繹的文論. *Hexi xueyuan xuebao* (2006.3): 61–64.

Kōzen Hiroshi 興膳宏. "Kōen Ryō Gentei Shō Eki no shōgai to *Kinrōshi*" 講演梁元帝蕭繹の生涯と金樓子. *Rikuchō gakujutsukai kaihō* 2 (2001): 107–19.

Liu Linkui 劉林魁. Chonglun Xiao Yi de wenxue paibie guishu" 重論蕭繹的文學派別歸屬. *Baoji wenli xuebao, Shehui kexue ban* (2004.5): 52–56.

Liu Mao 劉晟. "Xiao Yi *Jinlouzi* 'Liyan' zhuzhi bianzheng" 蕭繹金樓子立言主旨辯正. *Hua'nan shifan daxue xuebao, Shehui ke xue bao* (2002.2): 45–52.

Liu Yuejin 劉跃進. "Guanyu *Jinlouzi* yanjiuzhong de jige wenti" 關於金樓子研究中的幾個問題. In *Gudian wenxue wenxianxue conggao* 古典文學文獻學叢稿. Beijing: Xueyuan chubanshe, 1999.

Miyakawa Hisashi 宮川尚志. "Ryō Gentei—Shina kokin jimbutsu ryakuden" 梁元帝—支那古今人物略伝. *Tōyōshi kenkyū* 6.5 (1941): 48–62.

Moriya Mitsuo 守屋美都雄. "Rikuchō jidai no kakun ni tsuite" 六朝時代の家訓について. *Nihon gakushi-in kiyō* 10.3 (1952): 270.

Otonari Aya 音成彩. "Ryō Gentei *Kinrōshi* ni tsuite" 梁元帝金搜子について. *Kyūshū tōyōshi ronshū* 34 (2006): 50–70.

Shimizu Norio 清水凱夫. "Ryō Gentei Shō Eki *Kinrōshi* chū no jijohen ni tsuite— 'Fu-kan jūichi,' 'dai-kan ko-iso' no kaishaku" 梁元帝蕭繹金樓子中の自序篇について—'不閑什一','大寬小急'の解釈. *Gakurin* 40 (2004): 26–53.

Umino Yōhei 海野洋平. "Ryō Butei no ōji kyōiku" 梁武帝の皇子教育. *Shūkan Tōyōgaku* 75 (1996): 23–42.

Wakatsuki Toshihide 若槻俊秀. "Ryō Gentei *Kinrōshi* kō" 梁元帝金樓子攷. *Bungei ronsō* 4 (1975): 43.

Wu Guangxing 吳光興. *Xiao Gang Xiao Yi nianpu* 萧綱蕭繹年譜. Beijing: Sheke wenxian chubanshe, 2006.

Zhong Shilun. "Xiao Yi yu Liangdai jingu wenti zhi zheng" 蕭繹與梁代今古文體之争. *Shehui kexue zhanxian* (1998.6): 126–31.

———. "*Jinlouzi* chengshu shijian kaobian" 金樓子成書時間考辨. *Beijing daxue xuebao, Zhexue shehui kexue ban* 41.5 (2004): 145–50.

———. "*Liang shu* bu dai *Jinlouzi* kao jian lun *Liang shu* bianzhuan wenti" 梁書不戴金樓子考兼論梁書編撰問題. *Sichuan daxue xuebao, Zhexue shehui kexue bao* (2004.3): 93–97.

Translations with discussion or commentary

Chen Kang 陳伉 and Zhang Enke 張恩科. *Jinyan* 金言. Huhehot: Neimeng renmin chubanshe, 1998. A translation into modern Chinese that includes a commentary on the text.

Spade, Beatrice. "The Life and Scholarship of Emperor Yuan (508–555) of the Liang as Seen in the *Chin-lou-tzu*." Ph.D. diss., Harvard University, 1981. This work contains the only major translation into English of sections of the *Jinlouzi*, which include almost all entries composed by Xiao Yi himself.

Beatrice Spade

Kong Zhigui ji 孔稚珪集

Introduction

Kong Zhigui, styled Dezhang 德璋 (447–501), is sometimes called by the abbreviated name Kong Gui 孔珪 (*Nan shi*, q.v., 49:1214–16). Born in Shanyin 山陰 district in Kuaiji 會稽 commandery, he came from a family claiming to be descended from Confucius. His biography in *Nan Qi shu*, q.v., 48:835–40, pictures him as a wine-loving eccentric who preferred to live in reclusion and was not interested in official service. The truth is that Kong Zhigui served both the Liu-Song and Qi dynasties, and that the majority of his preserved writings were written for official occasions, including the "Zou Wang Rong zui" 奏王融罪 (Condemnation of Wang Rong), a formal proposal to execute Wang Rong after his unsuccessful attempt to enthrone the Prince of Jingling in 493.

After the death of the Qi emperor Ming (Xiao Luan; r. 494–498), Kong served his nefarious successor Xiao Baojuan (483–501), known posthumously as Donghun hou. Among several prestigious positions that he held before being removed from office was that of supervisor to the household of the heir apparent (*taizi zhanshi* 太子詹事), hence the traditional title of his collection, *Kong Zhanshi ji* 孔詹事集.

Contents

The edition of the *Kong Zhanshi ji* in *juan* 79 of Zhang Pu's (1602–1641) *Han Wei Liuchao baisanjia ji*, q.v., contains all the surviving works of prose and poetry, with the exception of two short fragments included in Lu Qinli, *Xian Qin Han Wei Jin Nanbeichao shi**, "Qi shi" 2:1408–9. There are nineteen pieces of prose and poetry arranged in the following order:

1. Memorials (petitions), five
2. Presentations, two
3. Communication, one
4. Letters, three
5. Epitaphs, two
6. Dispatch (*yiwen* 移文), one
7. Offering, one
8. Lyric poems and *yuefu*, four

It is to be expected that most of the preserved writings are formal parallel prose compositions. Kong Zhigui had already begun his literary activities while holding office under the (Liu-)Song, and he was an important figure at the Southern Qi court. He was admired primarily as a brilliant author of parallel prose. The best known and most remarkable piece in the collection is "Beishan yiwen" 北山移文 (Dispatch to North Mountain). The *yiwen* is a kind of written communication exchanged between officials of the same rank serving in different locations; the translation of this term as "dispatch" seems most appropriate (Knechtges, *Wen xuan*, 46), although "proclamation" is the term that has been used in Western translations of the title. Kong's poems are in five-syllable form and include *yuefu*.

Sources of the work

The *Kong Zhanshi ji* is a typical "gathered-up collection" (*jiben* 輯本) in that it was reconstructed from items scattered in various sources. The bibliographic monograph of *Sui shu*, q.v., 35:1076, records that Kong Zhigui's collection had consisted of ten *juan*; this collection was lost by the Yuan. Individual writings by Kong were preserved in the *Yiwen leiju*, q.v., *juan* 54, the *Hongming ji*, q.v., *juan* 11 of the fourteen-*juan* edition, and in his *Nan Qi shu* biography. The "Beishan yiwen" is in *juan* 43 of Xiao Tong's (501–531) *Wen xuan*, q.v.

Authenticity and transmission of the text

Issues of authenticity are not in general raised about the fragment that survives of Kong's writings, although small differences exist among texts in various editions, particularly in the titles of some prose pieces. Most of his prose pieces deal with events that can be dated to the Southern Qi. The only seriously disputed work in the collection is the second of two *yuefu* verses titled "Bai ma pian" 白馬篇. The two poems are both found under Kong's name in *juan* 63 of the *Yuefu shiji*, q.v., but the second of them has elsewhere been attributed to Emperor Yang of the Sui dynasty. Lu Qinli suggests it was composed by a "northern dynasty poet" ("Qi shi," 2:1408). Cao Daoheng and Shen Yucheng (*Zhonggu wenxue shiliao congkao*, 427–28) also doubt it was written by Kong.

Principal editions

Besides the editions of Zhang Pu's anthology, the *Kong Zhanshi ji* was also included in the *Zeng ding Han Wei Liuchao biejie* 增訂漢魏六朝別解 printed by Ye Shaotai 葉紹泰 during the Chongzhen era (1627–1644). Kong's prose and poems may be found separately in *juan* 19 of the *Quan shanggu Sandai Qin Han Sanguo Liuchao wen*, q.v.

Traditional assessments

Zhong Rong 鍾嶸 praised Kong Zhigui's poetry for being more elaborate than poems by his older maternal cousin Zhang Rong 張融, yet placed both of them in the third and lowest section of his *Shi pin*, q.v.

The "Beishan yiwen" became a popular model of parallel prose during the Tang and has been typically included in annotated selections of parallel prose up to modern times. It was traditionally thought to be a satire targeting Kong

Zhigui's contemporary Zhou Yong 周顒 (d. ca. 485) for his hypocrisy in claiming to pursue the ideals of a recluse while at the same time striving for office. This view has been echoed by modern scholars but in considering that Zhou was a friend of Kong, some do not believe the essay was intended as a personal reproof but instead criticized a widespread contemporary practice.

Selected studies

Berkowitz, Alan J. *Patterns of Disengagement: The Practice and Portrayal of Reclusion in Early Medieval China*. Stanford, CA: Stanford University Press, 2000. Pp. 137, 144.

Cao Daoheng 曹道衡. "Beishan yiwen xin zheng" 北山移文新證. In *Han Wei Liuchao wenxue lunwenji* 漢魏六朝文學論文集, 222–27. Guilin: Guangxi shifan daxue chubanshe, 1999.

Cao Daoheng and Shen Yucheng 沈玉成. Four essays on Kong Zhigui's life and works, in *Zhonggu wenxue shiliao congkao* 中古文學史料叢考, 426–29. Beijing: Zhonghua shuju, 2003.

———. "Nanchao wenxue shi" 南朝文學史. In *Zhongguo wenxue tongshi xilie* 中國文學通史系列, 195–98. Beijing: Renmin wenxue chubanshe, 1991.

Hightower, James R. "Some Characteristics of Parallel Prose." In *Studies in Chinese Literature*, ed. John Bishop, 108–39. Cambridge, MA: Harvard University Press, 1965. Originally published in Søren Egerod and Else Glahn. *Studia Serica Bernhard Karlgren Dedicata*, 60–91. Copenhagen: E. Munskgaard, 1959.

Knechtges, David. *Wen xuan, or Selections of Refined Literature*. Princeton, NJ: Princeton University Press, 1982. Vol. 1, pp. 44, 46.

Kondō Izumi 近藤泉. "Lun 'Beishan yiwen' chuangzuo beijing he shoufa yuanyuan" 論北山移文創作背景和手法淵源. *Beijing daxue xuebao (zhexue shehui kexue ban)* (1993.1): 107–14.

Tan Jiajian 譚家健. "Beishan yiwen xin yi" 北山移文新義. *Qi Lu xuekan, She zhe ban* (2001.6): 5–10.

Wang Yunxi 王運熙. "Kong Zhigui de Beishan yiwen" 孔稚珪的北山移文. In *Han Wei Liuchao Tangdai wenxue lunji* 漢魏六朝唐代文學論集, 79–84. Shanghai: Shanghai guji chubanshe, 1981 (originally in *Wenhui bao*, 29 July 1961).

Wu Zhenglan 吳正嵐. "Lun Kong Zhigui de yinyi guannian he zongjiao xinyang de guanxi" 論孔稚珪的隱逸觀念和宗教信仰的關係. *Nanjing daxue xuebao, Zhexue, renwen kexue, shehui kexue* 38 (2001.6): 76–80.

Translations

English

Hightower, James R. "Proclamation on North Mountain." In "Some Characteristics of Parallel Prose." Reprinted without notes in *Anthology of Chinese Literature*, ed. Cyril Birch and Donald Keene, 169–73. New York: Grove Press,

1965; reprinted with notes in *Classical Chinese Literature: An Anthology of Translations*, vol. 1, *From Antiquity to the Tang Dynasty*, ed. John Minford and Joseph S. M. Lau, 609–13. Hong Kong: The Chinese University Press; New York: Columbia University Press, 2000.

European languages

Margouliès, Georges. "Proclamation de la montagne du nord." In *Anthologie raisonnée de la littérature chinoise*, 242–44. Paris: Payot, 1948. An earlier version appeared under the title "Ordre militaire de la Montagne du Nord" in *Le Kou-Wen Chinois, Recueil de textes avec introduction et notes*, 135–39. Paris: Paul Geuthner, 1926.

Zach, Erwin von. "Die auf dem Nordberg erlassene Kundmachung." In *Die chinesische Anthologie: Übersetzungen aus dem Wen hsüan*, ed. Ilse Martin Fong, 2:805–8. 2 vols. Harvard-Yenching Institute Studies 18. Cambridge, MA: Harvard University Press, 1958.

Modern Chinese

Cao Minggang 曹明綱 and Xu Lian 許槤. *Liuchao wenjie yizhu* 六朝文絜譯注. Shanghai: Shanghai guji chubanshe, 1999. Pp. 196–203.

Research aids

Mou Hualin 牟華林. "Kong Zhigui nianpu" 孔稚珪年譜. *Yibin xueyuan bao* (2002.3): 39–43.

Mu Kehong 穆克宏. *Wei Jin Nanbei chao wenxue shiliao shulüe* 魏晉南北朝文學史料述略. Beijing: Zhonghua shuju, 1997. Pp. 121–22.

Olga Lomová

Liang Jianwendi ji 梁簡文帝集

Introduction

Xiao Gang 蕭綱 (503–552) was the third son of Emperor Wu of the Liang. Born on 2 December 503, he was enfeoffed as Prince of Jin'an (Jin'an wang 晉安王) in early 506. After the untimely death of his elder brother Xiao Tong 統 (501–531), Xiao Gang was made heir apparent. He succeeded to the throne in 549 but remained under the power of the rebel general Hou Jing 侯景 through his two-year rule. In the autumn of 551, he was forced to abdicate and placed under house arrest. Xiao Gang reportedly composed several hundred poems and prose pieces during the forty-five days of his imprisonment; having no paper, he wrote on the walls and screens of his chamber. After he was murdered, all of these writings were effaced by Hou Jing's men; however, one of the men memorized a few pieces, two of which survive.

Contents

Xiao Gang was a prolific writer who composed in a variety of genres. Apart from his lecture notes and commentaries on the *Shi jing*, *Lao zi*, and *Zhuang zi* and various writings on specific subjects, his collection consists of lyric poetry and *yuefu*, rhapsodies, commands, instructions, petitions, memorandums, letters, prefaces, disquisitions, eulogies, inscriptions, epitaphic inscriptions (*bei ming* 碑銘), grave memoir inscriptions, elegies, sacrificial offerings, and other writings.

Sources of the work

A major source for Xiao Gang's poetry is the Liang anthology *Yutai xinyong*, q.v., compiled by Xu Ling (507–583) for an aristocratic female readership, which alone accounts for almost a third of Xiao Gang's extant poems. Other important sources for both poetry and prose include Tang and Song encyclopedias—the *Yiwen leiju*, q.v., compiled by Ouyang Xun (557–641), the *Chuxue ji*, q.v., by Xu Jian (659–729), and the *Taiping yulan*, q.v., by Li Fang (925–996); anthologies—the *Guang hongming ji*, q.v., compiled by the Buddhist monk Shi Daoxuan (596–667), the *Wenguan cilin** by Xu Jingzong (592–672), the *Wenyuan yinghua** by Li Fang, and the *Yuefu shiji*, q.v., by Guo Maoqian (fl. 1084); and dynastic histories—namely, the *Liang shu*, q.v., and the *Nan shi*, q.v.

Authorship

As different sources sometimes assign the same poem to different authors, a number of poems in Xiao Gang's collection have multiple attributions. In most cases it is impossible to determine which attribution is correct. One of the factors responsible for the confusion is that Xiao Gang and his elder brother Xiao Tong are both referred to as "crown prince" (*huangtaizi* 皇太子) in some of the sources. Since the two brothers have long been considered to represent, respectively, the orthodox aesthetics and the decadent, editors often make editorial decisions on an ideological basis rather than on a textual basis. For a detailed discussion of this point, see the work by Xiaofei Tian ("Xiao Tong and Xiao Gang: A Case Study," 144–50).

Transmission and early history of the text

According to Xiao Gang's biography in *Nan shi* 8:233, his literary collection amounted to one hundred *juan*. Reportedly, only one copy of Xiao Gang's collection remained after the fall of the new Liang capital Jiangling 江陵 (in modern Hubei) in late 554, and it was taken to the Western Wei imperial library in Chang'an 長安. In the early 560s, Xiao Gang's youngest son, Xiao Dahuan 大圜, at the time appointed an academician by the Northern Zhou court, gained access to this work and to the only copy that had survived of the collection of Emperor Wu. Xiao Dahuan set out to make copies of the writings of his father and grandfather, which took him a year to finish. The edition of Xiao Gang's works alone was in ninety *juan* (*Zhou shu*, q.v., 42:757). The discrepancy in the numbers of *juan* recorded in the *Nan shi* entry may be due to a partial loss of the collection after the Hou Jing Rebellion.

The bibliographic monograph of *Sui shu* (35:1076), q.v., records a *Liang Jianwendi ji* in eighty-five *juan* that was compiled (possibly with a preface) by Lu Zhao 陸罩 (517–?), whose biography is in *Nan shi* 48:1205. Xiao Gang's collection survived the Tang in much better shape than the writings of Emperor Wu. *Jiu Tang shu* 47:2052 and *Xin Tang shu* 60:1592 each record the collection in eighty *juan*. Pre-Tang poetry and prose, particularly parallel prose (*pianwen* 駢文), at which Xiao Gang excelled, largely fell out of favor, however, during the Song (except for Tao Yuanming's works); after the Song, only one *juan* of the collection remained (*Song shi* 208:5429).

Despite severe losses, the total number of Xiao Gang's extant poems (over 250 in all) is among the largest surviving oeuvres of pre-Tang poets. It testifies to both his prolific output and the popularity of his poetry, for in the age of manuscript culture, when the endurance of any text depended solely on hand-copying everything, the more times a text was copied, the better chance it stood of surviving; and the more a text was liked, the more likely it was copied over and over again.

Newly discovered manuscripts

The *Wenguan cilin* was a large compendium in one thousand *juan* completed in 658 by Xu Jingzong (592–672) et al. It was long lost in China, but old manuscript copies of the *Wenguan cilin* that have been dated to the ninth century, though fragmentary, are still preserved in Japan. Different parts of the *Wenguan cilin* continuously surfaced from the turn of the nineteenth century through the early decades of the twentieth century and were assembled and photo-reprinted in Japan in 1969, and a Chinese edition, *Ricang Hongren ben Wenguan cilin jiaozheng**, appeared in 2001. A number of Xiao Gang's instructions included in this edition are not found in any other source.

Principal editions

Xiao Gang's collection was reassembled and printed in the Ming. Notable single-genre collections include the following four compilations:

Liang Jianwendi ji in two *juan*, in *Liuchao shiji**, one of the earliest series of Six Dynasties poetic collections printed in the Ming, with a preface written by Xue Yingqi (*jinshi* 1535) and dated 1543. In *Xuxiu Siku quanshu** 1589:8–29.

Xiao Gang's poetry in three *juan*, in Feng Weine's (1513–1572) *Gushu ji** (also known as *Shi ji* 詩紀), *juan* 77–79, a monumental anthology of pre-Tang poetry finished in 1557.

Xiao Gang's prose in two *juan*, in Mei Dingzuo's (1549–1615) *Liang wen ji**, an anthology of Liang prose.

Liang Jianwen wenchao 梁簡文文鈔 in one *juan*, in *Badai wenchao* 八代文鈔, edited by Li Bin 李賓 and printed in the late Ming.

Other editions include both poetry and prose:

Liang Jianwendi ji in fourteen *juan*. It forms part of the *Wenxuan yiji qizhong* 文選逸集七種 edited by the scholar Yan Guangshi 閻光世 in the early seventeenth century. Another edition of the collection appears in the series Xiao Liang wenyuan wuzhong 蕭梁文苑五種, also edited by Yan Guangshi. One copy of the *Wenxuan yiji qizhong* is in the collection of Beijing's Capital Library (Shoudu tushuguan); another copy is apparently in Taiwan's National Library (Guojia tushuguan). As for the *Xiao Liang wenyuan*, there is a copy in the Nanjing Library.

Liang Jianwendi yuzhi ji 梁簡文帝御制集 in sixteen *juan*, compiled by Zhang Xie 張燮 (1574–1640) in *Lidai sasijia wenji* 歷代卅四家文集. Zhengzhou: Zhongzhou guji chubanshe, rpt. 1997. *Juan* 1 includes rhapsodies; *juan* 2–5, poetry; *juan* 7–16, prose writings in various genres.

Liang Jianwendi ji in two *juan*, included in Zhang Pu's (1602–1641) *Han Wei Liuchao baisanjia ji*, q.v. The first *juan* includes rhapsodies and prose pieces; the second *juan* is devoted to poetry. Zhang Pu's edition was subsequently reprinted many times.

There is no modern typeset edition of Xiao Gang's collection. For his poetry, one may consult Lu Qinli's *Xian Qin Han Wei Jin Nanbeichao shi**, "Liang shi," *juan* 20–22, 3:1901–80. For his prose, one may consult Yan Kejun's (1762–1843) *Quan shanggu Sandai Qin Han Sanguo Liuchao wen*, q.v., "Quan Liang wen," *juan* 8–14, which, however, does not contain the additional prose pieces discovered in the old Japanese manuscript copy of *Wenguan cilin* (see previous section).

Encyclopedias and dynastic histories often include only excerpts from poetry and prose pieces. As a result, many of Xiao Gang's writings preserved through encyclopedias and dynastic histories are fragmentary. In a few cases, the *Wenguan cilin* versions are fuller than the versions contained in encyclopedic sources like the *Yiwen leiju*.

Selected studies

Gong Xianzong 龔顯宗. *Lun Liang Chen sidi shi* 論梁陳四帝詩. Gaoxiong: Gaoxiong fuwen tushu chubanshe, 1995.

Gui Qing 歸青. *Nanchao gongtishi yanjiu* 南朝宮體詩研究. Shanghai: Shanghai guji chubanshe, 2006.

Hu Nianyi 胡念貽. "Lun gongti shi de wenti" 論宮體詩的問題. *Xin jianshe* (1964.5–6): 167–73.

Lin Dazhi 林大志. *Si Xiao yanjiu: Yi wenxue wei zhongxin* 四蕭研究: 以文學為中心. Beijing: Zhonghua shuju, 2007.

Marney, John. *Liang Chien-wen Ti*. Boston: Twayne Publishers, 1976.

Rouzer, Paul. *Articulated Ladies: Gender and the Male Community in Early Chinese Texts*. Cambridge, MA: Harvard University Asia Center, 2001.

Shen Yucheng 沈玉成. "Gongti shi yu *Yutai xinyong*" 宮體詩與玉台新詠. *Wenxue yichan* (1988.6): 55–65.

Shi Guanhai 石觀海. *Gongti shipai yanjiu* 宮體詩派研究. Wuhan: Wuhan daxue chubanshe, 2003.

Tian, Xiaofei. *Beacon Fire and Shooting Star: The Literary Culture of the Liang (502–557)*. Cambridge, MA: Harvard University Asia Center, 2007.

Wang Chunhong 汪春泓. "Lun fojiao yu Liangdai gongtishi de chansheng" 論佛教與梁代宮體詩的產生. *Wenxue pinglun* (1991.5): 40–56.

Wu Fusheng. *The Poetics of Decadence: Chinese Poetry of the Southern Dynasties and Late Tang Poetics*. Albany, NY: SUNY Press, 1998.

Wu Guangxing 吳光興. *Xiao Gang, Xiao Yi nianpu* 蕭綱, 蕭繹年譜. Beijing: Shehui kexue wenxian chubanshe, 2006.

Xiong Weihua 熊偉華 and Wang Tingsheng 王汀生. "Butong guji zhong de Liang Jianwendi 'Meihua fu'" 不同古籍中的梁簡文帝梅花賦. *Guangzhou shiyuan xuebao* 21.10 (2000): 70–74.

Xu Zhongyu 徐中玉. "Wenzhang qie xu fangdang" 文章且須放蕩. In *Gudai wenyi chuangzuo lunji* 古代文藝創作論集, 19–39. Beijing: Zhongguo shehui kexue chubanshe, 1985.

Zhao Changping 趙昌平. "'Wenzhang qiexu fangdang' bian" 文章且須放蕩辨. *Gudai wenxue lilun yanjiu* (1984.9): 92–98.

Translations

A large part of Xiao Gang's poetry has been translated into English by John Marney in *Beyond the Mulberries: An Anthology of Palace-Style Poetry by Emperor Chien-wen of the Liang Dynasty (503–551)*, published by the Chinese Materials Center, San Francisco, in 1982. Other English translations of Xiao Gang's poetry may be found in *New Songs from a Jade Terrace: An Anthology of Early Chinese Love Poetry*, trans. Anne Birrell (London: Allen and Unwin, 1982); *An Anthology of Chinese Literature: Beginnings through 1911*, ed. and trans. Stephen Owen (New York: W.W. Norton, 1996); and chapter 6, "Suppression of the Light: Xiao Gang, Prince and Poet," in Xiaofei Tian, *Beacon Fire and Shooting Star*.

Xiaofei Tian

Liang shu 梁書

Contents

The *Liang shu* is the history of the Liang dynasty, beginning with the early life of its founder, Xiao Yan 蕭衍 (464–549, r. 502–549) and ending with the seizure of power and the founding of the Chen dynasty by Chen Baxian 陳霸先 (r. 557–559), thus covering approximately fifty-five years. The *Liang shu*, as well as the *Chen shu*, q.v., is the work of Yao Silian 姚思廉 (557–637).

The *Liang shu* consists of fifty-six *juan*, with six basic annals (*benji* 本紀) and fifty accounts (*zhuan* 傳). As with the *Chen shu*, the *Bei Qi shu*, q.v., and the *Zhou shu*, q.v., all compiled during the same period, the *Chen shu* contains no tables (*biao* 表) or monographs (*zhi* 志) . The Chen, the Bei Qi, and the Zhou dynasties were treated collectively in the monographs integrated in the *Sui shu*, q.v., from a work titled *Monographs of the History of the Five Dynasties* (*Wudai shi zhi* 五代史志).

Date of compilation and authenticity

Yao Silian was commissioned in 629 by Li Shimin 李世民, the Tang emperor Taizong, to compile both the *Chen shu* and the *Liang shu* at the same time that other scholars were to compile the *Bei Qi shu*, *Zhou shu*, and *Sui shu*. The year 629 marks the establishment of the Historiography Institute (Shiguan 史館), created to supervise and control the writing of official historical works. The compilation of the five histories was under the direction of Fang Xuanling 房玄齡 (578–648) and Wei Zheng 魏徵 (580–643), but in fact only the latter supervised the work; he was even directly involved in some of the writing (e.g., *Liang shu* 6:150). The *Liang shu* and *Chen shu* were completed in 636. It is generally assumed that the text of the *Liang shu* as we have it is the original text.

Sources

The compilation of the *Liang shu* did not run a smooth course. Earlier, after the collapse of the Chen in 589, Sui Wendi had ordered Yao Cha 姚察 (533–606), a former Chen official, to write a history of the Liang. Yao Cha died before finishing the work, but he made a deathbed request for his son Yao Silian to complete it. During the reign of Sui emperor Yangdi, Yao Silian was officially given the task of completing the work at the suggestion to the throne by the official Yu Shiji 虞世基 (d. 618; *Chen shu* 27:354). In 622, Emperor Gaozu of Tang, while ordering Yao Silian to finish his *Chen shu*, directed three other scholars, Cui Shanwei 崔善為, Kong Shao'an 孔紹安 (b. 577), and Xiao Deyan 蕭德言 (558–654) to compile a *Liang shu* (*Tang huiyao* 63:1091; *Tang dazhaolingji* 81:466–67), but they did not complete the task. Yao Silian was charged to bring the *Liang shu* to completion by Taizong in 629 (*Tang huiyao* 63:1091). Although he may have used some of the drafts made by Cui, Kong, and Xiao, it is clear from the frequent inclusion of comments made by his father, introduced by the phrase "Yao Cha, secretary at the Ministry of Personnel of the Chen, says" (陳吏部尚書姚察曰; e.g., *Liang shu* 8:173, 9:184, and 10:201), that he made extensive use of his father's work.

Transmission of the text

The earliest printed edition of the *Liang shu* that survives is (a) the Shu 蜀 edition from the Song's Shaoxing era (1131–1162). Later editions include:

(b) Nanjian 南監 edition of 1575;

(c) Beijian 北監 edition of 1605;

(d) Mao Jin's 毛晉 *Jiguge* 汲古閣 edition of 1631;

(e) Wuying dian 武英殿, or the "Palace" edition, of 1739;

(f) *Siku quanshu* 四庫全書 edition of 1782;

(g) Jinling shuju 金陵書局 edition of 1874.

For an overall account of the textual history of this and the other Six Dynasties standard histories, see appendix IV, "Textual Transmission of the Standard Histories."

Modern editions

In the *Sibu congkan** series of 1936, the Shangwu yinshuguan issued a photolithographic reproduction of the Song dynasty's "Shu edition" (a); this is known as the Baina ben 百衲本 edition. The Zhonghua shuju in Beijing produced a punctuated edition in 1973 that was based upon the (a)–(e) and (g) editions; this is now the standard edition.

Studies and research aids

Cui Lindong 崔林東. *Zhongguo shixueshi—Wei Jin Nan Beichao Sui Tang shiqi* 中國史學史—魏晉南北朝隋唐時期. Shanghai: Shanghai renmin chubanshe, 2006. Pp. 137–38, 145–47.

Jiang Boliang 蔣伯良. "*Liang shu, Chen shu* chuanwu bian" 梁書, 陳書舛誤辨. *Ningbo daxue xuebao, Renwen kexue ban* (2003.3): 62–65.

Li Shaoyong 李少雍. "Yaoshi fuzi de wenbi yu shibi—du *Liangshu, Chenshu* zhaji" 姚氏父子的文筆與史筆—讀梁書, 陳書札記. *Wenxue yichan* (2002.6): 79–92.

MacMullen, David. *State and Scholars in T'ang China*. Cambridge: Cambridge University Press, 1988. Pp. 165–67.

Qian Yiji 錢儀吉. *Nanchao huiyao* 南朝會要. Shanghai: Shanghai guji chubanshe, 1996.
Twitchett, Denis. *The Writing of Official History under the T'ang*. Cambridge: Cambridge University Press, 1992.
Wechsler, Howard. *Mirror to the Son of Heaven: Wei Cheng at the Court of T'ang T'ai-tsung*. New Haven, CT: Yale University Press, 1974. Pp. 111–13.
———. "T'ai-tsung (Reign 626–49): The Consolidator." In *The Cambridge History of China*, vol. 3, *Sui and T'ang, 589–906*, part 1, ed. Denis Twitchett, 215–16. Cambridge: Cambridge University Press, 1979.
Wright, Arthur. *The Sui Dynasty: The Unification of China, A.D. 581–617*. New York: Alfred A. Knopf, 1978. Pp. 14–16.
Wu Tianren 吳天任. *Zhengshi daodu* 正史導讀. Taipei: Taiwan shangwu yinshuguan, 1990. Pp. 53–57.
Xiong Qingyuan 熊清元. "Yao shi fuzi yu *Liang shu*" 姚氏父子與梁書. *Huanggang shifan xueyuan xuebao* (2001.2): 8–15.
Yuan Yingguang 袁英光. *Nanchao wushi cidian* 南朝五史辭典. Ji'nan: Shandong jiaoyu chubanshe, 2005.
Zhao Jun 趙俊. "*Liang shu*, *Chen shu* de biancuan deshi" 梁書, 陳書的編纂得失. *Zhongguo shehui kexue yanjiushengyuan xuebao* (1994.3): 17–24.
Zhu Mingpan 朱銘盤. *Nanchao Liang huiyao* 南朝梁會要. Shanghai: Shanghai guji chubanshe, 2006.

Translations

Bielenstein, Hans. "The Six Dynasties, vol. I." *Bulletin of the Museum of Far Eastern Antiquities* 68 (1996): 191–225; this is based mainly on the annals sections of the *Liang shu*.
Frankel, Hans H. *Catalogue of Translations from the Chinese Dynastic Histories for the Period 220–960*. Chinese Dynastic Histories Translations, supplement no. 1, pp. 95–101. Berkeley: University of California Press, 1957.

Indices

Ershisishi renming suoyin 二十四史人名索引. Beijing: Zhonghua shuju, 1980.
Ershiwushi jizhuan renming suoyin 二十五史紀傳人名索引. Shanghai: Shanghai guji chubanshe and Shanghai shudian, 1990.
Ershiwushi kanxing weiyuanhui 二十五史刊行委員會, ed. *Ershiwushi renming suoyin* 二十五史人名索引. Shanghai: Kaiming shudian, 1935; Beijing: Zhonghua shuju, 1956.
Zhang Chenshi 張忱石. *Nanchao wushi renming suoyin* 南朝五史人名索引. Beijing: Zhonghua shuju, 1985.

Bibliography

Tang da zhaoling ji 唐大詔令集. Comp. Song Minqiu 宋敏求 (1019–1079). Beijing: Shangwu yinshuguan, 1959.

Tang huiyao 唐會要. Comp. Wang Pu 王蒲 (922–982). Beijing: Zhonghua shuju, 1955.

Damien Chaussende

Liang Wudi ji 梁武帝集

Introduction

Xiao Yan 蕭衍 (464–549) was born into a gentry family that immigrated to Wujin 武進 (in modern Jiangsu) from Lanling 蘭陵 (in modern Shandong) after the Western Jin dynasty collapsed in the early fourth century; Wujin was subsequently renamed South Lanling (Nan Lanling 南蘭陵) after the Xiaos' place of origin. Xiao Yan began his official career in the early 480s and was much admired for his talents. He was a frequent visitor to the salon of his kinsman Xiao Ziliang 子良 (460–494), Prince of Jingling (Jingling wang 竟陵王), a refined literature lover and devout Buddhist who sponsored many literary, scholarly, and religious activities. Of the men of letters gathering around the prince, the most illustrious were known as the "Eight Companions of the Prince of Jingling," with Xiao Yan being one of them. In the winter of 500, Xiao Yan's elder brother, Xiao Yi 懿, was forced to commit suicide by the current Qi emperor, Xiao Baojuan; a younger brother was also executed.

Upon learning of the deaths, Xiao Yan organized a military uprising and eventually took Jiankang, the capital. Xiao Baojuan was killed by insurgents from inside the imperial palace; a new Qi emperor was put in place. Soon afterward, the new emperor abdicated to Xiao Yan, who founded the Liang dynasty in 502. What followed was a peaceful and prosperous rule of forty-eight years, one of the longest in all Chinese history. Under Emperor Wu's rule, the Liang became a flourishing regime, and Jiankang 建康 (modern Nanjing) the world's most populous city in its day. Emperor Wu, toward the end of his reign, made the fatal mistake of accepting the surrender of a northern general, Hou Jing 侯景 (d. 552). Hou Jing rebelled in the autumn of 548, and his army quickly advanced to the capital. A bloody siege ensued. In the spring of 549, the palace city fell, and Emperor Wu died soon after at the age of eighty-five.

Contents

Emperor Wu was an accomplished and extremely prolific writer. According to his biography in *Liang shu*, q.v., *juan* 1–3, he had a collection in 120 *juan* besides works on music and chess and various commentaries he authored on the Buddhist, Confucian, and Daoist canons in several hundred *juan*. His extant collection includes poetry, rhapsodies, edicts, prefaces, letters, essays, inscriptions, admonitions, and writings in other genres.

Sources of the work

Like many pre-Tang literary collections, Emperor Wu's was lost and then reassembled from various sources in the Ming. Major sources include Tang and Song encyclopedias, such as the *Yiwen leiju*, q.v., compiled by Ouyang Xun (557–641) et al., the *Chuxue ji*, q.v., compiled by Xu Jian (659–729) et al., and the *Taiping yulan*, q.v., compiled by Li Fang (925–996) et al.; anthologies, such as the *Yutai xinyong*, q.v., compiled by Xu Ling (507–583), the *Guang hongming ji*, q.v., compiled by the Buddhist monk Shi Daoxuan (596–667), the *Wenguan cilin**, compiled by Xu Jingzong (592–672) et al., the *Gu wenyuan* 古文苑 (a Tang anthology), the *Wenyuan yinghua**, compiled by Li Fang et al., and the *Yuefu shiji*, q.v., compiled by Guo Maoqian (fl. 1084); and dynastic histories, where many of Emperor Wu's edicts and letters can be found.

Authorship

Some of the poems in Emperor Wu's collection have multiple attributions due to conflicting claims in different sources. For example, a *yuefu* poem titled "Lin gaotai" 臨高臺 is attributed to Emperor Wu in the *Yutai xinyong* but to his son Xiao Gang 綱 in the *Wenyuan yinghua* and *Yuefu shiji*. Most notably, a number of *yuefu* quatrains are attributed to Emperor Wu in *Yutai xinyong* but to a Wang Jinzhu 王金珠 in the *Yuefu shiji*. Wang may have been a court musician in the Liang. In this case, there is no telling which source is correct. Perhaps Wang created the music while Emperor Wu supplied the lyrics, or vice versa, the emperor being a gifted musician himself.

Transmission and early history of the text

According to *Zhou shu*, q.v., 42:757, only one copy of Emperor Wu's collection in forty *juan* survived the Hou Jing Rebellion. After the fall in late 554 of the new Liang capital Jiangling 江陵 (in modern Hubei), the collection was taken to Chang'an and stored in the imperial library of the Western Wei. In the early 560s, Xiao Dahuan, Emperor Wu's grandson, spent a year making a copy of it (and of his father's collection) when he was appointed an academician by the Northern Zhou court. The bibliographic monograph of *Sui shu*, q.v., 35:1076, records Emperor Wu's collection in twenty-six *juan* and notes that in the Liang there were thirty-two *juan*.

These numbers are all significantly smaller than the 120 *juan* recorded in *Liang shu* 3:96 and *Nan shi*, q.v., 7:223. However, the *Sui shu* also records a *Collection of the Poems and Rhapsodies of Emperor Wu of the Liang* (*Liang Wudi shi fu ji* 梁武帝詩賦集) in twenty *juan*, a *Collection of the Miscellaneous Prose of Emperor Wu of the Liang* (*Liang Wudi zawen* 梁武帝雜文集) in nine *juan*, and, finally, a "Table of Contents of Emperor Wu of the Liang's Collection" ("Liang Wudi bieji mulu" 梁武帝別集目錄) in two *juan*. It seems that Emperor Wu's writings were circulated in several different versions; but, if his poetry and *fu* alone span twenty *juan* (and this is most likely *not* a complete collection of his poetry and *fu*), it is hard to believe that all of Emperor Wu's writings, including all his edicts and correspondence written during a rule that lasted nearly half a century, would amount to no more than 40 *juan* altogether. The likely explanation is that the collection in 40 *juan* seen by Xiao Dahuan was already not the complete collection, which became partially lost in the Hou Jing Rebellion and the bibliocaust committed by his son Xiao Yi, Emperor Yuan of the Liang (for his collection, see *Liang Yuandi ji*), before the fall of Jiangling.

In the Tang, the collection suffered further losses. *Jiu Tang shu* 47:2052 and *Xin Tang shu* 60:1582 each record Emperor Wu's collection in no more than 10 *juan*. After the Song, the collection was no longer extant, until several Ming scholars reassembled Emperor Wu's scattered writings from various sources into a collection again.

Newly discovered manuscripts

The *Wenguan cilin** was a large compendium in one thousand *juan* completed in 658. It was long lost in China, but old manuscript copies of the *Wenguan cilin* dated the ninth century, though fragmentary, are still preserved in Japan. Different parts of the *Wenguan cilin* continuously surfaced from the turn of the nineteenth century through the early decades of the twentieth century and were assembled and photographically reprinted in Japan in 1969. It was not until 2001 that a Chinese edition of a reassembled *Wenguan cilin*, the *Ricang Hongren ben Wenguan cilin jiaozheng**, based on the 1969 reprinted Japanese edition, was published in Beijing. A number of Emperor Wu's edicts and memorandums included in this edition are not found in any other source.

Principal editions

In the sixteenth and seventeenth centuries there was a revival of interest in Six Dynasties literature. As a result a number of anthologies of Six Dynasties poetry and prose were compiled, and many include Emperor Wu's works. The *Liuchao shiji**, with a preface written by Xue Yingqi (*jinshi* 1535) and dated 1543, contains one *juan* of Emperor Wu's poems (*Xuxiu Siku quanshu** 1589:3–7). Another Six Dynasties poetic anthology, the *Liuchao shihui* 六朝詩匯, compiled by Zhang Qian 張謙 and Wang Zongsheng 王宗聖 and printed in 1552, also includes Emperor Wu's poetry. Feng Weine's (1513–1572) *Gushi ji** (also known as the *Shi ji* 詩紀), a monumental anthology of pre-Tang poetry finished in 1557, also includes Emperor Wu's poems in two *juan* (74–75). Mei Dingzuo's (1549–1615) *Liang wen ji**, an anthology of Liang prose, includes one *juan* of Emperor Wu's prose.

Yan Guangshi 閻光世, of the late Ming, edited a *Liang Wudi ji* 梁武帝集 in eight *juan* in the *Wenxuan yiji qizhong* 文選逸集七種 in the early seventeenth century; another edition appears in the series *Xiao Liang wenyuan wuzhong* 蕭梁文苑五種, also edited by Yan Guangshi. One copy of the *Wenxuan yiji qizhong* is in the collection of Beijing's Capital Library (Shoudu tushuguan); another copy is apparently in Taiwan's National Library (Guojia tushuguan). As for the *Xiao Liang wenyuan*, there is a copy in the Nanjing Library. Zhang Xie (1574–1640) put

Emperor Wu's poetry and prose together to assemble the *Liang Wudi yuzhi ji* 梁武帝御制集 in twelve *juan* in the series known as *Qishi'er jia ji** (reprinted in *Xuxiu Siku quanshu* 1585:577–671 and 1586:1–53). This is the base edition for the *Liang Wudi ji* in two *juan* included in Zhang Pu's (1602–1641) *Han Wei liuchao bai san jia ji*, q.v. Zhang Pu's edition became very influential, and there were subsequently many reprints, such as one reprinted by the Xinshu tang 信述堂 in 1879 and a modern reprint issued in Yangzhou in 1990.

There is no modern typeset edition of Emperor Wu's collection. For Emperor Wu's poetry, one may consult *juan* 1 of "Liang shi," in Lu Qinli's *Xian Qin Han Wei Jin Nanbeichao shi**, 2:1513–39. For Emperor Wu's prose one may consult *juan* 1–7 of "Quewan Liang wen" in Yan Kejun's (1762–1843) *Quan shanggu Sandai Qin de Han Sanguo Liuchao wen*, q.v., which, however, does not contain the additional prose pieces contained in the Japanese manuscript copy of the *Wenguan cilin* (see previous section).

Encyclopedias and dynastic histories often include only excerpts from poetry and prose pieces. As a result, many of Emperor Wu's writings preserved through encyclopedias and dynastic histories are fragmentary.

Selected studies

Gong Xianzong 龔顯宗. *Lun Liang Chen sidi shi* 論梁陳四帝詩. Gaoxiong: Gaoxiong fuwen tushu chubanshe, 1995.

Hu Dehuai 胡德懷. *Qi Liang wentan yu si Xiao yanjiu* 齊梁文壇與四蕭研究. Nanjing: Nanjing daxue chubanshe, 1997.

Lin Dazhi 林大志. *Si Xiao yanjiu, yi wenxue wei zhongxin* 四蕭研究: 以文學為中心. Beijing: Zhonghua shuju, 2007.

Lin Dazhi and Chang Hongmei 常紅梅. "Xiao Yan shi lunlüe" 蕭衍詩論略. *Taiyuan shifan xueyuan xuebao* (2006.5–6): 71–74.

Tian, Xiaofei. *Beacon Fire and Shooting Star: The Literary Culture of the Liang (502–557)*. Cambridge, MA: Harvard University Asia Center, 2007.

Xie Rubai 謝如柏. "Liang Wudi 'Li shenming cheng Fo yiji,' xingshen zhi zheng de zhongjie yu xiang Foxing sixiang de zhuanxiang" 梁武帝立神明成佛義記, 形神之爭的終結與向佛性思想的轉向. *Hanxue yanjiu* 22.2 (2004): 211–44.

Yang Decai 楊德才. "Lun Xiao Yan de yuefu shi" 論蕭衍的樂府詩. *Wenxue yichan* (1999.3): 28–34.

Yu Yingli 于英麗. "Liang Wudi Xiao Yan de sixiang yu qi fu zhi guanxi" 梁武帝蕭衍的思想與其賦之關係. *Fujian shifan daxue xuebao* 4 (2005): 49–52.

Xiaofei Tian

Liang Yuandi ji 梁元帝集

Introduction

Xiao Yi 蕭繹 (508–555) was the seventh son of Emperor Wu of the Liang. He was enfeoffed as Prince of Xiangdong 湘東 at the age of six. Throughout Emperor Wu's rule Xiao Yi served in a number of provincial posts. He spent the longest time in Jiangling 江陵 as governor of Jingzhou 荊州 (in modern Hubei). When the Hou Jing Rebellion broke out in 548, Xiao Yi was in Jiangling, and it was there he ascended the throne on 13 December 552, as his elder brother Xiao Gang had been murdered by Hou Jing's men in the previous year. Against his councilors' advice, Xiao Yi decided to remain in Jiangling instead of returning to the old capital Jiankang 建康 (modern Nanjing). In the winter of 554, the army of Western Wei besieged Jiangling. After the city fell, Xiao Yi was captured and then executed on 27 January 555. He was granted the posthumous title Emperor Yuan 元.

Contents

Xiao Yi was an accomplished and productive writer and scholar; he authored and supervised the writing or compilation of many works. His literary collection contains poetry, rhapsodies, edicts, commands, prefaces, letters, inscriptions, eulogies, grave memoirs, sacrificial offerings, stele inscriptions, and writings in other genres. Among longer works, his *Master of the Golden Tower* (*Jinlouzi* 金樓子) is discussed as a separate entry in this volume.

Sources of the work

The major sources of Xiao Yi's writings include Tang and Song encyclopedias, such as the *Yiwen leiju*, q.v., compiled by Ouyang Xun (557–641) et al., the *Chuxue ji*, q.v., compiled by Xu Jian (659–729) et al.; anthologies, such as the *Guang hongming ji*, q.v., compiled by the Buddhist monk Shi Daoxuan (596–667), the *Wenguan cilin**, compiled by Xu Jingzong (592–672) et al., the *Wenyuan yinghua**, compiled by Li Fang et al., the *Yuefu shiji*, q.v., compiled by Guo Maoqian (fl. 1084); and dynastic histories, most notably the *Liang shu*, q.v., and the *Nan shi*, q.v., and, to a lesser degree, the *Chen shu*, q.v., and the *Zhou shu*, q.v.

Authorship and date of composition

There are about 120 extant poems in Xiao Yi's collection. Eights poems are also variously attributed to Xiao Gang, Xiao Lun 綸 (507?–551), Wu Jun 吳均 (469–520),

Shen Yue 沈約 (441–512), and Xiao Zixian 子顯 (489–537) in different early sources. It is difficult to determine the correct attribution in all of the cases.

In Xiao Yi's collection assembled in Zhang Pu's (1602–1641) anthology, *Han Wei Liuchao baisanjia ji*, q.v., two rhapsodies are misattributed to Xiao Yi. They are "Qiuxing fu" 秋興賦 and "Linqiu fu" 臨秋賦, both being attributed to Xiao Gang in the *Yiwen leiju*, q.v., and having no known variant attribution.

The authenticity of a short work discussing landscape painting techniques, "Shanshui songshi ge" 山水松石格, attributed to Xiao Yi and included in the "Quan Liang wen" section of Yan Kejun's (1762–1843) *Quan shanggu Sandai Qin Han Sanguo Liuchao wen*, q.v., has been disputed. In the *Song shi*'s bibliographic monograph (207:5289), this work appears in one *juan* as an independent volume and is titled "Hua shanshui songshi ge" 畫山水松石格, attributed to Emperor Yuan of the Liang. The eighteenth-century *Siku quanshu* editors argue that Xiao Yi, though an illustrious painter, was best known for portraiture rather than for landscape paintings; they also point out that the work was recorded as late as in the fourteenth century and judge its style to be too "common and vulgar" to be from the Six Dynasties (*Siku quanshu zongmu tiyao** 22:2370).

Transmission and early history of the text

Xiao Yi's biographies in the dynastic histories both state that his literary collection was in fifty *juan* (*Liang shu* 5:136; *Nan shi* 8:246). The bibliographic monograph of *Sui shu*, q.v., 35:1076, which was compiled in the early seventh century, records a *Liang Yuandi ji* in fifty-two *juan* and a *Selected Collection of Emperor Yuan of the Liang* (*Liang Yuandi xiaoji* 梁元帝小集) in ten *juan*. The two additional *juan* as compared to the *juan* number specified in Xiao Yi's biographies is most likely because the *Liang shu* and *Nan shi* authors did not take into account the table of contents in the collection, which easily could have spanned two *juan* for a volume of fifty *juan*.

Centuries later, *Jiu Tang shu* 47:2052 recorded one *Liang Yuandi ji* in fifty *juan* and another in ten *juan*; *Xin Tang shu* 60:1593 likewise listed a *Liang Yuandi ji* in fifty *juan* and a *Xiaoji* in ten *juan*. This demonstrates that Xiao Yi's collection had survived the Tang more or less intact. As there was very little interest in Southern Dynasties poetry and prose in the Song, Xiao Yi's collection was most likely never printed and subsequently lost. The *Song shi*, compiled in the fourteenth century, contained no entry on Xiao Yi's collection. It was not until the late Ming that a new surge of interest in pre-Tang literature led to the reassembling—and printing—of Xiao Yi's collection from various sources.

Newly discovered manuscripts

The *Wenguan cilin* was a large compendium in one thousand *juan* completed in 658. It was long lost in China, but old manuscript copies of the *Wenguan cilin* dated the ninth century, though fragmentary, are still preserved in Japan. Different parts of the *Wenguan cilin* continuously surfaced from the turn of the nineteenth century through the early decades of the twentieth century and were assembled and photographically reprinted in Japan in 1969. It was not until 2001 that a Chinese edition of this work was published in Beijing with the title *Ricang Hongren ben Wenguan cilin jiaozheng**. A number of Xiao Yi's commands and one stele inscription included in this edition are not found in any other source.

Principal editions

Earliest printed editions date to the late sixteenth and early seventeenth centuries. Xiao Yi's poetry was collected into the *Liang Yuandi ji* in one *juan* in the *Liuchao shiji**, one of the earliest series of Six Dynasties literary collections printed in the Ming, with a preface written by Xue Yingqi (*jinshi* 1535) and dated 1543 (*Xuxiu Siku quanshu** 1589:30–38). This became the basis of Xiao Yi's poetry collected in Feng Weine's (1513–1572) *Gushi ji** (also known as the *Shi ji* 詩紀, *juan* 80–81, a monumental anthology of pre-Tang poetry finished in 1557). Xiao Yi's prose was collected in two *juan* in Mei Dingzuo's (1549–1615) *Liang wen ji**, an anthology of Liang prose.

Major editions of Xiao Yi's collection that include both poetry and prose are the following:

Liang Yuandi ji in eight *juan*, in the series known as *Wenxuan yiji qizhong* 文選逸集七種, edited by Yan Guangshi 閻光世 in the early seventeenth century. Another edition, also in eight *juan*, appears in the series *Xiao Liang wenyuan wuzhong*, edited by the same Yan Guangshi. One copy of the *Wenxuan yiji qizhong* is in the collection of Beijing's Capital Library (Shoudu tushuguan); another copy is apparently in Taiwan's National Library (Guojia tushuguan). As for the *Xiao Liang wenyuan*, there is a copy in the Nanjing Library.

Liang Yuandi yuzhi ji 梁元帝御制集 in ten *juan*, compiled by Zhang Xie (1574–1640) in the *Qishi'er jia ji** (reprinted in *Xuxiu Siku quanshu* 1586:282–377).

Liang Yuanwendi ji in one *juan*, included in Zhang Pu's *Han Wei Liuchao baisan jia ji*. There are many reprints of Zhang's edition, such as the one reprinted by the Xinshu tang 信述堂 in 1879 and a modern reprint issued in Yangzhou in 1990.

There is no modern typeset edition of Xiao Yi's collection. For his poetry, one may consult *juan* 25 of "Liang shi" in Lu Qinli's *Xian Qin Han Wei Jin Nanbeichao shi** 3:2031–61. For his prose, one may consult *juan* 15–18 of "Quan Liang wen" in Yan Kejun's collection *Quan shanggu Sandai Qin Han Sanguo Liuchao wen*, which, however, does not contain the additional prose pieces discovered in the old Japanese manuscript copy of the *Wenguan cilin* (see previous section).

Encyclopedias and dynastic histories often include only excerpts from poetry and prose pieces. As a result, many of Xiao Yi's writings preserved through encyclopedias and dynastic histories are fragmentary.

Selected studies

Cao Xu 曹旭. "Lun Xiao Yi de wenxueguan" 論蕭繹的文學觀. *Shanghai shifan daxue xuebao* 28.1 (1999): 15–21.

Dudbridge, Glen. *Lost Books of Medieval China*. The Panizzi Lectures, 1999. London: The British Library, 2000.
Gong Xianzong 龔顯宗. *Lun Liang Chen sidi shi* 論梁陳四帝詩. Gaoxiong: Gaoxiong fuwen tushu chubanshe, 1995.
Hu Dehuai 胡德懷. *Qi Liang wentan yu si Xiao yanjiu* 齊梁文壇與四蕭研究. Nanjing: Nanjing daxue chubanshe, 1997.
Lin Dazhi 林大志. "Liang Yuandi Xiao Yi shi lunlue" 梁元帝蕭繹詩論略. *Zhangzhou shifan xueyuan xuebao* (2005.3): 46–51.
———. *Si Xiao yanjiu: Yi wenxue wei zhongxin* 四蕭研究：以文學為中心. Beijing: Zhonghua shuju, 2007.
Tian, Xiaofei. *Beacon Fire and Shooting Star: The Literary Culture of the Liang (502–557)*. Cambridge, MA: Harvard University Asia Center, 2007.

Xiaofei Tian

Liuzi 劉子

Introduction

The *Liuzi* (Works of Master Liu) by Liu Zhou 劉晝 (514–565) is one of the few extant works from early medieval China that was classified under "Philosophical Writings" (*zi bu* 子部) in traditional Chinese bibliography. Since the Song dynasty, it has sometimes been identified as *Liuzi xinlun* 新論 (New discourse of Master Liu) or simply *Xinlun* in some Ming and Qing editions. Five other titles, including *Liuzi* 流子, *Deyan* 德言, *Shipaozi* 石匏子, *Yunmenzi* 雲門子, and *Kongzhaozi* 孔昭子, were also given to the same work in various catalogs and collectanea. The work is hardly mentioned in Western scholarship and is relatively unknown even to Chinese scholars outside the field. Nor was it exactly a celebrated text in Chinese history. The considerable attention it has received owes not so much to the originality of its contents as to its authorship and textual problems.

Authorship

Traditionally, Liu Xiang 劉向 (77–6 B.C.), Liu Xiaobiao 劉孝標 (462–521), Liu Xie 劉勰 (465–520), and Liu Zhou (514–565) were variously named as author of the *Liuzi*, but it was usually attributed to either Liu Zhou of the Northern Qi dynasty or Liu Xie of the Liang, author of the *Wenxin diaolong*, q.v., the famous work of literary criticism. However, neither figure's biography in the official histories mentions that he composed the work. On the basis of strong circumstantial evidence, modern scholarship largely concurs that Liu Zhou was the actual author. One of the major reasons is that the author is mentioned in the book as embracing Daoism, and numerous sections in the *Liuzi* indeed are philosophically grounded on that doctrine, whereas Liu Xie was known to have followed the teachings of the Buddha and was for some time an ordained Buddhist monk. In fact, the Daoistic character of the *Liuzi* even earned it inclusion in the Daoist Canon (*Daozang*). Nonetheless, two minority views persist—one argues adamantly for Liu Xie to be the author, and the other proposes that the *Liuzi* was written by someone in the Wei-Jin period (220–288). In the past decade, several other new candidates have been proposed, but the advocate of each has remained a lone voice, apparently without drawing any group of followers.

Liu Zhou was a poor orphan, but he loved to study even at a young age. He specialized in the three Confucian classics on the rites as well as the *Zuo*

Commentary according to the Later Han exegete Fu Qian's 服虔 interpretation. After he failed the examination for the *xiucai* degree for the first time, he regretted that he had not practiced literary composition. He then tried to learn the art and composed a rhapsody on the universe, of which he was exceedingly proud. In his reckoning, he had studied the Confucian classics for more than two decades but failed the examination, yet he could master the art of literary composition very quickly; he therefore lamented that Confucian learning required much labor but delivered little in return. He later submitted his rhapsody to Wei Shou 魏收 (506–572), who was famous for his literary skill. Because he did not bow to the writer *cum* historian, he was snubbed and ridiculed. Undaunted, Liu went on to show his work to another prominent writer, Xing Shao 邢邵 (496–?), who also humiliated him mercilessly.

Nevertheless, Liu had a high opinion of himself and was fervidly eager to join the officialdom to offer his services. Unfortunately, he never earned the *xiucai* degree in spite of his repeated attempts for more than ten years. For this failure, he wrote "Biography of an Eminent Talent Who Goes Unappreciated" ("Gaocai bu yu zhuan" 高才不遇傳). This apparently autobiographical piece was lost. In 560 and 561 Liu continually submitted memorials to the authorities, but they were deemed impractical and thus not heeded. He compiled the rejected memorials into a book called *Didao* 帝道 [The Way of the emperor], which presumably was also lost, although it has been speculated that the piece was incorporated into the *Liuzi*. Liu was never able to secure an official post although he often dreamed that he was appointed magistrate of Xingjun 興俊 district of Jiaozhou 交州 (near modern Hanoi). He died sometime between 563 and 569 at the age of fifty-two. About two weeks after his death, he reportedly spoke through his young daughter that in the other world he had indeed been appointed to the office about which he had dreamed.

Liu Zhou often bragged about his erudition and unusual talents and had said he would not trade his works being passed down to posterity even for the thousands of chariots of Duke Jing of Qi. Between 562 and 564, he composed a work titled *Jinxiang biyan* 金箱璧言 (Words carved in jade and stored in a golden case) in which he criticized the policies of the central government. Nothing was known about this work, yet one Qing scholar believed it is in fact the *Liuzi* itself, whereas a modern scholar suspected that section 54, titled "Garden of Sayings," which covers various aspects of life, constitutes parts of the *Jinxiang biyan*. Both theories are speculative. What is certain is that the *Liuzi* survives virtually intact today. Liu Zhou's biographies in *Bei Qi shu*, q.v., 44:589–90, and *Bei Shi*, q.v., 81:2729–30, are essentially identical.

Authenticity and textual history

There are four different fragmented manuscripts of the *Liuzi* from the Dunhuang caves, one of which came from pre-Tang times and the rest from the early to middle Tang. The *Liuzi* was first recorded in the bibliographical monographs of the *Jiu Tang shu* (47:2033) and *Xin Tang shu* (59:1534), both in ten *juan*, and ascribed to Liu Xie. It continued to be listed in numerous bibliographical catalogs, official and private alike, from the Song onward until the end of imperial times. Since the Song, the work has been recorded as having fifty sections in two, three, four, five, or ten *juan* in different catalogs, and the order of the sections has not always been identical. The authorship of the *Liuzi* has usually been attributed to Liu Zhou despite its controversy. Some scholars suspect that the received version as we have it today might have been slightly tampered with in the early Tang dynasty.

The *Liuzi* was a fairly popular text in Tang times and was excerpted in Emperor Taizong's *Di fan* 帝範 (Paradigms for emperors), Empress Wu Zetian's *Chen gui* 臣軌 (Models for officials), and Buddhist works. Perhaps the work's popularity inspired Yuan Xiaozheng 袁孝政 to write the first commentary on it. Virtually nothing is known about this commentator except that he appears to have held the position of administrative supervisor (*lushi canjun* 錄事參軍) of Bozhou 播州 (modern Zunyi, Guizhou) during the Tang; the personal names of emperors Taizong and Gaozong were avoided as taboo characters in his commentary. Yuan's commentary is unanimously considered to be of poor quality by traditional and modern scholars alike. Xi Keqian 奚克謙 of the Song dynasty composed two commentaries on the *Liuzi*, with one focusing exclusively on the phonetic glosses. Both were lost, and the commentator is otherwise unknown. However, since the edition of the *Liuzi* in the Daoist Canon contains phonetic glosses and philological annotations, it is suspected that they might in fact have come from Xi's two commentaries as they were not found in Yuan's, which was also included in the canon.

Contents

The *Liuzi*, since its classification in the *Jiu Tang shu* and *Xin Tang shu*, has invariably been listed as a work of "Eclecticism" (*zajia* 雜家) under "Philosophical Writings" in traditional bibliographical catalogs. Chao Gongwu's *Junzhai dushuzhi** (preface dated 1151), 12:517, summed up the work thus: "It talks about how to cultivate the mind and govern the body, but its language is rather conventional and shallow." Wang Yinglin (*Yu hai** 53:23b–24a, p. 1056) said of the *Liuzi*, "It discusses in general terms the essentials of state governance and self-cultivation but incorporates the ideas of the nine philosophical schools (*jiu liu* 九流 [literally, "nine tributaries"]) [of the Warring States period]." These two early synopses capture the philosophical essence of the *Liuzi* quite accurately. Liu was indeed intensely interested in state governance, and he was truly eclectic in his philosophical outlook, not limiting himself to Daoism alone as many scholars would lead us to believe.

Organized in fifty-five topical sections, the *Liuzi* concerns subjects such as self-cultivation, personal destiny, academic learning, social education, military affairs, agricultural concerns, legalistic practices, music, and so on. Running through the entire work is an unmistakably personal, even autobiographical investment. Numerous sections dwell on lack of appreciation, the importance of timely assistance and social connections, the stoic acceptance of fate, and other factors that could contribute to the neglect or rejection of genuine talents. Stylistically, the language of the *Liuzi* is quite unadorned, but it teems with literary parallelisms and historical allusions that reveal Liu's encyclopedic knowledge of a wide variety of topics. These might have been intended precisely to show off his talent. In fact, traditional and modern commentators alike have expended much of their energy in identifying the work's abundant allusions.

The fifty-five sections, despite their subsumption under different *juan* in modern editions of the *Liuzi*, remain the same and are listed in identical order as follows:

1. Qingshen 清神 — Purifying the spirit
2. Fangyu 防慾 — Guarding desires
3. Quqing 去情 — Eradicating emotions
4. Taoguang 韜光 — Concealing the light
5. Chongxue 崇學 — Honoring learning
6. Zhuanxue 專學 — Concentrating on studying
7. Bianyue 辨樂 — Distinguishing music
8. Lüxin 履信 — Keeping promises
9. Sishun 思順 — Remembering compliance
10. Shendu 慎獨 — Watching over solitude
11. Guinong 貴農 — Valuing agriculture
12. Aimin 愛民 — Loving the people
13. Conghua 從化 — Yielding to transformation
14. Fashu 法術 — Norms and art
15. Shangfa 賞罰 — Rewards and punishments
16. Shenming 審名 — Examining names
17. Biming 鄙名 — Disrespecting names
18. Zhiren 知人 — Knowing people
19. Jianxian 薦賢 — Recommending the worthy
20. Yinxian 因顯 — Prominence by virtue of others
21. Tuofu 託附 — Taking advantage of circumstances
22. Xinyin 心隱 — Secrets of the heart
23. Tongse 通塞 — Success and frustration

24.	Yu buyu 遇不遇	Appreciation and lack of appreciation
25.	Mingxiang 命相	Fate and physiognomy
26.	Wangxia 妄瑕	Mistaken shortcomings
27.	Shi cai 適才	Suitable talent
28.	Wen wu 文武	The civil and the martial
29.	Junren 均任	Suitable appointments
30.	Shen yan 慎言	Care with words
31.	Gui yan 貴言	Appreciating words
32.	Shang chan 傷讒	Grieving over slander
33.	Shen xi 慎隙	Being mindful of grudges
34.	Jie ying 戒盈	Guarding against self-conceit
35.	Ming qian 明謙	Explaining receptiveness
36.	Dazhi 大質	Great integrity
37.	Bian shi 辯施	Distinguishing favors
38.	Hexing 和性	Harmonious nature
39.	Shu hao 殊好	Peculiar predilections
40.	Bingshu 兵術	Military arts
41.	Yue wu 閱武	Military inspection
42.	Ming quan 明權	Understanding scaling
43.	Gui su 貴速	Respecting speediness
44.	Guan liang 觀量	Observing one's capacity
45.	Sui shi 隨時	Going along with the times
46.	Fengsu 風俗	Transformative influence and customary practices
47.	Lihai 利害	Gains and losses
48.	Huofu 禍福	Misfortune and fortune
49.	Tan'ai 貪愛	Greed and craving
50.	Leigan 類感	Responses in kind
51.	Zhengshang 正賞	Proper rewarding
52.	Ji tong 激通	Exhortation to success

53.	Xi shi 惜時	Treasuring time
54.	Yan yuan 言苑	Garden of sayings
55.	Jiu liu 九流	The Nine Tributaries

The first four sections, inspired by Daoism, tend to wax philosophical, and the final one is a succinct overview and critique of the nine major philosophical schools of thought of the Warring States period. Of the nine schools, the Daoist was listed first in order. For this reason, it is now unanimously considered a reflection of the author's basic preference for Daoism. Similarities can be found in the author's critique with that expressed in the bibliographical monograph of the *Sui shu*, q.v.; this leads some scholars to think that the author's view might have been consulted, if not adopted, by early Tang historians.

Principal editions

The earliest versions exist in fragmentary manuscripts discovered in Dunhuang. Pelliot 3562 consists of nine complete sections and two fragmentary ones, from the second half of section 4 ("Taoguang") to the beginning of section 14 ("Fashu"). Pelliot 3704 consists of six sections from section 46 ("Fengsu") to section 51 ("Zhengshang"). Pelliot 2546 begins with section 17 ("Biming") and ends with the first half of section 21 ("Tuofu"). Still, there is another fragment copied and published by Luo Zhenyu 羅振玉 (1886–1940) before it disappeared; it begins with the latter half of section 3 ("Quqing") and ends with the former half of section 9 ("Sishun"), with a total of five complete sections and two fragmentary ones.

The earliest printed edition in ten *juan* comes in fragmentary form from the Song; it was authenticated by two respected Qing scholars of textual criticism, Sun Xingyan 孫星衍 (1753–1818) and Huang Pilie 黃丕烈 (1763–1825). The first two *juan* were missing but supplemented with the corresponding parts from a Ming edition, while the remainder was full of lacunae and corrupted graphs. Another complete Song edition survives in a complete Ming reprint. Numerous editions date from the Ming, including the one in the *Daozang* that was completed in 1445. However, it should be noted that the compilation of the *Daozang* began in the reign of the Tang emperor Xuanzong; it is possible that the *Liuzi* was already included in the canon then, and the edition in the Ming Canon could, in some form, be its replica. A virtually complete list and précis of extant versions from premodern times is provided at the beginning of Lin Qitan and Chen Fengjin (*Liuzi jijiao*).

To date, there are only five modern editions, and they do not share a common premodern edition as their base text. Critical notes abound in modern scholarship; most take advantage of the discovery of the Dunhuang fragments. The most authoritative edition is arguably Wang Shumin's (1914–2008) *Liuzi jizheng*. It includes, in three appendices, fragments of the *Liuzi* from other sources; Liu Zhou's biography in the *Bei Qi shu* and *Bei shi*; prefaces and postfaces of Ming, Qing, and modern editions as well as annotated editions; and discussions and reviews by traditional and modern scholars including the *Siku quanshu* review.

Wang's preface, a scholarly study in itself, discusses issues of authorship, textual and philological criticisms, and comments on previous studies (including those listed in the next section). Since the original publication of his study, Wang has twice supplemented it with notes and annotations (see later).

Texts with commentaries and notes

Daozang 道藏. Beijing: Wenwu chubanshe; Shanghai: Shanghai shudian; Tianjin: Tianjin guji chuabanshe, 1988. Vol. 21, pp. 726–81.

Fu Yashu 傅亞庶. *Liuzi jiaoshi* 劉子校釋. Beijing: Zhonghua shuju, 1998. Fu argues for Liu Zhou as the author. He uses a Ming edition (published in either 1563 or 1624) as his base text because it contains, Fu says, fewer errors and is more available to the general reader.

Jiang Jianjun 江建俊. *Xinbian Liuzi xinlun* 新編劉子新論. Taipei: Taiwan guji chuban youxian gongsi, 2001. Jiang follows Wang Shumin in using the Daozang edition as his base text and includes in one of the appendices a chronology of Liu Zhou's life, although the years supplied for his birth and death are purely speculative. This book also contains a bibliography of secondary literature.

Lin Qitan 林其錟 and Chen Fengjin 陳鳳金. *Liuzi jijiao* 劉子集校. Shanghai: Shanghai guji chubanshe, 1985. The husband-and-wife team argues for Liu Xie as the author. They use the 1792 reprint of the Han Wei congshu 漢魏叢書 edition as their base text because they consider it most similar to the Song edition.

Sun Xingyan 孫星衍. *Liuzi*. The only extant but fragmented edition surviving from the Southern Song (1127–1279); authorship attributed to Liu Xie, with Yuan Xiaozheng's commentary. Sun's postface appears at the front. The text is in the Shanghai Library.

Wang Shumin 王叔岷. *Liuzi jizheng* 劉子集證. Zhongyang yanjiuyuan lishi yuyan yanjiusuo zhuankan 中央研究院歷史語言研究所專刊 44. Taipei: Tailian guofeng chubanshe, 1975 reprint (originally published 1961). Wang uses the Daozang as his base text.

Xiang Chu 項楚. *Zengding Liuxi jiaozhu* 增訂劉子校注. Chengdu: Ba Shu shushe, 2008. Xiang argues that Liu Zhou was the author of the Liuzi.

Commentaries and notes without the complete text

Lin Qitan and Chen Fengjin. *Dunhuang yishu Liuzi canjuan jilu* 敦煌遺書劉子殘卷集錄. Shanghai: Shanghai shudian, 1988. Lin and Chen identify the author as Liu Xie.

Lu Wenchao 盧文弨 (1717–1796). *Liu Zhou xinlun jiaozheng* 劉晝新論校正. Included in *Qunshu shibu* 群書拾補, in *Congshu jicheng xinbian**, 237–40. Taipei: Xinwenfeng chuban gongsi, 1984. Lu used Cheng Rong's 程榮 *Han Wei congshu* edition (preface dated 1592) and consulted the *Daozang* edition and

He Yunzhong's 何允中 *Guang Han Wei congshu* 廣漢魏叢書 edition (published between 1573 and 1679).

Luo Zhenyu 羅振玉. *Dunhuangben Liuzi canjuan jiaoji* 敦煌本劉子殘卷校記. Collected in *Luo Xuetang xiansheng quanji chubian* 羅雪堂先生全集初編. Taipei: Wenhua chuban gongsi, 1968. Its coverage begins with the second half of section 4 ("Quqing") and ends with the first half of section 9 ("Sishun") and includes the comments of Luo's friend that compare the variants found in different editions of the *Liuzi*. Recently, the same work was published with two other studies by the same author in Luo Zhenyu, *Baopuzi canjuan jiaoji, Liuzi canjuan jiaoji, Yao-Qin xieben Weimojiejingjie jiaoji* 抱朴子殘卷校記, 劉子殘卷校記, 姚秦寫本維摩詰經解校記. Hangzhou: Xileng yinshe chubanshe, 2005.

Yang Mingzhao 楊明照 (1909–2003). *Liuzi jiaozhu* 劉子校注. Chengdu: Ba Shu shushe, 1988. Yang uses a Ming edition (published in either 1563 or 1624) as base text. The bulk of the book, consisting of critical textual notes and annotations, was originally published in Wenxue nianbao 4 (1938). Two studies of its authorship were added: "Liuzi lihuo," originally published in Wenxue nianbao 3 (1937), and "Zai lun Liuzi de zuozhe," in *Wen shi* 30 (1988): 73–81. Yang argues for Liu Zhou as the author. An expanded, revised version by his student Chen Yingluan 陳應鸞, titled *Zengding Liuzi jiaozhu* 增訂劉子校注, was published by Ba Shu shushe under Yang's name in 2008. It too contains a fragment of the Liuzi recovered from another source; at the book's end, Chen added a useful list of aphorisms that occur in the Liuzi.

Selected studies

Cai Xin 蔡欣. "*Liuzi* wenyi sixiang yanjiu" 劉子文藝思想研究. Master's thesis, Jiangxi Normal University, 2005.

———. "*Liuzi* wenyi fanchou bianxi" 劉子文藝範疇辨析. *Jiaxing xueyuan xuebao* (2007.1): 80–85.

Chen Yingluan 陳應鸞. "*Liuzi* zuozhe bukao" 劉子作者補考. *Wenxue yichan* (2008.3): 31–35.

Chen Zhiping 陳志平. "Lun Sun Xingyan ba Nan Song xiaozi ben Liuzi" 論孫星衍跋南宋小字本劉子. *Guji zhengli yanjiu xuekan* (2006.6): 57–62.

———. "*Liuzi* zuozhe he chuangzuo shijian xinkao" 劉子作者和創作時間新考. *Guji zhengli yanjiu xuekan* (2007.7): 14–18. The author argues that the *Liuzi* was written by someone during the Wei-Jin period.

———. *Liuzi yanjiu* 劉子研究. Changchun: Jilin renmin chubanshe, 2008.

Chen Zhiping and Chen Minghua 陳明華. "Liuzi mingcheng kao" 劉子名稱考. *Huanggang shifan xueyuan xuebao* (2008): 38–43. This article examines the seven different titles the Liuzi was given over time.

Han Yulan 韓玉蘭. "*Liuzi* yu *Yanshi jiaxun* bijiao" 劉子與嚴 (sic) 氏家訓比較. *Qinghai minzu xueyuan xuebao* (1996.4): 114, 115–16. Han takes Liu Xie as the author of the Liuzi.

Kameda Masami 龜田勝見. "Ryūshi shōkō" 劉子小考. In *Tōyō: Hikaku bunka ronshū* 東洋: 比較文化論集, Miyazawa Masayori hakushi koki kinen *bunka ronshū* 宮澤正順博士古稀記念文化論集, ed. Miyazawa Masayori hakushi koki kinen bunka ronshū kankōkai 刊行会, 615–28. Tokyo: Seishi shuppan, 2004.

———. "Ryūshi to *Ryū Chū*" 劉子と劉晝. In *Sankyō kōshō ronsō* 三教交涉論叢, ed. Mugitani Kunio 麥谷邦夫, 437–60. Kyōto daigaku jinbun kagaku kenkyūjo kenkyū hōkoku 京都大學人文科學研究所研究報告. Kyoto: Kyōto daigaku jinbun kagaku kenkyūjo, 2010.

Li Zhenglin 李政林. "Liuzi zuozhe wei Liu Xie zhi shuo shangque" 劉子作者為劉勰之說商榷. *Nanchang daxue xuebao* (1999): 131–34. Li, a Korean scholar, argues for Liu Zhou being the author of the Liuzi.

Lin Qitan and Chen Fengjin. "Wujuanben Liuzi he Riben gudai xuezhe de lunshu" 五卷本劉子和日本古代學者的論述. *Wenxian* (1989.4): 269–72.

Yamazaki Makoto 山崎誠. "Wakokubon 'Ryūshi' kō—Nihonrettō ni denraiseru kango bunken 和刻本劉子攷—日本列島に伝来せる漢語文献. *Kokugo kokubun* (2006.9): 1–13.

Yang Weizhong 楊衛中. *Liuzi yanjiu* 劉子研究. Taipei: Yongwen chubanshe, 1985.

Yu Jiaxi 余嘉錫. "Liuzi shijuan bianzheng" 劉子十卷辯證. In *Siku tiyao bianzheng* 四庫提要辯證, 827–40. Taipei: Yiwen yinshuguan, 1985.

Translation

Jiang Jianjun. *Xinbian Liuzi xinlun* 新編劉子新論. Taipei: Taiwan guji chuban youxian gongsi, 2001.

Lo Yuet Keung

Lu Ji ji 陸機集

Introduction

The collection of Lu Ji (261–303), styled Shiheng 士衡, *hao* Pingyuan 平原, has also appeared as *Lu Shiheng ji*, *Lu Shiheng wenji*, *Lu Pingyuan ji*, and as one half of the *Er jun ji* 二俊集 (Collections of the two paragons), with that of his younger brother Lu Yun 雲.

Lu Ji was an outstanding writer and scholar of the Western Jin. His most important work is the great "Wen fu" 文賦 (Rhapsody on writing), one of the classic statements of Chinese literary theory. The "Wen fu" is an intricate work that examines the purposes, techniques, and genres of writing, and it is itself composed in rich parallel prose, a style that mirrors and exemplifies its arguments. It has been translated into Western languages over a dozen times, and its dazzling brilliance has perhaps overshadowed the craft of Lu's other writings (for instance, the *Indiana Companion* entry on Lu is devoted exclusively to this work). It should be seen in the context of Lu's entire oeuvre, where he applies the principles set forth in the "Wen fu."

Some twenty-five rhapsodies are preserved in Lu Ji's collection, along with fragments of over twenty more. He was also a prolific writer of *yuefu* and of imitation poems, most of which were modeled on poems included in the "Nineteen Old Poems." He was notably fond of certain specialized genres, as evident in his "Bai nian ge" 百年歌 (Centenarial song), containing ten stanzas of heptasyllabic verse, each stanza of which describes a decade of a man's life. He also wrote fifty pieces of rhymed parallel prose in the "linked pearls" form. A good example of Lu's prose style is the satirical "Hao shi fu" 豪士賦 (Rhapsody on distinguished gentlemen), whose lengthy preface, though not the *fu* itself, was included in the *Wen xuan*, q.v.

Lu Ji came from a prominent family of the southern Wu state, whose native place was Wu 吳 (modern Suzhou). Both his grandfather Lu Xun 遜 (183–245) and father, Lu Kang 抗 (226–274), led armies of Wu as chancellor and commander-in-chief, respectively. Lu Ji himself, along with Lu Yun and their older brothers, fought in defense of Wu, and two of the brothers died in battle. The Jin conquest was a devastating blow, and Lu Ji and Lu Yun spent the decade of the Taikang era (280–289) at their family estate in Huating 華亭 (modern Songjiang 松江 County, Shanghai; see Cao Daoheng, "Lu Ji de jiguan wenti"). According to Du Fu's poem

"Zui ge xing" 醉歌行, Lu Ji composed the "Wen fu" at the age of twenty, or precisely in 280, at the time of the Jin conquest. Jiang Liangfu (*Lu Pingyuan nianpu*) accepts this dating, but other scholars such as Chen Shih-hsiang (*Essay on Literature*) have contested it, dating the rhapsody toward the end of Lu Ji's life. Around 288, Lu Ji composed the "Bian wang lun" 辯亡論 (Disquisition explaining the fall), reflecting on the fall of Wu. After he and Lu Yun were summoned to Luoyang in 289, they were immediately recognized as promising talents. Zhang Hua 張華 (232–300) remarked that while most people were concerned about having too little talent, Lu Ji might have too much (quoted in Lu's biography, *Jin shu*, q.v., 54:1480, and in the commentary to the *Shishuo xinyu*, q.v., 4/84).

Lu Ji's several positions in Luoyang included editorial director in the Secretariat, where he was engaged in producing several historical works, including the *Huidi qiju zhu* 惠帝起居注 (Record of the daily activities of Emperor Hui). During the following decade, Lu was part of a coterie of writers and courtiers surrounding the wealthy patron Jia Mi 賈謐 (d. 300). Political struggles lead to the deaths of Jia Mi and Zhang Hua in 300, and in that year Lu Ji composed the "Tan shi fu" 歎逝賦 (Rhapsody on lamenting the departed), lamenting the deaths of these and other friends. At the end of Lu's life he was embroiled in the Insurrection of the Eight Princes, after he joined the staff of Sima Ying 司馬穎 (279–306), Prince of Chengdu, who appointed him administrator of Pingyuan 平原. He was appointed commander-in-chief of the vanguard, but, after being defeated in a campaign against Sima Yi 乂 (d. 303), he was sentenced to death along with his two sons and brother Lu Yun.

Contents

The most widely available edition is the *Lu Shiheng wenji* included in the *Sibu congkan**, which was based on the edition of Xu Minzhan 徐民瞻 (fl. 1200). It is essentially a compilation of Lu Ji's works that survived in other sources, arranged in ten *juan*. One notable feature is that *shi* poetry occupies only a single *juan*:

1–4. Rhapsodies

5. Lyric poems

6. Ancient-style poems (*nigu* 擬古) and *yuefu* poems

7. *Yuefu* poems and a centenarial song

8. Linked pearls and sevens compositions (*qi* 七)

9. Miscellaneous prose

10. Opinion, disquisitions, and a funerary inscription

Most other editions follow the same organization, with the principal exception of the *Lu Pingyuan ji* in two *juan* in Zhang Pu's (1602–1641) *Han Wei Liuchao baisan jia ji*, q.v., the first *juan* being devoted to prose pieces and the second to poetry.

Authenticity and transmission of the text

The Lu brothers were extremely prolific writers, and Ge Hong in the *Baopuzi*, q.v., mentions that the combined collection of Lu Ji and Lu Yun had over one hundred *juan* (cited in *Beitang shuchao*, q.v., Wenhai chubanshe edition, 100:3a). The bibliographic monograph of *Sui shu*, q.v., 35:1063, lists a collection in fourteen *juan* but also mentions that the collection had forty-seven *juan* in the Liang (combined with a table of contents in one *juan* and Lu Ji's "linked pearls" compositions in one *juan*, listed separately, there would be forty-nine *juan* in total). The *Jiu Tang shu* (47:2060) and *Xin Tang shu* (60:1584) bibliographies both list his collection in fifteen *juan*.

By the Song dynasty the surviving collections of Lu's works had only ten *juan*, according to the *Junzhai dushu zhi**, the *Zhizhai shulu jieti**, and the *Song shi* bibliography. Extant collections are all based on the Song dynasty collection of Xu Minzhan, who compiled the *Lu Shiheng wenji* together with Lu Yun's under the title *Er jun ji*, with ten *juan* allotted to each brother. Because of the problems in transmission, many works that were not included in the *Wen xuan* have textual problems and errors; Lu Ji's works are extremely well represented in the *Wen xuan*, so this is not as great a problem as it first appears. He is one of the best represented writers in the anthology, with two rhapsodies, fifty-two *shi* pieces, and seven works in other genres. Nearly all the pieces in Lu's collection come from the *Wen xuan* or *Yiwen leiju*, q.v., along with the *Chuxue ji*, q.v., *Yutai xinyong*, q.v., and his *Jin shu* biography. The major exceptions are in the seventh *juan*, which contains some *yuefu* pieces whose source is unclear.

Several pieces in the *Lu Shiheng wenji* were mistakenly attributed to Lu Ji. Jin Taosheng (*Lu Ji ji*) omits the fragmentary "Wu chengxiang Jiangling hou Lu gong lei" 吳丞相江陵侯陸公誄 (an elegy for his grandfather Lu Xun) from *juan* 9, since it is included in its entirety in Lu Yun's collection. The confusion of attribution between the two brothers could occur quite easily. A similar case is that of the two encomiums "Kongzi zan" 孔子贊 and "Wangzi Qiao zan" 王子喬贊, included in *juan* 9 of Lu Ji's collection, but also forming part of the series of "Deng xia song" 登遐頌 by Lu Yun. Also, the *yuefu* "Beizai xing" 悲哉行 from *juan* 7 may not be authentic, since it is also included in Xie Lingyun's 謝靈運 collection. The final piece in the collection, "Jin pingxi jiangjun xiaohou Zhou Chu bei" 晉平西將軍孝侯周處碑, refers to events as late as the year 319, but scholars such as Jiang Liangfu (*Lu Pingyuan nianpu*) and Liu Yunhao (*Lu Shiheng wenji jiaozhu*) have concluded that the main body of the inscription is authentic.

Principal editions

The *Lu Shiheng ji* in the *Congshu jicheng chubian** is followed by one *juan* of textual notes and fragmentary pieces (*zhaji* 札記). Jin Taosheng's *Lu Ji ji* has the same ten *juan* supplemented by three additional *juan* collecting works not preserved in the original *Lu Shiheng wenji*. Liu Yunhao's *Lu Shiheng wenji jiaozhu* similarly has the original ten *juan* followed by a supplemental section. He includes a number of pieces omitted in previous editions, such as the *Luoyang ji* 洛陽記 (Record of Luoyang).

Lu Shiheng wenji. Ten *juan*, in *Jin erjun wenji*. Originally compiled by Xu Minzhan in 1200. Printed by Lu Yuanda 陸元大 in 1519. This is the base text of all modern editions and is contained in the *Sibu congkan*.

Lu Pingyuan ji. Two *juan*, in *Han Wei Liuchao baisan mingjia ji*. Compiled by Zhang Pu.

Lu Shiheng ji. Ten *juan* plus one supplementary *juan* of notes and collected fragments, in *Congshu jicheng xinbian**, vol. 59. This is a facsimile of the *Xiao wanjuanlou congshu* 小萬卷樓叢書 edition collated by Qian Peiming 錢培名 in 1852.

Lu Ji ji. In *Quan shanggu Sandai Qin Han Sanguo Liuchao wen*, q.v., "Quan Jin wen," *juan* 96–99. Compiled by Yan Kejun (1762–1843).

Jin Taosheng 金濤聲, ed. *Lu Ji ji*. Beijing: Zhonghua shuju, 1957 (rpt., 1982).

Texts with commentary and notes

Hao Liquan 郝立權, ed. *Lu Shiheng shi zhu* 陸士衡詩注. Beijing: Renmin wenxue chubanshe, 1958.

Liu Yunhao 劉運好, ed. *Lu Shiheng wenji jiaozhu* 陸士衡文集校注. Nanjing: Fenghuang chubanshe, 2007. A thoroughly annotated edition in two volumes.

Zhang Shaokang 張少康, ed. *Wen fu ji shi* 文賦集釋. Beijing: Renmin wenxue chubanshe, 2002 (rpt., 2006).

Selected studies

Cao Daoheng 曹道衡. "Lu Ji de jiguan wenti" 陸機的籍貫問題. In *Zhonggu wenxueshi lunwen ji xubian* 中古文學史論文集續編, 380–81. Taipei: Wenjin chubanshe, 1994.

———. "Lu Ji de sixiang ji qi shige" 陸機的思想及其詩歌. *Zhongguo shehui kexue yuan yanjiushengyuan xuebao* (1996.1): 60–66.

Chen Enliang 陳恩良. *Lu Ji wenxue yanjiu* 陸機文學研究. Hong Kong: Guanghua shuju, 1969.

Chen, Shih-hsiang. *Essay on Literature*. Portland, ME: Anthoensen Press, 1953.

Gu Nong 顧農. "Lu Ji shengping zhuzuo kaobian santi" 陸機生平著作考辯三題. *Qinghua daxue xuebao* 20.4 (2005): 60–67.

Jiang Liangfu 姜亮夫. *Lu Pingyuan nianpu* 陸平原年譜. Shanghai: Shanghai guji chubanshe, 1957.

Knechtges, David R. "Han and Six Dynasties Parallel Prose." *Renditions* 33 and 34 (1990): 78–101. Includes translation of the "Bian wang lun."

———. "Sweet-Peel Orange or Southern Gold? Regional Identity in Western Jin Literature." In *Studies in Early Medieval Chinese Literature and Cultural History in Honor of Richard B. Mather and Donald Holzman*, ed. Paul W. Kroll and David R. Knechtges, 27–80. Provo, UT: T'ang Studies Society, 2003.

Kōzen Hiroshi 興膳宏. *Han Gaku Riku Ki* 潘岳陸機. Tokyo: Chikuma shobō, 1973.
Lai, Chiu-mi. "River and Ocean: The Third Century Verse of Pan Yue and Lu Ji." Ph.D. diss., University of Washington, 1990.
———. "The Craft of Original Imitation: Lu Ji's Imitations of Han Old Poems." In *Studies in Early Medieval Chinese Literature and Cultural History in Honor of Richard B. Mather and Donald Holzman*, 117–48.
Satō Toshiyuki 佐藤利行. *Sei Shin bungaku kenkyū: Riku Ki o chūshin to shite* 西晉文學研究: 陸機を中心として. Tokyo: Hakuteisha, 1995. Chinese trans.: Zhou Yanliang 周延良. *Xi Jin wenxue yanjiu* 西晉文學研究. Beijing: Zhongguo shehui kexue chubanshe, 2004.
Takahashi Kazumi 高橋和已. "Riku Ki no denki to sono bungaku" 陸機の傳記とその文學. *Chūgoku bungaku hō* 11 (1959): 1–57; 12 (1960): 49–84.
Yu Shiling 俞士玲. "Lu Yun 'Deng xia song' kaoshi" 陸雲登遐頌考釋. *Guji zhengli yanjiu xuekan* 4 (July 2005): 51–58.
———. *Lu Ji Lu Yun nianpu* 陸機陸雲年譜. Beijing: Renmin wenxue chubanshe, 2009.

Translations

English

Frodsham, J. D., with the collaboration of Ch'eng Hsi. *An Anthology of Chinese Verse: Han Wei Chin and the Northern and Southern Dynasties*. London: Oxford University Press, 1967. Pp. 89–91.

Japanese

Satō Toshiyuki 佐藤利行. *Riku Shikō shishū* 陸士衡詩集. Tokyo: Hakuteisha, 2001.

Modern Chinese

Wang Dehua 王德華, trans. and comm. *Xinyi Lu Ji shiwen ji* 新譯陸機詩文集. Taipei: Sanmin shuju, 2006.

Nicholas Morrow Williams

Lu Yun ji 陸雲集

Introduction

Lu Yun, styled Shilong 士龍 (262–303), was from a gentry family of south China that resided in Wu district (Wu xian 吳縣) in Wu commandery (modern Suzhou, Jiangsu Province). He was able to write poetry at an early age. Although his writings were conventionally said to be inferior to those of his elder brother Lu Ji 機 (261–303), his ability in debating and editing was superior. Lu Yun's personality was noted for the traits of gentleness, refinement, and delicacy. The fourth-century historian Zhang Yin 張隱 claimed, "Lu Yun's nature was magnanimous and placid, and he was admired by other gentlemen and friends."

The two brothers were very close and continually exchanged writings and gave advice to each other. In 274, after their father died, they were separated for the first time when Lu Ji assumed command of their father's army in Jingzhou 荊州 (modern Hubei Province). After the Wu kingdom fell in 280, Lu Yun and other gentry families were moved by the Jin emperor to Shouyang (Shanxi Province). Lu Yun's first recorded set of poems in response to Lu Ji was written in 281 before they retreated successively to the family estate in Huating 華亭 (modern Songjiang 松江 County, Shanghai). In late 289 or early 290, Lu Yun went to Luoyang to start his political service at the Jin court. He was inevitably trapped in the factional struggles among the princes of the royal household. After Lu Ji's army was defeated in a campaign against Sima Yi 司馬乂 (d. 303), Yun was accused of treason and executed by the order of Sima Ying 穎 (d. 307) on 8 November 303. Shortly before his execution, he completed his last work, the "Nanzheng fu" 南征賦 (Rhapsody on the southern expedition).

Contents

The predominant types of writing in the collection are prose letters and poems of "presentation and response" (*zengda* 贈答). These works reflect the importance of social communications and literary interactions during the Six Dynasties period. Lu Yun's thirty-five letters to Lu Ji are particularly worth mentioning because they reflect Lu Yun's literary values of clarity, brevity, and naturalness that ran counter to the fashion of his time. He opposed complexity and verbosity, and he wished to promote lucid styles of writing that focused upon feelings. Such views made a significant contribution to Chinese literary theory and criticism, and they enable us to better understand issues prior to the publication in the early sixth century of the *Shi pin*, q.v., and *Wenxin diaolong*, q.v. In the latter work, Liu Xie (ca. 465–ca. 522) noted Lu Yun's views on clarity and brevity, and in the section titled "Dingshi" 定勢 (Determination of momentum), he quoted Lu Yun's remarks about *qing* 情 (emotion).

The modern *Lu Yun ji* edited by Huang Kui 黃葵 (Beijing: Zhonghua shuju, 1988) contains twenty-nine verses (including fragments), some of which are poetic suites, "seven" rhapsodies, and other literary genres. It is divided into ten *juan*, as follows:

1. Rhapsody and admonition
2–3. Lyric poetry in four-character lines
4. Lyric poetry in five-character lines
5. Dirge
6. Eulogy, encomium, and ridicule (*chao* 嘲)
7. Elegy
8. Letter, personal
9. Communication
10. Collected letters (*shuji* 書集)

Juan 8 contains his letters to Lu Ji, and *juan* 10 his letters to friends. *Juan* 9 contains six communications, most likely dating from the year 296, that were written to admonish the Prince of Wu, Sima Yan 司馬晏 (d. 310), while Lu Yun served on his staff.

Transmission and early history of the text

Lu Yun's biography in *Jin shu*, q.v., 54:1481–86, notes that he wrote 349 literary works. The *Siku quanshu zongmu tiyao** catalog gives the approximation of 240-odd pieces extant (29:3106). The *Lu Yun ji* was first recorded in the bibliographic monograph of the *Sui shu*, q.v., as containing twelve *juan* (35:1063), and the *Tong zhi** of the Song dynasty also listed twelve *juan* (69:816b). The *Xin Tang shu* listed only ten *juan* (60:5a), and the *Chongwen zongmu** listed only eight (5:15a; p. 717).

Of Lu Yun's five "presentation and response" verses collected into the *Wen xuan*, q.v., one is a formal, four-syllable poem titled "Da jiangjun yanhui beiming zuo cishi" 大將軍宴會被命作此詩 (Poem composed by the order of the general-in-chief for his banquet) in *juan* 20. His other four verses in the anthology are pentasyllabic and contained in *juan* 25. These include a pair of verses erroneously titled "Wei Gu Yanxian zeng fu er shou" 為顧彥先贈婦二首 (Two poems written on behalf of Gu Yanxian for his wife). A note by Li Shan 李善 (d. 689) points out that the verses are actually written as responses from the wife to her husband. In the

Yutai xinyong, q.v., *juan* 3, the two poems appear within a set of exchanged verses reflecting the voices of both husband and wife and are titled "Wei Gu Yanxian zeng fu wangfan si shou" 為顧彥先贈婦往返四首. Lu Yun's other pentasyllabic poems in the *Wen xuan* are "Da xiong Ji" 答兄機 (In reply to elder brother Ji) and "Da Zhang Shiran" 答張士然 (In reply to Zhang Shiran).

Principal editions

The Song dynasty *Lu Shilong wenji* 陸士龍文集, compiled with a preface dated 1200 by Xu Minzhan 徐民瞻, provided the basis for modern editions. Xu's collection of Lu Yun's works was part of his *Jin erjun wenji* 晉二俊文集 (Collected literary works of the two talents of the Jin dynasty), which contained ten *juan* for each of the two brothers, Yun and Ji. A postscript was written by a Xiang Yuanbian 項元汴. In a later postscript, dated 1859, the Qing scholar Weng Tongshu 翁同書 wrote that the *Jin erjun wenji* was collected into the *Zhibuzuzhai congshu* 知不足齋叢書 (comp. ca. 1776) by Bao Tingbo 鮑廷博 (1728–1814). It was later edited by Zhao Huiyu 趙懷玉 (1747–1824) in 1786 and was known as the "duplicated Song edition" (Ying Song ben 影宋本). In 1794, Lu Wenchao 盧文弨 (1717–1796) and Yan Yuanzhao 嚴元照 (1783–1817) finalized the edition.

A Ming edition of the *Jin erjun wenji* prepared by Lu Yuanda 陸元大 was based on a Song edition (probably that of Xu Minzhan) that was in the possession of the family of Du Mu 都穆 (1456–1525). Du Mu wrote a postscript dated 1519, and this edition was reproduced in the *Sibu congkan**. A second Ming edition, titled *Lu Qinghe ji* 陸清河集 (The collected works of Lu Qinghe), was included in Zhang Pu's (1602–1641) *Han Wei Liuchao baisanjia ji*, q.v. The epithet "Qinghe" in the title of the collection was from Lu Yun's appointment as royal administrator of Qinghe (Hebei Province), conferred on him by Sima Ying in 302.

The *Sibu beiyao** edition is a copy of the version in the *Han Wei Liuchao Ershi mingjia ji**, edited by Wang Shixian (dates unknown) of the Ming dynasty. It has also been reprinted in *Siku quanshu cunmu congshu buban** 27:571–641. The modern *Lu Yun ji* that was edited by Huang Kui provides an introduction to Lu Yun's life and the extant editions of his works. Appendices include a collection of texts of his biography from various sources, prefaces and postscripts of the Song, Ming, and Qing editions, and a review of these by the editors of the *Siku quanshu*.

Yan Kejun (1762–1843) included Lu Yun's fifty-four prose pieces in his *Quan shanggu Sandai Qin Han Sanguo Liuchao wen*, q.v., "Quan Jin wen," *juan* 100–104. Lu Qinli (1911–1973) collected Lu Yun's thirty-one poems in his *Xian Qin Han Wei Jin Nanbeichao shi**, "Jin shi," 6:697–719. Among the poems that survive as fragments, "Zeng Sun Xianshi shi" 贈孫顯世詩 and "Furong shi" 芙蓉詩 are not in Huang Kui's edition.

Selected studies

Cao Daoheng 曹道衡. "Shi lun Lu Ji, Lu Yun de 'Wei Gu Yanxian zengfu'" 試論陸機, 陸雲的為顧彥先贈婦. *Hebei shiyuan xuebao* (March 1989): 81–86. Rpt. in

Zhonggu wenxue shi lunwen ji xubian 中古文學史論文集續編, 65–76. Taipei: Wenjin chubanshe, 1984.

Cao Daoheng and Shen Yucheng 沈玉成. "*Jin shu* xu Lu Yun wei Zhou Jun congshi shici" 晉書敘陸雲為周浚從事失次 and "Lu Ji, Lu Yun xiongdi zengda shi shishou" 陸機, 陸雲兄弟贈答詩十首. In *Zhonggu wenxue shiliao congkao* 中古文學史料叢考, 119, 131–33. Beijing: Zhonghua shuju, 2003.

Dai Yan 戴燕. "Lu Yun de 'yongsi kunren' ji qi ta" 陸雲的'用思困人'及其他. *Chūgoku bungaku hō* 52 (1996): 23–36.

Hasegawa Shigenari 長谷川滋成. "Rikuchō bunjin den: Riku Ki, Riku Un (*Shin sho*)" 六朝文人傳: 陸機, 陸雲 (晉書). *Chūgoku chūsei bungaku kenkyū* 13 (1978): 35–72.

Jiang Jianyun 姜劍雲. "Lun Lu Yun 'Wen gui qingsheng' de chuangzuo sixiang" 論陸雲文貴清省的創作思想. *Shanghai shifan daxue xuebao, Zhexue shehui kexueban* 31.4 (2002): 94–98.

Kamatani Takeshi 釜谷武志. "Riku Un 'Ani e no shokan,' sono bungaku ron kōsatsu" 陸雲兄への書簡, その文學論考察. *Chūgoku bungaku hō* 28 (1977): 1–31.

Lin Fenfang 林芬芳. *Lu Yun ji qi zuopin yanjiu* 陸雲及其作品研究. Taipei: Wenjin chubanshe, 1997.

Mei Jialing 梅家玲. "Er Lu zengda shi zhong de ziwo shehui yu wenxue chuantong" 二陸贈答詩中的自我社會與文學傳統. In *Han Wei Liuchao wenxue xinlun: Nidai yu zengda pian* 漢魏六朝文學新論: 擬代與贈答篇, 235–94. Taipei: Liren shuju, 1997.

Satō Toshiyuki 佐藤利行. "Ni Riku no bunshō kan" 二陸の文章觀. *Nihon Chūgoku gakkaihō* 37 (1985): 75–88.

———. *Riku Un kenkyū* 陸雲研究. Tokyo: Hakuteisha, 1990.

Ueki Hisayuki 植木久行. "Rikuchō bunjin no besshū no ikkeitai—Riku Un shū no shoshigaku teki kōsatsu" 六朝文人の別集の一形態—陸雲集 の書誌學的考察. *Nihon Chūgoku gakkaihō* 29 (1977): 76–90.

———. "Sohan *Riku Un shū* ni tsuite" 宋版陸雲集について. *Kodai kenkyū* 8 (1977): 76–81.

Wang Yongping 王永平. "Lun Lu Ji, Lu Yun xiongdi zhi si" 論陸機, 陸雲兄弟之死. *Nanjing Xiaozhuang xueyuan xuebao* 18.3 (September 2002): 18–26.

Wu, Sujane. "The Biography of Lu Yun (262–303) in *Jin shu* 54." *Early Medieval China* 7 (2001): 1–38.

Xiao Huarong 蕭華榮. "Lu Yun 'qingsheng' de meixue guan" 陸雲'清省'的美學觀. *Wen shi zhe* (1982.1): 41–43.

Translations

English

Birrell, Anne, trans. *New Songs from a Jade Terrace: An Anthology of Early Chinese Love Poetry*. London: George Allen and Unwin, 1982. Pp. 94–95.

Wu, Fusheng. "Praising a Ruler at a Dangerous Time: Two Poems by Lu Yun for Sima Ying." *Early Medieval China* 16 (2010): 51–66.

Wu, Sujane. "Clarity, Brevity, and Naturalness: Lu Yun and His Works." Ph.D. diss., University of Wisconsin-Madison, 2001. Selections of poems, rhapsodies, and letters.

———. "The Last Word? Lu Yun's 'Nanzheng fu.'" *Early Medieval China* 17 (2011): 2–21.

Watson, Burton. *Chinese Lyricism: Shih Poetry from the Second to the Twelfth Century*. New York: Columbia University Press, 1971. Pp. 95–96.

Japanese

Satō Toshiyuki. *Riku Un kenkyū* 陸雲研究. Tokyo: Hakuteisha, 1990. Translation of the letters to Lu Ji.

Sujane Wu

Luoyang qielan ji 洛陽伽藍記

Introduction

The *Luoyang qielan ji* (Record of Buddhist monasteries in Luoyang) by Yang Xuanzhi 楊/羊/陽衒之 (fl. early sixth century) grew out of Yang Xuanzhi's 547 visit to Luoyang, a city lying in ruins in the wake of the civil war that split the Northern Wei into two rival states. With nostalgia, Yang, who had been a low-ranking official at the Northern Wei court, retold the story of Luoyang's Buddhist community that rose and fell with the fate of the city, which had served as the capital of the Northern Wei from 494 to 534. Yang's motive to write this book was twofold: to preserve the memory of the Buddhist monasteries and the city that hosted them before they sank into oblivion, and to tell a cautionary tale against the hubris of a Buddhist community that, under the patronage of the nobility, set up extravagant monastic structures and encroached on the common masses.

Contents

The book is divided into five chapters:

Chapter 1: Inner city

Chapter 2: Eastern suburb

Chapter 3: Southern suburb

Chapter 4: Western suburb

Chapter 5: Northern suburb

The decision by Emperor Xiaowen to relocate the capital to Luoyang was made in late 493. The architects Li Chong 李沖 (450–498) and Dong Jue 董爵 were then ordered to build a new city (later known as Northern Wei Luoyang) on the old site. In the tenth month of 494, Xiaowen bid farewell to his palace in the old capital Pingcheng 平城 and personally escorted the spirit tablets of the dynastic ancestors to Luoyang. Thus, 494 can be regarded as the starting date of Luoyang as the Northern Wei capital (*Weishu*, q.v., 7B.173, 175).

Of a total of 1,367 Buddhist monasteries in and around the city, Yang selects for coverage forty major ones and more than forty medium and small ones, with particular attention to their founding, locations, structures (such as pagodas and pavilions), scenic spots (such as ponds and woods), and sculptures and paintings.

Between the entries on the monasteries, which seem to function as the matrix of the book, are interspersed a host of additional related or unrelated accounts, including descriptions of city landmarks (such as residential wards, markets, mansions, bridges, and official buildings), biographical sketches, records of domestic and foreign social customs, narratives of palace intrigues, miracle tales, and ghost stories. Chapter 5 contains a long travelogue (see later), which is an oddity even by the lax organizational standards of the book. Following an age-old historiographical tradition, the text is interlaced with poems and stelae inscriptions. Chapter 2 even records the rhapsody "Shan fu" 山賦 (Fan Xiangyong, *Luoyang qielan ji jiaozhu*, 100). So, this book can be read at multiple levels: as a general account of the Buddhist monastic community in Luoyang, as an urban history, as a political history of the late Northern Wei that complements the standard histories (especially the *Wei shu* and *Bei shi*, q.v.), as a social history, and as a source of literature.

Of special interest to historians are the racy accounts of such major historical figures as Erzhu Rong 爾朱榮 (493–530) and Emperor Xiaozhuang (528–530), and on key events such as the Heyin Incident (*Heyin zhi bian* 河陰之變; 528). But the section that has garnered most scholarly attention in the West is the travelogue, a detailed account of Song Yun's 宋雲 and Huisheng's 惠生 journey to the Western Regions from 518 to 522, which took them as far west as present-day Afghanistan and Pakistan and preserves precious information on a number of Central Asian states.

Textual transmission

Initially, the book was composed of two distinct parts: the main text and the author's commentary. The distinction was maintained during the Tang (*Shi tong** 5:136). In the post-Tang period, the textual history of the book became murky, and no Song or Yuan edition has survived. The earliest edition extant dates back only to the middle Ming: the Ruyintang 如隐堂 edition. Later reproduced in the *Sibu congkan**, it is considered the best early edition. Another Ming edition of a different textual ancestry is the *Gujin yishi* 古今逸史 edition produced by Wu Guan 吳琯.

Principal editions

The Ming editions, unlike their predecessors, conflate the text with the commentary. In modern times, efforts were made by Wu Ruozhun 吳若準 (Qing) in his *Luoyang qielan ji jizheng* 洛陽伽藍記集證 (*Sibu beiyao** edition) and Tang Yan 唐晏 (early twentieth century) in his *Luoyang qielan ji gouchen* 洛陽伽藍記鉤沈 (*Longxi jingshe congshu* 龍谿精舍叢書 edition) to restore the commentary following the example of Quan Zuwang 全祖望 in his textual research of the *Shuijing zhu*, q.v. However, the restored textual arrangements are not widely accepted by academe. Zhang Zongxiang 張宗祥, for example, in his *Luoyang qielan ji hejiao* 洛陽伽藍記合校 (Beijing: Shangwu yinshuguan, 1930), makes a convincing case against them. More recently, another effort at textual rearrangement was made by Yang Yong 楊勇 in his *Luoyang qielan ji jiaojian* 洛陽伽藍記校箋 (Taipei: Zhengwen shuju, 1982).

In addition, there are more than a dozen editions, the more accessible of which include those in the *Siku quanshu** and *Taishō shinshū Daizōkyō** no. 2092 (51:999–1022).

Editions with commentaries

Fan Xiangyong 范祥雍. *Luoyang qielan ji jiaozhu* 洛陽伽藍記校注. Shanghai: Shanghai guji chubanshe, 1958.

Xu Gaoruan 徐高阮. *Luoyang qielan ji chongkanben* 洛陽伽藍記重刊本. Nangang: Zhongyang yanjiuyuan lishi yuyan yanjiusuo, 1960.

Yang Yong 楊勇. *Luoyang qielan ji jiaojian* 洛陽伽藍記校箋. Taipei: Zhengwen shuju, 1982.

Zhou Yannian 周延年. *Luoyang qielan ji zhu* 洛陽伽藍記注. Wanjie Studio (Wanjie zhai 萬潔齋) edition, 1937.

Zhou Zumo 周祖謨. *Luoyang qielan ji jiaoshi* 洛陽伽藍記校釋. Beijing: Kexue chubanshe, 1958.

The first annotated version was Zhou Yannian's *Luoyang qielan ji zhu*, published in 1937. In 1958, two annotated editions were published in mainland China: Fan Xiangyong's *Luoyang qielan ji jiaozhu* and Zhou Zumo's *Luoyang qielan ji jiaoshi*. While both are major academic achievements by top textual scholars, Fan's commentary is more substantial. In 1960, Xu Gaoran 徐高阮 published his annotated version in Taiwan. The Xu edition is known for its meticulous textual criticism.

Selected studies

Jenner, W. J. F. "*Lo-yang ch'ieh-lan chi.*" In *The Indiana Companion to Traditional Chinese Literature*, ed. William Nienhauser Jr., 597–98. Bloomington: Indiana University Press, 1986.

Lai, Whalen. "Society and the Sacred in the Secular City: Temple Legends of the Lo-yang *ch'ieh-lan-chi*. In *State and Society in Early Medieval China*, ed. Albert E. Dien, 229–68. Hong Kong: Hong Kong University Press; Stanford, CA: Stanford University Press, 1990.

Lin Jinshi. 林晉士. *Luoyang qielan ji zhi wenxue yanjiu* 洛陽伽藍記之文學研究. In *Zhongguuo fojiao xueshu lundian* 中國佛教學術論典, 108, 119–488. Kaohsiung, Taiwan: Foguang wenjiao jijinhui, 2004.

Wang Meixiu 王美秀. *Lishi, kongjian, shenfen: Luoyang qielan ji de wenhua lunshu* 歷史, 空間, 身份: 洛陽伽藍記的文化論述. Taipei: Liren shuju, 2007.

Xiao Hong 蕭紅. *Luoyang qielan ji jufa yanjiu* 洛陽伽藍記句法研究. In *Zhongguo Fojiao xueshu lundian* 中國佛教學術論典, 63:241–459. Kaohsiung, Taiwan: Foguang wenjiao jijinhui, 2002.

Ye Yongheng 葉永恆 (Yip, Wing-hang Eric). "Cong *Luoyang qielan ji* yanjiu Bei Wei houqi (A.D. 493–534) de zhengzhi, shehui, jingji yu fojiao" 從洛陽伽藍

記研究北魏後期 (A.D. 493–534) 的政治, 社會, 經濟與佛教. Master's thesis, University of Hong Kong, 1992.

Zdun, Genowefa. *Matériaux pour l'étude de la culture chinoise du Moyen Age: Le Lo-yang k'ie-lan ki*. Warsaw: Editions scientifiques de Pologne, Varsovie, 1982.

Translations

English

Beal, Samuel, trans. *Travels of Fah-Hian and Sung-Yun: Buddhist Pilgrims, from China to India (400 A.D. and 518 A.D.)*. A translation of the travelogue in chapter 5 of the *Luoyang qielan ji* is included. London: Susil Gupta, 1964.

Jenner, W. J. F. *Memories of Loyang: Yang Hsüan-chih and the Lost Capital (493–534)*. Oxford: Clarendon Press; New York: Oxford University Press, 1981.

Wang, Yi-t'ung (Wang Yitong), trans. and annot. *A Record of Buddhist Monasteries in Lo-yang*. Princeton, NJ: Princeton University Press, 1984.

Chinese

Liu Jiuzhou 劉九洲 and Hou Naihui 侯迺慧, trans. *Xinyi Luoyang qielan ji* 新譯洛陽伽藍記. Taipei: Sanmin shuju, 1994.

Wang Yitong 王伊同 and Cao Hong 曹虹, trans. *Luoyang qielan ji* 洛陽伽藍記, *A Record of Buddhist Monasteries in Luo-yang*. Beijing: Zhonghua shuju, 2008. Wang's English translation of Yang Xuanzhi's work is accompanied by a Chinese retranslation by Cao.

Zhou Zhenfu 周振甫. *Luoyang qielan ji yizhi* 洛陽伽藍記譯注. Nanjing: Jiangsu jiaoyu chubanshe, 2006.

Japanese

Iriya Yoshitaka 入矢義高, trans. *Rakuyō garanki* 洛陽伽藍記. Tokyo: Heibonsha, 1990.

Nagasawa Kazutoshi 長沢和俊, trans. and annot. *Hokken den, Sōun kōki* 法顕伝, 宋雲行紀. Tokyo: Heibonsha, 1971. A translation of the travelogue in chapter 5 of the *Luoyang qielan ji* is included.

Victor Cunrui Xiong

Nan Qi shu 南齊書

Introduction

The eighth of the standard histories, the *Nan Qi shu* (History of the Southern Qi) by Xiao Zixian 蕭子顯 (489–537), although made an official history under the Tang, was later overshadowed by Li Yanshou's *Nan shi*, q.v., a development fostered by Song criticism of the text. Though largely formal, these criticisms should not be ignored; of greater concern to the modern scholar, however, is the value of the *Nan Qi shu* for understanding the period. Used in conjunction with other sources, the *Nan Qi shu* offers an invaluable window into the political, social, intellectual, and cultural history of the time, especially the activities of the ruling Xiao family.

Contents

The *Nan Qi shu* contains fifty-nine *juan* and covers a regime noted for its brevity and internecine conflict. The Southern Qi lasted but twenty-three years (479–502), making the *Nan Qi shu* one of the shortest of the standard histories. Like most of its antecedents, the *Nan Qi shu* is of the composite (*jizhuan* 紀傳) format: it includes eight *juan* of annals, eleven of monographs (ritual, music, astrology, administrative geography, the bureaucracy, chariots and dress, omens and auguries, and the five phases), and forty of accounts.

Authorship

The *Nan Qi shu* was compiled during the Liang dynasty (502–556) by Xiao Zixian, whose background, personality, and motives are important to understanding the nature and shortcomings of the text. A scion of the Qi imperial family, Xiao was no disinterested observer. As a grandson of Xiao Daocheng 道成, founder of the Qi, Xiao Zixian's position under the Liang was rather sensitive. But, he was also distantly related to Xiao Yan 衍, Emperor Wu, founder of the Liang. He cut an impressive figure—eight *chi* (185 cm) tall and elegant in appearance—he had a love of learning, was a skilled writer and a good host, and "unafraid of spirits." Shen Yue 沈約 (441–513) classed his "Rhapsody on Swans in Formation" ("Hongxu fu" 鴻序賦) with Ban Gu's "Rhapsody on Communicating with the Hidden" ("Youtong fu" 幽通賦). But Xiao Zixian was also haughty, and he placed himself as high as eminent literary figures of the past. Aside from honorary ranks received because of his pedigree, Xiao initially held low-ranking positions such as historiographer, and he compiled a history of the Later Han derived from already existing histories.

The *Nan Qi shu* was probably completed between 515 and 520 and submitted to Emperor Wu, who ordered it placed in the imperial library. Having been noticed by the emperor, Xiao won his favor through literary talent and sycophancy. He compiled a collection of the emperor's writings and wrote a history of his northern campaigns—"Record of Northern Campaigns of the Putong Era" ("Putong beifa ji" 普通北伐記). Xiao's other writings include "Accounts of the Noble and Mean" ("Guijian zhuan" 貴儉傳) and his own collected works in twenty *juan*. Only the *Nan Qi shu* and some of his poetry remain. Following his death, Emperor Wu bestowed on him the posthumous sobriquet Jiao 驕, that is, "Vainglorious" (*Liang shu*, q.v., 35:511–12; *Nan shi* 42:1072–74.)

Sources

For the modern scholar, the *Nan Qi shu* is primary material, but it should more properly be treated as a secondary work compiled from various sources. At this remove it is barely possible to compare the *Nan Qi shu* with the original sources, but we can still know something about their nature and application and thus judge how to use the text. Although no statement of Xiao Zixian's historiographical principles or methodology remains, it is possible to gain some understanding of his sources and how he might have compiled his history from the example of Wu Jun 吳均 (469–520), who had previously sought to compile a history of the Qi dynasty, for which he requested access to court diaries (*qijuzhu* 起居注) and dossiers of conduct (*xingzhuan* 行狀) of officials. Emperor Wu refused. The events of the Qi were widely known, he said, and those who witnessed them could be interviewed (*Shi tong** 12:355). Xiao, because of his connections, potentially had court diaries, personnel dossiers, and informants available to him. He might also have borrowed from the histories of others, an accepted practice. There were Qi histories by Tan Chao 檀超 (fl. 481), Jiang Yan 江淹 (444–505), and Shen Yue.

It has been suggested that Xiao consulted Wu Jun's history, which circulated despite Emperor Wu's ordering it destroyed; comparison of existing fragments, however, reveals significant differences. Tang and Song bibliographies list other Qi histories as well. To produce the annals, he perhaps used court diaries, and, for the accounts, he must have turned to dossiers of conduct, local archives, regional histories, and the writings of his subjects. Lack of census data in the administrative geography chapters, *juan* 14 and 15, suggests he may not have used official archives. Xiao said that because of the arcane nature of astronomy, he did not himself attempt a disquisition on the subject but merely limited those chapters to a record of ominous and favorable omens. Yet, the contents of *juan* 12 and 13 are primarily astronomical observations only occasionally related to terrestrial occurrences, and there are a number of his explanations that delve into astronomical topics, introduced by *shichen* 史臣 (Gao Sisun 高似孫, *Shi lue*, 2:35). How Xiao handled these various sources determined the reliability of his history.

Court diaries might be used selectively, and biographical materials often shaded into hagiography. These possibilities must be considered.

Transmission of the text

The present *Nan Qi shu* is indubitably the original text; problems in transmission are relatively minor. The preface by Zeng Gong 曾鞏 (1019–1083) to the *Nan Qi shu* (pp. 1037–38) says that he and his colleagues corrected some errors but does not specifically mention missing text. Neither does the Song bibliography *Chongwen zongmu** of 1034–1041 by Wang Xiaochen, 3:4a, note any lacunae, though it does for other works. By the Ming, however, most editions were missing a few scattered graphs and had pages missing from one or more of *juan* 15, 35, 44, and 58. The *Siku quanshu** editors also suspected that an introductory section was missing from *juan* 52 (*Siku quanshu zongmu tiyao** 10:993).

An unresolved question is a possible missing *juan*. Several sources state that the *Nan Qi shu* contained sixty *juan*, while the present version has fifty-nine. The discrepancy was noted as early as the writing of the Tang histories—the *Jiu Tang shu* (46:1990) has fifty-nine but the *Xin Tang shu* (58:1456) has sixty—and later scholars have speculated about the contents of the missing *juan*. Some, most notably the editors of the *Siku quanshu*, suggested that it might have been an "author's postface" (*xuzhuan* 敘傳) presenting the author's familial and intellectual antecedents, similar to those of Sima Qian and Ban Gu. They believed a fragment of an "author's preface" (*zixu* 自序) preserved in Xiao's *Liang shu* account (35:512) was from such a postface, explaining that such materials were often dropped from later editions of a text (*Siku quanshu zongmu tiyao** 10:993). This view was cogently rejected by Yu Jiaxi (1884–1955), whose discussion of the text is the best evaluation of traditional critiques. Yu ("*Nan Qi shu* wushijiu juan," 3:147–50) concluded that the missing *juan* was probably a preface that contained Xiao's memorial of presentation, a fragment of which is found in Gao Sisun's *Shi lue*, 34–35.

Principal editions

Xiao Zixian (489–537). *Nan Qi shu*. Baina ben *Ershisishi* 百衲本二十四史. Shanghai: Shangwu yinshuguan, 1930–1937. *Sibu congkan**.

———. *Nan Qi shu*. Collated by Zhao Yongxian 趙用賢 and Zhang Yigui 張一桂. Nanjing Guozijian 南京國子監, 1590 (Wanli 18).

———. *Nan Qi shu: Wushijiu juan* 南齊書: 五十九卷. Changshu: Mao Jin Jiguge 毛晉汲古閣, 1637 (Chongzhen 10). *Nan Qi shu buji* 南齊書補緝, 1652 (Shunzhi 9).

———. *Nan Qi shu*. Qinding *Ershisishi* 欽訂二十四史, vols. 155–62. Shanghai: Tongwen shuju, 1884.

———. *Nan Qi shu*. Renshou ben *Ershisishi* 仁壽本二十四史. Reprint of the Song Shaoxing jian [1131–1162] Jiangnan ed. (宋紹興間江南重刊). Taipei: Ershiwushi biankanguan, 1955–1956.

———. *Nan Qi shu: Wushijiu juan* 南齊書: 五十九卷. By Wang Zugeng 王祖庚 (1700–1765) et al. Includes *Nan Qi shu kaozheng* 南齊書考證. Qianlong

Wuyingdian kanben 乾隆武英殿刊本, 1745. Rpt., Taipei: Yiwen yinshuguan, 1950.

The most complete early edition is the "Shu Large Characters" (*Shu dazi* 蜀大字) edition of the Song period, which was adopted for the Baina ben collection published by Shangwu yinshuguan (Shanghai, 1930–1937). This edition became the base text for the Zhonghua shuju punctuated edition (Shanghai, 1972, 3 vols.). Collation and compilation of the Zhonghua edition was done by the eminent Six Dynasties scholar Wang Zhongluo 王仲犖 (1913–1986), whose first task was to achieve a definitive and complete text. This was accomplished by comparing all editions of the *Nan Qi shu* to the *Dazi ban* version and emending the latter where appropriate. Wang also consulted texts that quoted the *Nan Qi shu*, corroborative material, and the writings of Song, Ming, and Qing scholars. The scope and care of Wang's effort are obvious from the endnotes. He probably restored the text as close to its original form as could be expected, though subsequent scholars have identified possible errors and alternative readings.

For an overall account of the textual history of this and the other Six Dynasties standard histories, see appendix IV, "Textual Transmission of the Standard Histories."

Traditional assessments

The *Nan Qi shu* has generally not been highly regarded. Tang historiographer Liu Zhiji 劉知機 (661–721) was ambivalent about it. His criticisms are based on formal criteria—some of the accounts ought to have been hereditary families (*shijia* 世家) chapters à la the *Shi ji*, the monographs should have been placed after the accounts as in the *Hou Han shu*, and Xiao's writing style in his chapter prefaces was awkward though the content was good. Liu thought Xiao was the most successful at *duanxian* 斷限, that is, adhering to temporal limits on his material (*Shi tong** 3:59, 3:67, and 4:82).

Attitudes toward the text became less positive in the Song, however. Zeng Gong, who collated the *Nan Qi shu* and wrote a preface for the imperial library, mentioned earlier, criticized Xiao for his precious style and weak content and for failing to expose the monstrous behavior of the Qi rulers as a lesson to the world. To have such views forcefully expressed in what became the standard preface to the *Nan Qi shu* surely undermined the work's credibility. Although Wang Yinglin 王應麟 (*Wengzhu Kunxue jiwen* 13:32b–33a) suggested that Xiao had little choice but to gloss over the sins of the Qi and Liang rulers, later writers followed Zeng's critique. Wang Zugeng (1700–1765), author of the *Nan Qi shu kaozheng* (see *Nan Qi shu: Wushijiu juan*), faulted him for twisting events, emphasizing Buddhism over Ruism, focusing on trivialities, failing to include household and population figures, and dealing only with anomalies and omens in the chapter on astronomy (*Nan Qi shu kaozheng* 59:1a–b). The *Siku quanshu* editors agreed and added other failings, including errors of fact (*Siku quanshu zongmu tiyao** 10:992–93). Qian Daxin 錢大昕 (1728–1804) rebutted some of these (*Nian'ershi kaoyi* 25:1a–4b). Zhao

Yi 趙翼 (1727–1814), while enumerating cases where Xiao had glossed over the actions of his ancestors, praised his facility in "associative narration" (*leixu fa* 類敘法), the technique of including in an individual's account mentions or descriptions of others who shared a notable characteristic with the main subject (*Nian'ershi zhaji* 9:117–18). The traditional criticisms have been insightfully evaluated by Yu Jiaxi ("*Nan Qi shu* wushijiu juan," 3:147–50).

Modern scholars have tended to follow the critiques of Zeng and his supporters. For example, Taiwan historiographer Du Weiyun says it would be difficult to call Xiao a "good historian" and faults him for being evasive, covering up the misdeeds of his ancestors, glossing over Xiao Yan's usurpation, and devoting excessive space to his own family (2:140–42). Mainland scholar Zhao Jihui condemns Xiao for promoting the idea of karma, the existence of gods, and Buddhist thought; for allowing considerations of family to interfere with objectivity; and for superficiality, for example, omitting population figures (Zhao Jihui, "*Nan Qi shu*," 1:347–62). While these criticisms have some basis and are understandable according to the lights of traditional Chinese historiography, they fail to consider Xiao's purposes. There is no reason to believe that he would have been interested—conditions permitting—in producing a precise, detailed history; his lack of concern about the household and population figures and about the astronomical data suggest the contrary. Rather, his history appears intended to put his ancestors in a good light, gain the notice of Liang Wudi, and assure the emperor of his loyalty. In all these, he succeeded. After presenting his history to the emperor, Xiao was appointed secretary to the heir apparent, the first of a series of appointments that led to that of palace attendant, bringing him in proximity to the emperor.

Major recensions

Wang Zugeng (1700–1765) et al. *Nan Qi shu kaozheng* 南齊書考證. Included in the Yiwen yinshuguan edition of *Nan Qi shu* (see later).

Xiao Zixian. *Nanseisho* 南齊書. Glossed by Sorai Ogyū 荻生徂徠. Preface by Kikuya Nagasawa 長澤規矩也. Tokyo: Kyūko shoin, 1970. *Kanbun* version with pronunciation, punctuation, and diacritical and syntactic markers prepared by Sorai Ogyū (1666–1728), based on the Ming Wanli Nanjian 明萬曆南監 edition.

———. *Nan Qi shu xuanyi* 南齊書選譯. Trans. and annot. Xu Keqian 徐克謙. Chengdu: Ba Shu shushe, 1994.

Traditional comments printed without text

Gao Sisun (*jinshi* 1184). *Shi lue, Zi lue* 史略, 子略. Collated and punctuated by Zhang Yanyun 張艷雲 and Yang Zhaoxia 楊朝霞. Shenyang: Liaoning jiaoyu chubanshe, 1998.

Qian Daxin (1728–1804). "*Nan Qi shu*." In *Nian'ershi kaoyi* 廿二史考異. Dakezi ben 大刻字本, 25:1a–14b. Taipei: Dezhi chubanshe, [1963?].

Shen Mingsun 沈名蓀 (*juren* 1690). *Nan Bei shishi xiaolu* 南北史識小錄. Wulin: Wu shi Qinglaitang, 1871 (Tongzhi *xinwei* 同治辛未).

Zhang Ruyu 章如愚 (*jinshi* 1196). *Qunshu kaosuo* 群書考索. Liu shi Shenduzhai jiaoke 劉氏慎獨齋校刻, 1508 (Zhengde *wuchen* keben 正德戊辰刻本), 134:7a–b. Rpt., Taipei: Xinxing shuju, 1969, 1:421–22.

Zhao Yi (1727–1814). *Nian'ershi zhaji, fu buyi* 廿二史劄記, 附補遺. Shanghai: Shangwu yinshuguan, 1937.

Secondary studies/recent studies

Chen Yanjia 陳延嘉. "*Nan Qi shu* dian jiao bu zheng" 南齊書點校補正. *Guji zhengli yanjiu xuekan* (1993.2): 38–39.

Ding Fulin 丁福林. "*Nan Qi shu* jiaodian zhaji" 南齊書校點札記. *Wenjiao ziliao* (1996.2): 82–90.

_____. "*Nan Qi shu juan* wushiqi 'Suolu zhuan' jiaoyi" 南齊書卷五十七'索虜傳'校議. *Yancheng shifan xueyuan xuebao* 27.3 (June 2007): 118–24.

_____. "*Nan Qi shu* kaoyi" 南齊書考疑. *Jianghai xuekan* (1998.2): 77, (2) (1998.3): 87, (3) (1998.4): 117, (4) (1998.5): 165, (5) (2004.4): 124, (6) (2004.5): 25, (7) (2004.6): 159, (8) (2005.3): 183, (9) (2005.4): 49, (10) (2005.5): 81, (11) (2005.6): 47, (12) (2006.1): 148, (13) (2006.2): 105, (14) (2006.3): 67, (15) (2006.4): 193, (16) (2006.5): 83, (17) (2006.6): 166, (18) (2007.1): 32, (19) (2007.2): 80, (20) (2007.3): 173, (21) (2007.5): 106.

Ding Qian 丁謙 (1843–1919). *Nan Qi shu "Yi Mo zhuan" dili kaozheng* 南齊書夷貊傳地理攷證. Zhejiang tushuguan congshu 浙江圖書館叢書, 4:3. Hangzhou: Zhejiang tushuguan, 1915.

Du Weiyun 杜唯運. *Zhongguo shixueshi* 中國史學史. Taipei: Sanmin shuju, 2002. Vol. 2, pp. 140–42.

Pan Xianghui 潘祥輝. "Zhonghua shuju ben *Nan Qi shu* jiaokan shangque, buyi shi li" 中華書局本南齊書校勘商榷, 補遺十例. *Jiangxi jiaoyu xueyuan xuebao*, *Shehui kexue* 24.5 (2003): 97–99.

Peng Yilin 彭益林. "*Nan Qi shu*: 'Tianwen zhi' bujiao" 南齊書天文志補校. *Guji zhengli yanjiu xuekan* (1988.3): 19–22.

Wang Yinglin (1223–1296). *Wengzhu Kunxue jiwen* 翁注困學紀聞. *Sibu beiyao**.

Yu Jiaxi 余嘉錫 (1884–1955). "*Nan Qi shu* wushijiu juan" 南齊書五十九卷. In *Siku tiyao bianzheng* 四庫提要辯證, 3:147–50. Hong Kong: Zhonghua shuju, 1974.

Zhao Jihui 趙吉惠. "*Nan Qi shu*." In *Zhongguo shixue mingzhu pingjie* 中國史學名著評介, ed. Cang Xiuliang 倉修良, 1:347–62. Taipei: Liren shuju, 1992.

Zhou Yiliang 周一良. "*Nan Qi shu* zhaji" 南齊書札記. In *Wei Jin Nanbeichao shi zhaji* 魏晉南北朝史札記, 216–66. Beijing: Zhonghua shuju, 1985.

_____. "*Nan Qi shu* 'Qiu Lingju zhuan' shishi jian lun Nanchao wenwu guanwei ji qingzhuo" 南齊書丘靈鞠傳試釋兼論南朝文武官位及清濁. *Wei Jin Nanbeichao shi lunji* 魏晉南北朝史論集, 102–26. Beijing: Beijing daxue chubanshe, 1997.

Zhu Jihai 朱季海. *Nan Qi shu jiaoyi* 南齊書校議. Beijing: Zhonghua shuju, 1984.

Research aids

"Bu *Nan Qi shu* 'Yiwen zhi'" 補南齊書藝文志. In *Ershiwushi bubian* 二十五史補編. Rpt., Taipei: Kaiming shudian, 1959 [1936–1937], 3:4323–45.

Wan Sitong 萬斯同 (1638–1702). "Qi zhuwang shibiao" 齊諸王世表. In *Ershiwushi bu bian* 二十五史補編. Rpt., Taipei: Kaiming shudian, 1959 [1936–1937], 3:4309–10.

———. "Qi jiangxiang dachen nianbiao" 齊將相大臣年表. In *Ershiwushi bubian* 二十五史補編. Rpt., Taipei: Kaiming shudian, 1959 [1936–1937], 3:4311–16.

———. "Qi fangzhen nianbiao" 齊方鎮年表. In *Ershiwushi bubian* 二十五史補編. Rpt., Taipei: Kaiming shudian, 1959 [1936–1937], 3:4317–22.

Yuan Yingguang 袁英光, editor-in-chief. *Nanchao wushi cidian* 南朝五史辭典. Ji'nan: Shandong jiaoyu chubanshe, 2005.

Translations

English

Tian, Xiaofei. *Beacon Fire and Shooting Star: The Literary Culture of the Liang (502–557)*. Harvard Yenching Institute Monograph Series 65. Cambridge, MA: Harvard University Asia Center, 2007. Translates Xiao Zixian's important statement on literature found in his commentary to the "Biographies of the Men of Letters" (*Nan Qi shu* 52:907–908).

Modern Chinese

Xie Shengming 謝聖明 and Huang Liping 黃立平, eds. *Nan Qi shu*. In *Baihua Ershisishi* 白話二十四史, 6:3–193. Beijing: Zhonghua huaqiao chubanshe, 1999.

Index

Zhang Chenshi 張忱石. *Nanchao wushi renming suoyin* 南朝五史人名索引. Beijing: Zhonghua shuju, 1985.

William Gordon Crowell

Nan shi 南史

Introduction

In eighty *juan*, the *Nan shi* 南史 (History of the south) records the history of the four regimes that held power in the south of China between 420 and 589: Song, Qi, Liang, and Chen. Though primarily associated with the name of Li Yanshou 李延壽 (d. 680), it was in fact the work of both Li Yanshou and his father, Li Dashi 李大師 (570–628).

Contents and arrangement of the text

The *Nan shi* was first conceived of as a chronicle; in its final form, it follows an annals-biography (*ji zhuan* 紀傳) structure. Its eighty *juan* consist of ten *juan* of annals and seventy of biographies and accounts. The biographical chapters appear to follow a broadly chronological sequence. The picture is more complex than this, though: Li Yanshou grouped individuals by their genealogical relationships; biographies of individuals from the same clan who lived in different periods may appear together. The *Nan shi* covers the following topics:

1–3. Song annals

4–5. Qi annals

6–8. Liang annals

9–10. Chen annals

11–12. Biographies of empresses and consorts

13–14. Biographies of members of the Song imperial family

15–40. Other Song biographies

41–44. Biographies of members of the Qi imperial family

45–50. Other Qi biographies

51–54. Biographies of members of the Liang imperial family

55–64. Other Liang biographies

65. Biographies of members of the Chen imperial family

66–69. Other Chen biographies

70. Biographies of obedient officials (*xunli* 循吏)

71. Biographies of Confucian scholars (*rulin* 儒林)

72. Biographies of litterateurs (*wenxue* 文學)

73–74. Biographies of filial and virtuous individuals (*xiaoyi* 孝義)

75–76. Biographies of recluses (*yinyi* 隱逸)

77. Biographies of royal favorites (*enxing* 恩幸)

78–79. Accounts of foreign states and peoples (*yimo* 夷貊)

80. Biographies of rebellious ministers (*zeichen* 賊臣)

Authorship and date of composition

The Lis claimed descent from the Guzang 姑臧 branch of the Longxi 隴西 Lis in the northwest; their immediate place of origin was Xiangzhou 相州 (at modern Anyang, Henan). Li Yanshou's ancestors had held official positions under the Northern Dynasties. His father, Li Dashi, had served under the Sui dynasty in a number of provincial appointments before taking office under a warlord rival to the Tang dynastic house; as a result, he spent some time in exile where he began to compile the history. Li Dashi planned his work as a chronicle along the lines of the *Wu Yue chunqiu* 吳越春秋. His professed aim was to transcend regional biases in existing accounts of the period and to correct their oversights. Between 626 and 628, after returning to the capital from exile, Li Dashi edited his earlier findings by consulting materials in his own library. After Li Dashi died in 628 without having completed his history, Li Yanshou inherited his father's research. Li Yanshou worked on official historiographical projects commissioned by Emperors Gaozu and Taizong; he served as an assistant (*zhi guo shi* 直國史) and, later, as a compiler (*xiu guo shi* 修國史) in the Institute of Historiography (Shi guan 史館) under Emperors Taizong and Gaozong. He supplemented his father's writings and rearranged them from their original chronological form into the annals-biography structure. He also divided Li Dashi's single work into two separate histories of the Southern and Northern Dynasties. It was in this form that, in 659, after correction by Assistant Director of the Palace Library Linghu Defen 令狐德棻 (583–666), Li Yanshou presented to the throne the *Nan shi* and *Bei shi*, q.v.

Despite Li Dashi's professed intention to accord even weight of analysis to the states of the south and the north—and despite his objections to earlier regional biases in historiographic accounts of the period—the Lis' northern background still makes itself felt in the *Nan shi* and *Bei shi*. The relative lengths of each work are suggestive: the *Nan shi* contains eighty *juan* compared to the *Bei shi*'s hundred. This is explained in part by the chronological scope of each history: the *Nan shi* covers 170 years to *Bei shi*'s 233 years. But there is also a difference of detail: already in the late twelfth to thirteenth centuries, Zhang Ruyu 章如愚 (*jinshi* 1196) drew a distinction between the sharp focus in Li Yanshou's accounts of the Northern Dynasties and his sketchier coverage of the south (*Qunshu kaosuo* 群書考索 14.10a; photolithographic reproduction of 1508 edition, Taipei: Xinxing shuju, 1969). Within the fabric of the *Nan shi*'s text, too, a negative representation of southern regimes at times appears.

Sources

In expanding Li Dashi's work, Li Yanshou drew on the existing official record—from recently compiled individual histories of the Southern and Northern Dynasties, as well as Wei Shou's earlier *Wei shu*, q.v. Comparison between the *Nan shi*'s length and that of its sources suggests a process of tight editing. Li Yanshou abridged or omitted altogether the texts of many court documents quoted at length in the earlier official histories, for example. Yet, he also added material gathered from over a thousand *juan* of "miscellaneous histories" (*zashi* 雜史). This even resulted in the inclusion of whole biographies that did not find direct parallels in the official record; the biographies of Wang Lin 王琳 and Zhang Biao 張彪 (in *juan* 64) offer two such examples. With the historians' comments inserted into the *Nan shi*, too, Li Yanshou offered individual interpretations of the past that diverged from his sources: a comparison of the biographies of Emperor Wu in the *Liang shu*, q.v., and the *Nan shi* is particularly suggestive. Li Yanshou was also able to draw on more recent historical research to inform his judgments. In his discussion of the ancestry of the ruling Xiao house of Southern Qi, for example, he used research on the *Han shu* by the scholar Yan Shigu 顏師古 (581–645) to refute claims of a genealogy that traced to Han senior ministers Xiao He 蕭何 (d. 193 B.C.) and Xiao Wangzhi 蕭望之 (d. 47 B.C.); see *Nan shi* 4:127.

Early reception of the text

After the *Nan shi* was submitted to the throne in 659, responses to it were mixed. Emperor Gaozong supplied a preface to Li's two works (*Tang hui yao* 唐會要 63:1092). The full text of that imperial document did not survive into the eleventh century, though. By the middle of the eighth century, the *Nan shi* was even proposed for inclusion in the civil service examination curriculum (*Tong dian*, q.v., 17:423; Zhonghua shuju, 1988). Yet it seems that because of Li Yanshou's youth and relatively low status, his work received an indifferent reception from many contemporaries. It attracted only slight attention from the famous critic Liu Zhiji (661–721) in his *Shi tong**.

The ambivalent critical reception continued after the Tang. On the one hand, the *Nan shi* drew praise in the eleventh-century *Xin Tang shu*, where it is noted that the Lis' histories "have a fair degree of orderliness about them; they go far beyond the sources in cutting out cluttered phrasing" (102:3986). Also during the Song, Sima Guang 司馬光 (1019–1086), Hong Mai 洪邁 (1123–1202), and Ye Shi 葉適 (1150–1223) were broadly positive in their assessments of the *Nan shi*; Hong Mai even produced a six-*juan Nan chao shi jingyu* 南朝史精語. On the other hand, the historian Liu Shu 劉恕 (1032–1078) pointed up a lack of rhetorical sophistication and an excess of structural complexity in the *Nan shi* and *Bei shi*. He also identified their lack of thematic monographs as a particular weakness. In the twelfth century, Chen Zhengmin 陳正敏 (fl. 1100–1110) claimed that Li Yanshou had "delighted in describing the demonic and the strange, auspicious omens, hearsay, and prophecies, which were particularly numerous" (*Dunzhai xianlan* 遯齋閒覽, according to the *Lei shuo* 類說 by Zeng Zao 曾慥 [fl. 1136–1147], photolithographic reproduction of 1626 edition, *Beijing tushuguan guji zhenben congkan* [Beijing: Shumu wenxian chubanshe, 1988], vol. 62, 47:11a–b). Other critics of the time included Luo Mi 羅泌 (1131–?) and Huang Zhen 黃震 (1213–1281), who saw the *Nan shi* as vulgar and at times unreliable. Yet in the twelfth century, as bibliophile Chao Gongwu (fl. mid-1100s) noted, the Lis' works circulated more widely than the official histories on which they were based (*Junzhai dushu zhi** 6:241).

After the Song, scholarship on the *Nan shi* falls into three broad types. First are compilations of excerpts. These made an appearance at least as early as the ninth century, in Sun Yuru's 孫玉汝 (*jinshi* 844) *Nan Bei shi lian xuan* 南北史練選. Similar works continued to be compiled into the nineteenth century. Extant examples include Hong Mai's *Nanchao shi jing yu*, Zhou Shiya's 周詩雅 (*jinshi* 1619) *Nan Bei shi chao* 南北史鈔, Shen Mingsun 沈名孫 (*juren* 1690) and Zhu Kuntian's 朱昆田 (1652–1699) *Nan shi shi xiaolu* 南史識小錄, Zhou Jiayou's 周嘉猷 (1751–1796) *Nan Bei shi junhua* 南北史捃華, and Liang Yusheng's 梁玉繩 (1745–1819) *Nan shi zhailüe* 南史摘略.

Second, supplements to and commentaries on the *Nan shi* were particularly popular during the Qing. In 1783, Zhou Jiayou 周嘉猷 produced a series of chronological tables in the *Nan Bei shi nianbiao* 南北史年表, *Nan Bei shi diwang shixibiao* 南北史帝王世系表, and *Nan Bei shi shixibiao* 南北史世系表. The *Nan Bei shi buzhi* 南北史補志 of 1848–1849 and the *Bu Nan Bei shi Yiwen zhi* 補南北史藝文志 of 1930 also sought to make up for a lack of thematic monographs—a common criticism of Li Yanshou's works. The most substantial commentary on the *Nan shi* is Li Qing's 李清 (1602–1682) *Nan Bei shi hezhu* 南北史合注, which he modeled upon Pei Songzhi's commentary to the *Sanguo zhi*, q.v., by drawing on a range of texts to provide textual parallels and variants for selected passages from the *Nan shi* and *Bei shi*. Though this work was praised for its detail by the eighteenth-century compilers of *Siku quanshu** (but ultimately excluded from that collection), passages quoted in the *Nan Bei shi hezhu* at times diverge from Li Yanshou's original text.

Third, scholarly attention, particularly during the eighteenth and nineteenth centuries, focused on text-critical studies of the *Nan shi*. In the first half of the eighteenth century, for example, Wang Maohong 王懋竑 (1668–1741) identified the *Nan shi*'s textual and historiographical errors in his *Du Nan shi jiyi* 讀南史記疑. His near-contemporary Zhang Zeng 張燧 (1705–1750) collated in his *Dushi juzheng* 讀史舉正 alternatives to Li Yanshou's version of events. In 1780, Qian Daxin 錢大昕 (1728–1804) gave over three *juan* of his *Nian'ershi kaoyi* 廿二史考異 to discussion of the *Nan shi*. On several points, Qian Daxin praised its clarity and directness (26.511), but his response to the *Nan shi* was more often negative. Wang Mingsheng 王鳴盛 (1722–1797) also devoted ten *juan* of his *Shiqishi shangque* 十七史商榷 to a text-critical study of the *Nan shi*, as well as to analyses of historical events of the Southern Dynasties that took the *Nan shi* as their starting point. Like Qian, Wang was broadly critical in his judgments. In 1790 or 1791, Zhao Yi 趙翼 (1727–1814) was more commendatory than his contemporaries in his reading notes titled *Gaiyu congkao* 陔餘叢考 (8.1b), praising Li Yanshou's two works as "excellent histories"; he also offered a broadly positive assessment of the *Nan shi* in his *Nian'ershi zhaji* 廿二史札記. In the nineteenth century, Hong Yixuan's 洪頤煊 (1765–1837) *Zhushi kaoyi* 諸史考異 and Li Ciming's 李慈銘 (1830–1894) *Yuemantang riji* 越縵堂日記 included comments on the *Nan shi*.

Behind these varied judgments lies a surprisingly unstable sense of just what type of work the *Nan shi* was: its bibliographic identity shifted repeatedly during its early history. The bibliographic monographs of both the *Jiu Tang shu* and *Xin Tang shu* list it as an official history (*zhengshi* 正史). Song references to "the seventeen official histories" also imply a fixed corpus that included the *Nan shi*. In 1042, though, a descriptive catalog of the imperial library, *Chongwen zongmu**, still had the *Nan shi* among "miscellaneous histories." Chao Gongwu used the same classification in the middle of the twelfth century. Yet two of Chao Gongwu's contemporaries, You Mao 尤袤 (1124–1193) and Zheng Qiao 鄭樵 (1104–1162), continued to identify it as an official history. In the early thirteenth century, yet another bibliographic category emerged: bibliophile Chen Zhensun 陳振孫 recorded the *Nan shi* as an "alternative history" (*bieshi* 別史). In the early fourteenth century, Ma Duanlin repositioned the work among official histories in his *Wenxian tongkao**. Here was a tension with the *Nan shi*'s appearance in the *Song shi*'s bibliographic monograph of 1345 as, once again, an "alternative history." Only with the imperial catalogs of the Ming and Qing, *Wenyuange shumu* 文淵閣書目 and *Siku quanshu zongmu**, was the *Nan shi* decisively identified as an official history.

For an overall account of the textual history of this and the other Six Dynasties standard histories, see appendix IV, "Textual Transmission of the Standard Histories."

Principal editions

Song woodblock editions. The National Library in Beijing (中國國家圖書館) and the Liaoning Provincial Library (遼寧省圖書館) both have incomplete sets of Song woodblock editions. A photolithographic reproduction of a 29-*ce* witness held by the National Library was published in 2003 in the *Zhonghua zaizao shanben* 中華再造善本 series.

Yuan edition of 1306, produced by the Xinzhou Circuit school (信州路儒學). This edition was used for the Bainaben *Ershisishi* series (see later). A revised edition was printed in 1522.

Jiajing 嘉靖 (1522–1566) edition, printed by the Southern Directorate of Education (南國子監). A number of editions were printed with revisions during the seventeenth and into the eighteenth centuries.

1603 edition, printed by the Northern Directorate of Education (北國子監). Gu Yanwu 顧炎武 (1613–1682) considered this edition superior in craftsmanship to that of the Southern Directorate of Education, yet full of text-critical errors.

1640 edition, by the bibliophile and publisher Mao Jin 毛晉 (1599–1659) in the Jiguge 汲古閣, Changshu 常熟 (modern Jiangsu). It draws on Song and Yuan imprints. Considered reliable, it was widely used as an alternative to the 1739 Palace edition (next item).

Wuying dian 武英殿, or "Palace edition," of 1739. Based on the editions produced by the Ming Directorates of Education in Nanjing and Beijing, textual lacunae and errors were corrected with reference to Song and Yuan editions. Though often considered inferior to the Jiguge and, later, Baina editions, it provided the basis of many subsequent editions: a Tongwen shuju edition of 1884, a 1916 edition by Shanghai shuangwu yinshuguan, a typeset edition of 1935 by Kaiming shudian, and a *Sibu beiyao** edition of 1936.

1872 edition, printed by the Jinling shuju 金陵書局 in Nanjing as part of an initiative to mend the effects of the Taiping Rebellion. It was based on the 1640 Jiguge edition, with corrections added.

1935 Baina edition, printed by Shanghai shangwu yinshuguan. It is a photolithographic reproduction of witnesses to the 1306 edition held in the National Beiping Library (國立北平圖書館) and the Hanfen lou 涵芬樓.

1975 typeset edition, published by Zhonghua shuju in Beijing. This punctuated and revised edition takes as its base text the Baina edition; it collates the Jiguge and Palace editions, and also makes use of the Southern and Northern Directorate of Education editions, and the Jinling shuju edition. It is now the standard edition.

Modern studies

Deng Wurong 鄧武蓉. "Shi lun *Nan shi* yu *Bei shi* de shizhuan wenxue chengjiu" 試論南史與北史的史傳文學成就. *Chuanshan xuekan* (2009.4): 174–77.

Ding Fulin 丁福林. "*Nan shi* kaoyi" 南史考異. *Jianghai xuekan* (2002–2011): multiple entries.

Enomoto Ayuchi 榎本あゆち. "*Nan shi* no setsuwateki yōso ni tsuite—Ryō shoō den o tegakari toshite" 南史の説話的要素について—梁諸王伝を手がかりとして. *Tōyō gakuhō* 70.3–4 (1989): 131–63.

———. "Futatabi *Nan shi* no setsuwateki yōso ni tsuite—Shō Junji no shi ni kansuru kiji o tegakari toshite" 再び南史の説話的要素について—蕭順之の死に関する記事を手がかりとして. *Rikuchō gakujutsu gakkaihō* 8 (2007): 81–96.

Fujiie Reinosuke 藤家礼之助. "*Nan shi* no kōsei—Sō hongi o megutte" 南史の構成—宋本紀をめぐって. In *Chūgoku seishi no kisoteki kenkyū* 中国正史の基礎的研

究, ed. Waseda daigaku bungakubu, Tōyōshi kenkyūshitsu 早稲田大学文学部, 東洋史研究室, 221–40. Tokyo: Waseda daigaku shuppanbu, 1984.
Gao Guokang 高國抗. "Yi bu qingxiang tongyi de zhengshi: Tang Li Yanshou de *Nan shi*, *Bei shi*" 一部傾向統一的正史: 唐李延壽的南史, 北史. *Ji'nan xuebao, Zhexue shehui kexue ban*) (1989.1): 55–65.
Gao Min 高敏. *Nan Bei shi duosuo* 南北史掇瑣. Zhengzhou: Zhongzhou guji chubanshe, 2003.
———. *Nan Bei shi kaosuo* 南北史考索. Tianjin: Tianjin guji chubanshe, 2010.
Gardiner, K. H. J. "Standard Histories, Han to Sui." In *Essays on the Sources for Chinese History*, ed. Donald Leslie, Colin Mackerras, and Wang Gungwu, 42–52, esp. 48–49. Canberra: Australian National University Press, 1973.
He Dezhang 何德章. "*Nan*, *Bei shi* zhi zhengtongguan" 南, 北史之正統觀. *Shixueshi yanjiu* (1990.4): 76–78.
Ji Rumei 季汝梅. "*Nan shi* kaozheng bu" 南史考證補. *Xue hai* (1944.10): 26–32.
Ma Zonghuo 馬宗霍. *Nan shi jiaozheng* 南史校證. Changsha: Hunan jiaoyu chubanshe, 2008.
Miyakawa Hisayuki 宮川尚志. "*Nan shi*, *Hoku shi* Bukkyō shiryō kō: Rikuchō seishi Bukkyō, Dōkyō shiryōshū no jūichi, jūni' 南史, 北史佛教史料稿: 六朝正史佛教, 道教史料集の十一, 十二 . *Tōkai daigaku kiyō, bungakubu* 43 (1985): 29–41.
Qu Lindong 瞿林東. *Nan shi he Bei shi* 南史和北史. Beijing: Renmin chubanshe, 1987.
Wang Shumin 王樹民. *Shibu yaoji jieti* 史部要籍解題. Beijing: Zhonghua shuju, 1981. Pp. 84–88.
Xie Baocheng 謝保成. "Qingxiang tongyi bu shi *Nan shi* yu *Bei shi* de zhuti" 傾向統一不是南史與北史的主題. *Beijing daxue xuebao, Zhexue shehui kexueban* (1990.2): 44–51.
Yu Jiaxi 余嘉錫. *Siku tiyao bianzheng* 四庫提要辨證. Beijing: Kexue chubanshe, 1958. Vol. 4, pp. 205–14.
Zhang Yuanji 張元濟. *Nan shi jiaokanji* 南史校勘記. In *Bainaben Ershisishi jiaokanji* 百衲本二十四史校勘記. Beijing: Shangwu yinshuguan, 2001.

Translations

Modern Chinese

Qi Zebang 漆澤邦. *Nan shi xuanyi* 南史選譯. Chengdu: Ba Shu shushe, 1989.
Xie Shengming 謝聖明 and Huang Liping 黃立平, eds. *Baihua Ershisishi* 白話二十四史. Beijing: Zhongguo huaqiao chubanshe, 1999. Vol. 8.
Yang Zhong 楊忠. *Nan shi quanyi* 南史全譯. In *Ershisishi quanyi* 二十四史全譯, ed. Xu Jialu 许嘉璐. Shanghai: Hanyu dacidian chubanshe, 2004.

Japanese

Hashida Kasumi 橋田佳純 and Saeki Masanori 佐伯雅宣. "Rikuchō bunjin den: Ka Son (*Ryōsho*, *Nan shi*)" 六朝文人伝: 何遜 (梁書, 南史). *Chūgoku chūsei bungaku kenkyū* 35 (1999): 73–85, esp. 81–85.

Nagasawa Kikuya 長澤規矩也, ed. *Nan shi* 南史. In *Wakokubon seishi* 和刻本正史. Tokyo: Kyūko shoin, 1972.

Sasaoka Emiko 笹岡恵美子 and Noguchi Mizue 野口瑞恵. "Rikuchō bunjin den: Go Kin (*Ryōsho, Nan shi*)" 六朝文人伝: 呉均 (梁書, 南史) *Chūgoku chūsei bungaku kenkyū* 34 (1998): 87–96, esp. 93–96.

Tanimoto Keiji 谷本圭司. "*Nan shi* Sha shi retsuden (1): Sha Kai" 南史謝氏列伝 (1): 謝晦. *Chūgoku chūsei bungaku kenkyū* 27 (1994): 49–89.

———. "*Nan shi* Sha shi retsuden (2): Sha Yū" 南史謝氏列伝 (2): 謝裕. *Chūgoku chūsei bungaku kenkyū* 29 (1996): 38–100.

Western languages

Hans Frankel has compiled bibliographic references to translations of the *Nan shi* into European languages before 1957, in *Catalogue of Translations from the Chinese Dynastic Histories for the Period 220–960* (Berkeley: University of California Press, 1957), 147–55. The translations that Frankel lists are of short fragments of the *Nan shi*'s text; none extends even to an entire *juan*. Since Frankel's list, there has been little progress: there are still no substantial translations from the *Nan shi* into Western languages.

Indices and other reference works

Ershiwushi jizhuan renming suoyin 二十五史紀傳人名索引. Shanghai: Shanghai guji chubanshe, 1990.

Liang Qixiong 梁啟雄, ed. *Niansishi zhuanmu yinde* 廿四史傳目引得. Shanghai: Zhonghua shuju, 1936; rpt., 1940.

Niu Jiqing 牛繼清 and Zhang Linxiang 張林祥. *Shiqishi yinianlu* 十七史疑年錄. Hefei: Huangshan shushe, 2007.

Wang Pu 王溥 (922–982). *Tang hui yao* 唐會要. Beijing: Zhonghua shuju, 1955.

Wu Shuping 吳樹平 et al., eds. *Ershisishi renming suoyin* 二十四史人名索引. Beijing: Zhonghua shuju, 1998.

Yuan Yingguang 袁英光 et al., eds. *Nanchao wushi cidian* 南朝五史辭典. Ji'nan: Shandong jiaoyu chubanshe, 2005.

Zhang Chenshi 張忱石 et al., eds. *Nanchao wushi renming suoyin* 南朝五史人名索引. Beijing: Zhonghua shuju, 1985.

Zhang Chenshi and Wu Shuping, eds. *Ershisishi jizhuan renming suoyin* 二十四史紀傳人名索引. Beijing: Zhonghua shuju, 1980.

Mark Strange and Jakub Hruby

Niu Hong ji 牛弘集

Introduction

Niu Hong, styled Liren 里仁 (545–610), has biographies in *Sui shu*, q.v., 49:1297–310, and *Bei shi*, q.v., 72:2492–504. He began his career under the Northern Zhou dynasty, and at one point he was responsible for drafting the imperial diary (*qijuzhu* 起居注), which may explain his interest in compiling a *Zhou shi* 周史 in eighteen *juan* (*Sui shu* 33:956) that has not, however, survived. He inherited the family rank of duke (*gong* 公) and received the prestige title of "general-in-chief unequaled in honor" (*da jiangjun kaifu yitong sansi* 大將軍開府儀同三司). When the Sui government was set up beginning in 581, Niu was made head of the Imperial Library, at which time he wrote a long memorial presenting the entire history of scholarship and archives since ancient times. In 582 he received the title of Duke of Qizhang 奇章, and, in 583, as head of the Ministry of Rites (*libu shangshu* 禮部尚書), he was commissioned to compile the *Wuli* 五禮 (Five Rites); his work in a hundred *juan* was well received. He also advocated the establishment of the Mingtang 明堂, or Numinous Hall, which was the traditional site of important ritual ceremonies.

By 589 Niu was thoroughly involved in court musicology and harmonics, and thus he wrote dozens of court ritual lyrics (see the "Monograph on Music" ["Yin yue" 音樂] section, part 2, of *Sui shu* 14:345, for his appointment to this task in 582). He also wrote opinions on the nature of pitch-standard harmonics, musical modes, and also the ritual to determine harmonics traditionally known as "watching the ethers" (*houqi* 候氣). This ritual was tried anew in Sui but not completely understood by the emperor Wendi, thus the project was not considered successful. Toward the end of Niu's life, under Sui Yangdi's reign, Niu was given honors and high offices. As with several other Six Dynasties writers, the life of Niu Hong is a crucial one for understanding the development of scholarship and court rituals under the Northern Zhou, Sui, and early Tang, and deserves a full analysis in the future.

Contents

Niu Hong's *wenji*, as it has come down to us, contains his treatises on technical matters of harmonics and other rituals, and it is especially well-larded with Niu's numerous lyrics for the various court musical events, both for high occasions (such as the imperial temple) and the relatively more festive ones. The fullest version of

Niu Hong's *wenji* is that contained in *juan* 117 of Zhang Pu's (1602–1641) *Han Wei Liuchao baisanjia ji*, q.v., which titles it *Niu Qizhang ji* 牛奇章集. As are many other Six Dynasties *wenji*, this is a collection of prose items in various genres, and verse items such as songs (or, chants, *ge* 歌) and poems. Niu's *wenji* contains a total of twenty-eight items; by genre, they are in the following order:

Petition, 1 title (Niu's memorial on the history of scholarship)

Presentation, 3 titles (including reports on court projects to edit the *Five Rites* and on lyrics for court ritual songs)

Disquisition, 1 title (report on harmonics)

Opinion, 3 titles (including a report on the history of the Mingtang)

Court songs (*yuege* 樂歌), 18 titles (these under several rubrics, some with subdivisions representing parts: "Jiaomiao geci" 郊廟歌辭 [Court lyrics for the imperial temple], "Yanshe geci" 燕射歌辭 [Court lyrics for feasting and archery], and "Guchui geci" 鼓吹歌辭 [Court lyrics for the drums and pipes]; these are traditional subgenres of lyric for court festal, saltatory, and temple ritual occasions)

Lyric poetry, 1 title

Yan Kejun's (1762–1843) "Quan Sui wen" 24:1a ff, in his larger *Quan shanggu Sandai Qin Han Sanguo Liuchao wen*, q.v., offers ten items: one petition, four presentations (one fewer than the number contained in the *Han Wei Liuchao baisanjia ji*), one disquisition, and four opinions. It does not contain the *Han Wei Liuchao baisanjia ji*'s "Tonglü duliang yi" 同律度量議, concerning metrology. Furthermore, one might expect that the short response to the Sui emperor by Niu (*Sui shu* 16:394) on the technical criterion used for interpreting the effects of the ether during the *houqi* tests would have been included in the "Quan Sui wen" because it is similar to many short court responses of this nature seen in Yan's compendium. This piece is translated in Bodde ("The Chinese Cosmic Magic Known as 'Watching for Ethers,'" 1981, p. 360).

Transmission and early history of the text

Niu Hong was one of the most learned bookmen, historiographers, and ritual experts of his era, especially influential in court discussions. However, as with other collections of this type, his *wenji* probably dropped out of circulation around the end of the Tang era, since, as we see next, the contents seem to have remained complete through the Tang. Niu's biography in *Sui shu* 49:1310 (completed 636), says merely that his *wenji* contained thirteen *juan* and was "current in his day," but the *Sui shu*'s bibliographic monograph (completed 656), 35:1081, says that the *Niu Hong ji* had twelve *juan*. The bibliography in *Jiu Tang shu* 47:2072 (completed 945, but utilizing eighth-century records) also lists *Niu Hong ji* in twelve *juan*. The catalog in the *Jiu Tangshu* (completed 945, but using eighth-century records) also lists it as twelve *juan* (47:2072). His collected writings are not listed in the major Song catalogs, and it is possible to theorize that they dropped out of popular circulation from early Northern Song to Yuan-Ming, when Feng Weine (1513–1572) included one of Niu's poems in his monumental *Gushi ji** 133:12a–b (*Yingyin Wenyuange Siku quanshu** 1380:469), and then later the *wenji* was reconstituted and included in the *Han Wei Liuchao baisanjia ji*.

Principal editions

The only complete edition of the *Niu Hong ji* that has come down to us is the recension in the *Han Wei Liuchao baisan jia ji*; see *Yingyin Wenyuange Siku quanshu* 1416:254–76. See also the 1879 recarved edition (*chongkan ben* 重刻本) of the Xinshutang 信述堂 printing, which titles it *Niu Qizhang ji* (rpt., Jiangsu: Jiangsu guji shudian, 1990, 5:659–83). There are no modern, annotated editions.

Niu's biography in the Beijing Zhonghua edition (1973) of the *Sui shu* contains punctuated texts of three of his petitions and opinions carried in the *Han Wei Liuchao baisanjia ji* and *Quan Sui wen*: on the history of scholarship, the history of the Mingtang, and the nature of the sixty pitch-standards.

Texts with commentary and notes

Lu Qinli. *Xian Qin Han Wei Jin Nanbeichao shi**. See vol. 3, "Sui shi" 5:2690–91, for his poetry, and 9:2755–70 for his Music Bureau verse and lyrics for court songs.

Secondary studies

Bodde, Derk. "The Chinese Cosmic Magic Known as 'Watching for Ethers.'" Reprinted in *Essays on Chinese Civilization*. Princeton, NJ: Princeton University Press, 1981.

Guo Kangsong 郭康松. "Soufang yiji zhili dingyue: Lun Niu Hong de wenhua gongxian" 搜訪逸籍制禮定樂: 論牛弘的文化貢獻. *Hubei daxue chengren jiaoyu xueyuan xuebao* (2004.8): 19–21.

Howard L. Goodman

Pan Yue ji 潘岳集

Introduction

Pan Yue (247–300) was styled Anren 安仁 , and his last official position was as gentleman attendant of the Yellow Gate (*huangmen shilang* 黃門侍郎), so his collection has also appeared as *Pan Anren ji* and *Pan Huangmen ji*. He was a native of Zhongmou 中牟, Xingyang 滎陽 (modern Zhongmou County, Henan). A well-known description of him relates that he was so handsome that women would gather around him with their hands clasped together (*Shishuo xinyu*, q.v., 14/7); in another version of the anecdote, women would toss fruit at him until it filled his carriage (*Jin shu*, q.v., 55:1507).

Pan Yue's father and grandfather had been successful officials, and around the age of twenty Pan went to serve as assistant to the minister of works. In 268 he impressed the court with his "Ji tian fu" 藉田賦 (Rhapsody on the sacred field) on behalf of Emperor Wu 武, which was included in the *Wen xuan*, q.v. Pan was supported at the capital by his father-in-law, Yang Zhao 楊肇 (d. 275), but Yang was dismissed from office in 272 and died in 275. In 278 Pan wrote his "Qiuxing fu" 秋興賦 (Rhapsody on autumn inspirations), also included in the *Wen xuan*, which declaims his discontent with official life. From 279 to 286 he was demoted to local positions outside the capital. When Emperor Hui 惠 took the throne in 290, he appointed Yang Jun 楊駿 (d. 291), father of Empress Dowager Yang, as grand tutor, and Pan Yue joined his staff as master of records. In the following year, Yang Jun was assassinated, and Pan himself only barely escaped death, but he remained in the capital as a leading member of the Twenty-Four Friends of Jia Mi 賈謐 (d. 300).

During the years 295 to 297 Pan was retired from the capital, and he composed his famous "Xianju fu" 閑居賦 (Rhapsody on living in idleness). He did continue to socialize, though, and in 296 participated in the gathering at Shi Chong's 石崇 (249–300) estate in Golden Valley (Jingu 金谷). Pan Yue's is the only poem that survives from the gathering. This is a pentasyllabic piece preserved in the *Wen xuan*; there is also a tetrasyllabic couplet attributed to Pan Yue and preserved in the Liuchen commentary to the *Wen xuan* (see *Zengbu Liuchen zhu Wen xuan* 增補六臣註文選 [facsimile of Song ed.; rpt., Taipei: Huazheng shuju, 1974; rpt., 1980], 59:20a). In 297 Pan returned to the capital as gentleman writer and gentleman attendant of the cavalry. In 298 his wife, Lady Yang, died, and his mourning for her was to serve as the occasion for several of his last works.

There are two conflicting dimensions to Pan Yue's traditional reputation: first, he was a handsome courtier criticized for sycophancy and superficiality; second, he is admired for his writings in various genres lamenting the deaths of friends, family, and nobility. Later critics have followed his *Jin shu* biography in denouncing his careerist service to Shi Chong and Jia Mi, particularly in composing the treasonous letter falsely attributed to Sima Yu 司馬遹 (d. 300), Crown Prince Minhuai 愍懷 (*Jin shu* 53:1459). Other court pieces, such as the "Rhapsody on the Sacred Field" and the "Guanzhong shi" 關中詩 (Guanzhong poems), were admired and included in the *Wen xuan*.

Modern scholarship has tended to emphasize the sympathetic quality of his personal writings over the ethically dubious aspects of his career. A number of Pan Yue's literary compositions actually express his distaste for an official career, most famously the "Rhapsody on Living in Idleness." Even more of his works are devoted to mourning friends and relatives, an aspect of his achievement that is also mentioned in his *Jin shu* biography. Not only did he write rhapsodies and poems of this kind (the "Daowang fu" 悼亡賦 and "Daowang shi" 悼亡詩, for instance), but also numerous compositions in the genres of epitaph, lamentation, offering, and dirge. To take just one example of his works' popularity, the *Wen xuan* includes four separate dirges by Pan Yue, in *juan* 56 and 57.

Contents

The most popular edition of the collection is *Pan Huangmen ji* in the *Han Wei Liuchao baisan mingjia ji*, q.v., of Zhang Pu (1602–1641). The collection is organized by genre in the following order:

1. Rhapsody
2. Petition
3. Letter (which has the heading "Zhazuo minhuai taizi shu" 詐作愍懷太子書 but is omitted from the table of contents)
4. Opinion
5. Eulogy
6. Encomium
7. Admonition
8. Correction (*xun* 訓)
9. Epitaph
10. Lament
11. Offering
12. Dirge
13. Lyric poetry

The two modern editions with commentary, Dong Zhiguang's *Pan Yue ji jiao zhu* and Wang Zengwen's *Pan Huangmen ji jiaozhu*, are both based on the *Pan Huangmen ji* in the *Han Wei Liuchao baisan mingjia ji* and follow the same order in their arrangement.

There are other Ming editions with a different arrangement, such as the *Pan Huangmen ji* in the *Qishi'er jia ji** edited by Zhang Xie (1574–1640). This edition, available in *Xuxiu Siku quanshu** 1584:473–532, has six *juan* arranged as follows:

1–3. Rhapsodies

4. Lyric poems, letter, opinions, memorials

5. Eulogy, encomium, admonition, correction, epitaphs, lamentations, offerings

6. Dirges and appendices

The generic divisions of Pan Yue's collection fail to indicate that a large part of his extant works is occupied by funerary pieces. In addition to his few dozen rhapsodies and poems, in most genres Pan has only one or two pieces that survive, but among his extant compositions there are nine lamentations, three offerings, and eleven dirges.

One prose work omitted by most collections is the "Guanzhong ji" 關中記 (Record of Guanzhong). A reconstruction of this work is in Tao Zongyi's 陶宗儀 (fl. 1360–1368) *Shuo fu* 說郛, *juan* 61, and it has been reprinted in Zhou Guangpei 周光培, ed., *Han Wei Liuchao biji xiaoshuo* 漢魏六朝筆記小說 (Shijiazhuang: Hebei jiaoyu chubanshe, 1994), 812.

Authenticity and transmission of the text

All extant collections were reconstructed in the Ming. The bibliographies of the *Sui shu*, q.v., *Jiu Tang shu*, and *Xin Tang shu* all record a *Pan Yue ji* in ten *juan*. Perhaps the original collection had already been lost by the Song, since the *Song shi* bibliography (208:13785) lists a collection in seven *juan*, which is close to the size of the extant Ming collections.

There are few problems of authenticity or attribution regarding Pan Yue's works. Counting sets of poems individually, modern collections include about sixty-six works, and the *Wen xuan* contains twenty-two, or exactly one-third of his extant compositions. The other pieces in his collection were mainly copied from the *Yiwen leiju*, q.v., and *Wen xuan* commentaries. One piece has been falsely attributed to him: "Rhapsody on Pensive Roaming" ("Si you fu" 思遊賦), actually by Zhi Yu 摯虞 (d. 311). A special case is the poem in five stanzas that Pan Yue addressed to his cousin Wang Kan 王堪. Three couplets are quoted in *Shishuo xinyu*, q.v., 8/139, and some Ming editions include only one stanza, but the entire poem is preserved in *Wenguan cilin**152:2a, compiled by Xu Jingzong (592–672).

Principal editions

Although the basis for modern texts is the one-*juan* edition by Zhang Pu, the earliest extant was the *Pan Huangmen ji* in six *juan* compiled by Lü Zhaoxi 呂兆禧 (1573–1590) and Yao Shilin 姚士麟 (1561–?) and printed by Weng Shaolu 翁少麓; see Li Jiangfeng ("Lü Zhaoxi he ta de *Dongfang xiansheng ji*"). This was included in Wang Shixian's *Han Wei Liuchao ershiyi mingjia ji** compiled during the Wanli era (1573–1620). The same edition, with some additions and alterations, was included in the *Qishi'er jia ji* and reprinted in the *Xuxiu Siku quanshu*.

Ding Fubao 丁福保 (1874–1952) also compiled a *Pan Anren ji* in five *juan* as part of his *Han Wei Liuchao mingjia ji chu ke* 漢魏六朝名家集初刻 (Shanghai: Wenming shuju, 1911). Ding added some fragments and other pieces not included in earlier editions. For a brief discussion of all these editions, see Chen Shumei (*Pan Yue ji qi shi shiwen yanjiu*, 91–92). Pan Yue's prose was collected separately in Yan Kejun's (1762–1843) *Quan shanggu Sandai Qin Han Sanguo Liuchao wen*, q.v., "Quan Jin wen," *juan* 90–93.

Texts with commentary and notes

There are two modern editions with textual notes and commentary. An advantage of Wang Zengwen's edition is that textual notes and commentary are kept separate, while Dong Zhiguang's edition includes textual notes in its commentary without any differentiation. On the contrary, Dong Zhiguang has consulted a wider variety of textual variants, especially among different versions of Pan Yue's collection.

Dong Zhiguang 董志廣, ed. and comm. *Pan Yue ji jiaozhu* 潘岳集校注. 1993; rpt. and rev., Tianjin: Tianjin guji chubanshe, 2005.
Wang Zengwen 王增文, ed. and comm. *Pan Huangmen ji jiaozhu* 潘黃門集校注. Zhengzhou: Zhongzhou guji chubanshe, 2002.

Selected studies

Chen Shumei 陳淑美. *Pan Yue ji qi shiwen yanjiu* 潘岳及其詩文研究. Taipei: Wenjin chubanshe, 1999.
Fu Xuancong 傅璇琮. "Pan Yue xinian kaozheng" 潘岳繫年考證. *Wen shi* 14 (1982): 237–57.
Kōzen Hiroshi 興膳宏. *Han Gaku Riku Ki* 潘岳陸機. Tokyo: Chikuma shobō, 1973.
Knechtges, David R. "Sweet-peel Orange or Southern Gold? Regional Identity in Western Jin Literature." In *Studies in Early Medieval Chinese Literature and Cultural History in Honor of Richard B. Mather and Donald Holzman*, ed. Paul W. Kroll and David R. Knechtges, 27–80. Provo, UT: T'ang Studies Society, 2003.
Lai, Chiu-mi. "River and Ocean: The Third Century Verse of Pan Yue and Lu Ji." Ph.D. diss., University of Washington, 1990.
———. "The Art of Lamentation in the Works of Pan Yue: 'Mourning the Eternally Departed.'" *Journal of the American Oriental Society* 114.3 (1994): 409–25.
Li Jiangfeng 李江峰. "Lü Zhaoxi he ta de *Dongfang xiansheng ji*" 呂兆禧和他的東方先生集. *Guji zhengli yanjiu xuekan* 4 (2008): 63–68.
Lin Wen-yüeh 林文月. "Pan Yue de qizi" 潘岳的妻子. *Zhongwai wenxue* 17.5 (1988): 4–28.
Matsumoto Yukio 松本幸男. "Han Gaku no denki" 潘岳の傳記. *Ritsumeikan bungaku* 321 (1972): 1–40.
Takahashi Kazumi 高橋和巳. "Han Gaku ron" 潘岳論. *Chūgoku bungaku hō* 7 (1957): 14–91.

Xu Gongchi 徐公持. "'Ershisi you' yu Pan Yue" 二十四友與潘岳. In *Wei Jin wenxue shi* 魏晉文學史, 316–44. Beijing: Renmin wenxue chubanshe, 1999.

Translations

There is no book-length translation of Pan Yue's works but annotated translations of seven rhapsodies may be found in David R. Knechtges's *Wen xuan, or Selections of Refined Literature*. Contained in volume 2, *Rhapsodies on Sacrifices, Hunting, Travel, Sightseeing, Palaces and Halls, Rivers and Seas* (Princeton, NJ: Princeton University Press, 1987) are "Rhapsody on the Sacred Field," "Rhapsody on Pheasant Shooting" ("She zhi fu" 射雉賦), and "Rhapsody on a Western Journey" ("Xi zheng fu" 西征賦). In volume 3, *Rhapsodies on Natural Phenomena, Birds and Animals, Aspirations and Feelings, Sorrowful Laments, Literature, Music, and Passions* are "Rhapsody on Autumn Inspirations," "Rhapsody on Living in Idleness," "Rhapsody on Recalling Old Friends and Kin" ("Huai jiu fu" 懷舊賦), "Rhapsody on a Widow" ("Guafu fu" 寡婦賦), and "Rhapsody on the Mouth Organ" ("Sheng fu" 笙賦).

Some studies cited earlier include numerous translations. Lai ("The Art of Lamentation in the Works of Pan Yue") translates "Ai yongshi wen" 哀永逝文, "Daowang fu," "Daowang shi" nos. 1–3, "Yangshi qi ai shi" 楊氏妻哀詩, "Shang ruozi ci" 傷弱子辭, "Sizi shi" 思子詩, and "Jinlu ai ci" 金鹿哀辭. The last four of these are not included in the *Wen xuan*. Kōzen Hiroshi provides translations of "Huai xian zuo" 懷縣作 no. 1, "Heyang xian zuo" 河陽縣作 no. 1, "Xianju fu," "Jingu ji zuo shi" 金谷集作詩, "Qiuxing fu," "Neigu shi" 內顧詩 no. 1, and "Daowang shi" nos. 1–3. All of these are also included in the *Wen xuan*, except for "Neigu shi," which is from *Yutai xinyong*, q.v.

Nicholas Morrow Williams

Qieyun 切韻

Introduction

The *Qieyun* (preface dated 601) was compiled by Lu Fayan 陸法言 (fl. 589–618) in collaboration with eight other literati. It is one of the earliest comprehensive codifications of Chinese syllables (that is, words designated by a single written character), reflecting significant progress made in a century—from the late fifth to the early seventh century—in the study of Chinese phonetics. The *Qieyun*'s influence spread during the Tang dynasty, when it gained the attention of commentators and became a prescribed reference for the civil service examinations.[1] The format by which the compositors arranged the syllables also became a standard for the rhyme books (*yunshu* 韻書) that followed, especially those compiled with official sponsorship. Although commonly regarded as a "rhyme dictionary" to aid in composing poetry, the work's actual function in premodern times, which may have included assistance in reading and comprehending classical texts, is still not fully understood. As the only pre-Tang rhyme book still extant in several revised editions, it has been a major source for reconstructing and transcribing Medieval Chinese (usually defined as the language of the sixth century) in modern linguistic studies, but controversies surrounding the nature of the work are still unresolved. The *Qieyun*'s importance lies as much in its historical significance as in modern scholars' conflicting views about it.

Contents

The earliest Chinese lexicographies used either an arrangement of semantic categories, as in the *Shiming* 釋名, or one based on the graphs, as in the *Shuowen jiezi* 說文解字. During the Six Dynasties period each Chinese syllable, represented by a written character, came to be analyzed as consisting of two parts, initial and final, the final of which included the tone, being the rhyme (*yun* 韻). Pronunciation of syllables could be indicated by what was called the *fanqie* 反切 system, sometimes translated as dimidiative spelling, which used two other syllables, the first indicating the initial of the word in question, without regard to tone, and the second, the rhyme incorporating both the final and the tone. For example, the modern $hong^2$ 紅 might be "spelled" by 胡 + 龍, h[u] + [l]ong^2. A number of

---

[1] There are several anecdotes involving the use of the *Qieyun* in the examinations, for example, in *Jiu Tang shu* 126:3559 and *Song shi* 155:3605.

dictionaries using these rhymes as the organizing framework then came to be compiled.

The *Qieyun* of 601 is no longer extant; there are only some manuscript fragments found at Dunhuang and elsewhere. The most complete text is in the various versions that survive of a Tang edition prepared by Wang Renxu 王仁昫 (eighth century). Based on Lu's preface, preserved fully by later rhyme-book compilers, and comparative study of its Tang revised editions, including that by Wang Renxu, several generalizations about the *Qieyun* have been made. The work was in five *juan* arranged according to the "four tones" (*sisheng* 四聲; i.e., *ping* 平, *shang* 上, *qu* 去, and *ru* 入). Because of the number of syllables that fell under the *ping* (level) tone, it made up the first two *juan*; the other tones had one *juan* each. Within a *juan*, syllables were organized into rhyme groups in a set order across all tones. Syllables ending in -p, -t, and -k (surviving today only in dialects like Cantonese and Hokkien) composed the *ru* tone. These could be fit into the rhyme scheme sequence by considering -p to stand for -m in the other tones (-m has become -n in Mandarin), -t for -n, and -k for -ng. Within each rhyme, the initials were also arranged according to a set sequence, thus forming a grid into which every syllable of the language could be included. Not every rhyme was represented in every tone; some of the spaces in the imaginary grid would have remained empty. Most accounts give the total number of rhyme groups as 193. There were fifty-four *ping*-tone rhyme groups, fifty-one in the *shang*-tone, fifty-six in the *qu*-tone, and thirty-two in the *ru*-tone (Tang Lan, "Essay," in *Tang xieben Wang Renxu kanmiu buque Qieyun*, ed. Wu Cailuan). Each rhyme's name as used by linguists is the first syllable that appears in the group. For example, in *juan* 1, the first three rhymes are named Dong 東 (ancient *tong*), Dong 冬 (ancient *tuong*), and Zhong 鐘 (ancient *tśjwong*). There is no way to verify how much of Wang Renxu's edition genuinely reflects Lu Fayan's *Qieyun*, but the arrangement and content described therein are usually attributed to Lu Fayan. In the Wang Renxu and other Tang editions, there are also brief notes on the main pages, given in smaller writing below the name of each rhyme group, which supply the *fanqie* gloss for the names of the rhyme groups and identify earlier compilers who either agreed or disagreed with a specific rhyme group designation. Many believe these are Lu Fayan's notes or that they represent his and his collaborators' views (on the *Qieyun*'s structure and organization, see Pulleyblank, *Middle Chinese*, 136–43).

Does the *Qieyun* language reflect the actual speech of the medieval period? This is probably the single most important issue in modern *Qieyun* studies. Speculation on this issue not only determines how the *Qieyun* might be used and perceived as a source for the study of Medieval Chinese, but also has deep implications for our understanding of how the Chinese viewed language as a form of cultural refinement and canonization—a growing concern among the cultural elites of the Six Dynasties. There are four main lines of argument concerning the nature of the *Qieyun* language. The first two are (1) its basis was the speech of the Sui dynasty capital Chang'an (modern Xi'an); and (2) its basis was the speech of the cultural elites in the lower Yangzi region. The other two arguments, based on strong doubt about the homogeneity of the *Qieyun* language, propose that (3) it was based on an eclectic speech mixing northern and southern dialects; and (4) it aimed at an artificial speech (Malmqvist, "The *Chiehyunn* Problem Re-examined"). In any event, one may say that the *Qieyun* represents the first widely recognized codification of Chinese syllables based on the collective perception by medieval cultural elites about what the "canonized language" was or should be.

Authorship

Lu Fayan, known by his style name (his *ming* was Ci 詞 or 慈), is mentioned only briefly in the biography of his father, Lu Shuang 陸爽 (539?–591?), in *Sui shu*, q.v., 58:1420, and *Bei shi*, q.v., 28:1023. The only office he is known to have held is gentleman for attendance (*chengfeng lang* 承奉郎), a sinecure title. In 600, while he was still working on the *Qieyun*, Lu Fayan was stripped of his official title and banned from holding office as a result of a "posthumous punishment" ordered by Sui Wendi against his late father (*Bei shi* biography). Thereafter, he appears to have led a private and somewhat isolated life, teaching students and having no contact with former fellow officials (Lu Fayan, "Preface"; see Yu Naiyong, *Xinjiao huzhu Songben Guangyun*). Other than his authorship of the *Qieyun*, Lu Fayan is practically unknown in history. Perhaps sensitive to his own relative anonymity, Lu ended his *Qieyun* preface by humbly saying that his work "is not the unruly claim of a nobody but an account of the views left by the various worthies" ("Preface," 14). He was referring to the attendees at a gathering in his home about twenty years earlier. According to his account, these eight literati, all of whom were senior to him in age as well as in official rank, had become engaged in an extended and thorough discussion about various phonetic issues of the day. They then spontaneously conceived the idea of the compilation and put him in charge of note-taking. Even though Lu Fayan was the one to carry out the compilation over the next two decades, modern scholars often regard the *Qieyun* as a collective work, some even highlighting the authorship of his better-known collaborators over his. The eight literati were Liu Zhen 劉臻 (526?–598), Yan Zhitui 顏之推 (531–590s), Lu Sidao 盧思道 (535–586), Wei Yanyuan 魏彥淵 (fl. 581), Li Ruo 李若 (fl. 581), Xiao Gai 蕭該 (fl. 581), Xin Deyuan 辛德源 (fl. 550–602), and Xue Daoheng 薛道衡 (540–609).[2] Yan Zhitui, author of the *Yanshi jiaxun*, q.v., and Xiao Gai, one of the earliest commentators of the sixth-century anthology *Wen xuan*, q.v., appear to be the leaders at the gathering.[3] The fact that some of these literati originally came

---

[2] The version of Lu Fayan's preface in the *Guangyun* mentions only Liu Zhen's name but all eight officials are named in the version included in the *Tang xieben Wang Renxu kanmiu buque Qieyun*. For brief biographies of them, see Wang Shouming, *Lidai Hanyu yinyuexue wenxuan*, 16n3.

[3] Lu Fayan's preface notes that Xiao Gai and Yan Zhitui "made most of the decisions" (*duo suo jueding* 多所決定) in their collective attempt to select the "refined and precise" (*jingqie* 精切) sounds. The two works attributed to Xiao Gai are the *Hanshu yinyi* 漢書音義 and the *Wenxuan yinyi* 文選音義, both of which are now lost. Yan Zhitui's *Yanshi jiaxun* reveals some

from the south, while others were from the north, has also led to the perception that the *Qieyun* was the product of a collaboration aimed at bridging the north-south divide.

Origin and authenticity

The commonly told story about the *Qieyun* is that it was a work inspired by the reunification of China under the Sui, when the need to reconcile northern and southern accents became more urgent (Luo Changpei, *Qieyun yanjiu lunwenji*, 26–65). Lu Fayan no doubt had a vision of an "idealized sound" that would transcend regional divide, but, as already discussed, the nature of the language that he eventually prescribed is very much in question. Instead of using a place-name or a regional name to identify his idealized sound, Lu simply promised his audience the most refined (*jing* 精) and the most precise (*qie* 切), and he underscored this by naming his work the *Qieyun* (Precise rhymes). While Lu Fayan and his collaborators were clearly seeking to "correct" what they saw as "mistakes" in their contemporaries' use of language, they were also responding to the "problems" that they detected in earlier compilers' attempts to codify Chinese syllables. Lu directly names six earlier works, including the *Yunji* 韻集 by Lü Jing 呂靜 of the Jin dynasty and comments that "they contradict one another" (*geyou guaihu* 各有乖互; "Preface," 13). The fact that he appears to think he could reconcile not only the regional divide and the language mistakes of his contemporaries, but also the differences among rhyme books from past and present, suggests that "the idealized sound" that he envisioned was a universal one, transcending not only a spatial divide but also the temporal gap. The function of his *Qieyun* was also meant to be wide reaching: while evaluating the "strengths and weaknesses" of northern and southern accents, he stated that he required "all [his] epigoni who are possessed of literary elegance" (*fanyou wenzao* 凡有文藻) to "have a clear grasp of sounds and rhymes" (*ming shengyun* 明聲韻; "Preface," 13). In other words, his aim was not only to correct speech or recitation, but to guide literary composition as well.

Transmission of the text and early commentaries

The *Sui shu*'s bibliographical monograph does not list the *Qieyun*, and it is not until *Jiu Tang shu*, q.v., 46:1985, that it is first mentioned in the standard histories. We have no information on how the *Qieyun* was circulated before it gained broader attention in the Tang. The earliest known response to the work is a commentary (*jian* 箋) by Zhangsun Neyan 長孫訥言 from 677, about seventy-five years after the *Qieyun*'s completion; and Wang Renxu's "corrected and supplemented" edition has been dated to approximately 706, more than a century after Lu Fayan's preface (Tang Lan, "Essay"). By that time, according to Wang Renxu, the work was "highly

---

of his views on the language issues of the day and has been used a reference for understanding the *Qieyun*.

regarded by all" (*shisu gongzhong* 時俗共重) and "was indeed the canonized sound" (*cheng wei dianyin* 誠為典音; Wang Renxu, "Preface"). The survival of a few incomplete copies of other Tang revised editions further attests to its popularity during the Tang.[4] But the *Qieyun*'s influence began to wane following the publication of other officially sanctioned rhyme books, such as the *Tang yun* 唐韻 (Tang rhymes) and, later, the *Guangyun* 廣韻 (Broad rhymes).[5] These two works are the most significant of a number of works that were meant to correct and/or expand upon the *Qieyun*. Sun Mian's preface to the *Tang yun* points out that the purpose of this compilation was to amend (*kanzheng* 刊正) the "minor imperfections" (*xia xia* 瑕) of the *Qieyun* (*Xinjiao huzhu Songben*, 16). The imperial authorization (*chidie* 勅牒) that accompanied one publication of the *Guangyun*, on the contrary, describes the work of the compilers after Lu Fayan and his collaborators simply as "adding characters" (*zengjia zi* 增加字; *Xinjiao huzhu Songben*, 11–12). In truth, these later works had made more complex changes to the *Qieyun*. The number of rhyme groups in Lu Fayan's *Qieyun*, as indicated earlier, is usually cited as 193; in the Wang Renxu version, the number increased to 195; and in the *Guangyun*, it is 206 (Pulleyblank, *Middle Chinese*, 135–36). The original *Qieyun*, with every new compilation that claimed to improve on it, was probably buried deeper layer by layer. But the perception of a continuing *Qieyun* tradition was so strong that many scholars in the late imperial period treated the *Guangyun* as if it were the work of Lu Fayan, although his completion of the *Qieyun* was separated from the last known compilation of the *Guangyun* by about four hundred years. In fact, *Song shi* 202:5073 lists Lu Fayan as the compiler of the *Guangyun*. That a number of later rhyme books were also named *Qieyun* further added to the confusion. In the nineteenth century, the *Qieyun* was eventually recognized as a lost work and a few recensions became available; in the twentieth century, copies of a few Tang revised editions, particularly the Wang Renxu edition, caught the attention of scholars.

Principal editions

Tang xieben Wang Renxu kanmiu buque Qieyun 唐寫本王仁昫刊謬補缺切韻 [Tang manuscript copy of Wang Renxu's corrected and supplemented *Qieyun*]. Edited by Wu Cailuan 吳彩鸞. Beijing: Guoli Gugong bowuyuan, 1947; rpt., Taipei: Guangwen shuju, 1964. Essay by Tang Lan 唐蘭, unpaged, at end of volume.

---

[4] For these incomplete copies, see Ding Shan 丁山, "Tang xieben *Qieyun* canjuan ba" 唐寫本切韻殘卷跋 [Preface to the incomplete copies of the Tang manuscript *Qieyun*] and "Tang xieben *Qieyun* canjuan xuba" 唐寫本切韻殘卷續跋 [Second preface to the incomplete copies of the Tang manuscript *Qieyun*], in Luo Changpei, *Qieyun yanjiu lunwenji*, 57–59, 60–61.

[5] The *Tang yun* was compiled by Sun Mian 孫愐 (fl. 732). The *Guangyun*, completed in 1007 under the auspices of the Song emperor Zhenzong, was the most comprehensive and authoritative rhyme book in premodern times. Chen Pengnian 陳彭年 is usually listed as its main compiler.

Tang xie quanben Wang Renxu kanmiu buque Qieyun jiaojian 唐寫全本王仁昫刊謬補缺切韻校箋 *[Complete* Tang manuscript copy of Wang Renxu's corrected and supplemented *Qieyun*, collated and annotated]. Annotations by Long Yuchun 龍宇純. Hong Kong: Chinese University of Hong Kong, 1968.

Selected studies

Chen Li 陳澧 (1810–1882). *Qieyun kao* 切韻考. Taipei: Taiwan xuesheng shuju, 1972.

Li Rong 李榮. *Qieyun yinxi* 切韻音系. Beijing: Kexue chubanshe, 1956. This study of the sound system of the *Qieyun* has nine chapters. The first arranges the characters in the *Qieyun* by their sound elements; the second classifies the finals (*yunmu* 韻母) into different categories; the third and fourth discuss the *fanqie*; the fifth lists Karlgren's reconstruction of the *Qieyun* initials and finals; the sixth, seventh, and eighth chapters discuss sound value by considering Karlgren's reconstruction; the ninth chapter discusses tonality (*shengdiao* 聲調).

Liu Fu 劉復. *Shi yunhui bian* 十韻彙編. Beijing: Peking University, 1936. The several reprints include Taiwan (1963) and Beijing (2007). The preface by Wei Jiangong 魏建功 contains bibliographies of early dictionaries, discussion of rhymes, *fanqie*, Dunhuang finds, and so on. This a most useful work for combining on parallel horizontal registers a complete text of the *Guangyun* with what remains of the texts of the *Qieyun* and *Tang yun*, so that one may see at a glance differences among the various texts for those portions that survive. An index by rhymes is not ordinarily useful, but that by radical and stroke is. The reference in the latter index is to tone, rhyme, and line within the rhyme, rather than to a page number.

Luo Changpei 羅常培 et al. *Qieyun yanjiu lunwenji* 切韻研究論文集. Hong Kong: Shiyong shuju, 1972.

Malmqvist, N. G. D. "The *Chiehyunn* Problem Re-examined." *Papers of the CIC Far Eastern Language Institute*, vol. 4, ed. Richard B. Mather, 10–18. Ann Arbor, MI: Panel on Far Eastern Language Institutes of the Committee on Institutional Cooperation, 1973.

Shao Rongfen 邵榮芬. *Qieyun yanjiu* 切韻研究. Beijing: Zhongguo shehui kexue chubanshe, 1982.

Reference works

Karlgren, Bernhard. *Grammata Serica Recensa*. Reprinted from the *Bulletin of the Museum of Far Eastern Antiquities*. Stockholm, 1957. A dictionary of the author's reconstruction of "Archaic" and "Ancient" Chinese. Words are arranged by the phonetic that brings word families together. Various graphic variants, taken from oracle bones and bronzes, are included. The sources of the definitions of the graphs drawn from the various classics are indicated. Three pronunciations are given for almost all graphs: archaic (fifth century

B.C.), asterisked because Karlgren considered these to be tentative; ancient (sixth century A.D.), which he thought phonetically accurate; and the modern. The index is to the phonetic components of the graphs. The introduction (pp. 1–18) is very useful. Various alternatives to Karlgren's system, as proposed by E. G. Pulleyblank and others, may be found in the historical linguistics literature.

Pulleyblank, E. G. *Middle Chinese: A Study in Historical Phonology*. Vancouver: University of British Columbia Press, 1984.

Shen Jianshi 沈兼士. *Guangyun shengxi* 廣韻聲系 [The phonetic system of the *Guangyun*]. Beijing: Furen daxue, 1945; rpt., Beijing: Wenzi gaige chubanshe, 1960; Beijing: Zhonghua shuju, 1985. A very useful reference work that arranges characters by their phonetic elements, thus grouping them into word families. Beside each character is the *fanqie* and definition as given in the *Guangyun*, and in the margin the ancient pronunciation (according to Karlgren's reconstruction) along with the rhyme, "button" word (first character of the group of its homophones), and other notations referring to later Chinese phonetic research. The index to the volume lists each character, something that the Karlgren volume does not do.

Wang Shouming 汪壽明. *Lidai Hanyu yinyuexue wenxuan* 歷代漢語音韻學文選 [Selection of essays on Chinese phonology through the ages]. Shanghai: Shanghai guji chubanshe, 1986.

Yu Naiyong 余迺永, comp. *Huzhu jiaozheng Songben Guangyun* 互註校正宋本廣韻 [Interlocking commentaries and collations of a Song edition of the *Guangyun*]. Taipei: Lianguan chubanshe, 1974. A photolithographic reproduction of a Song edition, but with the use of red ink to highlight the *fanqie* spellings and number of graphs under each "button" word, as well as to indicate in roman script the initial of those words. The numbers of the rhymes in sequential count are added in red in the tables of contents. Footnotes, also in red, indicate textual notes included at the bottom of each page. Other useful features are an index of the characters arranged by radical and stroke, and a table comparing a number of phonetic spelling conventions in the reconstructions of Karlgren and others.

———. *Xinjiao huzhu Songben Guangyun* 新校互註宋本廣韻 [Song edition *Guangyun* in new collation and with multiple annotations]. Shanghai: Shanghai cishu chubanshe, 2000. Lu Fayan's "Preface" on pp. 12–14.

Meow Hui Goh

Qimin yaoshu 齊民要術

Introduction

The *Qimin yaoshu* (Essential techniques [or arts] for the common people) by Jia Sixie 賈思勰 (fl. ca. 530–544) is the earliest Chinese agricultural treatise to have come down to us more or less intact, and its influence has been enormous. Written in simple and vivid language, the *Qimin yaoshu* is comprehensive and clearly arranged. Technical discussions are interwoven with personal observations, anecdotes, recipes, and literary, philosophical, or historical quotations, to form a vivid tapestry of the rural landscape and activities in medieval north China. Repeating Jia Sixie's precepts centuries later, many later agronomists writing on farming in north China believed that the sophistication and efficacy of the techniques recommended in the *Qimin yaoshu* had never been surpassed. In another register of influence, the *Qimin yaoshu*'s systematic organization, and the clarity and precision of its technical language, set the pattern for the layout of later agronomic treatises and indeed for the way in which many farming issues were conceptualized. Freely copied and extensively quoted, from the Tang through to the Qing, the *Qimin yaoshu* was an obligatory point of reference for anyone writing on agriculture or attempting to raise local farming standards, whether in a private or an official capacity.

The *Qimin yaoshu* also occupies a significant place in modern scholarship and popular culture. It was a fundamental source and reference for the historical studies of East Asian agricultural technology and economy that flourished in China, Japan, and the West between the mid-1950s and mid-1980s. In China in the 1950s and 1960s, agricultural historians and scientists were particularly interested in what they saw as the pioneering protoscientific knowledge contained in the *Qimin yaoshu* and in its potential applications in the modern Chinese countryside. Among the techniques they tested in the laboratory or on the farm were systems of crop rotation and the use of green manures; pelleting seeds with extracts of animal bone and plant insecticides; and intensive cultivation of melons and vegetables in pits filled with compost. More recently, the *Qimin yaoshu* has come to serve as a kind of mystical sourcebook for devotees of soy-based diets or exotic health brews. Reflecting broader shifts in academic focus from production to consumption studies, its most prominent scholarly use today is as a source for historians of diet and cuisine, although it continues to be studied by economic and social historians, historical linguists, and ethnobotanists.

Authorship

Our only direct information about Jia Sixie, the author of the *Qimin yaoshu*, comes from ten characters at the beginning of the preface that refer to him as "prefect of Gaoyang 高陽 during the Later [Northern] Wei." Otherwise, as the foremost *Qimin yaoshu* scholar Miao Qiyu 繆啓愉 notes, the historical record is blank.

There were in fact two Northern Wei prefectures called Gaoyang, one in modern Hebei and one in Yidu 益都 district in the commandery of Qi 齊, in modern Shandong. Scholars since the Qing have used internal evidence to argue for each location, but it is difficult to draw conclusions on internal evidence alone since Jia Sixie makes it clear that he had served in different regions of northern China and had made it his business to observe, experiment with, and compare local farming practices wherever he found himself, as well as consulting colleagues on their personal experiences, the better to distill general principles of good husbandry.

More recently, historians have noted that the court officials listed in the *Wei shu*, q.v., include a Jia Sibo 賈思伯 (d. 525) and a Jia Sitong 賈思同 (d. 540), both from Yidu; it is now generally agreed that Jia Sixie was probably a member of the same generation of the Yidu Jia family. If the family estate was indeed in Yidu, this raises the possibility (supported by repeated allusions in the text to "Qi customs" and to "Qi people," Qi being the traditional name of that area) that the term *qimin* in the title of the work is used punningly to refer not simply to the "common people" in general but also to the farmers of Qi in particular.

Internal evidence for the dating of the *Qimin yaoshu* puts its completion at some time between 533 and 544.

Contents and sources

In his preface, explaining that he had written the *Qimin yaoshu* "to instruct the youngsters of my family," the author Jia Sixie notes: "I have gleaned material from traditional texts and from folk songs. I have enquired for information from old men and learned myself from practical experience. From ploughing to pickles there is no domestic or farming activity that I have not described exhaustively." He goes on to explain that he has organized the work in ninety-two *pian* 篇 (chapters), divided into ten *juan*, with a table of contents at the beginning of each *juan* in order to make the work easier to use.

Each chapter devoted to a crop or animal typically begins with a discussion of varieties or breeds and of their common or learned names, citing etymological works and encyclopaedias such as the *Erya* 爾雅 (perhaps of the third century B.C.) or the *Fangyan* 方言 by Yang Xiong 楊雄 (53 B.C.–A.D. 18). Jia Sixie then breaks tasks up into sequences, treating individual crops systematically from seed preparation, ploughing, sowing, and hoeing through to harvesting and storage. For all important procedures he offers general principles followed by specific advice matched to variations in climate, soil type, and weather. This format set the precedent for most later treatises intended for official use. An alternative format, the *yueling* 月令 (monthly ordinances, or farming calendar), in which all

Juan	Chapter	
		xu 序, preface
		za shuo 雜說, miscellaneous remarks
I	1	*geng tian* 耕田, clearing and tilling land
	2	*shou zhong* 收種, collection and treatment of seed grain
	3	*zhong gu* 種穀, cultivation of setaria millet
II	4–16	cultivation of field crops (cereals, beans, etc.)
III	17–29	cultivation of vegetables
	30	*za shuo* 雜說, miscellaneous remarks (including *yueling*, monthly ordinance)
IV	31	*yuan li* 園籬, planting hedges
	32	*zai shu* 栽樹, transplanting trees (general rules)
	33–44	fruit trees and Chinese pepper
V	45	*zhong sang zhe* 種桑柘, mulberry trees (with an appendix on sericulture [*yang can fu* 養蠶附])
	46–51	timber trees and bamboo
	52–54	dye plants
	55	*fa mu* 伐木, cutting timber
VI	56–61	animal husbandry (including poultry and fish)
VII	62	*huozhi* 貨殖, the profits of trade
	63–67	brewing
VIII	68–79	culinary preparations (soy sauces, vinegars, preserved meats, etc.)
IX	80–89	culinary preparations (meats, cereal dishes, candies, etc.)
	90–91	glue making, preparation of ink, brushes, etc.
X	92	grains, fruits, and vegetables not indigenous to north China

the farm and household activities typical of a particular month, from ploughing cereal fields to mending ropes, were grouped in a single chapter—facilitating the organization of time and labor—was more typical of farming treatises intended for private use.

The *Qimin yaoshu* set the pattern for the sections on crop plants in later works, yet comparison shows that farming treatises evolved significantly over time. One striking contrast is the gendering of Song and post-Song works, structured to reflect what they saw as an economically but also cosmologically crucial complementarity of labor reflected in the common expression "men plough, women weave" (*nan geng nü zhi* 男耕女織). Such works generally begin with a section on (male) farming tasks followed by chapters on (female) tasks of textile production. The *Qimin yaoshu* discusses the production of the raw materials for textiles but not their fabrication; unlike later agronomists, Jia Sixie apparently did not consider ploughing and weaving conceptually inseparable. Nor did he address themes of central importance in later treatises like Wang Zhen's 王楨 *Nongshu* 農書 of 1313, such as the construction of different types of field, irrigation methods, or the building and use of tools and machinery. Whereas print-era treatises like Wang

Zhen's work integrated illustrations into their explanations of technical practices, the *Qimin yaoshu* contains no graphics beyond the tables of contents.

Another important difference with later agronomic treatises is that a substantial portion of the *Qimin yaoshu* is devoted to household industries, including the preparation of foodstuffs and other household necessities (among them ink and rouge), and miscellaneous instructions on such tasks as dry-cleaning silk robes and killing bookworms. In later times the details of food processing and household industries no longer figured prominently in agricultural treatises but found their place, along with discussions of dietetics, in the domestic sections of popular encyclopaedias. The *Qimin yaoshu* contains roughly 280 recipes, ranging from pasta and breads to meat stews, scrambled eggs with chives, and steamed bear. It is an important source of excerpts from two earlier culinary works, the *Shi jing* 食經 (Classic of foods) and *Shi ci* 食次 (Order of dishes), now lost, and provides an unparalleled documentation of the many complex forms of food processing current at the time. From it we see, for example, that while soy sauces, relishes, and pickles (of meat, fish, or vegetables) abounded, bean curd as we know it today was not yet part of the dietary repertoire.

Perhaps the most atypical aspect of the *Qimin yaoshu* compared to later agronomic works is the prominence of animal husbandry and of milk products. From very early times, perhaps because of high population densities, typical Chinese peasant farms devoted almost all their land to cropping. Pigs and poultry were raised inside the farmyard; ducks lived in the rice paddies; the few indispensable draught animals were tethered on marginal land to graze. But the manorial enterprises of medieval north China differed in raising large numbers of livestock (Jia Sixie mentions a flock of two hundred sheep). They relied heavily on draught animals, including mules and donkeys as well as oxen. Horses figure prominently too: it was a time when the elite liked to ride horses for pleasure or everyday travel, as well as for military purposes. And finally, there was a widespread culture of milk consumption between the Han and the Tang. Jia Sixie was writing at a time when pastoral peoples from Central Asia had ruled north China for over a century, and foodstuffs derived from the milk of sheep and cows were very popular. He describes the preparation of many products that totally disappeared from the Chinese diet in later dynasties, including forms of smoked yogurt or cheese, clarified butter, and Tibetan-style mixtures of parched wheat powdered and mixed with dried fruits and milk products. Jia Sixie is very enthusiastic about these muesli-style mixtures, which he recommends as travel rations.

Over one hundred thousand characters in length, the *Qimin yaoshu* is at once a manual and an encyclopaedia. Typically for books of the period, about half the work consists of quotations, drawn from around 160 works spanning some seven centuries. No specialist agronomic works earlier than the *Qimin yaoshu* are extant today, but the wealth of sources Jia quotes makes it clear that he drew on a long and rich agronomic tradition. The bibliographical chapter of the *Han shu* contains a list of nine specialist agricultural works (*nongjia* 農家) totaling 114 chapters (*pian* 篇);

some are attributed to Warring States authors, others to writers of the Western Han. All are now lost except for scattered quotations, but most of them appear to have been known to Jia Sixie; in fact, quotations in the *Qimin yaoshu* are our main or only source for several of these works, most notably the Western Han *Fan Shengzhi shu* 氾勝之書 (Book of Fan Shengzhi), originally 18 *pian* in length. Another important work quoted extensively by Jia is the *Simin yueling* 四民月令 (Monthly ordinances for the four classes of people), written circa A.D. 160 by Cui Shi 崔寔.

Jia Sixie did not restrict his references to agronomic works but quoted liberally from histories; treatises on natural philosophy, cosmology, and divination; works on the divine and curious such as the *Shenxian zhuan* 神仙傳 attributed to the Daoist alchemist Ge Hong 葛洪 (284–363); and collections of natural knowledge such as the *Nanfang caowu zhuang* 南方草物狀, attributed to the Jin scholar Xu Zhong 徐衷, and now known only through quotations.

It has been debated whether the *Qimin yaoshu* was written with small peasant farmers in mind, as the title seems to imply, or intended as a handbook for the owners of large estates—in other words, whether Jia Sixie was writing as an official or as a landowner. But just as Jia explicitly states that he composed the work for the benefit of his own family, so too the scale of operations taken for granted in Jia's own text confirms that he was writing with large, centrally managed estates in mind. The scale of crop rotations, the reliance on large numbers of draught animals, and the advice to devote large amounts of land, labor, and capital to the commercial production of timber or brewing were all far beyond the scope of peasant households.

The *Qimin yaoshu* offers a conspectus of best farming practice in medieval north China, a region characterized by cold winters, hot summers, and low humidity. The main cereal crops were drought-resistant millets, and the multiple rounds of hoeing, the careful timing of operations, and the crop rotations, green manures, and mulches that Jia Sixie minutely describes were all designed to prevent evaporation and preserve moisture in the soil. Starting in the Tang, the rice-growing wetlands of the Yangzi Valley began to surpass the northern plains, first in agricultural productivity, then in economic and finally in social and political importance. Capital and expertise were increasingly invested in the south, and the rural north became a relative backwater where small landholders with few capital resources struggled to survive. Most later writers discussing northern farming bewailed the fall in standards from those set in the *Qimin yaoshu*; few recognized that no peasant farmer could hope to attain them.

Transmission of the text and principal editions

For full critical accounts of the transmission and editions of the *Qimin yaoshu* the reader is referred to Miao Qiyu's modern translation (*Qimin yaoshu jiaoshi*, 733–858) and his readers' guide (*Qimin yaoshu daodu*).

The *Qimin yaoshu* became well known soon after its completion. It was widely consulted by Tang officials. An expanded version titled *Yan Qiren yaoshu* 演

齊人要術 (An expansion of the *Qi[min] yaoshu*), now lost, was compiled by the academician Li Hengfeng 李淳風 (602–670). Quotations from the *Qimin yaoshu* constitute the major part of the *Sishi zuanyao* 四時纂要, compiled circa 750 by Han E 韓鄂. Jia Sixie's recommendations continued to provide the basic framework for discussion in most later works on farming in north China, many of them written by gentleman farmers for local consumption. Here we might cite the thirteenth-century *Hanshi zhishuo* 韓氏直說, preserved only in quotations, and the *Nongsang jing* 農桑經, completed in 1705 by the famous author Pu Songling 蒲松齡 (1630–1715).

Although the *Qimin yaoshu* was ostensibly written for private use, its scope, technical sophistication, and insistence upon general principles that could be translated into a variety of local contexts ensured its early incorporation into the official corpus of statecraft texts. Along with the *Sishi zuanyao*, it was printed and distributed to magistrates around the country on imperial order in the early eleventh century. It is extensively quoted in officially commissioned works such as the *Nongsang jiyao* 農桑輯要, presented to the Yuan throne in 1273 by Meng Qi 孟祺, and the *Shoushi tongkao* 授時通考, commissioned by the Qianlong emperor and completed under the direction of E'ertai 鄂爾泰 (1677–1745) in 1742. The *Nong shu* of 1313 by Wang Zhen 王禎 and the *Nongzheng quanshu* 農政全書 by Xu Guangqi 徐光啟 (1562–1633), published posthumously in 1639—the two most original and influential late imperial treatises, both written specifically for official use although neither was officially commissioned—both rely heavily on the *Qimin yaoshu* for their discussions of good farming practice in north China.

The earliest known printing of the *Qimin yaoshu* is the Northern Song imperial Chongwenyuan 崇文院 woodblock edition of the Tiansheng period (1023–1031). Only two *juan* (5 and 8) of this original edition have survived in complete form. Preserved in the library of Takayama Monastery (高山寺) in Kyoto, they were reprinted in facsimile in 1914 by Luo Zhenyu 羅振玉 (1866–1940) in his *Jishi'an congshu* 吉石庵叢書 collection. Nine *juan* of a Japanese transcription of the Chongwenyuan edition made in 1274 have been preserved in the Kanazawa archives (金澤文庫) and were published in facsimile in 1948.

During the Southern Song, in 1144, Zhang Lin 張轔 made a private reprinting of the Chongwenyuan edition in Longshu 龍舒 (modern Anhui), with a postface by Ge You 葛祐. All that survives of this printed edition is an incomplete set of proofs. During the Ming, however, a complete manuscript copy of Zhang Lin's edition was made by a Mr. Deng of Jiangning (寧江鄧氏). Preserved in the Qunbilou 群碧樓 collection, it was rediscovered in the early Republican period and published in facsimile by the Commercial Press in 1922 as part of their *Sibu congkan* collection. In 1936 the same text was printed in movable type in the *Guoxue jiben congshu* 國學基本叢書 collection. As probably the closest version to the earliest printed edition, the *Sibu congkan**edition is generally considered, along with the Kanazawa text, to be the most accurate of the many versions of the *Qimin yaoshu*.

During the Yuan, large sections of the *Qimin yaoshu* were incorporated into the *Nongsang jiyao* of 1273, with quite a few errors of transcription and omission. A

Yuan woodblock edition, since lost and of unknown provenance, provided the basic text for the earliest Ming woodblock edition, printed in Huxiang 湖湘 by Ma Zhiqing 馬直卿 in 1524. This in turn served as the basis for the *Mice huihan* 秘冊 汇函 edition of 1603, produced by Hu Zhenheng 胡震亨. Hu passed on his blocks to Mao Jin 毛晉, who used them to print the *Jindai mishu* 津逮秘書 edition in 1630. Several collections of excerpts from the *Qimin yaoshu* were also published during the Ming. No critical scholarship went into any of the Ming editions, however, and although they survived and provided the basis for various later reprints and facsimile editions in China and in Japan, judged by the standards of modern scholarship their quality is very poor.

Critical editions of the *Qimin yaoshu* multiplied during and after the Qing. The *Xuejin taoyuan* 學津討原 printing of 1804 by Zhang Haipeng 張海鵬 (1755–1816) was a new version of the 1603 edition, revised in light of a critical edition of the *Nongsang jiyao* excerpts by Huang Qinliu 黃琴六. In 1926 a thorough critical revision of this version, by Huang Tingjian 黃廷鑑 (b. 1762), was published using movable type in the *Sibu beiyao** series by the Zhonghua shuju. By no means identical to the *Sibu congkan* edition of 1922, it is nevertheless considered by modern critics to be a good edition.

Another valuable edition is the *Jianxi cunshe congkan* 漸西村舍叢刊 edition of 1896, printed by Yuan Chang 袁昶. Although Miao Qiyu considers the critical scholarship of the editors Liu Shouzeng 劉壽曾 and Liu Fuzeng 劉富曾 rather superficial, the importance of this version is that it is based upon the draft of an unpublished critical edition of circa 1821, by an otherwise unknown scholar called Wu Dian 吾點. According to Liu Shouzeng, Wu Dian was a bibliophile with a huge collection, including not only the 1630 Jindai edition of the *Qimin yaoshu* but also a copy of the Song edition. Miao Qiyu's meticulous comparison between the texts of the Northern and Southern Song editions, the Ming editions and the *Jianxi cunshe* edition confirms that Wu Dian's recension does indeed avoid many of the mistaken transcripts of the Ming editions. The *Jianxi cunshe* edition served as the basis for the 1917 Longxi jingshe 龍谿精舍 edition and for the Shangwu yinshuguan (Commercial Press) moveable type *Congshu jicheng** edition of 1936.

Modern critical editions, and full and partial translations of the *Qimin yaoshu* and the works it contains

Li Changnian 李長年. *Qimin yaoshu yanjiu* 齊民要術研究. Beijing: Nongye chubanshe, 1959.

Miao Qiyu 繆啓愉. *Qimin yaoshu jiaoshi* 齊民要術校釋. Beijing: Nongye chubanshe, 1982.

———. *Qimin yaoshu daodu* 齊民要術導讀. Chengdu: Ba Shu shushe, 1988.

Nishiyama Takeichi 西山武一 and Kumashiro Yukio 熊代幸雄. *Seimin yōjutsu* 齊 民要術. 2 vols. Tokyo: Ajya Keizai Press, 1957, 1959; rpt., 1969, 1 vol.

Shi Shenghan 石聲漢. *Qimin yaoshu jinshi* 齊民要術今釋. 4 vols. Beijing: Kexue chubanshe, 1957.

———. *A Preliminary Survey of the Book Ch'i Min Yao Shu, an Agricultural Encyclopaedia of the Sixth Century*. Beijing: Science Press, 1958.

———. *On the Fan Sheng-chih Shu, an Agriculturalist Book of China Written by Fan Sheng-chih in the First Century* B.C. Beijing: Science Press, 1959; rpt., 1974.

———. *Qimin yaoshu xuanduben* 齊民要術選讀本. Beijing: Nongye chubanshe, 1961.

———. *Simin yueling jiaozhu* 四民月令校註. Beijing: Zhonghua chubanshe, 1965.

———. *Ji Xu Zhong Nanfang caowu zhuang* 輯徐衷南方草物壯. Xi'an: Dongbei nongye daxue, 1973.

Secondary literature

Amano Motonosuke 天野元之助. *Chūgoku nōgyōshi kenkyū* 中国農業史研究. Tokyo: Ochanomizu shobō, 1962; revised and expanded editions, 1979, 1989.

———. "Kogi no Ka Shikyō *Seimin yōjutsu* no kenkyū" 後魏の賈思勰齊民要術の研究. In *Chūgoku no kagaku to kagakushi* 中国の科学學と科学史, ed. Yamada Keiji 山田慶兒, 369–570. Kyoto: Humanities Institute of Kyoto University, 1979.

Bray, Francesca. "Agricultural Development and Agrarian Change in Han China." *Early China* 5 (1980): 1–13.

———. "Agriculture." In *Science and Civilisation in China*, ed. Joseph Needham, vol. 6.2. Cambridge: Cambridge University Press, 1984.

———. "Tecniche essenziale per il popolo." In *La Scienza in Cina, Storia della Scienza*, ed. Karine Chemla, Francesca Bray, Fu Daiwie, Huang Yilong, and Georges Métailié, vol. 2, pp. 208–19. Rome: Istituto della Enciclopedia Italiana, 2001.

Dong, Kaichen. "A Preliminary Discussion of Chinese Agricultural Treatises in the Style of 'Monthly Ordinances' *yueling*." *Journal d'agriculture traditionnelle et de botanique appliquée* 28.3–4 (1981): 231–53.

Gao Min 高敏. *Wei Jin Nanbeichao jingji shi* 魏晉南北朝經済史. 2 vols. Shanghai: Shanghai renmin chubanshe, 1996.

Han Guopan 韓國磐. *Beichao jingji shitan* 北朝經済試探. Shanghai: Shanghai renmin chubanshe, 1958.

———. *Nanbeichao jingji shilue* 南北朝經済史略. Xiamen: Xiamen daxue chubanshe, 1990.

Harper, Donald. "The Cookbook in Ancient and Medieval China." Unpublished paper presented at the conference "Discourses and Practices of Everyday Life in Imperial China," Columbia University, October 2002.

Herzer, Christine. "Das *Ssu-min yueh-ling* des Ts'ui Shih: Ein Bauern-Kalender aus der späteren Han-Zeit." Ph.D. diss., University of Hamburg, 1963.

———. "Chia Szu-hsieh, der Verfasser des Ch'i-min yao-shu." *Oriens Extremus* 19.1–2 (1972): 27–30.

Hsu, Cho-yun. *Han Agriculture: The Formation of Early Chinese Agrarian Economy (206* B.C.–A.D. *220)*. Seattle: University of Washington Press, 1980.

Hu Daojing 胡道靜. "Shandong de nongxue chuantong" 山東的農學傳統. *Wen shi zhe* 2 (1962): 48–49.

———. *Nongshu, nongshi lunji* 農書, 農史論集. Beijing: Nongye chubanshe, 1985.

Huang, H. T. "Food Processing Technologies." In *Science and Civilisation in China*, ed. Joseph Needham, vol. 6.4. Cambridge: Cambridge University Press, 2000.

Huang, Philip C. C. *The Peasant Economy and Social Change in North China*. Stanford, CA: Stanford University Press, 1985.

Knechtges, David R. "Gradually Entering the Realm of Delight: Food and Drink in Early Medieval China." *Journal of the American Oriental Society* 117.2 (1997): 229–39.

Kolb, Raimund Th. "Kurze Einführung in die Bekämpfung agrarischer Schadinsekten im spätkaiserlichen China (1368–1911)." In *Beten, Impfen, Sammeln: Zur Viehseuchen- und Schädlingsbekämpfung in der frühen Neuzeit*, ed. Katharina Engelken, Dominik Hünniger, and Steffi Windelen, 191–232. Göttingen: Universitätsverlag Göttingen, 2007.

Kumashiro Yukio. "Recent Developments in Scholarship on the *Ch'i-min yao-shu* in China and Japan." *Developing Economies* 9.4 (1971): 422–48.

Li Changnian 李長年. *Nongsang jing jiaozhu* 農桑經校注. Beijing: Nongye chubanshe, 1982.

Li, Wenhua, ed. *Agro-Ecological Farming Systems in China*. Man and the Biosphere Series. London: Taylor and Francis, 2001.

Liang Jiamian 梁家勉. "*Qimin yaoshu* de zhuanzhe, zhuzhe he zhuanqi" 齊民要術的撰者, 注者和撰期. *Huanan nongye kexue* (1957.3): 92–98.

Lo, Vivienne, and Penelope Barrett. "Cooking Up Fine Remedies: On the Culinary Aesthetic in a Sixteenth-Century Chinese *Materia Medica*." *Medical History* 49 (2005): 395–422.

Sabban, Françoise. "Un savoir-faire oublié: Le travail du lait en Chine ancienne." *Zinbun* (Memoirs of the Research Institute for Humanistic Studies, Kyoto University) 21 (1986): 31–65.

———. "De la main à la pâte: Réflexion sur l'origine des pâtes alimentaires et les transformations du blé en Chine ancienne." *L'Homme* 30.113 (1990): 102–37.

———. "'Suivre le temps du ciel': Économie ménagère et gestion du temps dans la Chine du VIe siècle." In *Le temps de manger: Alimentation, emploi du temps et rythmes sociaux*, ed. Maurice Aymard, Claude Grignon, and Françoise Sabban, 81–108. Paris: Editions Maison des Sciences de l'Homme/Institut National de Recherche Agronomique, 1993.

Servanti, Silvano, and Françoise Sabban. *Pasta: The Story of a Universal Food*. Trans. Antony Shugaar. New York: Columbia University Press, 2003.

Tanaka Seiichi 田中静一, Kojima Reiitsu 小島麗逸, and Ota Yasuhiro 太田泰弘. *Seimin Yōjutsu— Genzon suru saiko no ryōrisho* 斉民要術—現存する最古の料理書. Tokyo: Yuzankaku, 1997.

Wang Chaosheng 王潮生, ed. *Zhongguo gudai gengzhi tu* 中國古代耕織圖. Beijing: Nongye chubanshe, 1995.

Wang Yuhu 王毓瑚. *Zhongguo nongxue shulu* 中國農學書錄. Beijing: Nongye chubanshe, 1979.

In recent years scholarly articles on the *Qimin yaoshu* have been published in China at the rate of a dozen or more a year, covering a range of themes from textual composition to linguistics, dietetics, brewing technology, and peasant-market relations; lists are available online.

Francesca Bray

Quan shanggu Sandai Qin Han Sanguo Liuchao wen
全上古三代秦漢三國六朝文

Contents

The *Quan shanggu Sandai Qin Han Sanguo Liuchao wen* (Complete prose of high antiquity, the Three Dynasties, Qin, Han, Three Kingdoms, and Six Dynasties), by Yan Kejun 嚴可均 (1762–1843), contains the writings of 3,497 authors of prose. The types of writing include the standard types of prose such as *fu* 賦 (rhapsody, or exposition), *qi* 七 (sevens), *zhao* 詔 (edict), *ling* 令 (command), *jiao* 教 (instruction), *cewen* 策文 (examination question), *biao* 表 (petition, or memorial), *shang shu* 上書 (letter presented to a superior), *qi* 啟 (communication), *zhang* 章 (declaration), *tanshi* 彈事 (accusation, letter of impeachment), *jian* 箋 (memorandum), *zou* 奏 (presentation), *yi* 議 (opinion), *shu* 書 (letter), *xi* 檄 (proclamation), *duiwen* 對文 (dialogue), *shelun* 設論 (hypothetical discourse), *xu* 序 (preface), *song* 頌 (eulogy), *zan* 贊 (encomium), *fuming* 符命 (mandate to rule based on prophetic signs), *shi lun* 史論 (disquisition from the histories), *lun* 論 (disquisition or treatise), *lianzhu* 連珠 (epigram), *zhen* 箴 (admonition), *ming* 銘 (inscription), *lei* 誄 (dirge), *ai* 哀 (lament), *beiwen* 碑文 (epitaph, stele inscription), *muzhi* 墓志 (grave memoir), *xingzhuang* 行狀 (conduct description), *diaowen* 弔文 (condolence), and *jiwen* 祭文 (offering).

The collection covers the pre-Qin through the Sui period: (1) "Quan shanggu Sandai wen" 全上古三代文; (2) "Quan Qin wen" 全秦文; (3) "Quan Han wen" 全漢文; (4) "Quan Hou Han wen" 全後漢文; (5) "Quan Sanguo wen" 全三國文; (6) "Quan Jin wen" 全晉文; (7) "Quan Song wen" 全宋文; (8) "Quan Qi wen" 全齊文; (9) "Quan Liang wen" 全梁文; (10) "Quan Chen wen" 全陳文; (11) "Quan Hou Wei wen" 全後魏文; (12) "Quan Bei Qi wen" 全北齊文; (13) "Quan Hou Zhou wen" 全後周文; (14) "Quan Sui wen" 全隋文; and (15) "Xian Tang wen" 先唐文. It includes short biographical sketches for each author.

Yan Kejun specifies the source for each piece. Many of the pieces included are fragments, making this a useful work for finding reconstructed texts. For example, this is one of the earliest sources for the reconstructed text of the *Xin lun* 新論 of Huan Tan 桓譚 (23 B.C.–A.D. 56).

Compilation

Yan Kejun was one of the leading textual scholars of the Qing dynasty. Disappointed that he was unable to participate in the compilation of the *Quan Tang wen* 全唐文 (Complete Tang prose), beginning in 1808 Yan undertook to prepare a collection of all of the extant prose writings from the pre-Tang period. He spent twenty-seven years on this labor, completing the manuscript of 746 *juan* in 1836. However, the book was not printed in Yan's lifetime. Jiang Rui 蔣叡 (d. ca. 1860) compiled the table of contents and biographies. These were printed separately in a 103-*juan* edition in 1879. Yan's full collection edited by Wang Yuzao 王毓藻 (*jinshi* 1863) and others, minus the five-*juan* table of contents, was published by the Guangya shuju 廣雅書局 in Guangzhou between 1887 and 1893 in 741 *juan*. A table of contents arranged by rhyme was compiled by Min Sunshi 閔孫奭 and printed in 1931.

Some scholars in the Qing claimed that Yan Kejun did not compile this work, but took it from a manuscript prepared by Sun Xingyan 孫星衍 (1753–1818), with whom Yan had worked before Sun's death in 1818. Recently Qian Zhongshu (*Guanzhui bian*, 3:853–54) has defended Yan Kejun against this accusation. For a detailed account of the collection, see Liu Yuejin, *Zhonggu wenxue wenxian xue*, 61–71.

Sources

The main sources for the work are the standard histories, collected works of individual writers, anthologies such as the *Wen xuan*, q.v., and *Guwen yuan* 古文苑, and encyclopedias such as the *Yiwen leiju*, q.v., *Chuxue ji*, q.v., and *Taiping yulan*, q.v. Yan Kejun also collected a large amount of inscriptions.

Editions

Quan shanggu Sandai Qin Han Sanguo Liuchao wen. Guangzhou: Guangya shuju, 1887–1893.

Quan shanggu Sandai Qin Han Sanguo Liuchao wen. Beijing: Zhonghua shuju, 1959; rpt., 1965.

Quan shanggu Sandai Qin Han Sanguo Liuchao wen. Taipei: Shijie shuju, 1960; rpt., 1982.

Quan shanggu Sandai Qin Han Sanguo Liuchao wen. Shijiazhuang: Hebei jiaoyu chubanshe, 1997. Punctuated edition in simplified characters.

Indices

Hung, William, et al., comps. *Quan shanggu Sandai Qin Han Sanguo Liuchao wen zuozhe yinde* 全上古三代秦漢三國六朝文作者引得. Harvard-Yenching Sinological Index, series 8. 1932; rpt., Taipei: Ch'eng-wen Publishing, 1966. Author index to the collection. Keyed to Guangya shuju edition.

Quan shanggu Sandai Qin Han Sanguo Liuchao wen pianming mulu ji zuozhe yinde 全上古三代秦漢三國六朝文篇名目錄及作者引得. Beijing: Zhonghua shuju, 1965. Author and title index to the collection. Keyed to the Zhonghua shuju edition.

The Research Centre for Ancient Chinese Texts (中國古籍研究中心) of the Chinese University of Hong Kong has included the *Quan shanggu Sandai Qin Han Sanguo Liuchao wen* in its electronic database, known by the acronym CHANT (Chinese Ancient Texts). Access is by paid subscription.

Bibliography

Liu Yuejin 劉躍進. *Zhonggu wenxue wenxian xue* 中古文學文獻學. Nanjing: Jiangsu guji chubanshe, 1997.

Qian Zhongshu 錢鍾書. *Guanzhui bian* 管錐編. 4 vols. Beijing: Zhonghua shuju, 1979.

David R. Knechtges

Renwu zhi 人物志

Introduction

A discussion of the interest in judging human character and talents from the Later Han to the Jin would not be complete without considering the *Renwu zhi* (The study of human character) by Liu Shao 劉劭/邵 (186?–245?). This is a book that details the ways of observing different types of character traits and abilities, as well as mistakes made in the judgment of human character. Containing three *juan*, the *Renwu zhi* is a relatively short text whose intended audience is the ruler. It reflects an ideal vision of government in which the sage-ruler plays a minimal but crucial role in identifying talent. Liu Shao believed that the ruler's ability to govern depends on the accurate judgment of men and their appropriate appointments. In describing the strengths and weaknesses of different sorts of talent, his book displays a functionalist and practical tendency as it acknowledges the difficulty of finding well-rounded individuals. In reflecting the need for better governance during the Later Han period, where the practice of *chaju* 察举 (to ascertain [ability] and raise [to office]) became fraught with flaws, the book also encapsulates an ideal vision of government during a period of disunity.

The *Renwu zhi* has often been described as the first book in Chinese history that specifically deals with the subject of observing human character and abilities. A point to be noted is that Liu Shao's source of inspiration could in fact be traced to an earlier text; there are similarities between the *Renwu zhi* and the "Wenwang guanren" 文王官人 chapter in the *Dadai Li ji* 大戴禮記, which also lists personality types and discusses the importance of appointing appropriate men. Yet distinct differences exist; a comparison between these two texts shows different standards in the evaluation of men.

Although the *Renwu zhi* deals with a rather specific theme, it has often been placed in the larger context of Wei-Jin history and thought. Scholars have drawn upon this text in their discussions of the sage, the debate on *caixing* 才性 (talent and innate nature), and comparisons of political thought and the changes in Wei-Jin character appraisal, and they regard this text as indicative of historical changes in intellectual currents of the Wei-Jin period.

Structure and arrangement of the text

The *Renwu zhi* is divided into twelve chapters, excluding Liu Shao's preface, as follows:

1. Jiuzheng 九徵 — The Nine Manifestations
2. Tibie 體別 — Types of personalities
3. Liuye 流業 — Categories of abilities
4. Caili 材理 — Principles of abilities
5. Caineng 材能 — Abilities
6. Lihai 利害 — Advantages and disadvantages
7. Jieshi 接識 — How men observe and understand others
8. Yingxiong 英雄 — The man of intellect and courage
9. Baguan 八觀 — Observing men from eight points of view
10. Qimiu 七繆 — Seven mistakes in observing men
11. Xiaonan 效難 — Difficulties in obtaining results
12. Shizheng 釋爭 — Resolving rivalries

The contents of the *Renwu zhi* can generally be classified into three broad parts. In the first chapter, Liu Shao provides a theoretical framework that sets the basis for discussion in the remaining chapters. The second, third, fourth, fifth, sixth, and eighth chapters discuss the different personality types, abilities, and respective positions for which different men are suited. To Liu Shao, most men would fall under the category of *piancai* 偏材 (limited talent), whose characteristic lies in possessing only a certain ability; this is unlike the more well-rounded *jiancai* 兼材 (broad talent), who has a number of well-developed abilities. Chapter eight is devoted solely to the discussion of *yingxiong* 英雄, an ideal character type who has both foresight and courage. Following this, the latter half of the book deals with practical applications in the judgment of men. Chapters seven, nine, ten, and eleven discuss the ways of observing men, and difficulties and mistakes made in the judging of character.

Authorship

There is generally no dispute concerning the authorship of the *Renwu zhi*. Scholars agree that this is the major surviving work by Liu Shao, who held several appointments from the Late Han's Jian'an era through the Wei government's Zhengshi era. His biography is in *Sanguo zhi*, q.v., 21:617–20. It was during the reign of Cao Rui 曹叡, Emperor Ming of the Wei (r. 226–239), that Liu Shao rose from a minor official to be the governor of Chenliu 陳留 and, later, cavalier attendant-in-ordinary (*sanqi changshi* 散騎常侍). He then became more politically engaged, and his advice on military decisions was sought on several occasions. It was also during this period that he was involved in the composition of works such as the *Wei fa* 魏法, the *Xinlü* 新律, and more notably the *Duguan kaoke* 都官考科, a work commissioned by Cao Rui for the purpose of examining and appointing officials, and therefore similar in nature to the *Renwu zhi*. Although those works together with his *Falun* 法論, *Yuelun* 樂論, and several others are lost, the titles offer us a glimpse of Liu Shao's scholarly pursuits.

Transmission and editions of the text

The earliest edition of the *Renwu zhi* was printed in the Song dynasty by Ruan Yi 阮逸 (*jinshi* 1027), who lamented in his preface that the work was much neglected despite its merits. Song Xiang 宋庠 (fl. 996–1066) added a section of excerpted parts from the biographies in the standard histories of Liu Shao and of Liu Bing 劉昞 (365?–440), who had written a commentary on the text. Wen Kuanfu 文寬夫 (1002?–1094?) corrected errors that had occurred during its transmission, based on a collation of editions available to him. Most of the Ming and Qing editions include the prefaces and postfaces by these three Song dynasty contemporaries.

Many editions derive from the "Longqing edition" (隆慶本) printed by Zheng Min 鄭旻 in the sixth year of the Ming dynasty's Longqing era (1572). In addition to Zheng's own inscription, it includes the complete commentary by Liu Bing, as well as the prefaces and postfaces by Ruan Yi, Song Xiang, Wen Kuanfu, and Wang Sanxing 王三省 (dates unknown). This is considered one of the better editions. The version in the *Liangjing yibian*, known as the Hushi Liangjing yibian edition (胡氏兩京遺編本), comp. Hu Weixin 胡維新 (*jinshi* 1559), has many errors and missing text; the editions of Wang Mo 王謨 in the *Zengding Han Wei congshu* 增訂漢魏叢書 (1791–1795) and of He Yunzhong 何允中 in the *Guang Han Wei congshu* 廣漢魏叢書 (1796) consist of Liu Bing's commentary for each chapter title but not the text itself. The *Sibu congkan** version of the *Renwu zhi* uses the Longqing edition despite the claim that it was based on a Zhengde (1505–1521) edition.

Commentaries

Chen Yinke commented that it is unlikely that Liu Shao's work would have been preserved if not for Liu Bing's commentary (*Sui Tang zhidu yuanyuan luelun gao*, 41). His is the only notable commentary on the *Renwu zhi*. There have been general remarks and comments made on the text, however. The first appendix in Fu Junlian's "*Renwu zhi* 'Jiuzheng' pian fawei" contains a list of comments from the Tang to Qing dynasties; these offer a general overview of how the text was received over this period of time.

Text with commentaries and notes

Fu Junlian 伏俊璉. *Renwu zhi yizhu* 人物志譯註. Shanghai: Shanghai guji chubanshe, 2008.

Guo Mo 郭模. *Renwuzhi ji zhu jiaozheng* 人物志及注校證. Taipei: Wen shi zhe chubanshe, 1987.

Wu Jiaju 吳家駒. *Xinyi Renwu zhi* 新譯人物志. Taipei: Sanmin shuju, 2003.

Secondary studies

Chen Yinke 陳寅恪. *Sui Tang zhidu yuanyuan luelun gao* 隋唐制度淵源略論稿. Shanghai: Shenghuo, dushu, xinzhi sanlian shudian, 1954; rpt., Taipei: Taiwan shangwu yinshuguan, 1996.

Cheng Youwei 程有為. "Shixi Liu Shao *Renwu zhi* de rencai xueshuo" 試析劉邵人物志的人才學說. *Zhengzhou daxue xuebao* 32 (1999): 18–23.

Cheng Zhaoxiong 程兆熊. "Liu Shao *Renwu zhi* yu Chen Xiang jingyan lunjian" 劉邵人物志與陳襄經筵論薦. *Xinya shenghuo* 16 (1960): 8–10.

Feng Chengji 馮承基. "*Sanguo zhi* Wei zhi Liu Shao zhuan zhiyi shulue" 三國志魏志劉邵傳滯義疏略. *Shumu jikan* 9 (1975): 13–17.

Feng Youlan (Yu-lan) 馮友蘭. "Wei Jin zhi ji guanyu mingshi, caixing de bianlun" 魏晉之際關於名實, 才性的辯論. *Zhongguo zhexueshi yanjiu* (1983.4): 3–12.

Fu Junlian 伏俊璉. "*Renwu zhi* 'Jiuzheng' pian fawei" 人物志九徵篇發微. *Gansu gaoshi xuebao* (2005.10): 28–30.

Lin Lizhen 林麗真. "Du *Renwu zhi*" 讀人物志. *Shumu jikan* 9 (1975): 25–33.

Mou Zongsan 牟宗三. "*Renwu zhi* zhi xitong de jiexi" 人物志之系統的解析. In *Caixing yu xuanli* 才性與玄理, 43–66. Taipei: Xuesheng shuju, 1989; rpt., 2002.

Qian Mu 錢穆. "Lueshu Liu Shao *Renwu zhi*" 略述劉邵人物志. In *Zhongguo xueshu sixiangshi luncong* 中國學術思想史論叢, 3:53–60. Taipei: Dongda tushu youxian gongsi, 1977.

Tang Yongtong 湯用彤. "Du *Renwu zhi*" 讀人物志. In *Wei-Jin xuanxue lungao* 魏晉玄學論稿, *Tang Yongtong quanji* 湯用彤全集 4:3–21. Shijiazhuang: Hebei renmin chubanshe, 2000.

Wang Baoxuan 王保玹. "Xuanxue renxinglun yu rencailun de xingcheng" 玄學人性論與人才論的形成. In *Xuanxue tonglun* 玄學通論, 569–615. Taipei: Wunan tushu chuban gongsi, 1996.

Wang Xiaoyi 王曉毅. "*Renwu zhi* xingcheng de zhengzhi wenhua beijing" 人物志形成的政治文化背景. *Dongyue luncong* 28 (2007): 86–91.

Wu Pi 吳丕. "*Renwu zhi* zhengzhi sixiang fenxi" 人物志政治思想分析. *Beijing daxue xuebao* (1989.3): 106–12.

Yu Yingshi (Ying-shih) 余英時. "Han Jin zhi ji xin zijue yu xin sichao" 漢晉之際新自覺與新思潮. *Zhongguo zhishi jieceng shilun* 中國知識階層史論, 205–327. Taipei: Lianjing chuban shiye gongsi, 1980.

Zhang Beibei 張蓓蓓. "Han Jin renwu pinjian yanjiu" 漢晉人物品鑒研究. Ph.D. diss., Guoli Taiwan daxue Zhongwen yanjiusuo, 1983.

Translations

English

Shryock, John Knight. *The Study of Human Abilities: The Jen Wu Chih of Liu Shao*. New Haven, CT: American Oriental Society, 1937.

Japanese

Okamura Shigeru 岡村繁. "*Jinbutsushi* Ryūchū kōsen" 人物志劉注校箋. Nagoya daigaku bungakubu kenkyū ronshū 9 (1961): 59–120.

Tada Kensuke 多田狷介. "*Jinbutsushi* yakukō (ue)" 人物志譯稿 (上). *Shisō* 20 (1979): 111–28.

———. "*Jinbutsushi* yakukō (shita)" 人物志譯稿 (下). *Shisō* 21 (1980): 65–87.

Indices

Bauer, Wolfgang, comp., and Robert L. Irick, ed. *A Concordance to the Jen-wu chih with a Text*. Chinese Materials Research Aids Service Center, Research Aids Series 12. San Francisco: Chinese Materials Center, 1974.

The text of the *Renwu zhi* is also included in the Chinese Text Project (accessible via Google) with a full-text search capability.

Goh Kailing

Sanguo zhi 三國志

Introduction

The *Sanguo zhi* (Records of the Three Kingdoms) is a history of the three contending states that arose at the end of the Han dynasty: Wei 魏 (220–265); Wu (222–280); and Shu, often referred to as Shu-Han 蜀漢 (221–263). The main text was written by Chen Shou 陳壽 (233–297) and bears an important commentary by Pei Songzhi 裴宋之 (372–451). Although the period covered by the book is essentially less than a century, this relatively short time span does not reflect the *Sanguo zhi*'s status or influence. It is the third of the standard histories (*zhengshi* 正史), following the *Shi ji* 史記 and the *Han shu* 漢書 and dating from well before the *Hou Han shu*, q.v. The period treated by the *Sanguo zhi* is one that left an indelible mark on Chinese culture, so that in addition to its importance as a history, the *Sanguo zhi* has exerted a powerful and lasting influence on literature, religion, and popular culture, not only in China but in other parts of East Asia as well.

Contents

As a history of three separate geopolitical entities, the *Sanguo zhi* differs from the other standard histories. The work is organized into sixty-five *juan* 卷: *juan* 1–30 constitute the *Wei shu* 魏書; *juan* 31–45 form the *Shu shu* 蜀書; and *juan* 46–65 are the *Wu shu* 吳書. These section titles are those used in the received text. Some scholars have thought that the three sections were originally separate works that were not combined until a Northern Song dynasty (960–1126) printing, but that cannot be the case. It is true that the bibliographical treatises of *Jiu Tang shu*, 46:1985, 1992, and *Xin Tang shu*, 58:1455, list separately a *Wei guo zhi* 魏國志, *Wu guo zhi* 吳國志, and *Shu guo zhi* 蜀國志, but the earlier bibliographical treatise of the *Sui shu*, q.v. (33:955), contains an entry for the *Sanguo zhi* by Chen Shou, with Pei Songzhi's commentary. Furthermore, works composed during the Tang dynasty refer to the history as the *Sanguo zhi*, and there is good evidence that the work has borne its present title since Western Jin times. It thus seems likely that the work existed in different physical forms before the Northern Song. The earliest extant printed editions of the *Sanguo zhi* come from the Song period. Short manuscript fragments from the early medieval and Tang periods exist, but there is the possibility that at least two of these are modern forgeries.

Emperor Wen (r. 424–453) of the Liu-Song dynasty ordered Pei Songzhi to write a commentary to the *Sanguo zhi* to supplement the information in the text.

The long commentary that Pei produced quotes from preserves more than 150 works from Wei-Jin times alone, and over 200 works in all. Even when the sources quoted are of dubious accuracy, they provide insights into the attitudes, events, and personages of the period. It is now generally acknowledged that earlier claims that the commentary is longer than Chen Shou's text are incorrect.

Of the three sections making up the *Sanguo zhi*, Wei is not only the longest and placed first, but its rulers are called emperors (*di* 帝), and their accounts are presented in the same chronological fashion as in the *benji* 本紀, or basic annals, of the emperors of the Han in the *Shi ji* and *Han shu*. This confers legitimacy on Wei as the successor of the Han and consigns the rulers of Shu and Wu, who are accorded only biographies (*zhuan* 傳), to a subordinate position. Other features of the history also support the primacy of Wei, a stance that has been criticized by writers at various times in Chinese history. Such critics viewed Wei as illegitimate and were generally either contemporary adversaries of Wei or citizens of later polities that, due to their own geopolitical circumstances, identified with Wei's rival state of Shu-Han.

In addition to challenges to the *Sanguo zhi* over its supposed bias toward Wei, there have been other, narrower criticisms of its handling of specific persons or events. Some of these criticisms are valid, others not. Certainly Chen Shou and the *Sanguo zhi* have received their share of praise, and on balance this is a skillfully written history that is a key source for understanding the Three Kingdoms period.

Authorship

Chen Shou was from Anhan 安漢 in Baxi 巴西 commandery of Shu. He studied with Qiao Zhou 譙周 (201–270), whose works also later influenced Chang Qu 常璩 (ca. 291–ca. 361), the author of the *Huayang guo zhi*, q.v. In his youth, Chen Shou learned the *Shu jing* 書經 (Classic of documents) and the commentaries to the *Chunqiu* 春秋 (Spring and Autumn annals) but took particular interest in the *Shi ji* and *Han shu*. He served in various posts as a Shu official but was removed from office more than once for refusing to serve the interests of the powerful eunuch Huang Hao 黃皓. After the fall of Shu, Chen Shou was out of government service for some years, apparently due to censure for having had a maid make some pills for him when he was ill during the mourning period for his father. Later he was recommended to the Jin court by the influential writer and official Zhang Hua 張華 (232–300). While serving as editorial director (*zhuzuo lang* 著作郎), he was charged with editing the works of Zhuge Liang 諸葛亮 (181–234), the famous Shu strategist and statesman. His *Zhuge Liang ji* 諸葛亮集 (Collected works of Zhuge Liang) in twenty-four *juan* was submitted to the throne in 274, but the work has long been lost. In addition to the *Sanguo zhi*, Chen Shou also authored two other histories: the *Yibu qijiu zhuan* 益部耆舊傳 (Biographies of the elders of Yi region) and the *Guguo zhi* 古國志 (Records of ancient states). Neither of these survives.

It is likely that Chen Shou began writing the *Sanguo zhi* after the fall of Wu in 280 and that he completed it before the end of the decade. This was not an officially sponsored project, and it was only after Chen Shou's death that Secretarial Court Gentleman (*shang shu lang* 尚書郎) Fan Yun 范頵 submitted a memorial to the throne extolling the *Sanguo zhi*. As a result, the emperor sent people to Chen Shou's home to copy out the history.

Pei Songshi was from an influential family that had moved south in the early fourth century. It is not known where he was born. By eight *sui*, he knew the *Lun yu* 論語 (Analects), the Mao version of the *Shi jing* 詩經 (Classic of poetry), and other texts. He served in office from age twenty, including in a provincial post under Liu Yu 劉裕 (363–422), the future founder of the Liu-Song dynasty. After Liu Yu ascended the throne, Pei Songzhi served in a series of important posts and had significant responsibility. As mentioned previously, under the third ruler of the Liu-Song, Emperor Wen, Pei was ordered to compose his commentary to the *Sanguo zhi*. He completed the work and submitted it to the emperor in 429. Pei retired from office in 437 but was given additional honors and responsibilities. He died in 452 of illness.

Printing history

The earliest recorded block-print edition of the *Sanguo zhi* was one published in the Northern Song by the Guozi jian, the Directorate of Education, in the sixth year of the Xianping reign (1006). There were also Southern Song editions published in the Shaoxing (1131–1162) and Shaoxi (1190–1194) reign periods. It is the Shaoxing and Shaoxi editions that were used to produce the Baina 百衲 edition of the *Sanguo zhi*: *juan* 1–3 are the Shaoxing text and *juan* 4–65 are the Shaoxi text. According to Su Jie (2006), the Shaoxing edition seems no longer to exist.

A Yuan dynasty edition of the *Sanguo zhi* was printed, but more important are the Ming editions. An official woodblock edition was published under Feng Mengzhen 馮夢楨 (1546–1605) by the Directorate of Education in Nanjing. This is sometimes referred to as the Feng edition (Feng ben 馮本) or the Southern edition (Nan ben 南本). Another official woodblock edition, which was published by the Directorate of Education in Beijing, was a revision of the Southern edition. There is also a Jiguge 汲古閣 edition from the famous bibliophile and publisher Mao Jin 毛晉 (1599–1659). This is sometimes called the Mao edition (Mao ben 毛本). A Xishuangtang 西爽堂 edition by Wu Guan 吳琯 (fl. 1568–1572) was the base text used by Yi Peiji 易培基 (1880–1937) for the *Sanguo zhi buzhu* 三國志補注.

The *Sanguo zhi* was, of course, among the dynastic histories printed by the Wuyingdian 武英殿, the Qing dynasty imperial printing office and bindery, in 1747. This is often called the Dian ben 殿本, or Palace edition, although Lu Bi 盧弼 (1876–1967) refers to it as the *guan ben* 官本 (official edition). For his *Sanguo zhi jijie* 三國志集解, Lu took a woodblock edition by Jinling shuju 金陵書局, called the Ju ben 局本, as his base text. Zhao Youwen 趙幼文, however, used a Chengdu shuju 成都書局 1871 re-carving of the Palace edition as the base text for the *Sanguo zhi jiaojian* 三國志校箋. Another important contribution from the Qing is a Jinling movable-type redaction of the Southern edition; this served as the base text for the modern Zhonghua shuju 中華書局 punctuated *Sanguo zhi* of Chen Naiqian 陳乃乾.

The Zhonghua shuju punctuated edition of the *Sanguo zhi* is clearly the most commonly used and cited recension of the history, although it is not error free. It was first published in 1959 and saw a series of reprintings before a revised edition was issued in 1982. The new edition has been reprinted, as well; readers should note that such reprints sometimes contain unannounced minor changes. To prepare the Zhonghua shuju edition, the Jinling movable-type edition was collated against the Baina edition published by Shangwu yinshuguan (Commercial Press) in the 1930s, the Palace edition, and a Jiangnan shuju 江南書局 redaction of the Jiguge edition. A newer redaction by Wu Jinhua, one of the leading authorities on the text of the *Sanguo zhi*, has been published by Yuelu shushe 岳麓書社. This is based on the Baina edition and incorporates numerous corrections, but unfortunately it is in simplified characters, a significant shortcoming that Wu, as indicated in the front matter of the book, has labored to overcome.

For an overall account of the textual history of this and the other Six Dynasties standard histories, see appendix IV, "Textual Transmission of the Standard Histories."

Important critical editions

Lu Bi 盧弼 (1876–1967), ed. *Sanguo zhi jijie* 三國志集解. Beijing: Beijing guji chubanshe, 1957. Numerous reprints. Punctuated ed., 8 vols. Shanghai: Shanghai guji chubanshe, 2012.

Sanguo zhi 三國志. Beijing: Zhonghua shuju, 1959. Rev. ed., 1982. Numerous reprints.

Wu Jinhua 吳金華, ed. *Sanguo zhi* 三國志. Changsha: Yuelu shushe, 1990.

Yi Peiji 易培基 (1880–1937), ed. *Sanguo zhi buzhu* 三國志補注. Taipei: Yiwen yinshuguan, 1955. This is a posthumous publication edited by Yi Suping 易涑平.

Zhao Youwen 趙幼文 (d. 1993). *Sanguo zhi jiaojian* 三國志校箋. Chengdu: Ba Shu shushe, 2001. This is a posthumous publication edited by Zhao Zhenduo 趙振鐸 et al.

Selected works of textual criticism and related studies

Cui Shuting 崔曙庭. "*Sanguo zhi* benwen queshi duo yu Pei zhu" 三國志本文確實多于裴注. *Huazhong shifan daxue xuebao* (1990.2): 122–26.

Cutter, Robert Joe, and William Gordon Crowell, trans. *Empresses and Consorts: Selections from Chen Shou's Records of the Three States with Pei Songzhi's Commentary*. Honolulu: University of Hawai'i Press, 1999. The "Prolegomenon" contains information on Chen Shou, Pei Songzhi, and the text.

Crespigny, Rafe de. *The Records of the Three Kingdoms*. Occasional Paper 9. Canberra: Australian National University Centre of Oriental Studies, 1970.

———. *Generals of the South: The Foundation and Early History of the Three Kingdoms State of Wu*. Asian Studies Monographs, n.s. 16. Canberra: Faculty of Asian Studies, Australian National University, 1990. See chapter 9 on texts and historiography. Available at http://www.anu.edu.au/asianstudies/decrespigny/gos_index.html/.

———. *Imperial Warlord: A Biography of Cao Cao, 155–220 AD*. Leiden: Brill, 2010. The first half of chapter 11 has information on historiography.

Fang Beichen 方北辰. "*Sanguo zhi* biaodian shangque" 三國志標點商榷. *Sichuan daxue xuebao, Zhexue shehui kexue ban* (1987.1): 90–97.

Farmer, J. Michael. "What's in a Name? On the Appellative 'Shu' in Early Medieval Chinese Historiography." *Journal of the American Oriental Society* 121.1 (2001): 44–59. Includes a good discussion of the issue of legitimacy as treated in the *Sanguo zhi* and other texts.

Leban, Carl. "Ts'ao Ts'ao and the Rise of Wei: The Early Years." Ph.D. diss., Columbia University, 1971. Chapter 1 has information on sources.

Li Chunjiao 李純蛟. *Sanguo zhi yanjiu* 三國志研究. Chengdu: Ba Shu shushe, 2002.

Liang Zhangju 梁章鉅 (1775–1849). *Sanguo zhi pangzheng* 三國志旁證. Edited by Yang Yaokun 楊耀坤. Fuzhou: Fujian renmin chubanshe, 2000.

Lu Yaodong 逯耀東. "Pei Songzhi yu Wei Jin shixue pinglun" 裴松之與魏晉史學評論. *Shihuo yuekan* 15.3–4 (September 1985): 93–107.

———. "*Sanguo zhi* zhu yu Pei Songzhi *Sanguo zhi* zizhu" 三國志注與裴松之自注. In Xu Zhuoyun 許倬雲 et al., eds., *Zhongguo lishi lunwen ji* 中國歷史論文集, 1:257–72. Taipei: Shangwu yinshuguan, 1986.

Miao Yue 繆鉞 (1904–1995). "Chen Shou yu *Sanguo zhi*" 陳壽與三國志. In *Zhongguo shixue shi lunji* 中國史學史論集, ed. Wu Ze 吳澤 and Yuan Yingguang 袁英光, 1:313–22. Shanghai: Renmin chubanshe, 1980. Miao Yue was a leading authority on the *Sanguo zhi*, and this chapter and the front sections of the following two works are informative.

Miao Yue et al. *Sanguo zhi daodu* 三國志導讀. Chengdu: Ba Shu shushe, 1988.

Miao Yue, ed. *Sanguo zhi xuan zhu* 三國志選注. Beijing: Zhonghua shuju, 1984. Rpt. in *Miao Yue quanji* 繆鉞全集, vol. 4, *Sanguo zhi yu Chen Shou yanjiu* 三國志與陳壽研究. Shijiazhuang: Hebei jiaoyu chubanshe, 2004.

Shen Jiaben 沈家本 (1840–1913). *Sanguo zhi zhu suoyin shumu* 三國志注所引書目. In *Gu shumu san zhong* 古書目三種. Beijing: Zhonghua shuju, 1963.

Su Jie 蘇傑. *Sanguo zhi yiwen yanjiu* 三國志異文研究. Ji'nan: Qi Lu shushe, 2006. A detailed study whose concise section on editions was very helpful for the discussion of editions in this entry.

Wu Jinhua 吳金華. *Sanguo zhi jiaogu* 三國志校詁. Nanjing: Jiangsu guji chubanshe, 1990.

———. *Sanguo zhi congkao* 三國志叢考. Shanghai: Shanghai guji chubanshe, 2000. Wu Jinhua is a leading scholar of the text of the *Sanguo zhi*.

Yang Yaokun 楊耀坤 and Wu Yechun 伍野春. *Chen Shou Pei Songzhi pingzhuan* 陳壽裴松之評傳. Nanjing: Nanjing daxue chubanshe, 1998.

Yang Yixiang 楊翼驤. "Pei Songzhi yu *Sanguo zhi* zhu" 裴松之與三國志注. In Wu Ze and Yuan Yingguang, eds., *Zhongguo shixue shi lunji* 中國史學史論集, 1:323–46. Shanghai: Renmin chubanshe, 1980.

Zhang Yuanji 張元濟 (1867–1959). *Sanguo zhi jiaokan ji* 三國志校勘記. Beijing: Shangwu yinshuguan, 1999.

Translations

The several translations of the *Sanguo zhi* into modern Chinese vary in quality, so only a few of the better ones will be listed here. In addition, there are some books of selections from the *Sanguo zhi* with *baihuawen* 白話文 translations, but except for the two under Miao Yue's name listed previously, none are included in this entry.

Chinese

Cao Wenzhu 曹文柱 et al., trans. *Baihua Sanguo zhi* 白話三國志. 2 vols. Beijing: Zhongyang minzu xueyuan chubanshe, 1994. This is the only translation to include both Chen Shou's text and Pei Songzhi's commentary; however, it sometimes omits parts of the commentary.

Fang Beichen 方北辰, trans. *Sanguo zhi zhuyi* 三國志注譯. 3 vols. Xi'an: Shaanxi renmin chubanshe, 1995. Fang Beichen studied with Miao Yue and is a leading expert on the *Sanguo zhi*. The notes to this translation are very good.

Su Yuanlei 蘇淵雷 et al., trans. *Sanguo zhi jinzhu jinyi* 三國志今注今譯. 3 vols. Changsha: Hunan shifan daxue chubanshe, 1992.

Tian Yuqing 田余慶 and Wu Shuping 吳樹平, trans. *Sanguo zhi jinyi* 三國志今譯. 2 vols. Zhengzhou: Zhongzhou guji chubanshe, 1991.

Japanese

Imataka Makoto 今鷹真, Inami Ritsuko 井波律子, and Kominami Ichiro 小南一郎, trans. *Sangoku shi* 三國志. 3 vols. Tokyo: Chikuma shobō, 1977–1989. Rev. ed. in 8 vols, Tokyo: Chikuma shobō, 1992–1993.

Maruyama Matsuyuki 丸山松幸 et al., trans. *Sangoku shi* 三國志. 6 vols. Tokyo: Tokuma shoten, 1979–1980.

English

To date no complete English translation of the *Sanguo zhi* exists. Relatively short portions of it are translated in books, articles, and dissertations. Hans H. Frankel, *Catalogue of Translations from the Chinese Dynastic Histories for the Period 220–960* (Berkeley: University of California Press, 1957), 11–55, contains numerous listings, but it includes passages as short as twenty-five graphs, so the overall amount is not large. It is also possible to find some translations online, but these latter will often be found on sites for video gamers and seldom demonstrate professional competence. When they do, they may have been copied, sometimes without credit, from published academic work. Although it is not practicable to provide here a list of all works that contain passages from the *Sanguo zhi* translated into English, both Achilles Fang and Rafe de Crespigny deserve mention. Fang translated many passages from the *Sanguo zhi* in Achilles Fang, trans., *The Chronicle of the Three Kingdoms (220–265): Chapters 69–78 from the Tzu chih t'ung chien of Ssu-ma Kuang (1019–1086)*, ed. Glen W. Baxter, 2 vols. (Cambridge: Harvard University Press, 1952–1965). Note, however, that Fang is translating from Sima Guang's *Zizhi tongjian*, so it is only when that work draws its words directly from *Sanguo zhi*, as well as in some of his notes, that Fang can be said to be translating the *Sanguo zhi*. De Crespigny has likewise translated numerous *Sanguo zhi* passages in his many publications. His book *To Establish Peace: Being the Chronicle of Later Han for the Years 189 to 220 AD as Recorded in Chapters 59 to 69 of the Zizhi tongjian of Sima Guang*, Asian Studies Monographs, n.s. 16, 2 vols. (Canberra: Faculty of Asian Studies, Australian National University, 1996) does not translate from the *Sanguo zhi* per se, but it does translate Sima Guang's text and indicates clearly corresponding *Sanguo zhi* passages.

Concordances and indices

The availability of Academia Sinica's Scripta Sinica Web site and other online resources, along with the widespread dissemination of e-texts of the *Sanguo zhi*, has largely obviated reliance on concordances and indexes. Yet, it may be useful to introduce some of the printed tools here.

Gao Xiufang 高秀芳, comp. *Sanguo zhi renming suoyin* 三國志人名索引. Beijing: Zhonghua shuju, 1980.

Li Bo 李波, Song Peixue 宋培學, and Li Xiaoguang 李曉光, comps. *Sanguo zhi suoyin fu Pei Songzhi zhu suoyin* 三國志索引附裴松之注索引. Beijing: Zhongguo guangbo dianshi chubanshe, 2002.

Sanguo zhi ji Pei zhu zonghe yinde 三國志及裴注綜合引得 (Combined indices to San Kuo Chih and the Notes of P'ei Sung-chih). Harvard-Yenching Institute Sinological Index Series 33. 1938; rpt., Taipei: Ch'eng-wen, 1966; Shanghai: Shanghai guji chubanshe, 1986.

Wang Tianliang 王天良, comp. *Sanguo zhi diming suoyin* 三國志地名索引. Beijing: Zhonghua shuju, 1980.

Wong Fook-luen 黃福鑾, comp. *Sanguo zhi suoyin* 三國志索引. Taipei: Datong shuju, 1986. This is keyed to the *Sibu beiyao** and *Sibu congkan** editions.

Dictionary

Zhang Shunhui 張舜徽, Cui Shuting 崔曙庭, and Wang Ruiming 王瑞明, comps. *Sanguo zhi cidian* 三國志辭典. Ji'nan: Shandong jiaoyu chubanshe, 1992.

Supplemental texts

Miao Yue has suggested that the reason the *Sanguo zhi* lacks the treatises found in other dynastic histories is that there was a lack of sufficient information. Although this may be true, Carl Leban thinks it may be because the conventions of history writing were still in flux. Certain Qing dynasty works attempt to provide the "missing" *zhi* 志 and *biao* 表 for the *Sanguo zhi*.

Sanguo zhi bubian 三國志補編. Beijing: Beijing tushuguan chubanshe, 2005. This reprint from the original *Ershiwu shi bubian* 二十五史補編 (Shanghai: Kaiming shudian, 1936) has been reprinted elsewhere, and it contains a number of supplements to the *Sanguo zhi*.

Tao Yuanzhen 陶元珍. *Sanguo shihuo zhi* 三國食貨志. Shanghai: Shangwu yinshuguan, 1935. Rpt., Taipei: Shangwu yinshuguan, 1989.

Robert Joe Cutter

Shanghan lun 傷寒論

Introduction

The *Shanghan lun* (Treatise on cold pathogenic diseases) was authored by Zhang Ji 張機 (ca. 150–219), who is most often referred to by his style name, Zhongjing 仲景. This is the oldest text to explain the method of combining remedies to form a prescription, as well as changes to the remedy that are generated by the evolution of a disease. It is in fact concerned with only one type of pathology: the *shanghan*, or pathogenic disease caused by coldness, a pathological rubric that covers symptoms as diverse as chills, comas, and fevers induced by typhoid or malaria. Since the tenth century the *Shanghan lun* has been the much-commented-upon standard work for the theoretical basis of teachings related to pharmacological therapy. Although the work did not apply to the analysis of other pathologies, it nevertheless furnished an analytic model of recipes.

Authorship

Zhang Zhongjing was not a doctor. He states in his preface that following the decimation of his family by fevers and epidemic diseases, he researched prescriptions to cure these illnesses and started writing his book in 196, finishing it ten years later. He was born in Nanyang 南陽 district, Henan, during a period of troubles with resulting famine and epidemics. The only facts known about him are provided by Huangfu Mi's 皇甫謐 (215–282) preface in the *Zhenjiu jiayi jing* 針灸甲乙經, and by a biography of He Yu 何禺, who seems to have been an intimate friend of Zhang (*He Yu biezhuan* 何禺別傳, in *Taiping yulan** 444:2043). Zhang learned medicine from a certain Zhang Bozu 張伯祖 who practiced in Nanyang district. A recently discovered stele confirms that he was once governor of Changsha between 202 and 205/207 (see Zhou Yimou 周貽謀, "Zhang Zhongjing guan zhi Changsha taishou kao" 張仲景官至長沙太守考, *Zhonghua yishi zazhi* 37.2 [2007]: 108–11).

Contents

The *Shanghan lun* is composed of six *juan* of different lengths. Each is dedicated to one of the six modalities of *yin* and *yang* (*taiyang*, *yangming*, *shaoyang*, *taiyin*, *shaoyin*, and *jueyin*), and for each the text outlines a basic clinical sketch, with the various observed symptoms and the sequence of their appearance. A medical recipe that often incorporates its "sovereign" remedial ingredient within its title is provided; that is to say, it responds to the principal symptom, and then to other remedies. Nearly a hundred different substances are used as remedies in some hundred recipes. The remedies utilized most often are ginger, licorice, cinnamon, shrubby horsetail, peony, angelica, gardenia, bupleurum, *Poria cocos* (a fungus), Chinese coptis, and skullcaps. Normally, a recipe has from two to nine ingredients, although there is one that has fourteen and two that have twelve. Each prescription includes a list of symptoms to be treated; a list of ingredients, with the quantities required; the mode of preparation of some of the ingredients; the mode of preparation of the medicine; and, in the majority of cases here, the decoctions and dosages.

The pharmacopeia of the Han dynasty classified remedies in several categories: the "sovereign" remedy that acted against major symptoms, "minister" remedies, and "assistant" remedies. In the *Shanghan lun*, most of the titles of the recipes include the name of the "sovereign" remedy. Thus, the "Decoction of Cinnamon" ("Guizhi tang" 桂枝湯) has the "sovereign" remedy of cinnamon but contains five ingredients in total: cinnamon, licorice, peony, jujube, and ginger. Other recipes are based upon this decoction, but they are modified according to the evolution of symptoms on the clinical table and take the title of the plants added, such as the "Decoction of Cinnamon and Aconite" ("Guizhi jia fuzi tang" 桂枝加附子湯), composed of six ingredients.

In general overview, the focus of each *juan* is as follows:

Juan 1: maladies of *Taiyang* 太陽 (178 articles). The principle symptoms are disorders due to wind and coldness, which affect only the exterior of the body (*biao* 表). The "sovereign" remedy here is cinnamon and the basic therapy is sweating;

Juan 2: maladies of *Yangming* 陽明, the symptoms of heat in the interior parts of the body;

Juan 3: maladies of *Shaoyang* 少陽 (10 articles), harmonization of the energies;

Juan 4: maladies of *Taiyin* 太陰 (8 articles), excess of coldness and an empty spleen;

Juan 5: maladies of *Shaoyin* 少陰 (46 articles), a lack of *yang*, an excess of coldness, and an insufficiency of nourishing *qi*;

Juan 6: maladies of *Jueyin* 厥陰 (46 articles), other symptoms within the interior parts of the body.

Sources

Given the small amount of surviving medical literature from the Han, it is difficult to determine the precise sources of this text. According to the preface, Zhang Zhongjing used as sources the *Suwen* 素問, *Jiujuan* 九卷 (*Lingshu* 靈樞), *Bashiyi nan* 八十一難 (*Nanjing* 難經), *Yinyang dalun* 陰陽大論 (The grand discourse on the *yin* and *yang*), *Tailu yaolu* 胎臚藥錄 (Annals of remedies and their principles), and *Pingmai bianzheng* 平脈辯證 (Analysis and argumentation on pulses evaluation), of which the last three works are lost. The *Shanghan lun* is often cited in the medical writings of the Sui and Tang, either under its title or introduced by "Zhang Zhongjing has said" (*Zhang Zhongjing yue* 張仲景曰).

Transmission of the text

Zhang Zhongjing had in his preface originally titled his work *Shanghan zabing lun* 傷寒雜病論 in sixteen *juan*, as attested to in a Song edition. The text has been revised several times. Its original contents have been divided into the illnesses caused by the cold (*shanghan* 傷寒), which is the properly present *Shanghan lun*, and the various illnesses (*zabing* 雜病) found in the *Jingui yaolue* 金匱要略, which, according to its preface, is an abridgement of the first *Shanghan lun* that was made in order to facilitate the diffusion of recipes. One must mention a third work, the *Jingui yuhan jing* 金匱玉函經, the contents of which correspond mostly to the present *Shanghan lun* and in part to the *Jingui yaolue*. Zhang Zhongjing's complete work contained, then, sections on the pulses' diagnosis and the *shanghan* (the present *Shanghan lun*), and other sections found partially in the present *Jingui yaolue*—miscellaneous illnesses, women and children's illnesses, and forbidden food. For example, if one compares what is quoted from Zhang Zhongjing in the *Waitai biyao* 外臺秘要 of Wang Tao 王濤 (ca. 752), the quotes in *juan* two to eleven correspond to the text of the present *Shanghan lun* while those in *juan* fourteen to eighteen correspond to the *Jingui yaolue*. The *Shanghan lun*'s original structure was not based on the six *yin* and *yang* modalities but on therapeutic methods (sweating, vomiting, purge, warming, puncture, and so on), and when one could apply them or not. This change was already perceived at the time of Sun Simiao 孫思邈 (582?–681?) and appears to have been systematic in the reshuffling of contents when, in 1057, the Song emperor Renzong placed Lin Yi 林億 and others in charge of a bureau responsible for editing and republishing medical treatises.

According to the bibliographic monograph of the *Sui shu*, q.v., 34:1042, there had been a *Zhang Zhongjing bian shanghan* 張仲景辯傷寒 in ten *juan* and a *Zhang Zhongjing pingbing yaofang* 張仲景評病要方 in one *juan* during the Liang but these were lost. For the Sui, we have the *Zhang Zhongjing fang* 張仲景方 in fifteen *juan* (34:1041) and the *Zhang Zhongjing liao furen fang* 張仲景療婦人方 in two *juan* (34:1045). In *Xin Tang shu* 59:1567, we have the title *Shanghan cubing lun* 傷寒卒病論 in ten *juan* under the name of Zhang Zhongjing and also that of Wang Shuhe who is supposed to have written down the text; the preceding entry is the *Wang Shuhe Zhang Zhongjing yaofang* 王叔和張仲景葉方 in fifteen *juan*. It can be said that the three texts, the *Shanghan lun*, *Jingui yuhan jing*, and *Jingui yaolue*, revised by the Lin Yi medical team of the Song dynasty, are evolutions of the original text.

In fragmentary condition, a few *Shanghan lun* manuscripts remain: two Tang dynasty Dunhuang manuscripts (P.3287, S.202); a fragment from the year 805 that was copied in 1143 by a Japanese monk with 65 articles and a facsimile and is kept in the Academia Sinica (Taiwan); and a partial copy of 1063 by the assistant doctor Tamba Masatada 丹波雅忠 (see Ma, *Zhongyi*, 132–34).

Editions

(A) Northern Song and Jin

Gao Jichong 高繼冲 edition. Edited in 992 in the *Taiping shenghui fang* 太平聖惠方 (*juan* 8 to 14).

Northern Song edition in ten *juan*, revised by the medical board in 1065 and preserved in Japan.

Jin dynasty edition of 1172, now lost, that likewise was in ten *juan*, with commentary by Cheng Wuji 成無己. This differed in many places from the copy in Japan; according to the opinions of a number of commentators, it contained numerous errors.

(B) Yuan

1304 edition with commentary by Cheng Wuji (lost).

Undated edition, with commentary by Cheng Wuji; preserved in the Seikadō bunko and the Peking University library.

(C) Ming

1599 edition of Zhao Kaimei 趙開美 in *Zhongjing quanshu* 仲景全書; based on the 1065 edition.

(D) Qing

There were numerous editions during the nineteenth century (see Ma, *Zhongyi*, 123–27).

Citations in other texts

The forty-eight entries of Zhang Zhongjing cited by Su Song 蘇頌 (1020–1101) in his *Bencao tujing* 本草圖經 (1061), and included in the *Jingshi zhenglei beiji bencao* 經史証類備急本草 of Tang Shenwei 唐慎微 (eleventh–twelfth century), are not in surviving editions. Analysis of these quotations shows that the versions of Zhang Zhongjing's work consulted by Su Song were of two kinds. One version contained both exopathogenic cold and miscellaneous diseases, which is rather likely the ancient version of the *Shanghan zabing lun* or *Jingui yuhan yaolue fang* 金櫃玉函要略方 discovered by Wang Zhu 王洙, a Hanlin scholar at the Northern Song court. The other version was the one that discussed miscellaneous diseases exclusively, which is most likely the sourcebook used by the officials commissioned by Emperor Renzong to revise the *Jingui yaolue*, among other medical works. Based on the literal features of the text cited in the *Bencao tujing*, and the lost texts of Zhang Zhongjing cited in other medical books that are not seen in current versions of the *Shanghan lun* and *Jingui yaolue*, it may be that the source used by Su Song was one that appeared earlier than that used by the Song officials when revising Zhang's medical book.

Commentaries

Liu Duzhou and his coeditors, in their *Shanghan lun cidian*, 585–98, listed a total of 439 commentaries, of which 252 were written between the Song and the Qing dynasties, 188 during the twentieth century, and seventeen that jointly treat the *Shanghan lun* and the *Jingui yaolue*. They also indicated that there are eighty-four Japanese commentaries. Certain commentaries insist upon the theoretical aspects of the text, others on the clinical aspects. Following are some of the more important commentaries.

Zhu Hong 朱弘 (*jinshi* 1088). *Shanghan baiwen* 傷寒百問 or *Huoren shu* 活人書.
Cheng Wuji. *Zhujie Shanghan lun* 註解傷寒論, written in 1144.
Ke Qin 柯琴. *Shanghan lun laisu ji* 傷寒論來蘇集, 1669.
Long Yi (Zaijing) 龍怡 (在涇) (ca. 1679–1749). *Shanghan lun guanzhu ji* 傷寒論貫珠集, 1729.
Wu Qian 吳謙. *Shanghan lun zhu* 傷寒論註, in his major work, the *Yizong jinjian* 醫宗金鑑, 1742.

Current editions

Jingui yaolue 金匱要略. Part of the *Shanghan zabing lun* of Zhang Zhongjing (beginning of the third century). References are to the modern edition *Jingui yaolue yishi* 金匱要略譯釋, ed. Li Keguang 李克光. Shanghai: Shanghai kexue jishu chubanshe, 1993.
Jingui yaoluefang 金匱要略方 of Zhang Zhongjing (beginning of the third century). *Siku quanshu**.
Jingui yaolue yulu 金匱要略語錄 of Zhang Zhongjing (beginning of the third century); modern edition by Zhongyi yanjiuyuan 中醫研究院. Beijing: Renmin weisheng chubanshe, 1973.
Shanghan lun 傷寒論. *Sibu congkan**.

Selected studies

Liang Yongxuan 梁永宣 and Wang Qingguo 王慶國. "*Bencao tujing* suoyin Zhang Zhongjing yixue yiwen kao" 本草圖經索引張仲景醫學佚文考. *Zhonghua yishi zazhi* 36.1 (2006): 3–6.
Liu Duzhou 劉渡舟, Li Xianfa 李憲法, Qin Kefeng 秦克楓, and Ren Hanyang 任漢陽, eds. *Shanghan lun cidian* 傷寒論辭典. Beijing: Jiefangjun chubanshe, 1988.
Lo, Vivienne. "*Shang Han Lun: On Cold Damage, Translation and Commentaries* by Craig Mitchell, Feng Ye, Nigel Wiseman" [book review]. *Journal of Asian Studies* 60.3 (2001): 843–45.
Ma Jixing 馬繼興. *Zhongyi wenxian xue* 中醫文獻學. Shanghai: Shanghai kexue jishu chubanshe, 1990.

Okanishi Tameto 岡西為人. *Sō izen iseki kō* 宋以前醫籍考. Rpt., Taipei: Nantian shuju, 1949. Vol. 4.
Otsuka Yoshinori 大塚敬節. *Shōkanron kaisetsu* 傷寒論解說. Tokyo: Takoguchi shoten, 1966; rpt., 1982.
Taki Genkan 多紀元簡. *Shōkanron shūgi* 傷寒論輯義. In *Kinsei kanpō igaku shūsei* 近世漢方醫學書集成, vols. 41–42. Tokyo: Meicho shuppan, 1980.
Yamada Narihiro 山田業廣. "*Kinki yōryaku* shūchū" 金匱要略集注 [article in Chinese]. In *Yamada Narihiro senshū* 山田業廣選集. Tokyo: Meicho shuppan, 1984.

Translations

Anon. *Synopsis of Prescriptions of the Golden Chamber: A Classic of Traditional Chinese Medicine*. [A translation of the *Jingui yaolue*.] Beijing: New World Press, 1987.
Craig, Mitchell, Feng Ye, and Nigel Wiseman. *Shang Han Lun: On Cold Damage, Translation and Commentaries*. Brookline, MA: Paradigm Publications, 1999.
Despeux, Catherine. *Shanghanlun: Traité des Coups de froid*. Paris: Editions de la Tisserande, 1985.

Catherine Despeux

Shennong bencao jing 神農本草經

Contents

The *Shennong bencao jing* (The classic of *materia medica* of the divine ploughman) is a medical text attributed to the mythical Shennong 神農. According to its preface, the work analyzes 365 substances, a symbolic number equal to the 365 degrees of the sidereal revolution. The actual number of substances included in the various editions is in fact greater than that number.

The preface explains that the remedies are classified in three categories. Those of the highest rank, numbering 120, serve to nourish the vital force (*ming* 命) and correspond to heaven. These are not toxic and can be used over long periods. The remedies of the middle category, also numbering 120, nurture one's nature (*xing* 性) and correspond to the earth. These substances are slightly toxic but can be used over long periods. The last and lowest category, numbering 125, may be used to treat illnesses and correspond to humankind. These are toxic and should not be used for extended periods. The substances included in the work are of mineral, vegetable, and animal origins; some derive from the human body, such as hair or urine. For each, the text first gives the name, then the taste (acidic, bitter, pungent, sweet, or salty), the intrinsic nature (hot, tepid, neutral, cool, or cold), the level of toxicity, and the effect on such and such a symptom. Occasionally there is information on other aspects of the substance, its place of origin, or when it can be harvested. For the remedies deriving from substances of the highest rank, the effects relate most frequently to the different types of spirit, the *shen* 神, *shenming* 神明, *jing* 精, *hun* 魂, and *po* 魄, that are soothed by these remedies, but also those that lighten the body and extend life (*qingshen yannian* 輕身延年).

Sources

The text was compiled in the Han. Many dates have been proposed. For Ma Jixing, it goes back at least to the end of the Warring States period (third century B.C.), while for Donald Harper, the manuscript would have been compiled around the first to second centuries A.D. (*Early Chinese Medical Literature*, 34). Franz Schmidt arrives at a similar date. But since there survives no manuscript of a pharmacopeia of a date earlier than the *Shennong bencao jing*, it is not possible to be more specific about its origins. There had been earlier pharmacopeia. The oldest known is that mentioned in Jia Gongyan's 賈公彥 (fl. seventh century) commentary to the *Zhou li* 周禮, the *Ziyi bencao jing* 子義本草經. Jia thought the Ziyi mentioned in the title was the same Ziyi who was a disciple of Bian Que 扁鵲, cited by Zheng Xuan 鄭玄 (127–200) in his commentary on the same passage of the *Zhou li* (5:219b and 5:219c).

Authenticity and authorship

The work is of anonymous authorship, probably a compilation of received knowledge in a milieu that knew more from masters of the craft of pharmaecology and alchemists than doctors, properly speaking, mainly because of the significant proportion of remedies to expel demons or of those that "lighten the body and extend life." The attribution to the mythical emperor Shennong must be because during the Han, a number of works report the legend that this eminent ruler had tasted all the plants in order to learn their flavor and toxicity.

Transmission of the text

The *Shennong bencao jing* was transmitted down to the Southern Song. It was used in the redaction of pharmacopeia after the Han, along with other pharmacopeia that have since disappeared. At the beginning of the third century, Wu Pu 吳普, a disciple of the celebrated Hua Tuo 華陀 (end of the second century), composed a *Wu Pu bencao* 吳普本草, of which there remain a few citations. To write this pharmacopeia he used a dozen manuscripts, including two different versions of the *Shennong bencao jing*: the *Shennong [bencao]* and the *Shennong bencao yijing* 神農本草一經 (Schmidt, "The Textual History of the Materia medica in the Han Period," 2006). These various manuscripts show divergencies in the flavor and nature of the remedies (Schmidt, "Textual History," 2006; Ma, *Zhongyi*, 257).

During the entire period between the Jin and the Tang, the text was transmitted under a number of different titles, sometimes without the name of Shennong. It was annotated many times, as attested by numerous documents, especially bibliographic catalogs. Further, if one compares the same citations of a passage of the *Shennong bencao jing* in different works, one finds examples of variants in the attributed taste of some remedy or other (Ma, *Zhongyi*, 250). During transmission, fragments of the commentaries had been jumbled with the original text, showing the confusion that reigned during the transmission of a text that was far from fixed.

The *Shennong bencao* is reported as having either four or eight *juan* in *Sui shu*, q.v., 34.1044, while in the *Jiu Tangshu* (47:2047), *Xin Tang shu* (59:1566), and *Tong zhi** (69:811a) it is said to be in three *juan*; it was finally lost during the Southern Song. One of the reasons was undoubtedly that Tao Hongjing's 陶弘景 (486–536) *Bencao jing jizhu* 本草經集注 came to serve as the basic text for pharmacological education; when the Tang government decided to edit official pharmacopeias, the first one was the *Xinxiu bencao* 新修本草, whose compilation under the direction of Su Jing 蘇敬 was completed in 659. Copies of the *Shennong bencao jing* decreased in number and circulated less widely.

The transmitted versions are therefore reconstituted in part from citations found in medical and nonmedical sources, primarily from Song pharmacopeias printed from the Kaibao (968–976) to Daguan (1107–1110) eras, that is, the *Kaibao bencao* 開寶本草, the *Jiayou bencao* 嘉佑本草 of 1056–1063, and the *Zhenglei bencao* 證類本草, ca. 1082; later came the *Bencao pinhui jingyao* 本草品匯精要 (1505) and the *Bencao gangmu* 本草綱目 (1593). The most complete source remains the *Zhenglei bencao*. Collections of prescriptions such as the *Qianjin yaofang* 千金要方 (ca. 652), the *Qianjin yifang* 千金翼方 (681) of Sun Simiao 孫思邈 (582?–681?), and the Japanese pharmacopeia *Honzō wamyō* 本草和名 of 918 are also composed of citations from that pharmacopeia. In the nonmedical literature some citations are found in the *Bowu zhi*, q.v., of Zhang Hua 張華 (232–300), and the *Qimin yaoshu*, q.v., (544) of Jia Sixie 賈思勰, and in encyclopedias such as the *Yiwen leiju*, q.v., (624) of Ouyang Xun 歐陽詢, the *Chuxue ji*, q.v., of Xu Jian 徐堅 (659–729), and the *Taiping yulan*, q.v., (984).

The oldest manuscript to include citations of the *Shennong bencao jing* is a Tang manuscript that contains a partial text of the *Bencao jing jizhu* of Tao Hongjing found at Dunhuang. There are also three copies of the Tang *Xinxiu bencao*, the official pharmacopeia of 659 cited previously. Two copies were found at Dunhuang, and one manuscript of 734, at the Shōsōin 正倉院 in Nara, Japan, was a donation made in 756 by the empress Kōmyō 光明 to the Tōdaiji 東大寺. But since these manuscripts from Dunhuang and the Shōsōin were only recently discovered, the Ming and Qing recensions were for the most part based on the pharmacopeias. The citations from the *Shennong bencao jing* differ greatly among such Tang medical texts as the *Qianjin yaofang* or the *Waitai biyao*, so the present-day versions are therefore very different from the ancient text, which certainly did not have a unified version.

Diverse editions

The first edition is that of the Southern Song, the *Bencao zheng jing* 本草正經, in three *juan*. We have only a summary and the preface in the *Shuangxi leigao* 雙溪類槀 by Wang Yan 王炎 (*juan* 25). Ma Jixing (*Zhongyi*, 252) lists seven main editions during the Ming and Qing (1616, 1687, 1799, 1844, 1854, 1885, 1892).

The most common edition is that of Sun Xingyan 孫星衍 (1753–1818) and Sun Fengyi 孫馮翼 (fl. 1801) in three *juan*, printed in 1799 as *Shennong bencao jing* 神農本草經. It was included in many medical compendia and in the *Sibu beiyao** and *Congshu jicheng**; almost every library in China has a copy. A facsimile was published by the Renmin weisheng chubanshe, Beijing, in 1955; there are numerous modern typeset editions. The Qing edition of Gu Guanguang 顧觀光 (1799–1826) in three or four *juan* of 1844 was also made widely available, first in the *Wulingshanren yishu* 武陵山人遺書 of 1883. A Japanese recension (1854) by Mori Yōchiku 森養竹 (1807–1885) was reprinted by Ariake shoten, Tokyo, 1980. For details on the editions and commentaries, see Ma (*Zhongyi*, 251–57).

Commentaries

Shennong benjing huitong 神濃本經會通 (1617), ten *juan*. Contains one thousand remedies of which many are not from the *Bencao jing*. A Ming edition is in the holdings of the Shehui kexueyuan 社會科學院, Beijing.

Miu Xiyong 繆希雍. *Shennong bencao jing shu* 神農本草經疏 (1625), thirty *juan*. Facsimile edition in the *Zhoushi yixue congshu* 周氏醫學叢書. Beijing: Zhongguo zhongyao chubanshe, 1997.

Zhang Zhicong 張志聰 and Gao Shishi 高世栻. *Bencao chongyuan* 本草崇原 (1663), three *juan*. Contained in the *Yilin zhiyue* 醫林指月 (1767) by Wang Qi 王琦.

Xu Dachun 徐大椿 (1693–1771). *Shennong bencao jing baizhong lu* 神農本草經百種錄 (1803), one *juan*. Taipei: Taiwan shangwu yinshuguan, 1983.

Chen Xiuyuan 陳修園 (a.k.a. Chen Nianzu 念祖; ca. 1753–ca. 1823); annota. Xiao Xinlang 蕭欽朗. *Shennong bencao jing du* 神農本草經讀. Fuzhou: Fujian kexue jishu chubanshe, 1982.

Current editions

Guang Guanguang 顧觀光. *Shennong bencao jing* 神農本草經. Beijing: Renmin weisheng chubanshe, 1955.

Huang Shuang 黃奭. *Shennong bencao jing* 神農本草經. Beijing: Zhongguo guji chubanshe, 1982.

Sun Xingyan and Sun Fengyi. (See earlier, under "Diverse editions.")

Bibliography

Harper, Don. *Early Chinese Medical Literature: The Mawangdui Medical Manuscripts, Translation and Study*. The Sir Henry Wellcome Asian Series 2. London: Paul Kegan International, 1998.

Fukane no Sukehito 深根輔仁 (898?–922?). *Honzō wamyō* 本草和名 (918). Tokyo: Nihon koten zenshū kankōkai, 1926–1927.

Ma Jixing 馬繼興. *Zhongyi wenxianxue* 中醫文獻學. Shanghai: Shanghai kexue jishu chubanshe, 1990.

Ma Jixing et al. *Shennong bencao jing jizhu* 甚濃本草經輯注. Beijing: Renmin weisheng chubanshe, 1995.

Mori Takeyuki 森立之 (fl. 1850). *Honzōkei kochū* 本草經考註. 3 vols. Taipei: Xinwenfeng chuban gongsi, 1987.

Shang Zhijun 尚志鈞. "Shennong bencao jing wenxian yuanliu kaozheng" 神農本草經文獻源流考證. In Shang Zhijun et al., Zhongyi ba da jingdian quanzhu 中醫八大經典全注, 246–310. Beijing: Huaxia chubanshe, 1994.

Schmidt, Franz-Rudolf A. "The Textual History of the Materia medica in the Han Period: A System-theoretical Reconsideration." *T'oung pao* 92.4–5 (2006): 293–324.

Unschuld, Paul. *Medicine in China—A History of Pharmaceutics*. Berkeley: University of California Press, 1986.

Wang Jiakui 王家葵. "Shennong bencao jing chengshu niandai kaozheng" 神農本草經成書年代考證. *Zhonghua yishi zazhi* 21 (1991): 56–59.

Watanabe Kōzō 渡邊幸三. *Honzōsho no kenkyū* 本草書の研究. Osaka: Takeda kagaku shinkō zaidan, 1987.

Zhouli zhushu 周禮注疏, in *Shisanjing zhushu* 十三經注疏, vol. 1. Beijing: Zhonghua shuju, 1980.

Catherine Despeux

Shenxian zhuan 神仙傳

Introduction

The *Shenxian zhuan* (Traditions [or Biographies] of divine transcendents), a work initially compiled by Ge Hong 葛洪 (283–343) just before the year 317, is the largest and most important collection of lives of transcendents, immortals, sennin, sylphs, or ascendants—however one prefers to render *xian* 仙 into English—written before the Tang dynasty. It followed upon a few earlier works in the same genre, most notably the *Liexian zhuan* 列仙傳 (probably dating to the first or second century A.D.), but included more accounts, with much greater length and detail. The best way to understand this work and others of its genre is as a compilation of narratives reflecting (while also attempting to shape) the collective memory of particular figures deemed by some people to have been successful practitioners of *xian* arts. The text is therefore a mine of information for the history of these forms of proto-Daoist practices, the people who practiced them, and the many other people who sponsored, patronized, beseeched, or otherwise interacted with the practitioners. The text also provides copious incidental glimpses of popular religion; cults of local gods; and modes of healing and divination as well as the relationships between practitioners of these arts and their clients.

The reception and impact of the *Shenxian zhuan* went far beyond the early fourth century. Only a few decades later, the spirit beings who reportedly vouchsafed the Shangqing 上清 revelations to the medium Yang Xi 楊羲 (330–386) offered numerous rewritings of the lives of some figures featured in the *Shenxian zhuan*. A century after the *Shenxian zhuan* was written, manuscript versions of it were "circulating rather widely in the world," according to Pei Songzhi in his 429 commentary to the *Sanguo zhi*, q.v. The text helped to inspire numerous compendia of hagiographical material on *xian* in the Tang and later periods. The *Shenxian zhuan* was heavily anthologized in such later Daoist hagiographical collections as the *Xianyuan bianzhu* 仙苑編珠 (early tenth century), *Xuanpin lu* 玄品錄 (fourteenth century), *Sandong qunxian lu* 三洞群仙錄 (twelfth century), and *Lishi zhenxian tidao tongjian* 歷世真仙體道通鑑 (ca. 1300) as well as in non-Daoist imperially sponsored encyclopedia such as the *Taiping yulan*, q.v. (completed in 983 but drawn almost entirely from earlier anthologies) and the *Taiping guangji* 太平廣記 (completed in 978).

Contents

Since no integral version of the *Shenxian zhuan* survived into the era of printing and since every extant version or edition (with one possible exception) is some sort of reconstruction based on now-lost sources, the size and precise contents of the text depend largely on how one chooses to reconstruct it or, in other words, which textual witnesses one chooses to accept as representing some early version of the *Shenxian zhuan* rather than being later interpolations or misattributed passages. Most editions include hagiographies of between eighty-four and ninety-two individuals. We do not know how Ge Hong arranged his material. The persons treated in extant passages attributed to the *Shenxian zhuan* range in their supposed date of birth from extremely ancient times (such as Peng Zu and Master Whitestone) to a generation or two before Ge Hong's time or even, in a very few cases, figures still active in Ge's own day (such as Guo Pu 郭璞; 276–324). Many are said to have lived during the Western or Eastern Han or in the decades following the collapse of the latter regime. A preface to the work also survives, though its authenticity has long been questioned.

Authorship

In the autobiography included in the *Baopuzi* 抱朴子 (Master who embraces the unhewn), q.v., Ge Hong says he compiled a text in ten scrolls titled *Shenxian zhuan*, information that is repeated in a fifth-century catalog of Daoist works, a sixth-century Daoist hagiographical collection (*Daoxue zhuan* 道學傳), Ge's official biography in the *Jin shu*, q.v. (72:1910–13), the bibliographic monograph of the *Sui shu*, q.v., and many other works. That he wrote such a text cannot reasonably be doubted. Yet, it is virtually certain that some passages attributed to the *Shenxian zhuan* in extant works were not in fact written by Ge Hong, just as it is also virtually certain that some or many passages that were included by him in the work are now completely lost. Thanks to his autobiographical essay, comments made elsewhere in the *Baopuzi*, and his official biography, we know a fair amount about his life and thought. By his own statement, he wrote both the *Shenxian zhuan* and the *Baopuzi* by 317 while still a relatively young man and before he had gained access to many of his master Zheng Yin's most esoteric teachings. Both of these works are therefore best seen as the enthusiastic writings of a supporter of the quest for transcendence but someone who was, at the time of writing, a relative novice in the practice of the esoteric arts often featured in the texts.

Composition

Like other works of the biography/hagiography genre in the period, the *Shenxian zhuan* was largely based on an assortment of previously existing narrative sources, naturally subject to the compiler's own selection and editing. It is rarely possible in any specific instance to identify these sources with a high degree of confidence and to compare them to the *Shenxian zhuan* text. But we know that Ge Hong, like other authors of texts of this and related genres (notably including histories and narratives of anomalies) in the early medieval period, drew on oral accounts as well as on letters, biographies of individuals, histories, essays, scriptural material, stele inscriptions, and earlier, now-lost hagiographical compilations.

Transmission of the text

The *Shenxian zhuan* is listed in many early bibliographic catalogs from the fifth century on, as mentioned previously. It continues to be listed, usually in ten scrolls, in the *Jiu Tang shu* and in the *Song shi*, and indeed it is even listed in a Japanese catalog dating to around 890. But no version of the text seems to be recorded as having been transmitted past the end of the Southern Song; no Ming-era catalog lists it, and the Ming Daoist Canon lists it as missing. Most modern scholars have concluded that all extant editions date only from the late Ming and were, although presented as if they were Ge Hong's own versions, in fact re-formed by compilers from quotations in older printed collectanea. One modern scholar, Benjamin Penny, believes that one early modern edition, that prepared by a certain Mao Jin 毛晉 (1599–1659) and included in the *Siku quanshu**, may represent, at least in part, a transmission of a version of the text from the Song rather than a Ming-era recomposition, but other scholars have expressed doubt on this point. All extant editions are probably much smaller than many pre-Song versions (although it is very risky to assume that, in a manuscript era, any version of *Shenxian zhuan* that anyone reports having seen was necessarily the same as or even closely similar to the one(s) Ge Hong himself wrote!); for example, a Tang Buddhist writer, Liang Su 梁肅 (d. 793), mentions that the *Shenxian zhuan* he had seen contained lives of some 190 persons. The relationships between extant editions and their earlier source texts are much too complex to be summarized here; they are well discussed in the articles by Stephan Bumbacher and Benjamin Penny listed in the bibliography herein. I am aware of no early manuscript versions of the text, whether from Dunhuang, an excavated Six Dynasties or early Tang tomb, or a Japanese Buddhist temple; the discovery of such a manuscript would be a major event in *Shenxian zhuan* scholarship.

Principal editions

All extant editions derive from two families of sources: (1) The *Longwei mishu* 龍威秘書, *Zengding Han Wei congshu* 增定漢魏叢書, *Shuoku* 說庫, and some other editions (some of them abridged); all are based on a text recompiled from older printed sources by He Yunzhong 何允中 in the compendium *Guang Han Wei congshu* 廣漢魏叢書 (1592), itself not widely available. (2) Some other modern editions are based on the text that was included in the *Siku quanshu* in its complete reprinting, which was based on a text printed by Mao Jin; this is sometimes referred to as the Jiguge 汲古閣 edition, after the name of Mao's studio. The former family of editions contains ninety-two hagiographies, the latter eighty-four. In the two families of texts these hagiographies are also arranged in different order, and, when they overlap, they often differ in content or wording.

Modern critical editions

Not only is there not a truly and strictly critical edition of the text; given the checkered and complex history of the transmission of the *Shenxian zhuan* and the ways in which texts were transmitted in manuscript in the era before printing became common, there is likely never to be one, or at least, if there is, it would be a mistake to assume—barring some surprising find of an early manuscript version—that it closely resembles the version(s) produced by Ge Hong himself in his lifetime. The closest thing we have to a critical or at least variorum edition is that included in the *Zhonghua daozang* 中華道藏 (ed. Zhang Jiyu 張繼禹 [Beijing: Huaxia chubanshe, 2004]), which takes the *Siku quanshu* edition as its basis but notes variata in the *Guang Han Wei congshu* edition. An edition by Zhou Qicheng 周啟成, *Xinyi Shenxian zhuan* 新譯神仙傳 (Taipei: Sanmin shuju, 2004), is similarly based on the *Siku quanshu* edition but annotates variata in the *Zengding Han Wei congshu* edition as well as noting variata in several pre-Ming witnesses to the text and providing a translation into modern Chinese. Campany, *To Live as Long as Heaven and Earth* (see later, in "Interpretive Works"), while it is not a critical edition and does not include a Chinese text, provides detailed notes on the content and differences among various textual witnesses and in many cases offers translations or synopses of early witnesses. It also offers thorough annotation to the translated passages (part 3, pp. 373–552). One fair critical assessment of the success of this venture may be found in the Barrett article listed in the following.

Major studies of the text and its history

Barrett, T. H. "On the Reconstruction of the *Shenxian zhuan*." Bulletin of the School of Oriental and African Studies 66 (2003): 229–35.

Bumbacher, Stephan Peter. "On the *Shenxian zhuan*." Asiatische Studien/Etudes Asiatiques 54 (2000): 729–814.

Fukui Kōjun 福井康順. "*Shinsenden* kō" 神仙傳考. *Tōhō shūkyō* 1 (1951): 1–20.

Kominami Ichirō 小南一郎. "*Shinsenden* no fukugen" 神仙傳の復元. In Iriya kyōju, Ogawa kyōju, taikyū ki'nen Chūgoku bungaku gogaku ronshū 久矢教授, 小川教授, 退休記念中國文學語學論集, 301–13. Kyoto: Iriya kyōju, Ogawa kyōju, taikyū ki'nenkai, 1974.

———. "Gishin jidai no shinsen shisō: *Shinsenden* o chūshin toshite" 魏晉時代の神仙思想: 神仙傳を中心として. In Chūgoku no kagaku to kagakusha 中国の科學と科學者, ed. Yamada Keiji 山田慶兒, 573–626. Kyoto: Kyōto daigaku jimbun kagaku kenkyūjo, 1978.

———. "Jinyaku kara zonshi e: Shinsen shisō to dōkyō shinkō to no aida" 尋藥から存思へ: 神仙思想と道教信仰との間. In Chūgoku ko dōkyōshi kenkyū 中國古道教史研究, ed. Yoshikawa Tadao 吉川忠夫, 3–54. Kyoto: Kyoto daigaku jimbun kagaku kenkyū hōkoku, 1991.

Penny, Benjamin. "The Text and Authorship of *Shenxian zhuan*." Journal of Oriental Studies 34 (1996): 165–209.

———. "*Shenxian zhuan.*" In *The Encyclopedia of Taoism*, ed. Fabrizio Pregadio, 887–88. London: Routledge, 2008.

Interpretive works on particular themes or hermeneutical methods

Campany, Robert Ford. "Secrecy and Display in the Quest for Transcendence in China, ca. 220 B.C.E.–350 C.E." *History of Religions* 45 (2006): 291–336.

———. *Making Transcendents: Ascetics and Social Memory in Early Medieval China.* Honolulu: University of Hawai'i Press, 2009.

Penny, Benjamin. "Jiao Xian's Three Lives." In *Religion and Biography in China and Tibet*, ed. Benjamin Penny, 13–29. Richmond, UK: Curzon, 2002.

On Ge Hong and his thought and writings

Arbuckle, Gary. "When Did Ge Hong Die?" *B.C. Asian Review* 2 (1988): 1–7.

Campany, Robert Ford. "Ingesting the Marvelous: The Practitioner's Relationship to Nature According to Ge Hong." In *Daoism and Ecology: Ways within a Cosmic Landscape*, ed. N. J. Girardot et al., 125–48. Cambridge, MA: Center for the Study of World Religions, Harvard Divinity School, 2001.

———. *To Live as Long as Heaven and Earth: A Translation and Study of Ge Hong's Traditions of Divine Transcendents*, 3–117. Berkeley: University of California Press, 2002.

———. "Two Religious Thinkers of the Early Eastern Jin: Gan Bao and Ge Hong in Multiple Contexts." *Asia Major*, 3rd ser., 18 (2005): 175–224.

Chen Guofu 陳國符. *Daozang yuanliu kao* 道藏源流考, 95–98. Beijing: Zhonghua shuju, 1963.

Hu Fuchen 胡孚琛. *Wei Jin shenxian daojiao: Baopuzi neipian yanjiu* 魏晉神仙道教: 抱朴子內篇研究. Beijing: Renmin, 1989; rpt., Taipei: Taiwan shangwu yinshuguan, 1992.

Knechtges, David R. "Ge Hong." In *Ancient and Early Medieval Chinese Literature: A Reference Guide*, part 1, ed. David R. Knechtges and Taiping Chang, 269–72. Leiden: Brill, 2010.

Lai, Chi-Tim. "The Taoist Vision of Physical Immortality: A Study of Ko Hung's *Pao-p'u tzu.*" Ph.D. diss., University of Chicago, 1995.

Liang Rongmao 梁榮茂. *Baopuzi yanjiu: Ge Hong de wenxueguan ji qi sixiang* 抱朴子研究: 葛洪的文學觀及其思想. Taipei: Mutong, 1977.

Liu Gusheng 劉固勝. *Ge Hong yanjiu lunji* 葛洪研究論集. Wuhan: Huazhong shifan daxue chubanshe, 2006.

Ōfuchi Ninji 大淵忍爾. *Shoki no dōkyō: Dōkyōshi no kenkyū* 初期の道教: 道教史の研究, 487–552. Tokyo: Sōbunsha, 1991.

Robinet, Isabelle. *Taoism: Growth of a Religion.* Trans. Phyllis Brooks. Stanford, CA: Stanford University Press, 1997. Pp. 78–113.

Shi Qiong 石瓊. "Ge Hong shenxian sixiang xiping" 葛洪神仙思想析評. In *Daojiao shenxian xinyang yanjiu* 道教神仙信仰研究, ed. Sichuan daxue zongjiao yanjiusuo, 277–88. Taipei: Zhonghua dadao wenhua, 2000.

Sivin, Nathan. "On the *Pao p'u tzu nei p'ien* and the Life of Ko Hung (283–343). *Isis* 60 (1969): 388–91.
Wang Liqi 王利器. "Ge Hong zhushu kaolue" 葛洪著述考略. *Wen shi* 37 (1993): 33–54.
Wang Ming 王明. "Lun Ge Hong" 論葛洪. *Daojia he daojiao sixiang yanjiu* 道家和道教思想研究, 55–79. Beijing: Zhongguo shehui kexue, 1984.
Wells, Matthew. "Self as Historical Artifact: Ge Hong and Early Chinese Autobiographical Writing." *Early Medieval China* 9 (2003): 71–103.
———. *To Die and Not Decay: Autobiography and the Pursuit of Immortality in Early China*. Ann Arbor, MI: Association for Asian Studies, 2009.
Yang Shihua 楊世華. *Ge Hong yanjiu erji* 葛洪研究二集. Wuhan: Huazhong shifan daxue chubanshe, 2008.

Translations in European languages

Campany, Robert Ford. *To Live as Long as Heaven and Earth*. See previous section.
Güntsch, Gertrud. *Das Shen-hsien chuan und das Erscheinungsbild eines Hsien*. Frankfurt am Main: Peter Lang, 1988.

Japanese annotations and translations

Fukui Kōjun 福井康順. *Shinsenden* 神仙傳. Tokyo: Meitoku, 1983.
Sawada Mizuho 沢田瑞穂. *Shinsenden* 神仙傳. In *Chūgoku koten bungaku taikei* 中国古典文学大系 8. Tokyo: Heibonsha, 1969.

Robert Ford Campany

Shi pin 詩品

Introduction

The *Shi pin* (Poetry gradings) by Zhong Rong 鍾嶸 (469?–518) is the first work of applied criticism in the Chinese tradition to deal extensively with earlier individual poets and their *shi* 詩 poetry. There had previously been short comments on individual writers, but Zhong Rong was the first to provide critiques of a large number of poets (well over one hundred) and gradings ("upper," "middle," and "lower") in which to place them.

The approach, terminology, and framework of the *Shi pin* were to have great influence on later Chinese poetics and culture. The "approach," that of characterizing a poet in language that could (and generally did) refer both to (a) the personality or character of the writer and (b) the writings of the author—as well as sometimes (c) the response, that is, the feeling or impression that the poetry engendered in readers—became common. Although writers and their works had earlier been considered inseparable, as attested in passages by Sima Qian 司馬遷 (135?–86? B.C.) and Yang Xiong 揚雄 (53 B.C.–A.D. 18)—Zhong Rong's extended application of the approach to letters made it the norm in this realm. Only in Song times is the distinction between the two questioned, and even then more by way of exception. The conflation of the two (or three) axes of reference is common in discussions of literature in Chinese criticism to this day.

The terminology used in the *Shi pin* especially lends itself to such dual (or tripartite) reference. This is particularly true when terms such as *feng* 風 ("air") and *qi* 氣 ("life-breath" or "vital force") are used. For example, in Zhong Rong's formulation "Liu Zhen's 劉楨 [d. 217] noble air (*gao feng* 高風) surpasses the common run" (1.5), the expression "noble air" can refer to Liu Zhen, his work, and/or the feeling the latter is said to inspire in his readers. Dual and occasionally triple reference is suggested by other compounds as well, such as *yidang* 逸蕩 ("unrestrained and unencumbered") and *yuanfang* 淵放 ("profound and untrammeled"), even in contexts that clearly refer to writing. Although some of the terminology used by Zhong Rong was original, his work developed out of a characterological tradition that had been common since the third century. It is in the terminology used to characterize poets and their poetry that Zhong Rong's influence was greatest. The phrasing he devised was used by later critics of calligraphy and painting, as well as in the classic statements of Japanese poetics in the *Kokinshū* prefaces (古今集序; 905), in the series of poems on poetry by Yuan

Haowen 元好問 (1190–1257), and in the *Xu Shi pin* 續詩品 (Poetry gradings: A continuation) by Yuan Mei 袁枚 (1716–1797). His phrasing inspired the *Ershisi shi pin* 二十四詩品 (Twenty-four poetic modes), ascribed to Sikong Tu 司空圖 (837–908) but probably composed centuries later; it became pervasive in the array of *shihua* 詩話 (causeries on poetry) appearing from the Song dynasty onward; and it is echoed in language used to this day. One should remember that the *Wenxin diaolong* (The essence of literature: Carved-dragon elaborations), q.v., by Liu Xie (ca. 465–ca. 521), a much more famous and lauded work today, was virtually ignored during the first millennium of its existence. The *Shi pin* was *the* influential work of Chinese literary criticism over the period.

The *Shi pin*'s framework of ranking individuals and their work according to three gradings reflected an earlier characterological tradition that had developed out of the need to rank officials (official ranks being simply a three-level system further subdivided into three tiers). In the Han dynasty there had been seven- and nine-part bibliographical and historical classifications. From the third century on, important works were written that reflected what James R. Hightower has called the "pastime of evaluating and categorizing people," but where primary interest remained "determining the fitness of a person for office." Liu Shao's 劉邵 (190?–265) *Renwu zhi* 人物志 (Treatise on personalities) and Zhong Hui's 鍾會 (225–264) *Siben lun* 四本論 (Treatise on the four basic relations [between natural ability and human nature]) provide prime examples. The literary criticism in Cao Pi's (187–226) "Essay on Literature" in *Critical Treatises* (*Dianlun*, "Lunwen" 典論論文) was in fact but a by-product of the same interest in characterization. The three- and nine-part scheme of classification was even extended to believers of Pure Land Buddhism.

Yet by the fourth century, characterological discussion had lost much of its political significance and became more of a rhetorical diversion. Liu Yiqing's (403–444) *Shishuo xinyu*, q.v., is reflective of the tendency. But the interest in character and the ready-to-hand framework were easily extended. Shortly prior to the writing of the *Shi pin*, two different *Qi pin* 棋品 (Gradings of chess players) appeared, by Shen Yue 沈約 (441–513) and by Liu Yun 柳惲 (465–517), as well as a *Shu pin* 書品 (Calligraphy gradings) by Yu Jianwu 庾肩吾 (487–551). Zhong Rong applied the framework to poets and their poetry. Shortly afterward, application of the practice to calligraphers and painters continued, with the *Gujin shuping* 古今書評 (Critiques of calligraphers ancient and modern) by Yuan Ang 袁昂 (d. 540; work dated 523) and the *Gu huapin lu* 古畫品錄 (Venerable record of gradings of painters) by Xie He 謝赫 (fl. 535).

Much has been made of the three gradings and the placement of certain poets in one category or another—particularly the "misplacement" of Tao Qian 陶潛 (365?–427), in the "middle" rather than "upper" grade of poetry. What has often been overlooked is that "middle grade" poets were deemed "very good," not middling. And the rhetorical nature of the gradings is generally misunderstood: namely, the higher the level of abstraction, inclusiveness, or indeterminacy in a value proposition, the less force as a proposition of value it has. Gradings are in fact summary value judgments that serve other ends; for example, those trying to persuade readers of the comparatively greater (moral, literary, social) value of some writers, and so which authors to emulate in one's own writing, and, by extension, which writers' epigones on the contemporary scene to cultivate or shun.

Much attention has also been focused on the way Zhong Rong assigns a filiation to the five-character lyrical poetry (*shi* 詩) he treats that, directly or indirectly, goes back to the *Shi jing* 詩經 (Classic of song) or *Chu ci* 楚辭 (Chu lyrics). As a rule, the more removed a writer is from these fonts of the poetic tradition, the poorer the rank he is likely to be assigned. Like the gradings, however, the filiations can be misunderstood. Although on one level they refer to influence, borrowing, and emulation, on another, like the nod to the metaphysical origins of poetry at the beginning of Preface A, they are part of an overall pattern of justification of the enterprise, first, of writing poetry, and, second, of evaluating it—both apparently still in need of justification. At a still more fundamental level, the filiations reflect a philosophical milieu (especially regarding scholarship on the *Yi jing* 易經 [Classic of change]) that emphasized the retrospective embrace of an original unity in the cosmos.

Contemporary social implications of the work are important but sometimes difficult to assess. In the salon culture of the time, where literature was a prime interest, an attack on a man's literary work could be tantamount to a personal or political attack and might be effected by criticizing the poets a person emulated. Status and patronage were important. Consciousness of status is especially in evidence in the headings to Zhong Rong's evaluations: wherever possible, poets are identified by their official title.

It has commonly been held that there were three rival groups of poets at the time: the "avant-garde" school headed by Xiao Gang 蕭綱 (503–551) and Xiao Yi 蕭繹 (508–554); the "conservative" or "archaic" school said to be championed by Pei Ziye 裴子野 (469–530); and the "eclectic" or "compromise" school led by Xiao Tong 蕭統 (501–531), Zhong Rong being counted among the conservatives. Scholarship in recent years has challenged this view and presented a more nuanced picture.

For several of the poets Zhong Rong treats, including famous ones, only a limited number of poems are extant; for many, especially those in the "lower grading," there are none. So, assessment of the evaluations is often difficult.

Contents

The *Shi pin* contains three prefaces and characterizes 123 poets and their poetry (plus *gushi* 古詩, anonymous "old poems") under sixty-two entries. The three gradings are termed *shangpin* 上品, *zhongpin* 中品, and *xiapin* 中品, which are best thought of as referring to "outstanding," "very good," and "fair to good" poets and their poetry, as all entrants are deemed to have merit. Only deceased poets are treated, "since it is only their work that can be properly evaluated" (Preface B). And only pentasyllabic poetry, said to hold "the strategic place in the world of letters" and to be "the most flavorful of all creative works" (Preface A), is discussed.

A preface heads each of the three poetry gradings, and the prefaces are followed by entries. The prefaces include general statements about poetry and poetics, the entries largely applied criticism. Although normative statements concerning what poetry should be like are found only in the prefaces, specific traits mentioned in the critiques are considered in conjunction with the general statements in the prefaces when determining the overall placement of a poet within a grading; hence the flexibility of the system. And the terms used for specific traits, in turn, over later centuries could serve as normative traits, positive or negative, for poetry writing and evaluation.

In Preface A, a few formulas from earlier critical theory (e.g., from the "Great Preface," "Da xu" 大序, to the *Shi jing*) are repeated to give belles lettres a degree of metaphysical underpinning and to justify the author's enterprise—questionable at the time, if not novel—of judging writers and writing by something other than didactic criteria. A terse history of antecedent poetry follows. The need for balance in the use of *fu* 賦 (description), *bi* 比 (comparison), and *xing* 興 (evocative image) in poetry is argued. Following is a litany of the occasions of poetic composition and finally an encomium to the reigning sovereign.

Preface B focuses on two points, one being the near reverse correlative of the other: the deleterious effect of the overuse of allusions in poetry, and the need for plain speaking in verse writing. Preface C is similarly devoted to one theme with two parts: that too much attention has been paid in recent years to the rules of tonal euphony associated with Shen Yue (i.e., awareness of the "four tones" [*sisheng* 四聲] and emphasis on the "eight defects" [*babing* 八病] of poetry); all that is necessary is that a poem read smoothly when recited aloud (or be adaptable to song). This last preface ends with another virtual litany, one listing "masterpieces of five-character verse" that also happen to predate formulation of the rules of tonal euphony in poetry.

Entries after each preface contain brief characterizations of poets and their poetry. "The arrangement within each of the categories is chronological; entries are not further classified in terms of relative merit" (Preface B). The twelve entries for "upper grade" poetry uniformly treat a single poet (or, in one case, *gushi*); one-third of the twenty-one entries characterizing thirty-nine "middle grade" poets/poetry treat two or more poets; and the great majority of the twenty-nine "lower grade" treatments of seventy-three poets and their poetry address multiple authors. Hence, the lower the grade assigned a poet, the more terse the characterization of the writer's poetry is likely to be.

The 123 poets (and *gushi*) are assigned to the three gradings in the following order: Upper Grade, *Shangpin* 上品 (one general entry plus eleven entrants)

1.1.	Gushi	古詩	
1.2.	Li Ling	李陵	d. 74 B.C.
1.3.	Ban Jieyu	班婕妤	48?–6? B.C.
1.4.	Cao Zhi	曹植	A.D. 192–232

1.5.	Liu Zhen	劉楨	d. 217
1.6.	Wang Can	王粲	177–217
1.7.	Ruan Ji	阮籍	210–263
1.8.	Lu Ji	陸機	261–303
1.9.	Pan Yue	潘岳	247–300
1.10.	Zhang Xie	張協	d. 307
1.11.	Zuo Si	左思	ca. 250–ca. 305
1.12.	Xie Lingyun	謝靈運	385–433

Middle Grade, *Zhongpin* 中品 (thirty-nine entrants)

2.1a.	Qin Jia	秦嘉	Han dynasty
2.1b.	Xu Shu	徐淑	Han dynasty
2.2.	Cao Pi	曹丕	187–226
2.3.	Xi Kang	嵇康	232–262
2.4.	Zhang Hua	張華	232–300
2.5a.	He Yan	何晏	190–249
2.5b.	Sun Chu	孫楚	218?–293
2.5c.	Wang Zan	王讚	fl. 290
2.5d.	Zhang Han	張翰	Jin dynasty
2.5e.	Pan Ni	潘尼	250?–311?
2.6.	Ying Qu	應璩	190–252
2.7a.	Lu Yun	陸雲	262–303
2.7b.	Shi Chong	石崇	249–300
2.7c.	Cao Shu	曹攄	d. 308
2.7d.	He Shao	何劭	236–301
2.8a.	Liu Kun	劉琨	270–317
2.8b.	Lu Chen	盧諶	284–350
2.9.	Guo Pu	郭璞	276–324
2.10.	Yuan Hong	袁宏	328–376
2.11a.	Guo Taiji	郭泰機	Jin dynasty

2.11b.	Gu Kaizhi	顧愷之	ca. 344–ca. 405
2.11c.	Xie Shiji	謝世基	d. 426
2.11d.	Gu Mai	顧邁	Liu-Song dynasty
2.11e.	Dai Kai	戴凱	Liu-Song dynasty
2.12.	Tao Qian	陶潛	365–427
2.13.	Yan Yanzhi	顏延之	384–456
2.14a.	Xie Zhan	謝瞻	387–421
2.14b.	Xie Hun	謝混	d. 412
2.14c.	Yuan Shu	袁淑	408–453
2.14d.	Wang Wei	王微	415–453
2.14e.	Wang Sengda	王僧達	423–458
2.15.	Xie Huilian	謝惠連	397–433
2.16.	Bao Zhao	鮑照	d. 466
2.17.	Xie Tiao	謝朓	464–499
2.18.	Jiang Yan	江淹	444–505
2.19a.	Fan Yun	范雲	451–503
2.19b.	Qiu Chi	丘遲	464–508
2.20.	Ren Fang	任昉	460–508
2.21.	Shen Yue	沈約	441–513

Lower Grade, *Xiapin* 下品 (seventy-three entrants)

3.1a.	Ban Gu	班固	32–92
3.1b.	Li Yan	酈炎	150–177
3.1c.	Zhao Yi	趙壹	Han dynasty
3.2a.	Cao Cao	曹操	155–220
3.2b.	Cao Rui	曹叡	204–239
3.3a.	Cao Biao	曹彪	d. 249
3.3b.	Xu Gan	徐幹	170?–217?
3.4a.	Ruan Yu	阮瑀	165?–212
3.4b.	Ouyang Jian	歐陽建	270–300

3.4c.	Ying Yang	應瑒	d. 217	
3.4d.	Xi Han	嵇含	263–306	
3.4e.	Ruan Kan	阮侃	Jin dynasty	
3.4f.	Xi Shao	嵇紹	253–304	
3.4g.	Zao Ju	棗據	Jin dynasty	
3.5a.	Zhang Zai	張載	fl. 285	
3.5b.	Fu Xuan	傅玄	217–278	
3.5c.	Fu Xian	傅咸	239–294	
3.5d.	Miao Xi	繆襲	186-245	
3.5e.	Xiahou Zhan	夏侯湛	243–291	
3.6a.	Wang Ji	王濟	245?–290?	
3.6b.	Du Yu	杜預	222–284	
3.6c.	Sun Chuo	孫綽	314–371	
3.6d.	Xu Xun	許詢	Jin dynasty	
3.7.	Dai Kui	戴逵	d. 395	
3.8.	Yin Zhongwen	殷仲文	d. 407	
3.9.	Fu Liang	傅亮	374–426	
3.10a.	He Changyu	何長瑜	d. 443	
3.10b.	Yang Xuanzhi	羊璿之	d. 459	
3.11.	Fan Ye	范曄	398–445	
3.12a.	Liu Jun	劉駿	430–464	
3.12b.	Liu Shuo	劉鑠	431–453	
3.12c.	Liu Hong	劉宏	434–458	
3.13.	Xie Zhuang	謝莊	421–466	
3.14a.	Su Baosheng	蘇寶生	d. 458	
3.14b.	Ling Xiuzhi	陵修之	Liu-Song dynasty	
3.14c.	Ren Tanxu	任曇緒	Liu-Song dynasty	
3.14d.	Dai Faxing	戴法興	414–465	
3.15.	Ou Huigong	區惠恭	Liu-Song dynasty	

3.16a.	Tang Huixiu	湯惠休	Qi dynasty
3.16b.	Feng/Bo Daoyou	馮(帛)道猷	Qi dynasty
3.16c.	Kang Baoyue	康寶月	Qi dynasty
3.17a.	Xiao Daocheng	蕭道成	427–482
3.17b.	Zhang Yong	張永	410–475
3.17c.	Wang Jian	王儉	452–489
3.18a.	Xie Chaozong	謝超宗	d. 483
3.18b.	Qiu Lingju	丘靈鞠	Qi dynasty
3.18c.	Liu Xiang	劉祥	Qi dynasty
3.18d.	Tan Chao	檀超	d. 480
3.18e.	Zhong Xian	鍾憲	Qi dynasty
3.18f.	Yan Ce	顏測	Qi dynasty
3.18g.	Gu Zexin	顧則心	Qi dynasty
3.19a.	Mao Xuan	毛玄	Qi dynasty
3.19b.	Wu Maiyuan	吳邁遠	d. 474
3.19c.	Xu Yaozhi	許瑤之	Qi dynasty
3.20a.	Bao Linghui	鮑令暉	Qi dynasty
3.20b.	Han Lanying	韓蘭英	Qi dynasty
3.21a.	Zhang Rong	張融	444–497
3.21b.	Kong Zhigui	孔稚珪	447–501
3.22a.	Wang Rong	王融	467–493
3.22b.	Liu Hui	劉繪	458-502
3.23a.	Jiang Shi	江祏	d. 499
3.23b.	Jiang Si	江祀	d. 499
3.24a.	Wang Jin	王巾	d. 505
3.24b.	Bian Bin	卞彬	d. 500
3.24c.	Bian Shuo	卞鑠	Qi dynasty
3.25.	Yuan Gu	袁嘏	d. 498
3.26a.	Zhang Xintai	張欣泰	456–501

3.26b.	Fan Zhen	范縝	450–510
3.27.	Lu Jue	陸厥	472–499
3.28a.	Yu Xi	虞羲	Liang dynasty
3.28b.	Jiang Hong	江洪	Liang dynasty
3.29a.	Bao Xingqing	鮑行卿	Liang dynasty
3.29b.	Sun Cha	孫察	Liang dynasty

Authorship, dating, and transmission of the text

There are biographies of Zhong Rong in *Liang shu*, q.v., 49:694–97, and *Nan shi*, q.v., 72:1778–79. They relate that he initially specialized in study of the *Yi jing*, was to remain a low-level bureaucrat, and wrote a work in which he "graded former and contemporary five-word poetry, discussing its strong and weak points." Only the *Nan shi* mentions that Zhong Rong was once rebuffed by Shen Yue and suggests that Zhong wrote the *Shi pin* upon Shen's death to reciprocate the slight. Other than the *Shi pin* and the text of two memorials submitted to the throne (included in the *Liang shu* biography), no other work by him is extant, although he apparently wrote poetry himself.

The *Shi pin* was written in the second decade of the sixth century. Since it treats only deceased poets, the latest being Shen Yue (d. 513), and Zhong Rong died in 518, the work was written (or completed) between 513 and 518.

It is possible that the *Shi pin* was accompanied by an anthology of poetry. The list of occasions prompting poems linked to specific authors, as well as the list of poems that ends the last preface, suggest so, even though there is no concrete evidence for such a collection. Many anthologies from the period are no longer extant.

Cao Xu (*Shi pin yanjiu*) outlines the history of the *Shi pin* and lists fifty-three pre-twentieth-century editions of the work (one Yuan, twenty Ming, twenty Qing, and two Japanese). As Takagi Masakazu (*Shō Kō Shihin*) notes, until the twentieth century it was quite exceptional for the *Shi pin* to appear as a separate title (there is one Ming edition in the 1959 listing of rare books in the Beijing Library). From the Yuan onward, the text has appeared in numerous collectanea; he lists no fewer than fifteen. The work appears in three *juan* in all but two of those *congshu* 叢書 (where it is one *juan*). The most famous collectanea in which the work appears is the *Lidai shihua* 歷代詩話 edited by He Wenhuan 何文煥 (1732–1809).

Earlier texts of the *Shi pin* are reproduced in several modern editions. For their concordance to the *Shi pin*, D. C. Lau et al. use as a base text the 1970 Taipei photolithographic reprint (published by Xinxing shuju 新興書局) of the 1508 Ming dynasty "Shantang qunshu kaosuo" 山堂群書考索 edition of the work. Cao Xu photographically reproduces as a frontispiece to his *Shi pin jizhu* a page from the earliest known printing of the *Shi pin*, the 1320 "Shantang qunshu kaosuo," which he confirms is ancestor to the 1508 edition. Takamatsu Kōmei (*Shō Kō Shihin*) photolithographically reproduces a section of the 1561 edition of the "Yinchuang zalu" 吟窗雜錄 text of the *Shi pin* held by the National Diet Library. This text, having originally been edited by Chen Yinghang 陳應行 (fl. 1194), may reflect an older editorial tradition. In the same lineage, Takagi Masakazu photographically reproduces a section of the 1861 edition of the "Yinchuang zalu" text, edited with *kaeriten* 返り点 by Shōhei Kō 昌平黌 and held by Tokyo University, which takes as its base text the aforementioned 1561 edition. Bernhard Führer (in *Chinas erste Poetik*) reproduces the *Lidai shihua* punctuated edition of the *Shi pin*, as found in a 1973 photolithographic reproduction (of a reprint) of a 1770 edition of the collectanea.

Modern scholarship in Chinese, annotated editions

Modern scholarship on the *Shi pin* dates from the 1920s, with the appearance of studies by Gu Zhi 古直 (1926), Chen Yan 陳衍 (1926), Chen Yanjie 陳延傑 (1929), and Ye Changqing 葉長青 (1933) that focus on annotation of the text (as well as Zhang Chenqing's 張陳卿 1926 study, whose scope was broader). Their work, together with similar material by later twentieth-century scholar-pioneers of the *Shi pin*—Ch'a Chu-hwan 車柱環 (1960), Xu Wenyu 許文雨 (1967), Yang Zuyu 楊祖聿 (1981), and Yi Hwi-gyo 李徽教 (1983)—is copiously reproduced in the work by Wang Shumin (*Zhong Rong Shi pin jianzheng gao*) cited here. Much of the scholarship by the two Koreans, Ch'a Chu-hwan and Yi Hwi-gyo, is in Chinese.

Other book-length volumes on the *Shi pin* that appeared in the modern period to circa 1985 include those by Du Tianmi 杜天縻 (1935), Wang Zhong 汪中 (1969), Chan Hing-ho (Chen Qinghao) 陳慶浩 (1978), Liao Dongliang 廖棟樑 (1986), and Xiang Changqing 向長清 (1986), as well as masters theses by Liu Chunhua 劉春華 (1963), He Shize 何士澤 (1969), and Chen Duanduan 陳端端 (1972). Later annotated editions of the work—without modern-language translation—include those by Lü Deshen 呂德申 (1986; 2nd ed., 2000), Zhang Huaijin 張懷堓 (1997), and Zhang Liandi 張連第 (2000). Most important, however, are the 1994 work by Cao Xu and the aforementioned contribution by Wang Shumin.

Annotated edition in Japanese

Noteworthy for meticulous detail is "Shōshi *Shihin* so" 鍾氏詩品疏 by Shihin kenkyūhan 詩品研究班, published in *Ritsumeikan bungaku* in nine installments, 1964–1971: issues 232, 241, 268, 272, 282, 300, 308, 309, and 314. They were reprinted in *Chūgoku kankei ronsetsu shiryō* 中国関係論説資料 (Tokyo: Ronsetsu shiryō hozonkai, 1965, 1968–1970, and 1972), in vols. 4.2 (two installments), 9.2, 10.2, 11.2.1, 12.2.1, and 14.2.1 (three installments). Much of the annotation is included in the Takagi Masakazu volume noted later.

Annotated Chinese-language translations

There are at least seven complete annotated translations of the *Shi pin* into modern Chinese, all dating from 1985 and later. These are by Zhou Weimin 周偉民 and Xiao Huarong 蕭華榮 (1985), Zhao Zhongyi 趙仲邑 (1987), Xu Da 徐達 (1990), Chen Yuansheng 陳元勝 (1994), Zhou Zhenfu 周振甫 (1998; rpt., 2006), Yang Ming 楊明 (1999), and Cheng Zhangcan 程章燦 (2003).

Annotated Japanese-language translations

There are three complete Japanese-language translations of the *Shi pin*: Takamatsu Kōmei (Takaaki) 高松亨明, *Shō Kō Shihin* 鍾嶸詩品 (1959); Kōzen Hiroshi 興膳宏, in Arai Ken 荒井健 and Kōzen Hiroshi, *Bungaku ronshū* 文学論集 (1972); and Takagi Masakazu 高木正一, *Shō Kō Shihin* 鍾嶸詩品 (1978). Additionally, there is a translation of just the three prefaces by Okamura Shigeru 岡村繁 in *Bungaku geijutsu ronshū* 文学芸術論集, edited by Mekada Makoto 目加田誠, 1984.

European-language translations

Führer, Bernhard. *Chinas erste Poetik: Das Shipin (Kriterion Poietikon) des Zhong Hong (467? –518)*. Dortmund: Projekt Verlag, 1995. Complete translation into German, drawing much (with acknowledgment) on the earlier versions by Wixted and Tökei; includes helpful annotation and bibliography.

Tökei, Ferenc. *Műfajelmélet Kínában a III–VI. szábzadban: Liu Hie elmélete a költői műfajokról*. Budapest: Akadémiai Kiadó, 1967. Includes a complete translation of the *Shi pin* into Hungarian (pp. 177–208 and 310–25), which is not provided in the English version of the book: *Genre Theory in China in the 3rd–6th Centuries (Liu Hsieh's Theory on Poetic Genres)* (Budapest: Akademiai Kiadó, 1971).

Wixted, John Timothy. "Appendix A: A Translation of the *Classification of Poets (Shih-p'in* 詩品) by Chung Hung 鍾嶸 (469–518)." In "The Literary Criticism of Yüan Hao-wen (1190–1257)." 2 vols. D.Phil. diss., Oxford University, 1976. Vol. 2, pp. 462–91. Translation of the three prefaces and all entries for "upper grade" and "middle grade" poets and poetry (with listing in 2:489–91 of earlier Western-language translations of discrete passages); revised versions of many passages appear in the Wixted book and articles cited later.

Wong, Siu-kit. "Preface to *The Poets Systematically Graded*, Zhong Rong (Liang)." In *Early Chinese Literary Criticism*, pp. 89–114. Hong Kong: Joint Publishing, 1983. Translation of the three prefaces as one (with introduction and notes).

Research aids

Cao Xu 曹旭. *Shi pin jizhu* 詩品集注. Shanghai: Shanghai guji chubanshe, 1994. Good edition of the text, with helpful listing of textual variants.

———. *Shi pin yanjiu* 詩品研究. Shanghai: Shanghai guji chubanshe, 1998. Extensive section on the history of text (19–71); good outline of the reception of the *Shi pin*, including that in Japan (206–319); bibliography of important titles, including early editions of the text, unpublished twentieth-century book manuscripts on the work, and many modern book-length studies published in China, Japan, and Korea (365–71).

———, ed. *Zhong-Ri-Han Shi pin lunwen xuanping* 中日韓詩品論文選評. Shanghai: Shanghai guji chubanshe, 2003. Reprints more than four dozen earlier articles on, prefaces to, and critiques of scholarship about the work by Chinese, Japanese, and Korean scholars (some in Chinese translation); includes a year-by-year listing from 1926 through 2000 of books and articles on the *Shi pin* by Chinese, Japanese, and Korean scholars (559–94); includes prefaces by Kōzen Hiroshi (7–14, in Japanese) reviewing the activities of the "Shihin kenkyūhan" (mentioned previously), and by Ch'a Chu-hwan outlining research on the *Shi pin* in Korea (15–21, in Korean).

Kōzen Hiroshi 興膳宏, ed. *Rikuchō shijin den* 六朝詩人傳. Tokyo: Taishūkan shoten, 2000. Includes Japanese-language translation and annotation of the official biographies of all of the important poets treated in the *Shi pin*, as well as important bibliographical information on modern (especially Japanese-language) studies of those poets.

Shimizu Yoshio 清水凱夫. "Chūgoku ni okeru 1980-nen ikō no Shō Kō 'Shihin' kenkyū gaikan" 中國における一九八〇年以降の鍾嶸'詩品'研究概觀. *Chūgoku bungaku hō* 44 (April 1992): 137–50, and 45 (October 1992): 123–50.

Wang Shumin 王叔岷. *Zhong Rong Shi pin jianzheng gao* 鍾嶸詩品箋證稿. Taipei: Zhongyang yanjiuyuan, Zhongguo wenzhe yanjiusuo, 1992; rpt., Beijing: Zhonghua shuju, 2007. Includes extensive quotation of many of the major twentieth-century commentators on the text, as well as comprehensive citation (413–643) of extant *shi* by those poets treated in the work.

Zhang Bowei 張伯偉. *Zhong Rong Shi pin yanjiu* 鍾嶸詩品研究. Nanjing: Nanjing daxue chubanshe, 1999. Among much useful material, chapter 8 includes sections on the Tang dynasty influence of the *Shi pin*, Song dynasty and later scholarship on the *Shi pin*, and scholarship in Japan, Korea, and the West.

Note that works by the following (referred to elsewhere in this entry) contain indexes to names, phrases, and/or works cited in the *Shi pin*: Kōzen Hiroshi (1972), Takagi Masakazu (1978), and Lü Deshen (1986; rev. ed., 2000). Moreover, the following provide helpful "filiation charts" for poets treated in the work: Takamatsu Kōmei (1959), E. Bruce Brooks (1968), Kōzen Hiroshi (1972), Takagi Masakazu (1978), Wang Shumin (1992), and Bernhard Führer (1995).

Among material available on the Internet is a downloadable and computer-searchable edition of the *Shi pin* (http://web2.cc.nctu.edu.tw/~lccpan/newpage311.htm) that reprints the text as found in Liao Dongliang (see "Modern Scholarship" section herein).

Among book-length studies of the *Shi pin*, those by Feng Jiquan 馮吉權 (1981), Yu Kekun 禹克坤 (1989), and Jiang Zuyi 蔣祖怡 (1995) are devoted to comparison of the work with the *Wenxin diaolong*. A volume by Shimizu Yoshio 清水凱夫

(Chinese ed., 1995) focuses on the *Shi pin* and the *Wen xuan*, q.v., and another by Xiao Shuishun 蕭水順 (Xiao Xiao 蕭蕭) (1993) outlines Chinese literary theory from Zhong Rong to Sikong Tu 司空圖 (837–908).

Other studies of the work include those by Li Daoxian 李道顯 (1968), Mei Yunsheng 梅運生 (1982), Luo Liqian 羅立乾 (1990), and Wang Faguo 王發國 (1993).

Western-language studies

Brooks, E. Bruce. "A Geometry of the *Shī Pĭn*." In *Wen-lin: Studies in the Chinese Humanities*, ed. Chow Tse-tsung, 121–50. Madison: University of Wisconsin Press, 1968.

Cha, Chu Whan 車柱環 (Ch'a Chu-hwan). "On Enquiries for Ideal Poetry: An Instance of Chung Hung." *Tamkang Review* 6.2–7.1 (October 1975–April 1976): 43–54.

Führer [Fuehrer], Bernhard. "Zur Biographie des Zhong Hong (467?–518)." *Acta Orientalia Academiae Scientiarum Hungaricae* 46.2–3 (1992–1993): 163–87.

———. "Apotheosis of Poets: Two *modi operandi* of the Reasoned Exercise of Literary Taste." *Tamkang Review* 24.2 (Winter 1993): 59–81.

———. "High Wind and True Bone, Defying Ice and Frost: Illustrative Remarks on the *Shipin* of Zhong Hong (467?–518)." *Bochumer Jahrbuch zur Ostasienforschung* 19 (1995): 51–70.

———. "Glimpses into Zhong Hong's Educational Background, with Remarks on Manifestations of the *Zhouyi* in His Writings." *Bulletin of the School of Oriental and African Studies* 67.1 (2004): 64–78.

Rusk, Bruce. "An Interpolation in Zhong Rong's Shipin." *Journal of the American Oriental Society* 128.3 (2008): 553–57.

Wilhelm, Hellmut. "A Note on Chung Hung and His *Shih-p'in*." In *Wen-lin: Studies in the Chinese Humanities*, ed. Chow Tse-tsung, 111–20. Madison: University of Wisconsin Press, 1968. (See the review by D. R. Jonker, *T'oung Pao* 59 [1973] for corrections of Wilhelm's translation of Zhong Rong's *Liang shu* biography.)

Wixted, John Timothy. "The *Kokinshū* Prefaces: Another Perspective." *Harvard Journal of Asiatic Studies* 43.1 (June 1983): 215–38. Outlines the influence of the *Shi pin* on the major early Japanese statements of critical theory.

———. "The Nature of Evaluation in the *Shih-p'in* (Gradings of Poets) by Chung Hung (A.D. 469–518)." In *Theories of the Arts in China*, ed. Susan Bush and Christian Murck, 225–64. Princeton, NJ: Princeton University Press, 1983.

———. *Poems on Poetry: Literary Criticism by Yuan Hao-wen (1190–1257)*. Wiesbaden: Franz Steiner, 1982; rpt., Taipei: Southern Materials Center, 1985. Includes translation of Zhong Rong's treatment of eight poets and traces, in reference to them, the *Shi pin*'s influence on intervening Tang- and Song-period criticism, on Yuan Haowen's evaluations, and on later literary thought.

———. "Zhong Rong 鍾嶸, from *Shih-pin* (Poetry Gradings)." In *Women Writers of Traditional China: An Anthology of Poetry and Criticism*, ed. Kang-i Sun Chang and Haun Saussey, 719–20. New Haven, CT: Yale University Press, 1999. Translation of Zhong Rong's evaluations of women writers: Ban Jieyu, Xu Shu, Bao Linghui, and Han Lanying.

Yeh, Chia-ying, and Jan W. Walls. "Theory, Standards, and Practice of Criticizing Poetry in Chung Hung's *Shih-p'in*." In *Studies in Chinese Poetry and Poetics*, ed. Ronald C. Miao, 1:43–80. San Francisco: Chinese Materials Center, 1978.

Zhang, A. D. (Aidong). "Zhong Rong's *Shipin* and the Aesthetic Awareness of His Times." *East Asia Forum* 2 (1993): 50–64.

———. "Zhong Rong's *Shipin* and the Aesthetic Awareness of the Six Dynasties." Ph.D. diss., University of Toronto, 1996.

John Timothy Wixted

Shiliuguo chunqiu 十六國春秋

Introduction

The *Shiliuguo chunqiu* (Spring and autumn annals of the Sixteen States), by Cui Hong 崔鴻 (478–525), was the first unified history of the Sixteen States, a designation for the succession of petty states founded by nomadic invaders who dominated northern China from A.D. 304 to 439. Cui Hong, an official and historian of the Northern Wei dynasty, drew inspiration from Chen Shou's *Sanguo zhi*, q.v., another unified account of a period when China was divided into multiple kingdoms. Cui's work has the virtue of recording the unvarnished views of a Chinese historian unfettered by the concern to be sensitive to issues of ethnicity, a concern that negatively affected the historiography of later historians of the period as well as historians of later conquest dynasties such as the Liao, Jin, and Yuan. The modern historian Ren Huaiguo terms Cui's frankness in writing under the Northern Wei an act of bravery.

Authorship

Cui Hong (style Yanluan 彥鸞) was born into a family of scholar-officials in Qinghe 清河 (modern Zibo 淄博, Shandong). His uncle Cui Guang 光 (d. 518) was a notable historian who had served as editorial director for the Northern Wei dynasty and helped to compile the state history (*guoshi* 國史) for most of his forty years in office. Cui Hong himself had served successfully in a variety of posts. In 520, he helped to edit the imperial diaries (*qijuzhu* 起居注) of both Emperors Xiaowen 孝文 (r. 471–499) and Xuanwu 宣武 (r. 500–515). Additionally, for a short time commencing in 524, he was recruited into the Historiography Institute to participate in compiling the state history.

Composition

In all, thirty different types of historical works on the Sixteen States period had been produced before Cui Hong's time (*Shi tong** 12.358 ff lists these histories). Most of the works were devoted to a single state, but a few grouped the states of Zhao 趙 and Han 漢 together. The composition of Cui's work rendered the others superfluous, and most of them slowly disappeared.

In 500, Cui Hong started collecting and copying historical materials relevant to the Sixteen States, especially those histories produced by the individual states themselves. This task was completed by 504. In 506, he produced a draft version in ninety-five *juan*, lacking only the five chapters he reserved for the history of the state of Cheng Han 成漢 (304–347). Cui hesitated to present these chapters because he lacked a copy of a work he felt was crucial for the accurate coverage of this state, Chang Qu's 常璩 *Shu shu* 蜀書, a work not to be found in northern China. After sixteen years of searching, he finally obtained a copy in 521; he thereupon finished his history by completing the last five chapters of the "Shulu" in 525 and died shortly thereafter. His memorial (*biao* 表) introducing his work to the throne is still extant (*Wei shu*, q.v., 67:1503–5; also "Quan Hou Wei wen" 25:1a–2b, in *Quan shanggu Sandai Qin Han Sanguo Liuchao wen*, q.v.). In it he describes his work as a historian as consisting of "differentiating between contemporary events and stitching them together to produce a basic record. [I] eliminated discrepancies and created a unified structure. Reducing reduplications, [I] also supplemented what was inadequate ... edited them into veritable records ... provided prefatory appraisals, and evaluations of either praise or blame" (*Wei shu* 67:1504). His grave was discovered in 1973; the epitaph is still extant and has been published (Shandongsheng wenwu kaogu yanjiusuo, 1984).

Cui Hong was the first historian to regard the period of the Sixteen States as an important stage in history. His work changed the historiography on nomadic peoples in a variety of ways. Traditional historical writings on non-Han peoples had consisted of accounts (*zhuan* 傳), such as the "Xiongnu zhuan" 匈奴傳 of the *Shi ji*, included in larger dynastic histories. By implication and through the use of pejorative terminology, these chapters indicated the low or illegitimate status of these peoples. Cui elevated the historiographical attitudes of historians toward these peoples with his work by providing the nomadic conquerors of this period with their own unified history and even regarded his history as part of the tradition of "official histories" (*zhengshi* 正史) devoted to legitimate dynasties. He also changed the technical terminology. Although basing his work on each kingdom's self-compiled "state documents" (*guoshu* 國書), he termed the historical treatment of each state a "record" (*lu* 錄), indicating that he considered the texts to be the equivalent of the "veritable records" (*shilu* 實錄) of fully independent and legitimate states. He further adopted the terminology of "annals" (*ji* 紀) for the chapters devoted to the monarchs of these states, the same terminology used in traditional "official histories" starting with the *Shi ji*.

Perhaps of most importance was Cui's decision to let each state retain its legitimacy in terms of its own independent existence. Thus, he adopted the reign titles of each state to date internal events. Where certain events were not datable by this method, that is, when discussing affairs among the Southern Xiongnu nomads before they founded a formal state, he adopted the perspective of the native Chinese dynasty, supplying the dates in terms of Jin reign titles.

Edition in one hundred *juan*

The original version in one hundred *juan* was supplied with a preface and a chapter of chronological tables. It was presented to the throne by Cui Hong's son

Cui Ziyuan 子元 in 528. The bibliographic monograph of the *Sui shu*, q.v., 33:963 (641–656) records the work as having one hundred *juan*, while *Jiu Tang shu* 46:1993 (940) and *Xin Tang shu* 58:1462 (1060) list it as being in 120 *juan*. Yu Jiaxi 余嘉錫 (1883–1955) regards the number 120 as an error for an original 102 (*Siku tiyao bianzheng*, 7:387). The full text of the original version, since it is not listed in the standard bibliographies of the Song, was by most accounts lost sometime during the Northern Song. Yu Jiaxi notes that what may well have been an incomplete version lingered on into the Southern Song, being recorded in the *Suichutang shumu** of You Mao (1127–1194) but without number of *juan* or author (674:447). Apparently, Sima Guang 司馬光 used a version of the work to compose his *Zizhi tongjian* 資治通鑒 of 1084, even occasionally quoting from the "appraisals" of Cui Hong. Machida Takayoshi concluded that Sima Guang had access only to some twenty *juan* of the work, indicating that perhaps it was at this time that it started to circulate in an incomplete form.

Chen Changqi and Zhou Qun ("*Shiliuguo chunqiu* sanyi kaolue," 3) recently provided two indications that an incomplete version was extant even later. First, during the Ming, Yang Sheng'an 楊升庵 (1488–1559) mentioned in an offhand way that he had read the work, and he died before either the hundred-*juan* reconstruction appeared in 1585 or the sixteen-*juan Bieben* edition appeared in 1592 (on these versions, see later). Second, during the Qing, Song Luo 宋犖 purchased a "truncated edition" (*canpian* 殘篇) at an old book mart in Beijing. These two tattered versions may very well be descendants of an incomplete version in more than twenty *juan* that Yu Jiaxi (387–388) says is mentioned in the *Yu hai** of Wang Yinglin (1223–1296). A Qing bibliography, the *Baijinglou cangshu tibaji* 拜經樓藏書題拔記 of Wu Shouyang 吳壽暘, based on the collection of his father, Wu Qian 吳騫 (1733–1813), and printed in 1847, mentions another incomplete version, this one in ten *juan* (2:48–49).

Abridged editions in sixteen *juan*

An abridged version in sixteen *juan* is preserved in the Song encyclopedia *Taiping yulan*, q.v., dating from 938, included under the section "Peripheral Warlords" ("Pianba" 偏霸; *juan* 119–27). It is slightly shorter than another sixteen-*juan* abridgement first included in the *Guang Han Wei congshu* 廣漢魏叢書, edited by He Yunzhong 何允中 in 1592. As Michael Rogers states, the former differs from the latter in only minor matters, and the two may have been based on two editions of an abridged version (*The Chronicle of Fu Chien*, 20). The latter resurfaced in the *Zengding* 增訂 *Han Wei congshu*, edited by Wang Mo 王謨 in 1791. Later collectanea to print this version include the *Congshu jicheng**, the *Guoxue jiben congshu* 國學基本叢書, and the *Sibu beiyao**. *Siku quanshu** 463:315–1174 includes it under the title *Bieben* 別本 *Shiliuguo chunqiu*; it is also known as the *Shiliuguo chunqiu bieben*.

The Qing scholar Tang Qiu 湯球 regarded a ten-*juan* summary (*zuanlu* 纂錄) that was listed in the *Sui shu* bibliographic monograph (33:963) to have been a digest of the original version in one hundred *juan* and as the source of these abridged versions in sixteen *juan*, an explanation that Rogers concludes "cannot be proven but may well be correct" (*The Chronicle of Fu Chien*, 20). The *Siku quanshu zongmu tiyao** (14:1430) suggests that perhaps the *zuanlu* is the version listed in the *Chongwen zongmu** (2:29a, though in only two *juan*) as the *Shiliuguo chunqiulüe* 十六國春秋略, or what Sima Guang in his *Zishi tongjian kaoyi* 考異 referred to as the *Shiliuguo chunqiuchao* 十六國春秋鈔. The fact that one manuscript listed in a catalog by Qu Yong 瞿鏞 (10:16) of the *Shiliuguo chunqiulüe* is in sixteen *juan* lends credence to this supposition. A rare manuscript version of the *lüe* is preserved in the Beijing Library (Beijing tushuguan 322) under the title *Cui Hong Shiliuguo chunqiulüe* in two *ce* 冊 with no division into individual *juan*.

Reconstructed versions

Two Ming scholars, Tu Qiaosun 屠喬孫 and Xiang Lin 項琳, reconstituted the hundred-*juan* version (actual count 103 *juan*) in 1585. According to Rogers (*The Chronicle of Fu Chien*, 20–21), this was "the product of interweaving of the chronicle texts with the relevant passages of Ssu-ma Kuang's *Tzu-chih t'ung-chien*." By "chronicle texts," he means the thirty *zaiji* 載記 chapters appended to the *Jin shu* that recount the history of the fourteen states that had been founded by non-Han conquerors, chapters indebted to the original *Shiliuguo chunqiu*. (The two states founded by Chinese, the Former Liang and the Western Liang, are treated in the body of the *Jin shu*.) This reconstructed version was dated according to the reign titles of the Jin and Liu-Song dynasties. The reconstructed version was itself edited in 1781 by Wang Rigui 王日桂, who changed the internal dating of the text from the Chinese states of Jin and Liu-Song back to that of the Sixteen States themselves, which gave the work a detailed chronological framework, one of its impressive features (*The Chronicle of Fu Chien*, 21).

Tang Qiu provided his own reconstructions of what he considered to be the contents of the *zuanlu*, which, as previously mentioned, he felt was the source of the sixteen-*juan* abridgments. This work is called the *Shiliuguo chunqiu zuanlu jiaoben* 十六國春秋纂錄校本 (found in both the *Guangya congshu* 廣雅叢書 and the *Congshu jicheng*) in ten *juan*, with an appended section of textual corrigenda (*jiaokanji* 校勘記) by Qing scholar Wu Yiyin 吳翊寅. This reconstituted *zuanlu* is in fact a collation of the *Taiping yulan* and *Bieben* versions. Another editorial reconstruction made by Tang Qiu was fleshing out the narrative of his reconstructed *zuanlu* with quotations from the *Jin shu* and scattered quotations preserved in various *leishu* 類書; this work was titled the *Shiliuguo chunqiu jibu* 十六國春秋輯補 (in *Guangya congshu* and *Congshu jicheng*), in one hundred *juan*, with one *juan* of chronological tables.

Contents

The abridged *Shiliuguo chunqiu* is divided into sixteen *juan*:

1. Qian Zhao lu   前趙錄   Record of the Former Zhao
2. Hou Zhao lu   後趙錄   Record of the Later Zhao

3.	Qian Yan lu	前燕錄	Record of the Former Yan
4.	Qian Qin lu	前秦錄	Record of the Former Qin
5.	Hou Qin lu	後秦錄	Record of the Later Qin
6.	Shu lu	蜀錄	Record of Shu
7.	Qian Liang lu	前涼錄	Record of the Former Liang
8.	Xi Liang lu	西涼錄	Record of the Western Liang
9.	Bei Liang lu	北涼錄	Record of the Northern Liang
10.	Hou Liang lu	後涼錄	Record of the Later Liang
11.	Hou Yan lu	後燕錄	Record of the Later Yan
12.	Nan Liang lu	南涼錄	Record of the Southern Liang
13.	Nan Yan lu	南燕錄	Record of the Southern Yan
14.	Xi Qin lu	西秦錄	Record of the Western Qin
15.	Bei Yan lu	北燕錄	Record of the Northern Yan
16.	Xia lu	夏錄	Record of Xia

The content of the Tu-Xiang reconstruction in one hundred *juan* (actual count 103 *juan*) is as follows, with some variation in the order of states:

1.	Qian Zhao lu	10 *juan*		9.	Qian Liang lu	6 *juan*
2.	Hou Zhao lu	12 *juan*		10.	Shu lu	5 *juan*
3.	Qian Yan lu	10 *juan*		11.	Hou Liang lu	4 *juan*
4.	Qian Qin lu	10 *juan*		12.	Xi Qin lu	6 *juan*
5.	Hou Yan lu	10 *juan*		13.	Nan Liang lu	3 *juan*
6.	Hou Qin lu	10 *juan*		14.	Xi Liang lu	3 *juan*
7.	Nan Yan lu	3 *juan*		15.	Bei Liang lu	4 *juan*
8.	Xia lu	4 *juan*		16.	Bei Yan lu	3 *juan*

Studies of the text

Chen Changqi 陳長琦 and Zhou Qun 周群. "*Shiliuguo chunqiu* sanyi kaolue" 十六國春秋散佚考略. *Xueshu yanjiu* 7 (2005): 95–100.

Gu Shi 顧實. *Chongkao gujin weishukao* 重考古今僞書考. Shanghai: Datong shuju, 1926. Pp. 11–12.

Nagasawa Kikuya 長澤規矩也. *Seian kanseki kaidai chōhen* 靜盦汉籍解題長編. 2 vols. Tokyo: Kyūko shoin, 1970. Vol. 2, pp. 1190–91.

Qian Daxin 錢大昕. *Shijiazhai yangxinlu* 十駕齋養新錄. Shanghai: Shanghai shudian, 1983. Pp. 299–300.

Quan Zuwang 全祖望. "Da Shi Xueting wen *Shiliuguo chunqiu* shu" 答史雪汀問十六國春秋書. In *Jieqitingji waipian* 鮚埼亭集外篇 (1776), *juan* 44.

Schrieber, Gerhard. "The History of the Former Yen Dynasty, Part I." *Monumenta Serica* 14 (1949): 381–86.

Shiliuguo chunqiu yiwen 十六國春秋佚文. In *Yuhan shanfang jiyishu xubian sanzhong* 玉函山房輯佚書續編三種, ed. Wang Renjun 王仁俊 (Qing). Shanghai: Shanghai guji chubanshe, 1989.

Wang Mingsheng 王鳴盛. *Shiqishi shangque* 十七史商榷. Shanghai: Shanghai guji shudian, 2005. Vol. 52, pp. 1a–7a.

Yu Jiaxi 余嘉錫. *Siku tiyao bianzheng* 四庫提要辯證. Beijing: Zhonghua shuju, 1980. *Juan* 7, pp. 385–89.

Modern editions

Modern punctuated editions are based on the *Shiliuguo chunqiu bieben* edition, and are available at many websites.

Qinding Siku quanshu huiyao Shiliuguo chunqiu 欽定四庫全書薈要十六國春秋. Changchun: Jilin chuban jituan youxian zeren gongsi, 2005.

Shiliuguo chunqiu bieben. In *Zhonghua yeshi* 中華野史, ed. Che Jixin 車吉心 et al., 1:593–632. Shandong: Taishan chubanshe, 2000.

Shiliuiguo chunqiu jibu. In *Ershiwu bieshi* 二十五別史, ed. Liu Xiaodong 劉曉東 et al., vol. 11. Ji'nan: Qi Lu shushe, 2000.

Bibliography

Beijing tushuguan, ed. *Beijing tushuguan guji shanben shumu* 北京圖書館古籍善本書目. Beijing: Shumu wenxian chubanshe, 1987.

Chen Changqi 陳長琦 and Zhou Qun 周群. "*Shiliuguo chunqiu*." In *Zhongguo shixue mingzhu pingjie* 中國史學名著評介, ed. Cang Xiuliang 倉修良, 1:387–99. Ji'nan: Shandong jiaoyu chubanshe, 2006.

Chen Shiren 陳識仁. "Bei Wei xiushi luelun" 北魏修史略論. In *Jiebiangang* 結編綱, ed. Huang Lianqing 黃連清 et al. Taipei: Dongda tushu gongsi, 1998.

Han Jie 韓傑. "Bei Wei shiqi shiliuguoshi de zhuanshu" 北魏時期十六國史的撰述. *Shixueshi yanjiu* (1989.3): 39–46.

Jin Yufu 金毓黼. *Zhongguo shixueshi* 中國史學史. Taipei: Hansheng chubanshe guoshi yanjiushi, 1973 (reprint of 1957 ed.).

Li Hu 李虎. "Cui Hong—Wei shaoshu minzu zhengquan xieshi" 崔鴻—為少數民族政權寫史. In *Zhonghua renwuzhi* 中華人物志, ed. Qu Lindong 瞿林東 and Yang Muzhi 楊牧之, 70–76. Beijing: Zhonghua shuju, 1988.

Lin Ruihan 林瑞翰. *Wei Jin Nanbeichao shi* 魏晉南北朝史. Taipei: Zhida gufen youxian gongsi, 1977.

Machida Takayoshi 町田隆吉. "*Shiji tsugan kōi* shoin *Jūrokukoku shunjū* oyobi *Jūrokukoku shunjū shō* ni tsuite: Shiba Kō ga riyōshita *Jūrokukoku shunjū* o megutte" 資治通鋻考異所引十六国春秋及び十六国春秋鈔について: 司馬光が利用した十六国春秋をめぐって [On the *Shiliuguo chunqiu* and the citations of the *Shiliuguo chunqiu* by Sima Guang in his studies in the differences in interpretation in the *Zizhi tongjian*]. *Kokusaigaku rebyū* 12 (2000): 33–54.

Qu Yong 瞿鏞. *Tieqin tongjianlou cangshu mulu* 鐵琴銅劍樓藏書目錄. Wujin Dongshi Songfenshi 武進董氏誦芬室 edition, 1897.

Ren Huaiguo 任懷國. "Shilun Cui Hong de shixue gongxian—Jianlun *Shiliuguo chunqiu* de jiazhi" 試論崔鴻的史學貢獻—兼論十六國春秋的價值. *Weifang xueyuan xuebao* 24 (2002.5): 79–82.

Rogers, Michael C. *The Chronicle of Fu Chien: A Case of Exemplar History*. Chinese Dynastic Histories Translations. Berkeley: University of California Press, 1968.

Shandongsheng wenwu kaogu yanjiusuo 山東省文物考古研究所, ed. "Linzi Beichao Cuishi mu" 臨淄北朝崔氏墓. *Kaogu xuebao* (1984.2): 221–41.

Wu Shouyang 吳壽暘. *Baijinglou cangshu tibaji* 拜經樓藏書題拔記. Shanghai: Guji chubanshe, 2007.

Wu Zhenqing 吳振清. "*Shiliuguo shixue pingshu*" 十六國史學評述. *Shixueshi yanjiu* (1989.3): 30–38.

Yong Rong 永瑢 (1744–1790) et al., eds. *Siku quanshu jianming shulu* 四庫全書簡明書錄. Shanghai: Shanghai guji chubanshe, 1985.

Yun Yuding 惲毓鼎. "Du *Shiliuguo chunqiu*" 讀十六國春秋. *Zhongguo xuebao* (1913.3): 9–14.

Zhu Xizu 朱希祖. "Shiluguo jiushi kao" 十六國舊史考. *Zhiyan* 13 (1936). 19 pp.

David Brian Honey

Shishuo xinyu 世說新語

Introduction

Compiled by the Liu-Song prince Liu Yiqing 劉義慶 (403–444) and his staff around the year 430, the *Shishuo xinyu* (A new account of tales of the world) consists of more than 1,130 anecdotes about elite life in the late Han (ca. 150–220) and Wei-Jin (220–420) periods. As a group, these beautifully written and artfully constructed anecdotes express what came to be known as the "Wei-Jin spirit," an outgrowth of new intellectual trends that emerged during one of the most creative and iconoclastic periods of Chinese imperial history.

Contents

The *Shishuo xinyu*'s anecdotes about late-Han and Wei-Jin elite life range from state affairs to philosophical and poetic gatherings, and from public relationships to trifling domestic matters. Most episodes focus not so much on recounting the details or progression of an event as on capturing the emotional and personal characteristics of the participants. The book's concern with human personality types is further elaborated in its overall structure, which classifies the anecdotes into thirty-six categories that are all related to the observation and evaluation of people: their physical appearance, innate abilities, moral qualities, psychological traits, and the emotions that emerge from political and social contact with others. This system of classification sets the *Shishuo xinyu* apart from any other collection of brief narratives in the Chinese literary tradition, thus establishing a genre known to later generations as the "*Shishuo* genre" (*Shishuo ti* 世說體), which focuses primarily on the categorization of human character types and of particular individuals. The thirty-six chapters of the work are titled as follows.

1.	Dexing 德行	*De* conduct
2.	Yanyu 言語	Speech and conversation
3.	Zhengshi 政事	Affairs of government
4.	Wenxue 文學	Literature and scholarship
5.	Fangzheng 方正	The square and the proper
6.	Yaliang 雅量	Cultivated tolerance
7.	Shijian 識鑒	Recognition and judgment

8. Shangyu 賞譽 Appreciation and praise
9. Pinzao 品藻 Ranking with refined words
10. Guizhen 規箴 Admonitions and warnings
11. Jiewu 捷悟 Quick perception
12. Suhui 夙慧 Precocious intelligence
13. Haoshuang 豪爽 Virility and vigor
14. Rongzhi 容止 Appearance and manner
15. Zixin 自新 Self-renewal
16. Qixian 企羨 Admiration and emulation
17. Shangshi 傷逝 Grieving for the departed
18. Qiyi 栖逸 Reclusion and disengagement
19. Xianyuan 賢媛 Virtuous and talented ladies
20. Shujie 術解 Technical understanding
21. Qiaoyi 巧藝 Ingenious art
22. Chongli 寵禮 Favor and veneration
23. Rendan 任誕 Uninhibitedness and eccentricity
24. Jian'ao 簡傲 Rudeness and arrogance
25. Paitiao 排調 Taunting and teasing
26. Qingdi 輕詆 Contempt and insults
27. Jiajue 假譎 Guile and chicanery
28. Chumian 黜免 Dismissal from office
29. Jianse 儉嗇 Stinginess and meanness
30. Taichi 汰侈 Extravagance and ostentation
31. Fenjuan 忿狷 Anger and irascibility
32. Chanxian 讒險 Slanderousness and treachery
33. Youhui 尤悔 Blameworthiness and remorse
34. Pilou 紕漏 Crudities and blunders
35. Huoni 惑溺 Delusion and infatuation
36. Chouxi 仇隙 Hostility and alienation

The *Shishuo xinyu* and its genre emerged from three aspects of Wei-Jin intellectual life: namely, the dominant ideology, *Xuanxue* 玄學 (Abstruse Learning), the practice of *renlun jianshi* 人倫鑒識 (judging and recognizing types of human character, commonly translated "character appraisal"), and the growth of self-awareness. From within these categories the anecdotes illustrate the ability to act firmly according to what one understands or feels is right, or what one takes as his or her right path, the Dao 道 (the Way). They also show that in the social, political, and cultural milieux of the Wei-Jin period, great value was placed upon a person's inner ability, and that there was a heightened sensitivity toward embodying *qing* 情 (which can variously mean emotion, passion, or affection) in human relationships and interactions. (For an extended analysis of the significance of the anecdotes, see Qian, *Spirit and Self in Medieval China*, 2001).

Authorship

Liu Yiqing was a native of Pengcheng 彭城 (today's Xuzhou 徐州, Jiangsu Province) and a member of the Liu-Song royal family. He inherited from his father the title of Prince of Linchuan 臨川, and he served at court and in local offices, in both civil and military posts. According to Liu Yiqing's biography in the *Song shu*, q.v. (51:1475–80), his important positions included nine years as the mayor of the capital, and eight years as the governor of Jingzhou 荊州, the border state on the upper Yangzi that possessed half of the court's resources. For his good services, he received high honorific titles such as "commander unequalled in honor" (*kaifu yitong sansi* 開府儀同三司).

The *Shishuo xinyu* was conventionally attributed to Liu Yiqing since its first official entry in the *Sui shu*'s bibliographic monograph, completed in 656. Liu's biography applauds his affection for literature but also says that he did not "accomplish much in creating refined words" (*wenci buduo* 文詞不多). Liu's writings are, moreover, not recorded in his biography. For this reason, later scholars have doubted his literary achievements. Lu Xun 魯迅 (1881–1936), for one, questioned Liu Yiqing's authorship of the *Shishuo xinyu* in his *Zhongguo xiaoshuo shilue* 中國小說史略 (A brief history of Chinese fiction). He suggested that Liu might only have sponsored the work of his staff since, also according to the Song history's author, Shen Yue 沈約 (441–513), Liu assembled men of letters from near and far, including talented figures such as Bao Zhao 鮑照 (d. 466), Lu Zhan 陸展, and He Zhangyu 何長瑜. Modern scholars have broadly accepted Lu Xun's argument.

Authenticity and transmission of the text

The *Shishuo xinyu* is listed in the *Sui shu* bibliographic monograph as *Shishuo* 世說 and has since remained in the category of *xiaoshuo* 小說 in the sense of "petty talk" or "minor persuasions" (in modern usage the term can mean "fiction" or "novel"). There are two entries for the *Shishuo*, one in eight *juan* and the other, expanded by Liu Jun's 劉峻 (462–521) extensive commentary, in ten *juan* (34.1011). These entries are repeated in the bibliographic monographs in the *Jiu Tang shu* and the *Xin Tang shu*. To distinguish it from an earlier work of the same name, now lost, by Liu Xiang 劉向 (ca. 77–6 B.C.), the title soon acquired the added words "new writing" (*xinshu* 新書) and became *Shishuo xinshu*, as cited in the ninth-century miscellany *Youyang zazu* 酉陽雜俎 (IV, 7a) by Duan Chengshi 段成式 (ca. 803–863). As Richard B. Mather points out, "This title is confirmed by the oldest surviving manuscript fragment of the work, the so-called 'Tang fragment' written in the calligraphic style of the eighth century and covering most of the sixth *juan* of the ten-*juan* version (chapters 10 through 13)" (*New Account*, 2nd ed., p. xxx). Mather has also pointed out that the current title seems to appear for the first time in the Tang historian Liu Zhiji's (661–721) *Shi tong**, published in 710. Liu Zhiji severely criticized the Tang compilers of the *Jin shu*, q.v., for having incorporated "inauthentic historical accounts" from the *Shishuo xinyu*. Liu Zhiji's argument confirmed the transmission of the text and the transformation of the name of the *Shishuo xinyu*, as well as its strong influence in his time. This present title, though mixed with the other two in the early Song, has remained consistent in later citations of the work. For a list of the principal editions in the transmission of the text, see Qian (*Spirit and Self in Medieval China*, 475–77).

Modern critical editions

Shishuo xinyu [buzheng] 世說新語 [補證]. Commentary by Wang Shumin 王叔岷. Banqiao, Taiwan: Yiwen yinshuguan, 1975.

Shishuo xinyu [huiping] 世說新語 [會評]. Collected commentary by Liu Qiang 劉強. Nanjing: Fenghuang chubanshe, 2007.

Shishuo xinyu [jianshu] 世說新語 [箋疏]. Commentary by Yu Jiaxi 余嘉錫. Beijing: Zhonghua shuju, 1983. 2nd ed., 2 vols. Shanghai: Shanghai guji chubanshe, 1993.

Shishuo xinyu [jiaojian] 世說新語 [校箋]. Commentary by Yang Yong 楊勇. Hong Kong: Dazhong shuju, 1969.

Shishuo xinyu [jiaojian] 世說新語 [校箋]. 2 vols. Commentary by Xu zhen'e 徐震堮. Beijing: Zhonghua shuju, 1984.

Early commentaries

The earliest extant commentary, by Jing Yin 敬胤 (ca. fifth century), is included in Wang Zao's "Kaoyi" (alternate readings), appended to his edition of the *Shishuo xinyu*. According to Wang Zao, Jing Yin commented on fifty-one entries, among which three are not included in the text proper of Wang Zao's edition. Jing Yin's commentary is very different from Liu Jun's. Because Jing Yin referred to people of the Song-Qi transition (late fifth century) as contemporaries (*jinren* 今人), Wang Zao believed he lived earlier than Liu Jun.

Liu Jun's commentary on the *Shishuo xinyu* is considered to be the best. According to Mather: "[It] cites relevant passages—passages which were often drastically abridged by eleventh-century editors—from over 400 works (unofficial histories and biographies, family registers, local gazetteers, etc.) from the Later Han through Liu Jun's own times. Since most of these works are now lost, the quotations from them in Liu's and other similar commentaries, such as Pei Songzhi's (372–451) commentary on the *Sanguo zhi* (History of the Three Kingdoms), provide valuable supplementary material and occasional corrections to the idiosyncratic accounts in the *Shishuo xinyu*" (*Indiana Companion to Traditional Chinese Literature*, 704, with some editorial changes).

Selected studies

The following works include thorough bibliographies concerning the *Shishuo xinyu*:

Mather, Richard. "*Shishuo xinyu*." In *The Indiana Companion to Traditional Chinese Literature*, ed. William H. Nienhauser Jr. et al., 704–5. Bloomington: Indiana University Press, 1986.

Qian, Nanxiu. *Spirit and Self in Medieval China*: *The Shih-shuo hsin-yü and Its Legacy*, 478–501. Honolulu: University of Hawai'i Press, 2001.
  For language and narrative in particular, see:

Mei Jialing 梅家玲. *Shishuo xinyu de yuyan xushi* 世說新語的語言與敘事. Taipei: Liren shuju, 2004.

Translations

Mather, Richard, trans. *Shih-shuo hsin-yü: A New Account of Tales of the World*. Minneapolis: University of Minnesota Press, 1976. 2nd ed., Michigan Monographs in Chinese Studies 95. Ann Arbor: University of Michigan, 2002. A complete translation into English of the text and Liu Jun's commentary, plus the translator's own annotation.

For a list of other translations in various languages, see Qian (*Spirit and Self in Medieval China*, 477–78).

Research aids

Shishuo xinyu yinde 世說新語引得. Beiping: Yanjing daxue Hafu Yanjing xueshe yinde bianzuanchu, 1933.

Zhang Wanqi 張萬起. *Shishuo xinyu cidian* 世說新語辭典. Shanghai: Shangwu yinshuguan, 1993.

Zhang Yongyan 張永言. *Shishuo xinyu cidian* 世說新語辭典. Chengdu: Sichuan renmin chubanshe, 1992. This text is included in the Chinese Text Project with a full-text search capability.

Evaluation

The *Shishuo xinyu* left to later generations a twofold legacy. It transmitted a spirit that continued to inspire Chinese intellectuals to find (and express) their authentic "self." It also created a literary genre that yielded dozens of imitations from the latter part of the Tang dynasty (618–907) to the early Republican era in the twentieth century. Most of these imitations were Chinese works, but a few were written by Japanese. These imitations dutifully categorized collections of historical anecdotes following the *Shishuo* system of classification. The authors also altered this model in order to conform in a more satisfactory way to their own understandings of "self" and their respective social environments and cultural purposes. The *Shishuo xinyu* thus offered to later generations and other societies something other than a piece of China's mute and passive cultural heritage; instead, it made the Wei-Jin spirit an active factor in the formation (or, at least, expression) of the cultural values and systems of later periods.

Qian Nanxiu

Shiyi ji 拾遺記

Introduction

The *Shiyi ji*, compiled by Wang Jia 王嘉 (styled Zinian 子年; d. before 393) and alternately titled *Shiyi lu* 拾遺錄 and *Wang Zinian Shiyi ji* 王子年拾遺記, is an unusual example of early *zhiguai* 志怪 (accounts of anomalies). As the title indicates, the purpose of the *Shiyi ji* was to gather up remnant materials at risk of being lost if not recorded. The surviving text of 126 items consists of ancient legends, anecdotes and unofficial biographies from successive dynasties, and accounts of fantastic mountains and marvelous flora and fauna.

Originality and beauty of language are two striking features of the *Shiyi ji*. Although many materials in the *Shiyi ji* never appeared in earlier *zhiguai* works, the collection does sometimes provide accounts of items found in other works. In contrast to the *Soushen ji*, q.v., the best known *zhiguai* work of the Six Dynasties, the *Shiyi ji*'s language is quite elaborate and includes elegant passages and poetry. The sentences are well structured and balanced. Many of its descriptions are detailed and lengthy; some contain in excess of five hundred characters. There are also descriptive passages that are sensuous, a rarity in early *zhiguai* texts. In addition, allusions and quotations from pre-Han texts often occur, in reflection of the author's erudition. Another feature distinguishing the *Shiyi ji* from other *zhiguai* is the addition of remarks (*lu* 錄) by Xiao Qi 蕭綺 of the Liang dynasty. These are appended to the ends of sections in each *juan*, and they function as a commentary. Not only their language, but also the opinions expressed are often different from the concerns of the original items. A preface by Xiao Qi, who edited the work in the early sixth century, provides a good summary of the *Shiyi ji*'s typical features.

Contents

The *Shiyi ji* is divided into ten *juan*, of which the first nine are chronologically arranged, beginning with the "Three August Ones and Five Lords" (*san huang* 三皇 and *wu di* 五帝) and proceeding through the dynasties to end with the Jin. The items mainly concern legendary rulers, but there are also anecdotes or unofficial biographies for historical emperors, empresses, scholars, officials, and concubines, as well as accounts about marvelous flora, fauna, products, emissaries, and tributes from remote lands surrounding China. The tenth *juan* is devoted to the fantastic geography of the nine mountains sacred to Daoism. Rarely does the *Shiyi ji* deals with ghosts and immortals, popular subjects of other *zhiguai* works. In a few items there are no fantastic elements.

Juan 1. Chunhuang Pao Xi 春皇庖犧, Yan Di Shen Nong 炎帝神農, Xuan Yuan Huangdi 軒轅黃帝, Shao Hao 少昊, Zhuan Xu 顓頊, Gao Xin 高辛, Tang Yao 唐堯, Yu Shun 虞舜

Juan 2. Xia 夏, Yin 殷, Zhou 周

Juan 3. Zhou Mu Wang 周穆王, Lu Xi Gong 魯僖公, Zhou Ling Wang 周靈王

Juan 4. Yan Zhao Wang 燕昭王, Qin Shihuang 秦始皇

Juan 5. Qian Han, *shang* 前漢, 上 [Former Han, part 1]

Juan 6. Qian Han, *xia* 前漢, 下 [Former Han, part 2]; Hou Han 後漢 [Later Han]

Juan 7. Wei 魏

Juan 8. Wu 吳, Shu 蜀

Juan 9. Jin shi shi 晉時事 [Jin-period events]

Juan 10. Kunlun shan 昆侖山, Penglai shan 蓬萊山, Fangzhang shan 方丈山, Yingzhou shan 瀛洲山, Yuanjiao shan 員嶠山, Daiyu shan 岱輿山, Kunwu shan 昆吾山, Dongting shan 洞庭山

Authorship and transmission

Traditionally attributed to Wang Jia, the *Shiyi ji* has some fifteen versions, all of which stem from Xiao Qi's edited version. Little is known about Xiao. He was possibly related to the Xiao royal family of the Liang. According to his preface, the original text contained nineteen *juan*, consisting of 220 *pian* 篇, and he organized them into ten *juan* and added remarks. The Ming critic Hu Yinglin 胡應麟 (1551–1602) argued that Xiao Qi was the actual author of the *Shiyi ji* (*Shaoshi shanfang bicong* 32:318), but there is no evidence for this claim. Modern scholars such as Meng Qingxiang and Shang Meishu (*Shiyi ji yizhu*, 1) attribute 126 *pian* to Wang Jia and 36 *pian* to Xiao Qi.

In the Sui, Tang, and Song dynasties there were at least three editions of the *Shiyi ji*. Under the heading of miscellaneous histories (*zashi* 雜史), the *Sui shu* lists a *Shiyi lu* (two *juan*) under Wang Jia's name, and a *Wang Zinian Shiyi ji* (ten *juan*) under Xiao Qi's name. The *Jiu Tangshu* lists a *Shiyi ji* (three *juan*) and a *Wang Zinian Shiyi ji* (ten *juan*); the *Xin Tangshu* lists a *Wang Jia Shiyi ji* (three *juan*) and a *Shiyi ji* (ten *juan*). Tao Zongyi's 陶宗儀 (fl. 1360) *Shuofu* 說郛 includes parts of the *Shiyi ji*. The *Shiyi ji* is also mentioned in the Tang encyclopedia *Yiwen leiju*, q.v., and two Song encyclopedias, the *Taiping guangji* 太平廣記 and the *Taiping yulan*, q.v. The *Wenxian tongkao* 文獻通考 lists a *Wang Zinian Shiyi ji* (ten *juan*) and a *Mingshan ji* 名山記 (one *juan*). Under the heading of "*xiaoshuo*," the *Song shi* lists a *Wang Zinian Shiyi ji* (ten *juan*).

The extant versions in ten *juan* can be found in three editions of the Ming's Wanli era (1573–1620) and in several Qing collectanea. The earliest and most reliable is the Shidetang edition (Shidetang ben 世德堂本), which contains a postface by a certain Gu Chun 顧春 dated 1534. Collated by Cheng Rong 程榮 (fl. late sixteenth century), the *Han Wei congshu* 漢魏叢書 edition contains a preface by Tu Long 屠龍 (*jinshi* 1577) dated 1592. Also included are Xiao Qi's preface and remarks, a postscript, and Wang Jia's biography from *Jin shu*, q.v. (95:2496–97). The version in the *Guang Han Wei congshu* 廣漢魏叢書 of He Yunzhong 何允中 (fl. late Ming) contains Xiao's preface and commentary but no postscript or notes. The *Baihai* 稗海 edition, compiled by Shang Jun 商濬 (fl. 1590–1620), contains neither preface nor postscript. The *Gujin yishi* 古今逸史 edition, compiled by Wu Guan 吳琯 (fl. 1568–1572), includes Xiao's preface and remarks, as well as a postscript consisting of Wang Jia's biography. The edition included in the *Zengding Han Wei congshu* 增訂漢魏叢書, compiled by Wang Mo 王謨 (*jinshi* 1578), has Xiao's preface and remarks, along with Wang's own comments. As for the *Baizi quanshu* 百子全書 edition, printed in 1875, scholars have pointed out that its ten *juan* differ significantly from other versions, an indication that it probably derives from a different tradition.

Principal editions

The primary edition is from the Shidetang. Nearly identical to this first edition are the *Han Wei congshu* and *Gujin yishi* editions.

Texts with commentaries and notes

Meng Qingxiang 孟慶祥 and Shang Weishu 商嫩姝. *Shiyi ji yizhu* 拾遺記譯注. Harbin: Heilongjiang renmin chubanshe, 1998.

Qi Zhiping 齊治平. *Guxiaoshuo congkan: Shiyi ji* 古小說叢刊: 拾遺記. Beijing: Zhonghua shuju, 1981.

Selected studies

Campany, Robert F. *Strange Writing: Anomaly Accounts in Early Medieval China*. Albany: State University of New York Press, 1996. Pp. 64–67.

Chen Lijun 陳麗君. "*Shiyi ji* xinci xinyi kaoshi" 拾遺記新詞新意考釋. *Ningbo daxue xuebao, Renwen kexue* (2006.2): 47–51.

Dun Songyuan 頓嵩元. "*Shiyiji* jiqi zuozhe" 拾遺記及其作者. *Huanghe keji daxue xuebao* (2003.1): 135–39.

Foster, Lawrence C. "The *Shih-i chi* and Its Relationship to the Genre Known as *Chih-kuai Hsiao-shuo*." Ph.D. diss., University of Washington, 1974. Foster provides a complete translation of the text, except for Xiao Qi's preface.

Hu Yinglin 胡應麟. *Shaoshi shanfan bicong* 少室山房筆叢. Beijing: Zhonghua shuju, 1958.

Li Jianguo 李劍国. *Tangqian zhiguai xiaoshuo shi* 唐前志怪小說史. Tianjin: Nankai daxue chubanshe, 1984. Pp. 323–32.

———. *Tangqian zhiguai xiaoshuo jishi* 唐前志怪小說輯釋. Taipei: Wen shi zhe chubanshe, 1995. Pp. 345–79.

Wang Jingbo 王晶波. "Lun *Shiyi ji* de weimei qingxiang" 論拾遺記的唯美傾向. *Lanzhou xibei shida xuebao, Shehui kexue* (2003.1): 44–49.

Wang Xingfen 王興芬. "*Shiyi ji* nüxing mingyun de wenhua toushi" 拾遺記女性命運的文化透視. *Beifang luncong* (2008.3): 21–24.

Xue Keqiao 薛克翹. "Du *Shiyi ji* zatan" 讀拾遺記雜談. *Nanya yanjiu* (1996.1): 62–68.

Xue Ruize 薛瑞澤. "*Shiyi ji* zhong Luoyang shishi xuyao" 拾遺記中洛陽史事述要. *Zhongzhou jingu* (1994.6): 47–48.

Yan Maoyuan 嚴懋垣. "Wei Jin Nanbei chao zhiguai xiaoshuo shulu fu kaozheng" 魏晉南北朝志怪小說書錄附考證. *Wenxue nianbao* 6 (1940): 45–72.

Zhang Kan 張侃. "Shitan Xiao Qi dui *Shiyi ji* de zhengli he piping: Cong xiaoshuo pipingshi de jiaodu jiayi kaocha" 試談蕭綺對拾遺記的整理和批評: 從小説批評史的角度加以考察. *Fudan xuebao, Shehui kexue* (1995.2): 82–87.

Japanese translations

Nagasawa Kikuya 長沢規矩也, ed. *Wakokubon Kanseki zuihitsushū* 和刻本漢籍随筆集. Tokyo: Kyūko shoin, 1972. Vol. 10.

Takeda Akira 竹田晃, Kuroda Mamiko 黒田真美子, and Sano Seiko 佐野誠子, eds. *Chūgoku koten shōsetsusen* 中国古典小説選. Tokyo: Meiji shoin, 2006. Vol. 2.

Lei Jin

Shu Xi ji 束皙集

Introduction

Shu Xi (styled Guangwei 廣微) hailed from Yangping 陽平 (modern Hebei) and lived from circa 263 to circa 302. From his biography in the *Jin shu*, q.v. (51:1427–34), it is known that he died at thirty-nine years of age. A wide-ranging writer in an era of increasing interest in arts and genres of all types, he became well known in subsequent centuries as a poet but, as discussed later, was also an important historiographer. Appointed to the office of assistant editorial director (*zuo zhuzuolang* 佐著作郎), and additionally conferred with the title of erudite (*boshi* 博士), he worked on history-writing tasks, including the imperial annals and treatises for a "Jin shu." (An excellent biography is given in Declerq, "The Perils of Orthodoxy," 34–37; on his historiography, see Fairbank, "Ssu-ma I," 82.)

Shu Xi was known as an expert in ancient calligraphy, and it is probably not a coincidence that he was given the extraordinary opportunity sometime after 294 of examining the original (not just the already transcribed) Ji Tomb (汲冢) Warring States texts, inscribed on bamboo slips, that had been discovered in 281. He was therefore able to make major emendations in the establishment of the resulting text of the Ji Tomb's *Zhushu jinian* 竹書紀年, a source of pre-Han history. (On Shu's second edition, deduced from brief quotations in a number of sources, see Shaughnessy, *Rewriting Early Chinese Texts*, 151 ff; also Goodman, *Xun Xu and the Politics of Precision*, 321–25.)

We know very little else about Shu Xi, other than that he returned home around 300, when factional violence had already taken the lives of several of his closest allies in government. His biography states (51:1434) that his historiographic works—the *Jin Imperial Annals* (*Jin shu diji* 晉書帝紀, in ten *juan*) and monographs (*zhi* 志)—were lost after the fall of Luoyang, but that he had other writings circulating in his day (for notes on his general output, see Liu Rulin, *Han Jin xueshu biannian*, 7:207–8).

Liu Xie (d. ca. 532), in his critical work on literature, *Wenxin diaolong*, q.v. (see section 15, "Humor and Enigma"), held Shu Xi's talents to be worthy, even if he disapproved of the lightness of the topic of Shu's rhyme-prose on pasta ("Bing fu" 餅賦). (See *The Literary Mind and the Carving of Dragons*, trans. and annot. Vincent Yu-chung Shih [Taipei: Chung Hwa Book Co., 1971], 110.) Shu's set of poems titled "Bu wangshi" were collected in the sixth-century *Wen xuan*, q.v.

Contents

The fullest coverage of the genres of Shu Xi's writings makes up *juan* 43 of Zhang Pu's (1602–1641) *Han Wei Liuchao baisanjia ji*, q.v., where the collection is titled *Shu Guangwei ji* 束廣微集 (*Yingyin Wenyuange Siku quanshu** 1413:247–57). The contents fall into the same general shape as many other *wenji* of writers in the Wei-Jin Nanbeichao period; there are items such as court opinions and petitions, letters, disquisitions, prose-poems, and verse. There is a total of twenty-five titles (some without any extant text) in the following order by genre:

Rhapsodies, 5 titles (all are noted as stemming from the text of the *Yiwen leiju*, q.v., compiled by Ouyang Xun, 557–641)

Disquisition, 1 title

Opinion, 5 titles (including one introduced as "You yi" 又議)

Responding opinion/*dui* 對, 1 title ("Sanri qushui dui" 三日曲水對 [Responding opinion about the Lustration Festival], which is not in Yan Kejun's "Quan Jin wen"; see later)

Presentation, 1 title ("Jian Wang Pu zou" 薦王僕奏 [Presentation on recommending Wang Pu]; termed "lost," no text given)

Personal letter, 1 title ("Da Jizhong zhushu nanshi shu" 答汲冢竹書難釋書 [A reply about solutions to objections (by Wang Tingjian) to (Shu's editing of) the Ji Tomb slips]; termed "lost," no text given)

Memorandum, 1 title ("Xie gongcao jian" 謝公曹牋 [Declining service in a ducal bureau]; not carried in "Quan Jin wen")

Condolence, 2 titles

Miscellaneous prose/*zawen* 雜文, 2 titles (of which "Ji yu" 集語 [Collected comments] is not carried in "Quan Jin wen")

Poetry, 6 titles (the six parts of "Bu wangshi" 補亡詩 [Lost odes supplied], following a preface)

For the prose alone, the "Quan Jin wen," *juan* 87 (4:1a–9b) of Yan Kejun's (1762–1843) *Quan shanggu Sandai Qin Han Sanguo Liuchao wen*, q.v., yields between nineteen and twenty-two items, depending on how they are counted. Differences from the texts or titles carried in Zhang Pu's anthology are as follows: (1) contains the presentation "Jian Wang Pu zou," listed as lost in Zhang Pu; (2) appends to the "Bihui yi" 避諱議 (On avoiding taboo words) the text that had come under "You yi" 又議 in Zhang Pu; (3) contains two opinions not found in Zhang Pu, "Sun wei shu zu chizhong yi" 孫為庶祖持重議 (On grandsons' all performing [the three years of] mourning for the grandfather) and "Jiupin yi" 九品議 (Opinion on the Nine Grades [of evaluating officials]); (4) places two other works in an order that differs from Zhang Pu's arrangement. It is difficult to number the "Quan Jin wen" items because some are titles without comment, source, or text. Also, among the rhyme-prose and opinions there are lexic variations. Although the number of rhapsodies and their names are the same in both editions, the texts in "Quan Jin wen" are in some cases quite different in overall length; for example, "Bing fu" in "Quan Jin wen" is over four hundred characters, but in the *Han Wei Liuchao baisanjia ji* it is only sixty-eight. Clearly, "Quan Jin wen" has stitched together disparate sources. The sparcity of the *Han Wei Liuchao baisanjia ji*'s items for the *Shu Xi ji* was in fact harshly criticized in *Siku quanshu zongmu tiyao** 38.4214.

Transmission and early history of the text

As in the cases of many Western Jin writers, there is no evidence to say who first collected and/or edited Shu Xi's *wenji*, nor when the collection fell out of wide circulation. Shu's biography in *Jin shu* (completed in 648) says only that his "collected works in several tens of scroll-bundles (*pian* 篇) all circulated in his time" (51:1434). The *Sui shu*, q.v., bibliographic monograph 35:1063 lists "Shu Xi ji" in seven *juan*; the pre-Sui commentary then says: "Liang had an edition in five *juan*, plus a record of contents in one *juan*." The bibliography in *Jiu Tang shu* 47:2061 (completed in 945, but utilizing eighth-century records) cites it in five *juan*; the mid-Yuan *Song shi* records one *juan* (208:5328). It may be deduced, based on the previous, that Shu Xi's *wenji*, given the chaos of the end of Western Jin, was not transmitted integrally, and passages were picked up in widespread sources. The *wenji*'s decline as a "book" thus seems to have started soon after Shu's death. Since there are no remarks on his *wenji* in the major Song-era catalogs, it is possible to say that it dropped out of popular circulation from late-Tang to Yuan, when what appears to be a fragment was mentioned in *Song shi*. Then, during Ming times, Feng Weine (1513–1572) included remarks on Shu Xi's "Bu wangshi" in his *Gushi ji** (completed 1557) 33.7a (in *Yingyin Wenyuange Siku quanshu* 1379:266–67), and subsequently the entire *wenji* was reconstituted by Zhang Pu.

Principal editions

There are many editions of the *Han Wei Liuchao baisanjia ji*. For a punctuated version of Zhang Pu's anthology, see the 1879 re-cut woodblock edition (rpt., Jiangsu: Jiangsu guji shudian, 1990), where Shu Xi's collected writings are in 2:489–502.

Shu's biography in the *Jin shu* gives modern punctuated versions of three prose pieces: the "Xuanju shi" 玄居釋 (Apology for living in seclusion), the "Guang nong yi" 廣農議 (On expanding farming), and the "Sanri qushui dui," the last in fuller form than that found in Zhang Pu's edition. For modern annotations of the "Bu wangshi" poems, see "Jin shi," *juan* 4 (1:639–41), in Lu Qinli's *Xian Qin Han Wei Jin Nanbeichao shi**.

Text with commentary and notes

Liu Yue 劉悦. "Shu Xi ji jiaozhu" 束晳集校注. Master's thesis, Dongbei shifan daxue, 2006. All items in the *wenji*, with original sources, are given, but this is not a learned annotation.

Selected studies

Declercq, Dominik. "The Perils of Orthodoxy: A Western Jin 'Hypothetical Discourse,'" *T'oung Pao* 80.1–3 (1994): 27–60. Contains a translation of "Xuan ju shi," 38–53.

Fairbank, Anthony Bruce. "Ssu-ma I (179–251): Wei Statesman and Chin Founder, An Historiographical Inquiry." Ph.D. diss., University of Washington, 1994.

Goodman, Howard L. *Xun Xu and the Politics of Precision in Third-Century* AD *China*. Sinica Leidensia 95. Brill: Leiden, 2010.

Ling Xun 凌迅. "Shu Xi wenxue lun" 束晳文學論. *Shandong shifan daxue xuebao, Renwen shehui kexue ban* (1981.6): 52–58.

Mao Zhenhua 毛振華. "Shu Xi 'Bu wangshi' kao lun" 束晳"補亡詩"考論. *Xi'nan jiaotong daxue xuebao, Shehui kexue ban* (2006.5): 28–31, 51.

Satake Yasuko 佐竹保子. "Soku Seki no bungaku" 束晳の文學. *Shūkan Toyōgaku* 76 (1996): 42–60.

———. "Soku Seki" 束晳. In *Seishin bungakuron: Gengaku no kage to keiji no akebono* 西晉文學論: 玄學の影と形似の曙, 208–49. Tokyo: Kyūko shoin, 2002.

Shaughnessy, Edward L. *Rewriting Early Chinese Texts*. Albany: State University of New York Press, 2006. Pp. 151–53.

Tan Jiajian 譚家健. "Shu Xi de sufu" 束晳的俗賦. *Liaoning shizhuan xuebao, Shehui kexue ban* (2000.6): 30–32.

Xu Gongchi 徐公持. *Wei Jin wenxue shi* 魏晉文學史. Beijing: Renmin wenxue chuban she, 1999. Pp. 317–19.

Translations

Cherniack, Susan. "Book Culture and Textual Transmission in Sung China." *Harvard Journal of Asiatic Studies* 54.1 (1994): 51–53. Translates "Du shu fu" 讀書賦.

Knechtges, David R. "Early Chinese Rhapsodies on Poverty and Pasta." *Chinese Literature* (Summer 1999): 103–13. Translates "Pinjia fu" 貧家賦.

———. "A Western Jin Poem on Pasta." In *Early Medieval China: A Sourcebook*, ed. Wendy Swartz and Robert F. Campany (New York: Columbia University Press, 2014). Translates "Bing fu"; see his appended note citing earlier translations.

Yang, Lien-sheng. "Notes on the Economic History of the Chin Dynasty." *Harvard Journal of Asiatic Studies* 9.2 (1946): 134. Rpt. in *Studies in Chinese Institutional History* (Cambridge, MA: Harvard University Press, 1961), 146. Translates "Quan nong fu" 勸農賦.

Zach, Erwin von. "Ersatz für sechs verlorengegangene Oden des *Shih king*" (sechs Gedichte). In *Die chinesische Anthologie: Übersetzungen aus dem Wen hsuan*, ed. Ilse Martin Fong, 1:268–72. Cambridge, MA: Harvard University Press, 1958. Translates "Bu wangshi."

Research aid

Liu Rulin 劉汝霖. *Han Jin xueshu biannian* 漢晉學術編年. Shanghai: Shangwu yinshuguan, 1935.

Howard L. Goodman

Shuijing zhu 水經注

Introduction

The *Shuijing zhu* (Guide to waterways with commentary) by Li Daoyuan 酈道元 (d. 527) with its forty chapters and more than 300,000 characters is the most comprehensive geographical source of the Six Dynasties period. This important work's composition is structured according to the courses of the river systems of China and, to a degree, to those of neighboring countries as well. Traditionally the *Shuijing zhu* is labeled as a commentary to the *Shuijing*, an anonymous text finished shortly after the Three Dynasties (220–265) at the earliest, but in the eyes of Zhong Xing 鍾惺 (1574–1624), the *Shuijing zhu* is one of three commentaries from the Six Dynasties period that could stand as an independent book in its own right, together with those on the *Sanguo zhi*, q.v., and the *Shishuo xinyu*, q.v. (Tan and Li, *Shuijing zhu xuan zhu*, 511). In content and length, Li Daoyuan's *zhu* exceeds the *Shuijing*'s text by far—the *jing* contains records of only 137 river courses, whereas we find 1,252 rivers in the *zhu*. Further, the *Shuijing* entries consist only of short accounts on the course of a river and the administrative division through which it flows, while the commentary's narratives cover a broad variety of topics. In the preface to the *Wangshi hejiao Shuijing zhu* 王氏合校水經注, the Qing scholar Wang Xianqian 王先謙 (1842–1918) saw Li Daoyuan's approach as a way to preserve knowledge of ancient times (*cun gu* 存古) by using the rivers as a basic framework. The study of the *Shuijing zhu*, known as *Lixue* 酈學, includes three fields: literature, geography, and history.

Contents

In most cases an account of a river starts at its source. The geographical descriptions follow the course of the river and are interrupted by passages on cultural or historical matters as the river passes specific locations. Topics like historical geography, historical events and persons, anthropology, architecture, and religion—the *mirabilia* of a geographical place—are portrayed and discussed, rather briefly in the majority of cases. Because it was not possible for Li Daoyuan to visit all the places he wrote about, many accounts in the *Shuijing zhu* are based on written sources, named and unnamed, that are incorporated into the text.

In the commentary, 437 different texts ranging over time as well as numerous stone inscriptions, about 300, are mentioned, but Li Daoyuan maintained a critical stance regarding his sources, and his comments reveal a command of the historian's craft.

Authorship

Li Daoyuan, a native of Fanyang 范陽 (close to modern-day Beijing), one of five sons of Li Fan 酈範, a Chinese official of the Northern Wei, was born sometime between 465 and 472. It is reported that already in his early years he loved learning and was well read. Of his service in a number of different official posts, he was described as a man who performed his administrative tasks with harshness, on the one hand, but on the other hand he enjoyed the reputation of being an upright, brave person. He lost his life near Chang'an in 527 during the uprisings that marked the last years of the Northern Wei (*Bei shi*, q.v., 27:996).

Little is known about Li Daoyuan's motivation to write the *Shuijing zhu*, but the idea of rectifying and preserving knowledge is omnipresent throughout the text. In his preface he states that earlier works were not all-encompassing or were written in a way that did not allow the reader to understand the relations or the importance of noteworthy information. Thus he claims to be straightening out the shortcomings of former records with his *Shuijing zhu*.

Authenticity and transmission of the text

The commentary on the *Shuijing*, in forty *juan*, by Li Daoyuan is first mentioned in *Wei shu*, q.v., 80:1926. It is then entered in the bibliographical monograph of *Sui shu*, q.v., 33:948, and thereafter in the bibliographies of the later dynastic histories. In Tang times it seems that the text was valued by such prominent authors as Liu Zhiji 劉知幾 (661–721) and was also used by early commentators as a source of geographical information. The scholar Li Jifu 李吉甫 (758–814), known for his *Yuanhe junxian tuzhi* 元和郡縣圖誌, disapproved of the legends and supernatural matters Li Daoyuan recorded. Hence he composed a shorter version leaving out such contents. It is listed in the *Xin Tang shu* (58:1506) as *Shan Shuijing* 刪水經 in ten *juan* but has not survived.

By the end of the Song dynasty five chapters of the *Shuijing zhu* had been lost, but later editors, by dividing existing chapters and reconstructing or adding new chapters, managed to maintain the original length of forty *juan*. At least nine versions were redacted during these times, but none of them has been fully handed down.

The first known scholarly work on the text was carried out during the Ming dynasty. The edition included in the *Yongle dadian** (1403–1408) is considered the most basic. This was also the only early version in which the preface of Li Daoyuan was preserved. Numerous commentaries and revised editions on the basis of Song editions were composed, especially in the second half of the Ming dynasty.

Scholarly activity concerning the *Shuijing zhu* reached its peak in the Qing dynasty. More than fifty commentaries and adaptations of the text were created—several of them deploying innovative approaches. Qing versions became the main sources for the newer editions composed in later times.

Principal editions

According to Wang Guowei 王國維 (1877–1927), the *Shuijing zhu* that was included in the fifteenth-century *Yongle dadian* (*juan* 11127–41) is the version that comes closest to the texts of Song times. The *Shuijing zhu jian* 水經注箋 from 1615, composed by Zhu Mouwei 朱謀㙔 (d. 1624), is often regarded as the most important edition of the Ming dynasty. In his work, Zhu was supported by Xie Beishen 謝北申 and Sun Rucheng 孫汝澄. They employed the *Shuijing zhu* of Wu Guan 吳琯 from 1585 as well as parts of Song-period editions and the version of Huang Xingzeng 黃省曾 (1490–1540) from 1534.

Since the text of the *jing*-entries and the *zhu*-commentary were intermingled in later times—a problem also for the *Luoyang qielan ji*, q.v.—many Qing scholars tried to separate the original text from the commentary. Historian Quan Zuwang 全祖望 (1705–1755), in his *Qi jiao Shuijing zhu* 七校水經注, used different-sized characters to distinguish the two, further subdividing the latter, again by the size of characters, to indicate text dealing with the course of a river as against the records of other topics.

Zhao Yiqing 趙一清 (1711–1764), inspired by his friend Quan Zuwang, also deployed differing sizes to make a clear distinction between *jing* and *zhu* in his *Shuijing zhu shi* 水經注釋 from 1754, and in addition he used bold type and lightface. His attempt to identify errors in earlier editions was a great success, and the commentator Bi Yuan 畢沅 (1730–1797) claimed that there was nothing untrustworthy or unclearly explained in Zhao's edition.

Twenty years later, in 1774, Dai Zhen 戴震 (1724–1777) finished his so-called Palace edition (Dian ben 殿本) of the *Shuijing zhu*. Because of its parallels to Zhao Yiqing's work, Dai Zhen was later sometimes accused of having copied from the Zhao edition. Dai intensively worked on the differences between *jing* and *zhu*. Focusing on the place-names, he drew the conclusion that the *Shuijing* was a work limited to a relatively short period of time, while in the commentary there are toponyms of different times. He also pointed out that in the *jing*-entries the verb *guo* 過 has the sense "to pass by," while in the commentary the verb *jing* 逕 is used instead.

Wang Xianqian completed his *Hejiao Shuijing zhu* in 1892. He used different commentaries and editions of earlier times and relied strongly on the work of Zhao Yiqing, which for him came closest to the original document. His version is contained in the *Sibu beiyao**.

In 1916 Wang Guowei began his work on the *Shuijing zhu jiao* 水經注校, which would occupy him for about ten years. It was his aim to create a text corresponding to the original and therefore he compared numerous old versions. In contrast to many of the other editions, Wang Guowei's did not differentiate between *jing* and *zhu* as did Dai Zhen. Hence, Wang's *jing*-entries differ in a great many cases from those of other editions. He favored the work of Zhu Mouwei and strongly relied on the *Yongle dadian* text.

Regarding older versions as inaccurate, Yang Shoujing 楊守敬 (1839–1915) and his disciple Xiong Huizhen 熊會貞 (1863–1936) composed the *Shuijing zhu shu* 水經注疏. After the death of Yang, Xiong continued the work alone; they spent a combined sixty years in its completion. For the most part they used the text of Zhu Mouwei and various Qing dynasty editions. Later Duan Xizhong and Chen Qiaoyi revised the *Shuijing zhu shu* and added several additional notes and corrections (see later).

Texts with commentaries and notes

Chen Qiaoyi 陳橋驛, ed. *Shuijing zhu jiao zheng* 水經注校證. Beijing: Zhonghua shuju, 2007. Includes a list of the important editions used for the collation; one of the few editions that marks place-names and personal names.

Duan Xizhong 段熙仲 and Chen Qiaoyi, eds. *Shuijing zhu shu* 水經注疏. Nanjing: Jiangsu guji chubanshe, 1989. 3 vols. Revision of the *Shuijing zhu shu* of Yang Shoujing and Xiong Huizhen.

Wang Guowei, ed. *Shuijing zhu jiao* 水經注校. Shanghai: Shanghai renmin chubanshe, 1984.

Wang Xianqian, ed. *Wangshi hejiao Shuijing zhu* 王氏合校水經注. Beijing: Zhonghua shuju, 2009. Reprint of Shanghai: Zhonghua shuju, 1920–34, 18 *ce*, *Sibu beiyao* ed.

Yongle dadian ben Shuijing zhu 永樂大典本水經注. 8 vols. Taipei: Taiwan shangwu yinshuguan, 1971. Reprint of the fifteenth-century *Yongle dadian* edition.

Commentaries and notes without the complete text

Ding Qian 丁謙. *Shuijing zhu zhengwu juli* 水經注正誤舉例. Beijing: Wenwu chubanshe, 1984. 4 vols. Reprint of a block-printed edition, *Qiushuzhai congshu* 求恕齋叢書 series.

Tan Jiajian 譚家健 and Li Zhiwen 李知文, eds. *Shuijing zhu xuan zhu* 水經注選注. Beijing: Zhongguo shehui kexue chubanshe, 1989. Rpt., Taipei: Jianhong chubanshe, 1994. Contains some shorter essays on the *Shuijing zhu*.

Zhong Fengnian 鍾鳳年. "*Shuijing zhu* jiao bu zhiyi" 水經注校補質疑. *Yanjing xuebao* 32 (1947): 1–96.

Selected studies

Akimoto Etsuko 秋元悅子. "Nihon ni okeru Suikeichū ni tsuite: Edo jidai o chūshin ni" 日本における水經注について: 江戸時代を中心に. *Chūō daigaku Ajiashi kenkyū* 20 (1996): 205–32.

Bielenstein, Hans. "Notes on the *Shui ching*." *Bulletin of the Museum of Far Eastern Antiquities* 65 (1993): 257–83.

Chen Li 陳澧. *Shuijing zhu xi'nan zhushui kao* 水經注西南諸水考. In *Congshu jicheng xubian* 叢書集成續編, *ce* 222. Taipei: Xinwenfeng, 1989. Reprint of the *Guangya congshu* 廣雅叢書 woodblock edition of 1889.

Chen Qiaoyi. *Shuijing zhu yanjiu* 水經注研究. Tianjin: Tianjin guji chubanshe, 1985.

———. *Shuijing zhu yanjiu er ji* 水經注研究二集. Taiyuan: Shanxi renmin chubanshe, 1987.

———. *Lixue xinlun—Shuijing zhu yanjiu zhi san* 酈學新論—水經注研究之三. Taiyuan: Shanxi renmin chubanshe, 1992.

———. *Li Daoyuan pingzhuan* 酈道元評傳. Nanjing: Nanjing daxue chubanshe, 1994.

———. *Shuijing zhu yanjiu si ji* 水經注研究四集. Hangzhou: Hangzhou chubanshe, 2003.

Chen Shiren 陳識仁. *Shuijing zhu yu Beiwei shixue* 水經注與北魏史學. Taipei: Hua Mulan wenhua gongzuofang, 2008.

Ding Shan 丁山. "Lixue kao xumu" 酈學考敘目. *Guoli zhongyang yanjiuyuan lishi yuyan yanjiusuo jikan* 3.3 (1932): 353–74.

Fan Wenlan 范文瀾. *Shuijing zhu xie jing wenchao* 水經注寫景文鈔. Beiping: Pu she, 1929.

Hu Shi 胡適. "Shuijing zhu jiaoben de yanjiu" 水經注校本的研究. *Zhonghua wenshi luncong* 10 (1979): 145–220.

———. "A Note on Ch'üan Tsu-wang, Chao I-ch'ing and Tai Chên —A Study of Independent Convergence in Research as Illustrated in Their Works on the *Shui-ching Chu*." In *Eminent Chinese of the Ch'ing Period*, ed. Arthur W. Hummel, 2:970–82. 2 vols. Washington, DC: U.S. Government Printing Office, 1943–1944. Rpt., Taipei: SMC Publishing, 2002.

———. *Hu Shi quan ji* 胡適全集. 44 vols. Hefei: Anhui jiaoyu chubanshe, 2003. Vols. 14–17 contain Hu Shi's work on the *Shuijing zhu*.

Miyagawa Hisayuki 宮川尚志. "Suikeichū ni mietaru shibyō" 水經注に見えたる祠廟. *Tōyōshi kenkyū* 5.1 (1939): 21–38.

Mori Shikazō 森鹿三. "Reki Dōgen ryakuden: Shina kokin jinbutsu ryakuden" 酈道元略傳:支那古今人物略傳. *Tōyōshi kenkyū* 6.2 (1941): 52–60.

———. *Tōyōgaku kenkyū: Rekishi chirihen* 東洋學研究: 歷史地理篇. Kyoto: Tōyōshi kenkyūkai, 1971.

Nagasawa Kazutoshi 長澤和俊. "Suikeichū maki ni no seiiki chiri" 水經注卷二の西域地理. *Shikan* 119 (1988): 2–15.

Nylan, Michael. "Wandering in the Ruins: The *Shuijing zhu* Reconsidered." In *Interpretation and Literature in Early Medieval China*, ed. Alan K. L. Chan and Yuet-Keung Lo, 63–101. Albany: SUNY Press, 2010.

Petech, Luciano. *Northern India according to the Shui-Ching-Chu*. Rome: Ist. Italiano per il Medio ed Estremo Oriente, 1950. Includes translations of passages from chaps. 1 and 2.

Reiter, Florian C. "Die Ausführungen Li Tao-yüans zur Geschichte und Geographie des Berges Lu (Chiang-hsi) im 'Kommentar zum Wasserklassiker,' und ihre Bedeutung für die regionale Geschichtsschreibung." *Oriens Extremus* 28 (1981): 15–29. Includes translation of passages from chap. 39.

Ren Songru 任松如. *Shuijing zhu yiwen lu* 水經注異聞錄. Shanghai: Qizhi shuju, 1934. Rpt., Shanghai: Shanghai wenyi, 1991.

Shi Zhecun 施蟄存. *Shuijing zhu bei lu* 水經注碑錄. Tianjin: Tianjin guji chubanshe, 1987.

Strassberg, Richard E. *Inscribed Landscapes: Travel Writing from Imperial China*. Berkeley: University of California Press, 1994. Pp. 77–90. Includes translations of passages from chaps. 4 and 34.

Wang Hui 王恢. *Shuijing zhu Han houguo jishi* 水經注漢侯國輯釋. Taipei: Zhongguo wenhua daxue chuban bu, 1981.

Wu Tianren 吳天任. *Lixue yanjiu shi* 酈學研究史. Taipei: Yiwen yinshuguan, 1991.

Yamada Katsuyoshi 山田勝芳: "Suikeichū inyō no Gi tochi ki ni tsuite" 水經注引用の魏土地記について. *Shūkan Tōyōgaku* 60 (1988): 114–25.

Zhao Yongfu 趙永復. *Shuijing zhu tongjian jinshi* 水經注通檢今釋. Shanghai: Fudan daxue chubanshe, 1985.

Zheng Dekun 鄭德坤. *Shuijing zhu yinshu kao* 注水經引書考. Taipei: Yiwen yinshuguan, 1974.

———. *Zhongguo lishi dili lunwenji* 中國歷史地理論文集. Taipei: Lianjing chuban shiye gongsi, 1981. Contains five essays on the *Shuijing zhu*.

Zheng Dekun and Wu Tianren 吳天任. *Shuijing zhu yanjiu shiliao huibian* 水經注研究史料匯編. 2 vols. Taipei: Yiwen yinshuguan, 1984.

Translations

German

Altenburger, Engelbert. *Historische Geographie des Jangtse—Kommentar zum Shuijing zhu*. [Ph.D. diss.] Augsburg: Eigenverlag, 1981. Includes passages of chaps. 33–35.

Japanese

Chūgoku koten bungaku taikei 中國古典文學大系, vol. 21, ed. Iriya Yoshitaka 入矢義高 et al. Tokyo: Heibonsha, 1974. Includes translations of chaps. 1–5, 15–19.

Suikei chūso yakuchū: Isui hen (jō) 水経注疏訳注：渭水篇 (上). Ed. Xiong Huizhen, Yang Shoujing, and Chūgoku kodai chiikishi kenkyūhan 中国古代地域史研究班. Tōyō bunko ronsō 71. Tokyo: Tōyō bunko, 2008. Includes an annotated translation of chaps. 17–18, in addition to some essays on the *Shuijing zhu*.

Chinese

Chen Qiaoyi et al. *Shuijing zhu quan yi* 水經注全譯. 2 vols. Guiyang: Guizhou renmin chubanshe, 1996. Rpt., 2008. Translation and annotation.

Zhao Wangqin 趙望秦 et al. *Shuijing zhu xuan yi* 水經注選譯. Chengdu: Ba Shu shushe, 1990. Translation and annotation.

Research aids

Yang Shoujing. *Shuijing zhu tu* 水經注圖. Taipei: Wenhai chubanshe, 1967. Reprint of Yidu Yang shi Guanhaitang 宜都楊氏觀海堂 edition of 1905.

Wang Shiduo 汪士鐸. *Shuijing zhu tu* 水經注圖. 2 vols. Ji'nan: Shandong huabao chubanshe, 2003. One volume of maps; one volume with explanations by Chen Qiaoyi.

Index

Shuijing zhu yinde 水經注引得. Ed. Hong Ye 洪業 (William Hong) et al. Harvard-Yenching Institute Sinological Index Series 17, Peking, 1934. Rpt., Taipei: Chinese Materials and Research Aids Service Center, 1966; Shanghai: Shanghai guji chubanshe, 1987.

J. Henning Huesemann

Shuyi ji 述異記

Introduction

The *Shuyi ji* (Narrating the unusual) by Ren Fang 任昉 (460–508), a distinguished writer especially of prose, is a work that belongs to the *zhiguai* 志怪 genre. It includes tales of strange people, places, and events similar to those of the *Bowu zhi*. The entries include people or events that go back as early as the beginning of time—to Pangu 盤古, the creator of the world in Chinese mythology—down to some that even postdate the death of Ren Fang, the attributed author.

Authorship and date of composition

There are two works by this title. The earlier one by Zu Chongzhi 祖沖之 (429–500) in ten *juan* is recorded in the bibliographic monograph of the *Sui shu*, q.v. (33:980), and in the *Jiu Tang shu* (46:2005) and *Xin tang shu* (59:1540), but no mention is seen after that, and the work was evidently no longer extant. Zu Chongzhi was active during the Liu-Song and Southern Qi dynasties. Apart from being an official, he was well known for his inventions and achievement in mathematics. His sense of curiosity no doubt led him to collect items of strange and sometimes supernatural things.

Ren Fang's work by the same title, in two *juan*, was first recorded only during the late Tang and in the Song, for example, in the *Chongwen zongmu*** (3:33a; 366) and Chao Gongwu's *Junzhai dushu zhi*** (13:546). The late date of its listing has been one of the factors in raising concerns as to its authenticity. An answer to this, suggested by Chao Gongwu, was that there was only one work of this title, and the listing of the work in the earlier bibliographies as being by Zu is an error. No one else seems to be convinced by this argument.

Authenticity

The editors of the *Siku quanshu zongmu tiyao*** (27:2962) maintained that since some of the entries are about events in the Northern Qi (550–577), it is clear that such entries were added after Ren Fang's lifetime (142:1214). The editors therefore concluded that this work emerged sometime from the middle Tang into the Song by culling entries from an original work by Ren Fang as quoted by various *leishu* such as the *Shanhai jing* 山海經, *Yi yuan* 異苑, *Liexian zhuan* 列仙傳, and other, later items. However, the modern scholar Li Jianguo insists that without solid evidence, one should not refute its authorship (*Tangqian zhiguai xiaoshuo shi*, 427–29). In the extant Ming edition, divided into two *juan*, the entries do not appear to be arranged in any special order.

Transmission and early history of the text

The earliest edition still extant seems to date to the Wanli reign period of the Ming, in a redaction by Cheng Rong 程榮 (fl. 1592), compiler of the *Han Wei congshu* 漢魏叢書, and reprinted in the *Gezhi congshu* 格致叢書, *Bai hai* 稗海, and other *congshu*. During the Qing's Kangxi and Qianlong periods, two emended and expanded editions appeared. The Qianlong text was included in the *Zengding Han Wei congshu* 增訂漢魏叢書.

Selected studies

Campany, Robert Ford. *Strange Writing: Anomaly Accounts in Early Medieval China*. Albany: State University of New York Press, 1996. Pp. 84–85 and passim.

Li Jianguo 李劍國. *Tangqian zhiguai xiaoshuo shi* 唐前志怪小說史. Tianjin: Tianjin jiaoyu chubanshe, 2005. Pp. 422–35.

Lu Xun 魯迅. *Gu xiaoshuo gouchen* 古小說鉤沉. Ji'nan: Qi Lu shushe, 1997. Pp. 99–120.

Wang Zhizhong 王枝忠. *Han Wei Liuchao xiaoshuo shi* 漢魏六朝小說史. Hangzhou: Zhejiang guji chubanshe, 1997. Pp. 238–51.

Lily Xiao Hong Lee

Song shu 宋書

Introduction

The *Song shu* (History of the Song dynasty) by Shen Yue 沈約 (441–513) is the standard dynastic history of the first of the medieval Southern Dynasties, the Song (420–479), also known as the Liu-Song to distinguish it from the later Song dynasty (960–1279). At a total of one hundred *juan*, it is the longest and most thorough of the histories of the Southern Dynasties, and the best regarded.

Authorship

Shen Yue was one of the most influential literary figures of the early medieval era. He was born into a wealthy but not high-status family in Wuxing 吳興, in the Yangzi delta area. His father, an aide to an imperial prince, was executed along with his patron as a result of the civil war of 453 that put Song Emperor Xiaowu (r. 453–464) on the throne. Shen Yue himself, only twelve at the time, would go on to serve three different dynasties, mastering the art of being seemingly unthreatening and compliant in the often treacherous world of southern court politics. He gained fame for his poetry, especially for his theory of poetics, which developed and advocated the use of rules for tonal euphony. These were tremendously influential in the poetry of the Southern Dynasties, Sui, and Tang. In addition to his poetry and miscellaneous prose writings, however, Shen also worked on the compilation of imperial history. He spent a good deal of his early years working on a history of the Jin dynasty, which was never completed (and is no longer extant), and he also worked as a recorder for the Southern Qi court, with responsibility for compiling the journal of the court's activities. In the spring of 487 he was appointed by Qi Emperor Wu (r. 483–493) to compile the history of the Song dynasty.

Contents

The collection of materials for the *Song shu* had begun at the direction of Song Emperor Wen in 439. He Chengtian 何承天 (370–447) drafted the initial annals and accounts and the monographs on calendrics and astrology, while other historians such as Shan Qianzhi 山謙之, Pei Songzhi 裴松之 (372–451), and Su Baosheng 蘇寶生 made lesser contributions. In 462 Xu Yuan 徐爰 began a substantial expansion of this work, covering the period from 405 to the Daming period (457–464). Shen Yue thus inherited a substantial body of material to work with, but he also had several additional decades to cover and a good deal of revision in terminology to do in light of the dynastic change to the Qi regime. He finished this task in less than a year and submitted to the throne a total of seventy *juan* of annals and accounts. These are noteworthy for their extensive profiles of literary figures such as Xie Lingyun 謝靈運 (385–433); for accounts of numerous military men from outside the capital elite; for four chapters of "theme" biographies on filial exemplars, meritorious officials, recluses, and exemplars of gratitude; and for chapters on the northern regimes and on southern and northern "barbarian" groups. The annals and accounts have also been criticized for the haste with which they were compiled, and for their politically noncommittal and evasive treatment of critical events.

The other thirty *juan* of the *Song shu* are made up of monographs on eight topics: pitch and calendrics, rituals, music, astrology, omenology, five phases, geography, and bureaucratic offices. Shen Yue continued to work on some of the monographs for many more years, into the reign of Liang Emperor Wu (r. 502–548), often reaching back to discuss precedents and developments from Wei and Jin times in an effort to be more comprehensive. Though criticized by the Tang historian Liu Zhiji 劉知幾 (661–721) and others for what was felt to be an excessive attention to omens and astrology, these exhaustive and technically proficient monographs, particularly the one on music, are an invaluable resource for modern researchers.

Transmission of the text

The *Sui shu*, q.v., bibliographic monograph (33:955) lists Shen Yue's *Song shu* in one hundred *juan*, as well as two other works of the same title, that by Xu Yuan and another by Sun Yan 孫嚴 (also an official of the Southern Qi dynasty), both in sixty-five *juan*. The other two works survived in the bibliographic monographs of both Tang histories with fewer numbers of *juan* (*Jiu Tang shu* 46:1989 and *Xin Tang shu* 58:1456), but by the Song bibliography both had disappeared, while Shen Yue's version was consistently represented with one hundred *juan*. By Northern Song times, however, the text had deteriorated considerably; for example, various bibliographers note deficiencies in the biographies of Zhao Lunzhi 趙倫之 (46:1389), Dao Yanzhi 到彥之 (*juan* 46, missing), and Xie Lingyun (67:1743–77). The Northern Song court under Emperor Renzong (r. 1022–1063) first ordered editorial work to fill out the text with parallel passages from Li Yanshou's *Nan shi*, q.v., and other materials; subsequent editions include these along with further editorial additions and emendations.

Editions

Ming dynasty editions of the *Song shu* are the Nanjing Guozijian 國子監 edition (1594), as well as Mao Jin's 毛晉 Jiguge 汲古閣 edition (1634). Many editions appeared during the Qing: the Wuyingdian 武英殿 ("Palace edition") of 1739; the Xinhui Chen Zhuozhi 新會陳焯之 edition of 1851; the Guangdong Zuogutang 廣東芷古堂 edition of 1869; the Jinling shuju 金陵書局 edition of 1872; the Hubei

Chongwen shuju 湖北崇文書局 edition of 1879; the Shanghai Tongwen shuju 上海同文書局 edition of 1884; the Shanghai tushu jicheng yinshuju 上海圖書集成印書局 edition of 1888; the Wulin Zhujianzhai 武林竹簡齋 edition of 1892; and the Wenlan shuju 文瀾書局 edition, published in Shanghai in 1902.

Two important editions were published during the early Republican period: (1) the *Sibu beiyao** edition, printed by Zhonghua shuju (Shanghai, ca. 1930), and (2) the Baina 百衲 edition, in the series *Ershisishi** (Shanghai, 1933). An edition of the *Song shu* known as the Renshou 仁壽 edition, but which was based on the Baina edition, was published in Taiwan in the mid-1950s and reprinted by Chengwen chubanshe (Taipei, 1971). The most widely used modern text is the punctuated edition issued by Zhonghua shuju in Beijing (1974). For an overall account of the textual history of this and the other Six Dynasties standard histories, see appendix V, "Textual Transmission of the Standard Histories."

Modern editions with notes

Ding Fulin 丁福林, ed. *Song shu jiaoyi* 宋書校譯. Shanghai: Shanghai guji chubanshe, 2002.

Su Jinren 蘇晉仁 and Xiao Lianzi 蕭煉子, eds. *Song shu—yuezhi jiaozhu* 宋書—樂志校注. Ji'nan: Qi Lu shushe, 1982.

Selected studies

Hao Yixing 郝懿行. *Bu Song shu Shihuo zhi* 補宋書食貨志. Shanghai: Shanghai yinshuguan, 1936.

———. *Bu Song shu Xingfa zhi* 補宋書刑法志. Shanghai yinshuguan, 1939.

Hu Axiang 胡阿祥. *Song shu Zhoujun zhi huishi* 宋書州郡志匯釋. Hefei: Anhui jiaoyu chubanshe, 2006.

Kishiro Miyako 稀代麻也子. *Sōsho no naka no Shin Yaku: Ikiru to iu koto* 宋書のなかの沈約: 生きるということ. Tokyo: Kyūko shoin, 2004.

Li Ciming 李慈銘. *Song shu zhaji* 宋書札記. Beiping: Guoli Beiping tushuguan, 1930.

Lin Jiali 林家驪. *Shen Yue yanjiu* 沈約研究. Hangzhou: Hongzhou daxue chubanshe, 1999.

———. *Yi dai ci zong—Shen Yue zhuan* 一代辭宗—沈約傳. Hangzhou: Zhejiang renmin chubanshe, 2006.

Liu Dianjue 劉殿爵 (D. C. Lau), Chen Fangzheng 陳方正, and He Zhihua 何志華. *Shen Yue ji zhuzi suoyin* 沈約集逐字索引. Hong Kong: Chinese University Press, 2000.

Mather, Richard. *The Poet Shen Yueh (441–513): The Reticent Marquis*. Princeton, NJ: Princeton University Press, 1988.

Olney, Charles D. "The Six Dynasties Poet Shen Yueh." Master's thesis, Columbia University, 1971.

Song Wenbing 宋聞兵. *Song shu ciyu yanjiu* 宋書詞語研究. Beijing: Zhonghua shuju, 2009.

Suzuki Torao 鈴木虎雄. *Shen Yue nianpu* 沈約年譜. Shanghai: Shanghai yinshuguan, 1935.
Yao Zhenli 姚振黎. *Shen Yue ji qi xueshu tanjiu* 沈約及其學術探究. Taipei: Wen shi zhe chubanshe, 1989.
Yoshikawa Tadao 吉川忠夫. "Shin Yaku no denki to sono seikatsu" 沈約の傳記とその生活. *Tōkai daigaku kiyo, Bungakubu* 11 (1968): 30–45.
———. "Shin Yaku no shiso—Rikuchō-teki shōkon" 沈約の思想—六朝的傷痕. In *Chūgoku chūseishi kenkyū* 中國中世史研究, ed. Kawakatsu Yoshio 川勝義雄, 246–71. Tokyo: Tōkai daigaku shuppankai, 1970.
Zhang Yajun 張亞軍. *Nanchao sishi yu Nanchao wenxue yanjiu* 南朝四史與南朝文學研究. Beijing: Shehui kexue chubanshe, 2007.
Zhang Yuanji 張元濟 (1867–1959). *Song shu jiaokan ji* 宋書校勘記. Beijing: Shangwu yinshuguan, 2001.

Andrew Chittick

Soushen ji 搜神記

Introduction

Gan Bao's 干寶 (d. 336) *Soushen ji* (A record of a search for the supernatural) is the classic example of a *zhiguai* 志怪, or "recounting of anomalies," text from the Six Dynasties, the period in which the genre first emerged and flourished. In its length, breadth, and variety of content and form, the *Soushen ji* is unrivaled. Its influence has been immense both in the way it explored and elevated the genre, and also in the materials it preserved, much of which continued to be cited, reworked, and adapted in a variety of texts, be they encyclopedias (*leishu* 類書) or literary works.

Contents

The *zhiguai* genre can be rather amorphous. It includes a variety of materials in a mix of styles that are united in their nonorthodox subject matter often focusing on encounters between human and "other" worlds, such as the underworld or the realms of ghosts, gods, or demons. A sampling of the range of topics can be found in the extant twenty-*juan* version of the *Soushen ji*, consisting of nearly five hundred entries. DeWoskin ("The *Sou-shen chi* and the *Chih-kuai* Tradition," 264–65) describes the contents of each *juan* (the following list is paraphrased):

1. Deities and immortals
2. Daoist adepts
3. Adepts in divination and medicine
4. Gods
5. Earth gods and shrines
6. Dynastic omens
7. Dynastic omens focusing on the Jin dynasty
8. Omens foretelling new dynasties
9. Omens pertaining to individuals
10. Dreams
11. Extreme sincerity, filial piety, and loyalty

12. Peculiar objects, peoples, and events
13. Places and remarkable objects
14. Strange marriages, births, and transformations
15. Rebirths after funerals and grave robberies
16. Ghosts
17. Animal spirits and demons
18. Poltergeists and animal spirits
19. Fish and reptile spirits
20. Rewards and retributions

Although Gan Bao was an official historian and author of the *Jin ji* 晉紀 (Jin annals), his *Soushen ji* takes us away from the classics and belletristic writings to worlds, creatures, beings, and objects usually ignored in high literature. The entries are generally in a plain, direct, informal prose style typical of the genre. Yet within this basic mode there is a variety of approaches. Thus the *Soushen ji* contains extremely terse entries as short as two or three sentences as, for example, the numerous records of dynastic omens, many of which appear to be directly copied from such histories as the *Han shu*. But there are also relatively lengthy stories, surely based on folk and urban tales, which are far more sophisticated in their narratives. Such examples point the way to the Tang dynasty's *chuanqi* 傳奇 tales and could be described as proto-fiction. The range in content and style reflects the fact that like most other *zhiguai* works, the *Soushen ji* is largely a compilation of materials from a variety of earlier and contemporary sources. Gan Bao also mentions interviewing, so at least some of the entries would appear to have been recorded from oral accounts. In addition, there are sections of discourse, for example, the discussion of possessions and anomalies that opens *juan* 6. Given the nature and condition of the text, it is sometimes difficult to distinguish to what degree Gan Bao actually shaped the entries; he could be called an author as against a compiler.

Why did Gan Bao write the *Soushen ji*? His biography records several personal experiences of a fantastic nature, themselves *zhiguai* incidents, which supposedly stirred him to compile his work. In one, the favorite maid of his father was buried alive with her master when he passed away, and years later she returned to the world of the living. More to the point is Gan Bao's preface to the *Soushen ji*, a part of which has been preserved in his biography in the *Jin shu*, q.v. (82:2150–51). It opens with a defense of the validity of his work and then the declaration: "it is enough to make clear that the spirit world is not a lie" (*yi zu yi ming shendao zhi bu wu* 亦足以明神道之不誣; translation DeWoskin, *In Search of the Supernatural*, xxvii). Most scholars have taken this statement to mean that Gan Bao is asserting the existence of the events and worlds he records, but the original Chinese is a bit ambiguous and perhaps deliberately layered in meaning. The sentence could also mean "it is enough to make clear the spirit world's not playing false." That is, Gan Bao may not be trying to demonstrate simply the existence of the spirit world, but also its moral role and significance in this world. Also important is how Gan Bao closes his preface by noting the ideas and thoughts evoked by these stories. He speaks of them as a way to "let one's mind roam, one's eyes gaze" (*youxin yumu* 游心寓目) and thus touches on the fundamental pleasures of the genre.

For modern readers the *Soushen ji* can be studied for a variety of reasons. It is a treasury of traditional religious beliefs, folk tales, myths, and legends. Thus, one can find in *Soushen ji*, juan 14, no. 354, one of the earliest examples in the world of the swan-maiden motif (Thompson motif D361.1; see Stith Thompson, *Motif-Index of Folk Literature*, 1932–1937; rev. ed., Bloomington: Indiana University Press, 1955–1958). Here also is a rich grouping of fox stories, which were at a crucial stage of development. The belief of some intellectuals in various forms of magic and esoterica and in folk beliefs regarding the afterlife are also reflected in many entries. Through portrayals of people, longings, beliefs, and matters neglected in more orthodox writings, this text offers glimpses into other sides of human nature and a fuller picture of medieval China. Aside from its role in literary history as the beginnings of Chinese fiction, the *Soushen ji* offers the delights of this peculiarly Chinese genre that would continue to flourish into the modern period. Although it deals with the strange and the marvelous, many of its greatest stories are examples of how the genre so often comes back to what is human: love, revenge, injustice, virtue rewarded, and evil punished. Blood flowing upward, defying gravity, testifies to the injustices and suffering of a woman (*juan* 11, no. 290); trees by two graves that join their branches after the deaths of the hero and heroine express the frustrations of thwarted love (*juan* 11, no. 294).

Authenticity and transmission of the text

Gan Bao's dates are highly uncertain, and estimates of the date of compilation of the *Soushen ji* have varied widely. Recently, however, several scholars have noted the statement in Xu Song's 許嵩 (eighth century) *Jiankang shilu*, q.v., that Gan Bao died in 336. Li Jianguo, the leading authority on the *Soushen ji*, consequently suggests that this work was completed around 335 or 336 (*Xin ji Soushen ji*, 46). In Gan Bao's *Jin shu* biography, the work is listed as containing thirty *juan* (82:2150), and it is so described in the bibliographies of the *Sui shu*, q.v., *Jiu Tang shu*, and *Xin Tang shu*, as well as in the *Jiankang shilu*. By the latter part of the Song dynasty, however, the *Soushen ji* fails to appear in important bibliographies. In the rare instances in which it does appear, the citation seems simply to repeat an earlier citation or the actual text referred to is unclear and most likely not Gan Bao's original work. This has led scholars to the conclusion that the original text was lost some time during the Song dynasty.

It should be noted that the *Soushen ji*'s textual history has been vastly complicated and confused by a number of texts that have borrowed the title of Gan

Bao's original work or have invented variations on it. In addition, there is a well known "sequel" to the work, the *Soushen hou ji* 搜神後記, attributed to Tao Qian 陶潛 (365–427), the text of which has sometimes been confused and mixed with that of the *Soushen ji*. This web of texts and their relationships has been the subject of much *Soushen ji* scholarship. Suffice it to say it is now generally recognized that these other titles have little direct link to Gan Bao's original.

The version closest to Gan Bao's work is the twenty-*juan* version. It first appears during the Ming dynasty in the collectanea *Mice huihan* 祕冊彙函 (1603), which was produced by Hu Zhenheng 胡震亨 (1569–1645) and Shen Shilong 沈士龍 (dates unknown). The text is clearly a Ming reconstruction drawn from earlier *leishu*, histories, and commentaries. Although the identity of the recompiler is not certain, a number of scholars have argued that it was first put together by the Ming scholar Hu Yinglin 胡應麟 (1551–1602), and then, later, materials were possibly added before it was published (*Xin ji Soushen ji*, 77–79). While the twenty-*juan* edition is organized roughly by content, there is not sufficient evidence to prove that the structure and arrangement reflects Gan Bao's original work in a significant way (at least, this is the consensus of most recent scholarship). In fact, the twenty-*juan* version is in very corrupt condition with many anachronistic entries that clearly cannot have been part of the original. In addition, many items were mistakenly included from other texts, and other items overlooked that should have been included in the recension.

Principal editions

All extant twenty-*juan* versions derive from the *Mice huihan* edition, which was later included in Mao Jin's 毛晉 (1599–1659) *Jindai mishu* 津逮秘書 collectanea. An important Qing edition, helpful for its occasional notes, is found in Zhang Haipeng's 張海鵬 (1755–1816) *Xuejin taoyuan* 學津討原 (1805). This version served as the basis for Wang Shaoying's modern edition. An easily available traditional version can be found in the *Congshu jicheng, chubian**. Whereas this version is based on the *Mice huihan* edition, the *Xuejin taoyuan* was consulted, and additional prefatory materials were included from that edition as well as from the *Jindai mishu*.

Texts with commentaries and notes

Huang Diming 黃滌明, ed. *Soushen ji quan yi* 搜神記全譯. Guiyang: Guizhou renmin chubanshe, 1991. Rev. ed., 2008. This is one of several modern editions that include detailed annotations as well as *baihua* translations of the text. The base text is the *Jindai mishu* edition, though Huang also consulted the *Xuejin taoyuan* version for its notes as well as Wang Shaoying. Appended materials are identical to those found in Wang Shaoying.

Huang Jun 黃鈞, ed. *Xin yi Soushen ji* 新譯搜神記. Taipei: Sanmin shuju, 1996. Includes extensive notes along with a *baihua* translation. The base text is that of the *Jindai mishu*; Huang also notes his debt to Wang Shaoying's modern edition. Additional matter includes a selection of unredacted items (eighteen) and an appendix with several prefaces and documents similar to those found in Wang Shaoying.

Li Jianguo 李劍國, ed. *Xin ji Soushen ji* 新輯搜神記; *Xin ji Soushen hou ji* 新輯搜神後記. 2 vols. Beijing: Zhonghua shuju, 2007. This recent edition, essentially a new redaction of the text arranged in thirty *juan*, is a landmark in the *Soushen ji*'s history. Li subjected the twenty-*juan* version to a fresh, rigorous scrutiny, eliminating many items that seem not to have been in Gan Bao's original and adding ones from sources not consulted by the first Ming dynasty recompiler and later editors. Li rearranged the items in a revised structure and order by content. In addition to the text itself, he includes a lengthy introduction, which has some of the most detailed and advanced work yet on Gan Bao's biography and the *Soushen ji*'s textual history. As in Wang Shaoying's edition, the annotations are primarily limited to collation notes and identification of sources and versions. Several appendices discuss Li's inclusion or exclusion of items and compare this new edition to earlier ones.

Wang Shaoying 汪紹楹, ed. *Soushen ji* 搜神記. Beijing: Zhonghua shuju, 1979. Until recently the single most important modern edition. The base text is from the *Xuejin taoyuan*. Annotations are limited, with the comments primarily consisting of collation notes and identification of sources. It includes a collection of unredacted items (thirty-four), and in an appendix: Shen Shilong's and Hu Zhenheng's "*Soushen ji* yin" 搜神記引, Mao Jin's "*Soushen ji* ba" 跋, and Yu Jiaxi's 余嘉錫 (1884–1955) *Siku quanshu tiyao bianzheng* 四庫全書提要辯證 (N.p.: Duyi jianshuzhai, 1937) discussion of the *Soushen ji*. Also included are Gan Bao's preface to the *Soushen ji* and a memorial requesting paper for his project (labeled "Jin *Soushen ji* biao" 進搜神記表).

Selected studies

Campany, Robert Ford. "Two Religious Thinkers of the Early Eastern Jin: Gan Bao and Ge Hong in Multiple Contexts." *Asia Major* 18 (2005): 175–224.

DeWoskin, Kenneth J. "The *Sou-shen chi* and the *Chih-kuai* Tradition: A Bibliographic and Generic Study." Ph.D. diss., Columbia University, 1974.

Fan Ning 范寧. "Guanyu *Soushen ji*" 關於搜神記. *Wenxue pinglun* (1964.1): 86–92.

Kominami Ichirō 小南一郎. "Kan Hō *Sōshin ki* no hensan (jō)" 干寶搜神記の編纂 (上). *Tōhō gakuhō* 69 (1997): 1–71.

Mathieu, Rémi. *Démons et merveilles dans la littérature chinoise des Six Dynasties: Le fantastique et l'anecdotique dans le Soushen ji de Gan Bao*. Paris: Editions You-Feng, 2000.

Taga Namisa 多賀浪砂. *Kan Hō Sōshin ki no kenkyū* 干寶搜神記の研究. Tokyo: Kindai bungeisha, 1994.

Toyoda Minoru 豐田穰. "*Sōshin ki, Sōshin kōki* genryū ko" 搜神記, 搜神後記源流考. *Tōhō gakuhō* 12.3 (1941): 43–66.

Zhou Shengya 周生亞. *Soushen ji yuyan yanjiu* 搜神記語言研究. Beijing: Zhongguo renmin daxue chubanshe, 2007.

Zhu Chuanyu 朱傳譽, ed. *Gan Bao yu Soushen ji* 干寶與搜神記. Taipei: Tianyi chubanshe, 1982.

Translations

English

Bodde, Derk. "Some Chinese Tales of the Supernatural: Kan Pao and his *Sou-shen chi.*" *Harvard Journal of Asiatic Studies* 6 (1942): 338–57.
———. "Again Some Chinese Tales of the Supernatural." *Journal of the American Oriental Society* 62 (1942): 305–8.
DeWoskin, Kenneth J., and J. I. Crump Jr., trans. *In Search of the Supernatural: The Written Record*. Stanford, CA: Stanford University Press, 1996.

French

Mathieu, Rémi, ed. *À la recherche des esprits (Récits tirés du Sou shen ji)*. Paris: Gallimard, 1992.

Japanese

Takeda Akira 竹田晃. *Sōshinki* 搜神記. Tokyo: Heibonsha, 1964.

Korean

Im Tong-sŏk 林東錫, trans. *Susin'gi* 搜神記. 2 vols. Seoul: Tongmunsŏn, 1997.

Index

Harada Taneshige 原田種成, comp. *Sōshinki goi sakuin* 搜神記語彙索引. N.p.: Daitō bunka daigaku bungakubu, 1983.

Daniel Hsieh

Sui shu 隋書

Contents

The *Sui shu* (History of the Sui dynasty), composed by a group of prominent scholars led variously by Wei Zheng 魏徵 (580–643), Linghu Defen 令狐德棻 (583–666), and Zhangsun Wuji 長孫無忌 (d. 659), is one of the eight standard histories dealing with the Six Dynasties period completed under imperial auspices in the early Tang period. It basically follows the dynastic, composite format (*duandai jizhuan ti* 斷代紀傳體) pioneered by Ban Gu 班固 (32–92) of the Eastern Han, with the notable exception of its multidynastic monographs (*zhi* 志) section. The chapters of the five basic annals (*benji* 本紀) constitute the chronological framework of the book. The first four are devoted to Yang Jian 楊堅, posthumously Wendi (r. 581–604), and his son and heir, Yang Guang 廣, posthumously Yangdi (r. 604–617). The much shorter fifth chapter is about Yang You 侑, posthumously Gongdi (r. 617–618), a puppet emperor set up by Li Yuan 李淵, who shortly afterward dethroned him and founded the Tang dynasty.

The *Sui shu*'s three component parts are as follows: basic annals (*juan* 1–5), monographs (*juan* 6–35), and biographies (*juan* 36–85). The bulk of the book is taken up by the fifty biography (*zhuan* 傳) chapters. A biography is either an individual biography or a collective biography of a foreign people or ethnic group. All but one of the biography chapters contain multiple biographies. In selecting personages for coverage, the authors favored influential court officials and military officers, and imperial relatives (princes, princesses, empresses, and imperial consorts). Toward the end of the book, there are a number of thematic biography chapters, grouping subjects with similar characteristics: loyal subjects, filial sons, law-abiding officials, cruel officials, Confucian scholars, eminent literary figures, occultists, recluses, imperial consort relatives, and exemplary women. The last group of biography chapters is on ethnic groups and foreign peoples such as Koryŏ 高麗 (Koguryŏ; present-day northern Korea), Yamato 倭國 (in present-day Japan), and the Tujue 突厥 (early Turks). The last biography chapter is reserved for a group of treasonous characters. In line with an age-old convention, the account chapters do not feature Buddhist or Daoist clerics with the exception of the Daoist adept Xu Ze 徐則, but he is treated as a recluse, not a Daoist, which justifies his entry in the chapter on "Yinyi" 隱逸 ("Recluses"); see *Sui shu* 77:1758. Normally, the biography chapters do not include accounts of commoners except for those of "Chengjie" 誠節 ("Loyal subjects"), "Xiaoyi" 孝義 ("Filial sons"), and "Lienü" 烈

女 ("Exemplary women"), in *juan* 71, 72, and 80, where one may encounter a few short biographies of nonelite members of society.

So far as the basic annals and biographies are concerned, the *Sui shu* is relevant to the study of the Six Dynasties in that the Sui, until its conquest of Chen in 589, was the northern rival of the Chen dynasty—the last of the "legitimate" Six Dynasties regimes. So the *Sui shu* offers a northern perspective on the last phase of the Six Dynasties era, a perspective that differs from the views in such southern histories as the *Liang shu*, q.v., *Chen shu*, q.v., and *Nan shi*, q.v., all compiled during the Tang.

The greatest value of the *Sui shu* for research on the Six Dynasties era, however, lies in the second component of the book, the monographs in thirty chapters that focus on the Liang, Chen, Northern Qi, Northern Zhou, and Sui dynasties and extend their chronological coverage back into the Eastern Jin and the Northern Wei. As such, they constitute essential sources of information during these dynastic periods on the following subjects: rites and ceremonies, music, measures and calendrics, astrology, the Five Phases, food and money, punishment and law, officialdom, geography, and bibliography. Particularly worth mentioning are the four chapters that make up the monograph on bibliography ("Jingji zhi" 經籍志). It was the first such monograph still extant after the "Yiwen zhi" 藝文志 of the *Han shu* 漢書 had been completed in the first century A.D., and the single most important bibliographical source for the period of the Eastern Han to the Sui dynasties.

Authorship

In 622, on the advice of Linghu Defen, the Tang court under Gaozu (r. 618–626) launched the first official Sui history project, but nothing came of it. A second attempt was made in 629 under Taizong (r. 626–649), which resulted in producing a *Sui shu* in 636, containing the basic annals and biography chapters. The main part of these chapters was written by Yan Shigu 顏師古 (581–645), Kong Yingda 孔穎達 (574–648), and Xu Jingzong 許敬宗 (592–672). Of these authors, both Yan and Kong were highly respected scholars. The third author, Xu, was known for his extensive learning, but his reputation was tarnished because of the questionable role he played in court politics later. The editor-in-chief was Wei Zheng, Taizong's close adviser and confidant, who also penned the prefatory and end remarks that frame each of these chapters. (In reflection of his important role, the credit for the authorship or compiling of the *Sui shu* is usually stated in bibliographic references as "Wei Zheng et alia." Linghu Defen is sometimes recognized as the secondary contributor to the work.)

In 641, ten years after the completion of the first version of the court-sanctioned *Sui shu*, an imperial edict commissioned a work of monographs covering five dynasties (Liang, Chen, Northern Qi, Northern Zhou, and Sui). The project was first under the supervision of Linghu Defen, and later Zhangsun Wuji. As brother of Empress Zhangsun (Taizong's wife), the latter was a powerful official in the middle of the seventh century, and his personal involvement in the project suggests that the court attached much weight to it. The authors include Vice President of the Department of State Affairs (*zuo puye* 左僕射) Yu Zhining 于志寧 (588–665), Grand Astrologer (*taishi ling* 太史令) Li Chunfeng 李淳風 (602–670), Editorial Director (*zhuzuo lang* 著作郎) Wei Anren 韋安仁, and Court Gentleman for the Imperial Seals (*fuxi lang* 符璽郎) Li Yanshou 李延壽. When the work was completed in 656, it had a total of ten monographs in thirty chapters. As a major decision-maker at court, Yu Zhining was probably only nominally involved in the project. Among the other authors, Li Chunfeng, the leading occultist of his day, was responsible for the three relevant monographs in eight chapters: "Lüli" 律曆 ("Measures and calendrics"), "Tianwen" 天文 ("Astrology"), and "Wuxing" 五行 ("The Five Phases"); this probably explains the relatively high quality of these chapters. The editors of the *Siku quanshu zongmu tiyao** (10:1000) suspected that these three monographs were not written by Li Chunfeng, a point rejected by the modern scholar Yu Jiaxi (*Siku tiyao bianzheng*, 202–3).

Initially, these monograph chapters circulated as a stand-alone work, titled *Wudai shi zhi* 五代史志 (Monographs of the history of the Five Dynasties). Only much later did they merge into the *Sui shu* to form the integrated version.

Textual transmission

The *Jiu Tang shu* (46:1990), completed in the Later Jin (936–946), lists the *Sui shu* in its bibliographic monograph as a work of eighty-five *juan* (see also *Xin Tang shu* 58:1457), indicating that the integrated version had already made its appearance by then. Since the *Jiu Tang shu*'s monograph only catalogs titles earlier than the Tianbao reign (742–756) (*Jiu Tang shu* 46:1966), we can date the appearance of the integrated version to no later than the early 740s.

The earliest block-printed edition of the *Sui shu* is that of 1024 (Tiansheng 2), but it is no longer extant except for the postface, which is appended to the Zhonghua shuju 中華書局 edition of the *Sui shu* (p. 1903). There are two incomplete early editions dating from the Song, and two complete ones from the Yuan (*Sui shu*, "Chuban shuoming" 出版說明, p. 6). A photolithographic copy of one of the Yuan printings was included in the Baina 百衲 edition of the Twenty-four Histories published by the Shanghai Commercial Press from 1930 to 1937. Other important editions include the following.

1. The Jiguge 汲古閣 Ming edition, which is part of a Seventeen Histories set published by the bibliophile Mao Jin 毛晉 (1599–1659);

2. The Beijing National Academy Ming edition (*jianben* 監本) (1595–1606);

3. The Nanjing National Academy Ming edition (*nan jianben* 南監本) (1594–1595);

4. The Wuyingdian 武英殿 Qing edition, which is part of a Twenty-four Histories set (1747; rpt., Taipei: Yiwen yinshuguan, 1956). This is based on

earlier editions, especially the two previously listed National Academy editions.

5. The Zhonghua shuju edition (Beijing, 1973). In preparing this modern edition, the collators rigorously consulted all the previously cited extant early editions and other relevant sources. The Zhonghua edition replaced the Baina text (see earlier) as the most often consulted edition, and to this day it remains the most available and convenient edition.

For an overall account of the textual history of this and the other Six Dynasties standard histories, see appendix IV, "Textual Transmission of the Standard Histories."

Studies of the text and supplements

Cen Zhongmian 岑仲勉. *Sui shu qiushi* 隋書求是. Beijing: Shangwu yinshuguan, 1958.

Ershiwushi bubian 二十五史補編, vol. 4. Beijing: Zhonghua shuju, 1955; rpt., Taipei: Kaiming shudian, 1959. This contains a series of six studies that deal with the chronology, careers of officials and princes, geography, and bibliography of the Sui, drawing largely on the *Sui shu* but adding material from other sources.

Gardiner, K. H. J. "Standard Histories, Han to Sui." In *Essays on the Sources for Chinese History*, ed. Donald D. Leslie, Colin Mackerras, and Wang Gungwu. Columbia: University of South Carolina Press, 1973.

Sui Tang Wudai zhengshi dingbu wenxian huibian 隋唐五代正史訂補文獻彙編. Beijing: Beijing tushuguan chubanshe, 2004.

Xiong, Victor Cunrui. Introduction to *Emperor Yang of the Sui Dynasty: His Life, Times, and Legacy*. Albany, NY: SUNY Press, 2006.

Yu Jiaxi 余嘉錫. *Siku tiyao bianzheng* 四庫提要辨證. Beijing: Zhonghua shuju, 1980. Pp. 195–203.

Zhong Weilie 仲偉烈. *Sui shu diji jianzhu gao* 隋書帝紀箋注稿. Taipei: Xinwenfeng chuban shiye youxian gongsi, 2004.

Translations

Modern Chinese

Sun Yongchang 孫雍長, trans. *Sui shu*. In *Ershisishi quanyi* 二十四史全譯, ed. Xu Jialu 許嘉璐 and An Pingqiu 安平秋. Shanghai: Hanyu dacidian chubanshe, 2004.

Western languages

Hans H. Frankel compiled a bibliography of Western-language translations in *Catalogue of Translations from the Chinese Dynastic Histories for the Period 220–960*

(Berkeley: University of California Press, 1957). The most significant item for the *Sui shu* is the following:

Balazs, Étienne. *Etudes sur la société et l'économie de la Chine médiévale*. Leiden: E. J. Brill, 1953–1954. This contains two of the author's works: *Le traité économique du Souei-chou*, first appearing in *T'oung Pao* 42.3–4 (1953): 113–329, and *Le traité juridique du Souei-chou*, Bibliothèque de l'Institut des hautes études chinoises 9. These are annotated translations of *juan* 24 and 25 of the *Sui shu*.

Index

Deng Jingyuan 鄧經元. *Sui shu renming suoyin* 隋書人名索引. Beijing: Zhonghua shuju, 1979.

Victor Cunrui Xiong

Sun Chuo ji 孫綽集

Introduction

Sun Chuo, styled Xinggong 興公 (ca. 314–ca. 371), was descended from a distinguished family of officials and scholars, the Suns of Zhongdu 中都 (modern Pingyao 平遙 District, Shanxi). Around 309 the family moved to the south and settled in the Kuaiji 會稽 region (central Zhejiang). As a youth, Sun Chuo spent more than ten years at leisure in this scenic region, keeping aloof from official involvement and developing an attachment to Daoist and Buddhist beliefs that lasted throughout his life. He had an especially close relationship with Xu Xun 許詢 (300?–356?); both men were skilled writers of a form of philosophical verse known as *xuanyan shi* 玄言詩 (metaphysical poetry). Another close associate was the renowned monk Zhi Dun 支遁 (314–366), who became Sun's guide in Buddhist thought. Once Sun entered official service, his success was swift. He was ennobled as marquis of Changle (Changle *hou* 長樂侯), and he successively held numerous provincial offices, as well as positions at court at the middle and upper ranks. Toward the end of his life, Sun achieved his highest position, chief minister for law enforcement (*tingwei qing* 廷尉卿), and this title was subsequently attached to his collected writings. He died at the age of fifty-eight *sui*.

Helmut Wilhelm has observed that the remarkably successful career of Sun Chuo was due above all to "his serious attempt to integrate in a consistent way the various trends of thought current in his period" ("A Note on Sun Ch'o," 265). In both his life and writings, Sun strove to combine Daoist and Buddhist ideas with Confucianist tenets, postulating the fundamental oneness of the Way in different spiritual traditions while doing justice to the peculiarities of the various schools. Sun Chuo's biography, in *Jin shu*, q.v., 56:1544–47, is appended to that of his grandfather Sun Chu 孫楚 (ca. 218–293) and draws heavily on numerous anecdotes contained in the *Shishuo xinyu*, q.v.

Contents

The earliest extant edition of the *Sun Tingwei ji* 孫廷尉集 in two *juan* is contained in the late-Ming anthology *Qishi'er jia ji** compiled by Zhang Xie (1574–1640). Another edition, in one *juan*, was included as *juan* 61 of Zhang Pu's (1602–1641) *Han Wei Liuchao baisanjia ji*, q.v. Zhang Xie's edition contains forty works arranged in the following generic order:

1. Rhapsodies, 3
2. Lyric Poems, including fragments, 7
3. Proposal to the Throne (*shu* 疏), 2
4. Disquisition, 1
5. Preface, 1
6. Epitaphs, 6
7. Eulogy, 1
8. Encomiums, 14
9. Inscriptions, 3
10. Dirges, 2

A short colophon (*tici* 題詞) by Zhang Xie precedes the collection. Appended are Sun Chuo's biography, anecdotes from the *Shishuo xinyu* and the *Jin shu*, and a selection of critical comments on his writings. This collection provided the basis for Zhang Pu's edition, which contains thirty-five pieces since he excluded five of the encomia on Buddhist monks. Zhang Pu prefaced the collection with a colophon and appended it with Sun Chuo's biography but arranged the genres somewhat differently, placing lyric poetry last.

Sun Chuo's best-known work is "You Tiantai shan fu" 遊天台山賦 (Rhapsody on roaming the Celestial Terrace Mountains), an account of a mystical ascent of the sacred mountains in eastern Zhejiang in which Daoist and Buddhist concepts and lore are smoothly blended together. His largest and most important prose piece is "Yudao lun" 喻道論 (Disquisition on elucidating the Way). In it, Sun expounds the idea of fundamental unity between Buddhism and Confucianism and attempts to reconcile the two traditions—on such topics as retribution, temporality, and filial piety.

Sun Chuo achieved considerable renown as an author of funerary texts and was commissioned to compose epitaphs and dirges for the most distinguished personalities of his day. Among the epitaphs preserved in the collection are those for the military strongman and Sun's early patron Yu Liang 庾亮 (289–340), for Wang Dao 王導 (276–339), and for Grand Marshal Chi Jian 郗鑒 (269–339).

Sources of the work

Ming editions of Sun Chuo's writings had been compiled through gathering up single works and fragments scattered in various sources. Most important of the pre-Tang sources are the *Wen xuan* anthology, q.v., which in *juan* 11 contains the complete "You Tiantai shan fu"; the sixth-century collection of Buddhist apologetic literature *Hongming ji*, q.v., which in *juan* 3 contains the "Yudao lun"; and the *Gaoseng zhuan*, q.v., by Hui Jiao (d. 554), *juan* 1, 4, and 5 containing Sun's encomia on Buddhist monks. The text of the "Jian yi du Luoyang shu" 諫移都洛陽疏 (Formal address admonishing against moving the capital to Luoyang) is included in Sun Chuo's biography. Further pieces of poetry and prose are contained in the Tang encyclopaedias *Yiwen leiju*, q.v., and *Chuxue ji*, q.v., and in the Song's *Taiping yulan*, q.v. The poetry section of the *Sun Tingwei ji* is based on the earlier Ming anthology *Gushi ji** by Feng Weine (1512–1572), where seven of Sun's poems are included in *juan* 42.5b–7b and 43.3b (*Yingyin Wenyuange Siku quanshu** 1379.342–43 and 350).

Authorship and date of composition

Cao Daoheng questions Sun Chuo's authorship of some of the encomia on Buddhist monks who died after his probable life dates ("Jindai zuojia liukao," 187–88). Of dubious authenticity according to him are the encomia for Shi Dao'an 釋道安 (d. 385), Zhu Daoyi 竺道壹 (d. between 397 and 401), and Zhu Fatai 竺法汰 (d. 387). Cao supposes that these encomia were written by Sun Chuo's nephew Sun Teng 騰, who also achieved the title of *tingwei* (biography in *Jin shu* 56:1544, following that of Sun Tong 統).

Transmission and early history of the text

The compositions gathered in the two Ming anthologies are only a small fragment of Sun Chuo's original corpus. The bibliographic monograph of the *Sui shu*, q.v. (35:1067), lists a *Sun Chuo ji* in fifteen *juan* but apparently a part of Sun's writings had already been lost, for the commentary mentions a Liang edition in twenty-five *juan*. In addition, *Sui shu* 34:1002 lists separately a Daoist work titled *Sunzi* 孫子 in twelve *juan*. In other sections of the bibliography, we find *Zhiren gaoshi zhuan zan* 至人高士傳讚 (Encomia on the lives of accomplished men and eminent gentlemen) in two *juan* (33:975), *Liexian zhuan zan* 列仙傳讚 (Encomia on the lives of arrayed immortals) in three *juan* (33:979), and a *Lun yu* commentary, *Jijie Lun yu* 集解論語 (Collected explanations of the *Lun yu*) in ten *juan*. The fifteen-*juan* edition of Sun's collected works, his commentary to the *Lun yu* and *Sunzi* in twelve *juan* are also entered in the *Jiu Tang shu*'s bibliographic chapters (47:2065, 46:1981, and 47:2029, respectively) and in the *Xin Tang shu* (60:1588, 57:1443, and 59:1516, respectively). The *Zhiren gaoshi zhuan zan* and the *Liexian zhuan zan* are not listed and probably had been lost during the Tang.

In addition, Sun Chuo is credited with composing the *Mingde shamen lun mu* 名德沙門論目 (Comments on famed and virtuous monks), a work mentioned in Sengyou's 僧祐 (445–518) *Chu sanzang ji ji* 出三藏記集 15:565 (Beijing: Zhonghua shuju, 1995). Liu Jun's 劉峻 (462–521) commentary to the *Shishuo xinyu* gives the variant title *Mingde shamen ti mu* 名德沙門題目 several times without, however, mentioning Sun's authorship ("Dong Jin shiren Sun Chuo kaoyi," 210). Another lost composition, the "Dao xian lun" 道賢論 (Disquisition on monks and sages), is quoted in the *Gaoseng zhuan*, *juan* 1 and 4. In this essay, Sun groups together seven famous Buddhists of his day and equates them with the "Seven Sages of the Bamboo Grove." *Gaoseng zhuan* 4 also cites Sun's lost "Zhengxiang lun" 正像論 (Disquisition on the correct image).

Principal editions

No modern edition of the *Sun Tingwei ji* as such exists. Widely available reissues of Sun's collection in anthologies include the following:

Sun Tingwei ji. Two *juan*; appendix, one *juan*. In *Qishi'erjia ji*, compiled by
    Zhang Xie. Late-Ming (1621–1644) woodblock edition held in the Beijing

Library, Library of the National Palace Museum (Taipei), and other rare book collections. Photofacsimile reprint of *Qishi'erjia ji* in *Xuxiu Siku quanshu* 1585:136–60.

Sun Tingwei ji. One *juan*. In *Han Wei Liuchao baisanjia ji*, compiled by Zhang Pu. Photofacsimile reprint of late-Qing woodblock edition (1879) published by Jiangsu guji chubanshe (6 vols., Nanjing, 2002), 3:205–24.

Sun Tingwei jixuan 孫廷尉集選. One *juan*. A selection of seven prose compositions in Wu Rulun's (1840–1903) *Han Wei Liuchao baisanjia jixuan* 漢魏六朝百三家集選, an anthology whose contents draw upon Zhang Pu's compilation. Originally published in 1917; rpt., 16 vols., Hangzhou: Zhejiang guji chubanshe, 1985.

Major recensions

Qing dynasty scholars added more surviving fragments to the Ming collections of Sun Chuo's writings. Yan Kejun (1762–1843) identified fragments of ten more compositions, which include twenty-three excerpts from the *Sunzi*, two excerpts from the *Mingde shamen lun mu*, six excerpts from the "Dao xian lun," and three opinions (*yi* 議); see "Quan Jin wen," *juan* 61–62, of *Quan shanggu Sandai Qin Han Sanguo Liuchao wen*, q.v. (punctuated, simplified-character edition by Shijiazhuang: Hebei jiaoyu chubanshe, 1997; 4:633–49). Thirty-one fragments from Sun's commentary on the *Lun yu* are contained in Ma Guohan's 馬國翰 (1794–1857) *Yuhan shanfang ji yishu* 玉函山房輯佚書, 1735–1741 (reprint of 1883 woodblock edition by Shanghai guji chubanshe, 1990). The complete text of Sun Chuo's "Jiangzhou dudu Yu Bing beiming" 江州都督庾冰碑銘 (Epitaphic inscription for Yu Bing, commander-in-chief of Jiangzhou), a mere fragment of which is provided by Zhang Xie, Zhang Pu, and Yan Kejun, is contained in the partially reconstructed Tang anthology *Wenguan cilin**, *juan* 457. *Wenguan cilin*, *juan* 157, additionally contains twenty-eight previously lost four-syllable poems by Sun: "Zeng Wen Qiao" 贈溫嶠 (Presented to Wen Qiao), five verses; "Yu Yu Bing" 與庾冰 (For Yu Bing), thirteen verses; "Da Xu Xun" 答許詢 (Response to Xu Xun), nine verses; and "Zeng Xie An" 贈謝安 (Presented to Xie An), one verse. Ding Fubao included these poems in "Quan Jin shi," 5:12a–15a (1:571–77) of *Quan Han Sanguo Jin Nanbeichao shi**. The most complete collection of Sun's lyrical poetry, amounting to thirty-seven pieces, is in "Jin shi," *juan* 13 (2:896–902) of Lu Qinli's *Xian Qin Han Wei Jin Nanbeichao shi**. A collection of all Sun's surviving prose and poetry, based upon the editions of Lu Qinli and Yan Kejun, but expanded with additional fragments and supplied with annotations, is in Jiang Xiaoli's 姜曉麗 unpublished master's thesis, "*Sun Chuo ji* jiaozhu" 校注 (Dongbei shifan daxue, 2005).

Traditional assessments

Sun Chuo was praised in his day as the "crown of literary men" and much admired for his broad learning and talent (*Jin shu* 56:1544, 1547). Together with Xu Xun, he was a major exponent of *xuanyan* poetry, the two becoming the "literary models for the entire age" (*yishi wenzong* 一時文宗). In the *Xu Jin Yangqiu* 續晉陽秋, Tan Daoluan 檀道鸞 (fl. fifth century) credited Sun with enriching contemporary *xuanyan* verse with Buddhist terminology and ideas. His appraisal was quoted in the commentary by Liu Jun to the *Shishuo xinyu*; see *juan* 4, no. 85, in Yu Jiaxi 余嘉錫, *Shishuo xinyu jianshu* 世說新語箋疏, 262 (Beijing: Zhonghua shuju, 1983); also, trans. Richard B. Mather, *Shih-shuo Hsin-yu: A New Account of Tales of the World*, 145 (2nd ed., Ann Arbor: Center for Chinese Studies, University of Michigan, 2002).

When this philosophical type of verse fell out of fashion a century later, however, Sun's poetry began to be judged unfavorably. In the *Shi pin*, q.v., Zhong Rong relegated Sun to the third and lowest ranking, which reflected his low opinion of *xuanyan* verse in general. Numerous comments on Sun's writings and personality are contained in the *Shishuo xinyu*. A selection of these, as well as comments from the *Wenxin diaolong*, q.v., and *Xu Jin yang qiu*, were appended to Zhang Xie's *Sun Tingwei ji*. The colophons to Sun's collection by Zhang Xie and Zhang Pu also provide assessments. For the "You Tiantai shan fu," which was included in *juan* 11 of the *Wen xuan*, traditional commentaries to that anthology are an important resource.

Selected studies

Cao Daoheng 曹道衡. "Jindai zuojia liukao" 晉代作家六考. *Wen shi* 20 (1983): 185–94.

Fukunaga Mitsuji 福永光司. "Son Shaku no shisō—Tōshin ni okeru Sankyō kōshō no ichi keitai" 孫綽の思想—東晉における三教交渉の一形態. *Aichi gakugei daigaku kenkyū hōkoku, Jimbun kagaku* 10 (1961.2): 131–44.

Hachiya Kunio 蜂屋邦夫. "Son Shaku no shōgai to shisō" 孫綽の生涯と思想. *Tōyō bunka* 57 (1977): 65–100. Chinese translation: "Sun Chuo de shengping he sixiang" 孫綽的生平和思想. In *Daojia sixiang yu fojiao* 道家思想與佛教, 114–53. Shenyang: Liaoning jiaoyu chubanshe, 2000.

Hasegawa Shigenari 長谷川滋成. "Son Shaku shōden" 孫綽小伝. *Chūgoku chūsei bungaku kenkyū* 20 (1991): 74–91.

———. *Son Shaku no kenkyū: Risō no 'michi' ni akogareru shijin* 孫綽の研究: 理想の道に憧れる詩人. Tokyo: Kyūko shoin, 1999.

Kirkova, Zornica. "Distant Roaming and Visionary Ascent: Sun Chuo's 'You Tiantai shan fu' Reconsidered." *Oriens Extremus* 47 (2008): 192–214.

Li Wenchu 李文初. "Dong Jin shiren Sun Chuo kaoyi" 東晉詩人孫綽考議. *Wen shi* 28 (1987): 207–20.

Mather, Richard B. "The Mystical Ascent of the T'ien-t'ai Mountains: Sun Ch'o's *Yu-t'ien-t'ai-shan fu*." *Monumenta Serica* 20 (1961): 226–45. Includes a well-annotated translation.

Wilhelm, Helmut. "A Note on Sun Ch'o and His Yu-tao-lun." *Sino-Indian Studies* 5 (1957): 261–71.

Zhao Li 趙莉. "Sun Chuo yanjiu" 孫綽研究. Master's thesis, Zhengzhou University, 2007.

Translations

English

Chang, Kang-i Sun. Translation of "Da Xu Xun," no. 1. In *Six Dynasties Poetry*, 5–6. Princeton, NJ: Princeton University Press, 1986.

Frodsham, John D. Translation of "Qiuri shi" 秋日詩. In "The Origins of Chinese Nature Poetry," *Asia Major* 8 (1960–61): 79.

Holzman, Donald. Translation of "Da Xu Xun," no. 3. In *Landscape Appreciation in Ancient and Early Medieval China: The Birth of Landscape Poetry*, 136–37. Hsin-chu, Taiwan: National Tsing Hua University, 1996. Rpt. in *Chinese Literature in Transition from Antiquity to the Middle Ages*. Aldershot, UK: Ashgate, 1998.

Knechtges, David R. "Rhapsody on Roaming the Celestial Terrace Mountains." In *Wen Xuan or Selections of Refined Literature*, 2:243–53. Princeton, NJ: Princeton University Press, 1987. Well-annotated.

Link, Arthur E., and Tim Lee. "Sun Ch'o's 'Yü-tao-lun': A Clarification of the Way." *Monumenta Serica* 25 (1966): 169–96.

Owen, Stephen. "Wandering to the Tian-tai Mountains." In *An Anthology of Chinese Literature: Beginnings to 1911*, 184–88. New York: Norton, 1996.

Watson, Burton. "Wandering on Mount T'ien-t'ai." In *Chinese Rhyme-prose: Poems in the Fu Form from the Han and Six Dynasties Periods*, 162–71. New York: Columbia University Press, 1971.

European languages

Boevaia, I. M., and E.A. Torchinov. "Sun Chuo's 'You Tiantai shan fu.'" In *Religii Kitaia: Khrestomatiia* [Religions of China: An anthology], ed. E. A. Torchinov, 89–96. Saint Petersberg, Russia: Evrazia, 2001.

Kubin, Wolfgang. Translation of "Qiuri shi." In *Der durchsichtige Berg: Die Entwicklung der Naturanschauung in der chinesischen Literatur*, 156. Stuttgart: Franz Steiner Verlag Wiesbaden GMBH, 1985.

Lomova, Olga. Translation of "Qiuri shi." In *Poselství krajiny: Obraz přírody v díle tchangského básníka Wang Weje*. Prague: DharmaGaia, 1999.

Zach, Erwin von. "Die Wanderung über den T'ien-t'ai-Berg." In *Die chinesische Anthologie: Übersetzungen aus dem Wen hsüan*, ed. Ilse Martin Fong, 1:159–62. 2 vols. Harvard-Yenching Studies 18. Cambridge, MA: Harvard University Press, 1958.

Japanese

Hasegawa Shigenari 長谷川滋成. *Son Shaku shi yakuchū, fu sakuin* 孫綽詩訳注, 附索引. Yashiro-chō, Hyōgo-ken, 1990. Translation and annotation of poetry with index.

———. *Son Shaku bun yakuchū* 孫綽文訳注. Higashi-Hiroshima: Hiroshima daigaku kyōikugakubu kokugo kyōikugaku kenkyūshitsu, 1996. Translation and annotation of prose.

Obi Kōichi 小尾郊一 and Hanabusa Hideki 花房英樹. Translation of "You Tiantai shan fu" in *Monzen* 文選, 2:65–67. 33 vols. Zenshaku Kanbun taikei 全釋漢文大系 26–32. Tokyo: Shueisha, 1974–1976.

Research aid

Mu Kehong 穆克宏. *Wei Jin Nanbeichao wenxue shiliao shulüe* 魏晉南北朝文學史料述略. Beijing: Zhonghua shuju, 1997. Pp. 77–78. Lists major editions of Sun Chuo's works.

Zornica Kirkova

Taiping yulan 太平御覽

Introduction

The *Taiping yulan* (Imperial digest of the reign of Great Tranquillity), compiled under the supervision of Li Fang 李昉 (925–996), belongs to a set of four major works commissioned during the reigns of emperors Taizong (r. 976–997) and Zhenzong (r. 998–1022). Two of these are *leishu* 類書 (encyclopedias), the *Taiping yulan* and the *Cefu yuangui* 冊府元龜, whereas the other two, the *Wenyuan yinghua** and the *Taiping guangji* 太平廣記, are viewed as anthologies. The *Taiping yulan* may be regarded as an effort to gather all knowledge from existing works that endured the turbulent period of the Five Dynasties, during which the survival of books and libraries had been precarious. It stands in a tradition of imperially commissioned encyclopedias that started with the *Huanglan* 皇覽 (ca. 220) and continued with the *Xiuwendian yulan* 修文殿御覽 (572), the *Yiwen leiju* (624), q.v., and the *Wensi boyao* 文思博要 (641).

One of the significant features of classical Chinese encyclopedias is their categorizing transmitted knowledge and preserving bits and pieces of works that otherwise have been lost. At the time of compilation, the scholars working on the *Taiping yulan* had only limited access to original texts due to the upheavals at the end of the Tang and during the Five Dynasties period that resulted in the destruction of books and libraries. Many of the old texts quoted in the *Taiping yulan* hence have been copied from entries found in previous encyclopedias. The major feature that the *Taiping yulan* shares with its predecessors is its arrangement of categories and subcategories in an attempt to describe and capture the known world in writing.

Contents

The *Taiping yulan*'s table of contents alone is fifteen *juan* in length. Starting with "Heaven" and ending with "Plants," it is arranged into fifty-five categories in one thousand *juan*. It provides information on such diverse topics as political and bureaucratic practices, religion, non-Chinese peoples, things metaphysical, animals, and plants. The main categories are heaven (*tian* 天), seasons (*shixu* 時序), earth (*di* 地), emperors and kings (*huangwang* 皇王), usurpers and hegemons (*pianba* 偏霸), the imperial family (*huangqin* 皇親), provinces and prefectures (*zhoujun* 州郡), lodgings (*juchu* 居處), enfeoffments (*fengjian* 封建), bureaucracy (*zhiguan* 職官),

the military (*bing* 兵), human affairs (*renshi* 人事), hermits (*yimin* 逸民), relatives (*zongqin* 宗親), ceremonies and rites (*liyi* 禮儀), music (*yue* 樂), literature (*wen* 文), study (*xue* 學), administration (*zhidao* 治道), law (*xingfa* 刑法), Buddhism (*shi* 釋), Daoism (*dao* 道), ceremonies (*yishi* 儀式), clothing (*fuzhang* 服章), accessories (*fuyong* 服用), divinatory, medical, and other techniques (*fangshu* 方術), diseases (*jibing* 疾病), handicraft (*gongyi* 工藝), utensils (*qiwu* 器物), miscellaneous things (*zawu* 雜物), vessels (*zhou* 舟), vehicles (*che* 車), appointing envoys (*feng shi* 奉使), barbarians (*siyi* 四夷), precious things (*zhenbao* 珍寶), cloth and silk (*bubo* 布帛), trade and agriculture (*zichan* 資產), cereals (*baigu* 百穀), beverages and food (*yinshi* 飲食), fire (*huo* 火), auspicious omens (*xiuzheng* 休徵), inauspicious omens (*jiuzheng* 咎徵), spirits and demons (*shengui* 神鬼), extraordinary phenomena (*yaoyi* 妖異), quadrupeds (*shou* 獸), feathered animals (*yuzu* 羽族), animals with scales (*linjie* 麟介), insects and worms (*chongzhi* 蟲豸), wood (*mu* 木), bamboo (*zhu* 竹), fruit (*guo* 果), vegetables (*cai* 菜), incense (*xiang* 香), medicines (*yao* 葯), and plants (*baihui* 百卉).

Authorship

The *Taiping yulan* was the product of the collaboration of several scholars who worked under the direction of Li Fang. Half of the compilers had been officials of the state of Jiangnan that the Song conquered in 975. Upon the death of the first Song emperor Taizu in the following year, and the accession of his younger brother, Emperor Taizong, southerners were given a chance to prove their qualities as officials of the Song. The southerners employed in the compilation of the *Taiping yulan* were Tang Yue 湯悅 (a.k.a. Yin Chongyi 殷崇義; dates unknown), Xu Xuan 徐鉉 (917–992), Zhang Ji 張洎 (937–997), Wu Shu 吳淑 (947–1002), Shu Ya 舒雅 (before 940–1009), Lü Wenzhong 呂文仲 (dates unknown), and Ruan Sidao 阮思道 (dates unknown). The northerners apart from Li Fang were Hu Meng 扈蒙 (915–986), Li Mu 李穆 (928–985), and Song Bai 宋白 (933–1009). Another collaborator was Chen E 陳鄂 (dates unknown), who had been in the service of the state of Later Shu that was subdued in 966. No personal information is available on Li Keqin 李克勤 and Xu Yongbin 徐用賓, who are also listed as participating in the compilation of the *Taiping yulan* (Wang, *Yu hai*, 54:40a–41b, p. 453).

Origin and authenticity

Soon after succeeding to the throne in 976, Taizong remarked that he needed a new guide for government since older works were cumbersome to use. In April 977 an imperial order commanded the compilation of a book of one thousand *juan* that was to be based primarily on previous encyclopedias, such as the *Xiuwen dian yulan*, *Yiwen leiju*, *Wensi boyao*, and other works, and a reorganization of material contained therein. It is because of the nature of the source material of the *Taiping yulan* that Chen Zhensun (fl. 1211–after 1249) critically remarked:

> Once someone said to me: "At the start of the [Song] dynasty many old books were not yet lost." This statement is based on the [*Taiping*] *yulan*

quoting old book titles. As a matter of fact that is not correct, for it does quote especially from previous encyclopaedias. This is apparent from the entry in the *Sanchao guoshi* 三朝國史. The books held by the imperial libraries and within the palace [archives] only numbered somewhat more than 36,000 *juan*.[1] Many of the books quoted in the *Taiping yulan* were not listed at all [neither in the imperial libraries nor in the palace archives]. That is quite evident. (*Zhizhai shulu jieti** 14:425)

The point made here by Chen Zhensun is important because the compilation work was done in the newly established imperial library, which really did not measure up to previous libraries. The work on the *Taiping yulan* began even before the library moved in 978 to new and more spacious premises. As a matter of fact, many of the books that the editors were working with originated from the libraries of conquered states in the south, such as Shu (in Sichuan) and Jiangnan. Chen Zhensun's statement also explains why the categories of the *Taiping yulan* appear to have been copied in their majority from earlier encyclopedias, especially the *Yiwen leiju*.

Transmission of the text

The most likely working title of the *Taiping yulan* was *Taiping zonglei* 太平總類. When the work was submitted on 5 January 984 (*Yu hai* 54:41b, p. 453), from the next day, Taizong started reading the work at a rate of three *juan* each day. He finished reading a year later; consequently, the encyclopaedia was given the present title on 25 January 985 and was shelved in the palace library (Qian, *Song Taizong shilu*, 19).

The text was first listed in *Chongwen zongmu** 3:52a (p. 402), the official catalog of the imperial library compiled between 1034 and 1041, as well as in catalogs of private book collections of the Southern Song such as the *Suichutang shumu** (24) and the *Zhizhai shulu jieti** (14:425), and encyclopedias such as the *Tong zhi** (69:814b) and the *Wenxian tongkao** (228:1828), from the early Yuan dynasty.

Principal editions

After the *Taiping yulan* had been placed in the palace library, a first printing of the encyclopedia may or may not have occurred during the reign of Emperor Renzong (r. 1022–1063). The earliest editions found are the Min 閩 edition, dating from before the Qingyuan era (1195–1200), and the Shu 蜀 edition, from slightly later. Both were incomplete and missing different *juan*. The scholar Zhang Jinwu 張金吾 (1787–1829) possessed fragments of a Song print of *juan* 201–205 as well as 211 that were believed to have come from the Min edition. These fragments were

---

[1] Li Tao 李燾 (1115–1184) refers to only 12,000 *juan* in 960; after the establishment of a new imperial library under emperor Taizong in 978, there were 80,000 *juan* including multiple copies of works and other documents. See *Xu zizhi tongjian changbian* 續資治通鑒長編 (Taipei: Shijie shuju, 1983), 19:2b–3a, p. 225.

thus incorporated into the Min edition, increasing its total number of *juan* to 357 (Hu, *Zhongguo gudai de leishu*, 129–33).

In 1928 Zhang Yuanji 張元濟 (1867–1959) of the Commercial Press in Shanghai went to Japan and found a Shu edition that was almost complete. He asked and received permission to copy the 945 *juan* preserved of the main work. At the Seikadō bunko 靜嘉堂文庫 he discovered another Song edition, the Jian 建 edition, and copied a total of twenty-nine *juan* (42–61, and 117–25) to supplement the *juan* he already had. To make up for the still-missing *juan*, Zhang turned to a movable type, printed edition from Ming times that had also been in Japan and closely resembled the Shu edition. In December 1935, the Commercial Press in Shanghai photolithographically published the resulting work in 136 volumes within the *Sibu congkan* sanbian* 三編. The Zhonghua shuju in 1960 reissued this edition in one thousand *juan*.

Bibliography and selected studies

Guo Bogong 郭伯恭. *Song si dashu kao* 宋四大書考. Shanghai: Shangwu yinshuguan, 1940.

Haeger, John W. "The Significance of Confusion: The Origins of the *T'ai-p'ing yü-lan*." *Journal of the American Oriental Society* 88 (1968): 401–10.

Hu Daojing 胡道靜. *Zhongguo gudai de leishu* 中國古代的類書. Beijing: Zhonghua shuju, 1982.

Kurz, Johannes L. "The Politics of Collecting Knowledge: The Compilations Project of Song Taizong." *T'oung Pao* 87.1 (2001): 289–316.

———. *Das Kompilationsprojekt Song Taizongs (reg. 976–997)*. Bern: Peter Lang, 2003. Pp. 51–87.

———. "The Compilation and Publication of the *Taiping yulan* and the *Cefu yuangui*." In *Extrême-orient, extrême-occident: Qu'était-ce qu'écrire une encyclopédie en Chine? (What did it mean to write an encyclopedia in China?)*, ed. Florence Bretelle-Etablet and Karine Chemla, 39–76. Saint Denis, France: Presses Universitaires de Vincennes, 2007.

Lewin, Günter. "*T'ai-p'ing yü-lan*." In *A Sung Bibliography (Bibliographie des Song)*, ed. Yves Hervouet, 319–20. Hong Kong: The Chinese University of Hong Kong, 1978.

Qian Ruoshui 錢若水 (960–1003) et al., comps. *Song Taizong shilu* 宋太宗實錄. Lanzhou: Gansu renmin chubanshe, 2005.

Wang Yinglin 王應麟 (1223–1296), comp. *Yu hai* 玉海. Shanghai: Shanghai guji chubanshe, 1992.

Zhou Shengjie 周生傑. *Taiping yulan yanjiu* 太平御覽研究. Chengdu: Ba Shu shushe, 2008.

Indices

T'ai-p'ing yülan yin-te 太平御覽引得. Harvard-Yenching Institute Sinological Index Series 23. Beijing, 1935; rpt., Taipei: Chengwen Publishing, 1966.

Taiping yulan suoyin 太平御覽索引. Comp. Ch'ien Ya-hsin 錢亞新. Shanghai: Shangwu yinshuguan, 1934.

Taiping yulan yinde, Taiping guangji yinde 太平御覽引得, 太平廣記引得. Comp. Nie Chongqi 聶崇岐 et al.. Shanghai: Shanghai guji chubanshe, 1990.

Translation

August Pfitzmaier translated various entries from the work in the 1860s and 1870s. These have been critically reviewed by Richard Trappl, "Pfitzmaiers Übersetzung der chinesischen Enzyklopädie *Taiping Yulan*," in *August Pfitzmaier (1808–1887) und seine Bedeutung für die Ostasienwissenschaften*, ed. Otto Ladstaetter and Sepp Linhart, 165–82. Vienna: Verlag der Österreichischen Akademie der Wissenschaften, 1990.

Johannes L. Kurz

Tao Yuanming ji 陶淵明集

Introduction

The *Tao Yuanming ji* is a collection of the writings of Tao Qian 陶潛, styled Yuanming (365?–427), a poet who lived toward the end of the Eastern Jin dynasty. According to his biography in *Song shu*, q.v., 93:2286–90, some sources said his name was Yuanming and his style name was Yuanliang 元亮. Tao was the great-grandson of Tao Kan 侃 (259–334), a native of south China and a powerful statesman and general. By Tao Yuanming's time the family had lost much of its former political influence, but it was still considered a prominent southern family, with many of its members holding official positions. Tao Yuanming himself was appointed to a number of minor official posts, at one point serving as the magistrate of Pengze 彭澤, a county not far from his native town, Xunyang 潯陽 (in modern Jiangxi). He was not happy there. In 405, at the death of his younger sister, he resigned and never again took another official post. He spent the rest of his life living in reclusion, although he kept up his social contacts as many Chinese recluses did. He associated with men who were either recluses like himself or local or court officials. One of his friends was Yan Yanzhi 顏延之 (384–456), a celebrated poet of the day who wrote a dirge for Tao Yuanming after he passed away.

Contents

The standard collection of Tao Yuanming's writings consists of three parts: poetry in four-syllable lines, poetry in five-syllable lines, and prose. Tao left about 130 poems, many of which are about his life in reclusion, and a handful of prose pieces. These prose pieces include, among other items, a famous account of the Peach Blossom Fount (*Taohua yuan ji* 桃花源記), a thinly-veiled autobiography, "The Biography of Master Five Willows" ("Wuliu xiansheng zhuan" 五柳先生傳), a letter to his sons, and a "Sacrificial Address to Myself" ("Ziji wen" 自祭文), a singular example in the genre of sacrificial address that is usually directed to some person other than oneself, and a deceased person at that.

Often dropped from modern editions of Tao Yuanming's collection, but included in many premodern editions, are two works whose authenticity came into question as late as the eighteenth century (see later discussion). These two works are *A Category of Fours and Eights* (*Siba mu* 四八目), also known as *A Record of Sages, Worthies, and Their Various Assistants* (*Shengxian qunfu lu* 聖賢群輔錄), and

The Biographies of Five Filial Pieties (*Wuxiao zhuan* 五孝傳). The first work is a list of famous (and, in a few cases, notorious) figures from antiquity down to the early fourth century. The personages are often grouped in fours or eights, such as "The Four Friends of Confucius"; hence, the title of the work. After listing their names, the author gives a brief description of who they were and cites the sources, such as "See the *Analects*." For those who lived into the fourth century, the author notes: "I have heard about them in recent years from the elders." *The Biographies of Five Filial Pieties* is a list of filial sons, divided into five sections: emperors, princes, ministers, gentry members, and commoners. In each section, the author briefly describes the filial sons and ends the section with an encomium (*zan* 贊) in four-syllable lines. An anomaly account, the *Xu Soushen ji* 續搜神記, is attributed to Tao Yuanming but usually exists independently from his collected writings (*ji* 集).

Sources of the work

While many early medieval literary writings are preserved in dynastic histories, encyclopedias, anthologies, and other sources, only reassembled together into independent collections in late imperial times, the collection of Tao Yuanming is one of the few pre-Tang literary collections that have survived more or less intact. All manuscript copies of Tao's collection from the pre-Song period (i.e., before printing began to flourish) are lost, but several Southern Song printed editions, believed to be based on Northern Song editions, which would in turn have been based on manuscript copies from the Tang dynasty, are still extant in the original form or as reprints or both.

Authorship and date of composition

There are only a few pieces in the collection whose authenticity can be questioned. Number 6 of "Returning To Dwell in Gardens and Fields" ("Gui yuantian ju" 歸園田居) has been widely recognized as an imitation by Jiang Yan 江淹 (444–505) that got mixed into Tao's famous poetic series. There is doubt about another poem, "Inquiring of the Messenger" ("Wen laishi" 問來使), since it mentions Mount Tianmu in Zhejiang Province as the poet's home region, a piece of information that does not fit Tao's biographical data. According to Cai Tao 蔡絛 (fl. 1124), this poem had appeared in a Southern Tang manuscript of unknown provenance, as well as one in the possession of Chao Jiong 晁迥 (951–1034). One of Li Bai's 李白 (701–762) poems, "Stirred by Autumn at Xunyang" ("Xunyang ganqiu shi" 潯陽感秋詩), echoes the last couplet of this poem and associates it with Tao Yuanming. If Li Bai was indeed alluding to "Inquiring of the Messenger" as some believe, then it demonstrates that as early as the eighth century this poem was already included in some editions of Tao Yuanming's collection. Interestingly, a Southern Song printed edition notes that this poem was forged in the late Tang, based on the aforementioned Li Bai poem. It is impossible to verify whether Li Bai's poem was based on what he believed to be a Tao Yuanming poem or whether a poem based on Li Bai's poem was attributed to Tao Yuanming.

Another poem, more precisely an encomium in five-syllable lines, "An Encomium on Shang Chang and Qin Qing" ("Shang Chang Qin Qing zan" 尚長禽慶贊), is attributed to Tao Yuanming in the early Tang encyclopedia *Yiwen leiju*, q.v., compiled in 624, but is not included in the standard Tao Yuanming collection, which is most likely incomplete.

One of the prose pieces in the ten-*juan* collection, *A Category of Fours and Eights*, though attributed to Tao as early as in the sixth century, was designated as inauthentic by the Qing emperor Qianlong, on the basis that some of the personages included in this list of "sages and worthies and their assistants" were rebels against the ruling dynasty, and as such they could not possibly have been endorsed by Tao Yuanming, himself a loyalist. His Majesty's view was eagerly followed by the editors of the *Siku quanshu* in their *Siku quanshu zongmu tiyao**, 29:3106–7. The *Siku* editors also disputed the authenticity of *The Biographies of Five Filial Pieties* for the reason that it is "vulgar and shallow." Once again, there is no good textual evidence to back up either claim. Circumstantial evidence in fact points to a high level of credibility for Tao's being the author.

A number of Tao Yuanming's writings are dated. In the case of some poems, the date of composition appears as part of the poem's title. This is an unusual practice; prior to Tao, except for poems composed on memorable occasions such as the third day of the third month, a traditional festival, poets rarely embedded the date of composition in a poem title. There have been numerous speculations and theories about the chronology of Tao's life as well as his dates, despite the fact that the year of his death and his age at death were recorded in his biography. The dates of composition that appear in his writings are often used to support or dispute such speculations. Sometimes textual variants complicate the problem of dating; other times, however, commentators and scholars resort to emending a text to corroborate a date they hypothesize.

Transmission and early history of the text

Tao Yuanming's writings were widely circulated in his lifetime and in the centuries after his death. In the pre-Tang period, there were a six-*juan* edition and an eight-*juan* edition, the latter described by Yang Xiuzhi 陽休之 (509–582) as "disorganized and incomplete." Xiao Tong (501–531), Crown Prince Zhaoming of the Liang, compiled a collection of Tao's writings in eight *juan* with a preface. Yang Xiuzhi himself compiled a ten-*juan* edition, to which he added a foreword. Xiao's preface and Yang's foreword are extant.

In the Tang, numerous copies of Tao Yuanming's collection were in circulation, although none is extant. In the Northern Song, with the rise of print culture, scholars began to collate the different editions. Song Xiang 宋庠 (996–1066) claimed that he owned "several dozens of copies" (which he considered a "paltry" number), and that he never knew "which was the correct version," a situation in which Northern Song scholars frequently found themselves as they faced the immense and messy manuscript legacy of the Tang. Song Xiang's edition, although now lost, was often used as a reference in later editions for marking textual variants in the form of "[X] also as 'Y' in Song's edition" (*Song ben zuo mou* 宋本作某). The presence is shadowy, yet powerful, as many textual variants from the age of manuscript culture are preserved this way. We do not know whether Song Xiang's edition was copied by hand or printed; the earliest known printed edition of Tao's collection can be traced to 1122, but that edition is lost. We do know, however, that there were many printed editions of Tao's collection in the Southern Song, a few of which have survived. They will be treated in the following section.

Principal editions

There are numerous editions of Tao's collection from late imperial and modern times, but Southern Song editions are most significant because of their proximity to the manuscripts received from the Tang and Five Dynasties. The first of these woodblock editions contains a colophon dated the tenth year of the Shaoxing era of the Southern Song (1140). Since the characters in this edition were written in the calligraphic style of Su Shi 蘇軾 (1037–1101), it is known as "the edition in Su's handwriting" (Su xie ben 蘇寫本) or the "Shaoxing edition" (Shaoxing ben 紹興本). The second Southern Song edition is "Zeng Ji's edition" (Zeng Ji ben 曾集本) with a colophon dated 1192. Zeng Ji printed this edition while he was serving as magistrate in Tao's home region. The most important feature of this edition is that it preserves by far the largest number of textual variants for Tao Yuanming's poetry. Zeng also included a small amount of critical material in this edition, which may be regarded as a precursor to the later critical editions with collected commentaries. A number of Qing and early Republican reprints of these two Southern Song editions are available.

The other two Southern Song editions survive in their original physical form. One is known as the "Jiguge edition" (Jiguge ben 汲古閣本), since it once belonged to the famous late-Ming book collector and publisher Mao Jin 毛晉 (1599–1659), who named his library "Jiguge." It is the base edition for a modern edition put together by Yuan Xingpei (see later). Several Qing editions derive from this edition, among which is one printed in 1861 with a colophon by the famous book collector Mo Youzhi 莫友芝 (1811–1871).

The other Southern Song edition was compiled by Tang Han 湯漢 (styled Boji 伯紀; 1203–1273) and bears Tang Han's preface dated 1241. This edition is titled *Tao Jingjie xiansheng shizhu* 陶靖節先生詩注. "Jingjie" was part of a posthumous title (Jingjie zhengshi 靖節徵士) given to Tao by Yan Yanzhi in his dirge. Except for two prose pieces, this edition contains only Tao's poetry. It is held in the collection of the Chinese National Library and was handsomely photo-reprinted by Zhonghua shuju of Beijing in 1987.

Another major edition from the Song-Yuan period is *Jianzhu Tao Yuanming ji* 箋注陶淵明集. It is often dubbed "Li Gonghuan's edition" (Li Gonghuan ben 李公煥本) because it contains comments made on Tao Yuanming by various Song literati that were collected together by a Li Gonghuan of Luling 廬陵 (in modern

Jiangxi). This is the first extant edition with collected commentaries on Tao and on individual poems, but it is almost entirely devoid of textual variants. It was subsequently reprinted many times. One version was the base for the Hanfenlou 涵芬樓 edition in the *Sibu congkan**; another version, printed in the Yuan dynasty, is photo-reprinted in *Xuxiu Siku quanshu** 1587:1–58.

Many editions appeared in the Ming and Qing dynasties. These are primarily useful to scholars for the commentaries contained therein, not for the number and substance of the textual variants.

Commentaries

A large number of traditional commentaries are included in two modern collections: *Tao Yuanming shiwen huiping* 陶淵明詩文彙評 (Taipei: Zhonghua shuju, 1969) and *Tao Yuanming yanjiu ziliao huibian* 陶淵明研究資料彙編 (Beijing: Zhonghua shuju, 1962). Other substantial premodern commentaries include Chen Longzheng's 陳龍正 (1585–1645) *Tao shi yan* 陶詩衍 (first printed in 1643, reprinted in vol. 16 of *Tianjin tushuguan guben miji congshu* 天津圖書館孤本秘籍叢書 in 1999); Jiang Xun's 蔣薰 (1610–?) critical edition of *Tao Yuanming shiji* 陶淵明詩集, reprinted several times in the Qing; and Wu Zhantai's 吳瞻泰 (1657–1735) edition titled *Tao shi huizhu* 陶詩彙注, first printed in 1705. There is also Wen Runeng's 溫汝能 (1748–1811) edition, which consists of two volumes titled *Tao shi huiping* 陶詩彙評 and *He Tao hejian* 和陶合箋. *He Tao hejian* is an annotated edition of Su Shi's poems that matched the rhymes of Tao Yuanming's lyrics, with a collection of commentaries. Each volume has a preface by Wen dated 1806. The last premodern edition worth mentioning was edited by Tao Shu 陶澍 (1778–1839) and printed in 1840. It aimed to be comprehensive in terms of collected commentaries; it also contains a chronology of biographical events, titled *Jingjie xiansheng nianpu kaoyi* 靖節先生年譜考異, attached at the end.

Editions with modern annotation or commentary

Ding Fubao 丁福保. *Tao Yuanming shi jianzhu* 陶淵明詩箋注. Shanghai: Yixue shuju, 1927.

Fang Zushen 方祖燊. *Tao Yuanming shi jianzheng jiaozhu lunping* 陶淵明詩箋證校注論評. Taipei: Lantai shuju, 1971.

Gong Bin 龔斌. *Tao Yuanming ji jiaojian* 陶淵明集校箋. Shanghai: Shanghai guji, 1996.

Gu Zhi 古直. *Tao Jingjie shi jian* 陶靖節詩箋. In *Cengbingtang wuzhong* 層冰堂五種. Taipei: Guoli bianyiguan, 1984 reprint.

Lu Qinli 逯欽立. *Tao Yuanming ji* 陶淵明集. Beijing: Zhonghua shuju, 1979.

Sun Junxi 孫鈞錫. *Tao Yuanming ji jiaozhu* 陶淵明集校注. Zhengzhou: Zhongzhou guji, 1986.

Wang Mengbai 王孟白. *Tao Yuanming shiwen jiaojian* 陶淵明詩文校箋. Harbin: Heilongjiang renmin chubanshe, 1985.

Wang Shumin 王叔岷. *Tao Yuanming shi jianzheng gao* 陶淵明詩箋證稿. Taipei: Yiwen yinshu guan, 1975.

Wang Yao 王瑤. *Tao Yuanming ji* 陶淵明集. Beijing: Zuojia chubanshe, 1956.

Yang Yong 楊勇. *Tao Yuanming ji jiaojian* 陶淵明集校箋. Hong Kong: Wuxingji shuju, 1971.

Yuan Xingpei 袁行霈. *Tao Yuanming ji jianzhu* 陶淵明集箋注. Beijing: Zhonghua shuju, 2003.

Selected studies

In modern times, Tao Yuanming has inspired thousands of articles and book studies in Chinese as well as in other languages. The study of Tao Yuanming is dubbed "Tao'ology" (Tao *xue* 陶學). Following is a small selection of secondary literature:

Ashmore, Robert. *The Transport of Reading: Text and Understanding in the World of Tao Qian (365–427)*. Cambridge, MA: Harvard University Asia Center, 2010.

Chang, Kang-i Sun. "T'ao Ch'ien: Defining the Lyric Voice." In *Six Dynasties Poetry*, 3–46. Princeton, NJ: Princeton University Press, 1986.

———. "The Unmasking of Tao Qian and the Indeterminacy of Interpretation." In *Chinese Aesthetics: The Orderings of Word, Image, and the World in the Six Dynasties*, ed. Zong-qi Cai, 169–90. Honolulu: University of Hawai'i Press, 2004.

Hightower, James Robert. "Allusion in the Poetry of T'ao Ch'ien." *Harvard Journal of Asiatic Studies* 31 (1971): 5–27.

Li Hua 李華. *Tao Yuanming xinlun* 陶淵明新論. Beijing: Beijing shifan daxue chubanshe, 1992.

Owen, Stephen. "The Self's Perfect Mirror: Poetry as Autobiography." In *The Vitality of the Lyric Voice*, ed. Lin Shuen-fu and Stephen Owen, 71–102. Princeton, NJ: Princeton University Press, 1986.

Tian, Xiaofei. "Qingxing de quanshi: Lun Tao Qian 'Shu jiu' shi" 清醒的詮釋: 論陶潛述酒詩. In *Zhongguo zhonggu wenxue yanjiu* 中國中古文學研究, ed. Zhao Minli and Satō Toshiyuki. Beijing: Xueyuan chubanshe, 2005.

———. *Tao Yuanming and Manuscript Culture: The Record of a Dusty Table*. Seattle: University of Washington Press, 2005.

Wang Guoying 王國瓔. *Gujin yinyi shiren zhi zong Tao Yuanming lunxi* 古今隱逸詩人之宗陶淵明論析. Taipei: Yunchen wenhua gongsi, 1999.

Yuan Xingpei 袁行霈. *Tao Yuanming yanjiu* 陶淵明研究. Beijing: Beijing daxue chubanshe, 1997.

For studies of the reception history of Tao Yuanming, see the following:

Li Jianfeng 李劍鋒. *Yuan qian Tao Yuanming jieshoushi* 元前陶淵明接受史. Ji'nan: Qi Lu shushe, 2002.

Liu Zhongwen 劉中文. *Tangdai Tao Yuanming jieshou yanjiu* 唐代陶淵明接受研究. Beijing: Zhongguo shehui kexue chubanshe, 2003.
Luo Xiumei 羅秀美. *Song dai Tao xue yanjiu: Yige wenxue jieshoushi ge'an de fenxi* 宋代陶學研究：一個文學接受史個案的分析. Taipei: Xiuwei zixun, 2007.
Swartz, Wendy. *Reading Tao Yuanming: Shifting Paradigms of Historic Reception (427–1900)*. Cambridge, MA: Harvard University Asia Center, 2008.
Zhong Youmin 鍾優民. *Taoxue fazhanshi* 陶學發展史. Changchun: Jilin jiaoyu chubanshe, 2000.

Translations

Chinese

Guo Weisen 郭維森 and Bao Jingcheng 包景誠. *Tao Yuanming ji quanyi* 陶淵明集全譯. Guiyang: Guizhou renmin chubanshe, 1992.
Meng Erdong 孟二冬. *Tao Yuanming ji yizhu* 陶淵明集譯注. Changchun: Jilin wenshi chubanshe, 1996.
Wei Zhengshen 魏正申. *Tao Yuanming ji yizhu* 陶淵明集譯注. Beijing: Wenjin chubanshe, 1994.

English

Davis, A. R. *T'ao Yuan-ming: His Works and Their Meaning*. 2 vols. Cambridge: Cambridge University Press, 1984.
Hightower, James Robert. *The Poetry of T'ao Ch'ien*. Oxford: Clarendon Press, 1970.
Hinton, David. *The Selected Poems of T'ao Ch'ien*. Port Townsend, WA: Copper Canyon Press, 1993.
Owen, Stephen. *An Anthology of Chinese Literature, Beginnings to 1911*. New York: W. W. Norton, 1996.

European languages

Guidacci, Margherita. *Due antichi poeti cinesi: Tao Yuan-ming e Tu Fu*. Milan: Scheiwiller, 1988.
Jacob, Paul. *Oeuvres complètes de Tao Yuan-Ming*. Paris: Gallimard, 1990.
Liang Tsong-tai, with preface by Paul Valéry. *Les poèmes de T'ao Ts'ien*. Paris: Lemarget, 1930.
Pohl, Karl-Heinz. *Der Pfirsichblütenquell: Gesammelte Gedichte*. Bochum: Bochumer Universitätsverlag, 2002.

Japanese

Ikkai Tomoyoshi 一海知義. *Tō Emmei* 陶淵明. Tokyo: Iwanami shoten, 1958.
Matsueda Shigeo 松枝茂夫 and Wada Takeshi 和田武司. *Tō Emmei zenshū* 陶淵明全集. Tokyo: Iwanami shoten, 1990.
Shiba Rokurō 斯波六郎. *Tō Emmei shi chūyaku* 陶淵明詩注譯. Kyoto: Tōmon shobō, 1951.

Korean

Ch'a Chu-hwan 車柱環. *Hanyŏk To Yŏn-myŏng chŏnjip* 韓譯陶淵明全集. Seoul: Sŏul taehakkyo ch'ulp'anbu, 2001.

Index

Horie Tadamichi 堀江忠道. *Tō Emmei shibun sōgō sakuin* 陶淵明詩文總合索引. Kyoto: Ibundō shoten, 1976.

Xiaofei Tian

Tong dian 通典

Introduction

The *Tong dian* (Comprehensive canons), which may be characterized as an encyclopedic history of institutions, was the earliest representative of a genre, the administrative compendium, that remained important over the succeeding centuries. Written by the prominent scholar-official Du You 杜佑 (735–812) in the second half of the eighth century, its chronological coverage ranges from high antiquity (the age of the mythical sage kings) down to the author's own time. Not content with the simple transmission of inherited knowledge, Du used the *Tong dian* to promote his own ideas regarding the relationship of that heritage to practical problems of statecraft. Although of greatest value as a source for the history and institutions of the Tang dynasty, the book also contains much useful material bearing on the preceding period of division.

Contents

The *Tong dian* consists of two hundred *juan* and is divided into nine major sections, each dealing with a specific function or aspect of government:

1. Canon of Food and Goods, 食貨典 (*juan* 1–12)
2. Canon of Civil Service Examinations, 選舉典 (*juan* 13–18)
3. Canon of Government Offices, 職官典 (*juan* 19–40)
4. Canon of Ritual, 禮典 (*juan* 41–140)
5. Canon of Music, 樂典 (*juan* 141–47)
6. Canon of the Military, 兵典 (*juan* 148–62)
7. Canon of Punishments, 刑法典 (*juan* 163–70)
8. Canon of Administrative Geography, 州郡典 (*juan* 171–84)
9. Canon of Border Defense, 邊防典 (*juan* 185–200)

Each of these major sections is further divided into a fairly large number of subsections, and each of these subsections consists of one, several, or many passages drawn from earlier histories and other works. The military section, for example, has more than 120 subsections dealing with specific topics such as generalship, espionage, and attack by fire. The arrangement of passages within each subsection is basically chronological, proceeding from high antiquity down to the end of the emperor Xuanzong's reign in 756. After this date, "there is only a haphazard scattering of information from the 770s and early 780s, mostly incorporated as commentary" (Twitchett, *The Writing of Official History*, 107).

With the exception of material drawn from the standard histories (*zhengshi* 正史) of earlier dynasties, the national histories (*guoshi* 國史) of the Tang, and the veritable records (*shilu* 實錄) of individual Tang reigns, Du was usually careful to indicate the sources of the material he was copying into the *Tong dian*. The Canon of Ritual includes no less than thirty-five *juan* of material taken from the still-extant *Kaiyuan li* 開元禮 (Ritual code of the Kaiyuan period), dating from 732, though of much greater value to modern scholars are extensive extracts from lost works such as the *Li Jing bingfa* 李靖兵法, dating from early Tang, in the Canon of the Military, and the Sui *Xiyu tuji* 西域圖記 in the Canon of Border Defense (Twitchett, *The Writing of Official History*, 105; Huang, *Tang shi shiliao xue*, 67). Of particular interest to students of the era of division are the many essays from the Three Kingdoms and Six Dynasties periods preserved in the Canon of Ritual.

Although the vast majority of the some 1.5 million characters that make up the *Tong dian* consist of passages borrowed from earlier works, Du was able to express his own opinions in several ways; these included the large number of notes and comments he inserted into the text, the prefaces in each of the nine major sections, and the selection of texts for inclusion (or exclusion). The organizational scheme of the work, particularly the sequence of its major sections, is also highly significant. Du's decision to give pride of place at the beginning of the book to economic matters rather than ritual—a radical innovation at the time—reflected his conviction that successful government is founded on material prosperity (McMullen, *State and Scholars*, 155). In general, the *Tong dian* reflects Du's belief that history is shaped by administrative and institutional factors, rather than moral principles, and that institutions evolve over time, with different institutions and policies being appropriate for different times. Government should not be based on some ideal ancient pattern; instead, one "should adapt the essential truths of older writings to the needs of the present" (Pulleyblank, "Neo-Confucianism and Neo-Legalism," 99–100; also McMullen, *State and Scholars*, 261).

Authorship

Born into a prominent office-holding family in the Tang capital Chang'an, Du You entered government service through hereditary privilege in 752. He spent seven years (756–763) as vice magistrate (*xiancheng* 縣丞) of Shan 剡 (northern Zhejiang), and in 765 he joined the staff of Wei Yuanfu 韋元甫, an important territorial administrator in the lower Yangzi region. When Wei became military governor (*jiedushi* 節度使) of Huainan 淮南 in 768, Du accompanied him to his headquarters at Yangzhou 陽州, where he continued to work for the next eight years. Du subsequently served as prefect of Fuzhou 撫州 (in today's Jiangxi), director of the Treasury Bureau (*jinbu langzhong* 金部郎中) and the Expenditures Bureau (*duzhi langzhong* 度支郎中) of the Ministry of Revenue (Hubu 戶部), vice-minister of Revenue (*hubu shilang* 戶部侍郎), military governor of Lingnan 嶺南, and left vice-director of the Department of State Affairs (*shangshu zuo puye* 尚書左僕射). From 790 to 803, he was back in Yangzhou as military governor of Huainan—the post formerly held by his patron Wei Yuanfu—and he briefly returned to that city once again, in 805, as commissioner for Salt and Iron (*yantieshi* 鹽鐵使), the head of the government's salt monopoly. From 803 on, Du was a chief minister (*zaixiang* 宰相) at the courts of three successive emperors, Dezong 德宗, Shunzong 順宗, and Xianzong 憲宗 (*Jiu Tang shu* 147:3978–83 and *Xin Tang shu* 166:5085–90). Although experienced in many aspects of government administration, over his long career he acquired a reputation for particular expertise in financial matters (Guo Feng, *Du You ping zhuan*, chronology, 385–96).

Composition and dating

According to Du You's biographies in the two standard histories of the Tang, the *Tong dian* had its origin in an earlier work, the *Zheng dian* 政典 (Canons of government), compiled in the late 730s or 740s by the scholar-official Liu Zhi 劉秩, a son of the great Tang historian Liu Zhiji 知幾. This book of thirty-five *juan*, which no longer survives outside of the *Tong dian*, "seems to have been an ambitious political treatise, cast in historical form that, for the most part, was modeled on the subject of the traditional monographs [in the standard histories] and drew its material from a wide range of sources, both historical and non-historical" (Twitchett, *The Writing of Official History*, 103). As a young man, Du You read the *Zheng dian* and was inspired to embark upon a massive project of correction, reorganization, and augmentation that eventually yielded the *Tong dian*.[1] He added a vast amount of new material, expanding the work from thirty-five to two hundred *juan*, inserted his own notes and comments, and significantly altered Liu's original blueprint—a division into six major sections probably inspired by the six-office (*liu guan* 六官) scheme of the *Zhou li* 周禮. Du replaced this with an eight-section plan, which later became nine sections with the division of Punishments and the Military (originally forming a single section) into two separate canons (Huang Yongnian, *Tang shi shiliao xue*, 66). The date that Du began work on the *Tong dian* is highly uncertain, but it seems that the bulk of the writing was done in the middle and late 760s, when he was a member of Wei Yuanfu's entourage (Twitchett, *The Writing of Official History*, 105–6; Guo, *Du You pingzhuan*, 65–70). In about 771, when the

---

[1] Most scholars accept this account found in Du's biographies (*Jiu Tang shu* 147:3982; *Xin Tang shu* 166:5089–90). A dissenting view has recently been expressed by Guo Feng (*Du You ping zhuan*, 71–73), who argues that Du did not encounter the *Zheng dian* until much later, when he was prefect of Fuzhou, and that it did not have much influence on the writing of the *Tong dian* and for the most part was not incorporated into the text of the latter work.

prominent literatus Li Han 李翰 read a draft of the work and contributed a preface, the *Tong dian* already consisted of two hundred *juan* organized into eight major sections.² Between that time and 795, Du continued to fiddle with the text, making a few additions mostly in the form of notes and commentary. The *Tong dian* was presented to the throne in the tenth lunar month of 801, after Du, still at his post in Yangzhou, had sent a representative bearing the book to the capital with an accompanying memorial.³ Even after the book's presentation to the throne, minor additions and emendations were introduced into it, some as late as 820. It is possible, but by no means certain, that changes datable to the period 801–812 are the work of Du You himself. The *Tong dian* thus contains four layers of material: (1) the original *Zhengdian* of Liu Zhi, now indistinguishable from the other parts of the *Tong dian*; (2) the draft that Du completed by 770, accounting for the bulk of the material in the *Tong dian*; (3) the additions made by Du between that 770 and 801; and (4) additions made in the period between 801 and 820 (Twitchett, *The Writing of Official History*, 107).

Transmission of the text

It is reported that the *Tong dian* circulated widely after its presentation to the throne in 801 and received the approbation of the "scholars and gentlemen" of late Tang (*Jiu Tang shu* 147:3982; *Tang Huiyao* 36:660). Its existence is well attested in the surviving Northern Song bibliographies, including the *Xin Tang shu* monograph on literature, 59:1563, *Chongwen zongmu** 3:54a, p. 407, and Chao Gongwu's *Junzhai dushu zhi** 14:653. All three classify the *Tong dian* as an encyclopedia (*leishu* 類書), and all record the book as consisting of two hundred *juan*.

The earliest surviving copy of the text is a Northern Song woodblock edition. This and other early (Song and Yuan) specimens show only minor variations; comparison with later editions of the *Tong dian*, however, reveals that Ming and Qing redactors introduced numerous and often unwarranted emendations. A critical edition issued by Zhonghua shuju (1988) corrects these mistakes through collation with the earliest surviving editions (see later).

---

² Li Han's preface states that Du started work on the *Tong dian* at the beginning of the Dali period (766). The preface is reproduced at the beginning of the 1988 Zhonghua edition of the *Tong dian*.

³ *Jiu Tang shu* 13:395. There is also some evidence for presentation to the throne in 794 and 803, but following the arguments advanced by Wang Mingsheng 王鳴盛 in the eighteenth century, modern scholars generally accept 801 as the correct date; see Twitchett (*The Writing of Official History*, 106), and Qu ("Lun *Tong dian* de fangfa he zhiqu," 112–28). The memorial can be found in Du's biographies and at the beginning of the 1988 Zhonghua edition of the *Tong dian*.

Principal editions

A Northern Song edition held in Japan and available to researchers in the form of a microform copy (four reels) made during the late 1970s by the Takahashi Photo Service in Tokyo is:

Hokusō-ban tsūten: Kunaichō shoryōbu zō 北宋版通典：宮内廳書陵部藏 [The Northern Song edition of the *Tong dian*: Held by the Library of the Imperial Household Agency]. Edited by Nagasawa Kikuya 長澤規矩也 and Ozaki Yasushi 尾崎康. 9 vols. Tokyo: Kyūko shoten, 1980–1981. Photo-reprint of a mostly complete Northern Song woodblock edition, with twenty of the twenty-three missing *juan* filled in from an old Korean manuscript copy of the *Tong dian* (the *Chaoxian xieben* 朝鮮寫本).

The great repository of other early specimens of the *Tong dian* is the Beijing Library. Its collection includes other Song woodblock editions, some very fragmentary, that were revised (*dixiu* 遞修) in the Song or Yuan. These have recently been made more widely available by photolithographic reproduction in the series Zhonghua zaizao shanben 中華再造善本 by the Beijing tushuguan chubanshe. Among the Beijing Library's rare editions are the three surviving *juan* of a Yuan woodblock edition, by the Linru shuyuan 臨汝書院 of Fuzhou route (Fuzhou *lu* 撫州路); a microfilm copy is at the Library of Congress. Also in the Beijing Library collection is a very rough Ming manuscript copy of a Song edition of the *Tong dian*, missing text at many points. The 147 surviving *juan* of this Wu Silan 烏絲欄 manuscript copy have also been made available on microfilm by the Library of Congress. Finally, the Beijing Library holds a Ming Jiajing 嘉靖 (1522–1566) edition of the *Tong dian* that Fu Zengxiang (1872–1949) was able to collate with the incomplete text of a Southern Song Shaoxing 紹興 woodblock edition; the Song edition has since been lost, but Fu noted discrepancies with red ink in the Jiajing edition. Other notable editions, all in two hundred *juan*, are the following:

Tong dian. Also known as *Qinding Tong dian* 欽定通典 [Imperially authorized *Tong dian*] and *Wuying dianben* 武英典本, this "Palace" woodblock edition of 1747 was issued as part of the imperially sponsored *Jiutong* 九通 (Nine comprehensives) collection. It is based, albeit with many emendations, on the Ming Jiajing woodblock edition of Wang Deyi 王德溢 and Wu Peng 吳鵬.

Tong dian. Zhejiang shuju 浙江書局 woodblock edition, 1896. 50 *ce*. This edition is based on the 1747 palace edition and includes a one-*juan* appendix of text-critical comments (*kaozheng* 考證).

Tong dian. Shanghai: Tushu jicheng ju 圖書集成局 typeset edition, 1901.

Tong dian. Shanghai: Shangwu yinshuguan, 1935. Typeset edition issued as volume 1 in the *Shitong* 十通 collection, with index. It is based on the 1747 Palace edition and includes as a one-*juan* appendix the *Qinding Tong dian kaozheng* 欽定通典考證 of 1787. A facsimile reprint of the 1935 Shangwu edition of the *Tong dian* was issued by Zhonghua shuju in 1984.

Tong dian. 5 vols. Beijing: Zhonghua shuju, 1988. Punctuated and typeset edition based on the Zhejiang shuju edition but collated with several earlier editions; punctuation was done by a team of five scholars led by Wang Wenjin 王文錦. The assessment of the *Tong dian* from *Siku quanshu zongmu tiyao** 16.1695 is reprinted as an appendix, as is Wang Taiyue 王太岳 et al., *Tong dian kaozheng* 通典考證 (revised by Wang Wenjin and retitled *Tong dian kaozheng heshi* 通典考證覈實).

Studies of the text

Fu Zengxiang 傅增湘. *Tong dian jiaokanji* 通典校勘記. One *juan*. Beijing: Beijing tushuguan chubanshe, 2004. Photolithographic reproduction of the 1938 manuscript in the Beijing Library.

Selected studies

Guo Feng 郭鋒. *Du You ping zhuan* 杜佑評傳. Nanjing: Nanjing daxue chubanshe, 2004.

Kitagawa Shunshō 北川俊昭. "*Tsūten* hensan shimatsu kō" 通典編纂始末考 [Examination of the beginning and end of the compilation of the *Tong dian*]. *Tōyōshi kenkyū* 57.1 (June 1998): 125–48.

Liao Zhengxiong 廖正雄. *Du You Tong dian de bianzuan chuangxin ji qi shixue sixiang* 杜佑通典的編纂創新及其史學思想. In *Gudian wenxian yanjiu jikan, chu bian* 古典文獻研究輯刊, 初編, vol. 33. Yonghe, Taiwan: Hua Mulan wenhua gongzuofang, 2005.

McMullen, David. *State and Scholars in T'ang China*. Cambridge: Cambridge University Press, 1988.

———. "Du You, 735–812." In *RoutledgeCurzon Encyclopedia of Confucianism*, ed. Xinzhong Yao, 197. London: RoutledgeCurzon, 2003.

Niida Noboru 仁井田升. "*Tong dian* banben kao" 通典版本考. *Shixue xiaoxi* 1.8 (July 1937): 25–51.

Pulleyblank, Edwin G. "Neo-Confucianism and Neo-Legalism in T'ang Intellectual Life, 755–805." *The Confucian Persuasion*, ed. Arthur F. Wright, 77–114. Stanford, CA: Stanford University Press, 1960.

Qu Lindong 瞿林東. "Lun *Tong dian* de fangfa he zhiqu" 論通典的方法和旨趣. *Lishi yanjiu* (1984.5): 112–28.

———. *Du You pingzhuan: Chuang dianzhi tongshi, hui zhiguo liangmo* 杜佑評傳: 創典制通史, 匯治國良模. Nanning: Guangxi jiaoyu chubanshe, 1996.

Tamai Zehaku 玉井是博. "*Tong dian* de zhuanshu he liuchuan" 通典的撰述和流傳. *Shixueshi ziliao* (1980.1): 30–32.

Tao Maobing 陶懋炳. "Du You he *Tong dian*" 杜佑和通典. *Shixueshi ziliao* (1980.3): 9–19.

Twitchett, Denis. *The Writing of Official History under the T'ang*. Cambridge: Cambridge University Press, 1993.

Xie Baocheng 謝保成. "Lun *Tong dian* de xingzhi yu deshi" 論通典的性質與得失. *Zhongguo shi yanjiu* (1992.1): 131–43.

Zheng Hesheng 鄭鶴聲. *Du You nianpu* 杜佑年譜. Shanghai: Shangwu yinshuguan, 1934.

Evaluation

Huang Yongnian 黃永年. *Tang shi shiliao xue* 唐史史料學. Shanghai: Shanghai shudian chubanshe, 2002.

Qu Lindong. "*Tong dian.*" In Cang Xiuliang 倉修良, ed., *Zhongguo shixue mingzhu pingjia* 中國史學名著評價. Ji'nan: Shandong jiaoyu chubanshe, 1990.

David Graff

Wang Shuhe Maijing 王叔和脈經

Introduction

The *Maijing* (Classic on pulses), attributed to Wang Shuhe 王叔和, styled Xi 熙 (210–285?), is considered the first work that specializes on diagnosis by taking the pulse. Despite the title, its contents go beyond the simple subject of diagnoses by the pulse. The work concerns other methods of making diagnoses as well, including identifying diseases through an enumeration of the principal symptoms associated with the conduit vessels (*jingmai* 經脈), those symptoms of serious illnesses, and also those related to women and children. The text can in fact be regarded as a compilation of knowledge relating to diagnostics and to pathogeny that derives from many different traditions.

Author

There is no biography of Wang Shuhe in the standard histories. The preface of the *Zhenjiu jiayi jing* 針灸甲乙經 by Huangfu Mi 皇甫謐 (215–282) states that he was a native of Gaoping 高平 and held the office of imperial physician (*taiyiling* 太醫令) at a time close to that of Huangfu Mi. By the quality of his writings, he was considered the worthy successor of the doctor Zhang Zhongjing 張仲景 (fl. 200). A short biography in the *Mingyi lu* 名醫錄 by Gan Bozong 甘伯宗 of the Tang presents him as an expert in the art of diagnostics and someone who earned his livelihood by it.

There are a number of places in Shanxi and Shandong with the name Gaoping. The most likely locale is a place in southwestern Shandong now called Guolijizhen 郭里集鎮, near Zouxian 鄒縣, where a powerful Wang clan resided (Zhu and Liao, "Wang Shuhe jiguan kaocha," 205). The Wang clan had its start with Wang Bozong 伯宗, who had been born there in the district of Shanyang 山陽; he attained the office of defender-in-chief (*taiwei* 太尉) during the rule of the Han emperor Shun. His son Wang Chang 暢, styled Shumao (?–169), also attained high office, being named minister of works (*sikong* 司空) in 168 (*Hou Hanshu* 56:1819–22, 1823–26). In turn, his son Wang Qian 謙 held military posts, and his grandson Wang Can 王燦 (177–217), was a celebrated poet of the Jian'an era. When Wang Can left for Jingzhou 荊州 (to place himself under the protection of a Han royal family member, also from Gaoping but appointed as Jingzhou's provincial inspector), it is probable that the Wang clan members, including Wang Shuhe, followed him there.

Although the kinship connection between Wang Can and Shuhe is not known, there is a record in the *Zhenjiu jiayi jing* that relates that at the age of seventeen, Wang Can met Zhang Zhongjing in Jingzhou. Zhang told him that he had an illness for which he should take a decoction of the "Five Stones"; if he failed to do so, his eyebrows would fall out at the age of forty and he would die six months later. This account, in the *Zhenjiu jiayi jing*'s preface, is from the biography of He Yu 何顒, who, like Zhang Zhongjing, was from the commandery of Nanyang 南陽. That Jingzhou was near to Nanyang also makes the story relatively credible. Since Wang Can died in 217 at the age of forty-one, his meeting with Zhang would have taken place when he was twenty. Wang Shuhe could then well have received his teaching from Zhang. In any event he established a connection with Wei Fan 衛汛, a disciple of Zhang and author of many medical texts. According to Yu Jiaxi, since Wei Fan cites the words of Wang Shuhe, they would have been contemporaries (*Siku tiyao bianzheng*, 368).

Contents

The surviving text is in ten *juan*. The first is composed of fifteen separate and very short sections that provide diverse methods for analyzing the pulse according to its nature (these describe the twenty-four principal types of pulses [*mai*] that can be felt by the finger, according to the zone, age, size, or sex of the patient in order to reach a diagnosis).

Juan 2 treats the twenty-four principal pulses that one can sense in the three channels at the wrist and the pulse of eight separate vessels (*qijing bamai* 奇經八脈). *Juan* 3 presents in five sections the differing qualities of the pulses corresponding to the five viscera and their related receptacles. *Juan* 4 focuses on the prognostication of life or death for the patient.

Juan 5 is divided into five sections that deal with the knowledge of each of three eminent doctors of the past: Zhang Zhongjing, Bian Que 扁鵲, and Hua Tuo 華陀. The symptoms, often presented in a single line, concern for the most part the prognoses of life or death by the examination of the pulse. The pulses described here are not just those of the twenty-four types enumerated in *juan* 1, but come from multiple and varied perceptions taken from people's daily habits.

Juan 6 lays out the symptoms and pathologies of the twelve conduit vessels associated with the eleven organs (known also as the five viscera and six vessels), in the order of their pairing: liver with vesicular receptacle, heart with small intestine, spleen with stomach, lungs with large intestine, kidney with bladder, and, then, the three warming vessels. Missing is the twelfth conduit vessel, which is associated with "covering of the heart" (*xinbao* 心包) or with "master of the heart" (*xinzhu* 心主) in the traditional system, within which it is paired with the three warming vessels. The number of eleven conduit vessels and of eleven organs corresponds to an ancient tradition attested notably by a Mawangdui manuscript that enumerates only eleven vessels (Harper, *Early Chinese Medical Literature*, 192–212), and by a chapter of the *Suwen* that mentions only eleven organs (*Huangdi neijing Suwen* 3.9, 61–62, *Sibu congkan**). There are twelve conduits in other *juan* of the *Maijing*, a difference that shows clearly the heterogeneity of the text's sources.

Juan 7 contains twenty-four sections that recount the symptoms of illness that are curable or not; symptoms due to an excess of "heat" (epidemics); symptoms for which one can or cannot use a sweating cure, and those that can appear after a sweating cure is wrongly applied; symptoms when one can cause vomiting or where one ought purge or not, and illnesses for which one can use warm remedies; symptoms for which one can or cannot use cupping, whether one can prick the patient or not; symptoms for which one can use moxibustion and acupuncture, whether one can use water or fire; symptoms that foretell death when the symptoms of *yin* and *yang* are mixed up in a heat sickness, and the *shaoyin* and the *jueyin* are exhausted, or prognostication of death when there is too much *yang* and too much *yin*. Also discussed are symptoms to foretell the day of death in a heat sickness; those of the ten adversities in heat sickness; those to prognosticate the date of death when the breath of the five viscera are blocked; prognoses of death when one feels excessive pulse in heat illness, and those when the pulse is faint.

Juan 8 is divided into sixteen sections that lay out the symptoms and pathologies of serious illnesses: sudden comas, diarrhea and dysentery, attacks by the Wind, the stages of exhaustion and fatigue, the tightness of blood, jaundice, tightness of the thorax, buildup in the five viscera, vomiting, the etiolation of the lungs, the furuncles of the lungs, abscesses, bubos, and so forth.

Juan 9 is composed of nine sections that treat the symptoms and illnesses of women and children. It is to be noted that Sun Simo 孫思邈 (581–682) is often attributed with having drawn attention to the details of the illnesses of women and children and had dedicated to that topic the first *juan* of his magisterial *Qianjin yaofang* 千金要方, but, as has been recently shown, he was more concerned to assert a lineage than to give attention to women and children. On the contrary, Wang Shuhe's *Maijing* and, later, Chao Yuanfang's 巢元方 *Zhubing yuanhoulun* 諸病原候論 (610) dedicate many *juan* to the illnesses of women and children, although admittedly these discussions are at the end and not the beginning of their works.

Textual sources

In the preface, the author claims to have compiled the essential formulae for the pulses transmitted from Qibo 歧伯 (an instructor of the Yellow Emperor in the *Huangdi neijing* 黃帝內經) down to Hua Tuo 華陀 (d. 208?). The *Maijing* is in essence a compilation of early sources, some of which are known and others not.

The most ancient texts about the taking of the pulse are two documents from archaeological sites. The first is a manuscript found in Tomb No. 3 at Mawangdui 馬王堆 (Changsha, Hunan) dating to 168 B.C., the year the tomb was sealed. The other is a manuscript from Zhangjiashan 張家山 in Hubei. Of the received literature, the oldest mention of the pulse is in *Shi ji* 105 (translation by Hsu, *Pulse Diagnosis*), a chapter of the *Shanghan lun* 傷寒論 combined with the *Jingui yaolüe* 金

匱要略 of Zhang Zhongjing, as well as the *Nanjing* 難經, an anonymous text of the Later Han attributed to Bian Que.

None of these are mentioned by title in the *Maijing*, but they were used by Wang Shuhe. When the text includes a dialogue introduced by the phrases, "Huangdi *wen yue*" 黃帝問曰 or "Qibo *yue*" 歧伯曰, this implicitly refers to the *Huangdi neijing* (*juan* 1.13, pp. 10–11; *juan* 4.1 and 4.5, pp. 47, 59; *juan* 6.2, p. 91). Dialogue introduced by the words, "it was asked" (*wen yue* 問曰) and "the master replied" (*shi yue* 師曰), refers to the words of Wang Shuhe's teacher, Zhang Zhongjing; this pattern corresponds to a passage of the *Jingui yaolüe* by Zhang Zhongjing (*Maijing*, *juan* 8, p. 151; *juan* 15, p. 170). Finally, a passage introduced by "it is said in the canon" (*jing yan* 經言) corresponds to a passage from the *Nanjing*.

It is difficult to assess what parts were written by Wang Shuhe because the author rarely cites his sources, but one can nevertheless largely identify them by comparison with the existing literature. A third of the content of the *Maijing* comes from the old *Shanghan lun*'s manuscript of Zhang Zhongjing. According to Okanishi Tameto (*Sō izen iseki kō*, 126), in section 3 of *juan* 1, the passage introduced by "newly composed" (*xinzhuan* 新撰) corresponds to the additions by Wang, while the citation in the same *juan* to a *Sishi jing* 四時經 corresponds to the *Sanbu sishi wuzang zhense jue shimai* 三部四時五臟診色決事脈, which is listed in the bibliographic monograph of the *Sui shu*, q.v. (34.1044). This is, of course, a hypothesis, but nonetheless Bian Que, Hua Tuo, and Zhang Zhongjing are cited in the titles of the sections of *juan* 5.

Transmission and early history of the text

Most of the Sui to Song bibliographies list the *Maijing* in ten *juan* (*Sui shu*, q.v., 34.1040; *Xin Tang shu* 59.1565; *Tong* zhi* 69.810), but the *Jiu Tang shu* (47.2047) states two *juan*. Under the Song, Lin Yi 林億 and his team revised medical texts, using three versions of the *Maijing* to put it in order. Some citations of the *Maijing* are preserved in the *Yiqie jing yinyi* 一切經音義 by the Tang monk Huilin 慧琳 and in the *Xu yiqie jing yinyi* 續一切經音義 by the Song monk Xilin 希麟 (*Taishō shinshū Daizōkyō** 54:2128–29). These do not correspond with the text transmitted by Lin Yi, but citations of the work made by Pang Anshi 龐安時 in his *Shanghan lun* 傷寒論 and by Xu Shuwei 許叔微 in his *Shanghan lun baizheng ge* 傷寒論百證歌 do correspond to it (Ma, *Zhongyi*, 146). Dunhuang manuscript S.8289 contains the *Maijing*'s preface and *juan* 1.

Editions

The oldest surviving examples are two editions that date from the Northern Song. The first of these was revised by an official board in 1068. Printed in large characters, it consists of ninety-seven sections distributed over ten *juan*. The second edition, printed in small characters, was published by the Guozijian 國子鑑 in 1096. Four editions were issued during the Southern Song, but all have been lost (Ma, *Zhongyi*, 146). These are (a) undated edition of the Jianyang shufang 建陽書坊

(Fujian); (b) reprint of the Fujian edition in 1209 by Guangxi's Bureau of Transport (Caosi 漕司), (c) 1217 edition by He Daren 何大任, a physician of the imperial medical board (Taiyiju 太醫局), after the Guozijian version; (d) an undated edition.

Two main editions of the Yuan are (a) the Long Xingdao 龍興道 text (1327), a reprint of the Bureau of Transport edition; (b) the Guangqintang 廣勤堂 edition (1330) by Ye Rizeng 葉日增, after that of He Daren, which is held in the National Library, Beijing, and reproduced in facsimile in 1919 and 1935 (*Sibu congkan*), and again in 1956 (Renmin weisheng chubanshe).

During the Ming, the He Daren and Long Xingdao editions were both reprinted. The former attracted the attention of the literati and best approximates the Song text. Three Ming copies of He Daren's edition have survived: (a) that of the Bisonglou 皕宋樓 of Lu Xinyuan 陸心源, now in the Seikadō bunko 靜嘉堂 in Japan, which was reproduced in facsimile in 1981, in *Nihon tōyō yigaku zenbon sōsho* 日本東洋善本醫學叢書; (b) that of the Neikaku bunko 內閣文庫 in Japan; (c) a copy purchased in Japan by Yang Shoujing 楊守敬 (end of the nineteenth century), now in the library of the Palace Museum (Gugong bowuyuan 故宮博物院) in Taipei. Long Xingdao's edition was reprinted by Bi Yu 畢玉 ("Bi Yu shi kanben" 畢玉氏刊本) in 1474 and by Yuan Biao 袁表 ("Yuan Biao shi kanben" 袁表氏刊本) in 1575; of the latter, there is a movable-type Japanese edition of 1596–1661.

Among Qing dynasty editions, the most popular is the so-called *Maijing zhenben* 脈經真本, edited by Shen Liyi 沈禮意 (1812), and frequently re-edited (1833, 1856, 1862, 1890, 1892, 1899, 1930). For a detailed history of the editions, see Ma, *Zhongyi wenxianxue*, 148–50.

Commentaries

Liao Ping 廖平. *Maijing kaozheng* 脈經考證. In *Liuyiguan yixue congshu* 六譯館醫學叢書, vol. 64 in *Liuyiguan congshu* 六譯館叢書. Chengdu: Sichuan cungu shuju, 1921.

Sun Dingyi 孫鼎宜. *Maijing chao* 脈經鈔. In *Sunshi yixue congshu* 孫氏醫學叢書 (1932). Shanghai: Zhonghua shuju, 1936.

Bibliography

Harper, Donald. *Early Chinese Medical Literature: The Mawangdui Medical Manuscripts*. London: Kegan Paul International, 1998.

Hsu, Elisabeth. "Pulse Diagnostics in the Western Han: How *mai* and *qi* Determine *bing*." In *Innovation in Chinese Medicine*, ed. Hsu, 51–91. Cambridge: Cambridge University Press, 2001.

———. *Pulse Diagnosis in Early Chinese Medicine: The Telling Touch*. Cambridge: Cambridge University Press, 2010.

Ma Jixing 馬繼興. *Zhongyi wenxianxue* 中醫文獻學. Shanghai: Shanghai kexue jishu chubanshe, 1990.

Mayanagi Makoto 真柳誠 and Kosoto Hiroshi 洋小曽戶, eds. *Tōyō igaku zempon sōsho* 東洋醫學善本叢書. Osaka: Oriento shuppansha, 1987–89.

Okanishi Tameto 岡西為人. *Sō izen iseki kō* 宋以前醫籍考. 4 vols. Taipei: Jinxue shuju, 1969.
Rouquet de la Robertie, Catherine. *Wang Shuhe et le "Classique du pouls."* Ph.D. diss., Institut National des Langues et Civilisations Orientales, 1991.
Ru Dongmin 茹東民, Li Fuhua 李富華, and Zhang Shengmin 張生民. "Wang Shuhe shengping liji kao" 王叔和生平里籍考. *Shandong zhongyi xueyuan xuebao* 13.2 (1989): 107–8.
Yu Jiaxi 余嘉錫 (1884–1955). *Siku tiyao bianzheng* 四庫提要辯證. Beijing: Kexue chubanshe, 1958.
Zhu Hongming 朱鴻銘 and Liao Ziyang 廖子仰. "Wang Shuhe jiguan kaocha" 王叔和籍貫考察. *Zhonghua yishi zazhi* 15.4 (1985): 205–8.

Catherine Despeux

Wei shu 魏書

Introduction

The *Wei shu*, by Wei Shou 魏收 (505–572), is the history of the Northern Wei dynasty (384–535), from the appearance of the Tuoba 拓跋 people as a proto-state along the northeastern border in the early fourth century to the breakup of their unified rule over north China two centuries later. The *Wei shu* is the first of the standard histories that takes as its subject a "conquest dynasty." The history was compiled not long after the dynasty's demise, and, partly owing to the difficulty of navigating the contentious politics of the post-Wei period, the *Wei shu* and its author were criticized severely for bias and favoritism. The criticism carried over into the Sui and Tang periods and resulted in efforts to edit and rewrite the history. Despite that, the *Wei shu* represents the earliest and most complete available record of the Northern Wei dynasty, as all of the earlier or closely contemporaneous such histories have either been lost or, as in the case of the *Bei shi*, q.v., directly derived from the *Wei shu*.

Contents

The *Wei shu* consists of 130 *juan*, including the prefatory annals of the pre-Wei Tuoba rulers (*xu ji* 序紀), thirteen imperial annals (*di ji* 帝紀), ninety-six *juan* containing biographies of notable personages of the ruling family, scholars, officials, women, eunuchs, and accounts of foreign peoples (*liezhuan* 列傳), and twenty monographs (*zhi* 志) on various topics. Notable among the latter are monographs on economics (*shihuo zhi* 食貨志) and on Buddhism and Taoism (*shilao zhi* 釋老志).

Authorship

In the year 551, Wei Shou was commissioned by the Northern Qi ruler Gao Yang 高洋, posthumous name Wenxuandi (r. 550–559), to compile the official history of the Northern Wei dynasty. For the project, Wei Shou was able to draw on the work of several Northern Wei officials who had earlier been commissioned to edit the contemporary record of the state. During the rule of the Northern Wei founder, posthumous name Daowudi (r. 377–409), Deng Yuan 鄧淵 had compiled ten or more *juan* on the history of early Tuoba rule, titled *Dai ji* 代記, Dai having been the original name of that state. In the 440s, Cui Hao 崔浩 (381–450) and Gao Yun 高允 (391–487) rewrote the dynastic record, bringing it to thirty *juan* that, it was claimed, emphasized the primacy of Chinese institutions over Tuoba traditions and ostensibly led to Cui's arrest and execution. Li Biao 李彪 (444–501) and Cui Guang 崔光 (451–523), beginning in 487, brought the record up through the reign of Tuoba Hong, posthumous name Xianwendi (r. 466–470). Na Luan 那巒 (dates unknown), Cui Hong 崔鴻 (d. ca. 527?), and others compiled the historical record of the years during which the Northern Wei capital was Luoyang. Incorporating the previous work, their compilation was in the *jizhuan* 紀傳 (composite) style, consisting of annals, tables, monographs, and biographies/accounts. Wei Shou himself had participated, toward the end of the Northern Wei, in the compilation of the state history.

In contrast with later official dynastic histories, for which committees of scholars were appointed to the task of writing under the direction of a lead author or editor, and in contrast with previous such histories, which are thought to have been privately initiated and written, the newly commissioned compilation of a *Wei shu* was assigned to Wei Shou alone. He was given much editorial support by the Northern Qi history editing office, but the work was immediately criticized for biases in the treatment of some families of his contemporaries, and he was ordered four times to revise the text. Still, the original work was largely the product of Wei Shou's editorial hand, although it earned the title of being a "foul history" (*huishi* 穢史).

Dissatisfaction with Wei Shou's history continued after the fall of the Northern Qi. The founding ruler of the Sui dynasty commissioned a new history of the Northern Wei, the *Wei shi* 魏史, compiled by Wei Dan 魏澹 (dates unknown), that would not be slanted in favor of the Northern Qi, and with the charge of "correcting Wei Shou's errors." Tang Taizong later dealt with the matter of its bias, as well as that of the several other histories of the period of division, by ordering the compilation of the *Bei shi* and *Nan shi*, q.v. Later yet, the Tang historiographer Liu Zhiji 劉知幾 (661–721) revived the charge of bias against the *Wei shu*, but more for its pro-north/anti-south slant. His broader criticism was that Wei Shou was too subservient to his ruler, making the argument that it is the role of the historian to tell the strict truth, regardless of personal risk (*Shi tong** 12:356; Chaussende, "Un historien sur le banc des accusés," 2010).

Transmission of the text

By the Song dynasty, 30 of the 130 *juan* in the *Wei shu* were missing or incomplete. In the eleventh century, a team of scholars was commissioned to collate several histories from the Six Dynasties period, including the *Wei shu*. Such eminent scholars as Liu Ban 劉攽 (1023–1089), Liu Shu 劉恕 (1032–1078), An Dao 安燾 (1034–1108), and Fan Zuyu 范祖禹 (1041–1098) drew on Wei Dan's *Wei shi* and the *Bei shi*, as well as other sources, in order to make up a complete history. The resulting text was printed sometime between 1111 and 1118; this edition had a limited distribution, and no copies have survived. Another edition was printed in Sichuan during the Southern Song period, in 1144. No original copy of this edition itself has survived, but it was reprinted, along with some editorial changes, in both the Yuan and Ming periods. This printing has survived and is referred to as the Sanchao edition (Sanchao ben 三朝本). Two editions dating from the Ming Wanli 萬曆 reign (1573–1619), one printed in Nanjing—the Nan edition (Nan ben 南本)—and the other in Beijing—the Bei edition (Bei ben 北本)—have survived, as has another Ming edition printed by the Jiguge 汲古閣 in about 1636, known as the Ji edition (Ji ben 汲本). The 1739–1747 edition printed at the Wuyingdian 武英殿, within the Imperial Palace, survives and is known as the Dian ben 殿本, or Palace edition. Prior to the 1930s, almost all subsequent printings of the *Wei shu* were reprints of this 1739 Palace edition, the one exception being one published by the Jinling shuju in 1872, known as the Ju edition (Ju ben 局本).

For an overall account of the textual history of this and the other Six Dynasties standard histories, see appendix IV, "Textual Transmission of the Standard Histories."

Principal editions

The Commercial Press published an edition of the *Wei shu*, the Baina edition, between 1930 and 1937, that was primarily a photolithographic reproduction of the Sanchao edition, referring to it as the Song Sichuan edition. A limited number of corrections were nevertheless made to the text, so it was not an exact reproduction. The Kaiming shudian 開明書店 published the *Ershiwushi* in 1935, including an edition of the *Wei shu* known as the Kaiming edition. A list of references to various aids to the text—a genealogical chart of Northern Wei rulers, tables of imperial relatives and officials, and corrections and supplements to a few of the monographs—was attached at the end of each history. These supplementary materials were subsequently published separately in volume 4 of *Ershiwushi bubian* 二十五史補編 (Shanghai: Kaiming shudian, 1936–1937).

The Zhonghua shuju 中華書店 published a punctuated edition of the *Wei shu* in 1974, based on a close comparison of the Baina edition with the six extant pre-1900 editions, the last five of which were ultimately derived from the first, the Sanchao edition, each with some editorial changes. An electronic text version of the *Wei shu*, based on the Zhonghua shuju edition, can be accessed through the Twenty-five Histories (*Ershiwu shi* 二十五史) link at http://www.sinica.edu.tw/ftms-bin/ftmsw3/.

Selected studies

Blue, Rhea C. "The Argumentation of the Shih-Huo Chih Chapters of the Han, Wei, and Sui Dynastic Histories." *Harvard Journal of Asiatic Studies* 11.1/2 (1948): 1–118.

Chaussende, Damien. "Un historien sur le banc des accusés: Liu Zhiji juge Wei Shou." *Etudes chinoises* 29 (2010): 141–80.

Chen Lianqing 陳連慶. "*Jin shu* 'Shihuozhi' jiaozhu"; "*Wei shu* 'Shihuozhi' jiaozhu" 晉書食貨志校注；魏書食貨志校注. Changchun: Dongbei shifan daxue chubanshe, 1999.

Dien, Albert E. "Wei Tan and the Historiography of the *Wei shu*." In *Studies in Early Medieval Chinese Literature and Cultural History: In Honor of Richard B. Mather and Donald Holzman*, ed. Paul Kroll and David R. Knechtges, 399–466. Provo, UT: T'ang Studies Society, 2003.

Eberhard, Wolfram. *Das Toba-Reich Nordchinas: Eine soziologische Untersuchung*. Leiden: E. J. Brill, 1949.

———. "Objektivität und Parteilichkeit in der offiziellen chinesischen Geschichtsschreibung vom 3. bis 11. Jahrhundert." *Oriens Extremus* 5 (1958): 133–44.

Gardiner, Kenneth Herbert James. "Standard Histories, Han to Sui." In *Essays on the Sources for Chinese History*, ed. Donald D. Leslie, Colin Mackerras, and Wang Gungwu, 42–52. Canberra: Australian National University Press, 1973.

Holmgren, Jennifer. "Women and Political Power in the Traditional T'o-pa Elite: A Preliminary Study of the Biographies of Empresses in the *Wei-shu*." *Monumenta Serica* 35 (1981–1983): 33–74.

———. "Northern Wei as a Conquest Dynasty: Current Perceptions; Past Scholarship." *Papers on Far Eastern History* 40 (September 1989): 1–50.

Huang Yunhe 黃雲鶴. "Cong *Wei shu* Lizhi di yi juan kan Tuoba Xianbei jisi de Hanhua" 從魏書禮志第一卷看拓跋鮮卑祭祀的漢化. *Guji zhengli yanjiu xuekan* (2002.2): 50–53.

Ma Yanhui 馬艷輝. "Lun *Wei shu* shilun de tedian ji jiazhi" 論魏書史論的特點及價值. *Heilongjiang minzu congkan* 93 (2006): 88–94.

Qian Song 錢松. "*Wei shu* jiaokan zhaji" 魏書校勘札記. *Guji zhengli yanjiu xuekan* (2006.3): 54–59.

Wang Zhaoyi 王昭義. "Suichao chongxiu *Wei shu* shulue" 隋朝重修魏書述略. *Longdong xueyuan xuebao, Shehui kexue ban* 18.1 (2007): 83–85.

Ware, James Roland. "Notes on the History of the Wei-shu." *Journal of the American Oriental Society* 52.1 (1932): 35–45.

Zhang Li 張莉. "*Wei shu* zai minzushi zhuanshushang de chengjiu" 魏書在民族史撰述上的成就. *Shanxi daxue xuebao, Zhexue shehui kexue ban* 28.4 (2005): 92–97.

———. "*Wei shu* bianzhuan xingzhi kaolun" 魏書編撰性質考論. *Jinyang xuekan* (2006.1): 81–84.

———. "*Wei shu* 'Hui Shi' shuo bixu tuifan" 魏書穢史說必須推翻. *Yuncheng xueyuan xuebao* 24.1 (2006): 44–49.

Zhou Yiliang 周一良. "Wei Shou zhi shixue" 魏收之史學. In *Wei Jin Nanbeichao shilunji* 魏晉南北朝史論集, 236–72. Beijing: Zhonghua shuju, 1935; rpt., 1963.

Translations

Hans H. Frankel provides a bibliography of translations from the *Wei shu* in his *Catalogue of Translations from the Chinese Dynastic Histories for the Period 220–960* (Berkeley: University of California Press, 1957), 105–17. The following items are in addition to those in his bibliography.

European languages

Bokshchanin, A. A. *Materialy po ekonomicheskoi istorii Kitaia v rannee srednevekov'e: Razdely "shi kho chzhi" iz dinastiinykh istorii*. Moscow: Izd-vo "Nauka," Glav. red. vostochnoi litry, 1980. Translation from *juan* 110 [economics].

Holmgren, Jennifer. *Annals of Tai: Early T'o-pa History; An Annotated Translation of Chapter 1 of Wei shu*. Canberra: The Australian National University, 1982. Translation of *juan* 1 [pre-Wei Tuoba rulers].

Holzman, Donald. Review of Leon Hurvitz, "Wei Shou, Treatise on Buddhism and Taoism: An English Translation of the Original Chinese text of *Wei Shu* CXIV and the Japanese Annotation of Tsukamoto Zenryū." In *Yun-kang: The Buddhist Cave Temples of the Fifth Century A.D. in North China*, vol. 16. Kyoto: Kyoto University, Institute of Humanities, 1956. Also in *Journal of Asian Studies* 17.3 (1958): 474–76.

Japanese

Tsukamoto Zenryū 塚本善隆. *Gisho Shaku-Rō shi no kenkyū* 魏書釈老志の研究. Tokyo: Daitō shuppansha, 1974. Translation from *juan* 114 [Buddhism and Taoism].

———. *Gisho Shaku-Rō shi* 魏書釈老志. Tokyo: Heibonsha, 1990. Translation from *juan* 114 [Buddhism and Taoism].

Uchida Tomoo 内田智雄. *Yakuchū Chūgoku rekidai keihō shi* 譯注中國歷代刑法志. Tokyo: Sōbunsha, 1964. Translation from *juan* 111 [punishments/penal code].

Modern Chinese

Wang Zichen 王咨臣. *Lidai shihuozhi jinyi: Jin shu shihuozhi, Wei shu shihuozhi, Sui shu shihuozhi* 歷代食貨志今譯: 晉書食貨志, 魏書食貨志, 隋書食貨志. Nanchang: Jiangxi renmin chubanshe, 1986.

Indices

Chen Zhong'an 陳仲安 et al. *Beichao sishi renming suoyin* 北朝四史人名索引. 2 vols. Beijing: Zhonghua shuju, 1988.

Ershisishi renming suoyin 二十四史人名索引. 2 vols. Beijing: Zhonghua shuju, 1998.

Jian Xiuwei 簡修煒. *Beichao wushi cidian* 北朝五史辭典. 2 vols. Ji'nan: Shandong jiaoyu chubanshe, 2000.

Liang Qixiong 梁啓雄. *Ershisishi zhuanmu yinde* 二十四史傳目引得. Shanghai: Zhonghua shuju, 1936. Index to the Kaiming edition.

Kenneth Klein

Wei Wendi ji 魏文帝集

Introduction

Cao Pi 曹丕 (187–226), whose works are collected in the *Wei Wendi ji*, was the second son of Cao Cao 操 (155–220) and the elder brother of Cao Zhi 植 (192–232). After Cao Cao's death, Cao Pi deposed Emperor Xian of the Han (r. 189–220) and founded a new dynasty, the Wei. After ruling for six years, he died of illness in Luoyang in 226. Cao Pi is also known by his posthumous name, Wendi.

Contents

Cao Pi's extant literary work includes over thirty rhapsodies (*fu*), some of which have survived only as fragments. He was a versatile poet and wrote poems in various line lengths, including two *yuefu* titled "Ballad of Yan" ("Yan ge xing" 燕歌行), which are believed to be the earliest compositions in the seven-syllable line by a known author. His oeuvre includes forty poems in the five-syllable line, which was then emerging to become the most popular poetic form.

His literary talents are often compared with those of his brother Cao Zhi, but this comparison is almost always made in the context of the conflict between them over the issue of political succession. With very few exceptions, such as the judgments made by Liu Xie 劉勰 (ca. 460s–520s) and Wang Fuzhi 王夫之 (1619–1692), Cao Pi received a much lower evaluation than his brother. Despite a certain basis on literary and aesthetic grounds, the relative ranking of the brothers appears to owe also to sympathy for Cao Zhi as the losing party. Zhong Rong (fl. 502–519) ranks Zhong Pi in the middle category in the *Shi pin*, q.v. Noting a lack of refinement in his poems, Zhong comments that they are "low and plain like private conversation" (鄙質如偶語).

Cao Pi is also known for writing literary criticism. Although his important work *Dian lun* 典論 does not survive in its entirety, an excerpt from its chapter "On Literature" ("Lun wen" 論文) is preserved in the *Wen xuan*, q.v. Here, he discusses compositions of contemporary writers, noting their different literary styles and distinctive qualities in various literary genres. Cao Pi held literary accomplishments in high esteem and claimed them to be "a grand enterprise in managing a state and an enduring accomplishment" (經國之大業,不朽之盛事).

Another place where Cao Pi expounds some of his thoughts on literature is in two letters to his friend Wu Zhi (*Yu Wu Zhi shu* 與吳質書). In these letters he looks back and comments, with sad nostalgia, upon his friendship with talented contemporaries and their literary gatherings before a plague took the lives of several among them in 217. Here and in the chapter "On Literature," we see the emergence of the notion of the "Seven Masters of the Jian'an Period" (*Jian'an qizi* 建安七子), Jian'an being the last reign era of the Han dynasty's Emperor Xian. Although Cao Pi and Cao Zhi are often counted among the accomplished writers of the Jian'an reign, many of their works were actually written in the early years of the following Wei dynasty. In "On Literature," Cao Pi's evaluations of the strengths and skills in various genres of the Seven Masters show a new attention to discernible individual styles that are closely associated with personalities.

The self-image that he projected in his own writings, of being a royal patron and judge of literature, was reinforced in Xie Lingyun's 謝靈運 (385–433) series of poems titled "In Imitation of the Crown Prince of Wei's Collection at Ye" ("Ni Wei taizi Yezhong ji" 擬魏太子鄴中集). Depending on the interpretation of the character *ji* 集, which can mean either "gathering" or "collection," the title may indicate that there originally existed a "collection" of verses composed by Cao Pi and his friends. In the middle of several important military campaigns with his father, Cao Pi was able to spend most of his time between 204 to 219 in the city of Ye. According to *Sanguo zhi*, q.v., 21:599, after Cao Pi was appointed to the office of leader of court gentlemen for miscellaneous uses (*wu guan zhonglang jiang* 五官中郎將) in 211, he and his brother Cao Zhi frequently hosted literary gatherings with writers such as Wang Can 王粲 (177–217), Xu Gan 徐幹 (171–218), Chen Lin 陳琳 (d. 217), and Liu Zhen 劉楨 (d. 217). These gatherings often involved the composing of poems. In "Imitation," Xie Lingyun wrote poems in the personae of the famous Jian'an writers, preceded with a preface in Cao Pi's voice. The preface laments the loss of glory, a sentiment that strongly resonates with Cao Pi's own prose writings.

Sources of the work

There is no doubt that Cao Pi's extant writings are only a small portion of his original oeuvre. In the *Shi pin*, Zhong Rong singled out for praise a poem of his beginning with the line: "In the northwest there are floating clouds," and "more than ten other pieces" of like kind that had probably been grouped with it ("*Xibei you fuyun*" *shi yu shou* 西北有浮雲十餘首). Only the specific poem mentioned and one other piece have survived, thanks to their inclusion in the section for "miscellaneous poems" (*zashi* 雜詩) in the *Wen xuan*. The "Monograph on Music" ("Yue zhi" 樂志) of the *Song shu*, q.v., preserves some of Cao Pi's *yuefu* poems. The bibliographic monograph in the *Sui shu*, q.v., lists a collection in ten *juan* and notes that in the Liang it consisted of twenty-three *juan*. The same source also records the *Dian lun* in five *juan* and a *Record of Anomalies* (*Lie yi zhuan* 列異傳) in three *juan*. Most of these works have been lost. In the Ming dynasty, Zhang Xie (1574–1640) included a ten-*juan Wei Wendi ji* in his *Qishi'er jia ji**. Zhang Pu's (1602–1641) *Han Wei liuchao baisanjia ji*, q.v., contains a *Wei Wendi ji* in two *juan*, upon which most modern editions of Cao Pi's collected works are based. Ding Fubao 丁福保 (1874–1952) edited a six-*juan Wei Wendi ji* in his *Han Wei Liuchao mingjia ji* 漢魏六朝名家集.

Principal editions

Huang Jie 黃節. *Wei Wudi Wei Wendi shi zhu* 魏武帝魏文帝詩注. Beijing: Renmin wenxue chubanshe, 1958.

Xia Chuancai 夏傳才 and Tang Shaozhong 唐紹忠, eds. *Cao Pi ji jiaozhu* 曹丕集校注. Zhengzhou: Zhongzhou guji chubanshe, 1992.

Zheng Xuetao 鄭學弢, ed. *Lieyi zhuan deng wuzhong* 列異傳等五種. Beijing: Wenhua yishu chubanshe, 1988.

Selected studies

Bing Chen 炳宸. "Cao Pi de wenxue lilun" 曹丕的文學理論. In *Wenxue yichan xuanji* 文學遺產選集, 3:128–34. Beijing: Zuojia chubanshe, 1960.

Cai Yingjun 蔡英俊. "Cao Pi *Dianlun* 'Lunwen' xilun" 曹丕典論論文析論. *Zhongwai wenxue* 8.12 (May 1980): 124–45.

Cai Zhongxiang 蔡鍾翔. "*Dianlun* 'Lunwen' yu wenxue de zijue" 典論論文與文學的自覺. *Wenxue pinglun* (1983.5): 19–25.

Chen Bohai 陳伯海. "Cao Pi de wenxue piping biaozhun youguan wenti" 曹丕的文學批評標準有關問題. *Gudai wenxue lilun yanjiu* (July 1980): 141–54.

Chen Tianyi 陳恬儀. "Lun Cao Pi, Cao Zhi shige zhi jicheng yu chuangxin" 論曹丕曹植詩歌之繼承與創新. *Fuda Zhongyansuo xuekan* (1995.5): 177–97.

Fusek, Lois Mckim. "The Poetry of Ts'ao P'i (187–226)." Ph.D. diss., Yale University, 1975.

Goodman, Howard L. *Ts'ao P'i Transcendent: The Political Culture of Dynasty-Founding in China at the End of the Han.* Seattle: Scripta Serica, 1998.

Hu Ming 胡明. "Guanyu san Cao de pingjia wenti" 關於三曹的評價問題. *Wenxue pinglun* (1993.5): 30–41.

Knechtges, David. "The Rhetoric of Imperial Abdication and Accession in a Third-Century Chinese Court: The Case of Cao Pi's Accession as Emperor of the Wei Dynasty." In *Rhetoric and the Discourses of Power in Court Culture: China, Europe, and Japan*, ed. David R. Knechtges and Eugene Vance, 3–35. Seattle: University of Washington Press, 2005.

Leban, Carl. "Managing Heaven's Mandate: Coded Communication in the Accession of Ts'ao P'i, A.D. 220." In *Ancient China: Studies in Early Civilization*, ed. David T. Roy and Tsien Tsuen-hsuin, 315–42. Hong Kong: The Chinese University Press, 1978.

Lü Wuzhi 呂武志. "Liu Xie *Wenxin diaolong* yu Caoshi xiongdi wenlun" 劉勰文心雕龍與曹氏兄弟文論. *Guowen xuebao* 26 (June 1997): 107–36.

San Cao ziliao huibian 三曹資料彙編. Beijing: Zhonghua shuju, 1980.

Wang Meng'ou 王夢鷗. "Cong Dianlun canpian kan Cao Pi siwei zhi zheng" 從典論殘篇看曹丕嗣位之爭. *Zhongyanyuan shiyusuo jikan* 51.1 (1980): 97–114.

Zhang Keli 張可禮. *San Cao nian pu* 三曹年譜. Ji'nan: Qi Lu shushe, 1983.

Zhang Junli 張鈞莉. "Cong youxianshi kan Caoshi fuzi (Cao Cao, Cao Pi, Cao Zhi) de xingge yu fengge" 從遊仙詩看曹氏父子 (曹操, 曹丕, 曹植) 的性格與風格. *Zhongwai wenxue* 20.5 (1991): 95–121.

Zhang Xinjian 章新建. *Cao Pi* 曹丕. Hefei: Huangshan shushe, 1985.

Translations

Demiéville, Paul. *Anthologie de la poésie chinoise classique*. Paris: Gallimard, 1962. Pp. 115–17.

Holzman, Donald. "Literary Criticism in China in the Early Third Century A.D." *Asiatische Studien* 28 (1974): 113–49. [Translations of Cao Pi's *Dianlun lunwen* and letters to Wu Zhi.]

Owen, Stephen. "A Discourse on Literature." In *Readings in Chinese Literary Thought*, 57–72. Cambridge, MA: Harvard University Press, 1992.

———. *An Anthology of Chinese Literature: Beginnings to 1911*. New York: W. W. Norton and Company, 1996. Pp. 194–97, 262, 265–70, 282, 614.

Tian, Xiaofei. "A Discourse on Literature." [An annotated translation of Cao Pi's *Dianlun lunwen*.] In *Hawaii Reader of Traditional Chinese Culture*, ed. Victor H. Mair, Nancy S. Steinhardt, and Paul R. Goldin, 231–33. Honolulu: University of Hawai'i Press, 2005.

Qiulei Hu

Wei Wudi ji 魏武帝集

Introduction

Cao Cao 曹操 (155–220), whose writings are contained in the *Wei Wudi ji*, was a great warlord and powerful minister. He entered government service in 174 through recommendation, but his advance in power owed to his active participation in the military suppression of peasant revolts, among which the most critical was the Yellow Turban (*huang jin* 黃巾) Rebellion that broke out in 184. While he was the actual power holder for a long time, Cao Cao never claimed the throne. It was only after his death that his son Cao Pi 丕 (187–226) deposed the Han emperor and established the Wei dynasty. Cao Cao was posthumously named Emperor Wu of the Wei. By this point, the chaos at the end of the Han dynasty had considerably weakened the central government and enhanced the power of local warlords. As a result, the country divided into three states: Wei 魏 (220–265) in the north, Shu 蜀 (221–263) in the southwest, and Wu 吳 (222–280) in the southeast, resulting in the Three Kingdoms period of Chinese history.

Cao Cao was a great patron of literature. The Jian'an reign (196–220) of the last Han emperor is conventionally associated with the literary activities of the Cao family and the writers who gathered under its patronage. Besides the three Caos—Cao Cao and his sons Cao Pi and Cao Zhi 植 (192–232)—the representative writers of the Jian'an period include the so-called Seven Masters (*qi zi* 七子), a notion largely formulated in Cao Pi's essay "On Literature" ("Lun wen" 論文). They are usually listed as Ying Yang 應瑒 (d. 217), Liu Zhen 劉楨 (d. 217), Wang Can 王粲 (177–217), Chen Lin 陳琳 (d. 217), Ruan Yu 阮瑀 (ca. 165–212), Xu Gan 徐幹 (171–218), and Fan Qin 繁欽 (d. 218). Sometimes the list includes Kong Rong 孔融 (153–208), an important literary figure of an earlier generation, in place of Fan Qin.

Contents

The standard modern edition of Cao Cao's collection, known also as the *Cao Cao ji* 曹操集, includes twenty-two poems, 152 prose works, and a commentary to the *Sun zi* 孫子, a military manual. Cao Cao's poetic works were not highly regarded by his contemporaries. Until around the sixteenth century, his image in literature had often been more of a powerful patron than an accomplished writer. Only two of his poems were included in the literary anthology *Wen xuan*, q.v. Zhong Rong (fl. 502–519) ranked him in the lowest category of the *Shi pin*, q.v., and commented that his poems were "ancient in style and straightforward" (*gu zhi* 古直). Later readers of Cao Cao's poetry, however, often appreciated his straightforwardness and lack of refinement, traits that came to be seen as admirable characteristics of "ancient *yuefu*" (*gu yuefu* 古樂府).

All of Cao Cao's extant poems are *yuefu*, primarily preserved in the "Monograph on Music" ("Yue zhi" 樂志) in *Song shu*, q.v., 21:603–24, as part of the court music repertoire. Differing from most early *yuefu* poems, Cao Cao's poems often refer to historical events that he had experienced and thus have a certain specificity in time and place. This feature earned him Shen Deqian's 沈德潛 (1673–1769) comment: "The practice of borrowing old topics to describe contemporary events began with Lord Cao" (借古題寫時事始於曹公).

Among works included in Cao Cao's collection is a set of poems in four-syllable lines titled "Ballad on Stepping out of the Xia Gate" ("Bu chu Xiamen xing" 步出夏門行). The poems in this set describe places he passed through and seasonal changes he witnessed during the course of one of his military campaigns. Another famous piece is the "Short Ballad" ("Duan ge xing" 短歌行) that begins with the line, "Facing ale, one should sing" (對酒當歌). The poem is a variation on the motif of hosting a banquet and greeting honored guests, and in it Cao Cao cites a passage verbatim from "Deer Cry" ("Lu ming" 鹿鳴), a famous banquet poem in the *Shi jing* 詩經. Taking on the role of the Duke of Zhou (Zhou gong 周公), he expresses the wish to seek worthy men. This poem was later associated in popular imagination (most remarkably in the novel *Romance of the Three Kingdoms*, *Sanguo zhi yanyi* 三國志演義) with the famous battle at Red Cliff (*Chibi zhi zhan* 赤壁之戰), during which Cao Cao's attempt to conquer the territory south of the Yangzi River was crushed by the allied armies of Liu Bei 劉備 (161–223) of Shu and Sun Quan 孫權 (182–252) of Wu.

Cao Cao's extant prose writings consist of letters and documents that served practical and political purposes, most of which are preserved in his biography in the *Sanguo zhi*, q.v., and Pei Songzhi's 裴松之 (372–451) commentary. A large number of the prose essays belong to the genre of the command (*ling* 令). In "Divesting the Prefectures and Clarifying My Intents" ("Rang xian ziming benzhi ling" 讓縣自明本志令), dated 210, Cao Cao responds to suspicions about his ambition to usurp the throne and declares his loyalty to the Han court. As in his "Short Ballad," he claims to model himself on the Duke of Zhou and takes on the responsibility of protecting the emperor. There are several commands recruiting talented men, such as "Seeking Worthies" ("Qiu xian ling" 求賢令), dated 210, and "Not Being Restricted by Moral Qualities in Recommending Worthies" ("Ju xian wu ju pinxing ling" 舉賢勿拘品行令), dated 217. These documents reinforce the image of a charismatic leader created in the "Short Ballad."

Cao Cao wrote extensively on military strategy and tactics. The bibliographic monograph in the *Sui shu*, q.v., lists eight different kinds of his writings and commentaries on this topic, most of which have been lost. The only extant work is his commentary to the famous book of military strategy *Sun zi*, which circulated as an independent text. The earliest edition of the commentary, the *Wei Wudi zhu*

Sun zi 魏武帝注孫子 in three *juan* produced in the Song dynasty, is also the earliest annotated edition of the *Sun zi* that has survived. Owing to Cao's own success in the battlefield and reputation as a military strategist, his commentary was held in high regard.

Authorship and date of composition

Because Cao Cao's poems often deal with contemporary issues and seem to have certain connections with his own experience, later readers tended to view them as direct reflections and faithful records of crucial moments in his life. The association of the poem "Short Ballad" with the battle at Red Cliff is a case in point. Although this contextualization is often problematic because of the lack of external evidence, it provides Cao Cao's poems with a historical and cultural significance beyond literary and aesthetic value. Unlike most of his prose writings, which can be precisely dated, the time and context of composition remain uncertain for most of his poems.

In general, the relatively conservative nature of the major sources of Cao Cao's poems and prose, that is, the "Monograph on Music" in the *Song shu* and the *Sanguo zhi*, allows a certain level of confidence in the authenticity of the current collected works of Cao Cao.

Sources of the work

The earliest source of most of the extant poems is the "Monograph on Music" of the *Song shu*. The *Wen xuan* also includes two of Cao Cao's *yuefu* poems. Aside from the prose preserved in his biography in the *Sanguo zhi* and Pei Songzhi's commentary, some pieces can be found in encyclopedias such as the *Yiwen leiju*, q.v., and the *Taiping yulan*, q.v.

Transmission and early history of the text

The bibliographic monograph of the *Sui shu* (35:1059) records the *Wei Wudi ji* in twenty-six *juan* and notes that in the Liang it consisted of thirty *juan*, plus one *juan* that was a record of the contents. Both *Jiu Tang shu* 47:2052 and *Xin Tang shu* 60:1578 list a *Wei Wudi ji* in thirty *juan*. Most of the contents of this thirty-*juan* collection were lost by the Song dynasty. In the Ming dynasty, Zhang Xie (1574–1640) included a five-juan *Wei Wudi ji* in his *Qishi'er jia ji**. Zhang Pu (1602–1641) collated from early sources 145 poems and prose pieces into a one-*juan Wei Wudi ji* in his *Han Wei Liuchao baisan mingjia ji*, q.v. The Qing scholar Yao Zhenzong 姚振宗 (1842–1906) thoroughly researched the textual history of Cao Cao's works in the *Sanguo yiwen zhi* 三國藝文志, which is included as an appendix in the Zhonghua shuju edition of the *Cao Cao ji*. Ding Fubao's 丁福保 (1874–1952) *Han Wei Liuchao mingjia ji* 漢魏六朝名家集 includes a *Wei Wudi ji* whose four *juan* contain more works than Zhang Pu's collation. Ding's collection provided the base text for the standard modern edition of the *Cao Cao ji* published by Zhonghua shuju in 1959.

Principal editions

Cao Cao ji 曹操集. Ed. Zhonghua shuju bianji bu. Beijing: Zhonghua shuju, 1959; rpt., 1974.

Ding Fubao. *Wei Wudi ji*. In *Han Wei Liuchao mingjia ji*. Shanghai: Saoye shanfang, 1915.

Huang Jie 黃節 (1873–1935). *Wei Wudi Wei Wendi shi zhu* 魏武帝魏文帝詩注. Beijing: Renmin wenxue chubanshe, 1958.

Xia Chuancai 夏傳才, ed. *Cao Cao ji zhu* 曹操集注. Zhengzhou: Zhongzhou guji chubanshe, 1986.

Selected studies

Balazs, Etienne. "Cao Cao, zwei Lieder." *Monumenta Serica* 2 (1936–1937): 410–20. English translation by H. M. Wright: "Two Songs by Cao Cao." In *Chinese Civilization and Bureaucracy*, ed. Arthur F. Wright, 173–86. New Haven, CT: Yale University Press, 1964.

Chen Feizhi 陳飛之. "Lun Cao Cao shige de yishu chengjiu" 論曹操詩歌的藝術成就. *Wenxue pinglun* (1983.5): 27–33.

Chen Xiezhi 陳協志. "Cao Cao shige fengge zhi tanxi" 曹操詩歌風格之探析. *Fuda Zhongyansuo xuekan* 5 (September 1995): 161–75.

Inami Ritsuko 井波律子. "Sō Sō ron" 曹操論. *Chūgoku bungakuhō* 23 (October 1972): 1–27.

Owen, Stephen. *The Making of Early Classical Chinese Poetry*. Cambridge, MA: Harvard University Press, 2006. Pp. 139–77, 197–200.

Qiu Fuxing 邱復興. *Cao Cao jinlun* 曹操今論. Beijing: Beijing daxue chubanshe, 2003.

Ueki Hisayuki 植木久行. "Sō Sō gafushi ronkō" 曹操樂府詩論考. In *Mekada Makoto hakase koki kinen Chūgoku bungaku ronshū* 目加田誠博士古稀紀念中國文學論集, 99–120. Tokyo: Ryūkei shosha, 1974.

Zhang Keli 張可禮. *San Cao nianpu* 三曹年譜. Ji'nan: Qi Lu shushe, 1983.

Zhang Xiaohu 張嘯虎. "Cao Cao wenzhang yu Jian'an fenggu" 曹操文章與建安風骨. *Shehui kexue jikan* (1981.4): 126–31.

Zhang Zuoyao 張作耀. *Cao Cao zhuan* 曹操傳. Beijing: Renming chubanshe, 2000.

Translations

Demiéville, Paul. *Anthologie de la poésie chinoise classique*. Paris: Gallimard, 1962. Pp. 111–14.

Kroll, Paul. "Portraits of Ts'ao Ts'ao: Literary Studies on the Man and the Myth." Ph.D. diss., University of Michigan, 1976. Translation of some of Cao Cao's edicts in chap. 1 (pp. 1–47); translation of poems in chap. 2 (pp. 48–118) and appendix 1 (pp. 249–70).

Steinen, Diether von den. "Poems of Cao Cao." *Monumenta Serica* 4 (1939–1940): 130–81.

Qiulei Hu

Wen xuan 文選

Introduction

The *Wen xuan* (Selections of refined literature), compiled under the auspices of Xiao Tong 蕭統 (501–531), Crown Prince Zhaoming 昭明 of the Liang, is the earliest extant Chinese anthology arranged by genre. It is one of the most important sources for the study of Chinese literature from the Warring States period to the Qi (479–501) and Liang. Although the bibliographic monograph of the *Sui shu*, q.v., records the titles of 249 anthologies that were compiled from the Western Jin to the Sui period (265–618), nearly all of these works have been lost. The *Wen xuan* is the only one to survive intact.

Contents

The *Wen xuan* contains 761 pieces of prose and verse by 130 writers. The most commonly used version divides the works into thirty-seven genres: *fu* 賦 (exposition, or rhapsody), *shi* 詩 (lyric poetry), *sao* 騷 (elegy), *qi* 七 (sevens), *zhao* 詔 (edict), *ce* 冊 (patent of enfeoffment), *ling* 令 (command), *jiao* 教 (instruction), *cewen* 策文 (examination question), *biao* 表 (petition), *shang shu* 上書 (letter presented to a superior), *qi* 啟 (communication), *tanshi* 彈事 (accusation), *jian* 箋 (memorandum), *zouji* 奏記 (note), *shu* 書 (letter), *xi* 檄 (proclamation), *duiwen* 對文 (dialogue), *shelun* 設論 (hypothetical discourse), *ci* 辭 (song, or rhapsody), *xu* 序 (preface), *song* 頌 (eulogy), *zan* 贊 (encomium), *fuming* 符命 (mandate to rule based on prophetic signs), *shi lun* 史論 (disquisition from the histories), *shi shu zan* 史述贊 (evaluation and judgment from the histories), *lun* 論 (disquisition), *lianzhu* 連珠 (epigram), *zhen* 箴 (admonition), *ming* 銘 (inscription), *lei* 誄 (dirge), *ai* 哀 (lament), *beiwen* 碑文 (epitaph, stele inscription), *muzhi* 墓志 (grave memoir), *xingzhuang* 行狀 (conduct description), *diaowen* 弔文 (condolence), and *jiwen* 祭文 (offering). Some versions of the *Wen xuan* have thirty-eight categories with the addition of *yi* 移 (dispatch) between *shu* and *xi*. In the woodblock edition of Chen Balang 陳八郎 of the Southern Song, a thirty-ninth category, the *nan* 難 (refutation), is added.

The *fu* and *shi* sections, which are divided into subcategories, contain the most pieces. The *fu* section has fifteen subcategories, such as "Jingdu" 京都 (Metropolises and capitals), "Jiao si" 郊祀 (Sacrifices), and "Tianlie" 田獵 (Hunting). The *shi* section has twenty-three subcategories, among which those containing more than twenty pieces are "Yong shi" 詠史 (Poems on historical themes), "You lan" 游覽

(Sightseeing), "Zeng da" 贈答 (Exchange poems), "Xinglü" 行旅 (Travel), "Yuefu" 樂府 (Ballads), "Za shi" 雜詩 (Unclassified lyric poems), and "Za ni" 雜擬 (Diverse imitations). Works in each genre are arranged chronologically.

Xiao Tong explains in his preface the principles of compilation and the standards of selection. Four kinds of writing were excluded: (1) works traditionally attributed to the Duke of Zhou and Confucius, that is, works that are usually included in the *jing* 經, or "classics," category; (2) the writings of Laozi, Zhuangzi, Guanzi, and Mencius, meaning the works of the *zi* 子, or "masters," group; (3) the speeches of worthy men, loyal officials, political strategists, and sophists, which are found in such works as the *Guo yu* 國語 and *Zhanguo ce* 戰國策; and (4) historical narratives and chronicles. The last two types belong to the *shi* 史, or "history," category. Xiao makes a clear distinction between what he called *wen* 文, or "literary" works, and nonliterary works. By literary, he meant writing that displays "verbal coloration intricately arranged" and "literary ornament carefully organized," or works "whose matter is the product of profound thought, and whose principles belong to the realm of literary elegance." He considered the style of the classics, histories, and masters plain and simple, and their function primarily practical. Some later scholars faulted Xiao for much too narrow a definition of literature. The *Wen xuan* in fact does contain some pieces that belong to the excluded categories. For example, such works as "Preface to the *Shang shu*," "Preface to the Mao Version of the *Classic of Songs*," and the "Preface to the *Zuo shi Chunqiu*" by Du Yu 杜預 (222–284) all are from the standard version of the classics.

Compilation of the Text

The *Wen xuan* was compiled in the Eastern Palace, the residence of Xiao Tong. Xiao had a large library, which must have contained numerous collections of individual writers' works as well as earlier anthologies such as the *Wenzhang liubie ji* 文章流別集 compiled in the Western Jin by Zhi Yu 摯虞 (d. 312).

Much of the work of compiling the *Wen xuan* was done by members of Xiao Tong's staff. The most likely participants include Liu Xiaochuo 劉孝綽 (481–539), Wang Yun 王筠 (481–549), and Liu Xie 劉勰 (ca. 465–532). The *Bunkyō hifuron* 文鏡秘府論 by the Japanese Buddhist monk Kūkai 空海 (774–835) cites the early Tang scholar Yuan Jing 元兢, who says that Xiao Tong, Liu Xiaochuo, and others compiled the *Wen xuan*. The Song dynasty catalog *Zhongxing guange shumu* 中興館閣書目, compiled in 1178, mentions Xiao Tong's co-compilers as "He Xun 何遜 [d. ca. 518] and others." Most modern scholars believe that it is very likely that Liu Xiaochuo participated in the compilation of the *Wen xuan*. Shimizu Yoshio ("*Wen xuan* Li Shan zhu de xingzhi") has strenuously argued that Liu Xiaochuo is the primary compiler. It is unlikely that He Xun was involved in the project, for he died in 518 or 519, before the compilation of the *Wen xuan*.

According to Dou Chang 竇常 (756–825), who is cited in the Song dynasty private catalog *Junzhai dushu zhi** 20:1054, the compilers of the *Wen xuan* include in the anthology only writings by persons no longer living. The most recently deceased writer included in the *Wen xuan* is Lu Chui 陸倕, who died in 526. Thus, many scholars believe that the final compilation of the *Wen xuan* could not have been earlier than 526 or 527. Some scholars date it as late as 528. Recently, Wang Liqun ("Qingdai *Xuan* xue") published a book-length study in which he argues that the *Wen xuan* was compiled somewhat earlier, between 522 and 526.

Transmission and early history of the text

Almost immediately after compilation, the *Wen xuan* began to circulate widely. The original version was arranged in thirty *juan*. The earliest known commentary to the *Wen xuan* was actually done by a member of the Xiao family, Xiao Gai 該 (second half of sixth century). Xiao Gai was the grandson of Xiao Hui 恢 (476–526), who was a younger brother of Xiao Yan 衍 (464–549), Xiao Tong's father. Thus, Xiao Gai would have been a cousin once removed of Xiao Tong. Xiao Gai participated in the compilation of the famous dictionary *Qie yun*, q.v. His commentary to the *Wen xuan* was titled *Wen xuan yin yi* 文選音義. Although it is no longer extant, based on the title it must have been a philological commentary that explained the meaning and pronunciation of words in the text. Wang Zhongmin (*Bali Dunhuang canjuan xulu*, 2:3.12a–b) claimed to have discovered a fragment of this work among the Dunhuang manuscripts, but Zhou Zumo ("Lun *Wen xuan yin*") has disputed Wang's conclusion.

Already in the Sui and early Tang, *Wen xuan* scholarship began to flourish. The first important *Wen xuan* expert in this period was Cao Xian 曹憲 (fl. 605–649), a famous scholar from the Yangzhou area. He also wrote a commentary to the work titled *Wen xuan yin yi*. During the Tang, candidates for the *jinshi* (presented scholar) examinations were tested on their ability to compose *fu* and *shi*. Because the *Wen xuan* contained model examples of these two forms, it became one of the most important texts studied by degree candidates. Cao Xian taught the *Wen xuan* to younger scholars, including Xu Yan 許淹, Gongsun Luo 公孫羅, and Li Shan 李善 (d. 689). Li Shan divided the *Wen xuan* into sixty chapters. He also wrote a detailed commentary in which he cites from over 1,700 books. His preface to the *Wen xuan* does not state his principles of explication, but he did insert in his commentary remarks about his method of citation. One of Li's chief concerns was to illustrate the meaning of a particular graph or phrase by citing parallel examples from other texts. In most places, Li's commentary consists of providing the locus classicus so as to show the "origin" of a term. Li Shan also makes use of earlier commentaries on certain pieces. According to the *Zixia ji* 資暇集 of Li Kuangyi 李匡義 (Tang), Li Shan's commentary went through four revisions. He presented the final version to Emperor Gaozong in 658.

During the Tang, the *Wen xuan* was a very popular text (Wang, *Sui Tang Wenxuan xue yanjiu*). Du Fu, for example, urged his son "thoroughly to master the principles of the *Wen xuan*," and the *Chaoye qianzai* 朝野簽載 by Zhang Zhuo 張鷟 (ca. 660–ca. 740) mentions that even rural schools gave instruction in the *Wen xuan*. A number of manuscripts containing portions of the *Wen xuan* that have been discovered at Dunhuang and Turfan testify to its popularity. Although Li Shan's commentary provides detailed explanation of names, difficult words, and unusual terms, it does not contain extended paraphrases of the general meaning of many passages. Thus, in the Tang scholars wrote a new commentary that consists of a paraphrase that in effect "translates" the *Wen xuan* into Tang dynasty Chinese. In 718 Lü Yanzuo 呂延祚 presented to Emperor Xuanzong a text that consisted of the commentary of five scholars: Lü Xiang 呂向, Lü Yanji 呂延濟, Liu Liang 劉良, Zhang Xian 張銑, and Li Zhouhan 李周翰. This work, which was titled *Wuchen zhu* 五臣注, was more widely used than Li Shan's commentary, at least until the eleventh or twelfth centuries. Other versions of the *Wen xuan* are preserved in Japan. The most important of these is the *Wen xuan jizhu*, or *Monzen shūchū* 文選集注. The work originally consisted of 120 *juan* but only twenty-four *juan* survive.

During the Song, the *Wuchen* and Li Shan commentaries were combined into a single work known as the *Liuchen zhu Wen xuan* 六臣注文選. This is now regarded as a printing with many defects, the most serious of which was the frequent mingling of the Li Shan and *Wuchen* commentaries to the point that Li Shan's original commentary often could not be identified. There was, however, one carefully prepared edition of Li Shan's commentary printed by the Song scholar You Mao 尤袤 (1127–1181). This edition became the basis for the standard edition of the Li Shan commentary prepared under the direction of Hu Kejia 胡克家 (1757–1816). This version is generally regarded as the standard edition of the *Wen xuan*.

Principal editions

The *Wuchen* version of the *Wen xuan* was printed quite early. The earliest known printing was done in Sichuan during the Wudai period (906–960). Printings of the *Wuchen* commentary are now quite rare. The National Central Library in Taiwan has a Southern Song woodblock of the *Wuchen Wen xuan* prepared by Chen Balang in Shaoxing 紹興 31 (1161). This was printed by the Chonghua shufang 崇化書坊 in Jianyang 建陽. This edition is commonly referred to as the Chen Balang edition. Subsequently, the *Wuchen* commentary was printed together with Li Shan's commentary. This version was known as the *Liujia* 六家 version. In this arrangement, the *Wuchen* commentary precedes the Li Shan commentary. Like the Li Shan version, it is in sixty *juan*. It was long thought that the earliest known printing of this version was the Guangdu Pei shi 廣都裴氏 woodblock that was printed in Sichuan between 1106 and 1111. There was a reprint of this by Yuan Jiong 袁褧 (1502–1547) in the period 1534–1549. This is usually referred to as the Yuan ben 袁本. There is a recently discovered Korean printing of the *Liujia Wen xuan* dated 1428 that is held in the Kyujanggak 奎章閣 Library of Seoul National University. However, it is based on a printing done in Xiuzhou 秀州 (modern Jiaxing 嘉興, Zhejiang) in 1094. The Xiuzhou edition is the earliest known printing to combine the *Wuchen* and Li Shan commentaries. The *Wuchen* portion of the text is actually based on a printing done in Pingchang 平昌 (modern Anqiu 安邱, Shandong) before 1026. This makes it earlier by more than a hundred years than the Chen Balang edition. The Li Shan commentary is based on the edition prepared by the Guozijian 國子監 and presented to the Northern Song emperor in 1031. Another printing of the *Liujia Wen xuan* was done in the Southern Song in Mingzhou 明州 (modern Ningbo, Zhejiang). The original printing no longer exists. The earliest extant printing is a revised version dated Shaoxing 28 (1158).

The earliest printing of the more common version of the *Wuchen* and Li Shan commentary, called the *Liuchen zhu Wen xuan* 六臣注文選, was done in Ganzhou 贛州 (modern Jiangxi) and probably dates from 1162. This edition is held in the Zhongguo guojia tushuguan, Beijing. In this version, the Li Shan commentary precedes the *Wuchen* commentary. The so-called Chaling 茶陵 edition is the most commonly cited printing of the Ganzhou edition. Titled *Zengbu Liuchen zhu Wen xuan* 增補六臣注文選, it was edited with additional commentary by Chen Renzi 陳仁子 and first printed in Chaling in 1299. The Hong Pian 洪楩 woodblock of this work, originally issued in 1549, has been reprinted by the Huazheng shuju 華正書局 (Taipei, 1974). At the end of the Southern Song, another *Liuchen zhu Wen xuan* based on the Ganzhou edition was printed in Jianzhou 建州. It is estimated that the date of printing was between 1195 and 1200. This edition served as the basis for the photo-reproduction issued in the *Sibu congkan** in 1919. In 1987 the Zhonghua shuju in Beijing issued a three-volume reprint of the *Sibu congkan* edition.

The most famous Song printing of the Li Shan edition is the version prepared by You Mao in Chunxi 淳熙 8 (1181). The printing was done by the Chiyang jun zhai 池陽郡齋. Chiyang is the ancient name for Guichi 貴池 in Anhui. The You Mao edition has long been hailed as the earliest version of the Li Shan text that was not contaminated by the *Wuchen* readings. However, based on recent studies, we now know that the You Mao version does not represent a "pure" Li Shan text but actually shows signs of interpolations from the *Wuchen* version. There were multiple versions of the You Mao edition printed in the Southern Song, and there is a photographic reproduction of it:

Wen xuan 文選. Beijing and Hong Kong: Zhonghua shuju, 1974; Taipei: Shimen tushu youxian gongsi, 1976; *Zhonghua zaizao shanben* 中華再造善本. Beijing: Beijing tushuguan, 2004.

Throughout the Yuan and Ming the most commonly printed edition of the *Wen xuan* was the *Wuchen/Liuchen* text. In the Qing period, Hu Kejia was able to obtain a printing of You Mao's edition from the Wu area, and, wishing to make available a good edition of Li Shan's commentary, he requested the scholars Gu Guangqi 顧廣圻 (1776–1835) and Peng Zhaosun 彭兆孫 (1769–1821) to collate the text and prepare it for printing. As part of their collation work, Gu and Peng compiled a ten-*juan* variorum called the *kaoyi* 考異, which was appended to the text. This was printed in 1809 and has become the standard edition of the Li Shan *Wen xuan*. Some of the more commonly known printings are the following:

Wen xuan. Taipei: Yiwen yinshuguan, 1957. Rpt. of 1809 edition.

Wen xuan. Taipei: Zhengzhong shuju, 1971.

Wen xuan. Beijing: Zhonghua shuju, 1977.

There is a recent punctuated and typeset edition:

Wen xuan. 6 vols. Shanghai: Shanghai guji chubanshe, 1986.

Textual history

Fan Zhixin 范志新. *Wen xuan banben lungao* 文選版本論稿. Nanchang: Jiangxi renmin chubanshe, 2003.

Fu Gang 傅剛. *Wen xuan banben yanjiu* 文選版本研究. Beijing: Beijing daxue chubanshe, 2000.

Shiba Rokurō 斯波六郎. "*Monzen* shohon no kenkyū" 文選諸本研究. In *Monzen sakuin* 文選索引, 1:3–105. Kyoto: Kyōto daigaku jimbun kagaku kenkyūjo, 1959. Two translations of Shiba Rokurō into Chinese are (a) Dai Yan 戴燕, "Dui *Wen xuan* gezhong banben de yanjiu" 對文選各種版本的研究, in *Zhongwai xuezhe Wen xuan xue lunji* 中外學者文選學論集, ed. Yu Shaochu 俞紹初 and Xu Yimin 許逸民, 849–961 (Beijing: Zhonghua shuju, 1998); and (b) Huang Jinhong 黃錦鋐 and Chen Shunü 陳淑女, *Wen xuan zhuben zhi yanjiu* 文選諸本之研究 (Taipei: Fayan chubanshe, 2003).

Shimizu Yoshio 清水凱夫. "*Wen xuan* Li Shan zhu de xingzhi" 文選李善注的性質. In *Wen xuan yu Wen xuan xue* 文選與文選學, ed. Zhongguo *Wen xuan* xue yanjiu hui 中國文選學研究會, 709–24. Proceedings of the Fifth International *Wen xuan* Conference held in Zhenjiang in 2002. Beijing: Xueyuan chubanshe, 2003.

Wang Xibo 汪習波. *Sui Tang Wenxuan xue yanjiu* 隋唐文選學研究. Shanghai: Shanghai guji chubanshe, 2005.

Wang Zhongmin 王重民. *Bali Dunhuang canjuan xulu* 巴黎敦煌殘卷敘錄. Beijing: Guli Beiping tushuguan, 1936–1937.

Zhou Zumo 周祖謨. "Lun *Wen xuan yin* canjuan zhi zuozhe ji qi yin fan" 論文選音殘卷之作者及其音反. *Furen xuezhi* 8.1 (1939): 113–25; rpt. as "Lun *Wen xuan yin* canjuan zhi zuozhe ji qi fangyin" 方音, in *Wenxue ji* 問學集, 1:177–91 (Beijing: Zhonghua shuju, 1966); rpt. in *Zhongwai xuezhe Wen xuan xue lunji*, 45–58.

Translations

English

Knechtges, David R. *Wen xuan, or Selections of Refined Literature*. Vol. 1, *Rhapsodies on Metropolises and Capitals*. Princeton, NJ: Princeton University Press, 1982. Vol. 2, *Rhapsodies on Sacrifices, Hunting, Travel, Sightseeing, Palaces and Halls, Rivers and Seas*. Princeton, NJ: Princeton University Press, 1987. Vol. 3,

Rhapsodies on Natural Phenomena, Birds and Animals, Aspirations and Feelings, Sorrowful Laments, Literature, Music, and Passions. Princeton, NJ: Princeton University Press, 1996.

European languages

Margouliès, Georges. *Le "Fou" dans le Wen-siuan: Étude et textes*. Paris: Paul Geuthner, 1926.

Zach, Erwin von. *Die Chinesische Anthologie: Übersetzungen aus dem Wen Hsüan*, ed. Ilse Martin Fong. 2 vols. Harvard-Yenching Institute Studies 18. Cambridge, MA: Harvard University Press, 1958.

Japanese

Kōzen Hiroshi 興膳宏 and Kawai Kōzo 川合康三. *Monzen* 文選. Tokyo: Kadokawa shoten, 1988.

Nakajima Chiaki 中島千秋. *Monzen: Fuhen* 文選: 賦篇. Shinshaku Kambun taikei 79. Tokyo: Meiji shoin, 1977.

Obi Kōichi 小尾郊一 and Hanabusa Hideki 花房英樹, trans. *Monzen*文選. 7 vols. Zenshaku Kambun taikei 26–32. Tokyo: Shūeisha, 1974–1976.

Uchida Sennosuke 内田泉之助 and Ami Yuji 網祐次. *Monzen: Shihen* 文選: 詩篇. 2 vols. Shinshaku Kambun taikei 14–15. Tokyo: Meiji shoin, 1963–1964.

Chinese

Chen Hongtian 陳宏天, Zhao Fuhai 趙福海, and Chen Fuxing 陳復興, eds. and comm. *Zhaoming wenxuan yizhu* 昭明文選譯注. 6 vols. Changchun: Jilin wenshi chubanshe, 1987–1993.

Li Jingying 李景濚, ed. *Zhaoming wenxuan xinjie* 昭明文選新解. 6 vols. Tainan: Jinan chubanshe, 1990–1993.

Zhang Baoquan 張葆全, ed. Fan Yunkuan 樊運寬, comm. and trans. *Xinbian jinzhu jinyi Zhaoming wen xuan* 新編今注今譯昭明文選. 6 vols. Taipei: Liming wenhua shiye gongsi, 1995.

Zhang Qicheng 張啟成 et al., eds. *Wen xuan quan yi* 文選全譯. 5 vols. Guiyang: Guizhou renmin chubanshe, 1994.

Zhou Qicheng 周啟成, Cui Fuzhang 崔富章, Zhu Hongda 朱宏達, Zhang Jinquan 張金泉, Shui Weisong 水渭松, and Wu Fangnan 伍方南, comm. and trans. *Xinyi Zhaoming Wen xuan* 新譯昭明文選. 4 vols. Taipei: Sanmin shuju, 1997.

Bibliographies and surveys

Kang Dawei 康達維 (David R. Knechtges). "Ershi shiji de Ou Mei 'Wen xuan xue' yanjiu" 二十世紀的歐美'文選學'研究. *Zhengzhou daxue xuebao* (1994.1): 54–57.

Knechtges, David R. "*Wen xuan* Studies." *Early Medieval China* 10–11.1 (2004): 1–22.

Liu Yuejin 劉躍進. "*Wen xuan* xue" 文選學. In *Zhonggu wenxue wenxian xue* 中古文學文獻學, 21–26. Nanjing: Jiangsu guji chubanshe, 1997.

Wang Liqun 王立群. "Qingdai *Xuan* xue yu ershi shiji xiandai *Xuan* xue" 清代選學與20世紀現代選學. *Henan daxue xuebao, Shehui kexue ban* 42.4 (2002): 14–20.
———. *Xiandai Wen xuan xue shi* 現代文選學史. Beijing: Zhongguo shehui kexue chubanshe, 2003.
Wei Shuqin 魏淑琴, Wu Qiong 吳窮, and Jiang Hui 姜蕙, eds. *Zhongwai Zhaoming Wen xuan yanjiu lunzhu suoyin* 中外昭明文選研究論著索引. Changchun: Jilin wenshi chubanshe, 1988.

Concordances and indices

Shiba Rokurō 斯波六郎. *Monzen sakuin* 文選索引. 4 vols. Kyoto: Kyōto daigaku jimbun kagaku kenkyūjo, 1957–1959. Rpt., Taipei: Zhengzhong shuju, 1972.
Wen xuan zhu yinshu yinde 文選注引書引得. Harvard-Yenching Institute Sinological Index Series 26. Cambridge, MA: Harvard University Press: 1935. Rpt., Taipei: Chengwen, 1966.

David R. Knechtges

Wenxin diaolong 文心雕龍

Introduction

The *Wenxin diaolong* by Liu Xie 劉勰 (fl. late fifth to early sixth century) is the most important early medieval work of literary theory, acclaimed for its deep understanding, elegant diction, and singularly comprehensive approach. The *Wenxin diaolong* addresses a broad scope of questions, from the lofty workings of the literary imagination down to the depths of typology, illustrated throughout by perceptive, critical references to a vast number of texts through the ages that reveal Liu Xie's outstanding erudition. Although the *Wenxin diaolong* had already been held in high regard since the Tang, its reputation soared in the course of the twentieth century. Today, it is widely quoted as an authoritative voice in studies on Chinese literature of all periods and genres, and it has inspired more research than any other Chinese treatise on literature, giving rise to the designation "Dragon studies" (*long xue* 龍學). The extensive scholarly interest in the *Wenxin diaolong* testifies not only to the text's magnitude and complexity but also to the philological and interpretative problems posed by the author's sophisticated and often arcane parallel prose.

Among the aspects of the text that elude definitive interpretation is its subtle and without doubt intentionally ambiguous title. The words *wenxin diaolong* are commonly understood to express the complementary relation, or balance, of the spirit and the craft of literature. However, the exact meaning of the title's two components as well as their syntactic relationship have been interpreted in manifold ways, such as "the literary mind and the carving of dragons," "the literary mind carves dragons," "carving a dragon at the core of literature," "carving the dragon of the literary mind," "literary creativity and ornate rhetoric," and so forth.

Details about Liu Xie's life come mainly from his brief biographies in *Liang shu*, q.v., 50:710–12, and *Nan shi*, q.v., 72:1781–82. Neither source is explicit regarding family status and the years of his birth and death. Nor can we find in the postface to the *Wenxin diaolong* information about when he completed this major work, which has led to an abundance of hypotheses.

It is generally assumed that Liu Xie, styled Yanhe 彥和, was born between 460 and 480 in Jingkou 京口 near Jiankang (present Nanjing) into a distinguished but impoverished family whose members had formerly served in high ranks. The family may have been distantly related to the reigning house of the Han dynasty. Orphaned at an early age, Liu was devoted to learning. He did not marry, but depended on the eminent Buddhist monk Sengyou 僧祐 (445–518), who edited such important works as the *Chu sanzang ji ji* 出三藏記集 (Collected notes on the production of the *Tripiṭika*) and *Hongming ji*, q.v. Liu stayed with Sengyou at the Dinglin 定林 Temple on Mount Zhong 鐘 north of Jiankang for more than a decade, assisting him with the cataloging and collation of Buddhist scriptures. There is no consensus as to whether Liu was still an impressionable boy when he entered the temple or was already a young man with a solid Confucian education. Nor do we know whether his motive was utilitarian or religious. Such questions are often discussed by critics in order to claim Liu for Confucianism and to deny that he held any genuine Buddhist beliefs. It is quite certain, however, that Liu became thoroughly familiar with Buddhist scriptures, teachings, and practice during this decade, if not earlier. Like many of his contemporaries, he obviously did not assume the incompatibility of Confucianism and Buddhism.

Structure and arrangement of the text

The *Wenxin diaolong* is unusually extensive for a text of literary thought. Containing more than 38,000 characters, its length may be compared, for example, with the approximately 6,000 characters of the contemporaneous *Shi pin*, q.v. Another distinguishing feature of the *Wenxin diaolong* is its systematic organization that, given Liu Xie's expertise in Buddhist literature and thought, has led to the assumption that its structure was influenced by Indian epistemological and analytical models, especially the *śāstras*. Yet the organization of the work can actually be explained by an indigenous concept embodied in a venerated canonical book of Confucianism: the *Wenxin diaolong*'s fifty chapters (*pian* 篇) correspond to the cosmologically significant number of yarrow stalks used in divination according to the *Zhou yi* 周易 (Changes of Zhou). Disregarding the last chapter, which is a postface—just as during divination one of the yarrow stalks would be left out—we see that the composition of the *Wenxin diaolong* is essentially tripartite. The thematic units, discussed next, are *pian* 1–5, *pian* 6–25, and *pian* 26–49.

In the first five *pian*, Liu expounds his basic literary concepts. He opens with a treatise about the origin of civilization, writing, and literature in the metaphysical and absolute Way (*dao* 道), to turn directly to the core of the Confucian tradition in *pian* 2 and 3, which concern the literary impact of the sages, and the overarching importance of the Confucian canonical writings as models for all later literature, the *Zhou yi* being of key importance among them. Interestingly, *pian* 4 and 5 are then dedicated to the apocrypha and the *Chuci* 楚辭 (Elegies of Chu), respectively, which had acquired quasi-canonical significance by the late fifth century. In subsequent sections of the *Wenxin diaolong*, Liu Xie constantly refers back to the notions outlined in this introductory part, called the "pivot of literature" (*wen zhi shuniu* 文之樞紐) in his postface.

1. Yuan dao 原道   The Way as the source
2. Zheng sheng 徵聖   Evidence from the sages

3.	Zong jing 宗經	The canon as the ancestor
4.	Zheng wei 正緯	Rectifying the apocrypha
5.	Bian sao 辨騷	Distinguishing the elegies

Each *pian* in this section, as well as throughout the work, concludes with a rhymed encomium (*zan* 贊).

The next typological section consists of twenty *pian* that "discuss patterned [texts] and describe unpatterned [writings]" (*lun wen xu bi* 論文敘筆), again according to Liu's postface. *Pian* 6–25 feature an all-embracing range of literary genres and subgenres, by far superseding any former attempt at genre classification in China. Due to terminological and typological problems, the actual number of genres that are either introduced or mentioned in passing is controversial, but it is much larger than suggested by the titles of the *pian*, as some individually cover more than a dozen genres. The detailed introduction of the major genres follows a pattern described by Liu Xie in his postface: first, he traces the genre back to its origin in the Confucian canon and explains the genre's name; second, he outlines the genre's historical development from antiquity to his own day, mainly through critical references to exemplary works, and mentions subgenres.

6.	Ming shi 明詩	Elucidating lyric poetry
7.	Yuefu 樂府	Music Bureau poetry
8.	Quan fu 詮賦	Explaining rhapsodies
9.	Song zan 頌讚	Eulogies and encomia
10.	Zhu meng 祝盟	Prayers and covenants
11.	Ming zhen 銘箴	Inscriptions and admonitions
12.	Lei bei 誄碑	Dirges and epitaphs
13.	Ai diao 哀弔	Laments and condolences
14.	Za wen 雜文	Miscellaneous patterned texts
15.	Xie yin 諧讔	Humor and riddles
16.	Shi zhuan 史傳	Historical traditions
17.	Zhu zi 諸子	The masters
18.	Lun shuo 論說	Disquisitions and discourses
19.	Zhao ce 詔策	Edicts and patents of enfeoffment
20.	Xi yi 檄移	War proclamations and dispatches
21.	Feng shan 封禪	The sacrifices to heaven and earth

22.	Zhang biao 章表	Declarations and petitions
23.	Zou qi 奏啟	Presentations and communications
24.	Yi dui 議對	Opinions and answers
25.	Shu ji 書記	Written records

The third group of *pian* is dedicated to a variety of basic questions concerning the creative process, rhetoric, prosody, and so forth, summed up in Liu Xie's postface as "the analysis of feelings and the examination of coloration" (*pou qing xi cai* 剖情析采). Some of its twenty-five *pian* are among the most celebrated treatises of Chinese literary thought, such as *pian* 26 about the workings of imagination in writing, 27 about the formative power of an author's personality and its interaction with normative categories, 28 about the aesthetic concepts "wind" and "bone" as necessary qualities of a superior literary work, and 48 about questions of the reader's response to literature. Together with the five introductory chapters, this part of the *Wenxin diaolong* has been the source of greatest fascination for readers, scholars, and translators.

26.	Shen si 神思	Spirit thought
27.	Ti xing 體性	Style and personality
28.	Feng gu 風骨	Wind and bone
29.	Tong bian 通變	Continuity and change
30.	Ding shi 定勢	Determination of momentum
31.	Qing cai 情采	Actual condition and ornamentation
32.	Rong zai 鎔裁	Casting and tailoring
33.	Sheng lü 聲律	Prosody
34.	Zhang ju 章句	Paragraph and period
35.	Li ci 麗辭	Parallel phrasing
36.	Bi xing 比興	Comparison and affective image
37.	Kua shi 夸飾	Hyperbole
38.	Shi lei 事類	Allusion and reference
39.	Lian zi 練字	Elaborate characters
40.	Yin xiu 隱秀	Latent and salient
41.	Zhi xia 指瑕	Pointing out flaws
42.	Yang qi 養氣	Nourishing vitality

43. Fu hui 附會	Fluency and coherence
44. Zong shu 總術	The general technique
45. Shi xu 時序	Chronological order
46. Wu se 物色	The appearance of things
47. Cai lüe 才略	Survey of talent
48. Zhi yin 知音	The one who knows the tone
49. Cheng qi 程器	Weighing the vessel

Pian 50, titled "Xu zhi" 序志 (Exposition of my intentions) is a postface in the early and early medieval tradition of attaching an often autobiographically inspired statement to one's collection of writings. Liu's postface, while doing justice to its title in explaining his reason to write the *Wenxin diaolong* as well as aspects of his descriptive procedures, provides very little information about his life.

Date of composition

The date of the *Wenxin diaolong* is not known. According to one theory, Liu Xie completed the work during the last years of the Qi dynasty (479–502), toward the end of his stay with Sengyou. The *Liang shu* biography relates that Liu Xie approached Shen Yue 沈約 (441–513) in the way of a hawker to present him with his book, and that Shen Yue highly appreciated its contents. The anecdote is often regarded to be dubious, though, not the least because there is no indication of the book's wider reception or influence before the Tang. Some critics believe that Liu Xie did not come from an upper-class family but was a commoner who managed to rise to imperial recognition through his connection with Sengyou and the recommendation of Shen Yue.

After the founding of the Liang dynasty (502), Liu was appointed to various minor offices at court and beyond. The most noteworthy of these positions was interpreter-clerk of the Eastern Palace (*donggong tongshi sheren* 東宮通事舍人) in the service of heir-apparent Xiao Tong 蕭統 (Zhaoming taizi 昭明太子; 501–531), sometime during the early Liang and probably between 506 and 513. The prince enjoyed Liu Xie's company and may have been influenced by him in the compilation of his *Wen xuan*, q.v. An alternate theory about the date of the *Wenxin diaolong*'s composition presumes that the book was completed during Liu's term at the prince's residence, when he had access to an extensive library. On imperial command, Liu later resumed editorial work at the Dinglin Temple, a move commonly thought to have occurred either in the wake of Sengyou's death in 518 or that of Xiao Tong in 531. Having completed his assignment at the temple, Liu Xie asked for and was granted permission to become a monk. He took religious vows, adopted the name Huidi 惠地, and died within a year's time. Depending upon the presumed year of Liu Xie's second move to the Dinglin Temple as well as the duration of his editorial tasks there, his death has been dated to "520 or later" or to "532 or later."

The collected writings mentioned in Liu Xie's *Liang shu* biography were lost by the Tang dynasty. Apart from the *Wenxin diaolong*, only two other texts have survived to this day. One is a stele inscription (a genre in which Liu reportedly excelled) and is titled "Liang Jian'an wang zao Shanshan Shicheng si shixiang bei" 梁建安王造剡山石城寺石像碑 (Epitaph on the stone statue [of Maitreya] erected by the Liang Prince of Jian'an at Shicheng Temple on Mount Shan). The Prince of Jian'an was Xiao Wei 蕭偉 (476–533), who erected the statue in the year 516. The other text is a Buddhist apologetic, titled "Mie huo lun" 滅惑論 (Disquisition on the elimination of doubts). It remains an open question whether Liu Xie authored the politico-philosophical text *Liuzi xinlun* (Master Liu's new disquisitions).

Transmission

A *Wenxin diaolong* in fifty *pian* is first mentioned in Liu Xie's *Liang shu* biography. Starting with *Sui shu*, q.v., 35:1082, the work is listed in the standard histories' bibliographical monograph as consisting of ten *juan*, which should not be regarded to indicate a different length of the text. The *Wenxin diaolong* appears to have been in wide circulation during the Tang dynasty, as it is mentioned and cited in a number of texts, among them Kūkai's 空海 (774–835) *Bunkyō hifuron* 文鏡祕府論 (Discussion of the secret store of the *Mirror of Writing*). Citations and references to the *Wenxin diaolong* continue after the Tang, a prominent example being the *Taiping yulan* (comp. 978), q.v. Although the transmission of the *Wenxin diaolong* thus appears to have been uninterrupted, the earliest known commentary, by Xin Chuxin 辛處信 (listed in *Song shi* 209:5408) is presumed lost, as are all other Song dynasty editions of the text itself. The oldest surviving woodblock print, which is slightly damaged, dates from 1355 (Zhizheng 15) of the Yuan dynasty.

Yuan kanben Wenxin diaolong 元刊本文心雕龍. Shanghai: Shanghai guji chubanshe, 1993. Photomechanical reproduction of the Yuan print stored in Shanghai Library.

Zhou Zhenfu 周振甫 (1911–2000). *Wenxin diaolong cidian* 文心雕龍辭典. Beijing: Zhonghua shuju, 1996. Pp. 615–799 include an annotated edition of the Yuan print ("Yuan Zhizheng ben *Wenxin diaolong* huijiao" 元至正本文心雕龍匯校).

Newly discovered manuscripts

The oldest manuscript version, a fragment in the form of a butterfly-bound paper booklet containing the partly damaged first fifteen *pian*, dates from the Tang. It was found in Dunhuang and is kept in the British Museum in London (catalog no. S.5478). High-resolution images of the manuscript are available online through the International Dunhuang Project, at http://idp.bl.uk/. For a study of this manuscript, see the following:

Lin Qitan 林其錟 and Chen Fengjin 陳鳳金. *Dunhuang yishu Wenxin diaolong can juan ji jiao* 敦煌遺書文心雕龍殘卷集校. Shanghai: Shanghai shudian, 1991. Annotated photomechanical reproduction of the manuscript, with an appendix of those excerpts from twenty-three *pian* that were quoted in *Taiping yulan*.

Principal editions

Starting with a Ming printing in moveable type, prepared by Feng Yunzhong 馮允中 in 1504, dozens of late imperial editions of the *Wenxin diaolong* have survived. The most important or widely available are the following:

Zhang Zhixiang 張之象 (1579); reproduced in *Sibu congkan**.
Hu Weixin 胡維新 (1582); included in *Congshu jicheng chubian**.
He Yunzuhong 何允中 (1592); included in *Han Wei congshu* 漢魏叢書.
Wang Weijian 王惟儉. *Wenxin diaolong xungu* 文心雕龍訓詁 (1611). Based on a punctuated version by Yang Sheng'an 楊升庵, among other texts, and incorporating Mei Qingsheng's 梅慶生 phonetic annotations (*yinzhu* 音註); frequently reprinted (6th reprint in 1622).
Gujin tushi jicheng 古今圖書集成 (1726). Various sections of this work include the complete text of *Wenxin diaolong*, chapter by chapter.
Huang Shulin 黃叔琳 (1674–1756). *Wenxin diaolong jizhu* 文心雕龍輯注 (1741). This is the most influential premodern annotated edition; based on the commentaries by Mei Qingsheng, Wang Weijian, and others; copied into the *Siku quanshu* (1782; *Yingyin Wenyuange Siku quanshu** 1478:1–70) and later printed in *Sibu beiyao** and *Wanyou wenku* 萬有文庫 (Changsha: Shangwu yinshuguan, 1939).
Ji Yun 紀昀 (1724–1805). A revision of Huang Shulin's *Wenxin diaolong jizhu* printed in 1833.

Commentaries

In this selection of modern commentaries, those prepared by Fan Wenlan, Yang Mingzhao, and Zhou Zhenfu are most often used as standard editions.

Fan Wenlan 范文瀾 (1893–1969). *Wenxin diaolong zhu* 文心雕龍註. 2 vols. Beijing: Renmin wenxue chubanshe, 1958. Based on Fan's earlier *Wenxin diaolong jiangshu* 文心雕龍講疏 (1929–1931) and *Wenxin diaolong zhu* (1936); full text accessible online through Academia Sinica (Taipei).
Li Yuegang 李曰剛 (1906–1985). *Wenxin diaolong jiaoquan* 文心雕龍斠詮. 2 vols. Taipei: Guoli bianyiguan Zhonghua congshu bianshen weiyuanhui, 1982. Extensive commentary; among materials in the appendices are a study by Liu Yusong 劉毓崧 (Qing), "Shu *Wenxin diaolong* hou" 書文心雕龍後, with commentary by Meng Chuanming 蒙傳銘, subcommentary by Li Yuegang; a biographical study and a discussion of important editions.

Liu Yongji 劉永濟 (1887–1966). *Wenxin diaolong jiaoshi* 文心雕龍校釋. Beijing: Zhonghua shuju, 1962 (a revision of his first edition, Shanghai: Zhengzhong shuju, 1948).

Wang Gengsheng 王更生. *Wenxin diaolong duben* 文心雕龍讀本. 2 vols. Taipei: Wen shi zhe chubanshe, 1985. Appendices include a biographical essay and catalog of important editions.

Wang Liqi 王利器 (1912–1998). *Wenxin diaolong xinshu* 文心雕龍新書. Bali daxue Beijing Zhong Fa Hanxue yanjiusuo tongjian congkan 巴黎大學北京中法漢學研究所通檢叢刊 15. Beijing: Université de Paris Centre d'Études Sinologiques de Pékin, 1951. Appendices include collections of prefaces and assessments, collections of references to *Wenxin diaolong* in premodern texts, editorial remarks on Wang Weijian's *Wenxin diaolong xungu*, and Yang Mingzhao's glosses on Liu Xie's biography (see later).

———. *Wenxin diaolong jiaozheng* 文心雕龍校證. Shanghai: Shanghai guji chubanshe, 1980. Rev. ed. of the 1951 book. Rpt., *Wenxin diaolong jiaozhu* 校註. Taipei: Mingwen shuju, 1982.

Yang Mingzhao 楊明照 (1909–2003). *Wenxin diaolong jiaozhu* 文心雕龍校注. Shanghai: Gudian wenxue chubanshe, 1958. Modern typeset edition based on Huang Shulin's edition; commentaries by Huang and Li Xiang 李詳 (1859–1931) in *Wenxin diaolong buzhu shiyi* 文心雕龍補注拾遺 (1909–1911), followed by Yang Mingzhao's commentary; numerous valuable appendices: "*Liang shu* 'Liu Xie zhuan' jianzhu" 梁書'劉勰傳'箋註 (from *Wenxue nianbao* 7 [1941]: 91–96); Liu Xie's two other extant writings; collections of references to *Wenxin diaolong* in premodern texts (listings in bibliographies, historical appraisals, attributed and nonattributed quotations); a collection of prefaces to *Wenxin diaolong* editions, and descriptions of extant editions. See also Yang Mingzhao in "Commentary without the Text."

Zhan Ying 詹鍈. *Wenxin diaolong yizheng* 文心雕龍義證. 3 vols. Shanghai: Shanghai guji chubanshe, 1989. Most extensive commentary, with descriptive catalog of extant editions. Available online at Academia Sinica.

Zhou Zhenfu. *Wenxin diaolong zhushi* 文心雕龍註釋. Beijing: Renmin wenxue chubanshe, 1981. Contains an annotated version of Liu Xie's *Liang shu* biography.

Commentary without the text

Huang Kan 黃侃 (1886–1935). *Wenxin diaolong zhaji* 文心雕龍札記. Beijing: Wenhua shushe, 1927. Annotations to chapters 1–9, 24–44, and 50; incorporated into Fan Wenlan's commentary.

Yang Mingzhao. *Wenxin diaolong jiaozhu shiyi* 文心雕龍校注拾遺. Shanghai: Shanghai guji chubanshe, 1982. Contains revised and supplemented version of Yang Mingzhao's 1958 commentary *Wenxin diaolong jiaozhu* (384 pp.) and appendices (490 pp.).

―――. *Wenxin diaolong jiaozhu shiyi buzheng* 文心雕龍校注拾遺補正. Nanjing: Jiangsu guji chubanshe, 2001. Commentary further revised and supplemented.

Zhang Lizhai 張立齋. *Wenxin diaolong kaoyi* 文心雕龍考異. Taipei: Zhengzhong shuju, 1974. Available online at Academia Sinica.

Selected studies

Wenxin diaolong scholarship is a vast field. Qi Liangde's bibliography (later) collects more than six thousand titles published between 1907 and 2005—including a meager twenty-six works in Western languages. The following list is thus highly selective and gives priority to Western scholarship.

Cai, Zong-qi, ed. *A Chinese Literary Mind: Culture, Creativity, and Rhetoric in Wenxin diaolong*. Stanford, CA: Stanford University Press, 2001.

Fu Zhi 甫之 and Tu Guangsheng 涂光生, eds. *Wenxin diaolong yanjiu lunwen xuan* 文心雕龍研究論文選, *1949–1982*. 2 vols. Ji'nan: Qi Lu shushe, 1987.

Gibbs, Donald, A. "Liu Hsieh: Author of the *Wen-hsin tiao-lung*." *Monumenta Serica* 29 (1970/1971): 117–41. Based on the author's Ph.D. diss., "Literary Theory in the Wen-hsin tiao-lung," University of Washington (Seattle), 1970.

Jullien, François. "Théorie du parallélisme littéraire, d'aprés Liu Xie." *Extrême-Orient, Extrême-Occident* 11 (1989): 99–109.

Kōzen Hiroshi 興膳宏. *Xingshan Hong Wenxin diaolong lunwenji* 論文集. Trans. Peng Enhua 彭恩華. Ji'nan: Qi Lu shushe, 1984.

Lavoix, Valérie. "Un dragon pour emblème: Variations sur le titre du *Wenxin diaolong*." *Études chinoises* 19.1–2 (2000): 197–247. Based on the author's dissertation, "Liu Xie (ca. 465–ca. 521): Homme de lettres, bouddhiste laïque et juge des poètes," Institut National des Langues et Civilisations Orientales (Paris), 1998.

Lomová, Olga, ed. *Recarving the Dragon: Understanding Chinese Poetics*. Prague: Charles University, Karolinum Press, 2003.

Richter, Antje. "Notions of Epistolarity in Liu Xie's *Wenxin diaolong*." *Journal of the American Oriental Society* 127.2 (2007): 143–60.

Rao Zongyi 饒宗頤, ed. *Wenxin diaolong yanjiu zhuanhao* 文心雕龍研究專號. Hong Kong: Xianggang daxue Zhongwen xuehui, 1962.

Toda Kōgyō 戶田浩曉, trans. Cao Xu 曹旭. *Wenxin diaolong yanjiu* 文心雕龍研究. Shanghai: Shanghai guji chubanshe, 1992.

Tőkei, Ferenc (1930–2000). *Genre Theory in China in the 3rd–6th Centuries (Liu Hsieh's Theory on Poetic Genre)*. Budapest: Akadémiai Kiadó, 1971.

Wang Gengsheng. *(Chongxiu zengding) Wenxin diaolong yanjiu* (重修增訂)文心雕龍研究. Taipei: Wen shi zhe chubanshe, 1989. Revision of the 1977 ed.; includes detailed chronological table; study of early prints of *Wenxin diaolong*.

Wang Yuanhua 王元化 (1920–2008). *Wenxin diaolong chuangzuo lun (xiudingben)* 文心雕龍創作論(修訂本). Shanghai: Shanghai guji chubanshe, 1984. Revision of the 1979 ed.

Zhongguo *Wenxin diaolong* xuehui 中國文心雕龍學會, ed. *Wenxin diaolong xuekan* 文心雕龍學刊 . Ji'nan: Qi Lu shushe, 1983–1992 (six issues). Continued as *Wenxin diaolong yanjiu* 文心雕龍研究. Beijing: Beijing daxue chubanshe, 1995– (seven issues). Proceedings of *Wenxin diaolong* conferences organized by the association.

———, ed. *Lun Liu Xie ji qi Wenxin diaolong* 論劉勰及其文心雕龍. Beijing: Xueyuan chubanshe, 2000.

Translations

English

Owen, Stephen. "Wen-hsin tiao-lung." In *Readings in Chinese Literary Thought*, 183–298. Cambridge, MA: Harvard University Press, 1992. Extensively annotated translations of *pian* 1, 3, 26–32, 34–36, 40, 43–44, 46, 48, 50.

Shih, Vincent Yu-chung (Shi Youzhong 施友忠; 1902–2001). *The Literary Mind and the Carving of Dragons: A Study of Thought and Pattern in Chinese Literature*. Hong Kong: Chinese University Press, 1983. Revision of the first ed. (New York: Columbia University Press, 1959). Reviewed by James R. Hightower, *Harvard Journal of Asiatic Studies* 22 (1959): 280–88, and by Donald Holzman, *Artibus Asiae* 23 (1960): 136–39.

Wong, Siu-kit, Allan Chung-hang Lo, and Kwong-tai Lam. *The Book of Literary Design*. Hong Kong: Hong Kong University Press, 1999. Sparsely annotated.

Yang, Guobin, and Zhenfu Zhou. *Dragon-Carving and the Literary Mind*. 2 vols. Library of Chinese Classics Chinese-English. Beijing: Foreign Language Teaching and Research Press, 2003. Sparsely annotated translation into English and modern Chinese. Reviewed by Eugene Chen Eoyang, *China Review International* 12.2 (2005): 587–89.

European languages

Král, Oldřich. *Duch básnictví řezaný do draků*. Prague: Brody, 2000. Annotated.

Lavagnino, Alessandra C. *Il tesoro delle lettere: Un intaglio di draghi*. Grandi Pensatori d'Oriente e d'Occidente: Le Tradizioni 3. Milan: Luni Editrice, 1995. Annotated.

Li Zhaochu. *Traditionelle chinesische Literaturtheorie: Wenxin diaolong—Liu Xies Buch vom prächtigen Stil des Drachenschnitzens (5. Jh.)*. Edition Cathay 25. Dortmund, Germany: Projekt Verlag, 1997. Annotated translation of chaps. 26–50.

Relinque Eleta, Alicia. *El corazón de la literatura y el cincelado de dragones*. Granada: Comares, 1995.

Japanese

Kōzen Hiroshi. *Bunshin chōryō* 文心雕龍. Tokyo: Chikuma shobō, 1968. Annotated.

Mekada Makoto 目加田誠. *Bunshin chōryō* 文心雕龍. Tokyo: Ryūkei shosha, 1986. Annotated; first published in Mekada's *Bungaku geijutsu ronshū* 文學藝術論文集 (Tokyo: Heibonsha, 1974).

Toda Kōgyō 戶田浩曉. *Bunshin chōryō* 文心雕龍. 2 vols. Tokyo: Meiji shoin, 1974–1978. Annotated.

Modern Chinese

Feng Jiachu 馮葭初. *Yanwen duizhao Wenxin diaolong* 言文對照文心雕龍. 2 vols. Huzhou: Wuzhou shuju, 1927.

Li Jingrong 李景濚. *Wenxin diaolong xinjie* 文心雕龍新解. Tainan: Hanlin chubanshe, 1968.

Lu Kanru 陸侃如 (1903–1978) and Mou Shijin 牟世金. *Wenxin diaolong yizhu* 文心雕龍譯註. Ji'nan: Qi Lu shushe, 1981.

Zhang Deng 張燈. *Wenxin diaolong xinzhu xinyi* 文心雕龍新注新譯. Guiyang: Guizhou jiaoyu chubanshe, 2003.

Zhou Ming 周明. *Wenxin diaolong jiaoshi yiping* 文心雕龍校釋譯評. Nanjing: Nanjing daxue chubanshe, 2007.

Zhou Zhenfu. *Wenxin diaolong jinyi* 文心雕龍今譯. Beijing: Zhonghua shuju, 1986.

Reference works and research aids

Qi Liangde 戚良德. *Wenxin diaolong xue fenlei suoyin* 文心雕龍學分類索引, *1907–2005*. Shanghai: Shanghai guji chubanshe, 2005. Lists 6,517 studies (or editions), thematically arranged, with author index and information about textual history of many editions.

Yang Mingzhao, ed. *Wenxin diaolong xue zonglan* 文心雕龍學綜覽. Shanghai: Shanghai shudian chubanshe, 1995.

Zhang Shaokang 張少康 et al., eds. *Wenxin diaolong yanjiu shi* 文心雕龍研究史. Beijing: Beijing daxue chubanshe, 2001.

Zhang Wenxun 張文勛. *Wenxin diaolong yanjiu shi* 文心雕龍研究史. Kunming: Yunnan daxue chubanshe, 2001.

Zhou Zhenfu. *Wenxin diaolong cidian* 文心雕龍辭典. Beijing: Zhonghua shuju, 1996. Contains separate sections explaining difficult words and phrases, technical terms, authors, literary titles, secondary criticism and authors, disputes regarding the *Wenxin diaolong*; appendices include annotation of the Yuan dynasty print, collection of *Wenxin diaolong* prefaces, and descriptive catalog of extant editions.

Indices

Okamura Shigeru 岡村繁, ed. *Bunshin chōryō sakuin* 文心雕龍索引. Hiroshima: Hiroshima Bunrika daigaku Kanbungaku kenkyūshitsu, 1950. Stroke-count arrangement, based on Huang Shulin's *Wenxin diaolong jizhu* as revised by Ji Yun; no text included.

Wang Liqi, ed. *Wenxin diaolong xinshu tongjian* 文心雕龍新書通檢. Bali daxue Beijing Zhong Fa Hanxue yanjiusuo tongjian congkan 15. Beijing: Université de Paris Centre d'Études Sinologiques de Pékin, 1952. Stroke-count arrangement; supplementary indexes by EFEO romanization and Wade-Giles; the included text is Wang Liqi, *Wenxin diaolong xinshu*.

Zhu Yingping 朱迎平, ed. *Wenxin diaolong suoyin* 文心雕龍索引. Shanghai: Shanghai guji chubanshe, 1987. Stroke-count arrangement; four separate parts for sentences, personal names, titles, literary terms; supplementary indexes by four-corner system and *pinyin*; the included text is based on Fan Wenlan's *Wenxin diaolong zhu* (1958). This text is included in the online Chinese Text Project with a full-text search capability.

Antje Richter

Wu Jun ji 吳均集

Introduction

Wu Jun, styled Shuxiang 叔庠 (469–520), was a prolific and versatile writer in many genres. His biographies in *Liang shu*, q.v., 49:698–99, and *Nan shi*, q.v., 72:1780–81, relate that he was born into a poor family from Guzhang 故鄣, Wuxing 吳興 commandery (Anji, Zhejiang) but say nothing of his activities during the Southern Qi. It is thought he may have supported himself during his youth by his swordsmanship, and possibly spent five or six years in the garrison town of Shouchun 壽春 (alternate name: Shouyang 壽陽, Anhui) in the hope of making a name for himself there (Cao and Shen, *Nanbeichao wenxue shi*). More than any poet since Bao Zhao 鮑照 (ca. 414–466), he used the *yuefu* genre to focus upon the hardships suffered by soldiers on campaign and to celebrate their courage and stoicism.

The titles of Wu's occasional poems establish that he lived for a while in Guiyang 桂陽 (Chenzhou, Hunan), where he formed friendships with officials posted there from the central government. He also visited the capital Jiankang (modern Nanjing), where his literary ability favorably impressed Shen Yue 沈約 (441–513). During the early Liang, when the well-respected poet and official Liu Yun 劉惲 (465–517) was appointed grand warden of Wuxing, he invited Wu to be a recorder on his staff. Through Liu Yun's recommendation, he successively held positions in other local administrations and, around the year 513, was introduced at court and named an audience attendant (*chaojing* 朝請). A biography preserved by Zheng Qiao (1104–1162) gives the additional information that before going to the capital, while Wu served Xiao Wei 蕭偉 (476–533), the Prince of Jian'an 建安, in Jiangzhou (in modern Jiangxi), he held the office of gentleman attendant of the domain (*guoshi lang* 國侍郎); see *Tong zhi** 176:2819a–b.

At the Liang court Wu wrote light verses of which twenty-six pieces were included in the *Yutai xinyong*, q.v. He also popularized the subject of martial heroism. A major endeavor no longer extant is his annotation in ninety *juan* to the *Hou Han shu*, q.v. Another lost work is his *Qi Chunqiu* 齊春秋 (Chronicles of the Qi dynasty). This history's account of the support that the reigning Emperor Wu of the Liang (r. 502–549) had earlier given the murderous usurper Xiao Luan (known posthumously as Qi Mingdi) so offended the emperor that he dismissed Wu from office and ordered the work destroyed (*Nan shi* 72:1781). The task of writing the previous dynasty's history was then entrusted to a royal family member, Xiao

Zixian 蕭子顯 (489–537). After a period of retirement, Wu was recalled to court and reinstated in the lowly position of audience attendant, the office that occurs in some traditional editions of his collection.

Wu's extensive scholarship in local history, folklore, and geography is indicated in many other independent prose works of which only the titles or brief excerpts remain (Campany, *Strange Writing*, 178). A major collection of anomaly accounts (*zhiguai* 志怪) has survived, however.

Contents

The modern annotation by Lin Jiali 林家驪, *Wu Jun ji jiaozhu* 吳均集校注 (Hangzhou: Zhejiang guji chubanshe, 2005), contains the largest number of writings. Its contents, which are not divided by *juan*, are as follows:

Prose: rhapsodies, 5; memorial, 1; personal letters, 3; proclamations, 1; dispatch, 1; discourse, 1; epigrams, 2

Music Bureau poems (folk style): 38

Lyric poems: 106

Addendum: stories from a collection of anomaly accounts, 17; poem fragments omitted from traditional editions, 4; additional stories, 5

Wu's three letters have been acclaimed as outstanding early descriptions of natural scenery and travel. His originality is evident also in his humorous exploitation of genres that ordinarily had a serious purpose. The "Xi Jiangshen ze Zhou Muwang bi" 檄江神責周穆王璧 (Proclamation to the God of the Yangzi River, seeking the Jade Disc of King Mu of Zhou) is a parody of a proclamation of war. Other satires are a discourse (*shuo* 說) about ingredients to make the fillings for dumplings and a dispatch (*yi* 移) faulting a nobleman for not sharing the marvelous foods in his larder. The anomaly accounts belong to the *Xu Qi Xie ji* 續齊諧記 (A sequel to Qi Xie's records), which Wu evidently conceived as a continuation of the *Qi Xie ji* by Dongfang Wuyi 東方无疑 (fl. ca. 430). Lin Jiali's addendum presents the seventeen tales involving preternatural phenomena that had appeared in traditional editions and, in a separate section, five tales that modern scholars believe should have been included with the others.

Transmission and early history of the text

From the time of Wu Jun's biographies in the *Liang shu* and *Nan shi*, completed in 636 and 659, through the record in the *Jiu Tang shu* (47:2070), completed in 945, his collected works were said to consist of twenty *juan*. The *Jiu Tang shu*'s bibliographic monograph is thought, however, to rely upon a much earlier list drawn up in 721. Although the same number of twenty *juan* was reported in *Tong zhi** 69:819c, only ten *juan* were listed in *Xin Tang shu* 60:1594 (compiled in 1060), and in *Chongwen zongmu** 5:16a, p. 719, a roughly contemporaneous catalog of the Song imperial library. The *Song shi*'s bibliographic monograph, compiled during the middle of the Yuan, listed only three *juan* (208:5329). The *Xu Qi Xie ji* was first recorded in *Sui shu*, q.v., 33:980, as having one *juan*, the same length given in later bibliographic records with the exception of the *Chongwen zongmu* and the ninth-century catalog *Nihonkoku genzaisho mokuroku* 日本國見在書目錄, both of which noted three *juan*.

Principal editions

Ming dynasty scholars constructed the present collection. Feng Weine (1513–1572) assembled two *juan* of Wu's poetry in *Gushi ji**, *juan* 91–92, and Mei Dingzuo 梅鼎祚 (1549–1615) included eight pieces of his prose in the *Liang wen ji**. The collected works edited by Zhang Xie (1574–1640) for his *Qishi'er jia ji** was titled *Wu Chaojing ji* and contained three *juan* and an addendum; this has been reprinted in *Xuxiu Siku quanshu** 1587:368–400. The collation that has been the primary base for modern editions is Zhang Pu's (1602–1641) *Wu Chaojing ji* (one *juan*) in *Han Wei Liuchao baisan mingjia ji*, q.v. (Nanjing: Jiangsu guji chubanshe, 2002), 5:61–86.

No modern discoveries have enlarged the quantity of the five rhapsodies and nine prose pieces collected during the Ming. Naturally, there exist references to compositions now lost, as in Yan Zhitui's (531–after 591) mention of a "Pojing fu" 破鏡賦 (Rhapsody on a broken mirror) in *Yanshi jiaxun* (*juan* 4, section 9, "Wenzhang" 文章), q.v.; see also Lin, *Wu Jun ji jiaozhu*, 242. For texts of rhapsodies and prose alone, the standard edition is Yan Kejun's (1761–1843) *Quan shanggu sandai Qin Han Sanguo Liuchao wen** ("Quan Liang wen," *juan* 60).

The 101 lyric poems in Zhang Pu's edition were augmented by Ding Fubao (1874–1952) in "Quan Liang shi," *juan* 8 (2:1353–82) of the *Quan Han Sanguo Jin Nanbeichao shi**. Lu Qinli further added fragments of poems in "Liang shi," *juan* 10–11 (2:1719–54) of his *Xian Qin Han Wei Jin Nanbeichao shi**. Questions of authenticity account for minor differences in the editions' contents. For example, Zhang Pu and Lin Jiali both accept the lyric poem "Chun yuan" 春怨 as authentic, but Ding Fubao and Lu Qinli do not. This work had been ascribed to Wang Sengru 王僧孺 (d. 521) in *Yutai xinyong*, q.v., *juan* 6. Although Lin Jiali joins Lu Qinli to include "Lan gu shi" 覽古詩, Lin believes the poem actually belonged to a suite by Wu Yun 吳筠 (d. 778), as attributed in *Quan Tang shi* 全唐詩, *juan* 853 (Lin, "Foreword," p. 24). In the *yuefu* genre, Lin includes "Bo fu jiu" 白附鳩, which is given as an anonymous work in *Yuefu shiji*, q.v., *juan* 49, but immediately precedes Wu Jun's "Bo fu jiu" 白浮鳩. A note in the *Yuefu shiji* states that the first title is an alternate for the latter one. These are the only verses by either title in the anthology.

The *Xu Qi Xie ji*, a lost edition compiled by a certain Lu You 陸友 during the early Yuan, was probably the source for the text included by Gu Yuanqing 顧元慶 (1487–1565) in his *Wenfang xiaoshuo sishi'er zhong* 文房小說四十二種. This woodblock edition was reissued under the title *Yangshan Gushi wenfang xiaoshuo* 陽山顧氏文房小說 (Beijing: Beijing tushuguan chubanshe, 2004). Wu Guan 吳琯 also included the *Xu Qi Xie ji* in his *Gujin yishi* 古今逸史, published during the Wanli era (1573–1619). Many other editions were printed during the Ming and Qing. There are variations among them in the stories' narrative details. Critics long suspected that the *Xu Qi Xie ji* did not survive in complete form. The modern scholar Wang Guoliang has argued persuasively that five more tales that are variously attributed in encyclopedias and collectanea must have belonged to the original compilation. These are "Tiantai yu xian" 天台遇仙, "Wang Jingbo" 王敬伯, "Wuse shi" 五色石, "Wu Zixu" 伍子胥, and "Wanwen niang" 萬文娘.

Assessments

Contemporaries were struck by Wu Jun's "classical spirit," and imitators of his poetry's plain and straightforward diction coined the term "the Wu Jun style" (*Wu Jun ti* 吳均體). Wang Shizhen 王士禎 (1634–1711) credited him as a source for the development of "frontier works" (*biansai zhi zuo* 邊塞之作) during the High Tang.

The playwright Tang Xianzu 湯顯祖 (1550–1617) admired the *Xu Qi Xie ji*'s skillful narration and extraordinary contents, saying that their effect upon readers was "to make their bones fly and eyebrows dance" (*gufei meiwu* 骨飛眉舞). The stories have become recognized as some of the most sophisticated examples of the early *zhiguai* genre.

Selected studies

Cao Daoheng 曹道衡 and Shen Yucheng 沈玉成. "Wu Jun." In *Nanbeichao wenxue shi* 南北朝文學史, 206–12. Beijing: Renmin wenxue chubanshe, 1998.

Spring, Madeline K. "Recollections of a Fleeting Romance: The Wang Jingbo Narrative." *Early Medieval China* 10–11.2 (2005): 1–41.

Wang Guoliang 王國良. *Xu Qi Xie ji yanjiu* 續齊諧記研究. Taipei: Wen shi zhe chubanshe, 1987. A chapter of research about the collection precedes the annotation of twenty-two tales.

Wang Zhongling 王鍾陵. *Zhongguo zhonggu shige shi* 中國中古詩歌史, 715–29. Huaiyin: Jiangsu jiaoyu chubanshe, 1988.

Translations

Birrell, Ann. *New Songs from a Jade Terrace: An Anthology of Early Chinese Love Poetry, Translated with Annotations and an Introduction*. London: George Allen and Unwin, 1982. Pp. 160–65, 251, 279.

Campany, Robert Ford. "Ghosts Matter: The Culture of Ghosts in Six Dynasties *Zhiguai*." *Chinese Literature: Essays, Articles, Reviews* 13 (1991): 27–29.

Connery, Chris. "The Spirit of the Clear Stream Temple" and "The Scholar from Yang Hsien." In *Classical Chinese Tales of the Supernatural and the Fantastic: Selections from the Third to the Tenth Century*, ed. Karl S. Y. Kao, 159–63. Bloomington: Indiana University Press, 1985.

Hsieh, Daniel. *The Evolution of Jueju Verse*. New York: Peter Lang, 1996. Pp. 21, 198–200, 205.

Strassberg, Richard E. "Letter to Song Yuansi." In *Inscribed Landscapes, Travel Writing from Imperial China*, 31–32. Berkeley: University of California Press, 1994.

Research aid and concordance

Campany, Robert Ford. *Strange Writing: Anomaly Accounts in Early Medieval China*. Albany: State University of New York Press, 1996. Pp. 87–88. For stories not included in the *Xu Qi Xie ji*'s standard editions, Campany provides their locations in selected collectanea.

Go Kin shi sakuin 吳均詩索引. Edited by Satō Toshiyuki 佐藤利行, Morino Shigeo 森野繁夫, and Sasaoka Emiko 笹岡恵美子. Tokyo: Hakuteisha, 1999.

Cynthia L. Chennault

Xiao Tong ji 蕭統集

Introduction

Xiao Tong (501–531) is commonly known as Zhaoming taizi 昭明太子, or Crown Prince Zhaoming, a posthumous appellation that became incorporated into the title of the literary anthology that he compiled during the early half of the 520s. The *Zhaoming Wen xuan*, or simply *Wen xuan*, q.v., is the earliest fully extant anthology organized into thematic subgenres and arguably the most important and influential work to shape the development of Chinese literary tradition in the ensuing fifteen hundred years. Xiao Tong's name is first and foremost associated with this great literary monument.

Ironically, the intriguing life and literary mind of this learned man were somehow obscured by the *Wen xuan*'s monumentality. What we know of Xiao Tong as a thinker and man of letters is limited to the meager and biased information found in his official biographies. Xiao Tong's uniqueness as a historical personage lies in the fact that his birth coincided very closely with the founding of the Liang dynasty. The expectation that he would be the successor in a stable and long-ruling house was written into his name Tong, which can signify "unified and continuous reign." This turned out to be a failed promise, the cause of which is either glossed over or speculated upon by historians. One might wonder whether this prince, who had been given a conservative education and exerted circumspection throughout his life, came into conflict with his father's rather unconventional policies to promote the veneration of the Buddha.

A close reading of Xiao Tong's so-called religious poems discloses his uneasiness about the foreign religion's encroachment upon the state's economic and social order. This aspect of the Liang prince's thought was completely muffled due to obvious reasons. As he died at the unusually early age of thirty, it was probably natural for the court to attempt to protect his "good name," even if that meant shielding the truth from posterity. Readers of Xiao's biographies cannot but be left with a sense of dissatisfaction and puzzlement, as the Liang prince appears there to be a harmless Confucian who shared his father's passion for Buddhism. A study of Xiao's works may compensate for the inadequacy of the historical record, in addressing this puzzle and other questions about his thought.

Contents

Xiao Tong's collected writings are known as the *Zhaoming taizi ji* 昭明太子集 or *Zhaoming taizi wenji* 昭明太子文集. The modern *Zhaoming taizi ji jiaozhu* 昭明太子集校注, edited by Yu Shaochu 俞紹初 (Zhengzhou: Zhongzhou guji chubanshe, 2001), collates all existing editions and contains sixteen titles of dateable poems, ten titles of poems that cannot be dated (a majority of which are *yuefu*), five *fu*, and twenty-eight pieces of prose including letters, commands, memos, prefaces, notes, memorials, and encomiums. Additionally, there are disputable attributions of nine titles of palace-style poems, one *fu* on the cicada, one command, eight letters, one dirge, and one inscription.

Sources of the work

Xiao Tong's writings were first collected during his lifetime by Liu Xiaochuo 劉孝綽 (481–539), a friend and prominent poet of the Liang court. This collection, allegedly in ten *juan*, has long been lost. After Xiao Tong's death, his brother and successor Xiao Gang 綱 (503–551) collected his works into twenty *juan*, as first mentioned in Xiao Tong's biography in *Liang shu*, q.v., 8:165–71, and also recorded in the bibliographic monographs of the *Sui shu*, q.v., *Jiu Tang shu*, and *Xin Tang shu*. The twenty-*juan* collection became lost in the tenth century.

A *Zhaoming taizi ji* in five *juan* was listed in the *Song shi*'s bibliographic monograph, as well as in Chen Zhensun's (1211–1249) *Zhizhai dushu jieti**. These listings referred to a compilation made by Yuan Yueyou 袁說友 in 1181, which the *Sibu congkan** reproduced in five *juan*, on the basis of a Ming dynasty woodblock text held by the Xu 許 family of Wucheng 烏程. Another edition of the *Zhaoming taizi ji*, this time in six *juan*, was compiled by Ye Shaotai 葉紹泰 (fl. 1628–1644). This expanded edition contained many pieces that were clearly not by Xiao Tong but by his brother Xiao Gang, and the selection of this text for the *Wenyuange Siku quanshu** (1063:647–90) must have owed to insufficient scrutiny on the part of the editors.

Principal editions

Apart from the editions described previously, the following are also available in modern reprints.

Zhaoming taizi ji. Edited by Zhang Xie (1574–1670) in *Qishi'er jia ji**; rpt. in *Xuxiu Siku quanshu** 1586:54–119.
Liang Zhaoming ji. Edited by Zhang Pu (1602–1641) in *Han Wei Liuchao baisan mingjia ji*, q.v.; rpt., Nanjing: Jiangsu guji chubanshe, 2001, 4:125–64.
"Zhaoming taizi." Edited by Yan Kejun (1762–1843) in *Quan shanggu Sandai Qin Han Sanguo Liuchao wen*, q.v., "Quan Liang wen," *juan* 20–21.
"Liang Zhaoming taizi Xiao Tong." Edited by Lu Qinli in *Xian Qin Han Wei Jin Nanbeichao shi**, "Liang shi," *juan* 14 (2:1790–802).

Selected studies

Cao Daoheng 曹道衡 and Fu Gang 傅剛. *Xiao Tong pingzhuan* 蕭統評傳. Nanjing: Nanjing daxue chubanshe, 2001.

He Zhongshun 賀忠順. "Bainian wenyuan zhiji xu kong gu zu yin—ping Xiao Tong de *Tao Yuanming ji xu*" 百年文苑知己序空谷足音—評蕭統的陶淵明集序. *Changde shifan xueyuan xuebao, Shehui kexue ban* 27.6 (2002): 88–89, 101.

Hu Yaozhen 胡耀震. "Xiao Tong bian *Tao Yuanming ji* de shijian ji qi shiwen "wu sihao taixi Yuanming chu" 蕭統編陶淵明集的時間及其施文"無絲毫胎息淵明處." *Jiang Han luntan* (2004.11): 109–11.

Hu Zhiqiang 胡志強. *Lanling Xiaoshi jiazu ji qi wenxue yanjiu* 蘭陵蕭氏家族及其文學研究. Chengdu: Ba Shu shushe, 2008.

Lin Dazhi 林大志. *Si Xiao yanjiu—yi wenxue wei zhongxin* 四蕭研究—以文學為中心. Beijing: Zhonghua shuju, 2007.

Liu Jianguo 劉建國. "Xiao Tong jiguan kao" 蕭統籍貫考. In *Zhaoming Wen xuan yu Zhongguo chuantong wenhua*, ed. Wu Xiaofeng, 150–56. Changchun: Jilin wenshi chuban she, 2001.

Liu Zhongwen 劉中文. "Lun Xiao Tong dui Tao Yuanming de jieshou" 論蕭統對陶淵明的接受. *Qiushi xuekan* 30.2 (2003): 91–96.

Qi Yishou 齊益壽. "Xiao Tong ping Tao yu *Wen xuan* xuan Tao" 蕭統評陶與文選選陶. In *Wen xuan yu Wen xuan xue: Di wu jie Wen xuan xue guoji xueshu yantaohui lunwenji* 文選與文選學: 第五屆文選學國際學術研討會論文集, ed. Zhongguo Wenxuan xuehui 中國文選學會, 526–56. Beijing: Xueyuan chubanshe, 2003.

Wang, Ping. *The Age of Courtly Writing: Wen xuan Compiler Xiao Tong (501–531) and His Circle*. Leiden: Brill, 2012.

Wang Xipo 汪習波 and Zhang Chunxiao 張春曉. "Song Tao cang xinqu qian yibi xiongcai—lun Xiao Tong *Tao Yuanming ji xu* de ling yimian" 頌陶藏心曲謙抑避雄猜—論蕭統陶淵明集序的另一面. *Zhongzhou xuekan* 133.1 (2003): 59–62.

Wu Xiaofeng 吳曉峰. "Sanjiao heliu yi ru wei zhu de wenxueguan—cong Xiao Tong dui Tao Yuanming, Xie Lingyun shige de rentong tanqi" 三教合流以儒為主的文學觀—從蕭統對陶淵明, 謝靈運詩歌的認同談起. In *Zhaoming Wen xuan yu Zhongguo chuantong wenhua* 昭明文選與中國傳統文化, 455–63. Changchun: Jilin wenshi chuban she, 2001.

Yu Shaochu. "Zhaoming taizi Xiao Tong nianpu" 昭明太子蕭統年譜. *Zhengzhou daxue xuebao, Zhexue shehui kexue ban* 33.2 (2000): 66–78; rpt. in Yu Shaochu, ed., *Zhaoming taizi ji jiaozhu* (see the "Contents" section herein), 271–324.

Zhu Baoying 朱寶盈. "Xiao Tong, Liu Xiaochuo shi yu Qi Liang xinti zhi bijiao: Jianlun *Wen xuan* bianzuanzhe wenti" 蕭統, 劉孝綽詩與齊梁新體之比較: 兼論文選編纂者問題. *Zhongguo wenhua yanjiusuo xuebao* 52 (2011): 149–64.

Ping Wang

Xiaozi zhuan 孝子傳

Introduction

Xiaozi zhuan (Accounts of filial children) are collections of filial piety tales that became popular among literati during the Six Dynasties period. Our sole extant specimens of this type of work are preserved in Kyoto, Japan: the Yōmei bunko *Xiaozi zhuan* 陽明文庫孝子傳, along with its later cousin, the Funahashi *Xiaozi zhuan* 船橋孝子傳. These works provided both adults and children with models of filial behavior, and they flourished from the second to the seventh centuries. Officials, recluses, and even royalty compiled them; their authors included such notable people as Xu Guang 徐廣 (fl. 416) the historian, the famed poet Tao Yuanming 陶淵明 (365–372), Xiao Yan 蕭衍 and his son Xiao Yi 蕭繹, who were the Liang emperors Wudi and Yuandi, and Wu Zetian 武則天 (r. 690–705) of the Tang. The tales from these collections were so well known that images of the stories were everywhere: they adorned school and government office walls, daily goods, funerary couches, and sarcophagi.

Contents

The two manuscripts are obviously related; both are two-*juan* long and have the same forty-five filial piety stories in the exact same order. Even the tales' wording is largely identical; however, there are slight variations in content and omissions that lead scholars to believe that the Funahashi *Xiaozi zhuan* is later in date and pitched toward a slightly different audience. The texts themselves are relatively short—the Yōmei bunko *Xiaozi zhuan* consists of 6,194 Chinese characters, whereas the Funahashi *Xiaozi zhuan* has 5,852. Both texts have an introduction and the following forty-five tales:

1. Shun 舜
2. Dong Yong 董永
3. Xing Qu 邢渠
4. Han Boyu 韓伯瑜
5. Guo Ju 郭巨
6. Yuan Gu 原谷

7. Wei Yang 魏陽
8. Sanzhou yishi 三州義士 (Righteous Gentlemen of the Three Regions)
9. Ding Lan 丁蘭
10. Zhu Ming 朱明
11. Cai Shun 蔡順
12. Wang Juwei 王巨尉
13. Lao Laizi 老萊子
14. Zong Shengzhi 宗勝之
15. Chen Shi 陳寔
16. Yang Wei 陽威
17. Xiaonü Cao E 孝女曹娥 (Filial Daughter Cao E)
18. Mao Yi 毛義
19. Ou Shang 歐尚
20. Zhong You 仲由
21. Liu Jingxuan 劉敬宣
22. Xie Hongwei 謝弘微
23. Zhu Bainian 朱百年
24. Gao Chai 高柴
25. Zhang Fu 張敷
26. Meng Ren 孟仁
27. Wang Xiang 王祥
28. Jiang Shi 姜詩
29. Xiaonü Sheng Guangxiong 孝女升光雄 (Filial Daughter Sheng Guangxiong)
30. Yan Wu 顏烏
31. Xu Zi 許孜
32. Luguo yishi xiongdi 魯國義士兄弟 (Righteous Brothers of Lu)
33. Min Ziqian 閔子騫
34. Jiang Xu 蔣詡

35. Bo Qi 伯奇

36. Zeng Shen 曾參

37. Dong An 董黯

38. Shen Sheng 申生

39. Shen Ming 申明

40. Qin Jian 禽堅

41. Li Shan 李善

42. Yang Gong 羊公

43. Dongjing jienü 東京節女 (Virtuous Woman of the Capital)

44. Meijianchi 眉間赤 (Red Mark between the Eyebrows)

45. Ciwu 慈烏 (Compassionate Crows)

After identifying the subject, each biography presents an anecdote or anecdotes that describe the subject's exemplary filiality. Some of these accounts are quite short—the pithiest has only twenty-one characters, while other narratives are quite substantial. The account of Dong An is the longest, at 505 characters.

Authorship

The identity of the authors of these works is unknown. Some educated guesses have been made on what type of people they were. According to Nishino Teiji 西野貞治, since the author of the Yōmei text probably culled most of his material from other miscellaneous biographies rather than the classics, philosophers, or the secular histories, he probably had the learning only of a village scholar. Since the Funahashi text has many Buddhist and colloquial terms, Nishino believes that a Buddhist priest or layman edited it to be read to an audience. Nevertheless, since the author of the Yōmei text drew his accounts from at least twenty-nine sources and was aiming his work toward readers who had some familiarity with the classics, it was probably composed by a literatus who had access to a good library and was hoping to address other scholars. Since the author of the Funahashi version considerably simplifies the text and its language, he might have been a village teacher writing for his young charges.

Authenticity and transmission of the text

The authenticity of both of these documents appears manifestly questionable. The original Chinese manuscripts from which the Yōmei bunko *Xiaozi zhuan* and Funahashi *Xiaozi zhuan* were copied no longer exist. In the case of the former, what we have is a Japanese copy that was made sometime during either the Kamakura period (1185–1333) or the Muromachi period (1392–1573), which was then stored at the Yōmei bunko, a private archive. The Funahashi *Xiaozi zhuan* was copied by Kiyohara Edakata 清原枝賢 (1520–1590), who was the grandson of a great Confucian scholar named Kiyohara Nobukata 清原宣賢 (1475–1550). No written record exists of how and when either of the *Xiaozi zhuan* made its way to Japan. All of this information naturally raises the concern that these were in fact Japanese fabrications, rather than copies of Chinese originals.

In the past, Japanese scholars of Chinese literature, such as Yoshikawa Kōjirō 吉川幸次郎 and Nishino, largely used internal evidence to date and authenticate these two texts. Looking at the style of the two manuscripts' language, both Yoshikawa and Nishino posited that they were indeed copies of Chinese medieval texts. Based on the sources of the tales, Nishino thought that the Yōmei bunko *Xiaozi zhuan* was compiled sometime during the sixth century, while the Funahashi *Xiaozi zhuan*'s use of certain Tang colloquial expressions, such as *anzhi* 安置 and *aniang* 阿孃, suggests that it was composed sometime between the mid-Tang and the Song dynasty. In the past decade, by assiduously combing through early Japanese documents looking for quotations from these two *Xiaozi zhuan*, a group of Japanese scholars, known as the Yōgaku no Kai 幼學の會 (Children's literature research group), headed by Kuroda Akira of Bukkyō University, have endeavored to date more precisely the entry of these texts into Japan. Based on such evidence, the group believes that the Funahashi *Kōshiden* was already in Japan by 700, whereas the Yōmei bunko *Kōshiden* reached its shores by 733. Kuroda has also searched for echoes of the two Kyoto manuscripts in early medieval images of filial piety tales and their inscriptions. Due to the two manuscripts' ability to explain iconographical details of the filial piety images better than any other text, Kuroda believes that the manuscripts are bona fide Six Dynasties texts. Moreover, because the sequence of tales on Northern Wei artifacts and the language used in their inscriptions closely mirror that of the Yōmei bunko *Xiaozi zhuan*, he thinks that this text, or its ancestor, was the basis of the Northern Wei images of filial piety stories. Hence, he thinks that the Yōmei bunko *Xiaozi zhuan* was probably composed sometime during the Taihe reign period (477–499) of the Northern Wei.

Principal editions and Japanese translations

Kōshiden 孝子傳. Ed. Yoshikawa Kōjirō 吉川幸次郎. Kyoto: Kyōto daigaku fuzoku toshokan, 1959. Includes a photographic reproduction of the Funahashi *Xiaozi zhuan*, as well as a Japanese translation.

Kōshiden chūkai 孝子傳注解. Ed. Yōgaku no kai 幼學の會. Tokyo: Kyūko shoin, 2003. Includes critical editions, Japanese translations, and photographic reproductions of both texts.

Studies of the text

Knapp, Keith N. *Selfless Offspring: Filial Children and Social Order in Medieval China*. Honolulu: University of Hawai'i Press, 2005.

———. "Ō-Bei ni okeru *Kōshiden* kenkyū no genjō" 欧米に於ける孝子伝研究の現状. *Setsuwa bungaku kenkyū* 42 (2007): 103–11.
Kuroda Akira 黒田彰. *Kōshiden no kenkyū* 孝子伝の研究. Kyoto: Sibunkaku shuppan, 2001.
———. *Kōshidenzu no kenkyū* 孝子伝図の研究. Tokyo: Kyūko shoin, 2007.
———. "Yōmeihon *Kōshiden* no seiritsu" 陽明本孝子伝の成立. *Kyōtō gobun* 14 (2007): 57–136.
Nishino Teiji 西野貞治. "Yōmeihon *Kōshiden* no seikaku narabini Seikebon to no kankei ni tsuite" 陽明本孝子傳の性格並びに清家本との關係について. *Jinbun kenkyū* 7.6 (1956): 22–48.
Tōno Haruyuki 東野治之. "Ritsuryō to Kōshiden—Kanseki no chokusetsu inyō to kansetsu inyō" 律令と孝子傳—漢籍の直接引用と間接引用. *Manyōshū kenkyū* 24 (2000): 289–308.
Wang Sanqing 王三慶. "Dunhuang bianwen ji zhong de *Xiaozi zhuan* xintan" 敦煌變文集中的孝子傳新探. *Dunhuangxue* 14 (1989): 189–220.

Studies on illustrations

Katō Naoko 加藤直子. "Hirakareta Kanbo—kōren to 'kōshi' tachi no senraku" ひらかれた漢墓—孝廉と孝子たちの戦略. *Bijutsushi kenkyū* 35 (1997): 67–86.
———. "Gi Shin Nambokuchō ni okeru *Kōshidenzu* ni tsuite" 魏晋南北朝における孝子伝図について. In *Tōyō bijutsushi ronsō* 東洋美術史論叢, ed. Yoshimura Rei hakushi koki kinenkai 吉村怜博士古稀紀念會, 114–33. Tokyo: Yūzankaku shuppan, 1999.
Kuroda Akira. *Kōshidenzu no kenkyū*. Tokyo: Kyūko shoin, 2007.
Lin Shengzhi 林聖智. "Hokuchō jidai ni okeru sōgu no zuzō to kinō—sekikanshō kakobyō no bonushishōzō to *Kōshidenzu* o rei toshite" 北朝時代における葬具の図像と機能—石棺庄囲屏の墓主肖像と孝子伝図を例として. *Bijutsushi* 52.2 (2003): 207–26.
Wang, Eugene. "Coffins and Confucianism—The Northern Wei Sarcophagus in the Minneapolis Institute of Arts." *Orientations* 30.6 (1999): 56–64.
Wu Hung. *The Wu Liang Shrine: The Ideology of Early Chinese Pictorial Art*. Stanford, CA: Stanford University Press, 1989.
Yamakawa Masaharu 山川誠治. "Sō San to Min Son—Murakami Eini shi Kandai *Kōshidenzu* gazōkyō ni tsuite" 曾參と閔損—村上英二氏漢代孝子伝図画像鏡について. *Bukkyō daigaku daigakuin kiyō* 31 (2003): 93–102.
Zhao Chao 趙超. "Guanyu Bo Qi de gudai xiaozi tuhua" 關於伯奇的古代孝子圖畫. *Kaogu yu wenwu* 3 (2004): 68–72.
Zou Qingquan 鄒清泉. *Bei Wei Xiaozi huaxiang yanjiu: Xiaojing yu Bei Wei Xiaozi huaxiang tuxiang shenfen de zhuanhuan* 北魏孝子畫像研究: 孝經與北魏孝子畫像圖像身份的轉換. Beijing: Wenhua yishu chubanshe, 2007.

Keith N. Knapp

Xie Huilian ji 謝惠連集

Introduction

Xie Huilian (407–433) was a prodigy able to compose writings at the tender age of ten *sui*. His talent was much admired by his older cousin Xie Lingyun 靈雲 (385–433), who was the greatest poet of the age. Maintaining a close friendship, they spent time feasting and composing poetry together. According to a frequently quoted story mentioned first by Zhong Rong (469?–518) in the *Shi pin*, q.v., Xie Lingyun was once helped in poetic composition by Xie Huilian in a dream, who dictated to him the famous line: "Chitang sheng chun cao" 池塘生春草 (see biography in *Nan shi*, q.v., 19:537).

Like his senior kinsman, Xie Huilian possessed an undisciplined temperament that caused problems for his career. During the mourning period for his father, Xie Fangming 方明 (380–426), he violated protocol by writing a suite of poems to an official of his native commandery of Kuaiji 會稽 (modern Shaoxing) with whom he enjoyed a homosexual intimacy. The scandal of this breach of propriety resulted in his being banished and barred from holding office. He was later restored to the emperor's good graces by a vice-director of the Department of State Affairs, who appreciated his talent and for this reason insisted that the verses had been falsely attributed to him. In the year 430, Xie Huilian was appointed adjutant of the law section (*facao canjun* 法曹參軍) of the establishment of the Prince of Pengcheng 彭城, Liu Yikang 劉義康 (409–451), who was then serving as minister of education. This minor post was Xie's highest office and later became part of a traditional title for his collected works. In addition to the *Nan shi* biography, Xie's life is recorded in *Song shu*, q.v., 53:1524–25.

Contents

The *Xie Facao ji* 謝法曹集 that is included in *juan* 71 of the *Han Wei Liuchao baisan jia ji*, q.v., compiled by Zhang Pu (1602–1641), consists of rhapsodies, a number of parallel-style prose compositions, and more than thirty poems including "Music Bureau" poems (*yuefu*). The collection is arranged in the following order:

Rhapsodies, 5

Encomiums, 6

Admonitions, 2

Linked pearls, 4

Offerings, 3

Yuefu poems, 13

Lyric poems, 22 (including fragments)

The best-known pieces in the collection are "Xue fu" 雪賦 (Rhapsody on snow), the poems "Dao yi" 搗衣 (Washing clothes) and "Qiu huai" 秋懷 (Autumn feelings), and the prose composition "Ji guzhong wen" 祭古塚文 (Offering at an old grave).

Sources of the work

Xie had been represented in the *Wen xuan*, q.v., by a selection of seven pieces in the genres of rhapsody, lyric poetry, and prose (*juan* 13, 22, 23, 25, 30, 60). The *Yutai xinyong*, q.v., also included three amorous poems by him (*juan* 3). Although there were several attempts during the Ming, prior to Zhang Pu's compilation, to reconstitute a collection of Xie's writings (Mu, *Wei Jin Nanbeichao wenxue*, 107), Zhang's anthology is the only surviving premodern edition of both prose and poems.

Transmission and early history of the text

According to the bibliographic monograph of the *Sui shu*, q.v., 35:1071, the original collection was titled *Xie Huilian ji* 謝惠連集 and consisted of six *juan*. From the Tang through the early Song, a five-*juan* collection circulated, but, according to the *Zhizhai shulu jieti** (19:556), which was compiled by Chen Zhensun circa 1235, only one *juan* remained by the end of the Southern Song.

Principal editions

Apart from the *Han Wei Liuchao baisan jia ji*, Xie Huilian's prose writings are contained in Yan Kejun's (1762–1843) *Quan shanggu Sandai Qin Han Sanguo Liuchao wen*, q.v., "Quan Song wen," *juan* 34. For his poems, one may consult Lu Qinli's *Xian Qin Han Wei Jin Nanbeichao shi**, "Song shi," *juan* 4 (2:1188–99).

Traditional assessments

Zhong Rong placed Xie Huilian in the middle (*zhong* 中) section of the *Shi pin* and mainly praised his "ornate songs" (*qili geyao* 綺麗歌謠), by which he most probably meant love songs. He also extolled "Dao yi" and "Qiu huai," which he found so "concentrated in its thoughts (*rui si* 銳思) that even Xie Lingyun would not surpass him." Later, Zhang Pu concurred in respect to the quality of the "Dao yi" and "Qiu huai," and he praised the "Ji guzhong wen" as "concise yet full of meaning" (簡而有意). It is generally held that Xie Huilian's premature death interrupted a promising literary career that would otherwise have yielded masterpieces surpassing those of most of his contemporaries.

Owing to Huilian's junior status relative to Lingyun, traditional critics sometimes called him "Xie the Younger" (Xiao Xie 小謝). This epithet was used also in reference to Xie Tiao 朓 (464–499), another member of the émigré lineage of the Xie from Chenjun 陳郡. Together with Lingyun and Tiao, Huilian was known as one of the family's finest lyric poets. He was represented in a combined anthology titled *San Xie shi* 三謝詩 that was edited by Tang Geng 唐庚 (1071–1121) and that consisted of the three authors' poems that had appeared in the *Wen xuan*.

Selected studies

Cao Daoheng 曹道衡. "Cong 'Xue fu,' 'Yue fu' kan Nanchao wenfeng zhi liubian" 從雪賦, 月賦 看南朝文風之流變. *Wenxue yichan* (1985.2): 1–7.

———. *Zhonggu wenxue shiliao congkao* 中古文學史料叢考. Beijing: Zhonghua shuju, 2003. Pp. 315–17.

Cao Daoheng and Shen Yucheng 沈玉成. *Nanchao wenxue shi* 南朝文學史. Beijing: Renmin wenxue chubanshe, 1991. Pp. 62–64.

Katō Masahiko 佐藤正光. "Sha Keiren no 'Setsufu' to Sha Sō no 'Getsufu' ni tsuite" 謝惠連の"雪賦"と謝莊の"月賦"について. In *Ritsumeikan bungaku* 598 (2007.2): 571–77.

———. "Sha Keiren seinen kō" 謝惠連生年考. In *Nishōgakusha daigaku jinbun ronsō* 37 (1987): 44–54.

Kozen Hiroshi 興膳宏. *Rikuchō shijinden* 六朝詩人傳. Vol. 34 of *Sō: Tō Emmei, Sha Keiren hoka* 宋: 陶淵明, 謝惠連ほか. Tokyo: Taishūkan shoten, 2000.

Morino Shigeo 森野繁夫. "Sha Reiun to Sha Keiren: Reiun zakki 2" 謝靈運と謝惠連: 靈運雜記 2. *Chūgokugaku ronshū* 8 (1994.7): 1–14.

Owen, Stephen. "Hsieh Hui-lien's 'Snow *Fu*': A Structural Study." *Journal of the American Oriental Society* 94.1 (1974): 14–23.

Wang Ren'en 王人恩. "Shi lun Xie Huilian de 'Ji guzhong wen'" 試論謝惠連的祭古冢文. *Longyuan xueyuan xuebao* 25.5 (2007): 10–15.

Translations

English

Knechtges, David R. "Rhapsody on Snow." In *Wen xuan or Selections of Refined Literature*, vol. 3: 21–30. Princeton: Princeton University Press, 1996.

Watson, Burton. "The Snow." In *Chinese Rhyme-Prose: Poems in the Fu form from the Han and Six Dynasties Periods*, 86–91. New York: Columbia University Press, 1971.

European languages

Bezhin, Leonid E. Утренний иней на листьях клёна (поэзия семейства Се) [Morning dew on the maple leaves (poetry of the Xie family)]. Moscow: Kniga, 1993. Pp. 119–58. Translation of "Xue fu" and a five-poem suite presented to Xie Lingyun, "Xiling yu feng xian Kangle" 西陵遇風獻康樂.

Chapuis, Nicolas. "Sentiments d'Automne." In *Tristes Automnes: Poétique de l'identité dans la Chine ancienne*, 96–98. Paris: You Feng, 2001. Translation of "Qiu huai" with commentary.

Lomová, Olga. "Xie Huilian: Popisná báseň o sněhu." *Studia Orientalia Slovaca* I (2002): 17–28. Translation of "Xue fu" with notes and commentary.

Lomová, Olga, and Yeh Kuo-liang. "Text obětovaný pro obyvatele starodávného hrobu." In *Ach běda, přeběda! Oplakávání mrtvých ve středověké Číně* [Wu hu ai zai! Mourning the dead in medieval China], 152–57. Prague: DharmaGaia, 2004. Translation with commentary of "Ji guzhong wen."

Margouliès, Georges. "La Neige." In *Anthologie raisonnée de la littérature chinoise*, 359–61. Paris: Payot, 1948. Abridged translation of "Xue fu."

Zach, Erwin von. "Der Schnee." In *Die Chinesische Anthologie: Übersetzungen aus dem Wen hsüan*, ed. Ilse Martin Fong, 1:195–98. 2 vols. Harvard: Yenching Institute Studies 18. Cambridge: Harvard University Press, 1958. Translation of "Xue fu."

Research aid

Mu Kehong 穆克宏. *Wei Jin Nanbeichao wenxue shiliao shulüe* 魏晋南北朝文學史料述略. Beijing: Zhonghua shuju, 1997. Pp. 106–8.

Olga Lomová

Xie Lingyun ji 謝靈運集

Introduction

Xie Lingyun (385–433), the Duke of Kangle 康樂, is generally regarded as the patriarch of Chinese landscape poetry. He was born into one of the most illustrious clans of the Six Dynasties, originally of Chen commandery (Chenjun 陳郡) in present-day Henan, and led a life of privilege and leisure. His grandfather Xie Xuan 玄 (343–388) was a nephew of Xie An 安 (320–385), and both were heroes of the crucial Battle of the Fei River in 383 against Fu Jian 苻堅 (r. 358–385) of the Former Qin. According to Xie Lingyun's biography in *Song shu*, q.v., 67:1743–87, he was quite the trendsetter at the capital, popularizing styles of poetry and even of clothes and personal ornaments. He is furthermore portrayed as temperamental, proud, and exceedingly talented.

Xie's ability to advance himself politically did not match his literary achievement. He found himself exiled in the prime of life after a rash and halfhearted attempt to promote the Prince of Luling, Liu Yizhen 劉義真 (407–424), to the throne. Liu Yifu, eldest son of the Liu-Song dynasty's founder, was installed instead, posthumously Emperor Shao (r. 422–424). In exile at Yongjia 永嘉, and subsequently in retirement at an ancestral estate in Kuaiji 會稽, commanderies both situated in regions of Yangzhou (modern Zhejiang) known for magnificent landscapes, Xie turned toward an aesthetic appreciation of nature and a spiritual quest for enlightenment. During his many adventures into mountains and across rivers, he produced a wealth of landscape poems that would become models of this subgenre for later writers.

Contents

The *Xie Lingyun ji* contains lyric verses and "music bureau" poems, that is, *yuefu*, as well as rhapsodies and various prose works. The description here of the collection's arrangement follows the *Xie Lingyun ji jiaozhu* 謝靈運集校注 annotated by Gu Shaobo 顧紹柏 (Zhengzhou: Zhongzhou guji chubanshe, 1987), which is the most complete and reliable edition:

   Lyric poems arranged by chronology

   Yuefu poems, arranged without chronological order

Prose pieces arranged by chronology

Prose pieces, arranged without chronological order

There are 139 titles in Gu's edition: ninety-seven poems (four of which are only titles, without extant text; seventy-five lyric poems, and eighteen *yuefu*) and forty-two prose pieces. The prose genres represented are the rhapsody, letter, encomium, dirge, memorial, inscription, discussion, monograph, response to a challenge (*da nan* 答難), response to a question (*da wen* 答問), memorandum, eulogy, commentary, preface, and sevens (*qi* 七).

A number of the texts, especially among the prose works, consist of mere fragments, sometimes only a line or two. As Xie is known primarily as a poet, less attention has been paid to his achievement as a prose writer. His notable prose works include "Shan ju fu" 山居賦 (Rhapsody on dwelling in the mountains), "Fo ying ming" 佛影銘 (Inscription on Buddha's shadow image), "Lushan Huiyuan fashi lei" 廬山慧遠法師誄 (Dirge for Dharma Master Huiyuan of Lu Mountain), "Wudi lei" 武帝誄 (Dirge for Emperor Wu [of the Liu-Song; r. 420–422]), and "Bian zong lun" 辨宗論 (Disquisition on essentials).

Transmission of the text

The transmission history of the current *Xie Lingyun ji* is brief, since versions of the original work were lost sometime after the Song, and editors from the Ming onward needed to reconstruct the work by culling through anthologies, encyclopedias, collectanea, and histories for citations. The dynastic bibliography in *Song shi* (comp. 1343–1345) 208:5329 lists the work in nine *juan*. Just under half of the twenty-*juan* work that existed in the Liang dynasty (502–557) had survived.

The earliest extant edition of a *Xie Kangle ji* 謝康樂集 was compiled in the Ming by Shen Qiyuan 沈啟原 and published by Jiao Hong 焦竑. The result was a four-*juan* collection, with 110 poems and prose works drawn from sources such as the *Wen xuan*, q.v., which had contained forty verses under thirty-two poems titles, the *Yuefu shiji*, q.v., and the *Song shu*. Not only was this edition far from complete, it also was marred by a number of misattributions. Zhang Pu's (1602–1641) *Han Wei Liuchao baisan mingjia ji*, q.v., included a *Xie Kangle ji* in two *juan* with 119 poems and prose works and improved upon Shen's edition, though there were still notable errors. Two compilations of the Qing dynasty, Yan Kejun's (1762–1843) *Quan shanggu Sandai Qin Han Sanguo Liuchao wen*, q.v., and Ding Fubao's (1874–1952) *Quan Han Sanguo Jin Nanbeichao shi**, "Quan Song shi" 3:1a–18a (2:797–831), added to the number of known works by Xie Lingyun. Modern editions have relied on the work of Yan Kejun and Ding Fubao.

Principal editions and commentaries

The 1583 edition by Shen Qiyuan was reproduced in *Xuxiu Siku quanshu** 1585:219–303. Also, a late-Qing woodblock printing of Zhang Pu's anthology was reproduced in five volumes by the Jiangsu guji chubanshe, Nanjing, in 2002; Xie Lingyun's collection may be found in vol. 3, pp. 321–87. For most of the twentieth century, the standard edition used for Xie Lingyun's poetry was Huang Jie's 黃節 (1874–1935) *Xie Kangle shi zhu* 謝康樂詩註 (preface dated 1924). This work was published by Renmin wenxue chubanshe (Beijing, 1958) and reprinted several times by Yiwen yinshuguan (Taipei, 1967–1987). Huang's annotations and comments often cite traditional readings and include a number of his own insights. The now-standard edition for all of Xie's writings, by Gu Shaobo, contains 139 works in poetry and prose (including four works that exist only as titles). Gu culled through all available anthologies, encyclopedias, and histories to produce the fullest and most accurate collection to date. His extensive and excellent annotations and comments on Xie's poems are indispensable for research on the poet. Although the prose pieces in Gu's edition are not accompanied by annotations, they appear with important contextual information as well as variants and textual corrections. Gu's edition also includes a helpful introduction to Xie and a number of useful appendices, including a biography in modern chronological format, a descriptive genealogy of members of the Xie clan, and selected traditional criticism.

Two modern selections of Xie's poems deserve mention: Ye Xiaoxue's 葉笑雪 *Xie Lingyun shi xuan* 謝靈運詩選 (Shanghai: Gudian wenxue chubanshe, 1957) and Hu Dalei's 胡大雷 *Xie Lingyun Bao Zhao shi xuan* 謝靈運鮑照詩選 (Beijing: Zhonghua shuju, 2005). The commentaries and annotations of both are concise, helpful, and often insightful.

Selected studies

Chang, Kang-i Sun. "Hsieh Ling-yün: The Making of a New Descriptive Mode." In *Six Dynasties Poetry*, 47–78. Princeton, NJ: Princeton University Press, 1986.

Frodsham, J. D. *The Murmuring Stream: The Life and Works of the Chinese Nature Poet Hsieh Ling-yün (385–433), Duke of K'ang-Lo*. 2 vols. Kuala Lumpur: University of Malaya Press, 1967. Volume 1 provides a detailed biography with excerpts from poems; pp. 106–72 contain full translations of poems; appendix 4 (179–81) is a translation of the "Inscription on the Buddha's Shadow." Volume 2 contains notes to the chapters and poem translations.

Ge Xiaoyin 葛曉音. "Cong Da Xie ti dao Xiao Xie ti" 從大謝體到小謝體. In *Shanshui tianyuan shipai yanjiu* 山水田園詩派研究, 32–69. Shenyang: Liaoning daxue chubanshe, 1993.

———. *Xie Lingyun yanjiu lunji* 謝靈運研究論集. Guilin: Guangxi shifan daxue chubanshe, 2001.

Hu Dalei. "'Bian zong lun' yu Xie Lingyun dui xuanyan shi de gaizhi" 辨宗論與謝靈運對玄言詩的改制. *Wenzhou shifan xueyuan xuebao* 25.1 (2004): 34–38.

Huang, Shizhong 黃世中. *Xie Lingyun yanjiu congshu* 謝靈運研究叢書. Guilin: Guangxi shifan daxue chubanshe, 2001.

Jian, Dunxian 簡敦獻. *Xie Lingyun shanshui shi yanjiu* 謝靈運山水詩研究. Hong Kong: Kehua tushu chuban gongsi, 2004.

Li Yan 李雁. *Xie Lingyun yanjiu* 謝靈運研究. Beijing: Renmin wenxue chubanshe, 2005.

Lin Wenyue 林文月. *Xie Lingyun* 謝靈運. Taipei: Guojia tushuguan, 1998.

Obi Kōichi 小尾郊一. *Sha Reiun: kodoku no sansui shijin* 謝靈運: 孤独の山水詩人. Tokyo: Kyūko shoin, 1983.

Qian Zhixi 錢志熙. "Xie Lingyun 'Bian zong lun' he shanshui shi" 謝靈運辨宗論和山水詩. *Beijing daxue xuebao* 5 (1989): 39–46.

Swartz, Wendy. "Landscape and Farmstead Poems." In *How to Read Chinese Poetry: A Guided Anthology*, ed. Zong-qi Cai, 121–40. New York: Columbia University Press, 2008.

———. "Naturalness in Xie Lingyun's Poetic Works," *Harvard Journal of Asiatic Studies* 70.2 (2010): 355–86.

Westbrook, Francis. "Landscape Description in the Lyric Poetry and 'Fuh on Dwelling in the Mountains' of Shieh Ling-yunn." Ph.D. diss., Yale University, 1972.

———. "Landscape Transformation in the Poetry of Hsieh Ling-yün." *Journal of the American Oriental Society* 100.3 (1980): 237–54.

Translations

Frodsham, J. D. *The Murmuring Stream* (see "Selected studies" section herein).

Hinton, David. *The Mountain Poems of Hsieh Ling-Yün*. New York: New Directions Publishing, 2001.

Wendy Swartz

Xie Tiao ji 謝朓集

Introduction

Xie Tiao, styled Xuanhui 玄暉 (464–499), belonged to the émigré Xie lineage from Chenjun (in modern Henan) that dominated the southern court of the late fourth century. During the Liu-Song dynasty, however, political misadventures across the branches of this talented family were a factor in the sharp reduction of its males in high office. In Xie Tiao's descent line, his two uncles and their maternal uncle Fan Ye 范曄 (399–446) were executed for treason. His father, Wei 緯 (b. ca. 430–?), was banished to Guangzhou, where he remained for a decade. Xie Tiao's marriage to the daughter of a powerful commoner, the general Wang Jingze 王敬則 (d. 498), may have been arranged to compensate for this disaster. His works often expressed dependence upon the favor of influential officials.

Xie, during his early career, helped lead a movement advocating the systematic use of tonal contrast. The new practice by Xie and his associates, most notably Shen Yue 沈約 (441–513) and Wang Rong 王融 (467–493), was dubbed the "Yongming style" (*Yongming ti* 永明體) for the reign of the Southern Qi emperor Wu (r. 483–493) and was exemplified in brief lyrics typically written on set themes at salon gatherings. Xie composed longer poems descriptive of natural scenery when serving in Jiangling 江陵 (Hubei) as literatus (*wenxue* 文學) to the prince Xiao Zilong 蕭子隆 (474–494). Later, the regent Xiao Luan, known posthumously as Emperor Ming, selected Xie to oversee the writings from his establishment. Following Xiao Luan's genocidal usurpation in 494, Xie was appointed grand warden (*taishou* 太守) of the commandery of Xuancheng 宣城 (Anhui). Poems from this governorship during 495 and 496 combined the concerns of a rural administrator with the pleasures of a reclusive way of life; they are among his best-known works.

In 498, while serving as grand warden of Nan Donghai 南東海 and concurrently as senior assistant to Emperor Ming's eldest son in Nan Xuzhou 南徐州 (Jiangsu), Xie reported the plan of his father-in-law to lay siege to the capital. The rebellion was quelled, and his loyalty rewarded by promotion to the position of gentleman of the Board of Civil Office (*libu lang* 吏部郎). In 499, after refusing to join a plot to overthrow Emperor Ming's heir, Xie was accused by the conspirators of spreading slander about the royal family; he subsequently died in prison. His biography is in *Nan Qi shu*, q.v., 47:825–28, and *Nan shi*, q.v., 19:532–35.

Contents

Modern collections, whether of the complete works or the poems alone, contain 175 verses of lyric poetry, *yuefu*, and linked verses that were gathered into a key collation of the Southern Song (see section following). They may additionally supply pieces not found in traditional editions. Cao Rongnan's 曹融南 annotated *Xie Xuancheng ji jiaozhu* 謝宣城集校注 (Shanghai guji chubanshe, 1991) is organized in five *juan* as follows:

1. Rhapsodies, 9; memorials, 4; memorandum, 1; communications, 3; instructions, 2; lament, 1; patent conferring a posthumous name (*shi cewen* 諡冊文), 1; grave memoirs, 4; offerings, 3; ritual *yuefu*, 8 (one suite of hymns, mainly trisyllabic verses); banquet poems on behalf of attendees, 28 (three suites of tetrasyllabic verses)

2. *Yuefu* poems, 30 (of which twenty are in two suites)

3. Lyric poems, 43

4. Lyric poems, 26

5. Lyric poems, 33; and couplets for linked verses under 7 titles

An appendix of works omitted from traditional collections (*yiwen* 佚文) adds five verses: two lyric poems, one *yuefu*, and two lyrical fragments. All poems from *juan* 2 through the appendix are pentasyllabic. Also appended is an excerpt from a memorial composed on behalf of the prince Xiao Qiang 鏘 (469–494), which Kūkai 空海 (774–835) preserved in his *Bunkyō hifuron* 文鏡祕府論 ("West" section, "Wen ershiba zhong bing" 文二十八種病).

As in the Southern Song collation, Xie Tiao's poems in *juan* 2, 4, and 5 are accompanied by forty verses that his contemporaries wrote on the same occasion, or as "harmonizing" works (*he shi* 和詩), or presentations and responses (*zengda* 贈答). Owing to the Song edition's flaws, however, Cao Rongnan used a recension by Wu Qian 吳騫 (1733–1813) for the base text of the poems.

Authenticity

Among the *yiwen*, "Bie Wang Sengru" 別王僧孺 (Parting from Wang Sengru) was attributed to Xie Tiao in the *Yiwen leiju* (comp. ca. 620), q.v., but to Wang Rong in the *Guwen yuan* 古文苑 by Zhang Qiao 章樵 (*jinshi* 1208). Also, the quatrain "Chun you" 春遊 (Springtime roaming) was attributed to Xie Tiao in Wu Zhaoyi's 吳兆宜 expanded *Yutai xinyong* (comp. 1675), q.v., but it is not found in any other source.

Early history and sources of the text

The *Yanshi jiaxun*, q.v., relates that Liu Xiaochuo 劉孝綽 (481–539) kept a collection of Xie Tiao's poems on a side table and recited them constantly (*juan* 4, section 9, "Wenzhang" 文章). The *Sui shu*, q.v., bibliography (35:1076) listed a *Qi libulang Xie*

Tiao ji 齊吏部郎謝朓集 in twelve *juan* and a collation omitted from the standard collection (*yiji* 逸集) in one *juan*. During the Tang there circulated a *Xie Tiao ji* in ten *juan* (*Jiu Tang shu* 47:2069; *Xin Tang shu* 60:1592). To identify persons mentioned by surname and office in some titles of Xie's twenty-one poems in the *Wen xuan*, q.v., Li Shan (ca. 630–689) used an edition that noted their given names. During the Song, Wang Yaochen's (1001–1056) *Chongwen zongmu** 3:15b (p. 718) listed a *Xie Xuanhui ji* in ten *juan*. None of these editions survived.

Copies of the collection were scarce by the Southern Song when Lou Zhao 樓炤 took advantage of an appointment as Xuanzhou's 宣州 governor to collate a new edition of the poems. (The surname is written 婁 in the *Sibu congkan** edition). According to Lou's preface of 1157, after seeking out works from locally held manuscripts and engravings, he discovered that these as well as verses in the *Wen xuan* and *Yutai xinyong* (the original of the latter contained sixteen items) had been incorporated into a collection of fifty-eight poems edited by a certain Jiang Zhiqi 蔣之奇. Yet it happened that Lou Zhao's family owned a rare copy in ten *juan* of Xie Tiao's works, and after setting aside the rhapsodies, *yuefu*, and linked verses, as well as pieces by other authors in the first five *juan*, Lou found them to yield the much larger quantity of 102 lyric poems. His preface states that he and a group of colleagues compared discrepancies in the works' transmissions and made many corrections. In the case of textual gaps that could not be filled with an alternate version, they let the lacunae stand. He then had woodblocks carved to issue a *Xie Xuancheng shiji* (Collected poems of Xie of Xuancheng).

An undated woodblock edition of the Ming, based upon a Song dynasty handwritten copy of Lou's collation, was reproduced by photolithography as an item of the Hanfenlou 涵芬樓 collection in the *Sibu congkan** (1926; rpt., Shanghai shudian, 1989; *Sibu congkan chubian*, vol. 100). There is reason to believe the contents are faithful to Lou's work. Lacunae throughout conform with his report of leaving gaps when these could not be filled by alternate sources at hand. Provided that the first *juan*'s tetrasyllabic suites of banquet poems are excluded, along with its trisyllabic hymns that Lou explicitly left out of the sum for being *yuefu*, the 102 lyric poems tally with the number stated in his preface. An unusual feature of the Lou Zhao/Hanfen lou text that is reproduced in most modern editions is the presence of companion pieces by Xie's associates in *juan* 2, 4, and 5. In the case of literary gatherings when multiple authors wrote upon an assigned topic, the verses are moreover arranged in the sequence of their composition. These poems' arrangement in sets exposes a competitive interplay of themes and images among the texts and allows an understanding of common structural features (Chennault, "Odes on Objects and Patronage during the Southern Qi").

Lou's edition included rhapsodies, but he decided not to print the last five *juan* of his family's manuscript, which consisted of prose compositions, on the grounds that "these all were utilitarian writings of the time, about the affairs of an age in decline" (*jie dangshi yingyong zhi wen, shuaishi zhi shi* 皆當時應用之文，衰世之事), and that the best examples had been preserved in Xie's biography or the *Wen xuan*. Most of the omitted prose writings probably dated from the apogee of Xie's career under Emperor Ming. The *Wen xuan* contains a letter of farewell to Xiao Zilong (*juan* 47) that is also in the Xie biography, as well as a lament for Emperor Ming's consort upon her reburial (*juan* 58).

Principal editions

Many copies of Lou Zhao's *Xie Xuancheng shiji* were printed. An appointee to Xuancheng sixty years later by the name of Hong Ji 洪伋 found the woodblocks so worn that the characters were barely legible. Hong's preface of 1220 says he engraved new blocks so that the library of the administrative center could perpetuate the poems' transmission. The first *juan* and a portion of the second from his *Xuanzhou junzhai chongkan ji* 宣州郡齋重刊集 are the oldest fragments of Xie Tiao's collection to survive in the original. For libraries holding this and other rare editions, see Li Zhifang (*Xie Xuancheng shi zhu*, 1–6, 178–85).

During the Wanli era (1573–1620), Wang Shixian added Xie Tiao's prose to the fifth and last *juan* of a *Xie Xuancheng ji* that he edited for his *Han Wei Liuchao ershiyi mingjia ji** and that has been reprinted in *Siku quanshu cunmu congshu bubian** 28:30–71. Besides the *Wen xuan* and *Yiwen leiju*, other early sources for individual pieces were the *Liang shu*, q.v., biography of Zhuge Qu 諸葛璩 (d. 508), the *Chuxue ji*, q.v., the *Jigu lu bawei* 集古錄跋尾 by Ouyang Xiu 歐陽修 (1007–1072), and the *Mengqi bitan* 夢溪筆談 by Shen Gua 沈括 (1031–1095).

A Ming printing of the rhapsodies and poems was issued from Xuancheng with a preface dated 1579 by Mei Dingzuo 梅鼎祚 (1549–1615); a copy of this text, of which only the first two *juan* remain, is held in the Beijing University Library. Zhang Pu (1602–1641) compiled Xie's complete works in the *Han Wei Liuchao baisan jia ji*, q.v., placing the prose writings at the head of a one-*juan* edition.

The Qing bibliophile Wu Qian undertook a thorough recension of the poems by examining two editions produced in Xuancheng during 1511 and 1537 (known by the editors' names as the "Liu Shao edition" [Liu Shao ben 劉紹本] and the "Li Chen edition" [Li Chen ben 黎晨本]) and versions of the poems in literary collectanea. He compared these with a Song dynasty manuscript of Xie's works (the provenance of which he did not describe, other than to name its owner) and with texts in anthologies such as the *Yuefu shiji*, q.v. In a colophon dated 1767 to his *Xie Xuancheng shiji*, Wu described examples of the errors he discovered in the Ming printings. His edition was later incorporated in the *Baijinglou congshu* 拜經樓叢書 (*Congshu jicheng xinbian** 69:599–617). In notes dated 1782 for the catalog of the *Siku quanshu**, whose text was of the poems only, the compilers remarked on the anomaly of Xie's collection being titled after his governorship in Xuancheng, since this was not his highest office (*Yingyin Wenyuange Siku quanshu** 1063:612).

As for selective editions, the *San Xie shi* 三謝詩 by Tang Geng 唐庚 (1071–1121) reproduced the sixty-four poems by Xie Tiao, Xie Lingyun 靈運 (385–433), and Xie Huilian 惠連 (397–433) contained in the *Wen xuan*. The *Xie Xuancheng ji xuan* by Wu Rulun 吳汝綸 (1840–1903), published posthumously with a preface dated 1918 by his student Yao Yonggai 姚永概, used Zhang Pu's edition for presenting six rhapsodies, four prose pieces, eleven *yuefu*, and sixty-two lyric poems with occasional notes (in *Han Wei Liuchao baisanjia ji xuan* 漢魏六朝百三家集選; rpt., Hangzhou: Zhejiang guji chubanshe, 1985).

Xie Tiao's poems are in "Qi shi," *juan* 3–4 (2:1413–57) of Lu Qinli's *Xian Qin Han Wei Jin Nanbeichao shi**. His rhapsodies and prose are in "Quan Qi wen," *juan* 23 of Yan Kejun's *Quan shanggu Sandai Qin Han Sanguo Liuchao wen*, q.v.

Modern annotations

Hao Liquan 郝立權. *Xie Xuancheng shi zhu* 謝宣城詩注. Ji'nan: Qi Lu daxue, 1936; rpt., Taipei: Yiwen yinshuguan, 1971.

Hong Shunlong 洪順隆. *Xie Xuancheng ji jiaozhu* 謝宣城集校注. Taipei: Chunghua Book Company, 1969. Hong uses the Hanfen lou edition as base text, with extensive notes on variants and commentary relating the works to Xie's career; he believes that this edition adds a few poems to Lou Shao's original ("Introduction," p. 35).

Li Zhifang (Lee Chik-fong) 李直方. *Xie Xuancheng shi zhu* 謝宣城詩注. Hong Kong: Universal Book Company, 1968. Follows Hong Ji's edition for *juan* 1.

Selected studies

Ami Yūji 網祐次. "Sha Chō no denki to sakuhin" 謝朓の傳記と作品. In *Chūgoku chūsei bungaku kenkyū: Nan Sei Eimei jidai o chūshin to shite* 中國中世文學研究: 南齊永明時代を中心として, 484–561. Tokyo: Shinjusha, 1960.

Cao Daoheng 曹道衡 and Shen Yucheng 沈玉成. *Nanbeichao wenxue shi* 南北朝文學史. Beijing: Renmin wenxue chubanshe, 1998. Pp. 142–61. Four essays on Xie Tiao's life and works.

———. *Zhonggu wenxue shiliao congkao* 中古文學史料叢考. Beijing: Zhonghua shuju, 2003. Pp. 396–414. Fifteen essays on Xie Tiao's life and works.

Chang, Kang-i Sun. "Xie Tiao: The Inward Turn of Landscape." In *Six Dynasties Poetry*, 112–44. Princeton, NJ: Princeton University Press, 1986.

Chen Qingyuan 陳慶元. "Lun Xie Tiao shige de sixiangxing" 論謝朓詩歌的思想性. *Xi'nan shifan xueyuan xuebao* 4 (1984): 77, 103–8.

Chennault, Cynthia L. "Lofty Gates or Solitary Impoverishment? Xie Family Members during the Southern Dynasties." *T'oung Pao* 85 (1999): 249–327. Section on Xie Tiao: 305–22.

———. "Odes on Objects and Patronage during the Southern Qi." In *Studies in Early Medieval Chinese Literature and Cultural History, in Honor of Richard B. Mather and Donald Holzman*, ed. Paul W. Kroll and David R. Knechtges, 331–98. Provo, UT: T'ang Studies Society, 2003.

Goh, Meow Hui. *Sound and Sight: Poetry and Courtier Culture in the Yongming Era (483–493)*. Stanford, CA: Stanford University Press, 2010.

Hsieh, Daniel. *The Evolution of Jueju Verse*. New York: Peter Lang, 1996. Pp. 169–75, 185–87, 191–98 passim.

Liang Sen 梁森. *Xie Tiao yu Li Bo guankui* 謝朓與李白管窺. Beijing: Renmin wenxue chubanshe, 1995.

Mao Jiapei 茆家培 and Li Zilong 李子龍, eds. *Xie Tiao yu Li Bo yanjiu* 謝朓與李白研究. Beijing: Renmin wenxue chubanshe, 1995.

Mather, Richard B. "Hsieh T'iao's 'Poetic Essay Requiting a Kindness.'" *Journal of the American Oriental Society* 110.4 (1990): 603–15.

———. "Ritual Aspects of Hsieh T'iao's Wardenship of Hsüan-ch'eng." *Early Medieval China* 6 (2000): 32–47.

Satō Masamitsu 佐藤正光. "Senjō jidai no Sha Chō" 宣城時代の謝朓. *Nihon Chūgoku gakkaihō* 41 (1989): 63–78.

Wei Gengyuan 魏耕原. *Xie Tiao shi lun* 謝朓詩論. Beijing: Zhongguo shehui kexue chubanshe, 2004.

Translations

English

Richard B. Mather provides thoroughly annotated translations of the complete lyric poems and *yuefu* in *The Age of Eternal Brilliance: Three Lyric Poets of the Yung-ming Era, 483–493*, 2 vols. (Leiden: E. J. Brill, 2003), 2:3–286. Selective translations into English include:

Birrell, Ann. *New Songs from a Jade Terrace: An Anthology of Early Chinese Love Poetry*. London: George Allen and Unwin, 1982. Pp. 124, 127–30.

Frodsham, J. D., with the collaboration of Ch'eng Hsi. *An Anthology of Chinese Verse: Han, Wei, Chin, and the Northern and Southern Dynasties*. Oxford: Clarendon Press, 1967. Pp. 159–64.

Japanese

Morino Shigeo 森野繁夫. *Sha Senjō shishū* 謝宣城詩集. Tokyo: Hakuteisha, 1991.

Research aids

Cao Daoheng. "Xie Tiao shiji shiwen xinian" 謝朓事迹詩文系年. In *Liuchao zuojia nianpu jiyao* 六朝作家年普輯要, 2 vols., ed. Liu Yuejin 劉躍進 and Fan Ziye 范子燁, 1:448–66. Harbin: Heilongjiang jiaoyu chubanshe, 1999.

Shiomi Kunihiko 塩見邦彥. *Sha Senjō shi ichiji sakuin* 謝宣城詩一字索引. Nagoya: Saika shorin, 1970.

Wu Shutang 吳叔儻. "Xie Tiao nianpu" 謝朓年普. *Xiaoshuo yuebao* (special issue titled "Zhongguo wenxue yanjiu" 中國文學研究) 16 (1927): 1–14.

Cynthia L. Chennault

Xu Gaoseng zhuan 續高僧傳

Introduction

The *Xu Gaoseng zhuan*, by Shi Daoxuan 釋道宣 (597–667), is modeled on Huijiao's *Gaoseng zhuan*, q.v., and picks up where that text left off, providing biographies of monks from the sixth century to the seventh. Like the *Gaoseng zhuan*, it was compiled privately, based on stele inscriptions, court documents, miracle tale collections, prefaces to scriptures, oral accounts, and, to a limited extent, personal observation. Although more independent accounts of monks are available for the period Daoxuan covers than for the period Huijiao covered in his work, the *Xu Gaoseng zhuan* remains the standard source for biographical information about monks for the late sixth and early seventh centuries. Unlike the *Gaoseng zhuan*, which is relatively weak in its coverage of the north, the *Xu Gaoseng zhuan* provides extensive information on monks from all parts of China. Although much of the work is concerned with monks who lived during the Tang era, it is an important source for the Six Dynasties as well, providing information on doctrinal developments, monasticism, state policy toward Buddhism, popular religion, and everyday life.

Assessment of the *Xu Gaoseng zhuan* has ranged from the nineteenth-century scholar Yang Shoujing 楊守敬, who praised its elegance (*Riben fangshu zhi* 日本訪書志, Linsuyuan 鄰蘇園 edition, 1897, 16:1a), to the twelfth-century monk Huihong 惠洪, who excoriated Daoxuan for what he considered a pedestrian style (*Shimen wenzi chan* 石門文字禪, *Sibu congkan** edition, vol. 112, 26:4a). Nonetheless, it has been widely read and cited from the time of its completion to the present day.

Contents

The *Xu Gaoseng zhuan* contains 485 major biographies with 219 subordinate biographies. Coverage extends from the first year of the Liang Dynasty (501) to the year 665. The biographies are divided into ten categories:

1. Yijing 譯經   Translators
2. Yijie 義解   Exegetes
3. Xichan 習禪   Practitioners of meditation
4. Minglü 明律   Elucidators of the regulations (scholars of the Vinaya)

5.	Hufa 護法	Defenders of the Dharma (monks who defended Buddhism at court)
6.	Gantong 感通	Resonance (devoted to miracle workers)
7.	Yishen 遺身	Those who sacrificed themselves (monks who sacrificed their bodies in acts of charity or devotion)
8.	Dusong 讀誦	Chanters
9.	Xingfu 興福	Benefactors (literally, the "generation of merit," for monks who solicited funds for or otherwise contributed toward Buddhist construction and other worthy enterprises)
10.	Zake 雜科	Miscellany

These categories are slightly different from those of Huijiao. Most of the changes are adjustments in nomenclature (*gantong* for *shenyi* 神異, *yishen* for *wangshen* 亡身, *dusong* for *songjing* 誦經). More substantially, Daoxuan eliminated the category of hymnodists (*jingshi* 經師) and introduced a chapter devoted to monks who "defended the Dharma." Following Huijiao, at the end of each section Daoxuan appended a "disquisition" (*lun* 論) in which he discusses the theme of the section. Biographies include accounts of leading monks of the period such as Zhiyi 智顗, Xuanzang 玄奘, and Sengchou 僧稠, as well as biographies of otherwise unknown monks. Since the Song dynasty, Daoxuan's chapter on "practitioners of meditation" has attracted special attention because it includes early biographies of figures such as Bodhidharma and Daoxin who were later held up as patriarchs in the Chan school.

Authorship

Daoxuan was one of the most versatile and prolific monks of his generation. The son of a prominent official, he lived for most of his life in the Tang capital at Chang'an, where he worked briefly at Xuanzang's translation center and later served as abbot of the Ximing Monastery (Ximing si 西明寺). His works include a catalog of Buddhist writings, various historical texts, numerous writings on the monastic regulations, and records of his visionary encounters with divine beings. His writings had an impact on all of these genres, but especially on historiography and the study of the monastic regulations.

Composition

As in the case of the *Gaoseng zhuan*, most of the biographies in the *Xu Gaoseng zhuan* are taken in large part or completely from previous sources. On occasion, Daoxuan cites his sources, and he also notes at times that he personally visited a place mentioned in the biography or met someone with information about the subject of the biography. In the majority of cases, however, it is not possible to determine his sources. In general, Daoxuan follows traditional Chinese principles of historiography, for instance, drawing attention to discrepancies in names and dates. At other times he employs Buddhist doctrines in his analysis of historical materials, noting, for example, the function of karma in history, or identifying which supernatural power a monk must have had according to Buddhist lists of such powers. His dense and erudite disquisitions at the ends of the chapters disclose his familiarity with the breadth of Buddhist writings and with Chinese Buddhist history.

Transmission of the text

After completing the *Xu Gaoseng zhuan*, Daoxuan continued to collect information and subsequently, shortly before his death, completed the *Houji Xu Gaoseng zhuan* 後集續高僧傳, which contained his supplementary material. After Daoxuan's death, this material was broken up and incorporated into the *Xu Gaoseng zhuan* in a clumsy fashion. Hence, while Daoxuan's preface to the *Xu Gaoseng zhuan* states that his work begins with the first year of the Liang dynasty and ends 144 years later in the nineteenth year of the Zhenguan era of the Tang (645), in fact, as mentioned earlier, the text goes up to 665. Similarly, the preface says that the text includes 331 major biographies and 160 subsidiary biographies, when in fact it includes 485 major biographies and 219 subsidiary biographies. All of this is owing to the incorporation of the *Houji Xu Gaoseng zhuan* into the text.

In Daoxuan's own catalog of scriptures, the *Neidian lu* 內典錄, the *Xu Gaoseng zhuan* is listed as containing thirty *juan* and the *Houji Xu Gaoseng zhuan* as having ten. But by 730, when the catalog *Kaiyuan Shijiao lu* 開元釋教錄 was compiled, only the *Xu Gaoseng zhuan* is recorded, suggesting that already at this time the two works had been combined. The *Xu Gaoseng zhuan* was included in printed versions of the Buddhist Canon from the early twelfth century, through many printings, into the twentieth century.

Principal editions

Modern editions of the *Xu Gaoseng zhuan* for the most part derive from the Zhaocheng 趙城 (1139–1172), the Qisha 磧砂 (1225–1233), or the Korean edition of the canon (1236–1251). The *Zhonghua dazang jing* 中華大藏經 edition (Beijing: Zhonghua shuju, 1984–1996), for instance, is based on the Zhaocheng, while the most commonly cited edition, the *Taishō shinshū Daizōkyō**, vol. 50, no. 2060, is based on the Korean printing, with annotation of discrepancies from some other editions in the notes. The *Taishō* edition is widely available in printed and digital forms. There is as yet no consensus among scholars as to which edition is superior.

Modern critical editions

We await an edition of the text that rigorously compares all of the major editions and explains all discrepancies. A new, punctuated edition of the text has, for more than a decade, been scheduled to appear in the Zhonghua shuju series of

Buddhist texts, but it has not yet been published. Dharma Drum Buddhist College is currently preparing an annotated digital version of the text.

Studies of the text

Fujiyoshi Masumi 藤善真澄. *Dōsenden no kenkyū* 道宣傳の研究. Kyoto: Kyōto daigaku gakujutsu shuppankai, 2002.

Kieschnick, John. *The Eminent Monk: Buddhist Ideals in Medieval Chinese Hagiography*. Honolulu: University of Hawai'i Press, 1997.

Shi Guodeng 釋果燈. *Tang Daoxuan Xu Gaoseng zhuan pipan sixiang chutan* 唐道宣續高僧傳批判思想初探. Taipei: Dongchu, 1992.

Shinohara, Koichi. "Two Sources of Chinese Buddhist Biographies: Stupa Inscriptions and Miracle Stories." In *Monks and Magicians: Religious Biographies in Asia*, ed. Phyllis Granoff and Koichi Shinohara, 119–228. London: Mosaic Press, 1988.

Wagner, Robin. "Buddhism, Biography, and Power: A Study of Daoxuan's *Continued Lives of Eminent Monks*." Ph.D. diss., Harvard University, 1995.

John Kieschnick

Xun Xu ji 荀勖集

Introduction

Xun Xu (styled Gongceng 公曾; ca. 221–289), a member of a distinguished family from Yingchuan 穎川 (modern central Henan), was a man of arts and letters who made his mark while serving the Western Jin court and its first emperor, Wudi (Sima Yan; 235–290; r. 266–290). Xun's biography is found in *Jin shu*, q.v., 39:1152–57.

Xun belonged to a generation of influential Western Jin peers including Zhang Hua 張華 (232–300), Chenggong Sui 成功綏 (232–273), and Du Yu 杜預 (222–284). They and others made significant contributions to classical commentary, ancient texts and orthographies, musicology, historical calendrics and computational astronomy, and portraiture and calligraphy, as well as genres of intimate poetic expression and florid rhyme-prose. (Xun's contributions are discussed in Goodman, *Xun Xu and the Politics of Precision*, passim; see also Liu Rulin, *Han Jin xueshu biannian*, 152–53.) Many of these men were political activists as well. On imperial order, Xun assembled the first team to analyze and transcribe the Ji Tomb (Ji zhong 汲冢) ancient texts discovered in 280. His transcription drew objections from Du Yu and others, and Xun's career suffered after about 283. (The Ji Tomb affair is studied in Shaughnessy, *Rewriting Early Chinese Texts*, 138–42; its scholarly networks examined in Goodman, *Xun Xu and the Politics of Precision*, chap. 6.) In 287 he was transferred out of the Imperial Library, where he had conducted years of technical research, and died filled with remorse in 289, as he watched his rival Zhang Hua taking over this and related offices.

Contents

As are many other Six Dynasties *wenji*, the *Xun Xu ji* is a collection of prose items such as petitions, letters, disquisitions, epitaphs, and rhyme-prose, and also verse items such as songs (or chants, *ge* 歌) and poems. The extant, and fullest, edition is titled *Xun Gongceng ji* 荀公曾集; it was assembled in the late Ming by Zhang Pu (1602–1641; *jinshi* 1631) for his large work titled *Han Wei Liuchao baisanjia ji*, q.v. The items in the *Xun Gongceng ji* total nineteen and are in the following order:

Rhyme-prose, 1 title (fragment of a piece on the grape plant)

Presentation, 1 title

Petition, 5 titles

Responding opinion (*dui* 對), 2 titles

Opinion, 2 titles

Personal letter, 2 titles

Preface, 1 title (preface to his transcription of the Ji Tomb text of the *Mu Tianzi zhuan* 穆天子傳)

Court songs (*yuege* 樂歌), 4 titles under the general rubric "Jin sixiang yuege" 晉四廂樂歌 [Songs for the Jin (palace) four side-rooms], some with subtitled parts. These are traditional subgenres of song, in principle accompanied by music, for court festal, saltatory, and temple ritual occasions.

Lyric poem, 1 title

Yan Kejun's (1762–1843) "Quan Jin wen," *juan* 31 (part of his *Quan shanggu Sandai Qin Han Sanguo Liuchao wen*, q.v.), gleans only the prose, resulting in sixteen pieces: the one rhyme-prose, five petitions, three presentations (one of them in the *Han Wei Liuchao baisanjia ji* being split into two), four opinions (including some alternative text for one of them); two letters, and one preface.

Transmission and early history of the text

The biography of Xun Xu in the *Jin shu* curiously does not mention the compilation or transmission of any of his writings. *Sui shu*, q.v., 35:1061, in a note merely says that "[in Liang] *Xun Xu ji* had three *juan*, plus a one-*juan* 'Record of Contents'; lost." The *Xun Xu ji* was in fact noted by later bibliographers. The *Jiu Tang shu* (completed in 945, but using eighth-century records) states that "*Xun Xu ji* is in twenty *juan*" (47:2058; Yao Zhenzong, *Sui shu jingji zhi kaozheng*, 915:692, believed that the word "ten" was a mistake, which would make this two *juan*). The major Song catalogs do not mention Xun's *wenji*, and, as in the cases of many of his Western Jin peers, Xun's poetry was first critically collected and annotated by Feng Weine (1513–1572), who compiled the *Gushi ji**, and from there the complete oeuvre was reconstituted as we know it (as *Xun Gongceng ji* or *Xun Xu ji*, depending on edition), in the *Han Wei Liuchao baisanjia ji*.

Principal editions

The most complete edition is *juan* 38 of the *Han Wei Liuchao baisanjia ji*; see *Yingyin Wenyuange Siku quanshu** 1413:121–32, and the 1879 re-cut woodblock print (rpt., Jiangsu: Jiangsu guji shudian, 1990), 2:335–51.

Texts with commentary and notes

There is no modern, punctuated, text-critical edition of Xun Xu's *wenji*, but certain of the items in it have received scholarly attention. For a modern, punctuated version of Xun's "Tiaodie wen Lie He zhulü yizhuang zou" 條牒問列和諸律意狀

奏 (Memorial about the transcription of a dialog with [flute master] Lie He on the intended structure for all the regulated pitches), see *Song shu* ("Lüli zhi," part 1) 11.212–15; an annotation of it is given in Wang Zichu 王子初, *Xun Xu dilü yanjiu* 荀勖笛律研究 (Beijing: Renmin yinyue chubanshe, 1995). Modern versions of three other items (namely, one petition, one responding opinion, and one opinion) are carried via Xun's *Jinshu* biography. For modern punctuated versions of Xun's court ritual songs, see *Song shu* ("Monograph on Music," "Yue zhi" 樂志, part 2) 20:583–87.

Lu Qinli's *Xian Qin Han Wei Jin Nanbeichao shi** provides annotated texts, with source notes, of Xun's court songs, in "Jin shi," *juan* 10 (1:817–20), and for Xun's one poem, "Cong Wudi Hualinyuan yanshi" 從武帝華林園宴詩 (A feasting poem for a gathering with Wudi at Hualin Park), see *juan* 2 (1:592), where Lu offers two versions, one in tetrameter and one in pentameter (the alternative not provided in the *Han Wei Liuchao baisanjia ji*). For all court songs, see also the *Yuefu shiji*, q.v., *juan* 13 and 52.

Selected studies

Goodman, Howard L. *Xun Xu and the Politics of Precision in Third-Century AD China*. Sinica Leidensia 95. Leiden: E. J. Brill, 2010.

Mathieu, Rémi. "Mu t'ien tzu chuan" 穆天子傳. In *Early Chinese Texts: A Bibliographical Guide*, ed. Michael Loewe, 343–44. Berkeley: Society for the Study of Early China and Institute of East Asian Studies, University of California, Berkeley, 1993.

Shaughnessy, Edward L. *Rewriting Early Chinese Texts*. Albany: State University of New York Press, 2006.

Wang Fuli 王福利. *Jiaomiao yanshe geci yanjiu* 郊廟燕射歌辭研究. Beijing: Beijing daxue chubanshe, 2009. Wang briefly discusses Xun's court lyrics, 212–16. This is one of very few modern studies that looks at the texts of this genre of post-Han lyric.

Translations

Howard Goodman's *Xun Xu and the Politics of Precision in Third-Century AD China* provides translations with annotation for the court ritual song "Zhengde wu ge" 正德舞歌 (Choreographed chants for [Jin's] Just Potency), 140–46; the lyric poem "Cong Wudi Hualin yuan yanshi," 286–90; the presentation "Tiaodie wen Lie He zhulü yizhuang zou," 232–56; and an untitled piece of prose for the Jin's new foot-rule (*Jin xinchi* 晉新尺), 191–93, an item not collected in the *Han Wei Liuchao baisanjia ji*. In *Rewriting Early Chinese Texts* (140, 172), Shaughnessy translates and annotates the "Preface to *Mu Tianzi zhuan*." Additionally, there are the following:

Goodman, Howard L., and Y. Edmund Lien. "A Third Century AD Chinese System of Di-Flute Temperament: Matching Ancient Pitch-Standards and Confronting Modal Practice." *Galpin Society Journal* 62 (April 2009): 3–24. A translation and annotation of a major portion of the "Xun Xu dilü" 荀勖笛律, which is not collected in the *Han Wei Liuchao baisanjia ji*.

Research aids

Liu Rulin 劉汝霖. *Han Jin xueshu biannian* 漢晉學術編年. Shanghai, 1935.
Yao Zhenzong 姚振宗 (1843–1906). *Sui shu jingji zhi kaozheng* 隋書經籍志考證. In *Ershiwushi bubian* 二十五史補編, 4:5730c. Shanghai: Kaiming shudian, 1937.

Howard L. Goodman

Yanshi jiaxun 顏氏家訓

Introduction

The *Yanshi jiaxun* (Family counsels of Mr. Yan) by Yan Zhitui 顏之推 (531–after 591) is a remarkable work that contains many observations about the social conventions of its time by a keen observer; it moved the French scholar Etienne Balazs to say it was an "ouvrage précieux pour ses nombreux renseignements sur les moeurs et la civilisation du VIe siècle" (*Le traité économique*, 211n110). Its author, Yan Zhitui, was of the eighth generation of a distinguished family line originally from Linyi 臨沂, Shandong, that had moved to the south in the face of the collapse of the Western Jin. Yan served the Liang dynasty in a number of official capacities, was brought north after the capture of Jiangling by the Western Wei in 554, escaped to the Northern Qi in 556 in a futile attempt to return to the south, served that state from 556 to 577 as an official, and was again brought back to Chang'an when the Northern Qi was conquered by the Northern Zhou. There he lived out the remainder of his life, dying at some time during the Sui (*Bei Qi shu*, q.v., 45:617–26; *Bei shi*, q.v., 83:2794–96; and Dien, *The Biography of Yen Chih-t'ui*). These experiences gave Yan a broad range of experiences and the opportunity to make astute remarks about and comparisons between the cultures of the north and south.

The tradition of presenting one's offspring with some well-chosen words is an old one in China; Confucius urging his son to study the *Odes* is one example. By the Han there are many works of this nature, usually termed *jie* 戒, telling younger progeny how to behave. Early in the Six Dynasties period, the terms *jiajie* 家戒 and *jiaxun* 家訓 came to be used interchangeably as the genre broadened to instruct as well as to admonish the youths. The need to pass on the family traditions in those troubled times is often mentioned as the motivation for such instructional manuals. The continuing significance of the text is indicated by the approximately three hundred citations of the work in a database covering books published in the People's Republic of China since 1949.

Contents

The *Yanshi jiaxun* is divided into the following twenty sections:

1. Xuzhi 序致   Prefatory remarks on the scope
2. Jiaozi 教子   Teaching children

3. Xiongdi 兄弟   Brothers
4. Houqu 後娶   Remarriage
5. Zhijia 治家   Regulating the family
6. Fengcao 風操   Manners and tenets
7. Muxian 慕賢   Emulating the worthy
8. Quanxue 勉學   Diligent study
9. Wenzhang 文章   Literature
10. Mingshi 名實   Reputation and reality
11. Shewu 涉務   Meeting responsibilities
12. Shengshi 省事   Reducing [extraneous] matters
13. Zhizu 止足   Knowing when to stop
14. Jiebing 誡兵   Warning about military involvement
15. Yangsheng 養生   Nourishing life
16. Guixin 歸心   Turning one's heart [to Buddhism]
17. Shuzheng 書證   Literary verification
18. Yinci 音辭   Pronouncing words
19. Zayi 雜藝   Miscellaneous arts
20. Zhongzhi 終制   Final arrangements

Each section deals with a different general topic, but running through the whole is an emphasis on personal responsibility, circumspection in conduct, correct usage in language, and dislike of ostentation and deception. The general discussion is peppered with anecdotes and personal observations, making the work a fascinating read.

Authenticity and transmission of the text

From internal evidence, the *Yanshi jiaxun* was written during the Sui dynasty after Yan's sixtieth year (591 or after). It is entered in *Jiu Tang shu* 47:2025 and *Xin Tang shu* 59:1511 as having seven *juan*. A family epitaph written by a descendant, the famous calligrapher Yan Zhenqing 真卿 (708–784), and dated 780, includes it among Yan Zhitui's works, in twenty sections. The *Yanshi jiaxun* is cited in a number of commentaries during the Tang, such as Li Shan's 李善 (d. 689) commentary to *Wen xuan*, q.v., 38:26b (Taipei: Yiwen yinshuguan, 1957), citing *Yanshi jiaxun* 6:14a–b (ed. Zhou Fagao; see later). Section 16, which concerns Buddhism, was included in the *Guang Hongmingji*, q.v., dated 664; *Taishō shinshū Daizōkyō** 52:107–8 and 294.

The *Yanshi jiaxun* continued to be cited in the Song, and it is listed in *Chongwen zongmu** (dated between 1034 and 1038) 3:27a–b, *Junzhai dushuzhi** (dated 1151) 10:442, and *Zhizhai shulu jieti** (ca. 1235) 10:305, all in seven *juan*.

Principal editions

Modern editions derive from the Song. Shen Kui 沈揆 (*jinshi* 1160) and associates produced a version by collating two earlier texts, referred to as Shu 蜀 and Min 閩, along with a chapter of commentary. The result, dated 1183, was in the Taizhou 台州 library (modern Linhai 臨海, Zhejiang), and that edition has been copied into the *Zhibuzuzhai congshu* 知不足齋叢書.

A Ming edition included in the *Han Wei congshu* 漢魏叢書 of Cheng Rong 程榮, preface dated 1592, was prepared by a member of a Yan 顏 family in Suzhou, based on a Song edition with another, unspecified, in the family's possession, and printed in 1575. Still in twenty sections, it is in two rather than seven *juan*.

A second Ming edition, also in two *juan*, was copied from one in the imperial archives in 1524 and given to Fu Taiping 傅太平 of Liaoyang to print. This is known as the Fu edition and was reproduced in the *Sibu congkan**, with some additional collation by Leng Zongyuan 冷宗元.

Lu Wenchao 盧文弨 (1717–1796) and associates produced an edition, preface dated 1789, that was meant to be definitive. The major part of the collational effort was by Zhao Ximing 趙曦明 (1705–1787), with notes by Duan Yucai 段玉裁 (1735–1815) and other eminent scholars. This edition is included as a part of the *Baojingtang congshu* 抱經堂叢書 in 1792. The *Sibu beiyao* 四部備要 version is a virtual copy of it. Despite the reputation for careful textual analysis of the Qing scholars, a careful comparison of this edition with others indicates that textual changes were too often made on the basis of what read well, allowing subjective judgments to tamper with the received text, a process that has been termed *ratio et res ipsa*.

Critical notes continued to be written over the years. The last major edition was that compiled by Zhou Fagao in his *Yanshi jiaxun huizhu* (1960). This is a work of grand proportions, including most of the commentorial scholarship that had preceded it. Zhao also included Yan's biography from the *Bei Qi shu*, a *nianpu* 年譜 (chronology) of Yan's life, a bibliography, prefaces and postfaces from earlier editions and commentaries, quotations from bibliographical works that cite the *Yanshi jiaxun*, a concordance, an index to works cited, and a final section of additional commentary.

Texts with commentaries and notes

Wang Liqi 王利器. *Yanshi jiaxun jijie* 顏氏家訓集解. Shanghai: Guji chubanshe,
    1980. Rpt., Beijing: Zhonghua shuju, 1993. Appendices: prefaces and postfaces of Song, Ming, and Qing editions, the *Siku quanshu** review and note from the *Junzhai dushuzhi*; annotated biography of Yan Zhitui from the *Bei Qi shu*.

Zhou Fagao 周法高, ed. *Yanshi jiaxun huizhu* 顏氏家訓彙注. 4 vols. Zhongyang yanjiuyuan lishi yuyan yanjiusuo zhuankan 中央研究院歷史語言研究所專刊 41. Taipei, 1960.

Commentaries and notes without the complete text

Chen Pan 陳槃. "Du *Yanshi jiaxun* zhaji" 讀顏氏家訓札記. In *Symposium of Chinese Studies Commemorating the Golden Jubilee of the University of Hong Kong, 1911–1961* (Xianggang daxue wushi zhounian jinian lunwenji 香港大學五十週年紀年論文集), 1:127–37. Hong Kong: Hong Kong University Press, 1961.

Liu Pansui 劉盼遂. "*Yanshi jiaxun* jiaojian" 顏氏家訓校牋[箋]. *[Nüshida] xueshu jikan* 1.2 (1930): 1–21.

———. "*Yanshi jiaxun* jiaojian buzheng" 顏氏家訓校牋[箋]補證." *[Nüshida] xueshu jikan* 2.1 (1931): 1–10.

Wang Shumin 王叔岷. "*Yanshi jiaxun* jiaozhu" 顏氏家訓斠注. In *Symposium of Chinese Studies Commemorating the Golden Jubilee of the University of Hong Kong, 1911–1961*, 1:65–125. Rpt., *Yanshi jiaxun jiaozhu* 顏氏家訓斠注. Taipei: Yiwen yinshuguan, 1975.

———. "*Yanshi jiaxun* jiaozhu bulu" 顏氏家訓斠注補錄. In *Qingzhu Zhu Jiahua xiansheng qishi sui lunwenji* 慶祝朱家驊先生七十歲論問集. Dalu zazhi tekan di'er ji 大陸雜誌特刊第二輯 15–16. Taipei: Dalu zazhi she, 1962.

———. "*Yanshi jiaxun* jiaozhu buyi" 顏氏家訓斠注補遺. *Wen shi zhe xuebao* 12 (1963): 39–43.

———. *Yanshi jiaxun jiaobu* 顏氏家訓斠補. Taipei: Yiwen yinshuguan, 1975.

Xie Mingliang 謝明良. "Du *Yanshi jiaxun*: Zhongzhi zhaji" 讀顏氏家訓: 終制札記. *Gugong xueshu jikan* 7.2 (1989): 107–20.

Xu Weixian 許惟賢. "*Yanshi jiaxun* de xungu" 顏氏家訓的訓詁. *Nanjing daxue xuebao, Zhexue shehui kexue* (1983.1): 33–38.

Zhou Fagao 周法高. "*Yanshi jiaxun* huizhu buyi" 顏氏家訓彙注補遺. In *Qingzhu Dong Zuobin xiansheng liushiwu sui lunwenji* 慶祝董作賓先生六十五歲論文集, 857–97. Taipei: Academia Sinica, 1961.

———. "Du *Yanshi jiaxun* zhaji" 讀顏氏家訓札記. *Dalu zazhi* 62.5 (1981): 43.

Selected studies

Balazs, Etienne. "Le traité économique du 'Souei-chou.'" *T'oung Pao* 42 (1953): 113–329. Rpt., Leiden: E. J. Brill, 1953.

Dien, Albert E. "Yen Chih-t'ui, A Buddho-Confucian." In *Confucian Personalities*, ed. Arthur Wright and Denis Twitchett, 44–64. Stanford, CA: Stanford University Press, 1962.

———. *The Biography of Yen Chih-t'ui (Pei Ch'i shu 45)*. Würzburger Sino-Japonica 6. Bern: Herbert Lang, 1976.

———. "Instructions for the Grave: The Case of Yan Zhitui." *Cahiers d'Extréme-Asie* 8 (1995): 41–58.

———. "Comments on Chapter Nine of the *Yanshi jiaxun*: Literary Compositions" [in Chinese]. In *Wei Jin Nanbeichao wenxue lunji* 魏晉南北朝文學論集, 599–613. Nanjing: Nanjing University, 1997.

———. "A Sixth-Century Father's Advice on Literature: Comments on Chapter Nine of the *Yanshi jiaxun*." *Asia Major* 13.1 (2002): 65–82.

Han Fu 翰府. "Yan Zhitui de wenzhangxue lilun" 顏之推的文章學理論. In *Beichao yanjiu* 北朝研究, ed. Zhongguo Wei Jin Nanbeichao shixuehui 中國魏晉南北朝史學會 and Datong Pingcheng Beichao yanjiuhui 大同平城北朝研究會, 294–302. Beijing: Beijing Yanshan chubanshe, 2000.

Katsumura Tetsuya 勝村哲也. "Ganshi kakun Kishinhen to Enkonshi o megutte" 顏氏家訓歸心篇と冤魂志をめぐつて. *Tōyōshi kenkyū* 26 (1968): 350–62.

Liu Guoshi 劉國石. "Bashi niandai yilai *Yanshi jiaxun* yanjiu gaishu" 八十年代以來顏氏家訓研究概述. *Zhongguoshi yanjiu dongtai* (1997.4): 19–23.

Miao Yue 繆鉞. "Yan Zhitui nianpu" 顏之推年譜. *Zhenli* 1 (1944): 411–22.

Tang Changru 唐長孺. "Du *Yanshi jiaxun*—Houqupian lun nanbei dishu shenfen de chayi" 讀顏氏家訓—後娶篇論南北嫡庶身分的差異. *Lishi yanjiu* (1994.1): 58–65.

Utsunomiya Kiyoyoshi 宇都宮清吉. "Gan Shisui" 顏之推. In [*Aoki Masaru hakushi kanreki kinen*] *Chūka rokujū meika genkōroku* [青木正兒博士還曆記念]中華六十名家言行錄, ed. Yoshikawa Kōjirō, 63–68. Tokyo: Kōbundō shobō, 1948.

———. "Hoku-Sei-sho Bun'enden chū Gan Shisui-den no issetsu ni oite" 北齊書文苑傳中顏之推傳の一節に就いて. *Nagoya daigaku bungakubu kenkyū ronshū* 41 (1966): 47–63.

———. "Ganshi kakun 'Kishinhen' oboegaki" 顏氏家訓'歸心篇'覺書. *Nagoya daigaku bungakubu kenkyū ronshū* 44 (1967): 27–33.

Wang Xiaoxin 王小莘. "*Yanshi jiaxun* zhong fanying Wei Jin Nanbeichao shidai tedian de yuci de yanjiu" 顏氏家訓中反映魏晉南北朝時代特點的語詞的研究. *Huanan shifan daxuei xuebao, Shehui kexue ban* (1993.4): 46–55.

———. "Cong *Yanshi jiaxun* kan Wei Jin Nanbeichao de qinshu chengwei" 從顏氏家訓看魏晉南北朝的親屬稱謂. *Gu Hanyu yanjiu* (1998.2): 59–62.

———. "*Yanshi jiaxun* zhong de binglieshi tongyi (jinyi, leiyi) ciyu yanjiu" 顏氏家訓中的並列式同義(近義, 類義)詞語研究. *Gu Hanyu yanjiu* (1996.3): 56–60, 76.

Wang Xin 王忻. "Cong *Yanshi jiaxun* guankui Wei Jin shiqi Hanyu cihui fuyinhua de fazhan" 從顏氏家訓管窺魏晉時期漢語詞彙複音化的發展. *Gu Hanyu yanjiu* (1998.3): 28–31.

Yoshikawa Tadao 吉川忠夫. "Gan Shisui shōron" 顏之推小論. *Tōyōshi kenkyū* 20 (1962): 353–81.

You Yazi 尤雅姿. *Yan Zhitui ji qi jiaxun zhi yanjiu* 顏之推及其家訓之研究. Taipei: Wen shi zhe chubanshe, 2005.

Zhou Rijian 周日健 and Wang Xiaoxin 王小莘, comps. *Yanshi jiaxun cihui yufa yanjiu* 顏氏家訓詞彙語法研究. Guangzhou: Guangdong renmin chubanshe, 1998.

Zhou Zumou 周祖謨. "*Yanshi jiaxun* yincipian zhubu" 顏氏家訓音辭篇注補. *Furen xuezhi* 12.1 (1943): 201–20.

Translations

English

Dien, Albert E. "Yen Chih-t'ui (531–591+): His Life and Thought." Ph.D. diss., University of California, Berkeley, 1962. Translation of chaps. 1–8.

———. "House Instructions of Mr. Yan (*Yanshi jiaxun*)." In *Sources of Chinese Tradition*, 2nd ed., comp. Wm. Theodore de Bary and Irene Bloom, 541–46. New York: Columbia University Press, 1999.

Lau, D. C. "Advice to My Sons." *Renditions* 1 (1973): 94–98. Translation of chaps. 1 and 2.

———. "Yan's Family Instructions: Excerpts." *Renditions* 33–34 (1990): 58–62. Selections from chaps. 3 and 4.

Teng, Ssu-Yü, trans. *Family Instructions for the Yen clan: Yen-shih chia-hsün*. Annotated full translation. T'oung pao monographie 4. Leiden: E. J. Brill, 1968.

Japanese

Uno Seiichi 宇野精一. *Ganshi kakun* 顏氏家訓. Tokyo: Meitoku shuppansha, 1982.

Utsunomiya Kiyoyoshi 宇都宮清吉. *Ganshi kakun: Chūkoku koten bungaku taikei* 顏氏家訓: 中國古典文學大系, 9:405–630. Tokyo: Heibonsha, 1969.

Chinese

Cheng Xiaoming 程小銘. *Yanshi jiaxun quanyi* 顏氏家訓全譯. Guiyang: Guizhou renmin chubanshe, 1993.

Index

This text is included in the Chinese Text Project with a full-text search capability.

Albert E. Dien

Yezhong ji 鄴中記

Introduction

The *Yezhong ji* (A record of Ye) by Lu Hui 陸翽 (ca. fourth century) describes the sumptuous lifestyle, lofty architecture, and seasonal festivals in the capital city Ye 鄴 during the reign of Shi Hu 石虎, a non-Chinese ruler of the Later Zhao dynasty (319–351). Though transmitted only in fragments, this work is one of the extremely rare sources for the material culture of early medieval China.

Ye was located on the Zhang 漳 River at the present-day Linzhang 臨漳 in Hebei Province. A major city from the time of Cao Cao 曹操 (155–220), though it is not often cited in the historical records from the fourth to the sixth centuries, whenever north China split into east and west polities, Ye always replaced Luoyang and served as the capital of the eastern polity due to its strategic importance militarily and in transportation. According to *Ancient Letter II* found by Sir Aurel Stein in the vicinity of Dunhuang (dated shortly after 311, before the fall of the Western Jin), Ye, together with Luoyang, was at that time already known to Sogdian merchants as far away as Samarkand.

In 334 Ye replaced Xiangguo 襄國 (the present-day Xiangtai 邢臺 in Hebei) as the second capital of the short-lived Later Zhao State, founded by Shi Le 石勒 (r. 319–333), who was of Jie 羯 stock, possibly of Europoid Central Asian origin. His successor, Shi Hu (r. 334–349), reconstructed Ye on the basis of Cao Cao's original city plan by erecting new palaces and imperial gardens. Ye became the center of much luxury, and the lavish lifestyle there was enviously copied by other foreign rulers, such as Li Shou 李壽 (r. 338–343) of Cheng-Han 成漢 (*Jin shu*, q.v., 121:3045; *Wei shu*, q.v., 96:2111). Extravagant products, such as complex silk and woolen cloths, and handicrafts in gold and silver, were either traded or manufactured in Ye, thus attracting foreign merchants into the city and most likely making it one of the major terminals of overland commerce. The massacre of up to tens of thousands of people with "Europoid features" (i.e., deep eye sockets and high noses) around 349 may give an idea of the high density of the Iranian inhabitants in the city, who either came with the ruling Shi ("Čač," lit., "Stone") family or had settled there already at the beginning of the fourth century.

After the Later Zhao, Ye served as a quasi-capital of the Northern Wei, then again as the capital of Eastern Wei (534–550) and Northern Qi (550–577). During the Northern Qi the city expanded to the south and formed a larger "southern city of Ye" (Ye nancheng 鄴南城) adjacent to the original Ye. The city lost its prominence after the conquest of the Northern Qi by the Northern Zhou in 577.

Whereas the *Yezhong ji* was often cited to recall the splendor of the ancient city, it is also often cited as a source for the state of technological development in early medieval China. For the studies of historical textiles, the *Yezhong ji* is a unique source concerning the production of diverse luxurious silk and woolen weaving after Han times. The *Yezhong ji* is also the locus classicus for certain popularly adopted terms in Tang literature such as "five-colored edicts" (*wuse zhao* 五色詔) and "female escorts" (*nü lubu* 女鹵簿).

Contents

Surviving passages of the *Yezhong ji* concretely deal in the first place with the happenings *within* the city, especially those that relate to Shi Hu and his empress. A smaller portion is dedicated to the description of the suburban area and the folk festivals. Major points of interest are as follows: (1) the city's physical features, including the city walls, the three fortified towers, the gates, the boulevards, canalizations in palaces and in the city, palatial buildings, and imperial gardens; (2) the court ceremonies of Shi Hu, and festivals in palaces and imperial gardens; (3) the entourage of Shi Hu and his empress, such as the female mounted bodyguard, the female palace attendants, the female ministers and civil servants, and Shi Hu's (male) mounted assault troop; attention is paid especially to their costumes, hair styles, armor, and weapons; (4) the personal belongings of Shi Hu, including his wardrobe, furniture, tableware, accessories, interior furnishings, and vehicles; (5) the state of art in technology, for example, a filter system for the bathing pool of the empress, a water-spouting mechanism, the "South-Pointing Cart," the hodometer, a mill driven by mechanical power, the processional carriage with mechanically moving wooden figurines, the hunting palanquin with a rotating seat, and various sorts of textiles from the imperial weaving workshops; and (6) domestic and exotic fruits and herbs (especially those of Iranian origin).

This small work is strikingly matter-of-fact and mundane. It contains neither the reproaches of Confucian critics concerning the extravagance of Shi Hu's building activities, nor philosophical discussions, but only a few religious and supernatural anecdotes. If the surviving passages of the *Yezhong ji* are any indication, it would seem that the author indulged himself in the material accomplishments of the day and filtered out politics, ethics, and racial conflicts between the Han and the newly arrived peoples.

Authorship and date of composition

Li Daoyuan (d. 527) was the first expressly to mention the *Yezhong ji* and its author. In his *Shuijing zhu*, q.v. (ca. 515–525), he called the work the "*Yezhong ji* of Mr. Lu" (*Lu shi Yezhong ji* 陸氏鄴中記). Zong Lin 宗懍 was the first to refer to Lu Hui as the author of the *Yezhong ji* in his *Jing Chu suishi ji*, q.v. (ca. 550). In addition, the seventh-century *Sui shu* bibliographic monograph (33:983) attributed to Lu Hui the title "assistant tutor of the young sons of the state of Jin" (*Jin guozi zhujiao* 晉國子助教). Although there is no other information about him, there seems to be no doubt about the authorship of the *Yezhong ji*, since the earliest sources all give his name as the author. The modern scholar Xu Zuomin (*Yedu yizhi ji jiaozhu*, 3) suspects that the name of a certain Sui Hui 隋翻, author of two works on Shi Le and Shi Hu mentioned in the *Xin Tang shu* bibliographic monograph (58:1462), may be a scribal error for Lu Hui 陸翻. While one may deduce that Lu Hui could have been at the court of the Later Zhao, there is no concrete indication of the existence of the *Yezhong ji* in the fourth century. Wang Jia (d. before 393) also described the luxurious lifestyle and the bathing pool in Shi Hu's palaces at Ye in his *Shiyi ji*, q.v. (*juan* 9), but his text seems independent of that of the *Yezhong ji*. A passage concerning the mystery of the phoenix on the Fengyang Gate of Ye in the *You ming lu* 幽明錄 of Liu Yiqing 劉義慶 (403–444) could have been inspired by the description of the same gate in the *Yezhong ji*. The relationship among the *Shiyi ji*, the *Youming lu*, and the *Yezhong ji* remains unclear.

The existence of the *Yezhong ji* as a source cited in other works becomes clearer during the first half of the sixth century, when passages of the *Yezhong ji* appear in the *Shiliuguo chunqiu*, q.v. (completed in 525), without mention of the source, and in the *Qimin yaoshu*, q.v. (composed ca. 533–544), which cites the title.

Transmission and authenticity

The *Sui shu*, q.v., bibliographic monograph (33:983) registers the *Yezhong ji* in two *juan*, under the geographical works (*dili lei* 地理類) of the history section (*shi bu* 史部). It is also listed with Liu Hui as author and as being in two *juan* in *Xin Tang shu* 58:1504. The popularity of the *Yezhong ji* can be observed in its wide citation in encyclopedic works such as the *Beitang shuchao*, q.v., of Yu Shinan (558–628), *Yiwen leiju*, q.v., compiled in 624 by Ouyang Xun, and *Chu xue ji*, q.v., compiled in 727 by Xu Jian. Li Xian 李賢 and Li Shan 李善 also used this text to annotate the *Han shu* and *Wen xuan*, q.v., around 625 to 628 and 658, respectively. The fact that the work is sometimes cited as *Shi Hu Yezhong ji* 石虎鄴中記 indicates that the work in its original form was narrowly limited to the period of Shi Hu and no further. The Song catalog by Chen Zhensun (fl. 1211–1249), *Zhizhai shulu jieti**8:243, lists the *Yezhong ji* in only one *juan*, and without naming an author, states that it is a record of the palaces when Ye served as capital from the Cao-Wei period to Northern Qi times. All of this would indicate that by the Southern Song at the latest the original text of the *Yezhong ji* had been lost.

The *Yongle dadian**, however, includes fragments of the *Yezhong ji*. Some carry the title "Lu Hui *Yezhong ji*," others simply "*Yezhong ji*." It is certain that not all the fragments are of the original work. The enlarged edition of the *Shuofu* 說郛 in 120 *juan*, by Tao Ting 陶珽 at the end of the Ming, contains on the whole thirty-five entries, from which thirty-three are organized under the title *Yezhong ji*, without the name of the author and no division into *juan*. This version also appeared in the

Xu baichuan xuehai 續百川學海 (*yi ji* 乙集) and *Wuchao xiaoshuo daguan* 五朝小說大觀 (fourth *bian*, first *ce* 四編第一冊).

The first effort to sort out authentic passages of the "original" *Yezhong ji* was made in the Qing. The version in the *Siku quanshu**, Wuyingdian *juzhenben* 武英殿聚珍本, abridged as *dianben* 殿本 (the Palace edition), was reconstructed from scattered passages contained in the Ming dynasty's *Yongle dadian* 永樂大典 (comp. 1407). Ji Yun 紀昀 wrote in his preface to this work in the *Siku quanshu zongmu tiyao** (14:1428–29) that it was possible to recover only one *juan* with seventy-four passages of text, of which eight were of doubtful origin (according to the compilers) and were attached to the main corpus as an appendix (*fu lu* 附錄).

It would seem that the main body of the *dianben* version was transmitted through the Song encyclopedia *Taiping yulan*, q.v. Nonetheless, a large portion of the passages concerning the city gates, the palaces, the fortress towers, the ice cellar, the imperial parks, court festivals and ceremonies, the mounted troops of Shi Hu, the female bodyguard of his empress, the female civil servants, the utensils of the court, the imperial wardrobe, the area around Ye, and two local festivals were all mentioned before the Tang and thus are most likely authentic. Certain passages, such as that describing the bathing pool of the empress, appeared in Tang times. The technical parts regarding mechanical and civil engineering and hydraulics were collected predominantly from the *Taiping yulan*, and though this is a Song source there is no reason to doubt that these passages are authentic. The changing range of citations also reflects interestingly the expanding foci of topics through the dynasties.

At the end of the Qing another comprehensive edition of the *Yezhong ji* was published, this one by Chen Yi 陳毅 of Xiangxiang 湘鄉, the son of the famous general Chen Shi 陳湜 of the Hunan Army (Xiang jun 湘軍). Chen Yi was a well-versed scholar, collector of antiquarian books, and editor-in-chief of the later Tongwenguan 同文館 (School of Combined Learning). He compiled eighty-eight entries and published this collection with his own press, which was named Queshenshi 闕慎室 after his private library. Access to this edition is, however, difficult. Apart from private collections, the title appears only in the catalog of the National Library in Beijing (Guojia tushuguan 國家圖書館). Xu Zuomin (see later), who evidently was able to examine a Queshenshi imprint, makes the point that the version of the *Taiping yulan* upon which Chen Yi heavily relied was not the best edition available in his time. This shortcoming led to numerous errors in the quotations, including erroneous characters. Some entries do not belong to the *Yezhong ji*, while other entries were omitted.

Principal edition

The *Siku quanshu* edition, reproduced in *Baibu congshu jicheng* 百部叢書集成, no. 27 (Taipei: Yiwen yinshuguan, 1964–1968), is a facsimile of the Wuyingdian *juzhenban* of 1776 that still serves as the best working base, even though more modern editions have been published. This edition is also reproduced in *Yingyin*

Wenyuange siku congshu* 463:305–14 and in *Siku quanshu zhenben bieji* 四庫全書珍本別輯, vol. 128 (Taipei: Taiwan shangwu yinshuguan, 1975). Note that this "Palace" edition merely refers to possible sources for specific passages, without giving confirming evidence or other information.

Modern critical editions

(1) Huang Huixian 黃惠賢, comp. "Jijiao *Yezhong ji*" 輯校鄴中記. *Wei Jin Nanbeichao Sui Tang shi ziliao* (1988.9/10): 132–81. Reprinted in *Yecheng ji Beichao shi yanjiu* 鄴城暨北朝史研究, ed. Liu Xinchang 劉心長 and Ma Zhongli 馬忠理, 368–440. Shijiazhuang: Hebei renmin chubanshe, 1991.

Huang's work is the first modern attempt at a recension of the *Yezhong ji*. Taking the *dianben* edition as the base text, he added not only the pre-Yuan text fragments but also corresponding passages from the *Yedu gongshi zhi* 鄴都宮室志, chapter 8 in the Jiajing 嘉靖 edition of the *Zhangde fu zhi* 彰德府志 by Cui Xuan 崔銑 (preface 1522). Parts of the *Yedu gongshi zhi* were derived from the Song dynasty *Xiangtai zhi* 相台志 of Chen Shenzhi 陳申之 (compiled between 1086 and 1094), which was already lost by the middle of the Ming. Altogether, ninety-three passages that Huang considers to belong to the original *Yezhong ji* are collated and reconstructed back into two *juan*. *Juan* 1 contains passages about Shi Hu and all related happenings within the city, arranged by contextual subjects (gates, palaces, terraces, parks, court ceremonies, the cold-food festival, the harem of Shi Hu, weaving workshops, the compass wagon, and the hodometer); *juan* 2 concerns everything outside the city (including royal parks, mausolea, hunting grounds, and suburban residences, as well as Shi Hu's bodyguards and hunting costumes).

The *Yedu gongshi zhi* supplies eight short passages not found in other sources, which Huang believes to belong to the original *Yezhong ji*. These are included in Huang's *juan* 2. The rest of the *Yedu gongshi zhi*, totaling twenty-eight entries, is obviously of later origin and divided by Huang into two categories: the "northern city of the Ye capital" (Yedu beicheng 鄴都北城) and "southern city of the Ye capital" (Yedu nancheng 鄴都南城). Huang provides a good geographically categorized picture of Ye's "inner" and "exterior" areas through coherent contextual texts that give the reader a concrete understanding of the city's construction during the Northern Dynasties. The Huang edition is punctuated and annotated with editorial notes but without translation into modern Chinese. Certain passages are accompanied by exegeses concerning their authenticity. Huang furthermore offers a thorough study of the history of the text's transmission.

(2) Xu Zuomin 許作民, comp. *Yedu yizhi ji jiaozhu* 鄴都佚志輯校注. Luoyang: Zhongzhou guji chubanshe, 1996.

Xu's compilation contains all the works relating to the city of Ye, with the *Yezhong ji* of Lu Hui as the earliest of them. Using the editions of the *dianben* and another by Chen Yi 陳毅 of the Qing's Guangxu 光緒 era (1875–1908) as base texts, Xu also extracted materials from encyclopedic works and collectanea. To avoid Chen Yi's mistakes, he carefully selected the editions of his sources. Yet, he still failed to notice copyists' errors in some passages. Xu either did not know the edition of Huang Huixian or purposely did not mention it. It is noteworthy that the section of Xu's *Lu shi Yezhong ji*, passages that Xu believes with confidence to be part of the original *Yezhong ji*, does not contain fragments from the *Yedu gongshi zhi*. Xu maintains that besides Lu Hui's *Yezhong ji*, there existed another *Yezhong ji*, probably by an anonymous Northern Song author who combined the material of Lu Hui's text with some later works about Ye. A major part of the information in the *Yedu gongshi zhi* attributed to the *Yezhong ji* comes, according to Xu, via the *Xiangtai zhi* from that anonymous *Yezhong ji*.

Xu attributes eighty-two passages to Lu Hui's original and fifty to the anonymous *Yezhong ji* (3–68, 89–134). A passage concerning the "Three [Fortified] Towers" has been sorted out from the Lu Hui *Yezhong ji* and allocated to the anonymous *Yezhong ji*. This passage (*dianben* no. 11), first cited in the Yuan source *Heshuo fanggu ji* 河朔訪古記, is the longest surviving fragment of the *Yezhong ji* of the *dianben* version and the only written source for the distance between the towers; the stated lengths of sixty paces (*bu* 步) correspond almost exactly to archaeological surveys. Thus, Xu's strictly separating an anonymous *Yezhong ji* from the Lu Hui *Yezhong ji* seems overly rigid. While the wording might give the impression of a later origin, the information contained in some later citations may still be genuine. Also, the inclusion of the mystic tale of the phoenix descending from the Fengyang Gate into the Zhang River in both the Lu Hui *Yezhong ji* (no. 2) and the anonymous *Yezhongji* (no. 1) is confusing. This passage must have stemmed from another source (see following). Xu did not attempt to reconstruct the text into the two *juan* originally recorded. He did, however, make an effort to reorganize the passages according to their context. This edition is punctuated, and it contains philological and editorial comments but no translations.

(3) Müller, Shing. *Yezhongji, Eine Quelle zur materiellen Kultur in der Stadt Ye im 4. Jahrhundert*. Münchner Ostasiatische Studien 65. Stuttgart: Franz Steiner Verlag, 1993.

Taking the *dianben* version as base text, Müller compared the passages with other transmitted texts in encyclopedic works and collectanea and was able to prove with confidence that the entries concerning the tale of a golden phoenix descending into the Zhang River, the story of Xi Shao, and, most obviously, the southern city of Ye of the Northern Qi are mingled into the *Yezhong ji* from other sources (Y3, Y70, Y69, Y71 in this edition). She also allocated twelve passages to the *dianben* version, thus making altogether eighty-two passages that she believes belong to the original Lu Hui *Yezhong ji*; the argumentation is in the commentaries. Müller excluded the *Yedu gongshi zhi* from the *Zhangde fu zhi*, on which Huang Huixian relied heavily. She maintains that several citations of the alleged *Yezhong ji* appeared for the first time in that Ming work. Because they were very much fragmented, it is impossible to prove the genuineness of the passages. For this reason, her edition contains fewer texts than that of Huang but has the same number of passages as Xu's edition. Since the bases for Müller and Xu differ, there are considerable variations in the text. Müller's work includes an index of the *Yezhong ji* passages.

Müller translated the text as literally as possible and provides a thorough textual analysis. Her book also contains a short history of the Later Zhao according to both the official history and archaeological finds. By relating passages to archaeological finds, when possible, in the annotations, she makes the work of interest to those who specialize in the period's material culture.

(4) Liu Jianzhong 劉建中, comp. *Wuhu Shiliuguo lunzhu suoyin* 五胡十六國論著索引. 2 vols. Hefei: Huangshan shushe, 2008. *Yezhong ji* in vol. 2, appendix 6, pp. 1942–52.

To the seventy-four passages in the *dianben* text, twenty-eight entries found in different works are attached, which Liu calls *shi lue* 拾略 (collecting the omissions). Some of these are only variations on passages in the main body and cannot be treated separately in a reconstruction. Liu's compilation has the advantage of being punctuated but lacks annotation, translation into modern Chinese, and any detailed study of cryptic expressions or textual transmission. Nor is the authenticity of the added items examined, but this was probably not Liu's intention. This version is useful for those interested in a quick overview of the nature and contents of the work.

Secondary literature

There are relatively few modern studies of the *Yezhong ji*. Digital collections of classical Chinese literature should make it easier in the future to find widely dispersed citations of the *Yezhong ji* and to advance the philological study of the text. Also, archaeological finds concerning the contact between medieval China and Western Regions may help in the reappraisal of certain passages whose meaning is problematic.

Huang Huixian. "Du Ji Yun deng ji *Yezhong ji* shu hou" 讀紀昀等輯鄴中記書後. *Wei Jin Nanbeichao Sui Tang shi ziliao* (1985.7): 5–9.
Murata Jirō 村田治郎. *Chūgoku no teito* 中國の帝都. Kyoto: Sōgeisha, 1981. See chap. 2, "Gyōto kōryaku" 鄴都考略, 60–69, for Ye during the Three Kingdoms and Northern Dynasties.
Wang Qing 王青. "Shi Zhao zhengquan yu Xiyu wenhua zai Zhongyuan de chuanbo" 石趙政權與西域文化在中原的傳播. *Xiyu yanjiu* (2002.3): 91–98.
Zhou Yiliang 周一良. "Du *Yezhong ji*" 讀鄴中記. *Neimenggu shehui kexue* (1983.4): 102–10. Reprinted in his *Wei Jin Nanbeichao shilunji xubian* 魏晉南北朝史論集續編, 151–66. Beijing: Beijing daxue chubanshe, 1991. Also in *Yecheng ji Beichao shi yanjiu* 鄴城暨北朝史研究, ed. Liu Xinchang 劉心長 and Ma Zhongli 馬忠理, 1–15. Shijiazhuang: Hebei renmin chubanshe, 1991.

Translations

Western languages

In addition to Müller's translation to German in the critical edition *Yezhongji, Eine Quelle zur materiellen Kultur in der Stadt Ye im 4: Jahrhundert* (1993), another full translation is Edward H. Schafer's "The *Yeh Chung Chi*," in *T'oung Pao* 76 (1990): 147–207. The basis for his translation was also the *dianben* version. As did Huang ("Jijiao *Yezhong ji*") and Xu (*Yedu yizhi ji jiaozhu*), Schafer grouped the passages according to contextual coherence and thus more or less "reconstructed" the text. His translation into English is unsurpassed in style and elegance. A textual study was not the priority of Schafer's article, although he did include a brief history of the textual tradition and made comparisons between editions in cases of ambiguity in wording. Thorough philological annotations are provided with the translation. This article also supplies a history of the Later Zhao according to the official history.

Partial and paraphrased translations

Franke, Otto. *Geschichte des chinesischen Reiches*. Berlin: Walter de Gruyter and Co., 1936. Vol. 1, p. 72. About Fotudeng and his tomb.

Needham, Joseph, and Wang Ling. *Science and Civilisation in China*. Cambridge: Cambridge University Press, 1965. Vol. 4, part 2, pp. 159–60, 256–57, 552. About the procession cart with Buddhist figurines, the compass machine and hodometer, and Shi Hu's hunting palanquin.

Pfizmaier, August. "Kunstfertigkeiten und Künste der alten Chinesen." In *Sitzungsberichte der kaiserlichen Akademie der Wissenschaften, Philosophisch-historische Klasse* (Vienna), vol. 69, nos. 1–3 (1871): 151–52. About the compass machine and hodometer.

Schafer, Edward H. "The Development of Bathing Customs in Ancient and Medieval China and the History of the Floriate Clear Palace." *Journal of the American Oriental Society* 76 (1956): 72. About the bathing pool of the empress.

Soper, Alexander C. *Literary Evidence of Buddhist Art in China*. Ascona, Switzerland: Artibus Asiae, 1959. Pp. 84–85. About the procession cart with Buddhist figurines.

Turban, Helga. "Das *Ching-ch'u sui-shih-chi*: Ein chinesischer Festkalender." Ph.D. diss., Ludwig-Maximilians-Universität München, 1971. P. 80. About the custom of mounting a hill on the fifteenth day of the first month.

Wright, Arthur F. "Fo-t'u-têng: A Biography." *Harvard Journal of Asiatic Studies* 11 (1948): 346n36; 365n115. About Buddha's bathing, and Fotudeng and his tomb.

Shing Müller

Ying Qu ji 應璩集

Introduction

Ying Qu (190–252), styled Xiulian 休璉, was in his day a celebrated poet, epistolist, and calligrapher. He came from a literary family from Nandun 南頓 in Runan 汝南 (modern Henan) and began his career in the reign of Cao Pi, Emperor Wen of the Wei (r. 220–226). Having served in several advisory positions, he fell briefly out of favor during Emperor Ming's rule (226–239), possibly due to criticizing the ruler's lavish lifestyle. He returned to court during the reign of Cao Fang (239–254), King of Qi, and retired at the age of 61 *sui* as palace attendant (*shizhong* 侍中). Following his death, he was awarded the posthumous title of chief minister for the Palace Garrison (*weiweiqing* 衛尉卿).

Ying Qu was best known for the "Baiyi shi" 百一詩 (A hundred and one poems), arguably the first set of admonitory *shi* written by a known poet in China, as well as for his intensely lyrical personal letters, which played a major role in shaping the epistolary tradition.

Contents

Most of Ying Qu's works no longer survive. The core of Ying's works in the electronic database CHANT (Chinese Ancient Database, produced by the Chinese University of Hong Kong and available at www.chant.org) is Yan Kejun's collection of Ying's prose, in *Quan shanggu Sandai Qin Han Sanguo Liuchao wen*, q.v., "Quan Sanguo wen," 30:1a–7b, and Ding Fubao's (1874–1952) collection of the poetry, in *Quan Han Sanguo Jin Nanbeichao shi**, "Quan Sanguo shi," 3.14b–15b, 1.277–8. The CHANT collection, titled *Ying Xiulian ji* 應休璉集, includes one *juan* of poetry (three poems from "Baiyi shi"), one *juan* of prose that consists of thirty-four complete prose works and prose fragments, as well as an appendix of twenty-nine poetry fragments from the "Baiyi shi" and other miscellaneous poems, primarily taken from Lu Qinli's *Xian Qin Han Wei Jin Nanbeichao shi**.

The extant poetry provides a glimpse of some prevalent social problems in north China during the third century. There are also more inwardly focused verses that reflect upon Ying's personal life. His correspondence includes official letters written to colleagues (reflecting views on policies and governing, and, at times, on a particular official); recommendation letters; notes of thanks; and letters to friends and relatives. The prose writings reveal a wide range of literary styles that paved the way for the fluorescence of Western Jin literature.

Transmission of the text

Until the Tang, Ying's collected works were known as *Wei Weiqing Ying Qu ji* 魏衛卿應璩集 (Collection of Ying Qu, chief minister of the Wei for the Palace Garrison). Since the title refers to Ying's posthumous office, the writings were presumably compiled after his death. The bibliographic monograph of the *Sui shu*, q.v., recorded that the collection had ten *juan*, as well as separate collections, both in eight *juan*, of his "Baiyi shi" and of his letters, *Shulin* 書林 (Forest of letters). By the early Song, when the bibliographic monograph of the *Xin Tang shu* was compiled, only the "Baiyi shi" collection was listed. By the Yuan and the Ming dynasties, none of Ying's collections were listed in any of the contemporary bibliographies. The *Wen xuan*, q.v., contained the most complete and reliable version of Ying's works. Fragments of his writings existed in Tang and Song anthologies, primarily the *Beitang shuchao*, q.v., *Yiwen leiju*, q.v., *Chuxue ji*, q.v., and *Taiping yulan*, q.v.; a few pieces were cited or summarized in the *Sanguo zhi*, q.v.

During the Ming, Feng Weine (1512–1572) provided a base for modern editions of Ying's poetic works by collecting them under the title *Ying Xiulian ji* in *Gushi ji** 27.2b–5a; see *Siku quanshu zhenben** (*shi ji*) 四庫全書珍本 (十集), vol. 4 (Taipei: Shangwu yinshuguan, 1980). Zhang Pu's (1601–1641) *Han Wei Liuchao baisan jia ji*, q.v., included both poems and prose in a collection that was titled *Wei Ying Qu ji* and which contained additional items. Lu Qinli's (1911–1973) collection of the poems, mentioned earlier, is the best modern source for the poems because of his work in noting character variants among different sources.

Assessments

Prior to the Song dynasty, when Ying Qu's works were still widely read, his poetry and prose were celebrated for different reasons. The "Baiyi shi" was so candid in critiquing contemporary affairs that it invited both approving comments and criticism. Zhang Fangxian 張方賢 of the Western Jin noted that when this group of verses first circulated, it shocked everyone, and some thought that Ying should burn the poems. Others, such as Li Chonghan 李充翰 (fl. 323), claimed that these verses "taught the proper Way by means of moral suasion" and "perhaps have the same aim as the poems in the *Shi jing*." A hundred years after Ying's time, the noted historian Sun Zheng 孫盛 (302–373) observed in his now-lost *Jin yangqiu* 晉陽秋 (Annals of Jin) that "Ying Qu composed 130 pentasyllabic poems that speak about contemporary affairs and offer considerable benefit and improvement. They have been circulated widely in the world." For these views, see *Wen xuan**, *juan* 21, quoted in the commentary.

Additionally, Ying Qu's letters attracted acclaim for their beauty, wit, and persuasiveness. For example, we know from both *Sanguo zhi* 31:604 and the *Wenzhang xulu* 文章敘錄 (cited in that history's commentary) that Ying was renowned for his prose writings (*wenzhang* 文章) and letters (*shu* 書). He was one of the examples of good letter-writing identified by Liu Xie (fl. late fifth to early sixth century) in his section titled "Shuji" 書記, *pian* 5 of the *Wenxin diaolong*, q.v.

Nonetheless, Liu thought that Ying "loved to get involved in things and paid much attention to polished phrasing; he is to be ranked as secondary [to Kong Rong]." In the *Shi pin*, q.v., Zhong Rong (469?–518) identified Ying as the poetic ancestor of Tao Qian 陶潛 (365–427).

Few modern scholars in China and the West have paid attention to Ying's works, perhaps due to their fragmented nature. What little scholarship exists has often examined him in relation to Tao Qian, a connection that has stirred heated debate among literary historians. Only recently have a few scholars (Hu Dalei, "Ying Qu *Baiyi shi*," 2006; Hong Yanlong, "*Bai yi shi* he *Wen xuan*," 2008; Lin, "Rediscovering Ying Qu," 2009; Knechtges, "The Problem with Anthologies," 2010) begun to venture into Ying's poetic and epistolary works in their own right.

Editions with commentaries

Commentaries to Ying Qu's works in the *Wen xuan* are the most important resource for understanding his writings. In the *Liuchen zhu Wen xuan*, complete texts are in *juan* 21:32a–34b and 42:35b–46b (*Siku quanshu* electronic editions: Hong Kong: Dizhi wenhua chuban youxian gongsi, 1999; Taipei: Hanzhen tushu suoying gongsi, 2006). Fragments of Ying's poetry or prose are cited in 18:34a; 21:30a; 23:42b; 24:23b; 25:43a; 26:33b, 46b, 50b; 30:16a, 33b–34a; 38:42b–43a; 40:15a; 54:24a, 32b; 55:20b; 60:18a. The *Xinyi Zhaoming Wen xuan* 新譯昭明文選, 4 vols., ed. Zhou Qicheng 周啟成 et al. (Taipei: Sanmin shuju, 1997; rpt., 2000) provides modern commentary and glosses in 2:915–17 and 3:1969–81. Additionally, annotations of the prose alone may be found in *Wei Jin quanshu* 魏晉全書, 2 vols., ed. Cao Shujie 曹書傑, Han Geping 韓格平, et al. (Changchun: Jilin wenshi, 2006), 2:132–42.

Selected studies

Hong Yanlong 洪彥龍. "*Bai yi shi* he *Wen xuan* de jieshou shi kaocha" 百一詩和文選的接受史考察. *Leshan shifan xueyuan xuebao* 樂山師範學院學報 23.4 (2008): 22–25.

Hu Dalei 胡大雷. "Ying Qu *Bai yi shi* yu xingming xue" 應璩百一詩與形名學. *Zhongguo shixue* 11 (2006). Reprinted in Hu Dalei, *Xuanyan shi yanjiu* 玄言詩研究. Beijing: Zhonghua shuju, 2007. Pp. 25–42.

Knechtges, David R. "The Problem with Anthologies: The Case of the Writings of Ying Qu (190–252)." *Asia Major*, 3rd series, 23.1 (2010): 172–99. Includes translations of many poems.

Lin, Pauline. "Rediscovering Ying Qu and His Poetic Relationship to Tao Qian." *Harvard Journal of Asiatic Studies* 69.1 (2009): 37–74.

Wen Zhihua 文志華. "*Wen xuan* zhi '*Baiyi shi*' yanjiu" 文選之百一詩研究. *Xin shiji luncong* (2006.3): 150–52.

Xu Gongchi 徐公持. *Wei Jin wenxue shi* 魏晉文學史. Beijing: Renmin wenxue chubanshe, 1999. Pp. 162–64.

Yoshikawa Kōjirō 吉川幸次郎. "Ō Kyo no Hyakuichi shi ni tsuite" 應璩の百一詩について. In *Kyōto daigaku bungakubu Gojisshūnen kinen ronshū* 京都大学文

学部五十週年記念論集, ed. Kyoto daigaku bungakubu, 811–42. Kyoto, 1956. Reprinted in *Yoshikawa Kōjirō zenshū* 吉川幸次郎全集. Tokyo: Chikuma shobō, 1968–1970. Vol. 7, pp. 142–75.

Pauline Lin

Yiwen leiju 藝文類聚

Introduction

The *Yiwen leiju*, often translated as the *Collection of Literature Arranged by Categories*, is one of the earliest Chinese *leishu* 類書 (classified writings) extant today. It consists of excerpts of discussions and well-turned phrases from all genres of literature on a wide variety of subjects and was originally conceived as a reference aid for composition. Scholars more recently have been using it to collate and reconstitute ancient works that have long been lost.

The Tang emperor Gaozu commissioned the compilation of a comprehensive *leishu* in 622, and the *Yiwen leiju* was the result. It was one of the several scholarly endeavors under imperial auspices at the time; the others being histories of preceding dynasties. The official Tang histories report that about a dozen leading scholars, including Linghu Defen 令狐德棻 (582–666), Chen Shuda 陳叔達 (d. 635), and Pei Ju 裴矩 (547–627), participated in the project. Ouyang Xun 歐陽詢 (557–641), a great classicist and even greater calligrapher, was likely the overseer. Although there survives no direct evidence of his being put in charge, he was the person who wrote the preface and submitted the finished product to the throne. The *Yiwen leiju* was completed in just three years, far more quickly than other contemporary projects. This feat might be a result of the fact that its compilers were simultaneously working on these other projects, for which many of the same source materials had already been assembled. The speed can also be attributed to the relative simplicity of the task—devising an organizational scheme and copying excerpts of primary sources into the appropriate categories.

Even so, the *Yiwen leiju* is an impressive work in terms of coverage, organization, and overall editorial quality. It contains more than one million characters divided into one hundred *juan* and includes excerpts from 1,431 ancient texts. Its compilers combine in one collection writings on facts (*shi* 事) and works of belles lettres (*wen* 文) that had thus far been anthologized separately. They arranged the contents into 46 categories and 727 subcategories. They systematically grouped excerpts by genre within each subcategory and identified the sources for every citation. These innovations were not lost on the later generations of compilers and remained the common organization for subsequent *leishu*. The compilers of the *Yiwen leiju* moreover were praised for their careful selection of materials and the accuracy of the original transcriptions. Its overall editorial standard held up favorably against the *Taiping yulan*, q.v., often translated as the *Imperial Overview of the Taiping Reign*, a *leishu* of a similar nature completed in 983. This fact alone has made the *Yiwen leiju* extremely valuable to scholars. It preserves, in excerpt, many ancient texts that were extinct by the tenth century, and only about 10 percent of the remaining survives to this day.

The *Yiwen leiju* does have shortcomings. The selection criteria were not consistent. Some excerpts were included due to their relevance to the subject; others were chosen only because their title contains the same word used as the theme. The editors of the *Siku quanshu** criticized the rationale behind the conceptualization of several subcategories and inconsistencies in grouping the contents (*Siku quanshu congmu tiyao** 26:2783–84). Some modern scholars maintain that what seemed ill-considered to the *Siku* editors reflects the changes in the worldview that took place in the millennium after the original compilation. Further, the inconsistencies in grouping, found only in a few categories, might just be due to idiosyncrasies of one or two of the original compilers. Whatever the case, it would seem that even the compilers of the *Yiwen leiju* could not always fit everything neatly into the categories they had devised.

It remains unknown how widely the *Yiwen leiju* circulated in part or in whole during the Tang dynasty. What is well documented is the length of time the *Yiwen leiju* has remained in circulation. Printed editions of varying quality still survive from as early as the first half of the twelfth century. As is the case with most works that were first circulated only in manuscript form, transcription errors were unavoidable. The inclusion of excerpts from literary works composed years after the original compilation, however, was most probably intentional. It suggests that the *Yiwen leiju* had been continuously used as a reference aid for composition and so was subject to updating.

Many scholars past and present have attempted to preserve and restore the integrity of the text. They collected, compared, collated, and cross-checked different versions in order to remove what they considered to be errors or alterations. Some of them were more earnest than able and likely distorted the text further. That the *Yiwen leiju* survives largely intact through the centuries separating us from its original compilers is a testament to its intrinsic value and the scholarly attention it continues to attract. The wealth of information it offers remains essential to any scholar who does research on early and medieval China.

Contents and organization

Leishu as a genre has customarily been referred to in Western scholarship as "encyclopedia," although "florilegia" is a more apt translation. To call the *Yiwen leiju*, or any *leishu* that similarly organizes excerpts from primary sources by subject, an "encyclopedia" could obscure the true nature of the work. It is first and foremost a writing aid. The compilers of the *Yiwen leiju* focused not on what men knew about the world but on how men have imagined it and reflected upon their place in the world through words. It was not an encyclopedia of "what is" but "what has been represented as." The human experience was at the center of every subject, and the eloquence in expressing that experience was what the compilers most wanted to preserve and showcase. In other words, the *Yiwen leiju* is a guide to the history of how certain topics had been written about and a collection of phrases considered worth recycling.

The overall structure of the *Yiwen leiju* reflects the medieval worldview. The compilers divided the contents loosely into four hierarchical strata—the three realms (heaven, earth, and man) and, lastly, the other life forms. Each stratum consists of categories, and each category in turn consists of subcategories. In general, within each stratum, the categories relating to natural subjects appear before those relating to cultural topics. The stratum of heaven, for example, includes two categories, heaven (*tian* 天) first and seasons and festivals (*suishi* 歲時) second. The category of heaven has thirteen subcategories: heaven, sun, moon, stars, clouds, wind, snow, rain, clearing, thunder, lightning, fog, and rainbow. The category of seasons and festivals has twenty-one subcategories: the first of which are the four seasons; the next ten are the major festivals, such as the New Year and the Cold Food festivals; and the last seven cover important seasonal sacrifices, climate, music, and calendar making. The conceptual connections between some subcategories and their parent category at first may appear tenuous, such as that between "music" and "seasons and festivals." This is often where the differences in worldviews become obvious. To the compilers of the *Yiwen leiju*, the musical tones resonated with and harmonized nature. Music therefore had to accord with the month in which it was played. For this reason, "music" fitted comfortably with the theme of "seasons and festivals."

The compilers also gave those categories that reinforced the political order prominent placement in each stratum. The first few categories in the stratum on man are heaven's mandate (*fuming* 符命), imperial rulers (*diwang* 帝王), imperial consorts (*houfei* 后妃), and imperial heirs (*chugong* 儲宮). Only after these did they turn their attention to humbler subjects, such as humans (*ren* 人) and the many aspects of human life, including rituals, social institutions, governance, wars, everyday life, and material culture. A close look at the category of humans and its subcategories can give us insight into how pre-Tang elites discussed humans in writing. The very first few subcategories are all body parts—the head, eyes, ears, tongue, hair, skeleton, and gallbladder. The last, interestingly, is the only internal organ treated in the *Yiwen leiju*. If we were to think that this had been an encyclopedia of what man knew, we would have to conclude that early Tang elite knew nothing about the other internal organs in the human body; nothing would be further from the truth. The remaining subcategories cover different types of people based on the virtue, vice, talent, or temperament for which they were known, and human emotions.

What made the *Yiwen leiju* innovative compared to its predecessors was how the compilers laid out the materials in each and every subcategory. Typically, they began by providing excerpts that helped explain the subject. For instance, the subcategory of sagaciousness (*sheng* 聖) begins with two excerpts from the *Book of Documents*: "Perspicacity" (*rui* 睿) manifests itself in sagaciousness" and "sagaciousness is manifested in regulation (*ze* 則)." Excerpts from other texts, such as the *Zhuangzi* 莊子, *Li ji* 禮記, *Bohu tong* 白虎通, and *Huainanzi* 淮南子 follow, each adding another layer to the concept of sagaciousness. One quotation from the *Zhuangzi* discusses the relationship between the ability and the action of a sage. A passage from the *Huainanzi* identifies the qualities that made sages of Confucius, Mozi 墨子, and the mythical emperors Shennong 神農, Yao 堯, Shun 舜, and Yu 禹. Ouyang Xun called these explanatory quotations "facts." After the section on facts are excerpts from famous pieces of belles lettres of various genres that are arranged in a set sequence. In the belles lettres section of "sagaciousness" for example, the compilers selected works of four genres: "eulogia" (*song* 頌), "encomia" (*zan* 贊), "stone inscriptions" (*bei* 碑), and "disquisitions" (*lun* 論). Included are excerpts from Zhang Chao's 張超 (fl. mid-second century) "Eulogy for Confucius" ("Nifu song" 尼父頌) and Sun Chu's 孫楚 (ca. 218–293) piece of the same name; Lu Ji's 陸機 (261–303) "Encomium for Confucius" ("Kongzi zan" 孔子贊) and Zhan Fangsheng's 湛方生 (fl. Eastern Jin) piece of the same name; Mi Heng's 禰衡 (173–198) inscription "The Epitaph for Master of Lu" ("Lu fuzi bei" 魯夫子碑); Kong Rong's 孔融 (153–208) "Disquisition on the Superiority and Inferiority of Sages" ("Shengren youlie lun" 聖人優劣論) and Shen Yue's 沈約 (441–513) "Disquisition on Defending Sages" ("Bian sheng lun" 辯聖論).

Other common genres represented in the *Yiwen leiju* include but are not limited to lyrical poetry (*shi* 詩), rhapsody (*fu* 賦), opinion (*yi* 議), epitaph (*zhi* 志), petition (*biao* 表), instruction (*jiao* 教), memorandum (*jian* 箋), communication (*qi* 啓), letter (*shu* 書), introduction (*yin* 引), recitation (*yong* 詠), and inscription (*ming* 銘). Never before had excerpts on matters of substance and on belles lettres been collected in one subcategory; nor had genres found in the histories, such as disquisitions and petitions, and those found in literary anthologies been presented side-by-side. As Ouyang Xun proudly announced in the preface, this arrangement would benefit both readers and writers tremendously as they would no longer need to consult multiple encyclopedias and anthologies to find a suitable reference.

It must be noted that the *Yiwen leiju* gathers views and opinions that are often contradictory to one another. An obvious attempt was made to claim universal authority over a multitude of cacophonous voices and to achieve it through a balanced and yet comprehensive representation of the different sides of an issue. The text provides readers with quick access to the pertinent parts of the corpus that had shaped the contour of classical learning and elite culture; by doing so, it also filters and subtly redefines just what civilization means. The *Yiwen leiju* demonstrates the new mastery of the ruling elite in defining reality through written words. It therefore is to be understood as an empire-building project. That it was compiled soon after the founding of the Tang dynasty bespoke the ambition of its imperial patron to command all under heaven.

Table of contents

	Categories	Juan	Subcategories
1	Tian 天 (Heaven)	1–2	Astronomical bodies, and atmospheric and meteorological phenomenon, such as the sun, clouds, snow, and the like
2	Suishi 歲時 (Seasons and festivals)	3–5	Seasons, major festivals, and almanacs
3	Di 地 (Earth)	6	Geography
4	Zhou 州 (Provinces)	6	Administrative information on provinces
5	Jun 郡 (Commanderies)	6	Administrative information on commanderies
6	Shan 山 (Mountains)	7–8	Famous mountains
7	Shui 水 (Waters)	8–9	Bodies of water
8	Fuming 符命 (Heaven's mandate)	10	Divine births and marks of dynastic founders
9	Diwang 帝王 (Imperial rulers)	11–14	Lives of dynastic founders and renowned rulers
10	Houfei 后妃 (Imperial consorts)	15	Lives of imperial consorts
11	Chugong 儲宮 (Imperial heirs)	16	Lives of notable heirs apparent, consorts of the heirs apparent, and imperial princesses
12	Ren 人 (Humans)	17–37	Human organs, and celebrated personalities, virtues, notable actions, and social classes
13	Li 禮 (Rituals)	38–40	State and family rituals
14	Yue 樂 (Music)	41–44	Music, ballads, dances, and musical instruments
15	Zhiguan 職官 (Government offices)	45–50	Government offices and duties

	Categories	Juan	Subcategories
16	Fengjue 封爵 (Ranks and titles)	51	Investitures of royal relatives, meritorious ministers and generals, abdicated heirs apparent, and the like
17	Zhizheng 治政 (Governance)	52–53	Methods in governance and diplomacy
18	Xingfa 刑法 (Laws and regulations)	54	Laws and regulations
19	Zawen 雜文 (Miscellaneous compositions)	55–58	Writings about writing in various genres, writing implements, and stationery
20	Wu 武 (Military)	59	Famous generals and battles
21	Junqi 軍器 (Weapons)	60	Weapons such as swords, diggers, bows, and arrows
22	Juchu 居處 (Dwellings)	61–64	Buildings, city layouts, and thoroughfares
23	Chanye 產業 (Livelihoods)	65–66	Common industries and commercial activities
24	Yiguan 衣冠 (Apparel)	67	Clothing and fashion accessories, such as belts, shawls, and the like
25	Yishi 儀飾 (Ritual implements)	68	Insignias and [oddly] the water clock
26	Fushi 服飾 (Furnishings and accessories)	69–70	Boudoir furnishings and women's combs, ornamental hairpins, and socks
27	Zhouju 舟車 (Boats and carts)	71	Boats and carts
28	Shiwu 食物 (Food and drink)	72	Various kinds of food, sauce, and liquor
29	Zaqiwu 雜器物 (Utensils and trinkets)	73	Cooking and dining wares
30	Qiaoyi 巧藝 (Skills and games)	74	Calligraphy, painting, and a number of competitive games such as archery and chess

(continued)

Table of contents *(continued)*

	Categories	Juan	Subcategories
31	Fangshu 方術 (Formulary techniques)	75	The arts of cultivating life, divination, prognostics, and medicine
32	Neidian 內典 (Buddhism)	76–77	Buddhist-themed literature including temple steles
33	Lingyi 靈異 (The supernatural)	78–79	Immortals, spirits, dreams, and souls
34	Huo 火 (Fire)	80	Lamps, stoves, fuels, ashes, and smoke
35	Yaoxiangcao 藥香草 (Medicines, fragrances, and herbs)	81–82	Medicinal and fragrant plants and vegetables
36	Baoyu 寶玉 (Precious stones and jewels)	83–84	Precious stones and jewels including pearls, hawksbill tortoiseshell, and copper
37	Bogu 百穀 (Grains)	85	Grains and hemp
38	Bubo 布帛 (Textiles)	85	Textiles
39	Guo 菓 (Fruits)	86–87	Fruits
40	Mu 木 (Trees)	88–89	Trees and bamboo
41	Niao 鳥 (Birds)	90–92	Birds
42	Shou 獸 (Beasts)	93–95	Domesticated and wild animals
43	Linjie 鱗介 (Aquatic animals)	96–97	Mythical and real aquatic animals ranging from dragons to clams
44	Chongzhi 蟲豸 (Insects)	97	Insects
45	Xiangrui 祥瑞 (Auspicious omens)	98–99	Auspicious omens and signs in nature
46	Zaiyi 災異 (Disasters)	100	Natural and man-made disasters

Traditional editions and recensions

The *Yiwen leiju* has survived in various printed forms. The transmitted versions do not, however, preserve the original contents in a pristine fashion. This is to be expected with texts that were circulated before the invention of printing. A significant amount of errors, omissions, and alterations were introduced into the text no later than in the Southern Song, judging from the sole printed edition that survives from that period. There have been suggestions that there is a Yuan edition, but so far none has turned up. One can only speculate about versions of the text that may have been floating around based on those that were printed in subsequent periods. Most early printed editions that are extant were published in the Ming dynasty.

Although many scholars and publishers have endeavored to collate and edit the versions of the text that they could find, and indeed managed to produce two high-quality editions, more mistakes were added to the text. The *Yiwen leiju* did not see the kind of popularity in the Qing dynasty that it had enjoyed earlier, the reasons for which have yet to be advanced by modern scholars. Only two printed editions appear to have been produced during that dynasty. One is collected in the *Siku quanshu* (see later). This recension is very different from all surviving Ming editions, leading modern scholars to conclude that it came from a separate line of transmission. Moreover, this particular version of the *Yiwen leiju* suffers from what other pre-Qing texts also underwent at the hands of the *Siku* editors—censorship. Sensitive words and passages were substituted or removed entirely, making this rare recension nearly useless to cross-check and collate withother versions of the text. The other surviving Qing edition used the worst Ming edition as its base text; it has very little scholarly value.

A. The Southern Song edition

This is a woodblock print circulated in the Zhejiang 浙江 area during the Shaoxing reign (1131–1162). It is the only Song edition extant and is now housed in the Shanghai Municipal Library. The publisher Zhonghua shuju issued a facsimile of it in 1959.

B. Ming editions

1. The Shenduzhai 慎獨齋 edition. This edition was produced by Liu Hong's 劉洪 publishing house, from which it takes its name. It was reprinted many times during the Zhengde reign (1505–1521). Some scholars in the nineteenth and early twentieth centuries had thought it might be based on an edition produced in the Yuan dynasty.

2. The Lanxuetang 蘭雪堂 moveable-character edition. This edition was published by Hua Jian 華堅 of Xishan 錫山 in 1515.

3. The Hu Zuanzong 胡纘宗 edition. It is a small-print edition published in 1527 based on a hitherto unknown Song or Yuan source text. Hu, a

native of Tianshui 天水, wrote a preface to it. Lu Cai 陸采 reprinted this edition in Suzhou adding his own postscript in 1528. Another reprint with an added postscript appeared in 1528 and was attributed to Wen Renquan 聞人詮. The latter was redacted.

4. The Zongwentang 宗文堂 edition. This edition was printed in the 1530s by a Mr. Zheng 鄭. There have been many speculations on which edition served as its base text. The most recent consensus is that this may be a redacted version of the Shenduzhai edition.

5. Zhang Song 張松 of Luoyang, a clerk of Pingyang prefecture (Pingyang fushi 平陽府事) in Shanxi, published an edition in small characters in 1549. Although a number of new prefaces were included, this was essentially the Hu Zuanzong edition.

6. Wang Yuanzhen 王元貞 published an edition in large characters in Nanjing in 1587. It has been widely acknowledged to be the worst in editorial quality as it is full of mistakes and omissions.

7. Feng Shu 馮舒 published his recension in 1637. He corrected many errors in the Wen Renquan reprint after consulting a Song edition he borrowed from a friend. This Song edition did not survive. Some scholars suggest that although not identical to the Shaoxing edition mentioned, it came from the same line of transmission. Since the Qing dynasty, scholars have held the Feng Shu recension as the best in editorial quality and often used it as a stand-in for the now-lost Song edition.

C. Qing editions

1. The *Siku quanshu* edition (*Yingyin Wenyuange Siku quanshu** 887:137–753 and all of vol. 888). This recension is based on unknown versions of the text collected only in the imperial library. None of them has survived. Modern scholars have noted the superior quality of these versions compared to the existing Ming editions. However, for reasons mentioned earlier, this edition has little scholarly value.

2. The Hongdatang 宏達堂 edition published in Chengdu in 1879. This edition was based on the Wang Yuanzhen edition. Modern scholars have dismissed it because they have dismissed its parent edition.

Modern critical editions

Modern printed editions generally collate the Song and the two best Ming editions to produce a superior version of the text. Among the three editions that are most commonly used—the Zhonghua shuju (China), Wenguang chubanshe (Taiwan), and Qinghua University Press (China) editions—the first remains the most popular. The *Yiwen leiju* has never been translated into other languages. However, Japanese scholars compiled some of the most useful indexes of the text.

Yiwen leiju. 2 vols. Collated and punctuated by Wang Shaoying 汪紹楹. Beijing: Zhonghua shuju, 1965. Rpt., 4 vols., Shanghai: Shanghai guji chubanshe, 1982. The reprinted edition includes an index compiled by Li Jianxiong 李劍雄 and Liu Dequan 劉德權. Wang corrected many mistakes found in the Song edition after consulting all the surviving Ming editions. This is the most widely used modern critical edition.

Yiwen leiju. Collated and punctuated by Yu Dacheng 于大成. In *Leishu huibian* 類書薈編, vol. 5. Taipei: Wenguang chubanshe, 1974. This contains a revised index by Nakatsuhama Wataru 中津濱涉 to works cited. Yu checked the Hu Zuanzong edition against Feng Shu's recension to create this critical edition. He considered these two Ming printed editions far superior to the rest.

Yiwen leiju. Edited by Dong Zhi'an 董治安. In *Tangdai sida leishu* 唐代四大類書, vol. 2. Beijing: Qinghua daxue chubanshe, 2003. This is an enhanced facsimile of the Song edition that Zhonghua shuju published in 1959. Ming (mainly Hu Zuanzong) and modern (Wang Shaoying) editions were consulted to fill in the blurred or missing characters. A chart is included that lists all the characters that have thus been repaired.

Recent studies and research aids

Bauer, Wolfgang. "The Encyclopedia in China." *Journal of World History* 9.3 (1966): 665–91.

Chen Xinli 陳信利. "*Yiwen leiju* yanjiu" 藝文類聚研究. Master's thesis, Fu Jen Catholic University, Taiwan, 2001. The author examines the *Yiwen leiju* in the context of the development of the *leishu* genre.

Cui Fengyuan 崔奉源. "*Yiwen leiju* yin shibu tuji kao" 藝文類聚引史部圖籍考. Master's thesis, National Chengchi University, Taiwan, 1975.

Fan Yishun 樊義順. "Ping *Yiwen leiju* jiansuo gudai keji wenxian de zuoyong" 評藝文類聚檢索古代科技文獻的作用. *Gaoxiao tushuguan gongzuo* 73 (1999): 66–67.

Guo Xing 郭醒. "*Yiwen leiju* yanjiu" 藝文類聚研究. Ph.D. diss., Nanjing University. The author focuses on the *Yiwen leiju*'s contributions to the study of pre-Tang literature.

Han Jianli 韓建立. "*Yiwen leiju* bianzuan yanjiu" 藝文類聚編纂研究. Ph.D. diss., Jilin University, 2008. The dissertation focuses on the editorial process of the *Yiwen leiju*. The author published various parts of this dissertation as journal articles.

Hu Daojing 胡道静. "*Yiwen leiju* jieti" 藝文類聚解題. In *Zhongguo gudai dianji shi jiang* 中國古代典籍十講. Shanghai: Fudan daxue chubanshe, 2004. This is the reprint of the preface to the critical edition collated and punctuated by Wang Shaoying.

Li Zhi 力之. "*Yiwen leiju* de wenti zhongzhong—*Yiwen leiju* yanjiu zhi yi" 藝文類聚的問題種種—藝文類聚研究之一. *Guji zhengli yanjiu xuekan* (1998.4–5): 13–19.

———. "*Yiwen leiju* Wang Shaoyin xiansheng jiaoyu shangdui" 藝文類聚汪紹楹先生校語商兌. *Sanxia daxue xuebao, Renwen shehui kexue ban* 29.3 (2007): 43–46.

———. "Zonglun *Wen xuan* fei cangzuo chengshu—jianyu *Yiwen leiju* qianshijuan bijiao" 綜論文選非倉促成書—兼與藝文類聚前十卷比較. *Nei Menggu shifan daxue xuebao, Zhexue shehui kexue ban* 37.2 (2008): 82–88.

———. "Guanyu 'Shiju....' suoshe yinwen zhi luexiang zhu wenti—*Yiwen leiju* yanjiu zhi san" 關於'事具.....'所涉引文之略詳諸問題—藝文類聚研究之三. *Qinzhou xueyuan xuebao* 25.2 (2010): 22–29.

Ōbuchi Takayuki 大渕貴之. "*Geimon ruijū* hensenkō" 藝文類聚編纂考. *Nihon Chūgoku gakkaihō* 62 (2010): 44–58.

Pan Shuguang 潘樹廣. "*Yiwen leiju* gaishuo" 藝文類聚概說. *Cishu yanjiu* 1 (1980): 256–59.

Pan Yijun 潘宜君. "*Yiwen leiju* yin shibu zhuanjilei tushu yanjiu" 藝文類聚引史部傳記類圖書研究. Master's thesis, Chinese Culture University, Taiwan, 2009. The thesis focuses on the excerpts of biographies that were included in the *Yiwen leiju*. Pan carefully compares the excerpts with the extant version from which they were supposed to have been taken.

Sun Qi 孫麒. "*Yiwen leiju* banben yanjiu" 藝文類聚版本研究. Ph.D. diss., Fudan University, 2008. The author published various parts of the dissertation as journal articles.

Wei Zhen 韋臻. "Dangdai *Yiwen leiju* yanjiu zhuangkuang zongshu" 當代藝文類聚研究狀況綜述. *Guangxi guangbo daxue xuebao* 21.1 (2010): 63–66.

Indices

Endō Mitsumasa 遠藤光正. *Geibun ruijū kundoku fu sakuin* 藝文類聚訓讀付索引. 15 vols. Tokyo: Daitō Bunka daigaku Tōyō kenkyūjo, 1990.

Li Jianxiong 李劍雄 and Liu Dequan 劉德權, eds. *Yiwen Leiju renming shuming pianming suoyin* 藝文類聚人名書名篇名索引. Taipei: Dahua shuju, 1980.

Nakatsuhama Wataru 中津濱涉. *Geimon ruijū insho intoku* 藝文類聚引書引得. Kyoto: Chūbun shuppansha, 1974.

———. *Geibun ruijū insho sakuin* 藝文類聚引書索引. Kyoto: Chūbun shuppansha, 1977.

Jessey J. C. Choo

Yu Xin ji 庾信集

Introduction

Yu Xin (513–581), styled Zishan 子山, in his time shared only with Wang Bao 王褒 (d. 577) the status of foremost literatus of the Northern Zhou. Indeed, he has been described as the greatest writer of that century, which may help explain why the corpus of his surviving works is the largest of any pre-Tang writer (Graham, *The Lament for the South*, 2). The original title of his collected works was simply *Yu Xin ji*, but that compilation has not survived. Subsequent collections are titled either by his style, as *Yu Zishan ji* 庾子山集, or as *Yu Kaifu ji* 庾開府集, the *kaifu* referring to the honorific office of commander unequalled in honor (*kaifu yitong sansi* 開府儀同三司) that the Northern Zhou court had bestowed on him.

The literary works of his early career were all but lost in the turmoil of those years; what survives are basically those written during his last three decades of life. His most famous work, the "Ai Jiangnan fu" 哀江南賦 (Lament for the south), a poetic survey of the course of the Liang dynasty, is said to be "characterized by extreme emotionalism coupled with the strictest stylistic formalism" (Nelson, "Yu Hsin," 943). This piece has attracted the most attention from later critics, but Yu was equally famed for his lyric verse, a form in which he was extremely gifted. The discussion of his poetic skills is treated with special sensitivity by Kang-i Sun Chang in "Yu Hsin: The Poet's Poet" (1986). As for his prose writings, these are exceptional examples of the skillful use of antithetical parallelism. The texts of the many epitaphs and stelae in his collected works testify to the recognition of his writing ability by the highest elite in the Northern Zhou state, and these have much value for the historian as well.

Yu's family originally stemmed from Xinye 新野 in Nanyang 南陽; Xinye, in southern Henan, was near the modern place of that name, while Nanyang still carries that name. His was one of the émigré elite families that moved to Jiankang (modern Nanjing) when the Jin lost control of the north in 316. Members of the Yu lineage continued to serve as high officials in the series of southern states. Yu Xin is described as being particularly bright and widely read, especially attracted to the *Chunqiu* and *Zuo zhuan*. He was very large in stature and girth. His literary abilities early attracted much attention, and, rising quickly in the ranks, he was appointed magistrate of Jiankang. But like many of his colleagues, the invasion by Hou Jing 侯景 in 547 and the fall of Jiankang to the rebels disrupted his promising career in the south.

Yu fled to Jiangling 江陵 (Hubei) where, after the Hou Jing forces were defeated in 552, the prince Xiao Yi 蕭繹 (508–554), known posthumously as Emperor Yuan, declared himself emperor (*di* 帝) and made Jiangling the new capital of the Liang. Yu was then sent in 554 as an envoy to the Western Wei, and he was still in that state's capital of Chang'an just as the Western Wei mounted a successful attack on Jiangling that cut short the reign of Emperor Yuan and led to the end of the Liang state. Thus, Yu was already in the Western Wei capital when many of his former colleagues were brought up from the south to serve the dynasty, which in 557 became the Northern Zhou. Yu was considered a great prize because of his fame and was treated very well. Still, yearning for his old home in the south, he wrote his famous "Ai Jiangnan fu," the text of which makes up most of his biography in *Zhou shu*, q.v., 41:733–42. His biography in *Bei shi*, q.v., 83:2793–94, is more informative about his career in the north, the high regard in which he was held, and how much in demand he was to write epitaphs for the Northern Zhou elite. His colleague Wang Bao complained about having to spend so much time writing these funerary pieces. Yu may well have felt the same. What he is particularly noted for is his poetry, in which he combined a deep sensibility with a sure command of the craft, bringing a freshness to the art though he was weighed down by the heavy hand of allusions demanded by the style of his day (Watson, *Chinese Rhyme-Prose*, 102–3).

The preface to Yu Xin's collection of writings in twenty *juan* was written during his lifetime by the Northern Zhou prince Yuwen You 宇文逌 (d. 580). Judgments of his writings were not by any means uniformly appreciative. Linghu Defen 令狐德棻 (583–666), in a postface to the biography in *Zhou shu*, q.v., 41:744, in an extraordinarily derogatory and severe critique, said his writings were licentious and more corruptive than even those of the infamous states of Zheng and Wei in antiquity. Citing the statement by Yang Xiong 楊雄 (53 B.C.–A.D. 18) that writers of *fu* use language that is beautiful but unrestrained (Knechtges, *The Han Rhapsody*, 95), Linghu maintained that Yu was a criminal even among *fu* writers. Yu did find champions in later times, such as Du Fu 杜甫 (712–770), who wrote an ode dedicated to him (Chang, "Yu Hsin," 179–80), and in time he came to be recognized as one of the great poets of the Six Dynasties period. By one count, over 210 articles and twelve books have been written about his work over the last hundred years (Ji Ding, *Yu Xin yanjiu*, 3), a testament to the high regard in which he is now held.

Contents

The *Yu Zishan ji zhu* 庾子山集注, with commentary by Ni Fan 倪璠 (*juren* 1705), was issued in 1687 as a woodblock print of the "Chongxiutang" 崇岫堂 and was included in the *Siku quanshu** collectanea of 1765. The *Siku* editors deemed Ni Fan's comments to be more detailed and meticulous, and also not so adulatory, in comparison with those of Wu Zhaoyi (cited in the following). Indeed, despite the complaints of some writers that Ni's comments were excessive and at times misleading, he explained allusions that do not appear even in Morohashi's *Daikanwa jiten*. His commentary is so extensive that it can serve as a dictionary for the period. This collection consists of sixteen *juan* of literary works, preceded by some additional material and followed by a general introduction.

A) Prefatory material: preface (*tici* 題辭) by Zhang Pu (1602–1641), from his *Han Wei Liuchao baisan jia ji*, q.v.; preface by Ni Fan; chronology of Yu Xin's life; additional note by Ni Fan; Yu Xin's genealogical chart; the *Bei shi* biography; and preface by Yuwen You, Prince of Teng 滕 (derived from the *Wenyuan yinghua** compiled by Li Fang [925–996] et al., 699.1a–4a; 4349–50).

B) Literary works, with *juan* organized by genre:

1–2. Rhapsodies, 15

3–4. Lyric poetry, 236

5. *Yuefu* (Music Bureau poetry), 21

6. Song lyrics (*geci* 歌辭), 66

7. Memorials, 12

8. Communications and letters, 17

9. Epigrams, 44

10. Encomiums, 28

11. Instructions, dispatches (*yiwen* 移文), prefaces, accounts (*zhuan* 傳), 6

12. Inscriptions, 12

13–14. Epitaphs, 14

15–16. Grave memoirs, 19

C) General introduction (*zongshi* 總釋) in one *juan*

The following is a selection of the editions of this work, of which the last four are widely available.

(a) "Chizaotang" *Siku quanshu huiyao* 摛藻堂四庫全書薈要 (ms. ed. of 1773). Edited by Yu Minzhong 于敏中 (1714–1780) et al.

(b) *Hubei xianzheng yishu* 湖北先正遺書 (1923 photo reproduction of Ni Fan's 1687 edition). Compiled by Lu Jing 盧靖 from "Mr. Lu's *Shenshijizhai*" ("Lu shi *Shenshijizhai*" 盧氏慎始基齋, Mianyang 沔陽.

(c) *Guoxue jiben congshu* 國學基本叢書. Shanghai: Shangwu yinshuguan, 1935 (typeset).

(d) *Sibu beiyao**. Typeset ed. of 1936. Shanghai: Zhonghua shuju. Rpt., 2 vols., photo reproduction, Taipei: Xinxing shuju, 1959.

(e) Taipei: Wenhua chuban gongsi, 1968.

(f) Punctuated by Xu Yimin 許逸民. 3 vols. Beijing: Zhonghua shuju, 1980.

Transmission of the text

The earliest collections of Yu Xin's writings were lost even during his lifetime. According to Yuwen You's preface, a collection in thirteen *juan* compiled while Yu was still in Jiankang was lost during the Hou Jing disturbances, and another in three *juan*, from his time in Jiangling, suffered the same fate during the invasion of the Western Wei in 554. Finally, a collection in twenty *juan* was apparently made before his death; there is a letter from him thanking Yuwen You for writing the preface. That twenty-*juan* collection is mentioned at the end of Yu's biography in *Bei shi* 83:2794. The bibliographic monograph of the *Sui shu*, q.v. (35:1080), lists twenty-one *juan* but with the note that an addition was incorporated into the total (*binglu* 幷錄); the added *juan* is thought by some to have included some additional material collected from the south after Yu's death. *Jiu Tang shu* 47:2071 and *Xin Tang shu* 60:1595 both list twenty *juan*.

Tong zhi* by Zheng Qiao (1104–1162), 70:821a, lists Yu Xin's collection in twenty *juan* but adds an abbreviated version (*lüeji* 略集) in three *juan*. Chao Gongwu's *Junzhai dushu zhi** (preface dated 1151) 17:825 has an entry for twenty *juan*, while Chen Zhensun's (fl. 1211–1249) *Zhizhai shulu jieti** 16:465 lists the title as *Yu Kaifu ji*, still in twenty *juan*. In an added note, Chen said the Jiankang collection was in forty *juan*, rather than Yuwen You's mention of thirteen. Finally, Jiao Hong 焦竑 (1541–1620), in the bibliographic monograph of his *Guo shi* 國史 (1594), in which he claimed to have listed only books that he had seen (although there is some doubt that this was true), listed the Yu Xin collection in twenty-one *juan*. At any rate, it can be seen that thus far there is mention of Yu Xin's collected writings in twenty, twenty-one, and three *juan*. In addition, his "Ai Jiangnan fu" is also listed in an independent *juan*. It would appear that from the middle of the Ming on, there is no mention of the original *Yu Xin ji* in twenty or twenty-one *juan* in the records of any of the famous collections. Instead, there appears a number of new recensions put together in the Ming and later.

Editions

Apart from the *Yu Zishan ji zhu* with Ni Fan's commentary, many other editions were produced during the Ming and Qing. Further details about the following selection may be found in the articles by Wang Xiao'ou ("Yu Zishan ji banben") and Zhang Liming ("Yu Xin ji banben kaoding").

Yu Kaifu shiji 庾開府詩集. Four *juan*, edited by Zhu Chengjue 朱承爵, Cunyutang 存餘堂 woodblock print of 1521. This is the earliest surviving compilation of Yu Xin's poetry alone. A Ming edition of the same name but in six *juan*, compiled by Zhu Rifan 朱日藩, was printed during the Jiajing period 嘉靖 (1522–1566). During this same period, Xue Yingqi (*jinshi* 1535) included in his *Liuchao shiji** a *Yu Kaifu ji* consisting of two *juan* of Yu's poetry; see *Xuxiu Siku quanshu** 1589:313–49. *Yu Zishan ji* 庾子山集. Sixteen *juan*, with punctuation by Tu Long 屠隆 (*jinshi* 1577). Wanli period (1573–1619). This is the earliest text of Yu's complete works to survive as a book in the original. It was reissued in 3 volumes by photolithography in the *Sibu congkan**, edited by Zhang Yuanji 張元濟 et al. Shanghai: Shangwu yinshuguan, 1919, 1929; 1936, reduced size.

Yu Kaifu ji 庾開府集. Twelve *juan*, compiled by Wang Shixian as part of his *Han Wei Liuchao ershiyi mingjia ji** of 1583; see also his *Han Wei zhumingjia ji* and his *Han Wei liuchao zhujia wenji* 漢魏六朝諸家文集. The anthology, containing works by twenty-one authors of the period, was reissued in *Siku quanshu cunmu congshu bubian** 28:207–324.

Yu Kaifu ji 庾開府集. Two *juan*, edited by Zhang Pu (1602–1641) in his *Han Wei liuchao baisan mingjia ji*, q.v. Zhang clearly consulted the *Yu Kaifu ji* compiled by Zhang Xie, which was printed in 1621 in sixteen *juan*, as part of his *Qishi'er jia ji**; this last has been reprinted in the *Xuxiu Siku quanshu** 1588.90–242.

Yu Kaifu ji jianzhu 庾開府集箋註. Ten *juan*, with commentary by Wu Zhaoyi 吳兆宜 (fl. 1672); Baohantang 寶翰堂 woodblock print. A manuscript copy was included in the *Siku quanshu* editions of 1765 and 1782. This contains the same material as the sixteen-*juan* edition with Ni Fan's commentary but adds a fragment of a rhapsody. There are different sequences within many of the genre groups, as well as some differences in characters. The Wenyuange copy was reproduced in the series *Siku quanshu zhenben* 四庫全書珍本, *siji* 四集, vols. 209–10. Taipei: Taiwan shangwu yinshuguan, 1973.

Yu Kaifu ji 庾開府集. Two *juan*, in Hu Fengdan 胡鳳丹, ed., *Liuchao sijia quanji* 六朝四家全集. Yongkang Hushi Tuibuzhai 永康胡氏退補齋 woodblock print, 1870. This edition is based upon Zhang Pu's compilation.

These by no means exhaust the many collections of Yu Xin's works, especially of his poetry, that have been compiled over time. Finally, there are individual pieces included in a wide range of anthologies.

Selected studies

Cao Daoheng 曹道衡 and Shen Yucheng 沈玉成. Four essays on Yu Xin's life and works, in *Nanbeichao wenxue shi* 南北朝文學史, 142–61. Beijing: Renmin wenxue chubanshe, 1998.

Graham, William T., Jr. "Yu Hsin and 'The Lament for the South.'" *Harvard Journal of Asiatic Studies* 36 (1976): 82–113.

———. *The Lament for the South: Yü Hsin's 'Ai Chiang-nan fu.'* Cambridge: Cambridge University Press, 1980.

Ji Ding 吉定. *Yu Xin yanjiu* 庾信研究. Shanghai: Shanghai guji chubanshe, 2007.

Knechtges, David R. *The Han Rhapsody: A Study of the Fu of Yang Hsiung (53 B.C.–A.D. 18)*. Cambridge: Cambridge University Press, 1976.

Kōzen Hiroshi 興膳宏 and Tan Jishan 譚繼山, trans. *Yu Xin: Zhuanji* 庾信: 傳記. Taipei: Wansheng chuban youxian gongsi, 1984.

Liu Wenzhong 劉文忠. *Bao Zhao he Yu Xin* 鮑照和庾信. Shanghai: Shanghai guji chubanshe, 1986. Rpt., Taipei: Guowen tiandi zazhi, 1991.

Lu Tongqun 魯同群. *Yu Xin zhuan lun* 庾信傳論. Tianjin: Tianjin renmin chubanshe, 1997.

Marney, John. *Liang Chien-wen Ti*. Boston: Twayne Publishers, 1976.

Tan Zhengbi 譚正璧 and Ji Fuhua 紀馥華. *Yu Xin shi fu xuan* 庾信詩賦選. Shanghai: Gudian wenxue chubanshe, 1958. Rpt., Hong Kong: Yixin shudian, 1973.

Wang Xiao'ou 王曉鷗. "Yu Zishan ji banben de zhengli yu kaoding" 庾子山集版本的整理與考訂. *Xibei shida xuebao* (2001.2): 12–17.

Xu Baoyu 徐寶余. *Yu Xin yanjiu* 庾信研究. Shanghai: Xuelin chubanshe, 2003.

Zhang Liming 張黎明. "Yu Xin ji banben kaoding" 庾信集版本考訂. *Beijing keji daxue xuebao, Shehui kexue ban* (2005.3): 95–98.

Translations and commentary

Bear, Peter M. "The Lyric Poetry of Yü Hsin." Ph.D. diss., Yale University, 1969.

Cao Daoheng 曹道衡. "Yu Xin 'Ai Jiangnan fu' sijie'" 庾信哀江南賦四解. In *Zhonggu wenxue shilun wenji* 中古文學史論文集, 441–47. Beijing: Zhonghua shuju, 2003.

Cao Daoheng et al. Annotations of "Xiao yuan fu" 小園賦, "Kushu fu" 枯樹賦, "Ai Jiangnan fu," "Xie Zhaowang lai sibu qi" 謝趙王賚絲布啟, and "Xie Zhaowang lai boluo paoku qi" 謝趙王賚白羅袍袴啟. In *Han Wei Liuchao cifu yu pianwen jingpin* 漢魏六朝辭賦與駢文精品, 405–59, 722–25. Jilin: Xinhua shudian, 1995.

Chang, Kang-i Sun. "Yu Hsin: The Poet's Poet." In *Six Dynasties Poetry*, 146–84. Princeton, NJ: Princeton University Press, 1986.

Ch'en, Shou-yi. *Chinese Literature: A Historical Introduction*. New York: Ronald Press, 1961. Pp. 223–27.

Frodsham, J. D., with the collaboration of Ch'eng Hsi. *An Anthology of Chinese Verse: Han, Wei, Chin, and the Northern and Southern Dynasties*. Oxford: Clarendon Press, 1967. Pp. 188–95.

Graham, William T., Jr. and James R. Hightower. "Yü Hsin's 'Songs of Sorrow.'" *Harvard Journal of Asiatic Studies* 43.1 (1983): 5–55.

Liu, James J. Y. *The Art of Chinese Poetry*. Chicago: University of Chicago Press, 1962. Pp. 107, 132–33.

Nelson, Rod Ivan. "Yu Hsin." In *The Indiana Companion to Traditional Chinese Literature*, ed. William H. Nienhauser Jr., 942–44. Bloomington: Indiana University Press, 1986.

Owen, Stephen. "Deadwood: The Barren Tree from Yü Hsin to Han Yü." *Chinese Literature: Essays, Articles, Reviews* 1 (1979): 157–79.
Watson, Burton. *Chinese Rhyme-Prose.* New York: Columbia University Press, 1971. Pp. 102–9.
Zach, Erwin von. *Die chinesische Anthologie: Übersetzungen aus dem Wen hsüan,* ed. Ilse Martin Fong. 2 vols. Harvard-Yenching Institute Studies 18. Cambridge, MA: Harvard University Press, 1958. Vol. 2, pp. 1047–66.

Albert E. Dien

Yuan Shu ji 袁淑集

Introduction

Yuan Shu, styled Yangyuan 陽源 (408–453), was the son of Yuan Bao 袁豹 (373–413), a literatus and high-ranking statesman of the Eastern Jin. Yuan Shu was still a child when his father died, but he distinguished himself early in life and consequently received the support of influential family members. He held various positions in the retinues of the Liu-Song princes, initially as adjutant libationer (*situ jijiu* 司徒祭酒) for the Prince of Pengcheng 彭城, Liu Yikang 劉義康 (409–451), and later as administrative adviser (*ziyi canjun* 諮議參軍) for the Prince of Linchuan 臨川, Liu Yiqing 義慶 (403–444). In 449, at the invitation of Emperor Wen 文, Yuan Shu composed the "Fangyu suolu yi" 防禦索虜議 (Opinion on preparing against and resisting the northern barbarians). After Crown Prince Liu Shao 劭 assassinated the emperor in 453 and took the throne, Yuan Shu boldly refused to shift his allegiance and was put to death. Later, Emperor Xiaowu (r. 454–464) bestowed praise on Yuan Shu and posthumously gave him the name Zhongxian 忠憲 (Loyal Exemplar) and the title of grand commandant (*taiwei* 太尉). Yuan's biography is in *Song shu*, q.v., 70:1835–42, and *Nan shi*, q.v., 26:698–700.

Contents

The present *Yuan Yangyuan ji* 袁陽源集 was compiled during the Ming dynasty by collecting works attributed to Yuan Shu. The one-*juan* edition in Zhang Pu's *Han Wei Liuchao baisan mingjia ji*, q.v. (Nanjing: Jiangsu guji chubanshe, 2002; 3:489–500), includes the *Song shu* biography and is organized as follows:

1. Rhapsodies, 2
2. Opinion, 1
3. Declaration, 1
4. Letters, personal, 2
5. Record (*zhuan* 傳), 1
6. Miscellaneous prose writings (*zawen* 襍文), 7
7. Lyric poems, 6

Transmission and early history of the text

Yuan Shu's biography says only that his writings were transmitted, without specifying the size of his collection. The bibliographic monograph of the *Sui shu*, q.v. (35:1073), lists a *Song taiwei Yuan Shu ji* 宋太尉袁淑集 in eleven *juan*. *Jiu Tang shu* 47:2068 and *Xin Tang shu* 60:1591 list a *Yuan Shu ji* in ten *juan*. A *Taiwei Yuan Shu ji* 太尉袁淑集 in eleven *juan* appears again in Zheng Qiao's (1104–1162) *Tong zhi** (69:818b), but this collection does not appear in other Song catalogs.

Early bibliographies list two independent texts by Yuan Shu apart from his collected writings (*wenji* 文集): the *Feixie wen* 誹諧文 (or *Paixie wen* 俳諧文), an anthology of satirical anecdotes variously in ten *juan* (*Sui shu* 35:1098; *Tong zhi* 70:828a) or fifteen *juan* (*Jiu Tang shu* 47:2079; *Xin Tang shu* 60:1620), as well as the *Zhenyin zhuan* 真隱傳 (Biographies of true recluses) in two *juan* (*Jiu Tang shu* 46:2002; *Xin Tang shu* 58:1481; *Tong zhi yiwen lue* 3:1560).

Principal editions

Zhang Pu's *Yuan Yangyuan ji* is the fullest extant edition of Yuan Shu's work. He based much of his compilation on material from the *Gushi ji** of Feng Weine (1513–1572), 63:10b–12a, and the *Song wen ji* 宋文紀 of Mei Dingzuo 梅鼎祚 (1549–1615). Selections of Yuan Shu's rhapsodies and prose appear together under the title *Yuan Zhongxian ji* 袁忠憲集 in one *juan*. This work was included in the collectanea titled *Qiankun zhengqi ji* 乾坤正氣集, which was compiled in 1848 by Yao Ying 姚瑩 (1785–1853) and Gu Yuan 顧沅, edited by Pan Xi'en 潘錫恩 (*jinshi* 1811, d. 1868), and printed in 1866. A lightly annotated edition in one *juan* of selected works by Yuan Shu appears in the *Han Wei Liuchao baisan jia ji xuan* 漢魏六朝百三家集選, compiled and annotated by Wu Rulun 吳汝綸 (1840–1903) and published in 1917 and 1918 (rpt., Hangzhou: Zhejiang guji chubanshe). Drawing on Zhang Pu's compilation, Wu Rulun sought to compile an anthology of model writings in the ancient (*guwen* 古文) style.

The standard recension of Yuan Shu's prose and rhapsodies is that of Yan Kejun (1762–1843), in *Quan shanggu Sandai Qin Han Sanguo Liuchao wen*, q.v., "Quan Song wen," 44:1a–6a. Yan includes several fragments of Yuan's writing that do not appear in the *Yuan Yangyuan ji* edited by Zhang Pu but which were cited in *Wen xuan*, q.v., commentary. Yan also identifies several pieces in the *Yuan Yangyuan ji* as fragments from the *Feixie wen* and the *Zhenyin zhuan*. These fragments' provenance had been identified in Tang and Song collectanea but were not given by Zhang Pu. Yuan's lyric poetry is in Lu Qinli's *Xian Qin Han Wei Jin Nanbeichao shi** 2:1211–13. Lu also includes fragments of a poem found in early collectanea but that do not appear in the *Yuan Yangyuan ji*.

Traditional assessments

Zhong Rong 鐘嶸 (468–518) placed Yuan Shu in the middle category of his *Shi pin*, q.v. (*Shi pin jizhu* [Shanghai: Shanghai guji chubanshe, 1994], 277), tracing his poetic style to Zhang Hua 張華 (232–300), and grouping him with Xie Zhan 謝瞻 (387–421), Xie Hun 謝混 (?–412), Wang Wei 王微 (415–453), and Wang Sengda 王僧達 (423–458). Zhong Rong commented on these poets' shared talent for cultivating delicacy, which he suggested led to their development of styles that were light and graceful. Zhang Pu, in his preface to the *Yuan Yangyuan ji*, praised not only Yuan Shu's moral character, but also his prose, stating that Yuan Shu's talent was not far behind that of writers such as Ban Gu 班固 (32–92) in his "Feng Yanran shan ming" 封燕然山銘 (Inscription for the commemoration on Mt. Yanran) and Ma Rong 馬融 (79–166) in his "Guangcheng song" 廣成頌 (Eulogy on Guangcheng [Park]). Zhang Pu also commented on Yuan Shu's success in capturing the Jian'an style in his imitative poems. Had Yuan not died at the hands of Liu Shao, Zhang believed he would have held his own with the likes of Xie Lingyun 謝靈運 (385–433) and Yan Yanzhi 顏延之 (384–456).

Yuan Shu was involved in other literary projects besides his own writing. *Sui shu* 35:1084 credits Yuan Shu along with Zhang Fu 張敷 (fl. 424) with compiling a supplement in one hundred juan to the *Shiji* 詩集, a poetry collection compiled originally by Xie Lingyun.

Selected studies

Kishiro Mayako 稀代麻也子. "Shin Yaku *Sōsho* no 'Bunshi' to Jin: Ō Bi den to En Shuku den no hikaku o tōshite" 沈約宋書の文史と仁: 王微伝と袁淑伝の比較を通して. Added English title: "A Study of Shen Yue's *Song shu*: An Analysis of Wang Wei and Yuan Shu." *Aoyama gakuin daigaku bungakubu kiyō* 41 (1999): 1–19.

Liu Jian 劉健. "Yuan Shu nigushi pingyi" 袁淑擬古詩評議. *Sanxia daxue xuebao, Renwen shehui kexue ban* (2007.2): 131–32.

Matsuura Takashi 松浦崇. "En Shuku no 'Haikaibun' ni tsuite" 袁淑の俳諧文について. *Nihon Chūgoku gakkai hō* 31 (1979): 90–104.

Yabuchi Takayoshi 矢淵孝良. "En Shuku to 'Sesetsu': 'Sesetsu no senja ni tsuite' horon" 袁淑と世説: 世説の撰者について補論. Added English title: "Yuan Shu and *Shishuo*: A supplementary study on compilers of *Shishuo*." *Gengo bunka ronsō* 3 (1999): 343–70.

Brigitta Lee

Yuefu shiji 樂府詩集

Introduction

The common association of the *yuefu* poetic genre (*yuefu shi* 樂府詩, "Music Bureau poetry") with the period of the Han and Six Dynasties was firmly established by the eleventh-century anthology *Yuefu shiji* (Anthology of Music Bureau poetry), compiled by Guo Maoqian 郭茂倩 (fl. 1084). This association between the genre and the Six Dynasties was largely constructed, however, in a post-Tang retrospective, for the *yuefu* genre was, at best, actually a fourth-century construction with no functioning status in the Han and early Six Dynasties periods. Of course there was the bureaucratic office, the Music Bureau, dating from the Han period, but we must not confuse the name of the office with that of the literary genre. In addition, the common association of the genre with early "folk" or anonymous poetry is largely overdrawn: most poems in the anthology are by named literati.

Another association promoted by the anthology is the linkage between the poems and their musicality. While that seems logical given the name of the genre and its subcategories, it is clear that by the time the bulk of this poetry was produced (from the late Six Dynasties to the Tang), musicality was only incidental to the genre—the poems may have very well been presented within a musical setting, but that setting did not establish any generic lineages or defining criteria.

Contents

The *Yuefu shiji* collects approximately 5,500 poems dating from the Han to the late Tang in one hundred *juan*. Of the collection, approximately 5 percent are "old" or anonymous lyrics (*guci* 古辭), while 80 percent are by named poets; the remainder are ritual poems associated with court culture. The anthology organizes the poems primarily by twelve categories of supposed musicality:

1. Jiaomiao geci 郊廟歌辭 (lyrics for suburban and temple ritual songs), *juan* 1–12
2. Yanshe geci 燕射歌辭 (lyrics for banquet songs), *juan* 13–15
3. Guchui quci 鼓吹曲辭 (lyrics to tunes for drums and winds), *juan* 16–20
4. Hengchui quci 橫吹曲辭 (lyrics to tunes for horizontal flute), *juan* 21–15
5. Xianghe geci 相合歌辭 (lyrics for songs with strings and bamboo winds), *juan* 26–43

6. Qingshang quci 清商曲辭 (lyrics for tunes in the *qingshang* key), *juan* 44–51
7. Wuqu geci 舞曲歌辭 (lyrics for songs and dance tunes), *juan* 52–56
8. Qinqu geci 琴曲歌辭 (lyrics for songs with lute tunes), *juan* 57–60.
9. Zaqu geci 雜曲歌辭 (lyrics of songs with miscellaneous tunes), *juan* 61–78
10. Jindai quci 近代曲辭 (lyrics for recent tunes), *juan* 79–82
11. Zageyao ci 雜歌謠辭 (lyrics for miscellaneous songs and ditties), *juan* 83–89
12. Xin yuefu ci 新樂府辭 (lyrics for new Music Bureau poems), *juan* 90–100.

Many of the terms in this nomenclature have a long history, but as a typology the list is clearly unsystematic and overlapping, providing little insight into the poetry under consideration. Within these categories, however, Guo Maoqian provides further, more useful divisions: the most important is by titular set (poems with identical or derived titles), further parsed chronologically. Thus, in *juan* 38 we find seventeen poems that share the title "Yinma changcheng ku" 飲馬長城窟; these date from a single anonymous *guci* up through literati poems of the Tang dynasty. Allen has argued that it is the practice of textual imitation (or intratextuality) that established the defining convention of the genre, and that convention is most visible within these titular sets.

Although a complex compilation, the *Yuefu shiji* exhibits few textual problems, especially since it was transmitted in a relatively complete Song edition, photoreprints of which are available in a Beijing edition issued in 1955 and in the *Gafu shishū no kenkyū* (1970). The text for most needs is, however, the Beijing 1979 typeset edition (standard characters), which is punctuated (including all notes and commentaries) and fully collated, with all variants and emendations noted. This edition also includes a substantial preface introducing the text, a detailed table of contents, and, most importantly, complete indices to author names and poem titles (by stroke count). The *Gafu shishū no kenkyū* also includes these indices (by Japanese pronunciation), along with photocopies of the prefaces to all previous editions, as well as a variety of pre-Song materials related to the genre.

In addition to the poems themselves, the *Yuefu shiji* also contains a history of commentary on the poetry—these comments occur primarily in the headnotes to the musical categories and titular sets. Since Guo Maoqian includes citations to a number of otherwise lost texts, this commentary is especially useful in reconstructing the lineage of the genre—see the *Gafu shishū no kenkyū* (p. 163) for a list of all texts cited by Guo.

There have been relatively few modern studies of the text or the genre in either Chinese or Western sources, and where we do have such studies these have largely been limited to a discussion of "folk" poems in the genre, reflecting a twentieth-century penchant for the anthropological analysis of anonymous Chinese texts. When literati *yuefu* poems are examined, this is carried out primarily within a biographical reading of the poetry, far removed from the poetics of imitation and intratextuality. Exceptions are found in Allen (*In the Voice of Others*), Owen ("*Yuefu* as a Generic Term"), Zhou ("The Legacy of the Han, Wei, and Six Dynasties *Yueh-fu* Tradition"), and the *Yuefu shi jianshang cidian* (1990).

Transmission of the text

We know that the *Yuefu shiji* represents the culmination of *yuefu* anthologies and studies that began in the late Six Dynasties and continued through the Tang, of which few are extant. With all those losses, the *Yuefu shiji* is especially valuable in its collection and preservation of these critical materials, along with the poems. A short list of *yuefu*-related titles found in the *Sui shu*, q.v., bibliographic monograph (35:1085), includes an eight-*juan* volume called *Gu yuefu* 古樂府. Note also the entry for a *Wu sheng ge ciqu* 吳聲歌辭曲 in two *juan*, under which are the titles of numerous *yuefu* collections that were extant in the Liang, but subsequently lost. These texts were probably destroyed in Xiao Yi's infamous burning of the Imperial Library in 554. The *Jiu Tang shu* bibliography (47:2080) contains several volumes from the *Sui shu* list but adds a few new ones, most notably an anthology edited by Xie Lingyun 謝靈運 (385–433). There are also several related volumes listed under the "Music" section of the bibliography (46:1975). When it comes to the Song, we find Guo Maoqian's anthology first listed in the Southern Song's *Zhizhai shulu jieti**, with only one other related volume (15:446). The *Yuefu shiji* is in the *Song shi* bibliography under the music category (202:5056) with numerous other *yuefu* titles—but by this time *ci* poetry was also sometimes called *yuefu*.

Editions and related classical texts

Cui Bao 崔豹 (fl. 290–306). *Gu jin zhu* 古今注. *Sibu congkan**. Notes on poetry and music.

Gafu shishū no kenkyū 樂府詩集の研究. Ed. Nakatsuhama Wataru 中津浜涉. Tokyo: Kyūko shoin, 1970. Photocopy of Song ed.

Wu Jing 吳競 (670–749). *Yuefu guti yaojie* 樂府古題要解. 2 *juan*. *Congshu jicheng xinbian**, vol. 81. *Siku quanshu cunmu congshu** (*jibu* 集部), vol. 415. Rpt., Tainan (Liying): Zhuangyan wenhua youxian gongsi, 1997; Ji'nan: Qi Lu shushe, 1997.

Yuefu shiji. Beijing: Wenxue guji kanxingshe, 1955. Photocopy of Song ed.

Yuefu shiji. Beijing: Zhonghua shuju, 1979. Typeset, punctuated, 7th printing, 2007.

Zuo Keming 佐克明. *Gu yuefu* 古樂府. In *Siku quanshu zhenben shi'er ji* 四庫全書珍本十二集, vol. 200. Taipei: Shangwu yinshuguan, 1982. Small Song anthology.

Selected studies

Allen, Joseph R. *In the Voice of Others: Chinese Music Bureau Poetry*. Ann Arbor: University of Michigan Center for Chinese Studies, 1992.

Birrell, Anne. *Popular Songs and Ballads of Han China*. London: Unwin Hyman, 1988.

Egan, Charles. "Were Yüeh-fu Ever Folk Songs? Reconsidering the Relevance of the Oral Theory and Balladry Analogies." *Chinese Literature: Essays, Articles Reviews* 22 (2000): 31–66.

Frankel, Hans. "Yüeh-fu Poetry." In *Studies in Chinese Literary Genres*, ed. Cyril Birch, 69–107. Berkeley: University of California Press, 1977.

Huang Jie 黃節. *Han yuefu fengjian* 漢樂府風箋. Beijing daxue chubanshe, 1923; rpt., Taipei: Hu Shi ji'nianguan, 1969.

Luo Genze 羅根澤. *Yuefu wenxue shi* 樂府文學史. Beijing: Wenhuaxue she, 1931. Rpt., Taipei: Wen shi zhe shuju, 1974.

Owen, Stephen. "*Yuefu* as a Generic Term." In *The Making of Early Chinese Classical Poetry*, 301–7. Cambridge, MA: Harvard University Asia Center, 2006.

Qi Tingting 亓婷婷. *Liang Han yuefu yanjiu* 兩漢樂府研究. Taipei: Xuehai chubanshe, 1980.

Wang Yunxi 王運熙. *Yuefushi luncong* 樂府詩論叢. Shanghai: Zhonghua shuju, 1962.

Yuefu shixuan 樂府詩選. Taipei: Zhengzhong shuju, 1991.

Yuefushi jianshang cidian 樂府詩鑒賞辭典. Beijing: Zhonghua shuju, 1990.

Yuefushi yanjiu lunwenji 樂府詩研究論文集. Beijing: Zuojia chubanshe, 1957.

Zhou, Zhenfu. "The Legacy of the Han, Wei, and Six Dynasties *Yueh-fu* Tradition and Its Further Development in T'ang Poetry." In *The Vitality of the Lyric Voice: Shih Poetry from the Late Han to T'ang*, ed. Shuen-fu Lin and Stephen Owen, 287–95. Princeton, NJ: Princeton University Press, 1986.

Joseph R. Allen

Yulin 語林

Introduction

The *Yulin* (Forest of conversations) by Pei Qi 裴啟 (fl. latter half of fourth century) is a collection of anecdotes and quotations related mainly to people from the Han to the Jin dynasty. It is a predecessor of the *Shishuo xinyu*, q.v., so the nature of the two is similar. Since it exists only in collated fragments, we are unable to determine its original structure and arrangement. As in the case of the *Shishuo xinyu*, its contents may well have been grouped under subject headings, a possibility suggested by the large number of its entries incorporated into the existing text of the *Shishuo xinyu*.

Sources of the work

According to the *Shishuo xinyu* and its commentary by Liu Jun 劉峻 (462–521), the author Pei Qi compiled the *Yulin* by collecting anecdotes and quotations from the Han to Jin, but his sources were not identified. It is said, however, that some of the material was derived from statements by Pei's contemporaries (Yu, *Shishuo xinyu jianshu*, 269–70, 843–45; Mather, *Shih-shuo Hsin-yü*, 138–39, no. 90, 437–38, no. 24).

Authorship and date of composition

The only information about Pei Qi and his work comes from the *Shishuo xinyu* and its commentary and from a genealogy attached to a Song edition of its text. Pei Qi was a descendent of the famous Pei clan, though a member of a distant branch. He was fond of the popular pastime of evaluating the respective merit of scholars. Presumably because of his family connections, he was acquainted with the famous scholars of his time, so he began to collect those of their utterances which he thought to be interesting and significant. It is said that during the Eastern Jin's Longhe reign (362–363) he committed these to writing (Yu, *Shishuo xinyu jianshu*, 844; Mather, *Shih-shuo Hsin-yü*, 438n1).

Authenticity

The three collations of this text are similar, and they all gather items from similar sources, that is, *leishu* 類書 such as the *Yiwen leiju*, q.v., so they are only as authentic as their sources. While these *leishu* are not considered completely reliable because they usually collect material outside of the official histories, they are often the only source available on a given subject and should not be ignored altogether. Ideally, one should try to corroborate facts in other sources and, when that is not possible, to point out the question of credibility.

An important source for the study of the *Yulin* text is Liu Jun's commentary to the *Shishuo xinyu*. Liu was active during the century after Pei's compilation; since the sources Liu quoted were mostly contemporary to Pei, these entries should at least be reliable as historical material. It is true that in the *Shishuo xinyu*, Xie An 謝安 (320–385) is quoted as saying that Pei made up material "out of whole cloth." According, however, to Liu's commentary, it was because Pei Qi included in his text a rhapsody (*fu*) composed by Xie's estranged relative by marriage, Wang Xun 王珣 (350–401), thereby popularizing it, that Xie denigrated Pei's work publicly, resulting in its fall into disrepute and demise (Mather, *Shih-shuo Hsin-yü*, 138, and 437–8n1).

Transmission and early history of the text

The text seems to have been lost since the Tang dynasty, since it is not mentioned in the bibliographic monograph of the *Sui shu*, q.v. Two efforts at collating its fragments from *leishu* were made in premodern times: one during the Yuan dynasty by Tao Zongyi 陶宗儀 (fl. 1360–1368) and the other during the Qing dynasty by Ma Guohan 馬國翰 (1794–1857). Lu Xun 魯迅 (1881–1936), perhaps unaware of the two earlier collations, made his own collation in the Republican period. The larger part of his work duplicates the earlier two editions.

Principal editions

Pei Qi Yulin 裴啟語林. In Tao Zongyi, *Shuofu* 說郛. Wanweitang 宛委堂 ed. Shanghai: Shanghai yinshuguan, 1930. Reissues of *Shuofu* include those by Xinxing shuju (Taipei) in 1963 and Shandong jiaoyu chubanshe (Ji'nan) in 1999. This edition's collation of *Yulin* contains 21 entries.

Pei Qi Yulin. Comp. Zhou Lengjia 周楞伽. Beijing: Wenhua yishu chubanshe, 1988. This collation contains 82 items.

Peizi Yulin 裴子語林. In Ma Guohan, *Yuhan shanfang ji yishu* 玉涵山房輯佚書. Xiangyuantang 湘遠堂, 1884. Reissues of *Yuhan shanfang ji yishu* include those by Langxuanguan (Changsha) in 1883, Wenhai chubanshe (Taipei) in 1967, and Shanghai guji chubanshe in 2002. This edition's collation of *Yulin* contains 151 entries.

Peizi Yulin. In Lu Xun, *Gu xiaoshuo gouchen* 古小說勾沉, 5–36. Beijing: Renmin wenxue chubanshe, 1951. This collation contains 180 entries.

Bibliography

Jiang Guangzhen 姜廣振. "Cong Pei Qi *Yulin* yishu kan Wei Jin mingshi Ren Dan zhi feng" 從裴啟語林一書看魏晉名士任誕之風. *Suihua xueyuan xuebao* 25.5 (2005): 73–75.

———. "Lüelun *Lunyu* dui Pei Qi *Yulin de yingxiang*" 略論論語對裴啓語林的影響. *Kaifeng jiaoyu xueyuan xuebao* 29.3 (2009): 5–7.
Lee, Lily Hsiao Hung. "*Yü-lin* and *Kuo-tzu*: Two Predecessors of *Shih-shuo hsin-yü*." In *Festschrift in Honour of Professor Jao Tsung-i on the Occasion of His Seventy-fifth Anniversary*, ed. Zheng Huxin 鄭會欣, 357–81. Hong Kong: Institute of Chinese Studies, Chinese University of Hong Kong, 1993.
Mather, Richard B., trans. *Shih-shuo Hsin-yü: A New Account of Tales of the World*. Minneapolis: University of Minnesota Press, 1976.
Xu Jun 許軍. "Pei Qi *Yulin* wangyi yuanyin kao" 裴啓語林亡佚原因考. *Dongnan daxue xuebao, Zhexue shehui kexue ban* 11.2 (2009): 81–86.
Yu Jiaxi 余嘉錫. *Shishuo xinyu jianshu* 世說新語箋疏. Beijing: Zhonghua shuju, 1983.

Lily Xiao Hong Lee

Yutai xinyong 玉臺新詠

Introduction

The *Yutai xinyong* (New songs for the jade terrace) is the third oldest extant anthology of poetry in China after the *Shi jing* 詩經 and the *Chu ci* 楚辭. Compiled by the court poet Xu Ling 徐陵 (507–583) under the patronage of Crown Prince Xiao Gang 蕭綱, later Emperor Jianwen of the Liang, the collection consists of amorous songs composed mostly in five-syllable lines. As the term *xinyong* 新詠 (new songs) indicates, the emphasis is on contemporary or near-contemporary poems that represent the avant garde of Liang literary taste. The compound *yutai* 玉臺 (jade terrace) carries several historical and mythological connotations. Here, it refers specifically to the inner quarters of palace ladies at the imperial or princely courts.

Apart from amorous themes and references to objects from the palace ladies' boudoir, as well as frequent use of pentasyllabic meter, sensuous folk songs from south China and the Western Regions are another novel feature of the collection. The brevity of these folk songs—a large number were quatrains—greatly appealed to the southern elite, a fascination that is reflected in the significant number of literati-style four- and eight-line poems included in the anthology. The selection of quatrains and octaves also mirrors contemporary fascination with the metrical and euphonic qualities of poetry, in particular the application of prosodic rules with which poets had been experimenting since the late fifth century.

According to Xu Ling's preface, the *Yutai xinyong* was compiled for the reading pleasure of palace ladies. As such, it marks a moment in Chinese literary history that saw the emergence of anthologies and encyclopedias explicitly addressing an educated female readership, thereby opening a literary space beyond the male-dominated public sphere. The *Yutai xinyong* asserted the independence of literature from the classical canon and rejected the traditional definition of poetry as a vehicle for moral instruction. Given that the *Yutai xinyong* is a poetic anthology not *of* or *by* palace ladies but *for* palace ladies, "New Songs for the Jade Terrace" instead of the conventional "New Songs of the Jade Terrace" might be the best translation of the title.

Traditionally, the *Yutai xinyong* has been regarded as *the* representative collection of palace-style poetry (*gongti shi* 宮體詩), the style associated with Xiao Gang and his literary salon. It has often been compared with and seen in opposition to the literary world of the slightly earlier *Wen xuan*, q.v. The pieces included in the *Wen xuan* became part of the literary canon, and the anthology itself was enthusiastically promoted by successive Tang emperors as the primary text studied in preparation for the official examinations. By contrast, the *Yutai xinyong* never held an honored place in the literary tradition. Although there is no evidence that would allow us to securely assess the impact and reception of the anthology in the sixth century, literary critics from the early seventh century onward dismissed the collection as an outflow of the decadence prevalent in the poetry of the Southern Dynasties. From the early Tang onward, Xiao has been accused of having divested poetry of its didactic function and moral concerns, promoting instead literary values that emphasize idle playfulness, pleasure, and the unbridled expression of feelings. The anthology's thematic focus on the royal palace, the sensuous description of female beauty, and luxurious objects associated with the world of palace ladies has even been held responsible for the devastation caused by the rebellion of Hou Jing 侯景 (548–552) and the subsequent fall of the Liang.

This traditional assessment of the *Yutai xinyong* and of Xiao's literary accomplishments has recently been challenged by Tian Xiaofei (*Beacon Fire and Shooting Star*). Individual scholars have drawn attention to the common literary values shared by Xiao Tong 蕭統 (501–531), Xiao Gang's elder brother and compiler of the *Wen xuan*, and Xiao Gang himself, thereby questioning the stark contrast commonly believed to exist between the two collections.

Furthermore, doubts have been cast on the assumption that the *Yutai xinyong* was meant to be the representative anthology of palace-style poetry. A much clearer understanding of the innovations of palace-style poetry has led to a reevaluation of the *Yutai xinyong* and Xiao's role in its compilation. Tian has demonstrated that palace-style poetry is not primarily concerned with the theme of love and the sensuous world of the female boudoir. Rather, it was informed by a Buddhist vision of the illusionary nature of the material world. Palace-style poetry seeks to expose the fundamental emptiness of even the most precious objects by subjecting them to a prolonged and focused gaze. Likewise, the reevaluation of Xiao's poetic work raises questions concerning his precise role in the compilation of the *Yutai xinyong*. If the anthology was not meant to be the signature work of palace-style poetry, it is unlikely that Xiao actively hid an agenda in the collection. It is even possible that he merely tacitly agreed to its compilation.

Contents

The *Yutai xinyong* contains poems from the second century B.C. to the sixth century A.D. by about 115 poets, of whom 14 were female and 54 were active during the sixth century or even beyond. These numbers can vary slightly since some of the attributions are not certain. Likewise, the number of poems included in the collection can vary between a minimum of 654 and a maximum of 843 pieces depending on the edition. Wu Zhaoyi 吳兆宜 (fl. 1675), who wrote the first commentary, claimed that Xu Ling originally collected 870 poems. This claim has been rejected by Liu Yuejin (*Yutai xinyong yanjiu*, 95–96) and other modern scholars as being without any basis. According to Liu, the *Yutai xinyong* as it was known during the Tang consisted of 670 poems. Liu further believes that we can safely assume around 650 to 660 poems in the anthology's Song editions, but none of these editions are extant. The value of the *Yutai xinyong* lies not the least in the fact that it preserves many poems that have otherwise been lost and that it provides the names of authors for poems that other collections treat as anonymous. Thus, it is a valuable source to supplement the collected works (*ji* 集) of individual poets, including Xiao Gang, whose works have not survived independently.

Although the pieces included in the *Yutai xinyong* cover a time span of roughly seven hundred years, the majority of poems, more than 60 percent of them, date from the Liang. The imperial family alone is represented with 166 poems; Xiao Gang has the most pieces at seventy-six poems, followed by Xiao Yan 蕭衍, Emperor Wu, at forty-one poems.

The *Yutai xinyong* is considered a single-genre anthology divided into ten untitled *juan*. Xu Ling, in his preface, states that he has "selected amorous songs, ten *juan* in all." The generic term *yange* 艷歌 (amorous songs), however, conceals a much greater variety of poetic subgenres represented in the collection, including folk material. The most common forms are the Han *yuefu* 漢樂府 (Han dynasty Music Bureau verses), *gushi* 古詩 (old-style poems), *tongyao ge* 童謠歌 (children's ditties and political broadsides), *ge* 歌 (songs), *gu chui qu* 鼓吹曲 (tunes for drums and pipes), *sao* 騷 (old elegies), *yange xing* 艷歌行 (amorous folk songs), *jindai Wu ge* 近代吳歌 (modern Wu songs), *xiqu ge* 西曲歌 (modern western songs), *xing* 行 (ballads), *jueju* 絕句 (quatrains), *lianju* 聯句 (linked verses), *zengda shi* 贈答詩 (presentation and reply poems), *yongwu shi* 詠物詩 (poems on things), and *nigu shi* 擬古詩 (imitation poems). The poems cover a large variety of themes ranging from love and courtship, and the relationship between art and reality, to naughty palace girls in Chinese history and homoerotic relationships (see Birrell, *Games Poets Play*, 285 and 294–95).

Among the genres that the *Yutai xinyong* deliberately excludes are the *jiaosi ge* 郊祀歌 (songs for suburban sacrifice), *fu* 賦 (rhapsody), and examples from the *Shi jing* and the *Chu ci*. In other words, Xu Ling excluded pieces that were already part of the orthodox poetic canon, thereby underscoring the anthology's claim to newness. It has, moreover, not escaped scholars' notice that the works of Xu Chi 徐摛 (474–551) are entirely missing from the *Yutai xinyong*. The conspicuous absence of the poet who was not only one of Xiao Gang's most loyal courtiers but also the one to whom the *Liang shu* historians attributed the designation "palace-style" (*Liang shu*, q.v., 30:447) has nourished doubts concerning the anthology's status as the representative collection of palace-style poetry.

Structure and arrangement of the text

It is generally accepted that the poems in the *Yutai xinyong* are "arranged more or less chronologically" (Tian, *Beacon Fire and Shooting Star*, 107), which means that both the division of the collection into ten *juan* as well as the sequence of poets within each *juan* follow chronological principles. Much harder, however, if not impossible, is determining what these principles exactly are. Is it the poems or the poets that are arranged chronologically? Does the death year of a poet determine his or her placement in the collection (not an entirely convincing organizing principle in an anthology with an emphasis on contemporary poetry)? Is a poet's main period of production, the dates of the poems, or some other criterion the structural principle behind the arrangement? One problem in answering these questions is the dating of anonymous pieces, another the fact that we have very little biographical information on a number of poets. In a few cases, the known dates of a poet contradict his position in the sequence of the *juan*. Court rank perhaps underlies the organization of *juan* 8, while in other *juan* there seems to be no discernable ordering pattern. Thus, any attempt to extract a coherent organizational scheme on the basis of the actual arrangement of the poems in the extant editions faces great problems. At the present stage of our knowledge, the safest conclusion is that there is no perceptible order to the arrangement of poems in the *Yutai xinyong* (Knechtges, "Culling the Weeds and Selecting Prime Blossoms," 241). At least there is no order that in any respect approaches the careful organization of the material into clearly labeled, interrelated literary groups that we find in the *Wen xuan*. With these caveats in mind, it is still possible and worthwhile to make some general observations on the individual sections of the anthology and their contents.

Juan 1 includes poems from the Han dynasty (206 B.C.–A.D. 220). All but one are in pentasyllabic lines. This section provides a historical reference point for the recent literary innovations promoted by Xiao Gang's salon. The old poems, especially the examples taken from the "Nineteen Old Poems" ("Gushi shijiu shou" 古詩十九首) at the beginning of the collection, connect contemporary poetry with a hallowed tradition and thus provide justification for and confer dignity on the anthology.

Juan 2 and 3 mostly, though not exclusively, contain poems by writers who died under the Wei and Jin dynasties.

Juan 4, 5, and 6 contain works of poets of the Southern Dynasties. *Juan* 4 includes poets who died during the fifth century, while *juan* 5 and 6 include poets who lived into the sixth century.

Juan 7 contains poems by members of the Liang imperial family, who are arranged in the order of their seniority: Xiao Yan (Emperor Wu; 464–549), Xiao Gang (503–551), Xiao Lun 綸 (507?–551), Xiao Yi 繹 (Emperor Yuan; 508–555), and Xiao Ji 紀 (508–553). All of them were still alive at time of compilation.

Juan 8 has poems by other contemporary poets who lived under the Liang dynasty, some of them even beyond. It is uncertain whether all were still alive when the collection was put together.

Juan 9 contains pieces in different subgenres and irregular meters from the second century B.C. to the sixth century A.D.

Juan 10 consists entirely of pentasyllabic quatrains up to the sixth century, among them many anonymous songs and folk songs from the south and the

Western Regions. This section also includes poems by Xiao Yan and Xiao Gang placed between works by other poets.

Sources of the work

It is generally accepted that Xu Ling is the compiler of the *Yutai xinyong*. The bibliographic chapter of the *Sui shu*, q.v., the collection of Tang anecdotes titled *Da Tang xinyu* 大唐新語 and compiled by Liu Su 劉肅 (fl. 806–821), as well as the early Tang encyclopedia *Yiwen leiju*, q.v., confirm Xu Ling as compiler. However, doubts concerning the role of Xu have been periodically expressed since the Ming dynasty, fueled by the fact that Xu's biography in *Chen shu*, q.v., *juan* 26, surprisingly does not make any mention of the *Yutai xinyong*. Zhao Jun 趙均 (fl. 1633–1638), according to his postscript to his 1633 edition, hoped that this edition would silence these doubts. However, the editors of the *Siku quanshu zongmu tiyao** (37: 4123–24) likewise felt compelled to refute doubts concerning Xu's role as compiler.

The precise dating of the *Yutai xinyong* is still very much under debate. The difficulties in resolving the problem are due less to the existence of contradictory textual evidence than to the fact that scholars interpret the few available sources differently, often relying on unproven assumptions. Useful summaries of the various attempts to date the anthology can be found in Liu Yuejin (*Yutai xinyong yanjiu*, 65–88), Birrell (*Games Poets Play*, 307–11), and Zhang Lei ("*Yutai xinyong yanjiu shuyao*," 73–74), among which Liu's account is the most detailed one.

The earliest evidence for the date of the compilation is given in Liu Su's *Da Tang xinyu*, which contains an important early account of Xu Ling's anthology. The passage relevant for the dating of the *Yutai xinyong* reads as follows:

> Previously, when Emperor Jianwen of the Liang was still the crown prince, he loved to write sensuous poetry. People were influenced by him, and so the writing of sensuous poetry prevailed. It was dubbed the Palace Style. In his later years, Emperor Jianwen reformed his ways, but it was already too late; so, he commissioned Xu Ling to compile *The Collection of the Jade Terrace* (*Yutai ji* 玉臺集) to glorify the style.

This ambiguous excerpt is part of a larger passage in which Liu Su tells the story of the Tang official Yu Shinan 虞世南, who remonstrated with Emperor Taizong (r. 626–649) about his having written a "romantic song for fun" (*xi zuo yanshi* 戲作艷詩). The emperor accepted his minister's criticism promptly and rewarded him publicly with fifty bolts of silk. Liu Su refers to Xiao Gang and Xu Ling as negative examples of a monarch who used his minister to cover up his youthful error of composing love poetry.

The quoted passage is generally understood by modern scholars as relating events from the period between 531 and 549, when Xiao Gang was still crown prince. This time span is further narrowed down by the fact that Xu Ling was sent on a diplomatic mission to the Northern Wei in 548. He never saw Xiao Gang again. Hence, most scholars date the compilation of the anthology to some time between 531 and 548.

Among the attempts made at dating the *Yutai xinyong*, the work of Kōzen Hiroshi (*"Gyokudai shin'ei no hensan ni tsuite"*; Chinese trans., *"Yutai xinyong cheng shu kao"*) has received the most attention. He proposes that 534, the sixth year of the Zhong Datong reign (529–535), is the most likely date for the compilation of at least two of the *juan*. Kōzen observed that the poets in *juan* 7 and 8 were arranged according to their social and official rank rather than chronologically, the living members of the imperial family, starting with Emperor Wu, being listed in descending order. Kōzen furthermore discovered that six poets included in *juan* 8 were also listed among the compilers of another text commissioned by Xiao Gang, the *Fabao lianbi* 法寶聯璧, which can safely be dated to 534. The sequence in which the six names appear in Xiao Yi's preface to the *Fabao lianbi* is identical to their arrangement in the *Yutai xinyong*. Although there is no apparent connection between the two works, the correlation in the arrangement of names has been interpreted by Kōzen as evidence that at least *juan* 7 and 8 can be dated around the same year as the compilation of the *Fabao lianbi*. Shen Yucheng has pushed Kōzen's theory even further and postulated that the entire *Yutai xinyong* was compiled around the years 533 and 534 (*"Gongti shi yu Yutai xinyong"*).

Liu Yuejin (*Yutai xinyong yanjiu*, 68–88), in his review of earlier attempts to date the anthology, cautions against any conclusion regarding the compilation date based on the contents or organization of the text. All currently available editions, he argues, do not represent Xu Ling's original compilation but are based on editions possibly "stitched together from fragments" in the late Northern Song, when it was extremely difficult to get ahold of a complete copy of the anthology, and further edited during the Ming. The organizing principles of individual *juan* of the anthology do not help either. First, it is doubtful whether the organization is identical to Xu Ling's original arrangement and, second, the arrangement of some *juan*, for instance nine and ten, does not seem to follow any coherent principle at all.

Transmission and early history of the anthology

The title of the anthology is not mentioned in the original preface by Xu Ling, nor does it appear in the standard histories covering its period of compilation (*Liang shu* and *Nan shi*, q.v.). Several major bibliographic catalogs do, however, mention the anthology. The first reference to a *Yutai ji* appears in Liu Su's *Da Tang xinyu*. A *Yutai xinyong* is listed in the bibliographic chapter of the *Sui shu*, q.v. (35:1084), compiled between 629 and 636, as well as in those of the *Jiu Tang shu* (47:2081) and *Xin Tang shu* (60:1621), which were compiled between 940 and 945 and 1043 and 1060, respectively. Although the *Yutai xinyong* was not included in the orthodox canon of literature, apart from the *Wen xuan*, it is the only anthology of the 147 anthologies listed in the *Sui shu*'s bibliographic chapter that is extant.

The transmission of the *Yutai xinyong* is problematic, reflecting the precariousness of survival due to political upheaval and the concomitant destruction of libraries, on the one hand, and the censorship of hostile critics on the other. Ji Rongshu 紀容舒 (fl. 1757), author of the second major commentary on the work, noted in the preface to his edition (dated 1757) that its transmission was "so murky and shadowy that it is extremely fortunate that it did not disappear without trace" (Birrell, *Games Poets Play*, 304). Unlike the *Wen xuan*, which became a core text in the preparation for the examinations and had attracted a commentary by a court scholar as early as 658, the *Yutai xinyong* never received official sanction. Its first complete edition appeared only in 1633, after which date scholarly research on the text started. Birrell presumes (*Games Poets Play*, 311) that its survival has to do with a variety of factors, including imperial patronage and an avid private readership, but it may also simply come down to mere chance.

The earliest surviving fragment of the *Yutai xinyong* was found in Dunhuang and dates to around 1035. It consists of seven complete and two incomplete poems from the end of *juan* 2 and was published in 1917 as part of Luo Zhenyu's 羅振玉 (1866–1940) *Mingsha shishi guji congcan* 鳴沙石室古籍叢殘. The sequence of poets and poems in the Dunhuang manuscript is identical to that of the earliest Ming edition by Zhao Jun, which itself preserves a Song edition of 1215, while there are a number of textual variants. This has been taken as confirmation of a manuscript tradition of transmission from Tang to Song as well as of editorial intervention at an early stage (Birrell, *Games Poets Play*, 313). A Tang edition of the *Yutai xinyong* is further mentioned by the Qing bibliographer Shao Yichen 邵懿辰 (1810–1861) in his *Siku quanshu jianming mulu biaozhu* 四庫全書簡明目錄標注. This edition circulated between 937 and 975 but is no longer extant.

A major event in the preservation and transmission of the *Yutai xinyong* was the attempt undertaken by the Southern Song scholar Chen Yufu 陳玉父 (fl. 1215) to prepare a complete edition of the anthology under the title *Yutai xinyong ji* 玉臺新詠集. This edition is no longer extant, but Chen Yufu's colophon, dated 1215, survived. It states that he pieced together the text from two incomplete printed editions and one manuscript copy. The fact that Chen found one of the printed editions in a pile of "discarded books" (*fei shu* 廢書) in the house of his father-in-law reveals the precariousness of the anthology's transmission at the start of the thirteenth century. The second woodblock edition that Chen consulted consisted of only five *juan* instead of the original ten, perhaps the result of an interruption in the printing process. The *Siku quanshu zongmu tiyao* confirms that three editions were in circulation in Chen's time. By the early seventeenth century, the Chen edition had become very rare and marred with errors. Several editions of the *Yutai xinyong*, including Song editions, were available during the Qing dynasty (Liu Yuejin, *Yutai xinyong yanjiu*, 3).

Principal editions

The earliest extant editions of the *Yutai xinyong* are from the Ming dynasty. Liu Yuejin (*Yutai xinyong yanjiu*, 3–41) has listed more than thirty different extant editions from the Ming, Qing, and Republican period (including a Japanese edition from 1806) that belong to either one of two distinct lines of textual transmission. The first goes back to the 1215 edition of Chen Yufu, the second derives from the earliest dated Ming edition, the Jiajing 嘉靖 19 (1540) edition of Zheng Xuanfu 鄭玄撫. The most relevant premodern editions, all belonging to the Chen tradition, are the following:

(A) *Wuyunxi guan tong huozi ben* 五雲溪館銅活字本. This edition bears no date, but may have originated in the late fifteenth or early sixteenth century. The bibliophile Feng Shu 馮舒 (1593–?) mentions in his colophon of 1629 that this edition was one of four current during his time. Reproduced in *Sibu congkan**. See Liu Yuejin, *Yutai xinyong yanjiu*, 5–7.

(B) *Han shan Zhao Jun fu Song ben* 寒山趙均覆宋本. A reproduction of the Song edition by Zhao Jun (fl. 1633–1638) of Hanshan. Also known as the *Zhaoshi Xiaowantang ben* 趙氏小宛堂本 or the *Zhaoshi ben* 趙氏本. This is the standard edition, dated 1633. Although it is often referred to as a Song edition, scholars in a position to compare Zhao Jun's edition with a Song edition praised Zhao's edition as a major advance in terms of editing and printing and as being the finest of all the Ming and Qing editions (Birrell, *Games Poets Play*, 318). Zhao Jun excluded the 179 poems interpolated in some Ming editions. This edition has been reproduced in *Zhongguo wenxue mingzhu* 中國文學名著 (Taipei: Wenxue guji kanxingshe, 1955).

(C) *Wu Zhaoyi zhuben* 吳兆宜注本. An annotated edition by Wu Zhaoyi, published in 1675. Wu provided the only premodern commentary to the *Yutai xinyong*. The commentary includes the loci classici for allusions in the poem texts, textual variants, glosses, explanations of titles, biographical information, and comparisons with the *Wen xuan*. Wu Zhaoyi included 179 additional pieces in various Ming editions so that the total number of poems in his collection is about 870. In his 1774 revision of Wu's edition, Cheng Yan 程琰 (fl. 1774–1780) corrected errata, revised Wu's commentarial apparatus, and removed the extra 179 poems from the body of the text and placed them at the end of each *juan*. Mu Kehong's *Yutai xinyong jianzhu* 玉臺新詠箋注 (1985) is the edited version of Cheng's revision that has also been printed in the *Sibu beiyao** and by Shijie shuju (Shanghai, 1936).

(D) *Yutai xinyong kaoyi* 玉臺新詠考異. Colophon dated 1757. Collated edition based on several earlier editions as well as poem versions in literary collections, encyclopedias, and historical works. The author of the preface is Ji Rongshu, who is generally named as the compiler of this work. Yet, Beijing University Library houses a manuscript titled *Yutai xinyong jiaozheng* 玉臺新詠校正 by Ji Rongshu's son Ji Yun 紀昀 (1724–1805). The preface to this manuscript, as well as the main text and the commentary, are almost identical to the edition containing Ji Rongshu's preface. It is therefore presumed that Ji Yun was the actual compiler of the *Yutai xinyong kaoyi* and attributed his own work to his father. Reprinted in *Siku quanshu** and *Congshu jicheng chubian**.

Modern critical editions

Fu Chengzhou 傅承洲 et al. *Yutai xinyong* 玉臺新詠. 2 vols. Beijing: Huaxia chubanshe, 1998.

Huang Gongzhu 黃公渚, annota. *Yutai xinyong*. Shanghai: Shangwu yinshuguan, 1934. Annotated selection.

Mu Kehong 穆克宏. *Yutai xinyong jianzhu* 玉臺新詠箋注. 2 vols. Beijing: Zhonghua shuju, 1985. Standard modern typeset edition based on the 1774 revisions (*shanbu* 刪補) by Cheng Yan and checked by Mu against other editions and material transmitted in encyclopedias; contains the commentary by Wu Zhaoyi as well as an appendix with forty prefaces or colophons (*xu ba* 序跋) to this and various other editions.

Yutai xinyong 玉臺新詠. Shanghai: Shanghai guji chubanshe, 2007. Includes the commentary by Wu Zhaoyi, Cheng Yan's revisions, and notes (*daodu* 導讀) by Cao Minggang 曹明綱.

Selected studies

Yutai xinyong scholarship is a rapidly growing field as the negative assessments of the collection's content and style have given way to a much more positive appreciation since the 1980s. Hence, for reasons of space, the following list gives preference to studies in Western languages and monographs in Chinese or Japanese while necessarily excluding a large number of Chinese and Japanese articles.

Birrell, Anne M. "The Dusty Mirror: Courtly Portraits of Woman in Southern Dynasties Love Poetry." In *Expressions of Self in Chinese Literature*, ed. Robert E. Hegel and Richard C. Hessney, 33–69. New York: Columbia University Press, 1985.

———. *Games Poets Play: Readings in Medieval Chinese Poetry*. Cambridge: McGuinness China Monographs, 2004. Chapter 9 contains a full translation and analysis of the *Yutai xinyong*'s preface. Chapter 10 contains valuable information on textual history and editions.

Hu Dalei 胡大雷. *Gongti shi yanjiu* 宮體詩研究. Beijing: Shangwu yinshuguan, 2004.

Knechtges, David R. "Culling the Weeds and Selecting Prime Blossoms: The Anthology in Early Medieval China." In *Culture and Power in the Reconstitution of the Chinese Realm, 200–600*, ed. Scott Pearce, Audrey Spiro, and Patricia Ebrey, 200–41. Cambridge, MA: Harvard University Press, 2001.

Kōzen Hiroshi 興膳宏. "*Gyokudai shin'ei* no hensan ni tsuite" 玉台新詠の編纂について. *Tōhōgaku* 63 (1982): 58–73. Chinese translation: "*Yutai xinyong* cheng shu kao" 玉臺新詠成書考. In *Zhongguo gudian wenxue congkao* 中國古典文學叢考, 1:341–60. Shanghai: Fudan daxue chubanshe, 1985.

Liu Yuejin 劉躍進. *Yutai xinyong yanjiu* 玉臺新詠研究. Beijing: Zhonghua shuju, 2000. The most comprehensive study to date of the anthology's textual history (editions, dating, original form). Includes biographical sketches of the Liang poets in the collection, 152–90. Part 2, "Xu Ling shiji biannian congkao" 徐陵事跡編年叢考, 219–400, contains extensive source material on the compilation of the work and the poets included in the collection arranged in chronological order.

Marney, John. *Liang Chien-wen ti*. Boston: Twayne, 1976.

Martin, François. "Le *Yutai Xinyong* et la nouvelle poésie: Une anthologie de la poésie galante en Chine au VIe siècle." Ph.D. diss., Université Paris VII, 1979.

———. "Pratique anthologique et orthodoxie littéraire: Le cas de deux anthologies parallèles en Chine au VIe siècle." *ExtrêmeOrient, Extrême Occident* 5 (1984): 49–74. A comparison between the *Wen xuan* and the *Yutai xinyong*.

Miao, Ronald. "Palace-Style Poetry: The Courtly Treatment of Glamour and Love." In *Studies in Chinese Poetry and Poetics*, 1–42. San Francisco: China Materials Center, 1978.

Shen Yucheng 沈玉成. "Gongti shi yu *Yutai xinyong*" 宮體詩與玉臺新詠. *Wenxue yichan* (1988.6): 55–65.

Tai, Earl S. "The Nineteen Ancient Poems: Reception and Canonization, 221–581 A.D." Ph.D. diss., Columbia University, 2003. Tai analyzes the role the Nineteen Old Poems play within the larger purposes of the anthology; includes a comparison between the *Wen xuan* and the *Yutai xinyong*; suggests a tripartite division of the anthology: general poems of pentasyllabic verse (*juan* 1–8); poetry of varied meter (*juan* 9); short pentasyllabic verse (*juan* 10).

Tian, Xiaofei. *Beacon Fire and Shooting Star: The Literary Culture of the Liang (502–557)*. Cambridge, MA: Harvard University Press, 2007. Pp. 104–9, 144–49, 186–95.

Yan Zhiying 顏智英. *Zhaoming Wenxuan yu Yutai xinyong zhi bijiao yanjiu* 昭明文選與玉臺新詠之比較研究. Taipei: Hua Mulan wenhua chubanshe, 2008.

Zhan Ying 詹鍈. "*Yutai xinyong* san lun" 玉臺新詠三論. *Dongfang zazhi* 40.6 (1944): 52–57. Zhan argues that Lady Xu, wife of Liang Yuandi (Xiao Yi), compiled the *Yutai xinyong*.

Zhang Lei 張蕾. *Yutai xinyong lungao* 玉臺新詠論稿. Beijing: Renmin chubanshe, 2008.

Translations

English

Many if not all of the individual pieces that make up the anthology have been translated several times into European and East Asian languages. Yet, the only complete translation of the anthology in a European language is Anne M. Birrell's *New Songs from a Jade Terrace: An Anthology of Early Chinese Love Poetry* (London: Allen and Unwin, 1982), reprinted by Penguin, 1986, with J. H. Prynne's essay "Chinese Figures," which originally appeared as a review of the first edition in *Modern Asian Studies* 17 (1983): 671–704. A revised version was published by Penguin in 1995 under the title *Chinese Love Poetry: New Songs from a Jade Terrace—A Medieval Anthology*. Birrell follows the Zhao Jun edition.

Xu Ling's "Preface" was translated by James R. Hightower in "Some Characteristics of Parallel Prose," *Studies in Chinese Literature*, ed. John L. Bishop, 125–35 (Cambridge, MA: Harvard University Press, 1965). Translations of the preface that include an analysis are:

Lim, Chang Mee. "The Poetry of Hsu Ling." Ph.D. diss., Stanford University, 1984. See chapter 3.

Rouzer, Paul. *Articulated Ladies: Gender and the Male Community in Early Chinese Texts* (partial translation and discussion, 132–37). Cambridge, MA: Harvard University Press, 2001.

Japanese

Ishikawa Tadahisa 石川忠久, trans., and Tōdō Akiyasu 藤堂明保, ed. *Gyokudai shin'ei* 玉台新詠. Chūgoku no koten 25. Tokyo: Gakushū kenkyūsha, 1986. Accompanied by a supplement of 183 pages containing the Chinese text with *kunten* 訓点.

Suzuki Torao 鈴木虎雄. *Gyokudai shin'ei shū* 玉台新詠集. 3 vols. Iwanami bunko 岩波文庫 4975–4986. Tokyo: Iwanami shoten, 1953–1956. Translation is based on a Japanese block-printed edition of 1806 (Bunka 3) that reproduces the Zhao Jun edition. It includes the original Chinese text (with *kunten*) but does not include Xu Ling's preface; it does include explanatory notes on the title (*tijie* 題解) and interpretation (*yijie* 義解), as well as on words and phrases in each poem; author index.

Uchida Sennosuke 内田泉之助. *Gyokudai shin'ei* 玉台新詠. 2 vols. Shinshaku Kanbun taikei 新釈漢文大系 60–61. Tokyo: Meiji shoin, 1974–1977. Translation into modern Japanese based on Wu Zhaoyi's original commentary and Ji Rongshu's *Yutai xinyong kaoyi*. It includes the original Chinese text (with *kunten*) and notes on poem titles and poets plus extensive explanations of the poem text; Xu Ling's preface is translated and copiously annotated; there is an index of personal names and phrases from the poems and explanations.

Modern Chinese

Zhang Baoquan 張葆全. *Yutai xinyong yizhu* 玉臺新詠譯注. Guilin: Guangxi shifan daxue chubanshe, 2007. First complete annotated translation into modern Chinese.

Reviews of research

Xu Yuru 徐玉如. "Jin ershinian *Yutai xinyong* yanjiu" 近二十年玉臺新詠研究. *Huaiyin shifan xueyuan xuebao* 23.2 (2001): 225–29.

Zhang Lei. "*Yutai xinyong* yanjiu shuyao" 玉臺新詠研究述要. *Hebei shifan daxue xuebao* 27.2 (2004): 72–76. Useful research report with a focus on studies done in the People's Republic of China since the 1980s.

Chronological biographies of Xu Ling, Xiao Gang, and Xiao Yi

Liu Yuejin. "Xu Ling shiji biannian congkao" 徐陵事跡編年叢考 (see "Selected Studies"; Liu Yuejin, *Yutai xinyong yanjiu*, 219–400). This is the most comprehensive chronology for it incorporates material from five earlier *nianpu* 年譜.

Liu Yuejin and Fan Ziye 范子燁. *Liuchao zuojia nianpu jiyao* 六朝作家年譜輯要. Harbin: Heilongjiang jiaoyu chubanshe, 1999. 2 vols. Vol. 2, pp. 350–51, contains an abbreviated version of Liu's "Xu Ling shiji biannian congkao."

Wu Guangxing 吳光興. *Xiao Gang Xiao Yi nianpu* 蕭綱蕭繹年譜. Beijing: Shehui kexue wenxian chubanshe, 2006.

Zhou Jianyu 周建渝. "Xu Ling nianpu" 徐陵年譜. *Zhongguo wenzhe yanjiu jikan* 10 (1997.3): 105–82.

Concordance

Obi Kōichi 小尾郊一 and Takashi Masao 高志眞夫, comps. *Gyokudai shin'ei sakuin, fu Gyokudai shin'ei senchū* 玉臺新詠索引, 附玉臺新詠箋註. Tokyo: Yamamoto shoten, 1976. In addition to a table of all pieces arranged in the sequence in which they appear in the anthology (including the 179 interpolated poems), this concordance contains an index of poem titles and an author index as well as a reproduction of the Qianlong 39 (1774) edition of the *Yutai xinyong jianzhu* with Wu Zhaoyi's commentary.

Thomas Jansen

Yuzhu baodian 玉燭寶典

Introduction

The *Yuzhu baodian* (Precious canon of the jade candle), completed circa 581 by Du Taiqing 杜臺卿 (d. ca. late 590s), is an encyclopedic compendium of textual citations and sparse authorial commentary relating to seasonal observances, especially ritual. It is the richest single repository of Han and Six Dynasties textual material on this subject, surviving in more complete and reliable form than its better known contemporary *Jing-Chu suishi ji*, q.v. The material ranges broadly from the ancient "classical" to the contemporary "popular," while attempting (often unsuccessfully) to maintain a clear hierarchic distinction between them.

Contents

Du Taiqing describes his methodology and the work's structure as follows:

> In the past, when free from official duties, I would examine and collate literary works. The *Record of Ritual*'s (*Li ji* 禮記) "Monthly Ordinances" ("Yueling" 月令) is the most comprehensive, so I divide it according to month, and make each the crown of a chapter. I begin by quoting the orthodox classics, then reach further to their various explanations, inscribing each in sequence beneath the month, to broaden the currents. The historical biographies and hundred schools of thought are drawn upon from time to time. Verses and rhapsodies are [overly] embroidered; in them, ornament outweighs meaning. Except for the truly outstanding, none are [here] adopted.
>
> Works recording local folkways embody the people's lives and collect customs; those discussing errant customs hope to foster knowledge of correct models. I begin with the month of *mengzou* 孟陬 [first month] and conclude with that of *tailü* 太呂 [twelfth month], with the center (*wuji* 戊己) appended at the end of the final month of summer.[1] There are twelve *juan* in all, making up a single work. Where an individual term appears frequently, but the language is not transparent, I elucidate it with

---

[1] Han cosmographers inserted the fifth "central" season to facilitate correlation with the five phases. It corresponded to the last ten days of the sixth lunar month. *Wu* and *ji* are, respectively, the earthly branch and heavenly stem coordinates of this "month" within the "Monthly Ordinances" system.

the annotation "Note." If a matter is in doubt, its threads encapsulating everything from the Yellow to the Han Rivers, then it is explicated separately as a "Correct Explanation." As for festivals observed in the popular realm, even if they are without veritable precedents, I verify them with relevant dictums of the elders, as found in the classics and histories. I put these under the heading "Supplementary Explanations." There is also a "Prefatory Explanation" and "Final Chapter" to cap the head and tail [of the work] (*Yuzhu baodian* 1:2–5).

In other words, to each of the luni-solar calendar's twelve months (that for the ninth month is now lost), Du dedicates a chapter (each of a single *juan*), and he subdivides each chapter according to cultural register, that is, by degree of canonicity. Specifically, each chapter includes the components I to III (listed next). The category labels are those Du uses in his preface. Headings II and III, but not heading I, also appear in the text of each chapter. Predictably, there are numerous difficulties and inconsistencies in implementing such classifications (Chapman, "Carnival Canons," 125–26).

I. Orthodox classics and assorted explanations (*zhengjing* 正經, *zhongshuo* 衆説)

   A. *Li ji* "Yueling" (*Record of Ritual*, "Monthly Ordinances"): full text.

   B. Cai Yong's 蔡邕 (131–192) *Yueling zhangju* 月令章句 (Sections and phrases of the "Monthly Ordinances"): full text of Cai's commentary to the "Yueling."

   C. Other "Yueling" exegesis: citations relating to individual phrases of "Ordinances" text, or to annual rites Du considers "classical" but that are not mentioned in the "Ordinances." Includes citations from other classics, "apocrypha" (*weishu* 緯書), politico-philosophical works, and histories, as well as the occasional piece of verse or short prose. The vast majority are pre–Six Dynasties. These relate solely to climate, phenology (the seasonal cycles of animals and plants), and ritual: there is no mention of the administrative duties that form a very large proportion of the "Yueling" itself.

   D. Cui Shi's 崔寔 (ca. 103–ca. 170) *Simin yueling* 四民月令 (Monthly ordinances for the four walks of life): full text.

II. Correct explanations (*zhengshuo* 正説)

Du cites examples from a wide array of texts on one or more points he deems problematic and offers his own very brief comments. These may relate to issues raised in the "Classics" section or venture into contemporary domains. That for the fourth month, for example, is devoted entirely to confusion surrounding the correct date of the Buddha's birthday.

III. Supplementary explanations (*fushuo* 附説)

The "festivals observed in the popular realm" (*shisu suo xingjie* 世俗所行節) treated in this section are mostly contemporary festivals; the proportion of Six Dynasties texts, including *zhiguai* 志怪 accounts, is relatively high. It seems likely that Zong Lin's *Jing-Chu ji*, q.v., provided an unacknowledged template for at least some of these sections (Chapman, "Carnival Canons," 184–93).

In addition, Du sprinkles his own commentary throughout the text. Medieval encyclopedias and extant editions display this portion in small characters. Encyclopedia citations indicate that modern editions do not preserve all of Du's commentary, which was probably quite extensive.

I will comment briefly on two interrelated facets of Du's approach, although much else about his work is noteworthy: first, his recasting of the "Yueling" as a ritual calendar focusing on festivals; and, second, his arguments regarding the cultural uniformity of an empire in the process of reunification. The "Yueling" is one example of a type of calendar current in the Warring States and early Han that provided advice, primarily for rulers, on how to synchronize human activity with seasonal cycles. It is the most complex and bureaucratized of extant ordinance calendars from that period. Incorporation within the *Li ji* elevated this particular calendar to canonical status. The "Yueling" and similar texts offer instruction on a wide range of activities, including ritual, jurisprudence, agriculture, construction, crafts, education, diet, and clothing. Cui Shi's second-century calendar for landed patriarchs, the *Simin yueling*, is similarly diverse in its concerns. Zong Lin's mid-sixth century *Jing-Chu ji* adapts the Ordinances' textual format for a calendar of festival customs but makes little attempt to draw upon its actual text. Du Taiqing's *Yuzhu baodian* follows the *Jing-Chu ji*'s lead in focusing on periodic ritual, especially festivals, but firmly installs the original "Yueling" as its foundational text. In so doing, in a sense it reinvents the latter as a festival calendar, largely ignoring its other aspects.

Grounding contemporary custom in classical orthodoxy serves Du's purpose of demonstrating the essential unity of contemporary regional cultures. He views contemporary mores as sharing an "ancient mandate." This concords with his relatively tolerant stance toward popular custom: he may silently censure by omission but never directly criticizes a practice. His assertion of uniformity also embodies an argument for imperial legitimacy, implying that diverse regions are bonded by more than military conquest. Imperial reunification indeed forms an important backdrop to the work.

Sources

As mentioned earlier, the *Yuzhu baodian* is on one level an extended exegesis of the "Yueling." Though Du rarely cites it by name, Zong Lin's *Jing-Chu ji* seems to have been an important source for the "Supplementary Explanations" sections on contemporary festival customs. Essentially a carefully ordered compilation of citations, the *Yuzhu baodian* is a valuable resource for collecting fragments of lost texts or interrogating transmitted editions (Niimi, "*Gyokushoku hōten* ni tsuite,"

97–98; Cui and Zhu, "*Guyi congshu* ben," 145). Scholars have in fact made more use of it for bibliographic reconstruction than for researching medieval ritual. It incorporates three texts more or less in their entirety, providing the most complete surviving versions of the latter two: the "Yueling," Cui Shi's *Simin yueling*, and Cai Yong's *Yueling zhangju*. It also cites extensively from Han "apocryphal" writings, a class of texts entirely extinguished by successive imperial bans.

Authorship and date of composition

Du Taiqing's family was from Quyang 曲陽 district in Boling 博陵 commandery (modern Baoding, Quyang County, Hebei). His birth date is uncertain (Niimi, "*Gyokushoku hōten* ni tsuite," 74–75; "ca. 536"). One account states he died "some years" after his retirement from office in 594 (*Sui shu*, q.v., 58:1421), while another suggests he died in the mid-580s (*Bei Qi shu*, q.v., 24:354). Du held several positions in the central bureaucracy of the Northern Qi, whose capital was at Ye 鄴 (modern Anyang, Henan). Du probably compiled much of the *Yuzhu baodian* during a "sabbatical" from 577, when his native state of Northern Qi fell to the Chang'an-based Northern Zhou, until 581, when he was summoned to serve the Northern Zhou's successor, the Sui. He presented the work to Sui Emperor Wen soon after arriving in Chang'an, for which he was rewarded with two hundred bolts of heavy silk (*Sui shu* 58:1421). Though he may have begun work on the project while still serving the Northern Qi (Ishikawa, *Gyokushoku hōten*, 6–7), it seems likely that he did most of the compilation work during his four years in retirement from 577 to 581 (Niimi, "*Gyokushoku hōten* ni tsuite," 83).

Transmission and early history of the text

Shortly after *Yuzhu baodian*'s compilation, Du Taiqing's own nephew Du Gongzhan 杜公瞻 (fl. 600s–610s) drew extensively on it in preparing a commentary to Zong Lin's *Jing-Chu ji*, probably titled *Jing-Chu suishiji*. The *Yuzhu baodian* is cited and cataloged in works from the Sui to the Ming (Niimi, "*Gyokushoku hōten* ni tsuite," 92–94). Scholars believe it had become rare by the late Ming and had disappeared from China by the early Qing (Niimi, "*Gyokushoku hōten* ni tsuite," 94–95; Moriya, *Chūgoku kosaijiki no kenkyū*, 7–8; Cui and Zhu, "*Guyi congshu* ben," 144–45). Scholars consistently cite Chen Di's 陳弟 (1541–1617) *Shishantang shumu* 世善堂書目 (full title *Shishangtang cangshu mulu* 世善堂藏書目錄) as the last Chinese catalog to list the work.

Principal editions

Fortunately, the text had made its way to Japan, possibly as early as the eighth century, but by the late ninth century at the latest (Cui and Zhu, "*Guyi congshu* ben," 147). It came to attention in Japan in 1827 when Mōri Takanaka 毛利高翰 presented to the Bakufu a manuscript of the text held by his family (Niimi, "*Guyi congshu* ben," 95; Ishikawa, "Kaisetsu," 8–10). This was in fact a copy of an older manuscript in the collection (now the Sonkeikaku bunko 尊経閣文庫) of the ruling Maeda 前田 family of the Kaga domain. The Maeda manuscript consists of six scrolls (Cui and Zhu, "*Guyi congshu* ben," 145). The *Yuzhu baodian* appears on the recto side, while various Japanese texts appear on the verso (on the verso texts, see Imae, *Maeda-bon Gyokushoku hōten*). The only reliable date on the recto *Yuzhu baodian* manuscript is 1348; others from verso-side writings fall in the 1336–1347 range. *Yuzhu baodian*'s ninth *juan*, corresponding to the ninth month, is missing, as it is from the Moori manuscript, copied from the Maeda scrolls (Ishikawa, "Kaisetsu," 8–9).

Awareness of the existence of Japanese editions enabled the *Yuzhu baodian*'s return to China. Yang Shoujing 楊守敬 (1839–1914) and Li Shuchang 黎庶昌 (1837–1896), members of He Ruzhang's 何如璋 diplomatic mission to Japan, came upon a *Yuzhu baodian* manuscript in the early 1880s in the course of their search for lost Chinese texts surviving in Japan (Niimi, "*Gyokushoku hōten* ni tsuite," 96–97; Ishikawa, "Kaisetsu," 8). From this, Li prepared a moveable-type edition, which he included in his 1884 collection *Guyi congshu* 古逸叢書.

Manuscripts (and facsimile prints thereof)

At least five manuscripts survive in Japan, all based directly or indirectly on the Maeda manuscript. All lack the ninth *juan* from a total of twelve. Only the Maeda text is available in printed facsimile form.

1. Maeda MS, ca. 1348.

Six scrolls; housed in the Sonkeikaku bunko, Megoro-ku, Tokyo. It is difficult to determine how complete or reliable this edition is, since it is the sole surviving exemplar. The entire ninth *juan* is missing, and Tang-Song encyclopedia citations reveal occasional minor omissions. But the surviving eleven *juan* are voluminous and seem intact in structure, at least in the main text. Overall, commentary is sparse in the Maeda edition. There are numerous errors, and unusual orthography tends to produce others in transcription and interpretation. Facsimiles are published in the following:

Sonkeikaku sōkan 尊経閣叢刊. Ed. Kōshaku Maedake Ikutoku zaidan 侯爵前田家育德財団. Tokyo: Ikutoku zaidan, 1943. Vol. 1.

Suishi xisu ziliao huibian 歲時習俗資料彙編. Taipei: Yiwen yinshuguan, 1970. Vol. 1.

2. Mōri Takanaka MS, ca. 1827. Concertina book; housed in the National Archives of Japan. Copied from the Maeda MS.

3 and 4. *Gyokushoku hōten kōshō* 玉燭宝典攷証. Annota. Yoda Toshimochi 依田利用, ca. 1840.

This includes Du Taiqing's text, based on the Maeda MS, and Yoda's commentary. Yoda suggests numerous textual revisions, partly based on comparison with modern editions of cited works (Cui and Zhu, "*Guyi congshu* ben," 146, 149–50). There are two slightly different versions, both probably in the author's hand; one is held at Tokyo's National Diet Library and the other at the Tōyō Bunken: Iwasaki 岩崎 collection; 6 vols. (Ishikawa, "Kaisetsu," 9–10).

5. Mori Tatsuyuki 森立之, Mori Yakushi 森約之 MS, 1854–1866.

Four volumes; in the collection of Senshū 専修 University Library. Edited version (including some erroneous emendations) based on the Moori MS (Ishikawa, "Kaisetsu," 9; Cui and Zhu, "*Guyi congshu* ben," 146, 147–48).

Typeset editions

Congshu jicheng*, *chubian* 初編, vols. 1338–39 (1939). Based on the *Guyi congshu* edition.

Guyi congshu 古逸叢書. Ed. Li Shuchang 黎庶昌 and Yang Shoujing 楊守敬. Tokyo: Zunyi Li shi, 1884. Published by Li Shuchang under the appellate Zunyi Li shi. Cui Fuzhang and Zhu Xinlin argue that this earliest surviving printed edition of the *Yuzhu baodian* is based on the manuscript produced by Mori Tatsuyuki et al., and they cite Mori's record of Yang Shoujing inquiring after and borrowing his manuscript in 1881 (Cui and Zhu, "*Guyi congshu* ben," 146–49). Facsimile reprints are available in several other collections; for example, *Xuxiu Siku quanshu** 885.1–110.

Gyokushoku hōten. Ed. and trans. Ishikawa Misao. Tokyo: Meitoku shuppansha, 1988. Currently the only punctuated edition of the text. It is based on the Maeda manuscript but makes numerous emendations based partly on the Yoda and Mori editions (Ishikawa, "Kaisetsu," 10), only some of which are indicated in the text. It omits Du Taiqing's own annotations.

Commentary

Gyokushoku hōten kōshō. Annota. Yoda Toshimochi. Ca. 1840 (see preceding).

Selected studies

Over a century after the *Yuzhu baodian*'s repatriation to China and publication in print, relatively little research has been done on the text, and attention has focused on its bibliographic rather than historiographic value. The following works include substantial discussion of the text:

Chapman, Ian D. "Carnival Canons: Calendars, Genealogy, and the Search for Ritual Cohesion in Medieval China." Ph.D. diss., Princeton University, 2007. Pp. 116–37, 184–93.

Cui Fuzhang 崔富章 and Zhu Xinlin 朱新林. "*Guyi congshu* ben *Yuzhu baodian* diben bianxi" 古逸叢書本玉燭寶典底本辨析. *Wenxian* (2009.3): 144–50.

Huang Liming 黃麗明. "*Yuzhu baodian* yanjiu" 玉燭寶典研究. Master's thesis, Shanghai shifan daxue, 2010.

Imae Hiromichi 今江廣道. *Maeda-bon Gyokushoku hōten shihai monjo to sono kenkyū* 前田本玉燭宝典紙背文書とその研究. Tokyo: Zoku gunsho ruiju kanseikai, 2002.

Ishikawa Misao 石川三佐男. "Kaisetsu" 解説. In Ishikawa, ed., *Gyokushoku hōten* 玉燭宝典, 5–12. Tokyo: Meitoku shuppansha, 1988.

———. "*Koitsu sōsho* no hakubi *Gyokushoku hōten* ni tsuite" 古逸叢書の白眉玉燭宝典について. In *Akita Chūgoku gakkai 50 shūnen kinen ronshū* 秋田中国学会50周年記念論集, ed. Akita Chūgoku gakkai 50 shūnen kinen ronshū henshū i-inkai 秋田中国学会50周年記念論集編集委員会. Akita: Akita Chūgoku gakkai, 2005.

Moriya Mitsuo 守屋美都雄. *Chūgoku kosaijiki no kenkyū; shiryō fukugen o chūshin to shite* 中國古歲時記の研究; 資料復元を中心として. Tokyo: Teikoku shoin, 1963.

Niimi Hiroshi 新美寛. "*Gyokushoku hōten* ni tsuite" 玉燭寶典について. *Tōhō gakuhō* 13.3 (1943): 73–98.

Yang Shoujing 楊守敬. *Yuzhu baodian zhaji* 玉燭寶典札記. Unpublished MS, n.d., held at Beijing's Palace Museum. Cataloged in Li Xueqin 李學勤 et al., eds. *Siku dacidian* 四庫大辭典. Changchun: Jilin daxue chubanshe, 1996.

Yoshikawa Kōjirō 吉川幸次郎. "*Gyokushoku hōten* kaidai" 玉燭宝典解題. Appended to the *Sonkeikaku sōkan* 尊經閣叢刊 edition of *Yuzhu baodian*. Tokyo: Ikutoku zaidan, 1943; rpt. in *Yoshikawa Kōjirō zenshū (zōho)* 吉川幸次郎全集(増補), 7:552–57. Tokyo: Chikuma shobō, 1974. For a translation into Chinese, see Lin Wenyue 林文月, "*Yuzhu baodian* jieti" 玉燭寶典解題. Appended to the *Suishi xisu ziliao huibian* (vol. 1) edition of the *Yuzhu baodian*.

Japanese translation

Ishikawa Misao, ed. and trans. *Gyokushoku hōten* 玉燭寶典. Tokyo: Meitoku shuppansha, 1988. Includes translations of all but the last two surviving fascicles.

Ian Chapman

Zhang Hua ji 張華集

Introduction

Zhang Hua, styled Maoxian 茂先 (232–300), whose biography is in *Jin shu*, q.v., 36:1068–78, lived in an innovative era in terms of literature and the arts. He and many of his associates during the Western Jin dynasty (266–317), for example, Xun Xu 荀勖 (d. 289), Fu Xuan 傅玄 (217–278), and Zuo Si 左思 (d. 306), were in many cases powerful political actors but also influential scholars. These scholars wrote in many widely utilized late-Han literary genres, but they also wrote on such things as antiquities, natural philosophy, engineering, logistics of various kinds, astronomy, and medicine—indicating skills passed down within their own families or acquired recently, based on a general revival of interest.

Zhang Hua was of this type—capable and inventive in many genres and skills, even military matters. His collected writings provide important historical documents of private and court life during the Western Jin. The great literary critic Liu Xie 劉勰 (d. ca. 520) praised Zhang's writing, specifically the court memorials and *fu* compositions (Greatrex, *The Bowu zhi*, 18). The sixth-century *Wen xuan*, q.v., included Zhang's "Jiaoliao fu" 鷦鷯賦 (Rhapsody on the wren), a suite of nine lyric poems titled "Li zhi shi" 勵志詩 (Strengthening one's determination), and five additional lyric poems.

Zhang was also one of the most powerful courtiers of his day: he took part in formulating important policies of the Western Jin, both as a military planner of the Wu War (280) and as a molder of the Jin literary and historiographical offices (especially the Imperial Library and Palace Writers, the leadership of which had been a point of contention with Xun Xu). Eventually rising to the top level of the political echelon as minister of works (*sikong* 司空), he became one of early China's most effective patrons of young writers such as Zuo Si and Lu Ji 陸機 (261–303). Zhang Hua himself collected a large number of texts and antiquities and was, probably from about 285 to his death, responsible for keeping and organizing official documents of the Western Jin court. A work that achieved fame beginning soon after his own day is the *Bowu zhi* 博物志, q.v., a large collection of notices and anecdotes on various topics. For a list of all of Zhang's writings as cited in early sources, see Liu Rulin, *Han Jin xueshu biannian*, 7:205.

Contents

Over the centuries, Zhang's *wenji* underwent changes in content, in title, and in number of *juan*. It has never received a modern, critical edition. The extant, and fullest, edition of choice, with the title *Zhang Maoxian ji* 張茂先集, is the version collected in the late Ming by Zhang Pu (1602–1641; *jinshi* 1631) for his large work titled *Han Wei Liuchao baisanjia ji*, q.v. As with many other Six Dynasties *wenji*, it is a collection of prose items such as petitions, letters, disquisitions, epitaphs, and rhyme-prose; also verse items such as songs (or chants, *ge* 歌) and poems. The items in the *Zhang Maoxian ji* total sixty-four and are in the following order:

Rhapsody, 8 titles

Petition, 2 titles

Opinion, 3 titles, including a long discussion on the Fengshan 封禪 sacrifice

Lament, 2 titles

Dirge, 3 titles

Admonition, 4 titles

Inscription, 2 titles

Personal letter, 3 titles

Inquiry (*wen* 問), 1 title

Preface, 1 title, to the *Bowu zhi*

Encomium, 1 title

Court songs (*yuege* 樂歌), 12 titles under the general rubric "Jin sixiang yuege" 晉四廂樂歌(Songs for the Jin [palace] four side-rooms), some with subdivisions representing parts; these are traditional subgenres of lyric for court festal, saltatory, and temple ritual occasions

Poems, 23 titles, some with subdivisions

Transmission and early history of the text

On the transmission of Zhang Hua's writings, his biography in the *Jin shu* (completed in 648) says only that his "*Bowu zhi* in ten *juan* as well as his literary writings (*wenzhang* 文章) were known in the world [of that time]" (36:1077). This remark was careful to distinguish Zhang's *Bowu zhi* from his general writings—works that became collected in the *wenji*. The *Sui shu*, q.v., bibliographic monograph, subsection on "Private Collections" ("Bie ji" 別集) lists a *Jin sikong Zhang Hua ji* 晉司空張華集 in ten *juan*. This is the first record of Zhang Hua's *wenji*. The *Sui shu* commentary states that Zhang's *wenji* had earlier contained a "Record of Contents" (*lu* 錄) in one *juan* (*Sui shu* 35:1062; Yao Zhenzong, *Sui shu jingji zhi kaozheng*, 5734c).

The *Jiu Tang shu*, completed in 945, but using eighth-century records, lists the *Zhang Hua ji* as containing ten *juan* (47:2060); the ninth-century catalog *Nihonkoku genzaisho mokuroku* 日本國見在書目錄 does the same. The *Junzhai dushu zhi** (1151) 17:815 states that it contained three *juan*, giving 120 for the number of poems and only 3 for rhyme-prose. The bibliographical treatise carried in the mid-Yuan *Song shi* (208:5328) lists a *Zhang Hua ji* in two *juan* and, "in addition, one of verse" (for the earlier references to later catalogs, see Yao Zhenzong, *Sui shu jingji zhi kaozheng*, 915:697). Zhang's *wenji* is one of only a few Western Jin *wenji* mentioned in Song catalogs, which indicates its popularity. But the transmission of the *wenji* was fraught with lapses after Tang times, and the number of *juan* diminished. Han and Six Dynasties *wenji* were finally reconstituted by several Ming-era scholars based on Song and Yuan recensions available to them, and, like many Western Jin *wenji*, today's commonly used edition of the *Zhang Hua ji* is that found in Zhang Pu's *Han Wei Liuchao baisan jia ji*, where it is titled *Zhang Maoxian ji* 張茂先集. An eminent Qing-era collectanea, Yan Kejun's (1762–1843) *Quan shanggu Sandai Qin Han Sanguo Liudai wen*, q.v., devotes "Quan Jin wen," *juan* 58, to the prose of Zhang and differs slightly from the prose items collected in the *Han Wei Liuchao baisan jia ji*.

Principal editions

The most complete edition, titled *Zhang Maoxian ji*, is found in *juan* 40 of *Han Wei Liuchao baisanjia ji*. The unpunctuated *Siku quanshu** edition, which is quite reliable relative to all the early *Han Wei Liuchao baisanjia ji* editions, is in *Yingyin Wenyuange Siku quanshu** 1413:186–211. There is also the 1879 traditionally punctuated edition, photo-facsimile reprinted by the Jiangsu guji shudian, 1990 (2:409–441). An 1848 edition titled *Zhang Sikong ji* 張司空集 by Pan Xi'en 潘錫恩, included in Pan's large collectanea *Qiankun zhengqi ji* 乾坤正氣集 (rpt., Taipei: Huanqiu shuju, 1966), contains only the rhyme-prose and prose, matching their number and order as seen in the *Han Wei Liuchao baisanjia ji*.

There is no modern punctuated, text-critical edition of Zhang Hua's entire *wenji*; only certain of its items have received such attention. First, for the title "Jiaoliao fu," see the modern, punctuated version in *Jin shu* (36:1069); second, the best critical, annotated version of Zhang's poetry is that in Lu Qinli's *Xian Qin Han Wei Jin Nanbeichao shi**, "Jin shi," *juan* 3 (1:610–23), which contains several poetry fragments not found in the *Han Wei Liuchao baisanjia ji*; and for his court lyrics, see "Jin shi," *juan* 4 (1:820–22, 825–26). For "Li zhi shi," there is an extant Dunhuang manuscript in Meng Liefu 孟列夫 (L. N. Menshikov) and Qian Bocheng 錢伯城, editors-in-chief, *E cang Dunhuang wenxian* 俄藏敦煌文獻, 15 vols. (Shanghai: Shanghai guji chubanshe, 1992–), vol. 4, and also in Luo Guowei 羅國威, *Dunhuang ben Zhaoming wen xuan yanjiu* 敦煌本昭明文選研究 (Harbin: Heilongjiang jiaoyu chubanshe, 1999), 153–61.

Texts with commentary and notes

Fang Shungui 方順貴. "Zhang Hua shige jiaozhu" 張華詩歌校注. Master's thesis, Sichuan daxue, 2007. Commentary on the poetry only.

Ma Hongyan 馬鴻雁. "Zhang Hua ji jiaozhu" 張華集校注. Master's thesis, Dongbei shifan daxue, 2005. This is a punctuated and annotated text of all of the prose and verse items, as found in the *Han Wei Liuchao baisanjia ji*, but it is not a learned annotation.

Selected studies

Fang Shungui 方順貴. "*Wen xuan* Zhang Hua 'Li zhi shi' bianzheng" 文選張華勵志詩辨證. *Mudanjiang jiaoyu xueyuan xuebao* 99 (2006): 3–4.

Liao Weiqing 廖蔚卿. "Zhang Hua yu Xi Jin zhengzhi zhi guanxi" 張華與西晉政治之關系. *Wen shi zhe xuebao* 22 (1973): 13–88.

Mukōjima Narumi 向嶋成美. "Chō Ka no shi ni tsuite" 張華の詩について. *Tōkyō kyōiku daigaku bungakubu kiyō* 87 (1972): 77–107.

Shaughnessy, Edward L. *Rewriting Early Chinese Texts*. Albany: State University of New York Press, 2006.

Wang Fuli 王福利. *Jiaomiao yanshe geci yanjiu* 郊廟燕射歌辭研究. Beijing: Beijing daxue chubanshe, 2009. Pp. 216–23. Brief discussion of Zhang's court lyrics. One of very few modern studies that looks at the texts of this genre of post-Han lyric.

Translations

Farmer, J. Michael. "On the Composition of Zhang Hua's 'Nüshi zhen.'" *Early Medieval China* 10–11, part 1 (2005): 151–76. Translates "Admonition of the Female Scribe" ("Nüshi jian" 女史箴).

Greatrex, Roger. *The Bowu zhi: An Annotated Translation*. Skrifter utgivna Fürningen für Orientaliska Studier 20. Stockholm: Akademitryck AB, Täby, 1987.

Knechtges, David R. *Wen xuan, or Selections of Refined Literature*. Princeton, NJ: Princeton University Press, 1996. Vol. 3, pp. 57–63. Translates "Rhapsody on the Wren" (*Wen xuan*, juan 13).

Straughair, Anna. *Chang Hua: A Statesman-Poet of the Western Chin Dynasty*. Australian National University, Faculty of Asian Studies, Occasional Paper 15. Canberra: Australian National University, 1973. Pp. 24–72, 74–119. Translates Zhang Hua's *Jin shu* biography (excluding "Rhapsody on the Wren") and nineteen verses of the lyric poetry category from the *Zhang Maoxian ji*.

Zach, Erwin von. "Der Schneidervogel," "Ermunterung zu fleissigem Studium," "Zwei Gedichte in Antwort auf das Gedicht des Ho Shao," "Gedicht ohne besonderen Titel." In *Die chinesische Anthologie: Übersetzungen aus dem Wen hsuan*, ed. Ilse Martin Fong. 2 vols. Cambridge, MA: Harvard University Press, 1958. Vol. 1, pp. 201–3, 277–79, 390–91, 532. In the *Wen xuan*, these are

"Rhapsody on the Wren," "Strengthening One's Determination" (*juan* 19), "Replying to He Shao" ("Da He Shao" 答何劭, two poems; *juan* 24), and "Miscellaneous Poems" ("Zashi" 雜詩, three poems; *juan* 29).

Reference works, research aids, concordances

Jiang Liangfu 姜亮夫. *Zhang Hua nianpu* 張華年譜. Shanghai: Gudian wenxue chubanshe, 1957.

Liao Weiqing. "Zhang Hua nianpu" 張華年譜. *Wen shi zhe xuebao* 27 (1978): 1–96.

Liu Rulin 劉汝霖. *Han Jin xueshu biannian* 漢晉學術編年. Shanghai: Shangwu yinshu guan, 1935; rpt., 1991. Chap. 7, pp. 204–5.

Yao Zhenzong 姚振宗 (1843–1906). *Sui shu jingji zhi kaozheng* 隋書經籍志考證. In *Ershiwushi bubian* 二十五史補編, 6 vols., 4:5734c–5735b. Shanghai: Kaiming shudian, 1937.

Howard L. Goodman

Zhang Rong ji 張融集

Introduction

Zhang Rong, styled Siguang 思光 (444–497), was descended from a leading southern family, the Zhang clan of Wu commandery, that for generations had distinguished itself in scholarship and literary writings. Anecdotes in the *Shishuo xinyu*, q.v., furthermore show the expertise of family members in "mysterious learning" (*xuanxue* 玄學) and the art of "pure conversation" (*qingtan* 清談). This brought them respect from the northern émigré elite and opened doors for some to top official careers. Despite the success of the Wujun Zhang lineage as a whole, Zhang Rong's biography in *Nan Qi shu*, q.v., 41:721–30, records that he grew up in poverty and, even after he received office, he did not possess the proper attire for presenting himself at court, so Emperor Qi Taizu on one occasion gave him his own robes.

The Zhangs were traditionally followers of the Teaching of the Celestial Masters (Tianshi dao 天師道). There were also generations of family members who revered the Buddha, as Zhang Rong himself pointed out in his "Disquisition about the [Different] Schools" (see later). Zhang's personality bore traces of his family tradition, including the proclivity for a recluse's lifestyle and ostentatious nonconformity. As described in his biographies in the *Nan Qi shu* and *Nan shi*, q.v., 32:833–37, he was short and ugly in appearance, yet eloquent in learning, speech, and literary ability, as well as a skilled calligrapher in the cursive form. In the *Shu pin* 書品, Yu Jianwu (487–551) ranked him in the lower middle category (*xia zhongpin* 下中品).

The biographies recount Zhang Rong's extraordinary skills bestowed on him by a Daoist master, his deeds of filial piety and loyalty to friends, and his eccentric behavior and neglect of formal propriety. His eclectic learning is evident in his famous "Testament" ("Yi ling" 遺令), in which he instructed his family to bury him with the *Xiao jing* and the *Lao zi* in his left hand and the *Aṣṭasāhasrikā Prajñāpāramitā Sutra* and the Lotus Sutra in the right. The "Testament" also requested only a simple burial and asked that his two concubines not mourn for him after his death, but soon return to their families. Unlike many other illustrious men of similar family background and social position who, being involved in politics and court intrigues, met violent deaths, Zhang peacefully died of illness at the age of fifty-four *sui*. He had served in several offices in the provinces and at court during the Song and Qi. The highest position to which he was promoted was senior administrator in the Ministry of Education (*situ zuo zhangshi* 司徒左長史) in the service of Xiao Ziliang 蕭子良, the Prince of Jingling (460–494)—hence, the traditional title of his collection, *Zhang Zhangshi ji* 張長史集.

Contents

The edition of the *Zhang Zhangshi ji* in *juan* 78 of Zhang Pu's (1602–1641) *Han Wei Liuchao baisanjia ji*, q.v., contains fourteen pieces of poetry and prose arranged in the following order:

1. Rhapsody, 1
2. Memorandum, 1
3. Letter (personal), 5
4. Disquisition, 1
5. Preface, 1
6. Warning (*jie* 誡), 1
7. Lyric poem, 4 (including fragments)

The best-known literary piece in the collection is the "Hai fu" 海賦 (Rhapsody on the sea), which Zhang composed early in his career, between 454 and 457, when he traveled by sea to take up his appointment as district magistrate of Fengxi 封溪 (about 25 kilometers northwest of modern Hanoi). The work has been acknowledged as a masterpiece of the Six Dynasties among rhapsodies on objects (*yongwu fu* 詠物賦) and valued for its spontaneity, originality, and powerful expression based on direct observations of the sea. Some critics, however, have had reservations and consider this *fu* to be derived from an earlier "Hai fu" by Mu Hua 木華 (fl. ca. 290). It was Mu Hua's work, not Zhang Rong's, that was included in the *Wen xuan*, q.v. (Cao and Shen, *Nanchao wenxue shi*).

The collection's largest and most important prose piece is the "Men lun" 門論 (Disquisition on the [different] schools), an exposition of the unity between Daoism and Buddhism (*fo dao tong yuan* 佛道通源). Zhang Rong's correspondence with Zhou Yong 周顒 (d. ca. 485) on this issue, which consisted of the latter's rebuttal of Zhang's ideas and Zhang's reply, is also preserved in the collection.

Zhang's lyric poetry was unpolished, even crude, very much unlike the Yongming style (*Yongming ti* 永明體) fashionable during the rule of Emperor Wu of the Qi (r. 483–493). In his "Men lü zixu" 門律自序 (Authorial preface to the house rules), Zhang proudly spoke about his idiosyncratic literary style, declaring: "Now how could literature have a routine form? When it attains a form, it becomes routine" (夫文豈有常體,但以有體為常). He also criticized contemporary taste for being too preoccupied with formal elaboration and outward beauty at the expense of individual expression. Originality and personal style were Zhang's highest values.

Sources of the work

Zhang Pu's edition of Zhang Rong's writings is a typical "gathered-up collection" (*jiben* 輯本), in that it was reconstructed from surviving items scattered in various sources. *Nan Qi shu* 41.730 mentions that Zhang Rong compiled his own collection and gave it the title *Yu hai* 玉海 (Jade sea) to represent the moral integrity of Confucian teachings (jade) and the all-embracing compassion of Buddhism (sea). The bibliographic monograph of the *Sui shu*, q.v., records that Zhang's collection had consisted of twenty-seven *juan* but that only ten were extant. It mentions a *Yu hai* in ten *juan* separately, as well as other shorter collections, that have been lost. The "Hai fu" was preserved in Zhang Rong's *Nan Qi shu* biography as well as in *Yiwen leiju*, q.v., *juan* 8. The "Men lun" and exchange with Zhou Yong over the relationship between Buddhism and Daoism was included in *Hongming ji*, q.v., *juan* 6 of the ten-*juan* edition. All the remaining prose texts may be found in his biographies.

Authenticity and transmission of the text

Only a small fragment survives of Zhang Rong's work, and the texts as we now have them are not always reliable. In his biography, we already find the remark that there are "many omissions and mistakes" in the "Hai fu" (*Nan Qi shu* 41:726).

The relationship between the "Men lun" and the "Men lü zixu" has been a subject of debate. Indeed, both works have variant titles. "Men lun" is the title given in Ming texts of the *Hongming ji*, but it is titled *Men lü* 門律 elsewhere, including in modern Japanese editions. As for the "Men lü zixu," it was preserved in the *Nan Qi shu* as the "Wen lü zixu" 問律自序. It is thought, however, that *wen* 問 may have been a scribe's error for *men* 門, and "Men lü zixu" is now generally accepted as the correct title. Although these two texts concern different topics and Zhang Pu had distinguished them as separate writings, modern editors and critics have supposed that the preface belonged to the "Men lun" (*Foguang dacidian*, 4:3605, 5:4546). A closer look into historical sources suggests, however, that not only was Zhang Pu correct in perceiving the works as distinct from each other but also that they were probably written at different times. While the "Men lun" is a disquisition about religious matters and probably dates from before the year 448, the "Men/wen lü zixu" belongs to the genre of family instructions and was likely composed at the end of the Yongming era (Cao Daoheng, *Zhonggu wenxue shiliao congkao*, 422–23).

Principal editions

Apart from editions of Zhang Pu's anthology, Zhang Rong's collected writings were included in the *Siku quanshu**. In the photolithographic reproduction, *Yingyin Chizaotang Siku quanshu huiyao* 影印摛藻堂四庫全書薈要 (Taipei: Shijie shuju, 1986), these are in vol. 471 (collected works no. 124), 33–44. There are no modern editions of the *Zhang Zhangshi ji*; his prose and poems may separately be found in the following anthologies:

Lu Qinli. "Qi shi," juan 2, pp. 1409–10. *Xian Qin Han Wei Jin Nanbeichao shi**.
Yan Kejun 嚴可均. "Quan Qi wen," 15.1a–8b. *Quan shanggu Sandai Qin Han Sanguo Liuchao wen*, q.v.

Traditional assessments

Zhong Rong praised Zhang Rong's poetry as "untrammeled" (*bu jucu* 不局促) and ranked him along with his younger maternal cousin, the renowned recluse Kong Zhigui 孔稚珪 (447–501), in the third and lowest section of his *Shi pin*, q.v. One may consult Zhang Pu's preface to the *Zhang Zhangshi ji* for a brief discussion of Zhang Rong's personality and evaluation of his achievement.

Selected studies

The following secondary scholarship concerns individual writings by Zhang Rong or his religious views.

Cao Daoheng 曹道衡. *Zhonggu wenxue shiliao congkao* 中古文學史料叢考. Beijing: Zhonghua shuju, 2003. Pp. 422–26.

Cao Daoheng and Shen Yucheng 沈玉成. *Nanchao wenxue shi* 南朝文學史. *Zhongguo wenxue tongshi xilie* 中國文學史系列. Beijing: Renmin wenxue chubanshe, 1991. Pp. 193–95. A description of Zhang Rong's life and works.

Foguang dacidian 佛光大辭典. 8 vols. Ed. Xingyun dashi 星雲大師 et al. Gaoxiong: Foguang chubanshe, 1988. Vol. 4, p. 3605, and vol. 5, p. 4546.

Gao Lintao 郜林濤. "Wujun Zhangshi ji Nanchao shizu de Fojiao sixiang" 吳郡張氏及南朝士族的佛教思想. *Xinzhou shifan xueyuan xuebao* 17.1 (2001): 26–28, 72.

Ji Zhichang 紀志昌. "Nan Qi Zhang Rong de Dao Fo jiaoshe siwei shi shi—yi Menlü, Tongyuan zhong yu Zhou Yong de duihua wei zhu" 南齊張融的道佛交涉思維試釋—以門律, 通源中與周顒的對話為主. *Zhongguo wenzhe yanjiu jikan* 35.9 (2009): 45–88.

Qian Zhongshu 錢鍾書. *Guanzhui bian* 管錐編, 4 vols. Beijing: Zhonghua shuju, 1979. Vol. 4, "Quan Qi wen," 15.1342–46. For discussion of the "Hai fu" and "Men lun."

Tan Jiajian 譚家健. "Han Wei Liuchao shiqi de 'Hai fu'" 漢魏六朝時期的海賦. *Liaocheng shifan xueyuan xuebao* (2000.2): 84–89.

Wakamizu Suguru 若水俊. "Chō Yū yo sono shisō" 張融とその思想. *Ibaraki joshi tanki daigaku kiyō* (Added title: *Bulletin of Ibaraki Women's Junior College*) 7 (1980): 10–41.

———. "Chō Yū no dōkyō shisō ni tsuite" 張融の道教思想について. *Ibaraki joshi tanki daigaku kiyō* 9 (1982): 1–18.

Translation

A Japanese translation of Zhang Rong's polemic with Zhou Yong is available in *Gumyō shū kenkyū* 弘明集研究, 3 vols., edited by the Kyōto daigaku jinbun kagaku kenkyūjo, Kyoto: Kyoto University Institute for Research in Humanities, 1973–1975. Vol. 3, pp. 358–76.

Olga Lomová

Zhou shu 周書

Introduction

The *Zhou shu* 周書 (History of the Zhou) is the main textual source for the history of the sixth-century Chang'an regime comprising the Western Wei and Northern Zhou dynasties, which gave way to the Sui usurpation in 581 and from which ultimately grew the Tang empire. It contains fifty chapters—eight annals and forty-two biographies and accounts—and mentions almost three hundred individuals. The monographs (*zhi* 志) in the *Sui shu* include coverage of this period (McMullen, *State and Scholars in T'ang China*, 167).

History of the text

There are three major phases in the history of the book's composition. The initial period of compilation and composition began in the Western Wei and stretched into the Sui. Work began with Liu Qiu 柳虯 (501–554; biographies in *Zhou shu* 38:680–82, *Bei shi*, q.v., 64:2278–89), a member of one of those gentry families on the north-south border in the Luoyang region who joined the nascent Chang'an regime. In 548 Liu was appointed vice-director of the Palace Library (*mishu cheng* 祕書丞), which institution from this time began to be involved in history-keeping; in 550 he was additionally assigned to compile the imperial diary (*qijuzhu* 起居注). There is no mention of Liu Qiu's work in the *Sui shu*, q.v., bibliographic monograph; the first explicit mention of him as an early participant in the compiling of the *Zhou shu* is by the Tang historian Liu Zhiji 劉知幾 (661–721) in *Shi tong** 12:369.

Liu Qiu was succeeded by Niu Hong 牛弘 (545–610), a man of the northwest who first served the Northern Zhou as editor of the imperial diary, and then, under the Sui, became director of the Palace Library (*mishu jian* 祕書監) and was later advanced to other offices (biographies in *Bei shi* 72:2492, *Sui shu* 49:1297–310). Niu initiated a successful campaign to build up the Sui imperial library by offering rewards for contributed books. Also during the Sui, Niu compiled an unfinished history of the Western Wei and Northern Zhou in eighteen *juan*, the *Zhou shi* 周史 (*Sui shu* 33:956; *Shi tong* 12:369), apparently drawing upon the work of Liu Qiu; it seems likely that Niu had simply picked up the work in progress, building on Liu's work. It is not clear what exactly the organization of the eighteen-*juan* work was; the subsequent *Zhou shu* has just eight *juan* of annals, so Niu's *Zhou shi* may have been a combination of annals and an incipient biography section, including biographies of major palace figures such as the empresses. The sources for the history of the Western Wei–Northern Zhou regime may have been very limited. In fact, as a quick scan of the pertinent section of the *Sui shu* monograph on bibliography (*juan* 33) confirms, nothing much existed beyond Niu's eighteen-*juan* draft. In the imperial diary section of the monograph, though we know that both Liu and Niu worked on such records for the Zhou, nothing of the sort survives nor is there a separate chronological history. The only item listed for Zhou is "Commands of Yuwen Tai" ("Hou Zhou Taizu haoling" 後周太祖號令; *Sui shu* 33:965).

The second stage in the history of the *Zhou shu* is its actual compilation by a commission appointed in 629 by the Tang emperor Taizong (r. 626–649), headed by Linghu Defen 令狐德棻 (583–666). Linghu Defen was himself a man of a prominent northwestern lineage. Under the Tang founder, Li Yuan (r. 618–626), he served as imperial diarist, and then as assistant director of the Palace Library (*mishu cheng* 祕書丞); he eventually rose to be chancellor of the National University (*guozi jijiu* 國子祭酒). Known as an active and productive scholar, with a special interest in music and ritual, he worked on the *Jin shu*, q.v., and other important projects, as well as the *Zhou shu*. Another member of the *Zhou shu* commission, Cen Wenben 岑文本 (595–645), was also a well-known literary figure; he wrote most of the postfaces to each *juan*. Finally, Cui Renshi 崔仁師, whose offices reached that of attendant gentleman of the Secretariat (*zhongshu shilang* 中書侍郎), ran the operation (editors' preface, *Zhou shu*, Zhonghua shuju edition, 2). The completed *Zhou shu* was presented to the throne in 636.

The fall of the Tang in 906 led yet again to chaos and the scattering of texts. In the early Song we see another phase in the effort to recover and repair texts, the third in the history of the *Zhou shu*. The editors of the Zhonghua shuju imprint of the *Zhou shu* (1971) suggest that *juan* 18, 24, 26, 31, 32, and perhaps 36 were completely lost, though the last may have retained a half of the original; largely lost was *juan* 21 (editors' preface, *Zhou shu*, 8; Wang, *Shibu yaoji jieti*, 79). These were partially restored during the Song by drawing on surviving Tang-era texts that had originally drawn on the *Zhou shu*, though with substantial abridgment and emendation. These texts would include the *Bei shi* as well as the *Gaoshi xiaoshi* 高氏小史, an early ninth-century book by Gao Jun 高峻 (fl. 806–820). Losses to the *Zhou shu* continued to occur in the Song even after repairs were made, for there are quotations from the *Zhou shu* in the encyclopedia *Cefu yuangui* 冊府元龜, compiled 1005, of parts of *juan* 6 and 39 that are missing in the current text (editors' preface, *Zhou shu*, 8).

Evaluation

Liu Zhiji, in his *Shi tong*, was particularly critical of the *Zhou shu*. He felt that "the style of writing was refined, but not sincere; elegant but unrestrained. Traces of genuineness are very rare; the courteous treatment was especially vexing" (17:500). The complaint was clearly based in part on a dislike of the sixth-century archaic literary style used by Liu Qiu and Niu Hong, and perpetuated by Linghu Defen. In addition, according to Liu, it was not a true record (17:501). Biographies of some men may have been included because their descendants held prominent office in the Tang (editors' preface, *Zhou shu*, 4; other examples are given by Wang, *Shibu yaoji jieti*, 78). However, various scholars have said that despite its flaws the text is useful in different ways. The editors of the Zhonghua shuju edition of the *Zhou shu* (editors' preface, 6) point out that among the book's strengths are its accounts of the regime's founding; its power struggles; and its three wars against Eastern Wei–Northern Qi. Chai (*Shiji juyao*, 86) adds to these suggestions the book's importance for examining the origins of the "equal fields" (*juntian* 均田) land distribution program and the *fubing* 府兵 military system.

Transmission of the text

The *Zhou shu* was first printed between 1068 and 1074, but this imprint did not survive. It was printed again in 1174, in Sichuan at Meishan; this is the oldest edition, though it is not complete, and it was supplemented in the Yuan and Ming. For more detail on the Song, Ming, and Qing editions upon which the Zhonghua shuju edition is based, see the editors' preface (9–10). For an overall account of the textual history of this and the other Six Dynasties histories, see appendix IV, "Textual Transmission of the Standard Histories."

Principal editions

Zhou shu. 50 *juan*. Linghu Defen et al. Photolithographic reproduction of the Song dynasty's Shu Large Character edition, supplemented with a Yuan and Ming repaired imprint. Shanghai: Shangwu yinshuguan, 1936. Included in the series *Baina ben ershisishi* 百衲本二十四史 ["Hundred patches" edition of the twenty-four standard histories]. *Sibu congkan**.

Zhou shu. 50 *juan*. 3 vols. Linghu Defen et al. Beijing: Zhonghua shuju, 1971.

Selected studies

Chai Degeng 柴德賡. *Shiji juyao* 史籍舉要. Beijing: Beijing chubanshe, 1982.

McMullen, David. *State and Scholars in T'ang China*. Cambridge: Cambridge University Press, 1988.

Qian Daxin 錢大昕 (1728–1804). *Nian'ershi kaoyi* 廿二史考異. Shanghai: Shanghai guji chubanshe, 2002. *Juan* 32.

Wang Shumin 王樹民. *Shibu yaoji jieti* 史部要籍解題. Beijing: Zhonghua shuju, 1981.

Zhao Zheng 趙政. "*Zhou shu* kaolun" 周書考論. *Wuyi daxue xuebao* 3.1–2 (1989): 30–37.

———. "*Zhou shu* kaolun, xu" 周書考論, 續. *Wuyi daxue xuebao* 4.1 (1990): 25–31.

Translations

For translations of portions of the *Zhou shu*, see Hans H. Frankel, *Catalogue of Translations from the Chinese Dynastic Histories for the Period 220–960*. Chinese Dynastic Histories Translations, supplement no. 1, 121–24. Berkeley: University of California Press, 1957. In addition, see:

Dien, Albert E. *Biography of Yü-wen Hu*. Chinese Dynastic Histories Translations 9. Berkeley: University of California Press, 1962. Translates 11:165–77, 181–82.

Miller, Roy Andrew. *Accounts of Western Nations in the History of the Northern Chou Dynasty [Chou shu 50.10b–17b]*. Chinese Dynastic Histories Translations 8. Berkeley: University of California Press, 1959. Translates 50:914–20.

Indices

Chen Zhongan 陳仲安 et al., eds. *Beichao sishi renming suoyin* 北朝四史人名索引. 2 vols. Beijing: Zhonghua shuju, 1988.

Huang Huixian 黃惠賢, ed.-in-chief. *Ershiwushi renming da cidian* 二十五史人名大辭典. 2 vols. Zhengzhou: Zhongzhou chubanshe, 1997.

Scott Pearce

Zuo Si ji 左思集

Introduction

Zuo Si (ca. 253–ca. 307), a native of Linzi 臨淄 (modern Zibo 淄博, Shandong), was a famous literary figure of the Western Jin. He was styled Taichong 太沖 (alternately written 泰沖). His father, Zuo Yong 左雍 (elsewhere, Zuo Xi 熹), served in the capital as an attendant censor responsible for surveillance over palace personnel (*dianzhong shiyushi* 殿中侍御史). In 272, when Zuo Si's sister Zuo Fen 芬 (alternately, 棻; ca. 255–300) was chosen for her literary talent to be a lady of the imperial harem, the whole family moved to Luoyang. Zuo Si occupied the positions of Palace Library assistant (*mishu lang* 秘書郎) and libationer (*jijiu* 祭酒). He taught the *Han shu* to the Palace Library's director, Jia Mi 賈謐 (d. 300), and joined his group of "Twenty-four Friends." In March of 300, his sister Zuo Fen died. In April of that year, the Prince of Zhao, Sima Lun 司馬倫 (d. 301), led a coup d'état, cast out Empress Jia 賈 (256–300), and killed Zhang Hua 張華 (232–300) and Jia Mi. Zuo Si withdrew from public life to Yichunli 宜春里, a town east of Luoyang, and focused on his literary writings. The Prince of Qi, Sima Jiong 司馬冏 (d. 302), offered him a position as record keeper (*jishi du* 記室督), but he declined it. When Zhang Fang 張方 (d. 306) attacked Luoyang in 303, Zuo Si's family moved to Jizhou 冀州 (the site of modern Jizhou in Hebei). He died of illness several years later. His biography is found in the "Wen yuan" 文苑 section of *Jin shu*, q.v., 92:2375–77, and is preserved in fragments from other versions of that history. Other accounts about him are in the *Shishuo xinyu*, q.v.

Contents

The one-*juan Zuo Taichong ji* 左太沖集 compiled by Ding Fubao 丁福保 (1874–1952) was included in his *Han Wei Liuchao mingjia ji chuke* 漢魏六朝名家集初刻 (Shanghai: Shanghai wenming shuju, 1911). This single *juan*, containing Zuo Si's biography from the *Jin shu*, rhapsodies, and poems, is organized as follows:

"Three Capitals Rhapsody" ("Sandu fu" 三都賦), a trilogy on the capitals of the states of Shu 蜀, Wu 吳, and Wei 魏, accompanied by a preface

"White Hair Rhapsody" ("Baifa fu" 白髮賦)

"Qi Capital Rhapsody" ("Qidu fu" 齊都賦), 5 fragments

"Seven Admonitions" ("Qi feng" 七諷), 1 fragment

"On My Pampered Daughters" ("Jiao nü shi" 嬌女詩), 1 poem

"On History" ("Yong shi" 詠史), 8 poems

"On the Theme of Summoning the Recluse" ("Zhao yin" 招隱), 2 poems

Miscellaneous poem (zashi 雜詩), 1 poem

Ding's edition does not contain "Grief at Parting: Two Poems Presented to My Younger Sister" ("Dao li zeng mei er shou" 悼離贈妹二首) and four lines from a poem on history that did not survive in its entirety. The *Wenguan cilin** (comp. 658), edited by Xu Jingzong (592–672), included the former in *juan* 152, and the *Beitang shuchao*, q.v., by Yu Shinan 虞世南 (558–638), contained the latter in *juan* 119.

Transmission and early history of the text

The *Jin shu* states that when Zuo Si was young, it took him only one year to compose the "Qi Capital Rhapsody." Later, however, he spent ten years composing the "Three Capitals Rhapsody." He showed it to Huangfu Mi 皇甫謐 (215–282), who offered to write a preface. According to the *Shishuo xinyu*, those who had previously belittled the work then sang its praises ("Letters and Scholarship," *juan* 4, no. 68). Zuo's contemporaries Zhang Zai 張載, Liu Kui 劉逵, and Wei Quan 衛權 all wrote commentaries. The *Wen xuan*, q.v., included this three-part rhapsody (*juan* 4–6), eight poems on history (*juan* 21), two poems on the theme of "Summoning the Recluse" (*juan* 22), and the miscellaneous poem mentioned previously (*juan* 29). The *Yutai xinyong*, q.v., included "On My Pampered Daughters" (*juan* 2).

Sui shu, q.v., 35:1063, mentions a *Jin Qiwangfu Jishi Zuo Si ji* 晉齊王府記室左思集 in two *juan*, with a note that a five-*juan* collection had existed during the Liang. Furthermore, the Sui bibliography lists a "Five Capitals Rhapsody" ("Wudu fu" 五都賦) in six *juan* that incorporates the "Three Capitals Rhapsody," and also a "Rhapsody on Miscellaneous Capitals" ("Zadu fu" 雜都賦) with a note mentioning a lost Liang edition of the "Qi Capital Rhapsody" in two *juan*. The Sui bibliography further notes (35:1083) an "Annotated Edition of Miscellaneous Rhapsodies" ("Zafu zhuben" 雜賦注本) with two lost annotated editions of the "Three Capitals Rhapsody" from the Liang. One had notes by Zhang Zai, Liu Kui, and Wei Quan collectively, and the other by Qiwu Sui 綦毋邃 (dates unknown); both were in three *juan*.

Jiu Tang shu 47:2060 and *Xin Tang shu* 60:1583 both list a *Zuo Si ji* in five *juan*. They also record a five-*juan* "Wudu fu," a three-*juan* "Sandu fu," and a one-*juan* "Qidu fu." Moreover, they note Li Gui's 李軌 one-*juan* "Phonetic Gloss on the Qi Capital Rhapsody" ("Qidu fu yin" 齊都賦音), and Qiwu Sui's one-*juan* "Phonetic Gloss on the Three Capitals Rhapsody" ("Sanjing fu yin" 三京賦音). The *Song shi*'s bibliographic monograph does not list Zuo Si's works.

Principal editions

Almost all of Zuo Si's extant works were preserved in anthologies or encyclopedias of the Six Dynasties and Tang. During the Ming, Hu Yinglin 胡應麟 (1551–1602) mentioned in his *Shi sou* 詩藪 (*waibian* 外編, *juan* 2) the experience of reading the *Taichong [Zuo Si] ji*, which indicates that the collection was still available then. Zuo Si's works were not included, however, in Zhang Pu's (1602–1641) *Han Wei Liuchao baisanjia ji*, q.v. The contemporary scholar Xu Chuanwu reviews information about all the works or surviving fragments by Zuo Si and his sister in the section of his book titled "Zuo Si Zuo Fen zuopin cunwang kao" 左思左棻作品存亡考 (21–31).

The standard edition for Zuo Si's rhapsodies is Yan Kejun's (1762–1843) *Quan shanggu Sandai Qin Han Sanguo Liuchao wen*, q.v., "Quan Jin wen," 74:1a–17b (Shijie shuju ed., vol. 4). For his poetry, see Lu Qinli's *Xian Qin Han Wei Jin Nanbeichao shi**, "Jin shi," *juan* 7 (1:731–36).

Traditional assessments

Zhang Hua, a contemporary of Zuo Si, praised the "Sandu fu" as being comparable to Ban Gu's 班固 (32–92) and Zhang Heng's 張衡 (78–139) capital rhapsodies (*Jin shu* 92:2377). Liu Xie (ca. 465–ca. 521) commented, "Zuo Si was a man of extraordinary talent, deeply accomplished in his literary works, and of profound vision. He was completely focused on writing the 'Three Capitals Rhapsody' and outstanding in his 'Poems on History'; he exhausted all his energy in them" (*Wenxin diaolong*, q.v., *juan* 47, "Cai lue" 才略). Zhong Rong (469?–518) placed Zuo Si's pentasyllabic poems in the top rank with this comment in the *Shi pin*, q.v.: "His poems originated in Gonggan [i.e., Liu Zhen 劉楨; d. 217] and used literary allusions to express his resentment. They were quite refined and precise, and attained the peak of admonition through allegory. Although he was less refined than Lu Ji 陸機 [261–303], he was more profound than Pan Yue 潘岳 [247–300]. Xie Kangle [i.e., Xie Lingyun 謝靈運; 385–433] once said, 'Zuo Taichong's and Pan Anren's [i.e., Pan Yue] poems are hard to match in both the past and present.'" Zhong Rong asserted furthermore that the aesthetic quality of the poetry of Tao Yuanming 陶淵明 (ca. 365–427) was influenced by Zuo Si: "It originates from Ying Qu and is guided by the affective force of Zuo Si" (translated by Wendy Swartz, *Reading Tao Yuanming: Shifting Paradigms of Historical Reception (427–1900)* [Cambridge, MA: Harvard University Asia Center, 2008], 152).

Shen Deqian 沈德潛 (1673–1769) said, "Taichong's poems on history do not exclusively sing of particular persons or events. He sings of the ancient people, yet his own nature and emotions are fully apparent. His poetry was the pinnacle of poetic perfection for a thousand years. Later only Mingyuan [i.e., Bao Zhao 鮑照; ca. 414–466] and Taibo [i.e., Li Bo 李白; 701–762] could write poems like him" (*Gushi yuan* 古詩源, commentary by Miao Hong 苗洪 [Beijing: Huaxia chubanshe, 1998], 305).

Selected studies

Jiang Jianyun 姜劍雲. *Taikang wenxue yanjiu* 太康文學研究. Beijing: Zhonghua shuju, 2003.

Kōzen Hiroshi 興膳宏. "Sa Shi to Eishi shi" 左思と詠史詩. *Chūgoku bungaku hō* 21 (1996): 1–56.

Kuriyama Masahiro 栗山雅央. "Sa Shi 'Santofu' wa naze Rakuyō no shika o takametaka" 左思三都賦は何故洛陽の紙価を貴めたか. *Chūgoku bungaku ronshū* 38 (2009): 20–33.

Lewis, Mark Edward. *The Construction of Space in Early China*. Albany: State University of New York, 2006. Pp. 238–44.

Pak Tong-sŏk 박동석 (朴東碩)."Chwasa wa Yŏngsasi" 좌사와 영사시 [左思和詠史詩]. *Chungguk munhak* 7 (1980): 22–32.

Wu Yun 吳雲. *Ershi shiji zhonggu wenxue yanjiu* 二十世紀中古文學研究. Tianjin: Tianjin guji chubanshe, 2004. Vol. 20, pp. 190–204.

Xu Chuanwu 徐傳武. *Zuo Si Zuo Fen yanjiu* 左思左棻研究. Beijing: Zhongguo wenlian chubanshe, 1999.

Xu Gongchi徐公持. *Wei Jin wenxue shi* 魏晉文學史. Beijing: Renmin wenxue chubanshe, 1999. Pp. 386–401.

Ye Riguang 葉日光. *Zuo Si shengping ji qi shi zhi xilun* 左思生平及其詩之析論. Taipei: Wen shi zhe chubanshe, 1979.

Yu Shiling 俞士玲. *Xi Jin wenxue kaolun* 西晉文學考論. Nanjing: Nanjing daxue chubanshe, 2008.

Translations

English

Birrell, Anne. "A Poem on a Dainty Girl." In *Chinese Love Poetry: New Songs from a Jade Terrace: A Medieval Anthology*, 100–101. London: Penguin Books, 1995.

Frodsham, J. D., with the collaboration of Cheng Hsi. "Summoning the Recluse" (nos. 1–2) and "Three Historical Poems" (nos. 2, 5, 6). In *An Anthology of Chinese Verse: Han, Wei, Chin and the Northern and Southern Dynasties*, 94–97. Oxford: Oxford University Press, 1967.

Knechtges, David. "Preface to the Three Capitals Rhapsody," "Shu Capital Rhapsody," "Wu Capital Rhapsody," "Wei Capital Rhapsody," and biographical sketch. In *Wen xuan, or Selections of Refined Literature*, 1:337–477, 483–84. Princeton, NJ: Princeton University Press, 1982.

Liu, James. "On History." In *The Chinese Knight-Errant*, 77–78. London: Routledge and Kegan Paul, 1967.

Owen, Stephen. "Calling to the Recluse" (no. 1). In *An Anthology of Chinese Literature: Beginnings to 1911*, 273. New York: W. W. Norton, 1996.

Schmidt, J. D. "Singing of History" (no. 6). In *Harmony Garden: The Life, Literary Criticism, and Poetry of Yuan Mei (1716–1798)*, 340. London: RoutledgeCurzon, 2003.

Waley, Arthur. "Day Dreams" (no. 1) and "The Scholar in the Narrow Street" (no. 8). In *Translation from the Chinese*, 74–75. New York: Alfred A. Knopf, 1941.

Warner, Ding Xiang. "Summoning the Recluse" (no. 1). In *A Wild Deer amid Soaring Phoenixes: The Opposition Poetics of Wang Ji*, 74–75. Honolulu: University of Hawai'i Press, 2003.

German

Zach, Erwin von, trans., and Ilse Martin Fang, ed. *Die chinesische Anthologie: Übersetzungen aus dem Wen hsüan*. 2 vols. Harvard-Yenching Institute Studies 18. Cambridge, MA: Harvard University Press, 1958. Vol. 1, pp. 44–92, 312–16, 332–33, 537.

French

Demiéville, Paul. *Anthologie de la poésie chinoise classique*. Paris: Gallimard, 1962. Pp. 131–32.

Chinese

Chen Hongtian 陳宏天, Zhao Fuhai 趙福海, and Chen Fuxing 陳復興. *Zhaoming Wen xuan yizhu* 昭明文選譯注. 6 vols. Changchun: Jilin wenshi chubanshe, 1988–1994. Vol. 1, pp. 222–365; vol. 3, pp. 146–60, 223–26, 980–81.

Zhang Baoquan 張葆全. *Yutai xinyong yizhu* 玉臺新詠譯注. Guilin: Guangxi shifan daxue chubanshe, 2007. Pp. 79–81.

Korean

Kang Pyŏng-ch'ŏl강병철 (姜秉喆). "Chwasa si yŏkchu"좌사시역주 [左思詩譯註]. *Chunggukŏmunhak yŏkch'ong* 4 (1996): 121–34.

———. "Chwasa pu yŏkchu"좌사부역주 [左思賦譯註]. *Chunggukŏmunhak* 5 (1996): 121–46.

Japanese

Obi Kōichi 小尾郊一 and Hanabusa Hideki 花房英樹. *Monzen* 文選. 7 vols. Tokyo: Shūeisha, 1974–1976. Vol. 1, pp. 233–365; vol. 3, pp. 180–96, 258–63; vol. 4, pp. 337–38.

Research aids

Liu Wenzhong 劉文忠. *Zuo Si, Liu Kun* 左思, 劉琨. Shenyang: Chunfeng wenyi chubanshe, 1999.

Zheng Xunzuo 鄭訓佐 and Zhang Chen 張晨. *Zuo Si yu Zuo Fen* 左思與左棻. Ji'nan: Shandong wenyi chubanshe, 2004.

Yue Zhang

APPENDIX I

Cross-References to Alternate Titles

Bao Canjun ji 鮑參軍集	*Bao Zhao ji* 鮑照集
Bao Mingyuan ji 鮑明遠集	*Bao Zhao ji* 鮑照集
Baoshi ji 鮑氏集	*Bao Zhao ji* 鮑照集
Bieben Shiliuguo chunqiu 別本十六國春秋	*Shiliuguo chunqiu* 十六國春秋
Cao Cao ji 曹操集	*Wei Wudi ji* 魏武帝集
Cao Zijian ji 曹子建集	*Cao Zhi ji* 曹植集
Cao Pi ji 曹丕集	*Wei Wendi ji* 魏文帝集
Chen Si wang ji 陳思王集	*Cao Zhi ji* 曹植集
Chenggong Zi'an ji 成公子安集	*Chenggong Sui ji* 成公綏集
Deyan 德言	*Liuzi* 劉子
Fu Chungu ji 傅鶉觚集	*Fu Xuan ji* 傅玄集
Fuzi 傅子	*Fu Xuan ji* 傅玄集
(Gaoseng) Faxian zhuan (高僧)法顯傳	*Foguo ji* 佛國記
Han Wei Liuchao baisan mingjia ji 漢魏六朝百三名家集	*Han Wei Liuchao baisanjia ji* 漢魏六朝百三家集
He Hengyangji 何衡陽集	*He Chengtian ji* 何承天集
He Jishi ji 何記室集	*He Xun ji* 何遜集
He Shuibu ji 何水部集	*He Xun ji* 何遜集
He Zhongyan ji 何仲言集	*He Xun ji* 何遜集
Huanyuan zhi 還冤志	*Huanyuan ji* 還冤記
Jianzhu Tao Yuanming ji 箋注陶淵明集	*Tao Yuanming ji* 陶淵明集

Cross-References to Alternate Titles

Jin Qiwangfu jishi Zuo Si ji 晉齊王府記室左思集   *Zuo Si ji* 左思集

Jin sikong Zhang Hua ji 晉司空張華集   *Zhang Hua ji* 張華集

Jin sili xiaowei Fu Xuan ji 晉司隸校尉傅玄集   *Fu Xuan ji* 傅玄集

Jing-Chu ji 荊楚記   *Jing-Chu suishi ji* 荊楚歲時記

Kong Zhanshi ji 孔詹事集   *Kong Zhigui ji* 孔稚珪集

Kongzhaozi 孔昭子   *Liuzi* 劉子

Liuzi 流子   *Liuzi* 劉子

Liuzi Xinlun 劉子新論   *Liuzi* 劉子

Liyou tianzhu jizhuan 歷遊天竺記傳   *Foguo ji* 佛國記

Lu Pingyuan ji 陸平原集   *Lu Ji ji* 陸機集

Lu Qinghe ji 陸清河集   *Lu Yun ji* 陸雲集

Lu Shiheng ji 陸士衡集   *Lu Ji ji* 陸機集

Lu Shiheng wenji 陸士衡文集   *Lu Ji ji* 陸機集

Maijing 脈經   *Wang Shuhe Maijing* 王叔和脈經

Niu Qizhang ji 牛奇章集   *Niu Hong ji* 牛弘集

Pan Anren ji 潘安仁集   *Pan Yue ji* 潘岳集

Pan Huangmen ji 潘黃門集   *Pan Yue ji* 潘岳集

Shi Hu Yezhong ji 石虎鄴中記   *Yezhong ji* 鄴中記

Shipaozi 石匏子   *Liuzi* 劉子

Shiyi lu 拾遺錄   *Shiyi ji* 拾遺記

Shu Guangwei ji 束廣微集   *Shu Xi ji* 束皙集

Song taiwei Yuan Shu ji 宋太尉袁淑集   *Yuan Shu ji* 袁淑集

Sun Tingwei ji 孫廷尉集   *Sun Chuo ji* 孫綽集

Tao Jingjie xiansheng shizhu 陶靖節先生詩注   *Tao Yuanming ji* 陶淵明集

Wang Zinian Shiyi ji 王子年拾遺記   *Shiyi ji* 拾遺記

Cross-References to Alternate Titles

Wei weiqing Ying Qu ji 魏衛卿應璩集
Wu Chaojing ji 吳朝請集
Xie Facao ji 謝法曹集
Xie Kangle ji 謝康樂集
Xie Xuancheng ji 謝宣城集
Xinlun 新論
Xun Gongceng ji 荀公曾集
Ying Xiulian ji 應休璉集
Yu Kaifu ji 庾開府集
Yu Zishan ji 庾子山集
Yuanhun zhi 冤魂志
Yuan Zhongxian ji 袁忠憲集
Yuan Yangyuan ji 袁陽源集
Yunmenzi 雲門子
Zhang Maoxian ji 張茂先集
Zhang Sikong ji 張司空集
Zhang Zhangshi ji 張長史集
Zhaoming taizi wenji 昭明太子文
Zuo Taichong ji 左太沖集

Ying Qu ji 應璩集
Wu Jun ji 吳均集
Xie Huilian ji 謝惠連集
Xie Lingyun ji 謝靈運集
Xie Tiao ji 謝朓集
Liuzi 劉子
Xun Xu ji 荀勖集
Ying Qu ji 應璩集
Yu Xin ji 庾信集
Yu Xin ji 庾信集
Huanyuan ji 還冤記
Yuan Shu ji 袁淑集
Yuan Shu ji 袁淑集
Liuzi 劉子
Zhang Hua ji 張華集
Zhang Hua ji 張華集
Zhang Rong ji 張融集
Xiao Tong ji 蕭統集
Zuo Si ji 左思集

APPENDIX II

Common Literary Genres

1. Admonition (*zhen* 箴)
2. Command (*ling* 令)
3. Communication (*qi* 啟)
4. Condolence (*diaowen* 弔文)
5. Declaration (*zhang* 章)
6. Dirge (*lei* 誄)
7. Discourse (*shuo* 說)
8. Disquisition (*lun* 論)
9. Edict (*zhao* 詔)
10. Elegy (*sao* 騷)
11. Encomium (*zan* 贊)
12. Epigram, linked pearls (*lianzhu* 連珠)
13. Epitaph (*bei* 碑, *bei wen* 碑文)
14. Eulogy or Hymn (*song* 頌)
15. Grave memoir (*muzhi* 墓誌, *muzhi ming* 墓誌銘)
16. Inscription (*ming* 銘)
17. Instruction (*jiao* 教)
18. Lament (*ai* 哀)
19. Letter, personal (*shu* 書); *see also* Memorandum
20. Linked verse (*lianju* 連句/聯句)
21. Lyric poetry (*shi* 詩)
22. Memorandum, official letter (*jian* 箋/牋)
23. Memorial: *see* Declaration; Petition

Common Literary Genres

24. Music Bureau poetry, ballad (*yuefu* 樂府)
25. Offering (*ji* 祭, *jiwen* 祭文)
26. Opinion (*yi* 議)
27. Petition (*biao* 表)
28. Presentation, note of presentation (*zou* 奏, *zou ji* 奏記)
29. Preface (*xu* 序)
30. Proclamation (*xi* 檄)
31. Rhapsody, rhyme-prose, exposition (*fu* 賦)

APPENDIX III

Frequently Cited Sources and Collectanea

The following titles are marked with an asterisk on their first occurrence in an entry. Imprint information is provided only in this appendix. The editions listed here were selected because they were the most conveniently available to the editors; they are not being recommended as the most authoritative.

Chongwen zongmu 崇文總目 (1034–1041), by Wang Yaochen 王堯臣 (1001–1056) et al.
   Recension prepared by Qian Dongyuan 錢東垣 (d. 1824) et al., Jiading Qin shi kanben 嘉定秦氏刊本, 1799.
   Taipei: Guangwen shuju, 1968. 2 vols. Facsimile reproduction of the Yueyatang congshu 粵雅堂叢書 ed. (1853), with notes (jishi 輯釋) by Qiao Yanguan 喬衍琯. In the Shumu xubian 書目續編 series.

Congshu jicheng 叢書集成 collectanea. Shanghai: Shangwu yinshuguan, 1935–1937. Over 4,100 titles in 3,467 volumes. Reprinted as *Congshu jicheng xinbian* 新編, Taipei: Xinwenfeng chubanshe, 1986.

Guoxue jiben congshu 國學基本叢書 series. Shanghai: Shangwu yinshuguan, 1929–1941. 400 titles. Reprint, Taipei: Taiwan shangwu yinshuguan, 1968.

Gushi ji 古詩紀 (1557), also titled *Shi ji* 詩紀, compiled by Feng Weine 馮惟訥 (1513–1572).
   Taipei: Taiwan shangwu yinshuguan, [1983]. In *Yingyin Wenyuange Siku quanshu**, 1379–80:1–702.

Han Wei Liuchao ershiyi mingjia ji 漢魏六朝二十一名家集, compiled by Wang Shixian 汪士賢 (dates unknown) during the Wanli era (1573–1620). Photofacsimile of 1583 ed. of *Han Wei Liuchao zhujia wenji* 漢魏六朝諸家文集/*Han Wei zhuming jiaji* 漢魏諸名家集.
   Reprinted in the *Siku quanshu cunmu congshu bubian**.

Junzhai dushu zhi 郡齋讀書志, compiled by Chao Gongwu 晁公武 (ca. 1104–1183), preface dated 1151. Additions by Yao Yingji 姚應績 (1249), addendum in 2 *juan* by Zhao Xibian 趙希弁 (fl. mid-thirteenth century), collation notes, table of contents, and erratum by Wang Xianqian 王先謙 (1842–1917).
   Shanghai: Shanghai guji chubanshe, 1990 (2006 printing), with Sun Meng's 孫猛 collation notes (*jiaozheng* 校證). 2 vols.

Liang wen ji 梁文紀, compiled by Mei Dingzuo 梅鼎祚 (1549–1615).
   In *Yingyin Wenyuange Siku quanshu**, vol. 1399.

Liuchao shiji 六朝詩集 (1543), compiled by Xue Yingqi 薛應旂 (*jinshi* 1535).

Frequently Cited Sources and Collectanea

Photo-facsimile of a Jiajing era (1522–1566) woodblock ed. *Xuxiu Siku quanshu**, vol. 1589.

Qishi'er jia ji 七十二家集, compiled by Zhang Xie 張燮 (1574–1640).
Photo-facsimile of a late-Ming woodblock ed. *Xuxiu Siku quanshu**, vols. 1583–88.

Quan Han Sanguo Jin Nanbeichao shi 全漢三國晉南北朝詩, compiled by Ding Fubao 丁福保 (1874–1952). Taipei: Yiwen yinshuguan, 1975. 3 vols.

Ricang Hongren ben Wenguan cilin jiaozheng 日藏弘仁本文館詞林校證 (658), compiled by Xu Jingzong 許敬宗 (592–672) et al., edited by Luo Guowei 羅國威. Beijing: Zhonghua shuju, 2001. This is a revised *Wenguan cilin**, based on additional material found in Japan.

Shi tong 史通, by Liu Zhiji 劉知幾 (661–721). *Shitong tongshi* 史通通釋, annotated by Pu Qilong 浦起龍 (1679–ca. 1762).
Shanghai: Shanghai guji chubanshe, 1978. 2 vols.

Sibu beiyao 四部備要 collectanea.
Shanghai: Zhonghua shuju, 1920–1933. Reprints: Taipei: Zhonghua shuju, 1966–1975; Shanghai: Zhonghua shuju, 1990. 336 titles, 2,500 *ce*. Typeset in an imitation Song-style font, which readily identifies the set.

Sibu congkan 四部叢刊 collectanea.
Shanghai: Shangwu yinshuguan: (1) *chubian* 初編, 1919–1922; (2) *xubian* 續編, 1934; (3) *sanbian* 三編, 1936. 504 titles in 3,112 *ce*. Photo-facsimiles of earliest editions all reduced to the same size.

Siku quanshu 四庫全書.

A multifaceted project begun in 1772, one result of which was the selection of 3,461 works considered to be the most important. Seven sets of handwritten copies were deposited at various sites in the empire. One of these, that of the Wenjinge 文津閣, is in the National Library, Beijing, while another, that of the Wenyuange 文淵閣, is in the Palace Museum, Taipei. The latter has been printed in facsimile but reduced size. See *Yingyin Wenyuange Siku quanshu*.

Siku quanshu cunmu congshu bubian 四庫全書存目叢書補編. Ji'nan: Qi Lu shushe, 2001.

Siku quanshu zhenben congshu 四庫全書珍本叢書. A selection of 231 of the rarest of the *Siku quanshu* titles reprinted by photo-facsimile reproduction; 105 of these are the collected writings of individuals.
Shanghai: Shangwu yinshuguan, 1934–1935. 231 titles in 1960 *ce*.

Siku quanshu zongmu 四庫全書總目.
See *Siku quanshu zongmu tiyao*.

Siku quanshu zongmu tiyao 四庫全書總目提要. Dai Zhen 戴震 (1724–1777) et al., 1782. An annotated bibliography of the 3,461 works included in the *Siku quanshu* as well as another 6,793 others, making 10,254 in all.
Taipei: Taiwan shangwu yinshuguan, 1968. In the *Guoxue jiben congshu* series.

Suichutang shumu 遂初堂書目, compiled by You Mou 尤袤 (1127–1194).
In *Yingyin Wenyuange Siku quanshu** 674:435–90.

Also in *Baibu congshu jicheng* 百部叢書集成, edited by Yan Yiping 嚴一萍. Taipei: Yiwen yinshuguan, 1965–1970.

Taishō shinshū Daizōkyō 大正新修大藏經, edited by Takakusu Junjirō 高楠順次郎 (1866–1945) and Watanabe Kaigyoku 渡邊海旭 (1872–1932). Tokyo: Taishō shinshū Daizōkyō kankōkai, 1924–1932; rpt., 1962 (85 and 15 vols.). Vols. 1–85, the Chinese Buddhist Canon; 86–100, supplementary materials by modern Japanese scholars. Photolithographic rpt., Taipei: Xinwenfeng chuban gongsi, 1983; rpt. with index (vol. 101), Taipei: Caituan faren Fotuo jiaoyu jijinhui, 2001. Digital text in SAT Daizōkyō Text Database and the Chinese Buddhist Electronic Text Association.

Tong zhi 通志, by Zheng Qiao 鄭樵 (1104–1162). 200 *juan*.
In the *Shitong* 十通, Wanyou wenku 萬有文庫 series, Shanghai: Shangwu yinshuguan, 1935–1937.

Wenguan cilin 文館詞林 (658), compiled by Xu Jingzong 許敬宗 (592–672) et al.
In *Xuxiu Siku quanshu** 1582:403–561. This is a reprint of the *Shiyuan congshu* 適園叢書 edition.

Wenxian tongkao 文獻通考, compiled by Ma Duanlin 馬端臨 (1254–1325).
In the *Shitong* 十通, Wanyou wenku 萬有文庫 series, Shanghai: Shangwu yinshuguan, 1935–1937.

Wenyuan yinghua 文苑英華, compiled 983–986 by Li Fang 李昉 (925–996) et al.
Taipei: Huawen shudian, 1965. Photo-offset from a 1567 woodblock edition, with additional material. 13 vols.

Xian Qin Han Wei Jin Nanbeichao shi 先秦漢魏晉南北朝詩, compiled by Lu Qinli 逯欽立 (1911–1973). Beijing: Zhonghua shuju, 1983. 3 vols.

Xuxiu Siku quanshu 續修四庫全書.
Shanghai: Shanghai guji chubanshe, 1995–2002. 1,800 titles and subtitles.
A collectanea of works not included in the original *Siku quanshu* as well as a selection of subsequent titles down to the end of the Qing.

Yingyin Wenyuange Siku quanshu 景印文淵閣四庫全書.
Taipei: Shangwu yinshuguan, 1983–1986. 1,500 vols.
Photo-facsimile of the Wenyuange copy of the *Siku quanshu* in the possession of the Palace Museum, Taipei. Each page represents two leaves of the original *Siku quanshu*.

Yongle dadian 永樂大典 (1403–1408), compiled by Xie Jin 解縉 (1369–1415), Yao Guangxiao 姚廣孝 (1335–1418), et al., 1403–1408. 22,877 and 60 *juan* in 11,095 manuscript volumes.
Ji'nan: Qi Lu shushe, 2001. 15 vols. Photo-facsimile of 742 surviving *juan*.

Yu hai 玉海, compiled by Wang Yinglin 王應麟 (1223–1296).
Taipei: Hualian chubanshe, 1964. 8 vols. This is a photo-facsimile of a 1337 woodblock edition, two double pages on one page.

Zhizhai shulu jieti 直齋書錄解題 (ca. 1235), compiled by Chen Zhensun 陳振孫 (fl. 1211–1249). 22 *juan*.
Shanghai: Shanghai guji chubanshe, 1987. Index to titles, 1–75; index to authors, 78–128.

Frequently Cited Sources and Collectanea

The standard histories

Shi ji	史記	Beijing: Zhonghua shuju, 1959. 10 vols.
Han shu	漢書	Beijing: Zhonghua shuju, 1962. 12 vols.
Hou Han shu	後漢書	Beijing: Zhonghua shuju, 1965. 12 vols.
Sanguo zhi	三國志	Beijing: Zhonghua shuju, 1962. 5 vols.
Jin shu	晉書	Beijing: Zhonghua shuju, 1974. 10 vols.
Song shu	宋書	Beijing: Zhonghua shuju, 1974. 8 vols.
Nan Qi shu	南齊書	Beijing: Zhonghua shuju, 1972. 3 vols.
Liang shu	梁書	Beijing: Zhonghua shuju, 1973. 3 vols.
Chen shu	陳書	Beijing: Zhonghua shuju, 1972. 2 vols.
Wei shu	魏書	Beijing: Zhonghua shuju, 1973. 8 vols.
Bei Qi shu	北齊書	Beijing: Zhonghua shuju, 1973. 2 vols.
Zhou shu	周書	Beijing: Zhonghua shuju, 1971. 3 vols.
Sui shu	隋書	Beijing: Zhonghua shuju, 1973. 6 vols.
Nan shi	南史	Beijing: Zhonghua shuju, 1975. 6 vols.
Bei shi	北史	Beijing: Zhonghua shuju, 1974. 10 vols.
Jiu Tang shu	舊唐書	Beijing: Zhonghua shuju, 1975. 16 vols.
Xin Tang shu	新唐書	Beijing: Zhonghua shuju, 1975. 20 vols.
Jiu Wudai shi	舊五代史	Beijing: Zhonghua shuju, 1976. 6 vols.
Xin Wudai shi	新五代史	Beijing: Zhonghua shuju, 1974. 3 vols.
Song shi	宋史	Beijing: Zhonghua shuju, 1977. 40 vols.
Liao shi	遼史	Beijing: Zhonghua shuju, 1974. 5 vols.
Jin shi	金史	Beijing: Zhonghua shuju, 1975. 8 vols.
Yuan shi	元史	Beijing: Zhonghua shuju, 1976. 15 vols.
Ming shi	明史	Beijing: Zhonghua shuju, 1974. 28 vols.

APPENDIX IV

Textual Transmission of the Standard Histories

There are few manuscript remains of the histories that predate the period of printing that began in the Song. Portions of Jin dynasty manuscripts of the *Sanguo zhi* have been found in Xinjiang; one of these manuscripts is reproduced in the Zhonghua shuju edition of that history. An abbreviated version of a portion of the *Jin shu* was recovered at Dunhuang by Aurel Stein. Full texts of the histories become available only with the advent of woodblock printing in the Song.

The Song Imperial Academy (Guozijian 國子監; termed the "Directorate of Education" by some authors), in addition to its other duties, was very active in printing books. By some counts over 140 titles were produced, but there were undoubtedly many more. The full range of books was included, and the histories were given full due. From the introduction of printing, some histories were printed individually, but the usual practice was to produce the standard histories in a set. The term "standard histories" (*zhengshi* 正史), used at least as early as the Liang, came into general use in the Song to designate the basic annals-account style. The early Song set of Fifteen Histories (Shiwushi 十五史) was produced in four stages. The first was completed from 994 to 999 (Chunhua 淳化 5 to Xianping 咸平 2) and included the *Shi ji* 史記, *Han shu* 漢書, and *Hou Han shu* 後漢書. During the next stage, 1000 to 1023 (Xianping 咸平 3 to Tiansheng 天聖 1), the *Sanguo zhi* 三國志 and *Jin shu* 晉書 appeared. In the third stage, 1024 to 1058 (Tiansheng 天聖 2 to Jiayou 嘉佑 3), the *Nan shi* 南史, *Bei shi* 北史, and *Sui shu* 隋書 were printed. Finally, in the fourth stage, the most productive, from 1059 to around 1072 (Jiayou 嘉佑 4 to Xining 熙寧 5), the printing of the *Song shu* 宋書, *Nan Qi shu* 南齊書, *Liang shu* 梁書, *Chen shu* 陳書, *Wei shu* 魏書, *Bei Qi shu* 北齊書, and *Zhou shu* 周書 was completed. In addition, two newly compiled histories, the *Xin Tang shu* 新唐書 and *Xin Wudai shu* 新五代史, both compiled by Ouyang Xiu 歐陽脩 (1007–1072), were printed in 1060 and 1072, respectively. This set, now of Seventeen Histories (Shiqishi 十七史), is often referred to simply as the 994 edition.

For the Song editions of the seven histories falling within the Six Dynasties period, the *Song shu*, *Qi shi*, *Liang shu*, *Chen shu*, *Bei Wei shu*, *Bei Qi shu*, and *Zhou shu*, the *Junzhai dushu zhi* 郡齋讀書志 by Chao Gongwu 晁公武, preface dated 1151 (Shaoxing 紹興 21), has additional information. According to Chao, in 1061 (Jiayou 嘉佑 6) manuscript copies of these seven histories that were stored in the imperial library, and in deplorable condition, were consigned to the officials of the learned academies who served in editorial and compilation capacities (*guange guan* 館閣官)

to repair, collate, and correct errors. Those involved in this effort included Zeng Gong 曾鞏 (1019–1083), who presented completed copies of the *Nan Qi shu*, *Liang shu*, and *Chen shu* from 1064 to 1067 (Yeping 治平 1–4), Liu Shu 劉恕 (1032–1078), who worked on the *Bei Wei shu*, and Wang Anguo 王安國 (1028–1074) and Lin Xi 林希, the *Zhou shu*, probably completed between 1068 and 1074 (Xining 熙寧 1–7). Although the capital of the Song was at Kaifeng, Wang Guowei maintained that most if not all of the actual printing was done at Hangzhou. It was only in the Zhenghe 政和 period (1111–1118) that the project was completed, the books had been printed for the first time, and copies were distributed to all the officials concerned with education in the provinces. Very few copies were made available to the general population, and perhaps for that reason none has survived.

In 1144 (Shaoxing 紹興 14), early in the Southern Song, Jing Du 井度 (styled Xianmeng 憲孟), an official in Sichuan, called on the various provincial offices untouched by the wars to forward to him the copies of the histories that had been distributed earlier. Even in that short time, the condition of the histories had deteriorated, but a complete set was put together, except for ten *juan* of the *Bei Wei shu*. Finally, a copy of that work with the missing part was found in the collection of a certain Yuwen Jimeng 宇文季孟, and the seven histories were complete. We know these details because the *Junzhai dushu zhi* by Chao Gongwu grew out of his catalog of Jing Du's own library. Blocks were then cut for these seven histories and printed at Meishan 眉山, a short distance southwest of Chengdu. This edition is known as the Song Shu edition (Song Shu ben 宋蜀本), or the Meishan Seven Histories edition (Meishan qishi ben 眉山七史本), and is also known as the "Shu Large Character" (*Shu dazi* 蜀大字) edition. That name was derived from the expansive format; in the case of the histories, only nine lines to the page with eighteen characters to the line, which made this set and other Meishan editions famous. In addition, these Southern Song Sichuan imprints were carefully collated, the characters finely cut in excellent style, and the ink an even color.[1] This seven histories edition was also included with other histories, which by now had grown to be a Seventeen Histories set.

The Yuan imprint of the Seventeen Histories was based on the Song dynasty Shu Large Character edition and begun in 1305, during the Dade 大德 era (1297–1307). The task of collating and printing the histories was distributed among nine of the routes (*lu* 路) under the Yuan's administration of Jiangzhe Province's Jiangdong Jiankang circuit (Jiangdong Jiankang dao 江東建康道). Whereas the original plan was to include all seventeen standard histories of the time, only nine were completed, of which five of those histories are covered in this bibliographic guide. The Ningguo 寧國 route, whose seat was in Xuancheng 宣城, Anhui, took on the *Hou Han shu*, Chizhou 池州, the *Sanguo zhi*, Raozhou 饒州, the *Sui shu*, and Xinzhou 信州, the *Bei shi*. The *Nan shi* was undertaken by the Tongchuan 桐川 Academy, which may have been in either the Guangde 廣德 or Qianshan 鉛善 route. The

---

[1] Guo Moruo 郭沫若, "Xinjiang xinchutu de Jinren xieben *Sanguo zhi* canjuan" 新疆新出土的晉人寫本三國志殘卷, *Wenwu* (1972.8): 2–6.

academic offices (*ruxue* 儒學) of these places occur in the names of the editions of the individual histories, which collectively are known as the Dade Nine Route (Dade jiulu 大德九路) imprint, although the final stage may have gone beyond the Dade period.[2] There were other cooperative printings during the Yuan. The Yuan's Jiangxi province's *Sui shu*, for example, was printed again in 1332 in the Ruizhou 瑞周 route, with nine lines per page, as against the ten of the Dade edition.[3]

As new histories were compiled under state sponsorship they were added to the official set. By 1346, in the late Yuan, the *Liao shi*, *Song shi*, and *Jin shi* had appeared.[4] In the Ming, a history of the Yuan was added, bringing the potential number to twenty-one.

In 1368, at the very start of the Ming, the Yuan imperial collection as well as the printing blocks were moved into the Imperial Academy in Nanjing. These of course included Song editions, among them that of the famous Meishan Seven Histories. By then the blocks had suffered much damage and had been repaired during the Yuan. The actual number of blocks for each history was recorded at the time.[5]

Shen Lin 沈麟 in 1528 (Jiajing 嘉靖 7) requested that a new edition of the standard histories be made on the basis of a wide search for excellent imprints, but this was considered inconvenient; instead, the old editions already in the Nanjing Academy collection were to be mended and printed, and the sets sent out for wide distribution.[6] This series consisted of the Seventeen Histories, among which were seven of the Meishan histories and ten of various routes of the Yuan academic offices. However, the dates of imprints of individual histories stretch on for as much as sixty years.[7] The set of the Twenty-one Histories as a whole was printed again

---

[2] Zhao Zhen 趙真, "Stein 1393 hao wenshu *Jin shu* liezhuan canjuanba" 斯坦因1393號文書晉書列傳殘卷跋, *Guji zhengli yanjiu xuekan* 6 (November 2007): 28–30.

[3] The preface to the Zhonghua shuju edition of the *Hou Han shu*, p. 3, speaks of the 994 edition and another of 1005 (Jingde 景德 2), neither of which included the thirty *juan* of monographs by Sima Biao 司馬彪 (240–306); these were added in a 1022 (Qianxing 乾興 1) edition. The *Hou Han shu* was included with the *Shi ji* and *Han shu* in the Three Histories (Sanshi 三史), or with the *Sanguo zhi* in the Four Histories (Sishi 四史); since they were considered the epitome of historical writing, they would have been printed more frequently than the other, later Six Dynasties histories.

[4] Cao Zhi 曹之, *Zhongguo guji banbenxue* 中國古籍版本學 (Wuhan: Wuhan daxue chubanshe, 1992; 2nd ed., 2007, p. 181). For another version of the composition of the Seventeen Histories, see Li Bohua 李伯華, *Zhengshi yuanliu kao* 正史源流考, in *Gudian wenxian yanjiu jikan* 古典文獻研究輯刊 33, p. 61 (Taipei: Huamulan wenhua gongzuofang, 2005).

[5] Recent edition: Taipei: Guangwen shuju, 1967; see especially 5.6a–b, but also passim. This is a facsimile reproduction of a Changsha edition with some additional notes by Wang Xianqian 王先謙 (1842–1917) and Qiao Yanguan 喬衍琯 and is in that press's Shumu xubian 書目續編 series. See also Endymion Wilkinson, *Chinese History: A Manual*, Harvard Yenching Institute Monograph Series 52 (Cambridge, MA: Harvard University Press, 2000), 450n8.

[6] For an impressive study of the nature of such collational efforts during the Song, see Susan Cherniack, "Book Culture and Textual Transmission in Sung China," *Harvard Journal of Asiatic Studies* 54.1 (1994): 5–125.

[7] Wang Guowei 王國維, *Liang Zhe gu kanben kao* 兩浙古刊本考, in his *Min Shu Zhe Yue*

between the years 1594 and 1606 (Wanli 萬曆 22–34) at the Northern Academy at Beijing and is known accordingly as the Beijian 北監.[8] There has been some criticism of the quality of the editions of the Northern Academy and Southern Academy in Nanjing.[9] Still, there were exceptions: their *Sanguo zhi* is considered excellent. Since there is a clear filiation of editions from the Song through the Yuan to the Ming, this set of the Twenty-one Histories has been labeled the Three Dynasties (Sanchao 三朝) edition.[10]

Publications by private, nonofficial individuals flourished in the Ming, and one of the most eminent such publishers was Mao Jin 毛晉 (1599–1659) at his Jiguge 汲古閣 Library. Among his numerous publications was a set of the Seventeen Histories printed during the years 1628 to 1644 (Chongzhen 崇禎 1–17) and reprinted with reconditioned blocks from 1648 to 1656 (Shunzhi 順治 5–13). Apparently, the Jiguge publication was based on the Ming Northern Academy edition; this is known as the "Ji edition" after the name of his library.

The Ming Imperial Academy editions of the histories continued to be printed in the Qing dynasty (1644–1912), with either the original blocks or those that were repaired. For example, Feng Rujing 馮如京 (1602–1669) had the Twenty-one Histories reprinted in 1650. Individual histories were printed individually as well, such as the *Liang shu* and the *Sui shu* in 1700.[11]

By the Qing, the number of dynastic histories had increased. In 1739, a new printing of the Twenty-one Histories was initiated at the Wuyingdian 武英殿 within the Imperial Palace, drawing on the Ming Northern Academy edition in the Imperial Academy, but two new histories were added, the *Ming shi* 明史 and the *Jiu Tang shu* 舊唐書, bringing the number to twenty-three; the set was printed by 1747.[12] The recovery by Shao Jinhan 邵晉涵 (1743–1796) of the *Jiu Wudai shi* 舊五代史 from the *Yongle dadian* 永樂大典 and other works added another history, printed by 1784, making this the Twenty-four Histories (*Ershisishi* 二十四史), referred to as the "Siku quanshu" or, alternatively, as the Dian ben or Palace edition. The Jinling shuju 金陵書局, Nanjing, and other branches of the consortium of the Wushengguan shuju 五省官書局 under the patronage of Zeng Guofan 曾國藩 (1811–1872) cooperated in publishing a set of the Twenty-four Histories from 1864 to 1875, based on the Jiguge texts with others added, and using where possible the

---

keshu congkao 閩蜀浙粵刻書叢考 (Beijing: Beijing tushuguan chubanshe, 2003), 142. Wang cites an edict dated 28 October 1061 that authorized this project.

[8] Liu Shaoquan 劉少泉, "Tang Song Shuke banben shulüe" 唐宋蜀刻版本述略, *Sichuan daxue xuebao* (1989.4): 108–9.

[9] Cao Zhi, *Zhongguo guji banbenxue*, 222–24.

[10] K. T. Wu, "Chinese Printing under the Four Alien Dynasties," *Harvard Journal of Asiatic Studies* 13 (1950): 464–69.

[11] Wu, "Chinese Printing under the Four Alien Dynasties," 472–73.

[12] Li Bohua, *Zhengshi yuanliu kao*, p. 61, citing Gu Yanwu 顧炎武 (1613–1682), *Rizhilu* 日知錄, *Guoxue jiben congshu* ed. (Taipei: Taiwan Shangwu yinshuguan, 1956), vol. 3, 3b; *juan* 18, p. 97. Li Mingjie 李明杰, "Mingdai Guozijian keshu kaolüe (*shang*)" 明代國子監刻書考略 (上), *Daxue tushuguan xuebao* 27.3 (2009): 87–88.

blocks surviving from the Song. The fourteen histories from the *Shi ji* through the *Bei shi* were assigned to the Jinling shuju; the Huainan shuju 淮南書局 handled the *Sui shu*, and the other three members of the consortium printed the later histories. This edition is sometimes designated the Wuzhou shuju 五洲書局 or Ju 局 edition, or the Jiangnan shuju 江南書局 edition, Jiangnan being a later name taken by the Jinling shuju.[13] What is now known as the Jinling edition is a movable-type production by that press. A lithographic reproduction of the Palace Twenty-four Histories by the Tongwen shuju 同文書局, Shanghai, 1894, introduced a new methodology in printing the histories. The preceding description by no means exhausts the various printings of the histories during the Qing dynasty; other designations refer to copies of this or that history included in private collections.

In more recent years, the Baina ben 百納本, or "Hundred Patch," edition of the Twenty-four Histories (taking its name from the "hundred patch" robes of Buddhist monks) was an ambitious project to reproduce by photolithography the oldest copy of each of the histories. This was published from 1930 to 1937 by the Shangwu yinshuguan (Commercial Press) as a part of its enormous *Sibu congkan* reprint series. The editions used are all Song and Yuan prints except, of course, for the last few items. The *Hou Han shu*, *Sanguo zhi*, and *Jin shu* simply say "Song edition" or "Shaoxing edition," the *Song shu*, *Nan Qi shu*, *Liang shu*, *Bei Wei shu*, *Bei Qi shu*, and *Zhou shu* all were of the Shu Large Character edition, while the *Sui shu*, *Nan shi*, and *Bei shi* were of the Yuan Dade edition. This is an excellent series and was long used by many scholars as the basic edition for *juan* and page references in their publications. For the Six Dynasties histories treated here, a Renshou 仁壽 edition, published in Taiwan from 1955 to 1956, differed from the Baina ben only for the *Hou Han shu* and *Jin shu*; the other histories were based on the Baina ben without giving proper credits, citing as their basis nomenclature for the editions that differed from the Baina ben when it was obvious they had simply photographed the Baina ben. For example, rather than using the term "Shu Large Character edition," the term used was "Shaoxing-period Jiangnan recut of the Northern Song Academy edition," which amounts to the same thing. It may be that it was felt the more expansive description was more meaningful. The sources listed in colophons by the two editions are as follows:

---

[13] Li Mingjie, "Mingdai Guozijian keshu kaolüe (shang)," 85. According to Li Bohua, *Zhengshi yuanliu kao*, 61, citing Gu Yanwu, at the beginning of the Jiajing era (1522–1566) the head of the Nanjing Academy Zhang Bangqi 張邦奇 (1484–1544) was also involved with the request to initiate the new printing. This initial project was completed and presented to the emperor in 1532; it is known as the Nanjian 南監 edition. Li Mingjie, "Mingdai Guozijian keshu kaolüe (shang)," 87, cites Liu Zhizheng 柳詒徵, "Nanjian shitan" 南監史談, in his *Liu Zhizheng shixue lunwenji* 柳詒徵史學論文集 (Shanghai: Shanghai guji chubanshe, 1991), 181–206, that the Imperial Academy edition of the Twenty-one Histories was printed from blocks that included seven of the histories from Song blocks, ten from the Yuan, two redone in the Ming from the Yuan, and two newly made in the Ming, blocks that were brought together from Jiangnan, Sichuan, Guangdong, and Beiping. Li has a table (p. 88) that gives in great detail the source of the blocks and their number, including how many were missing, for each of the Ming Imperial Academy Twenty-one Histories.

	Baina ben editions	Renshou editions
Hou Hanshu	Song Shaoxing 紹興 (1131–1162)	Southern Song Futang commandery academy (Futang junxiang 福唐郡庠) reprint of a Northern Song Chunhua 淳化 (990–994) Imperial Academy edition
Sanguo zhi	Song Shaoxi 紹熙 (1190–1194) edition, supplemented by a Shaoxing edition for a missing three *juan*	Southern Song Shaoxi edition with Shaoxing Quzhou 衢州 edition to supplement it
Jin shu	Song edition and Song edition of the Jiangsu Provincial Guoxue Library for the *zaji*	嘉業 (nonexistent period title) recut edition
Song shu	Song Shu Large Character edition supplemented with a Yuan-Ming repaired imprint	Shaoxing Jiangnan recut Northern Song Imperial Academy edition
Nan Qi shu	Song Shu Large Character edition	Shaoxing Jiangnan recut Northern Song Imperial Academy edition
Liang shu	Song Shu Large Character edition supplemented with a Yuan-Ming repaired imprint	Shaoxing Jiangnan recut Northern Song Imperial Academy edition
Wei shu	Song Shu Large Character edition	Shaoxing Jiangnan recut Northern Song Imperial Academy edition
Bei Qi shu	Song Shu Large Character edition supplemented with a Yuan-Ming repaired imprint	Shaoxing Jiangnan recut Northern Song Imperial Academy edition
Zhou shu	Song Shu Large Character edition supplemented with a Yuan-Ming repaired imprint	Shaoxing Jiangnan recut Northern Song Imperial Academy edition
Sui shu	Yuan Dade	Yuan Xinzhou route school (Xinzhou lu xue) 信州路學 edition
Nan shi	Yuan Dade	Yuan Dade
Bei shi	Yuan Dade	Yuan Xinzhou route school edition

There are a number of other printings that were meant to fit a niche for convenient and less-expensive editions. The Kaiming shudian 開明書店, Shanghai, in 1935 published the Twenty-five Histories (including the *Xin Yuanshi* 新元史 added in 1921) in nine volumes, with extremely small characters in four registers across the page, convenient for visually scanning text in the days before digital indexing. The set was reprinted by the same publisher in Taipei in 1965. The Yiwen Press in Taipei from 1956 to 1958 issued a photolithographed reprint of the Qing dynasty Wuyingdian edition of the Twenty-four Histories, in two registers per page. The same edition, but with punctuation added (hence the term *duanjuben* 斷句本 in the title), was issued by the Xinwenfeng chuban gongsi, Taipei, in 1975. Consecutive page numbers and some textual emendations were added. The discussion by Qian Daxin 錢大昕 (1728–1804), in his *Nian'er shi kaoyi* 廿二史考異, is appended to each appropriate history.

The most recent edition of the Twenty-five Histories, one that has become the standard for citations, is that published by the Zhonghua shuju in Beijing, 1959–1974 (see appendix III herein for a list of the histories with specific years of publication and number of volumes). This is a punctuated, fully collated text, with new introductions setting forth the history of each history. The traditional commentaries are included as well. While the introductions to the individual histories lay out in detail what editions and other sources were used in the collations, some contain the statement that differences among the various editions used in the collation are noted only when in the opinion of the collators such variations are significant. While the collation was directed by some of China's leading scholars, including Gu Jiegang 顧頡剛 (1893–1980), He Ziquan (Ho Tse-chuan) 何茲全 (1911–2011), Wang Zhongluo 王仲犖 (1913–1986), and others, decisions as to which text is correct are still a value judgment, and those using the histories for research may well want at times to check the various earlier editions and commentaries to make their own decisions. The latest development is the digitalization of the histories.

(A) Research Centre for Chinese Ancient Texts (Zhongguo guji yanjiu zhongxin 中國古籍研究中心) of the Chinese University of Hong Kong, under the direction of D. C. Lau, has produced an electronic database of hundreds of texts under the title "Chinese Ancient Texts," hence the acronym CHANT. While the corpus includes many Six Dynasty historical texts, the only standard histories are the *Hou Han shu*, *Sanguo zhi*, *Song shu*, *Nan Qi shu*, and *Wei shu*.

(B) Academia Sinica, Taiwan, maintains Scripta Sinica (Hanji dianzi wenxian ziliao ku 漢籍電子文獻資料庫), which includes all the standard histories.

(C) The *Siku quanshu* 四庫全書 has also been digitized and of course contains all the histories. See http://tw.subscriptionv3.skqs.com/skqs/download/.

Reference works

Wilkinson, *Chinese History*, p. 509, cites the following as important studies of the standard histories, commenting, comparing, and correcting. These are invaluable in helping to solve problems.

Wang Mingsheng 王鳴盛 (1722–1797). *Shiqishi shangque* 十七史商榷. 1787. Punctuated edition, Shanghai: Shangwu yinshuguan, 1937, and many reprints.

Zhao Yi 趙翼 (1722–1814). *Nian'ershi zhaji* 廿二史劄記. 1799. Shanghai: Shijie shuju, 1936. There are many reprints and also editions with critical notes by Wang Shumin 王樹民 and Du Weiyun 杜維運, both eminent historians.

Qian Daxin 錢大昕 (1728–1804). *Nian'ershi kaoyi* 廿二史考異. 1782. Shanghai: Shangwu yinshuguan, 1937. There are many other editions.

The works by Wang and Zhao are indexed in Saeki Tomi 佐伯富. *Chūgoku zuihitsu zatcho sakuin* 中國隨筆雜著索引. Tokyo: Nihon gakujutsu shinkōkai, 1954.

Finally, the *kanbun* edition of the Twenty-one Histories, with pronunciation, punctuation, and diacritical and syntactic markers, based on the Ming Southern Academy edition, and prepared by Ogyū Sorai 荻生徂徠 (1666–1728) and others is very useful: *Wakokubon seishi* 和刻本正史. Tokyo: Koten kenkyūkai, Kyūko shoin (hatsubai), 1971.

APPENDIX V

Non-Western Periodical Titles

Aichi gakugei daigaku kenkyū hōkoku, Jimbun kagaku 愛知学芸大学研究報告, 人文科学
Aichi kyōiku daigaku kenkyū hōkoku, Jimbun kagaku 愛知教育大学研究報告, 人文科学
Aichi shukutoku daigaku ronshū, Bungakubu (bungaku kenkyū kahen) 愛知淑徳大学論集, 文学部 (文学研究科篇)
Aoyama gakuin daigaku bungakubu kiyō 青山学院大学文学部紀要
Baoji wenli xueyuan xuebao, Shehui kexue ban 寶雞文理學院學報, 社會科學版
Beifang luncong 北方論叢
Beijing daxue xuebao, Zhexue shehui kexue ban 北京大學學報, 哲學社會科學版
Beijing keji daxue xuebao, Shehui kexue ban 北京科技大學學報, 社會科學版
Bijutsushi 美術史
Bijutsushi kenkyū 美術史研究
Bowuguan yanjiu 博物館研究
Bukkyō daigaku daigakuin kiyō 仏教大学大学院紀要
Bungei ronsō 文芸論叢
Changchun shifan xueyuan xuebao 長春師範學院學報
Changde shifan xueyuan xuebao, Shehui kexue ban 常德師範學院學報, 社會科學版
Chengdu daxue xuebao, Shehui kexue 成都大學學報, 社會科學
Chonnam sahak 全南史學
Chuanshan xuekan 船山學刊
Chūgoku bungaku hō 中国文学報
Chūgoku bungaku ronshū 中国文学論集
Chūgoku chūsei bungaku kenkyū 中國中世文學研究
Chūgoku-gaku ronshū 中国学論集
Chūgoku kodai shōsetsu kenkyū 中國古代小說研究
Chūgoku koten bungaku kenkyū 中国古典文学研究
Chungguk munhak 中國文學
Chunggukŏmunhak yŏkch'ong 中國語文學譯叢
Chūō Daigaku Ajiashi kenkyū 中央大学アジア史研究
Cishu yanjiu 辭書研究
Dalu zazhi 大陸雜誌
Daxue tushuguan xuebao 大學圖書館學報
Dao jiao xue tansuo 道教學探索
Dongfang wenhua 東方文化
Dongfang zazhi 東方雜誌

Dongnan daxue xuebao, Zhexue shehui kexue bao 東南大學學報, 哲學社會科學版
Dongyue luncong 東岳論叢
Dōshisha hōgaku 同志社法学
Dunhuang yanjiu 敦煌研究
Dunhuangxue 敦煌學
Faguang xuetan 法光學壇
Fuda Zhongyansuo xuekan 輔大中研所學刊
Fudan xuebao, Shehui kexue 復旦學報, 社會科學
Fujian shifan daxue xuebao 福建師範大學學報
Fujian xuekan 福建學刊
Fukuoka joshi tandai kiyō 福岡女子短大紀要
Furen xuezhi 輔仁學誌
Gakurin 學林
Gansu gaoshi xuebao 甘肅高師學報
Gansu shida xuebao, Zhexue shehui kexue 甘肅師大學報, 哲學社會科學
Gaoxiao tushuguan gongzuo 高校圖書館工作
Gengo bunka 言語文化
Gengo bunka ronsō 言語文化論叢
Guangxi guangbo dianshi daxue xuebao 廣西廣播電視大學學報
Guangzhou shiyuan xuebao 廣州師院學報
Gudai wenxue lilun yanjiu 古代文學理論研究
Gudian wenxianxue yanjiu 古典文獻學研究
Gugong xueshu jikan 故宮學術季刊
Gu Hanyu yanjiu 古漢語研究
Guji yanjiu 古籍研究
Guji zhengli yanjiu xuekan 古籍整理研究學刊
Guocui xuebao 國粹學報
Guoli Beiping tushuguan guankan 國立北平圖書館館刊
Guoli Zhongyang daxue wenxueyuan yuankan 國立中央大學文學院院刊
Guoli zhongyang yanjiuyuan lishi yuyan yanjiusuo jikan 國立中央研究院歷史語言研究所集刊
Guowen xuebao 國文學報
Hanguo xuebao 韓國學報
Hanxue yanjiu 漢學研究
Hebei shifan daxue xuebao 河北師範大學學報
Hebei shiyuan xuebao 河北師院學報
Heilongjiang minzu congkan 黑龍江民族叢刊
Henan daxue xuebao, Shehui kexue ban 河南大學學報, 社會科學版
Hexi xueyuan xuebao 河西學院學報
Hiroshima daigaku bungakubu kiyō 広島大学文学部紀要
Huaiyin shifan xueyuan xuebao 淮陰師範學院學報
Huagang wenke xuebao 華岡文科學報
Huanggang shifan xueyuan xuebao 黃岡師範學院學報
Huanghe keji daxue xuebao 黃河科技大學學報

Huanan nongye kexue 華南農業科學
Huanan shifan daxue xuebao, Shehui kexue ban 華南師範大學學報, 社會科學版
Huazhong shifan daxue xuebao 華中師範大學學報
Hubei daxue chengren jiaoyu xueyuan xuebao 湖北大学成人教育学院學報
Hunan keji daxue xuebao, Shehui kexue ban 湖南科技大學學報, 社會科學版
Ibaraki joshi tanki daigaku kiyō 茨城女子短期大学紀要
Indogaku bukkyōgaku kenkyū 印度學佛教學研究
Jianghai xuekan 江海學刊
Jiang Han luntan 江漢論壇
Jiangsu shengli guoxue tushuguan niankan 江蘇省立國學圖書館年刊
Jiangxi jiaoyu xueyuan xuebao, Shehui kexue 江西教育學院學報, 社会科学
Jiaxing xueyuan xuebao 嘉興學院學報
Jilin shifan xueyuan xuebao 吉林師範學院學報
Ji'nan xuebao, Zhexue shehui kexue ban 暨南學報, 哲學社會科學版
Jimbun kenkyū 人文研究
Jinri Hubei, Lilun ban 今日湖北, 理論版
Jinyang xuekan 晉陽學刊
Kagakushi kenkyū 科學史研究
Kaifeng jiaoyu xueyuan xuebao 開封教育學院學報
Kanbun gakkai kaihō 漢文学会会報
Kanbun kyōshitsu 漢文教室
Kan Gi bunka 漢魏文化
Kaogu yu wenwu 考古與文物
Kodai kenkyū 古代研究
Kokugo kokubun 国語国文
Kokusaigaku rebyū 国際学レブユ
Komazawa daigaku bukkyōgakubu ronshū 駒沢大学仏教学部論集
Kuntengo to kunten shiryō 訓点語と訓点資料
Kurume daigaku bungakubu kiyō 久留米大学文学部紀要
Kyōtō gobun 京都語文
Kyūshū tōyōshi ronshū 九州東洋史論集
Lanzhou beifang luncong 蘭州北方論叢
Lanzhou daxue xuebao, Shehui kexue ban 蘭州大學學報, 社會科學版
Lanzhou xibei shida xuebao, Shehui kexue 蘭州西北師大學報, 社會科學
Leshan shifan xueyuan xuebao 樂山師範學院學報
Liaocheng shifan xueyuan xuebao 聊城師範學院學報
Liaoning shizhuan xuebao, Shehui kexue ban 遼寧師專學報, 社會科學版
Lishi yanjiu 歷史研究
Longdong xueyuan xuebao, Shehui kexue ban 隴東學院學報, 社會科學版
Longyan xueyuan xuebao 龍岩學院學報
Manyōshū kenkyū 万葉集研究
Minsu yanjiu 民俗研究
Mudanjiang jiaoyu xueyuan xuebao 牡丹江教育學院學報
Nagoya daigaku bungakubu kenkyū ronshū 名古屋大学文学部研究論集

Nagoya daigaku bungakubu kenkyū ronshū, Shigaku 名古室大学文学部研究論集, 史學
Nanchang daxue xuebao 南昌大學學報
Nanjing daxue xuebao, Zhexue, renwen kexue, shehui kexue 南京大學學報, 哲學, 人文科學, 社會科學
Nanjing daxue xuebao, Zhexue shehui kexue 南京大學學報, 哲學社會科學
Nanjing shida xuebao, Shehui kexue ban 南京師大學報, 社會科學版
Nanjing Xiaozhuang xueyuan xuebao 南京曉莊學院學報
Nanjing Zhongyiyao daxue xuebao 南京中醫藥大學學報
Nanya yanjiu 南亞研究
Neimenggu shehui kexue 內蒙古社會科學
Nei Menggu shifan daxue xuebao, Zhexue shehui kexue ban 內蒙古師範大學學報, 哲學社會科學版
Nihon Chūgoku gakkaihō 日本中国学会報
Nihon gakushi-in kiyō 日本学士院紀要
Ningbo daxue xuebao, Renwen kexue ban 寧波大學學報, 人文科學版
Ningxia shehui kexue 寧夏社會科學
Nishōgakusha daigaku jimbun ronsō 二松学舎大学人文論叢
[*Nüshida*] *xueshu jikan* [女師大] 學術季刊
Ōsaka daigaku bungakubu kiyō 大阪大学文学部紀要
Pingdong jiaoyu daxue 屏東教育大學
Rikuchō gakujutsu gakkaihō 六朝学術学会報
Rikuchō gakujutsukai kaihō 六朝学術会会報
Qi Lu xuekan, She zhe ban 齊魯學刊, 社哲版
Qinghai minzu xueyuan xuebao 青海民族學院學報
Qinghua daxue xuebao 清華大學學報
Qinzhou xueyuan xuebao 欽州學院學報
Qiushi xuekan 求實學刊
Ritsumeikan bungaku 立命館文学
Sanxia daxue xuebao, Renwen shehui kexue ban 三峽大學學報, 人文社會科學版
Setsuwa bungaku kenkyū 説話文学研究
Shandong shifan daxue xuebao, Renwen shehui kexue ban 山東師範大學學報, 人文社會科學版
Shandong Zhongyi xueyuan xuebao 山東中醫學院學報
Shandong Zhongyiyao daxue xuebao 山東中醫藥大學學報
Shanghai jiaotong daxue xuebao, Zhexue shehui kexue ban 上海交通大學學報, 哲學社會科學版
Shanghai shifan daxue xuebao, Zhexue shehui kexue xuebao 上海師範大學學報, 哲學社會科學學報
Shanxi daxue xuebao, Zhexue shehui kexue ban 山西大學學報, 哲學社會科學版
Shehui kexue jikan 社會科學輯刊
Shehui kexue zhanxian 社會科學戰綫
Sheke zongheng 社科縱橫
Shenyang yinyue xueyuan xuebao 瀋陽音樂學院學報
Shidō bunko ronshū 斯道文庫論集

Shien 史苑
Shihuo yuekan 食貨月刊
Shijie zongjiao yanjiu 世界宗教研究
Shikan 史観
Shinagaku 支那学
Shiryō hihan kenkyū 史料批判研究
Shisō 史艸
Shiteki 史滴
Shixue niankan 史學年刊
Shixueshi yanjiu 史學史研究
Shixue xiaoxi 史學消息
Shixueshi ziliao 史學史資料
Shoshi gaku 書誌学
Shoudu shifan daxue xuebao, Shehui kexue ban 首都師範大學學報, 社會科學版
Shūkan Tōyōgaku 集刊東洋學
Shumu jikan 書目季刊
Sichuan daxue xuebao, Zhexue shehui kexue ban 四川大學學報, 哲學社會科學版
Sichuan daxue xuebao congkan 四川大學學報叢刊
Sichuan shifan daxue xuebao 四川師範大學學報
Suihua xueyuan xuebao 綏化學院學報
Taidong shizhuan xuebao 臺東師專學報
Taida zhongwen xuebao 臺大中文學報
Taidong shizhuan xuebao 臺東師專學報
Taiyuan shifan xueyuan xuebao 太原師範學院學報
Tianjin Zhongyiyao daxue xuebao 天津中醫藥大學學報
Tōa ronsō 東亞論叢
Tōhōgaku 東方学
Tōhō gakuhō 東方学報
Tōhō shūkyō 東方宗教
Tōkai daigaku kiyō, Bungakubu 東海大学紀要, 文学部
Tōhoku daigaku kyōiku gakubu, Jimbun kagakubu 東北大学教育學部, 人文科學部
Tokushima daigaku sōgō kagakubu kiyō 德島大学総和科学部紀要
Tōkyō kyōiku daigaku bungakubu kiyō 東京教育大学文学部紀要
Tōyō bunka 東洋文化
Tōyō gakuhō 東洋学報
Tōyōshi kenkyū 東洋史研究
Tōyō shien 東洋史苑
Tushuguan zazhi 圖書館雜志
Weifang xueyuan xuebao 濰坊學院學報
Wei Jin Nanbeichao Sui Tang shi ziliao 魏晉南北朝隋唐史資料
Wenjiao ziliao 文教資料
Wenyi lilun yanjiu 文藝理論研究
Wen shi 文史
Wen shi zhe 文史哲

Wen shi zhe xuebao 文史哲學報
Wenwu 文物
Wenxian 文獻
Wenxue nianbao 文學年報
Wenxue pinglun 文學評論
Wenxue yichan 文學遺產
Wenxue zazhi 文學雜誌
Wenzhou shifan xueyuan xuebao 溫州師範學院學報
Wuyi daxue xuebao 武邑大學學報
Xiaoshuo yuebao 小說月報
Xibei shidi 西北史地
Xibei shida xuebao 西北師大學報
Xibei shifan daxue xuebao, Shehui kexue ban 西北師範大學學報, 社會科學版
Xi'nan jiaotong daxue xuebao, Shehui kexue ban 西南交通大學學報, 社會科學版
Xi'nan shifan xueyuan xuebao 西南師範學院學報
Xin jianshe 新建設
Xinya shenghuo 新亞生活
Xinya xuebao 新亞學報
Xinyang shifan xueyuan xuebao, Zhexue shehui kexue ban 信陽師範學院學報, 哲學社會科學版
Xinzhou shifan xueyuan xuebao 忻州師範學院學報
Xiyu yanjiu 西域研究
Xuelin manlu 學林漫錄
Xue hai 學海
Xueshujie 學術界
Xueshu jilin 學術集林
Xueshu yanjiu 學術研究
Yancheng shifan xueyuan xuebao 鹽城師範學院學報
Yanjing xuebao 燕京學報
Yibin xueyuan bao 宜賓學院報
Youshi xuezhi 幼獅學誌
Yuncheng xueyuan xuebao 運城學院學報
Zhangzhou shifan xueyuan xuebao 漳州師範學院學報
Zaozhuang shifan zhuanke xuexiao xuebao 棗莊師範專科學校學報
Zhenli 真理
Zhengzhou daxue xuebao, Zhexue shehui kexue ban 鄭州大學學報, 哲學社會科學版
Zhiyan 制言
Zhongguo difangzhi 中國地方志
Zhongguo gudian xiaoshuo yanjiu zhuanji 中國古典小說研究專集
Zhongzhou jingu 中州今古
Zhongguo shehui kexue yanjiushengyuan xuebao 中國社會科學院研究生院學報
Zhongguo shi yanjiu 中國史研究
Zhongguoshi yanjiu dongtai 中國史研究動態
Zhongguo wenhua yanjiusuo xuebao 中國文化研究所學報

Zhongguo wenzhe yanjiu jikan 中國文哲研究集刊
Zhongguo xuebao 中國學報
Zhonghua yishi zazhi 中華醫史雜誌
Zhongguo zhexueshi yanjiu 中國哲學史研究
Zhongguo Zhongyi jizheng 中國中醫急症
Zhonghua wenshi luncong 中華文史論叢
Zhonghua yishi zazhi 中華醫史雜誌
Zhongshan daxue xuebao 中山大學學報
Zhongshan xueshu wenhua jikan 中山學術文化集刊
Zhongwai wenxue 中外文學
Zhongguo wenzhe yanjiu jikan 中國文哲研究集刊
Zhongyanyuan shiyusuo jikan 中研院史語所集刊
Zhongyiyao xuekan 中醫藥學刊
Zhongzhou xuekan 中州學刊
Zhongzhou jingu 中州今古

Subject Index

Works are listed under subject areas in chronological order by the year of completion or the dates of the author, compiler, or sponsor. The collected writings of individuals are in order of the author's dates.

Agriculture

Qimin yaoshu, Jia Sixie (fl. 530–544)

Anomaly accounts and ghost stories

Bowu zhi, Zhang Hua (232–300); *Soushen ji,* Gan Bao (d. 336); *Shiyi ji,* Wang Jia (d. before 393); *Shuyi ji,* attributed to Ren Fang (460–508); *Huanyuan ji,* Yan Zhitui (531–d. after 591)

Anthologies

multigenre: *Wen xuan,* Xiao Tong (501–531); *Han Wei Liuchao baisanjia ji,* Zhang Pu (1602–1641); **prose**: *Quan shanggu Sandai Qin Han Liuchao wen,* Yan Kejun (1762–1843); **poetry**: *Yutai xinyong,* Xu Ling (507–583); *Yuefu shiji,* Guo Maoqian (fl. 1080)

Biography

Buddhist: *Biqiuni zhuan,* attributed to Shi Baochang (ca. 495–528); *Gaoseng zhuan,* Shi Huijiao (497–554); *Guang Hongming ji,* Daoxuan (596–667); *Xu Gaoseng zhuan,* Shi Daoxuan (597–667); **Daoist**: *Shenxian zhuan,* Ge Hong (283–343); **filial paragons**: *Xiaozi zhuan,* anonymous (late fifth to early eighth century); **recluses**: *Gaoshi zhuan,* Huangfu Mi (215–282)

Buddhism, doctrine

Hongming ji, Sengyou (445–518)

Buddhism, history

Foguo ji (comp. 416), Fa Xian (ca. 337–422); *Luoyang qielan ji,* Yang Xuanzhi (fl. early sixth century). *See also* **Biography, Buddhist**

Character appraisal

Renwu zhi, Liu Shao (186?–245?); *Bowu zhi*, Zhang Hua (232–300); *Shishuo xinyu* (comp. ca. 430), Liu Yiqing (403–444)

Collected anecdotes or sayings

Bowu zhi, Zhang Hua (232–300); *Diaoyu ji* (comp. ca. 700); *Shishuo xinyu* (comp. ca. 430), Liu Yiqing (403–444); *Yulin*, Pei Qi (fl. latter half of fourth century)

Collected writings of individuals

Wei Wudi ji (155–220); *Wei Wendi ji* (187–226); *Ying Qu ji* (190–252); *Cao Zhi ji* (192–232); *Fu Xuan ji* (217–278); *Xun Xu ji* (ca. 221–289); *Zhang Hua ji* (232–300); *Chenggong Sui ji* (231–273); *Pan Yue ji* (247–300); *Zuo Si ji* (ca. 253–ca. 307); *Lu Ji ji* (261–303); *Lu Yun ji* (262–303); *Shu Xi ji* (ca. 263–ca. 302); *Sun Chuo ji* (ca. 314–ca. 371); *Tao Yuanming ji* (365?–427); *He Chengtian ji* (370–447); *Xie Lingyun ji* (385–433); *Xie Huilian ji* (407–433); *Yuan Shu ji* (408–453); *Bao Zhao ji* (414–466?); *Zhang Rong ji* (444–497); *Kong Zhigui ji* (447–501); *Xie Tiao ji* (464–499); *Liang Wudi ji* (464–549); *He Xun ji* (466?–519?); *Wu Jun ji* (469–520); *Xiao Tong ji* (501–531); *Liang Jianwendi ji* (503–552); *Liang Yuandi ji* (508–555); *Yu Xin ji* (513–581); *Niu Hong ji* (545–610)

Daoism

Baopuzi (*neipian*), and *Shenxian zhuan*, Ge Hong (283–343). **See also Biography, recluses**

Encyclopedias

Yiwen leiju, Ouyang Xun (557–641); *Beitang shuchao*, Yu Shinan (558–638); *Chuxue ji*, Xu Jian (d. 729); *Diaoyu ji* (comp. ca. 700); *Taiping yulan*, Li Fang (925–996); **political institutions**: *Tong dian*, Du You (735–812)

Family instructions

Yanshi jiaxun, Yan Zhitui (531–d. after 591)

Festivals and seasonal observances

Yuzhu baodian, Du Taiqing (d. ca. late 590s); *Jing-chu suishi ji*, Zong Lin (ca. 500–563)

Geography

Foguo ji (comp. 416), Fa Xian (ca. 337–422); *Shuijing zhu*, Li Daoyuan (d. 527)

Histories, local

Huayang guo zhi, Chang Qu (ca. 291–ca. 361); *Yezhong ji*, attributed to Lu Hui (ca. fourth century); *Jing-chu suishi ji*, Zong Lin (ca. 500–563); *Luoyang qielan ji*, Yang Xuanzhi (fl. early sixth century); *Jiankang shilu* (ca. 756)

Histories, standard

Sanguo zhi, Chen Shou (233–297); *Hou Han shu*, Fan Ye (398–446); *Song shu*, Shen Yue (441–513); *Nan Qi shu*, Xiao Zixian (489–537); *Wei shu*, Wei Shou (505–572); *Chen shu* and *Liang shu*, Yao Silian (557–637); *Bei Qi shu*, Li Baiyao (565–648); *Sui shu*, Wei Zheng (580–643); *Zhou shu* (636), Liu Qiu (501–554), Nin Hong (545–610), Linghu Defen (583–666); *Jin shu* (648); *Nan shi* and *Bei shi* (659), Li Yanshou (exact dates unknown)

Histories, unofficial

Diwang shiji, Huangfu Mi (215–282); *Shiliuguo chunqiu*, Cui Hong (478–525). *See also Buddhism, history; Local histories*

Literary criticism

Shi pin, Zhong Rong (469?–518); *Wenxin diaolong*, Liu Xie (fl. late fifth to early sixth century)

Literature

See **Anomaly accounts and ghost stories; Anthologies; Collected writings of individuals; Collections of anecdotes; Poetry**

Medicine

diagnostics: *Wang Shuhe Maijing*, attributed to Wang Shuhe (210–285?); **pharmacology**: *Shanghan lun*, Zhang Ji (ca. 150–219); *Shennong bencao jing*, anonymous, referenced by Wu Pu (early third century); *Ge xianweng Zhouhou beijifang*, Ge Hong (283–343)

Miscellany

Bowu zhi, Zhang Hua (232–300); *Shishuo xinyu* (comp. ca. 430), Liu Yiqing (403–444); *Yulin*, Pei Qi (fl. latter half of fourth century); *Jinlouzi* (553), Liang Yuandi (503–555)

Moral instruction

Baopuzi, Ge Hong (ca. 283–343); *Xiaozi zhuan* (comp. between late fifth and early eighth century); *Yanshi jiaxun*, Yan Zhitui (531–d. after 591)

Philosophy

Renwu zhi, Liu Shao (186?–245?); *Jinlouzi* (553), Liang Yuandi (503–555); *Liuzi*, Liu Zhou (514–565)

Phonology

Qieyun (preface 601), Lu Fayan (fl. 589–618)

Poetry, anthology

Yutai xinyong (comp. between 531 and 548), Xu Ling (507–583); *Yuefu shiji*, Guo Maoqian (fl. 1080); **criticism**: *Shi pin*, Zhong Rong (469?–518)

CHINA RESEARCH MONOGRAPHS (CRM)

50. Hershatter, Gail, Emily Honig, Susan Mann, and Lisa Rofel, comps and eds. *Guide to Women's Studies in China.* 1998.
51. Yeh, Wen-hsin, ed. *Cross-Cultural Readings of Chineseness: Narratives, Images, and Interpretations of the 1990s.* 2000.
52. Levine, Marilyn A., and Chen San-ching. *The Guomindang in Europe: A Sourcebook of Documents.* 2000.
53. Keightley, David N. *The Ancestral Landscape: Time, Space, and Community in Late Shang China (ca. 1200–1045 B.C.).* 2000.
54. Worthing, Peter. *Occupation and Revolution: China and the Vietnamese August Revolution of 1945.* 2001.
55. Guo, Qitao. *Exorcism and Money: The Symbolic World of the Five-Fury Spirits in Late Imperial China.* 2003.
56. Antony, Robert J. *Like Froth Floating on the Sea: The World of Pirates and Seafarers in Late Imperial South China.* 2003.
57. Fogel, Joshua A. *The Role of Japan in Liang Qichao's Introduction of Modern Western Civilization to China.* 2004.
58. Liu, Xin. *New Reflections on Anthropological Studies of (greater) China.* 2004.
59. Ho, Virginia Harper. *Labor Dispute Resolution in China: Implications for Labor Rights and Legal Reform.* 2004.
60. Kowallis, Jon Eugene von. *The Subtle Revolution: Poets of the "Old Schools" during Late Qing and Early Republican China.* 2006.
61. Esherick, Joseph W., Wen-hsin Yeh, and Madeleine Zelin, eds. *Empire, Nation, and Beyond: Chinese History in Late Imperial and Modern Times—A Festschrift in Honor of Frederic Wakeman.* 2006.
62. Strand, David, and Sherman Cochran, eds., Wen-hsin Yeh, general ed. *Cities in Motion: Interior, Coast, and Diaspora in Transnational China.* 2007.
63. Yeh, Michelle. *A Lifetime Is a Promise to Keep: Poems of Huang Xiang.* 2009.
64. Cheng, Weikun. *City of Working Women: Life, Space, and Social Control in Early Twentieth-Century Beijing.* 2011.
65. So, Billy K. L., and Ramon H. Myers, eds. *The Treaty Port Economy in Modern China: Empirical Studies of Institutional Change and Economic Performance.* 2011.
66. Henriot, Christian, and Wen-hsin Yeh, eds. *History in Images: People and Public Space in Modern China.* 2012.
67. Keightley, David N. *Working for His Majesty: Research Notes on Labor Mobilization in Late Shang China (ca. 1200–1045 B.C.), as Seen in the Oracle-Bone Inscriptions, with Particular Attention to Handicraft Industries, Agriculture, Warfare, Hunting, Construction, and the Shang's Legacies.* 2012.
68. Knoblock, John, and Jeffrey Riegel. *Mozi: A Study and Translation of the Ethical and Political Writings.* 2013.
69. Yeh, Wen-hsin, ed. *Mobile Horizons: Dynamics across the Taiwan Strait.* 2013.
70. Liu, Xun, and Vincent Goossaert, eds. *Quanzhen Daoists in Chinese Society and Culture.* 2013.

JAPAN RESEARCH MONOGRAPHS (JRM)

10. Rabson, Steve, trans. *Okinawa: Two Postwar Novellas by Ōshiro Tatsuhiro and Higashi Mineo.* 1989; revised 1996.
11. Tsukada, Mamoru. *Yobiko Life: A Study of the Legitimation Process of Social Stratification in Japan.* 1991.
12. White, James W. *The Demography of Sociopolical Conflict in Japan, 1721–1846.* 1992.
13. Davis, Winston. *The Moral and Political Naturalism of Baron Katō Hiroyuki.* 1996.
14. Gibbs, Michael H. *Struggle and Purpose in Postwar Japanese Unionism.* 2000.
15. Pereira, Ronan Alves, and Hideaki Matsuoka, eds. *Japanese Religions in and beyond the Japanese Diaspora.* 2007.
16. Clark, Paul H. *The Kokugo Revolution: Education, Identity, and Language Policy in Imperial Japan.* 2009.
17. Miller, Aaron L. *Discourses of Discipline: An Anthropology of Corporal Punishment in Japan's Schools and Sports.* 2013.